The Socratic Movement

The Socratic Movement

Edited by

Paul A. Vander Waerdt

Cornell University Press

Ithaca and London

First published 1994 by Cornell University Press.

Library of Congress Cataloging-in-Publication Data

The Socratic movement / edited by Paul Vander Waerdt.
    p.   cm.
  Includes bibliographical references and index.
  ISBN 0-8014-2585-9 (alk. paper). — ISBN 0-8014-9903-8 (pbk. : alk. paper)
  1. Socrates. I. Vander Waerdt, Paul A. II. Title.
B317.S643 1994
183'.2—dc20   93-43746

Contents

PART I   Socrates in the *Sōkratikoi Logoi*

PART II   The Hellenistic Heirs of Socrates

Preface

Six of the contributions in this book (Chapters 1, 5–7, 9, and 11) originated in a conference entitled "The Socratic Movement" held at Duke University on April 6–7, 1990, under the auspices of the Departments of Classical Studies, Philosophy, and Political Science. Funding for the conference was provided by the Office of the Dean of Arts and Sciences at Duke, the Patterson Endowment in Philosophy, the Department of Political Science, and the John M. Olin Foundation. On behalf of the participants in the conference, I would like to thank the three session chairs—Daniel Devereux, Michael Gillespie, and Phillip Mitsis—for their cooperation, as well as my research assistant, Darren Weirnick, for keeping the logistics of the conference running smoothly. With the exception of Chapter 3 (soon to be published as part of a larger study by the author) and Chapter 12 (an earlier version of which appeared in *OSAP* Suppl. Vol. 3 [1992]), here reprinted with a new afterword, the other contributions were specially commissioned for this volume. My editorial work on this collection has been aided by a grant from Duke's University Research Council. I am grateful to Clare Hall, Cambridge, for the hospitality it accorded me as a Visiting Fellow in 1992–93, when I completed work on this volume. Among my professional colleagues, I am especially indebted to Diskin Clay and Michael Gillespie of Duke University for their invaluable advice and steadfast friendship during the planning and execution of this volume; to Dirk Obbink of Barnard College, Columbia University, for his assistance with proofreading; to Bernhard Kendler at Cornell University Press, for his generous reception and encouragement of the project; and to Marian Shotwell for her skill and tact in imposing consistency across a volume with fourteen independent-minded contributors.

P. A. V. W.

San Francisco

Abbreviations

A&A	*Antike und Abendland*
AGP	*Archiv für Geschichte der Philosophie*
AJAH	*American Journal of Ancient History*
AJP	*American Journal of Philology*
ANRW	*Aufstieg und Niedergang der römischen Welt*
AP	*Ancient Philosophy*
APSR	*American Political Science Review*
BICS	*Bulletin of the Institute of Classical Studies of the University of London*
CA	*Classical Antiquity*
CErc	*Cronache ercolanesi*
CJ	*Classical Journal*
CP	*Classical Philology*
CQ	*Classical Quarterly*
CR	*Classical Review*
DG	*Doxographi Graeci*, ed. H. Diels (Berlin, 1879)
DHA	*Dialogues d'histoire ancienne*
DK	*Die Fragmente der Vorsokratiker*[6], ed. H. Diels and F. Kranz (Berlin, 1951)

GRBS	*Greek, Roman and Byzantine Studies*
ICS	*Illinois Classical Studies*
JHI	*Journal of the History of Ideas*
JHP	*Journal of the History of Philosophy*
JHS	*Journal of Hellenic Studies*
MH	*Museum Helveticum*
OSAP	*Oxford Studies in Ancient Philosophy*
PBACAP	*Proceedings of the Boston Area Colloquium in Ancient Philosophy*
PCG	*Poetae Comici Graeci*, ed. R. Kassel and C. Austin (Berlin, 1983–)
PCPS	*Proceedings of the Cambridge Philological Society*
PP	*La parola del passato*
PQ	*Philosophical Quarterly*
PR	*Philosophical Review*
RE	*Paulys Real-Enzyklopädie der klassischen Altertumswissenschaft*, ed. G. Wissowa (Stuttgart, 1893–)
REA	*Revue des études anciennes*
REG	*Revue des études grecques*
Rev Meta	*Review of Metaphysics*
RhM	*Rheinisches Museum für Philologie*
SO	*Symbolae Osloenses*
SSR	*Socratis et Socraticorum Reliquiae*[2], ed. G. Giannantoni (Naples, 1990)
SVF	*Stoicorum Veterum Fragmenta*, ed. H. von Arnim (Leipzig, 1904–23)
TAPA	*Transactions of the American Philological Association*
TGF	*Tragicorum Graecorum Fragmenta*, ed. R. Kannicht, B. Snell, and S. Radt (Göttingen, 1971–85)
TLS	*Times Literary Supplement*
YCS	*Yale Classical Studies*
ZPE	*Zeitschrift für Papyrologie und Epigraphik*

Introduction

Paul A. Vander Waerdt

According to a well-established ancient tradition, Socrates was the philosopher who "first called philosophy down from the heavens" and made the study of nature instrumental to human happiness.[1] Yet the assessment of Socrates' philosophical achievement presents obstacles more daunting than we face in the case of any other major philosopher. Socrates himself wrote nothing, apart from his poetic renditions of Aesop's fables and the hymn to Apollo that he composed while confined in prison during the last days of his life.[2] For firsthand information concerning his thought and life we must rely on three authors, each of whom poses formidable problems of literary interpretation. Only one of these authors wrote during Socrates' own lifetime, and he left his testimonial incompletely revised: this is Aristophanes' comic attack on Socrates in the *Clouds*. Our other two principal informants, Plato and Xenophon, wrote in the genre of literature that Aristotle named the Σωκρατικοὶ λόγοι and paired with the mimes of Sophron and Xenar-

---

[1]Cic. *Tusc.* 5.10–11; cf. Xen. *Mem.* 1.1.11–16; Pl. *Ap.* 19b–d; Arist., *Metaph.* 987b1–2; D.L. 2.16, 45. For the interpretation of this claim, see Chapter 2.

[2]Pl. *Phd.* 60c–61b; cf. D.L. 2.42; M. L. West, *Iambi et Elegi Graeci* (Oxford, 1972), 2:118–19. Socrates' turn to the writing of poetry in his last days appears to represent a reconsideration of the interpretation he put on the pronouncement of the Delphic oracle that no human being was wiser than he. At *Apology* 33b–c he claims that he has been ordered through oracles and dreams as well as by the original Delphic oracle to pursue his philosophical mission; hence his reconsideration of the meaning of the dream "make μουσική" (*Phd.* 60e) is tantamount to a reconsideration of the original interpretation he placed on the oracle, to the service of which he traces his condemnation.

chus as an unnamed genre of poetry or mimesis.[3] Our assessment of
the generic conventions with which Plato and Xenophon worked is
complicated by the loss of the earliest examples of these Socratic conversations, most regrettably the thirty-three dialogues that Simon the
Athenian cobbler composed based on Socrates' conversations in his
workshop.[4] For all practical purposes, the fragments of Aeschines'
seven works that displayed "the Socratic character" provide our only
substantial comparative material (D. L. 2.61).[5] Even so, there is every
reason to suppose that none of the authors of fourth-century *Sōkratikoi
logoi* sought to offer a portrayal that was of merely historical interest.[6]
One ancient reader found that Plato's dialogues represent a "Socrates
embellished and made new,"[7] while Xenophon's considerable literary
originality is evidenced in his authorship of such works as the *Cyropaedia, Memorabilia,* and *Anabasis,* each of which is without generic precedent in Greek literature.

The fact that Socrates is accessible to us only through the eyes of
three authors, each possessed of great literary ambition, inevitably
complicates philosophical evaluation, particularly when, as in this case,
none of our firsthand information about Socrates is merely doxographical in character, while none of our Socratic doxography derives
from sources clearly independent of the distinctive literary agendas of
Socrates' philosophical heirs.[8] Scholarship on Socrates has traditionally
taken as its objective the recovery of the "historical Socrates," the eponymous father of the fourth-century portraits that provide our closest
point of entry into Socrates' life and thought.[9] Yet the fictional char-

---

[3] See *Poet.* 1447b11; cf. *Rh.* 1417a20; *On Poets* fr. 72 Rose = Ath. 11.505c.

[4] See D. L. 2.122–23; and, for Simon's influence among later Socratics, see R. F. Hock,
"Simon the Shoemaker as an Ideal Cynic," *GRBS* 17 (1976): 41–54. For the discovery of
a workshop just outside the Agora that has been identified as Simon's, see Chapter 1,
note 19.

[5] For a survey of Aeschines' work, see A. E. Taylor, "Aeschines of Sphettus," in *Philo-
sophical Studies* (London, 1934), pp. 1–27; see also H. Dittmar, *Aischines von Sphettos:
Studien zur Literaturgeschichte der Sokratiker, Untersuchungen und Fragmente,* Philologische
Untersuchungen 21 (Berlin, 1912); B. Ehlers, *Eine vorplatonische Deutung de sokratischen
Eros: Der Dialog Aspasia des Sokratikers Aischines,* Zetemata 41 (Munich, 1966); reviewed by
K. Gaiser, *AGP* 51 (1969): 200–209; K Döring, "Der Sokrates des Aischines von Sphettos
und die Frage nach dem historischen Sokrates," *Hermes* 112 (1984): 16–30.

[6] For the fictional character of the Socratic memorial literature, see especially
A. Momigliano, *The Development of Greek Biography* (Cambridge, Mass., 1971), pp. 52–54.

[7] *Epistle* 2, 314c: the value of this testimony does not depend upon the authorship of
the *Epistle,* since its author (whether Plato or not) clearly had an intimate knowledge of
Plato's *Sōkratikoi logoi.*

[8] On Diogenes Laertius' biography of Socrates, see most recently G. Giannantoni,
"Socrate e i Socratici in Diogene Laerzio," in *Diogene Laerzio: Storico del pensiero antico,* a
special volume of *Elenchos* 7 (1986): 183–216.

[9] A. Patzer, ed., *Der historische Sokrates,* Wege der Forschung 585 (Darmstadt, 1987),
provides the most convenient point of entry into the scholarly discussion.

acter of the *Sōkratikoi logoi* may well render this objective unrealizable: if Aristophanes, Plato, and Xenophon each felt free to use the figure of Socrates as "the guide to territories as yet unexplored" (as Arnaldo Momigliano memorably put it), then we must give serious consideration to the possibility that none of these sources offers a historically reliable picture of Socrates. In that case the scholarly discussion formulated in terms of whether we should "prefer" Plato's account or Xenophon's in cases where they conflict is unlikely to generate tenable conclusions about the historical Socrates himself. It might be preferable, given the character of and limitations imposed by our surviving evidence about Socrates, to regard our chief objective as the understanding of the Socratic movement in all its diversity—in which case conflicting accounts among different Socratics arguably provide an excellent guide to authorial intent, even if they tell us little about Socrates himself. Alternatively, we might be principally concerned with the recovery of the most philosophically brilliant of the portraits of Socrates without regard to its historical status. There are strong and legitimate arguments for each of these approaches, and the present volume should aid scholars with either aim.

The Socratic movement that gives this volume its title refers in the first place to those of Socrates' associates who attempted to commemorate his life by recording his conversations for posterity. A remarkable number of these associates became authors of *Sōkratikoi logoi:* of the eighteen Socratics whom Plato's Phaedo mentions as being present or absent on Socrates' last day (cf. *Phd.* 59b-c), nine are attested to have written Socratic dialogues;[10] of the seven associates whom Xenophon names (*Mem.* 1.2.48) as consorting with Socrates for proper motives (in order to become gentlemen, καλοικἀγαθοί), three wrote *Sōkratikoi logoi* (Crito [D.L. 2.121], Simmias [D.L. 2.123], and Cebes [D.L. 2.125]), while a fourth, Hermogenes, is named as Xenophon's source for his *Apology of Socrates* (2, 27; *Mem.* 4.8.4–11). In later antiquity, Antisthenes, Aeschines, Plato, and Xenophon were singled out as the "chief" Socratics (D.L. 2.47), though the second edition of Gabriele Giannantoni's collection of the fragments of Socrates and the Socratics contains some seventy entries. In accordance with the common ancient practice of suppressing explicit reference to one's philosophical rivals, the four major Socratics scarcely mention one another by name,[11] although it is

[10]For the details, see Chapter 1.

[11]Thus Plato rigorously excludes his primary rivals among the Socratics from mention: while nearly all the other members of Socrates' circle (named, for example, at *Phaedo* 59b) are depicted in the course of his dialogues, Plato mentions Antisthenes—the most influential of the Socratics in his own day—only to confirm his presence at Socrates' death, Aristippus only to record his absence (*Phd.* 59c), and Aeschines only to

clear that they read and responded to one another's work and that the *Sōkratikoi logoi* constituted a distinct and lively literary genre. The existence of this genre also enabled others, who were not themselves associates of Socrates, to claim the mantle of his authority, provided that they could represent their philosophical position as a plausible development or interpretation of what Socrates held. In this broader sense the Socratic movement refers to the numerous fourth- and third-century philosophers—most important, the Stoic Zeno and Academic skeptic Arcesilaus, originators of the two most influential early Hellenistic schools—who recognized Socrates as their chief authority and who viewed their own philosophical activity as a continuation of his.

The terrain of the Socratic movement extends so far and in so many different directions that it is not clear what the best route is on which to set out to traverse it. We might begin with the rather modest goal of assessing Cicero's characterization of the philosophical revolution Socrates accomplished. The difficulty immediately arises that our three principal sources appear to contradict one another.[12] Our earliest and only contemporary source, Aristophanes, represents Socrates as an enthusiastic student of φυσιολογία, as the proponent of the explanation of all natural phenomena in terms of their material constituents—a philosophical position fully consistent with the kind of study of nature favored by contemporary Ionian φυσικοί. And so far from "calling philosophy down from the heavens" and making *physiologia* instrumental to human happiness, the Aristophanic Socrates first comes before us suspended aloft in a basket in order better to investigate the heavenly things (*Nub.* 217–33); he takes no interest in the ethical subjects favored by contemporary sophists and appears not to recognize the socially corrosive effects of his atheism or of his philosophical enquiries concerning the conventional bonds of human society. Aristophanes depicts Socrates as a comically transformed natural philosopher of his own time and place rather than as a philosopher who revolutionized the study of nature by making it serve the end of human happiness. Cicero's characterization of the Socratic revolution in fact presupposes

---

note his presence at Socrates' death and trial (*Ap.* 33e). Xenophon himself never receives mention, although he states in discussing Glaucon's education that Socrates took an interest in him "on Plato's account" (*Mem.* 3.6.1; cf. 1.2.48, where Plato does not figure among Socrates' associates), while Antisthenes features prominently in Xenophon's *Symposium*, and Aristippus in his *Memorabilia*.

[12] The fourth source commonly cited, Aristotle, is remarkably reticent on Socrates' philosophical achievement as assessed in the doxography cited above: in one passage he says that "Socrates concerned himself with ethics and not at all with nature as a whole" (*Metaph.* 987b1–2); but Aristotle does not grant Socrates recognition for the revolution he thereby effected in philosophy.

the correctness of his fourth-century apologists' presentation of his philosophy. Modern scholars, recognizing this discrepancy between Aristophanes' portrayal and that of Socrates' philosophical heirs, have usually been inclined to suppose that it is just so much to Aristophanes' discredit.

Yet careful examination of how Socrates' apologists treat his interest in the study of nature suggests that such a judgment is overly hasty. The two Platonic texts that might be adduced with greatest plausibility as evidence for Socrates' own philosophical development both are centrally concerned to respond to Aristophanes' portrayal. When Socrates undertakes to discredit the charges of impiety and of corruption of the youth circulated by Aristophanes and other unnamed "first accusers" (Pl. *Ap.* 18b–23e), he leaves the distinct impression that he never, even in his youth, engaged in the study of nature such as is parodied in the *Clouds* (cf. 19b).[13] Yet the "intellectual autobiography" in Plato's *Phaedo* (96a–99d) reports that Socrates, at a youthful stage in his philosophical development, enthusiastically pursued the study of nature and advocated materialistic explanations of natural phenomena along lines quite similar to those depicted by Aristophanes.[14] Hence Plato's testimony in important respects corroborates rather than discredits Aristophanes' portrayal;[15] and it is prima facie implausible, in any case, that Plato would devote such constant care to respond to the latter's comic attack of several decades earlier if it could be dismissed as a simple misrepresentation.

The evidence of Xenophon similarly corroborates the plausibility of the Aristophanic portrayal. Xenophon's account of Socrates' dismissal of the pre-Socratic study of nature in *Memorabilia* 1.1.11–16 is no less apologetically motivated, although more nuanced, than Plato's: defending Socrates from the charges of impiety and corruption, Xenophon claims that he "did not even converse about the nature of the cosmos" (after saying that no one ever heard him do or say anything

---

[13]G. Vlastos, *Socrates: Ironist and Moral Philosopher* (Ithaca, N.Y., 1991), pp. 160–62, takes these denials as a sufficient basis for dismissing Aristophanes' portrayal as "groundless" but takes no account of the evidence adduced below.

[14]The close connection between the two accounts, and an attempt to show how they might be explained in terms of Socrates' philosophical development, are retailed in Chapter 2.

[15]Plato implies, even in the *Apology* (21a), that Socrates had a pre-Socratic past, for otherwise it is difficult to see how the oracle at Delphi could have pronounced no man wiser than he, an event that on Socrates' own account precedes his public search for self-knowledge (but see now C. Reeve, *Socrates in the Apology* [Indianapolis, 1989], pp. 28–30, for the possibility that the oracle did not rely on evidence in pronouncing upon Socrates' wisdom). The fact that Socrates was a favored target of comic poets from 423 B.C. on certainly suggests that he had acquired a considerable reputation before reaching his philosophical maturity.

impious, *Mem.* 1.1.10); but his account of piety in *Memorabilia* 1.4 makes clear that Socrates' enquiry into "the human things"—his constant subject of discussion (*Mem.* 1.1.16)—does presuppose a teleological natural philosophy (see Chapter 10). Thus Xenophon's account, despite its apparent denial that Socrates ever engaged in the pre-Socratic study of nature, is fully compatible with the hypothesis that at some point in his intellectual development Socrates did so. Moreover, in the penultimate chapter of the *Memorabilia* (4.7), just before he recounts Socrates' noble conduct in the thirty days after his condemnation, Xenophon not only admits that Socrates was versed in the ancillary disciplines of natural science (Socrates was "not inexperienced" [οὐκ ἄπειρος] in the study of geometry, and "not ignorant" [οὐδὲ ἀνή-κοος] of astronomy), but also explains how Socrates regarded some knowledge of these disciplines as necessary to instill in his associates the free and self-sufficient disposition at which he aims. Xenophon thus restricts Socrates' disavowal of the study of nature to the kind of enquiry into causes favored by the pre-Socratics; but he affirms that Socrates regards some knowledge of *physiologia* as necessary to enquiry into the human things. His evidence thus is incompatible with Aristotle's claim (*Metaph.* 987b1–2) that Socrates abandoned entirely the study of nature for ethics.[16]

The Platonic and Xenophontic evidence on which Cicero's assessment of Socrates' philosophical achievement rests can hardly be said, therefore, to justify the wholesale rejection of Aristophanes' portrayal of Socrates as a natural philosopher. Only a careful consideration of the literary character and motivation of each of these sources would afford any basis for the development of a historically plausible account of Socrates' philosophical achievement.

The absence of a consistent and unproblematic portrayal of Socrates among our three principal sources is not the only serious obstacle to assessment of his philosophical significance. We might hope to find some basis for adjudicating the different portraits of Socrates offered by our three principal sources by turning to his immediate companions and philosophical heirs for guidance in recovering the substance of his thought. Yet these sources likewise represent Socrates' thought so differently that this approach offers no unproblematic resolution of the basic literary problems, as a brief inspection of the terrain will show.

During his lifetime and the century following his death, Socrates inspired a variety of philosophical movements, each of which claimed to

---

[16]Socrates' influence on contemporary *physiologia* is a neglected subject that merits investigation; but see now D. W. Graham, "Socrates, the Craft Analogy, and Science," *Apeiron* 24 (1991): 1–24.

trace its ancestry to him and to expound the authentic version of his philosophy.[17] The Socrates who is the nearly exclusive preoccupation of modern scholarship is that of Plato's "Socratic" dialogues—so much so that the claims advanced by other Socratics have almost entirely disappeared from the discussion. Yet in ancient doxography Plato's portrayal of Socrates was not accorded the primacy it receives in contemporary scholarship,[18] while in his own time and place Plato's was only one among several competing interpretations of Socrates' philosophy. Plato's competitors include figures as diametrically opposed in their interpretations of Socrates as Antisthenes, spiritual father of the Cynics and apparently the most influential of the Socratics during the first fifteen years after Socrates' death,[19] and Aristippus, the hedonist to whom the Cyrenaics traced their ancestry. There were also a host of other "minor Socratics," so grouped by tradition, although some were influential philosophers of the first rank.[20] During the following century, Socrates was adopted as the principal authority of the two most influential Hellenistic schools, the Stoics and the Academic skeptics— the former actually wishing to be called Socratics,[21] the latter claiming that their skeptical practice represented the proper interpretation of Socrates' dialectical practice.[22] Debate between these two schools often took the form of offering differing interpretations of certain Socratic premises and doctrines to which both subscribed.[23] Indeed, only the

---

[17]Much of the relevant evidence for the Socratics is assembled in G. Giannantoni's four-volume collection *Socraticorum Reliquiae* (Naples, 1983–85), now in its second edition with a new title, *Socratis et Socraticorum Reliquiae* (1990).

[18]As A. A. Long, "Socrates in Hellenistic Philosophy," *CQ* n.s. 38 (1988): 150–71 at p. 154, concludes in a survey of the ancient evidence: "Plato, or what we call Plato's Socratic dialogues, appear to have been widely regarded as neither more nor less authentic witnesses to Socrates than Xenophon's writings."

[19]This judgment is based upon Antisthenes' position as Isocrates' primary rival (cf. *Adv. Soph.* 1–8; *Helen* 1); see C. Euken, *Isokrates* (Berlin, 1983), pp. 25–27, 63.

[20]One might single out for mention the Dialectical school, which located Socrates' true importance not in ethical doctrine but in his dialectical practice. For its considerable influence on early Hellenistic philosophy, see D. N. Sedley, "Diodorus Cronus and Hellenistic Philosophy," *PCPS* n.s. 23 (1977): 74–120; more recently, K. Döring has argued against the separate existence of the Dialectical school: "Gab es eine Dialektische Schule?" *Phronesis* 34 (1989): 293–310.

[21]See Philod. *De Stoic.*, cols. 12–13, in the edition of T. Dorandi, *CErc* 12 (1982): 91–133.

[22]For Arcesilaus' appropriation of Socrates' authority, see Cic. *De or.* 3.67; *Fin.* 2.2, 5.10; *Acad.* 1:44; *Nat. d.* 1.11; he is attacked by his contemporary, the Epicurean Colotes, *apud* Plutarch, *Adversus Colotem* 1121e–1124c.

[23]For the Stoic appropriation of Socrates, see P. A. Vander Waerdt, "Politics and Philosophy in Stoicism," *OSAP* 9 (1991): 185–211; also chapters 9–11 below. For the Academic skeptic's interpretation, see M. Frede, "The Skeptic's Two Kinds of Assent and the Question of the Possibility of Knowledge," in *Philosophy in History*, ed. R. Rorty et al. (Cambridge, 1984), pp. 255–78; A. M. Ioppolo, *Opinione e scienza: Il dibattito tra Stoici e*

Epicureans among the major philosophical schools during this period rejected Socrates as an exemplum of the philosophical life.[24] The competing versions of Socrates' philosophy advocated both by his immediate disciples and by his Hellenistic heirs illustrate the range of basic alternatives available in interpreting his thought.

Yet Socrates' companions adopted such diametrically opposed views, on pleasure and its relation to virtue and happiness, for example,[25] that they fail to provide consistent testimony that would enable us to adjudicate the basic conflicts between our three principal authorities. The Academic skeptics and the Stoics, Socrates' most important Hellenistic heirs, construe his understanding of such central subjects as virtue as knowledge of good and evil so differently that it is clear that no consensus about the substance of Socrates' philosophy emerged over the century following his death. Hence we have no alternative, in assessing Socrates' principal philosophical achievements, but to revert to investigation of the literary questions to which we referred above.

If there is no independent evidence concerning "the historical Socrates" on which to adjudicate the conflicting claims of our three principal sources, these authors do provide abundant evidence for comparative treatment. We must begin by considering with care and impartiality basic questions about the nature of our principal sources. How do the generic characteristics of the *Sōkratikoi logoi* inform the presentation of Socrates offered by Plato and Xenophon? What constraints did the function of Athenian comedy as a vehicle for social criticism place upon dramatic anachronism in the case of Aristophanes' portrayal of Socrates? What is the relation of Xenophon's Socratic corpus to that of Plato? Although these obvious questions potentially admit of decisive answers, it can hardly be said that contemporary scholarship has arrived at a well-informed consensus about them. In fact, although the obvious point of entry into the evaluation of our conflicting sources of information about Socrates is the comparative analysis of how various Socratics represent similar doctrines or identical

---

Accademici nel III e nel II secolo a.c. (Naples, 1986), largely endorsed by J. Annas, "The Heirs of Socrates," *Phronesis* 33 (1988): 100–112. See also Long (above, note 18), pp. 150–71; chapters 12–13 below.

[24]For the origin of Epicurean interest in Socrates in Colotes' controversy with the Academic skeptic Arcesilaus, see P. A. Vander Waerdt, "Colotes and the Epicurean Refutation of Skepticism," *GRBS* 30 (1989): 225–67 at pp. 253–59; also M. T. Riley, "The Epicurean Criticism of Socrates," *Phoenix* 34 (1980): 55–68; K. Kleve, "*Scurra Atticus:* The Epicurean View of Socrates," in *Syzetesis: Studi sull' epicureismo greco e romano offerti a Marcello Gigante* (Naples, 1983), pp. 227–53.

[25]See Chapter 4.

events in his life, such study is rare.[26] The absence of such comparative study is particularly remarkable in view of the abundant parallel evidence between Plato and Xenophon.[27]

The explanation for this state of affairs lies principally in the vagaries of scholarly fashion. During the last two decades, the enormous body of scholarship devoted to the Platonic Socrates by philosophers working in the Anglo-American analytical tradition has clarified in important ways the philosophical methodology and commitments of the Socrates whom tradition has come to regard as the most compelling of the ancient portraits.[28] Yet the problematic but often unargued assumptions of this scholarship have tended to discourage the careful examination of our other evidence.[29] It is often assumed, though the assumption is rarely supported by detailed argument, that the "historical Socrates" is identical with the Socrates of Plato's early, "Socratic" dialogues.[30] Even if we could reconstruct a reliable chronology of Plato's dialogues and concede, generously, that this chronology exactly

[26] Two exceptions are Charles Kahn's recent assessment of how Plato's *Symposium* responds to earlier literature on Socratic eros by Aeschines and Antisthenes: "Plato as a Socratic," in *Hommage à Henri Joly*, Recherches sur la philosophie et le langage 12 (Grenoble, 1990), pp. 287–301; and my own attempt to show how Xenophon reconfigures discussion of Socrates' defense speech in accordance with his own understanding of Socrates' distinctive virtue and philosophical mission: "Socratic Justice and Self-Sufficiency: The Story of the Delphic Oracle in Xenophon's *Apology of Socrates*," *OSAP* 11 (1993): 1–48.

[27] Surprisingly, the best statement of the relation between the Platonic and the Xenophontic Socrates seems to remain that of J. Burnet in the introduction to his edition of Plato's *Phaedo* (Oxford, 1911), pp. ix–lvi (= Patzer [above, note 9], pp. 109–45).

[28] It is worth recalling, however, the extent to which scholarly fashion in this matter has varied: among Zeller's predecessors, "Xenophon has come to be regarded as the only perfectly trustworthy authority for the philosophy of Socrates; to all the others, Plato himself included, at most a supplementary value is allowed," a position that Zeller himself in the main endorses despite Schleiermacher's objections ("Über den Werth des Sokrates als Philosophen," *Abhandlungen der klg. Preussischen Akademie der Wissenschaften zu Berlin 1814/15* [1818]: 50–68 = Patzer [above, note 9], pp. 41–58), which strikingly resemble the arguments on which the contemporary reversal of this position rests (see Zeller, *Socrates and the Socratic Schools*, trans. J. Reichel [London, 1885], pp. 99–105 at pp. 100, 182–86). The present dismissive attitude toward Xenophon's testimony seems to have won out around the beginning of the present century; by 1916 W. W. Baker could write in his "Apologetic for Xenophon's *Memorabilia*," *CJ* 12 (1916–17): 293–309 at p. 293: "After constituting the supreme court of appeal on matters Socratic in some past generations, [Xenophon] has . . . not only been removed from the bench, but even at times quite thrown out of court and denied the right to appear either as advocate or witness."

[29] One of the most elegant critiques of the analytical approach to the study of Plato is that of Diskin Clay, "*Platonic Studies* and the Study of Plato," *Arion* n.s. 2 (1975): 116–32. For an attempt to explain the philosophical considerations that led Plato to adopt the dialogue form, see Michael Frede, "Plato's Arguments and the Dialogue Form," *OSAP* Suppl. Vol. 3 (1992): 201–19.

[30] Vlastos (above, note 13) argues in detail for this widely held view.

mirrors the development of Plato's own thought, it would not follow that we have any reliable criterion whereby to identify certain dialogues as "Socratic," if that term is understood to designate dialogues in which Plato's portrayal of Socrates is not fundamentally informed by his own philosophical preoccupations.[31] Nor is it at all clear, if the recovery of the historical Socrates is taken to be the objective of Socratic studies, that these dialogues should necessarily occupy their present privileged position in the discussion. Such an assumption could be justified only by detailed comparative study with the evidence provided by other Socratics—and it is precisely such study that is lacking in the contemporary scholarship. Indeed, one could turn around the question often used to justify the primacy of Plato in Socratic studies—How could Socrates have exercised such philosophical influence unless he was as Plato (not Xenophon or Aeschines or . . .) represented him?—and ask how we can understand who Socrates was without understanding how he was able to inspire such diverse philosophical movements. An unsurprising, but impoverishing effect of the recent scholarly preoccupation with the Platonic Socrates has been the exclusion of rival portraits of Socrates from serious study.

This impoverishment is nowhere clearer than in the current orthodoxy about our other two primary sources. The comic attack on Socrates in Aristophanes' *Clouds*, though it is the sole document we possess that dates from Socrates' own lifetime, is widely dismissed as the composite portrait of the "typical sophist,"[32] hence as irrelevant to the assessment of his philosophical significance. Yet this view, despite its popularity, is quite poorly supported by the text of the *Clouds*. There is in any case a great discrepancy between the dismissive attitude that contemporary scholars adopt toward Aristophanes' portrayal of Socrates and the great care that his chief apologists, Plato and Xenophon, took to answer his attack.[33] Certainly Aristophanes' portrayal

---

[31]This is certainly a minority opinion; for more conventional opinion, see, for example, W. K. C. Guthrie, *A History of Greek Philosophy* (Cambridge, 1975), 4: 39–66. Charles Kahn has questioned the assumption that the Socrates depicted in Plato's early dialogues is the historical Socrates, in "Did Plato Write Socratic Dialogues?" *CQ* n.s. 31 (1981): 305–20. Already in antiquity Cicero recognized that Plato attributes to Socrates his own philosophical preoccupations: see *Rep.* 1.15–16.

[32]This is the position of K. J. Dover in the standard Greek edition of the play, *Aristophanes' Clouds* (Oxford, 1968), pp. xxxii–lvi at p. xl; reprinted as "Socrates in the Clouds," in *The Philosophy of Socrates*, ed. G. Vlastos (New York, 1971), pp. 50–77 at p. 58. Dissent from such a view has been registered in a variety of quarters: see Chapter 2, note 21.

[33]Plato answers Aristophanes not only in the *Apology* (18b–23e) but also in the setting of his *Theages* (see T. L. Pangle, "Socrates on the Problem of Political Science Education," *Political Theory* 13 [1985]: 112–37). Xenophon suppresses Plato's distinction between Socrates' first and second accusers in his *Apology*, but in the *Oeconomicus* (11.18, 3; 3.7–10)

placed on the agenda of his fourth-century philosophical heirs the problem of providing a publicly defensible justification for philosophical activity that lays to rest objections of the kind raised by Aristophanes.

Xenophon's portrayal of Socratic ethics has been treated with similar disregard in both classical and philosophical circles, though the grounds most often stated in support have been amply discredited.[34] Xenophon has fared somewhat better at the hands of political theorists, who have tended to treat him with more sympathetic consideration, in part because of his influence on subsequent political thought.[35] But several considerations suggest that the careful and sympathetic study of Xenophon's account of Socratic ethics could enrich our understanding of the Socratic movement. In the first place, there is good reason to suppose that Xenophon held a less critical view of Socrates' philosophy than Plato did, hence that his presentation of that philosophy is less influenced by his own agenda than Plato's is likely to be. Although there is no general agreement about the relation of Plato's thought to that of his teacher, most contemporary treatments of the so-called middle and late dialogues presuppose that Plato is here developing his own philosophical project in critical reaction to perceived inadequacies in Socrates'.[36] Although the more narrowly focused apologetic purpose of Xenophon's presentation of Socrates complicates comparison of his corpus with that of Plato's, there is no evidence

---

he represents Socrates as going to the perfect *kaloskagathos,* Ischomachus, for instruction in *kalokagathia,* at a time at which he suffers from his Aristophanic reputation as an idle chatterer with his head in the air; and in the *Symposium* Xenophon portrays Socrates as responding to abuse from the Syracusan entertainer that specifically presupposes Aristophanes' attack (see 7.4). For further evidence and discussion see Chapters 1–2, 5, and 8.

[34]See D. R. Morrison, "On Professor Vlastos' Xenophon," *AP* 7 (1987): 9–22. Vlastos (above, note 13), pp. 99–106, makes a renewed attempt to confront Xenophon's testimony, but his discussion tends to be selective and unsympathetic, and it takes insufficient account of the literary agenda that informs Xenophon's presentation of Socratic philosophy.

[35]See T. L. Pangle, "The Political Defense of Socratic Philosophy: A Study of Xenophon's *Apology of Socrates to the Jury,*" *Polity* 18 (1985): 98–114; C. Bruell, "Xenophon," in *History of Political Thought,* ed. L. Strauss and J. Cropsey (Chicago, 1987), pp. 89–117; W. R. Newell, "Machiavelli and Xenophon on Princely Rule," *Journal of Politics* 50 (1988): 108–30. Leo Strauss's early work on Xenophon is especially helpful in exposing his complexity and subtlety: see "The Spirit of Sparta or the Taste of Xenophon," *Social Research* 6 (1939): 502–36, and *On Tyranny* (Glenco, Ill., 1950), now available in its third, enlarged edition (1991). Strauss's later books, *Xenophon's Socratic Discourse: An Interpretation of the Oeconomicus* (Ithaca, N.Y., 1970) and *Xenophon's Socrates* (Ithaca, N.Y., 1972), are less accessible; the clearest statement of his interpretation of Xenophon's Socrates known to me is that in "The Problem of Socrates: Five Lectures," in *The Rationalism of Classical Political Philosophy,* ed. T. L. Pangle (Chicago, 1989), pp. 103–83.

[36]This is a central claim, for instance, of Vlastos (above, note 13), esp. pp. 45–80.

of a sustained critical rejection of Socrates' philosophical methodology and views on the scale one finds in Plato. Second, even if one considers Plato our best source for Socrates' thought, Xenophon alone among the early Socratics provides extensive evidence parallel to Plato's that holds open the possibility of clarifying what is distinctive about the portrayal of each. Third, Xenophon offers an internally consistent and plausible account of Socrates' distinctive virtue and philosophical mission that differs considerably from Plato's, and consideration of these differences could lead to a better understanding of central features of Socratic ethics. Thus Xenophon does not accept the Platonic characterization of Socrates as the wisest of human beings on account of his knowledge of his own ignorance (the Xenophontic Socrates never disavows positive knowledge); he rather finds the foundation of Socratic virtue (κρηπῖδα ἀρετῆς, *Mem.* 1.5.4) to consist in ἐγκράτεια, or self-control, in a kind of self-sufficiency to which knowledge makes some, but perhaps not even the most important, contribution. The central differences in the Platonic and Xenophontic accounts of Socratic ethics—on such questions as the unity of virtue, the possibility of ἀκρασία, the relation of virtue to the goods of fortune—all are related to this fundamental difference. Fourth, Xenophon's interpretation of Socratic ethics provided a model that competed with Plato's for the allegiance of Socrates' Hellenistic heirs. Thus the Cynics follow Xenophon's model, while the Stoics and Academic skeptics principally develop Plato's—at the same time disagreeing vehemently about the interpretation of certain Socratic doctrines that both accept, such as that virtue is knowledge of good and evil, a debate that persisted over several centuries. In short, the early development of Hellenistic philosophy would be better understood if serious consideration were given to Xenophon's portrayal of Socratic ethics.[37]

The contemporary revival of interest in Hellenistic philosophy has very recently led to a better appreciation of Socrates' role as a philosophical authority among the early Hellenistic schools.[38] There is now general agreement that both the early Stoics and the Academic skeptics represented themselves as Socrates' true heirs, and that much of their debate centered on the proper interpretation of various Socratic doctrines. Yet work on this subject is still at an early stage; some of the fundamental questions that await satisfactory explanation are discussed in Part 2 of this book. The contents of Gabriele Giannantoni's

[37]I cannot accept the claim of Long (above, note 18), p. 154, that in the Hellenistic period "it was Plato's Socrates, rather than any other, that stimulated serious philosophy." Chapter 10 demonstrates that Xenophon's *Memorabilia* was a crucial source of reflection for early Stoic thinking on theology.

[38]See the literature cited above, note 31.

Socratis et Socraticorum Reliquiae likewise have only begun to be appreciated both in their own right and for their influence on early Hellenistic philosophy.

Despite the extraordinary importance of the Socratic revolution for the later history of philosophy, it has received remarkably little attention, either historical or philosophical, from modern scholars. There is, for instance, no satisfactory general survey of the Socratic movement, many of whose figures remain poorly understood even in the specialist literature.[39] Previous collections of essays on Socrates have tended to focus almost exclusively on Plato's portrayal of him.[40]

The present volume assembles essays that aim to clarify problematic and poorly understood aspects of the Socratic movement. It is in the nature of an exploratory project such as this to offer nearer the first word than the last—hence this book should be regarded as a stimulus for further investigation rather than as a comprehensive or definitive history. Several features of the volume's plan require comment.

First, since the volume's purpose is in part protreptical, the contributors were chosen with a view to offering diverse viewpoints, intellectual affiliations, and interpretive strategies. This diversity of approach is intended to foster dialogue between the different professional communities concerned with the study of classical philosophy, which have tended in recent years to adopt a rather insular view toward one another.

Second, for reasons of space and coherence, the scope of this book is restricted to those Socratics who flourished during Socrates' lifetime down to the early Hellenistic period. One could of course profitably extend study of Socrates' role as a philosophical authority through later antiquity to include such figures as Epictetus or the Neoplatonists.[41] Within the period delimited, the principles of inclusion are

---

[39]The best general account is probably that of Jean Humbert, *Socrate et les petits Socratiques* (Paris, 1967), but it excludes the Hellenistic schools and is rather weak on philosophical interpretation.

[40]The well-known collection edited by Gregory Vlastos (above, note 32) contains an introduction, a chapter surveying the sources for Socrates, a chapter on the *Clouds* reprinted from Dover's edition, and eleven chapters on Plato; the collection *Essays on the Philosophy of Socrates*, ed. H. H. Benson (Oxford, 1991), also focuses narrowly on Plato. *Der historische Sokrates* (above, note 9), as befits its title, is more catholic in both coverage and approach; the editor's "Einleitung" provides a useful survey of Continental discussion of the Socratic problem. There is also the volume *New Essays on Socrates*, ed. E. Kelly (Lanham, Md., 1984).

[41]See K. Döring, *Exemplum Socratis: Studien zur Sokratesnachwirkung in der kynisch-stoisehen Popularphilosophie der frühen Kaiserzeit und im frühen Christentum*, Hermes Einzelschriften 42 (Wiesbaden, 1979); J. Hershbell, "The Stoicism of Epictetus: Twentieth Century Perspectives," *ANRW* II.36.3 (Berlin, 1989), pp. 2153–55; also F. Schweingruber, "Sokrates und Epiktet," *Hermes* 78 (1943): 195–226; K. Döring, "Sokrates bei Epiktet," in *Studia Platonica*, ed. K. Döring and W. Kollman (Amsterdam, 1974), pp. 195–226.

intended to be generous. Aristophanes' *Clouds* does not, strictly speaking, form part of the genre of *Sōkratikoi logoi* that are the subject of Part 1 of this book (though Aristophanes certainly claims important affinities with Socrates in the parabasis of the *Clouds*); but its influence on that genre and its role, arguably, as a model for the earliest of the *Sōkratikoi logoi* make a chapter on it essential. Four chapters are devoted to Xenophon, partly because his evidence is so extensive and partly because his portrayal of Socrates and his manner of writing are so poorly understood by contemporary scholars. Among the Hellenistic schools, particular attention has been given to the Stoics, who most self-consciously saw themselves as developing Socratic theses in their own philosophy.

Third, an attempt has been made to restore the Platonic Socrates to his own time and place. Several of the chapters (1–4, 7, 9, 11–13) are centrally concerned with Plato's relation to other important figures in the Socratic movement. If no chapter is devoted solely to his portrayal of Socrates, that is because our principal concern is to investigate the less well known but not for that reason necessarily lesser Socratics.[42]

The volume is divided into two parts. Part 1 contains eight essays that seek to elucidate the origin, literary character, and philosophical contributions of the *Sōkratikoi logoi* outside the Platonic tradition. Part 2 consists of six essays that explore how the early Hellenistic schools employed Socrates as a philosophical authority in developing their own positions.

The volume opens with Diskin Clay's attempt to identify the character and sources of the *Sōkratikoi logoi* as a distinct literary genre. After a review of the literary activities of Socrates' companions and of the competing claims advanced in antiquity for the prize of having first invented the Socratic dialogue, Clay turns to the earliest imitations of Socrates, in Attic comedy, and advances the novel argument that comedy provided an important model for the earliest Socratic dialogues. He then turns to consider some of the important contributions Socrates' chief philosophical heirs made to the development of the narrative dialogue, with particular emphasis on the innovations Plato introduced into this genre of writing.

The investigation of the comic Socrates continues in Chapter 2, where I endeavor to clarify two central problems in Socrates' intellec-

---

[42]For guidance in the literature, see H. Cherniss, "Plato 1950–1957," *Lustrum* 4 (1959): 5–308, and 5 (1960): 321–648; H. Brisson, "Platon 1958–1975," *Lustrum* 20 (1977): 5–304; R. McKirahan, *Plato and Socrates: A Comprehensive Bibliography* (1958–73) (New York, 1978). On Platonic scholarship in antiquity, see now Harold Tarrant's *Thrasyllan Platonism* (Ithaca, N.Y., 1993).

tual biography. After arguing that Aristophanes parodies a specifically individuated portrayal of Socrates at a certain stage in his intellectual development rather than a composite figure to whom Aristophanes affixes objectionable traits of contemporary sophists, I undertake to show that Socrates in the *Clouds* is represented as being an enthusiastic advocate of the same kind of material explanations of natural phenomena to which the youthful Socrates described in the "intellectual autobiography" in Plato's *Phaedo* (96a–99d) was attached. The reconstruction of this philosophy offers numerous compelling parallels with the thought of his contemporary Diogenes of Apollonia. I then turn to the second problem, the motives that led Socrates to abandon his pre-Socratic past. After a detailed discussion of Aristophanes' criticism of Socrates' investigations into nature, which remarkably parallel the mature Socrates' view as reported by both Plato and Xenophon, I argue that Xenophon's account of the positive use to which Socrates believed the *kaloskagathos*, or gentleman, could put the ancillary disciplines of natural philosophy provides a plausible explanation for Socrates' abandonment of his pre-Socratic past.

In Chapter 3, Charles Kahn continues the investigation into the origins of the *Sōkratikoi logoi* begun in Chapter 1. Aeschines is known to have written seven Socratic dialogues, and the fragments of *Aspasia* and *Alcibiades* are extensive enough to enable us to form a relatively full picture of their form and content. Aeschines seems to have offered an innovative account of Socrates' eros and its role in the protrepic and educational aspects of his philosophy. This theme is traced out in detail as it relates to the two dialogues just mentioned. In an appendix Kahn attempts to situate their chronology in regard to other Socratic writings of related subject matter.

The role of pleasure in Socratic moral philosophy, the subject of Harold Tarrant's essay, is notoriously obscure, as Socrates' associates and philosophical heirs adopt opposing views on pleasure and its relation to virtue and happiness. Although Xenophon's Socrates is aware of the dangers of indiscriminate pursuit of pleasure, he sometimes regards pleasure as valuable in itself; the Platonic evidence is contradictory: at first sight, the *Protagoras* advocates hedonism, and the *Gorgias* opposes it. Tarrant undertakes to clarify the nature of Socrates' commitment to hedonism through a detailed analysis of the argument of the *Hippias major*, which represents an important contribution to the Academy's Socratic tradition, whether by Plato or not. Here Socrates is scathing about his feeble interlocutor's refusal to equate without qualification the noble, or τὸ καλόν, with the pleasant. The chapter concludes with a consideration of how the contrasting positions of Antisthenes and Aristippus represent different attempts to draw out the central threads of Socrates' philosophy, a subject to which we return in Chapter 14.

The next four chapters focus on Xenophon's portrayal of Socratic ethics. Thomas Pangle opens the discussion by attempting to situate Xenophon's *Sōkratikoi logoi* within his corpus taken as a whole and viewed as a "system," as suggested by Shaftesbury's discussion of Xenophon's manner of writing. The relation between politics and philosophy, reflected in the relation between the more strictly political writings and the Socratic writings, is the guiding thread of the discussion. Among the Socratic writings, particular attention is paid to the contrast developed in the *Oeconomicus* between Socrates and the gentleman Ischomachus, a contrast that clarifies the standard of *kalokagathia,* or gentlemanliness, that Socrates is especially concerned to instill in his associates. Among the political writings, the greatest attention is paid to the *Cyropaedia,* considered in light of Machiavelli's esteem and pointers toward a radical interpretation. Pangle argues that Xenophon's manifold corpus is best viewed as a kind of bipolar galaxy defined by Socrates in one hemisphere and Cyrus in the other.

In Chapter 6, David O'Connor explores Xenophon's account in the *Memorabilia* of Socrates' self-sufficiency as it relates to his friendships with his associates. Xenophon does not offer a straightforward account but proceeds by presenting a diverse collection of different interpretations of Socrates' self-sufficiency, from both admirers and detractors, leaving his reader to triangulate from these mistaken or partial views to the authentic interpretation. The chapter considers three such views: Alcibiades aspires to a political version of self-sufficiency, which draws him toward political leadership and ultimately toward tyranny; Aristodemus aspires to an atheistic version of self-sufficiency, which denies the relevance of divinities and divination to human life, so drawing him toward impiety; and Aristippus aspires to a transpolitical understanding of self-sufficiency, which involves a complete separation from political life, thus rendering him indifferent to politics. Each of these interpretations and imitations of Socratic self-sufficiency distorts some central aspect of his way of life. To see how this is so, O'Connor examines Socrates' defense against the charge of Antiphon that his way of life brings misery to himself and his associates. Socrates claims that his own life involves an erotic self-sufficiency that does not lead to tyranny, impiety, or political indifference, and the chapter closes with a consideration of the coherence of these claims.

One of Xenophon's chief purposes in the *Memorabilia* is to defend Socrates against the charge, leveled against him at his trial, of corrupting the youth. Donald Morrison offers a detailed examination of Socrates' education of Euthydemus in book 4, our most extensive account of how Socrates selects and educates his students. After considering how Socrates' tactics as a moral educator vary from case to case depending upon the character of his interlocutor, Morrison takes up the problem of Socrates as a teacher of virtue. Xenophon's Socrates, unlike Plato's, openly professes to be a moral educator. But the Platonic Socrates has substantive moral opinions and does influence the character and actions of his young associates; hence he too is a teacher of virtue in the ordinary sense. Both Plato and Xenophon are more acutely aware than their modern interpreters of the potentially corrupting effects of Socratic pedagogy, particularly his practice of the elenchus, on the young.

The *Oeconomicus* is the only Socratic work of Xenophon's that takes the form of a dialogue between Socrates and an interlocutor on a particular subject. John Stevens shows how Socrates attempts to instill a certain kind of self-sufficiency in Critoboulos by relating the story of his encounter with Ischomachus, who was widely reputed to be the *kaloskagathos*, or perfect gentleman. It is not at all clear, however, that Socrates intended Critoboulos to learn self-sufficiency by imitating Ischomachus. The wife of Ischomachus, whose training occupies much of the dialogue, is, it is argued, the woman whom Callias married in the scandalous affair reported by Andocides (*De myst.* 119ff.). Moreover, Socrates' characterization of his encounter with Ischomachus is cast as a response to the attack on Socratic education by Aristophanes in the *Clouds*. By presenting Critoboulos with an account of how a man merely "reputed" to be a gentleman manages his household with ruthless economy, Socrates suggests that the disrepute into which Ischomachus' wife later falls might be due to Ischomachus' failure to understand the "economy" of eros. Xenophon's portrayal of Socratic moral education reveals it to be inextricably linked with Socratic eros, a subject of more direct interest to the amorous and impractical Critoboulos.

In Part 2 we examine the Hellenistic appropriation of Socrates, beginning with three chapters that explore the early Stoics' complex relation to Socrates and his philosophical heirs.

In Chapter 9, Gisela Striker considers how the Stoics respond to Plato in developing their own account of Socratic ethics. Striker's thesis is that the Stoics try to make their account immune to Plato's criticism of Socratic theses they themselves accept; they in turn attack Plato where they think he has left Socratic ground, thereby producing an alternative version of certain doctrines that were developed by Plato in a different direction. Thus Socrates' influence on the Stoics is not limited to certain attractive theses they seek to establish on independent grounds; rather, they seek to clarify these theses through reflection on Plato's presentation. Striker supports this argument with a detailed examination of two connected examples: first, the thesis that virtue is sufficient for happiness; and second, that virtue is a kind of knowledge or craft, namely, knowledge of good and evil. Both ideas appear to be abandoned by Plato in his mature dialogues, and both are defended by the Stoics, in part by making more precise the reasoning employed by the Platonic Socrates.

The next two chapters develop the thesis that the early Stoic scholarchs arrived at their theory of natural law through critical reflection on Socratic arguments. Although Xenophon's influence in the early Hellenistic period has received little attention, Joseph DeFilippo and Phillip Mitsis argue in Chapter 10 that one crucial feature of the Stoic position originated in reflection on Xenophon's account of Socrates' natural teleology in *Memorabilia* 1.4, which provided Zeno and his followers with a Socratic warrant for their view of a rationally ordered nature structured by divine will. DeFilippo and Mitsis then consider how the Stoics interpreted Socrates as supporting a connection between divine law and moral principles and as taking such moral principles as his guide for action. They conclude that the origins of natural law theory may be placed firmly within the framework of the Socratic movement.

In Chapter 11, I attempt to identify the philosophical problems that Zeno sought to resolve in developing the theory of natural law that he presents in his *Republic,* the founding work of the natural law tradition. This theory, I argue, is intended to provide improved answers to questions Plato considered in his *Republic* by making more precise and explicit the teaching on natural justice that Plato gives to Socrates. The chapter first seeks to establish that the purpose of Zeno's *Republic* is to illustrate the way of life that accords with natural law, and that this explains its peculiar social structure and way of life. Next, I suggest that Zeno's purpose in offering an account of his best regime, a "dream or image of a philosopher's well-regulated regime" (in the words of Plutarch in *De virtute Alexandri* 329a–b), corresponds quite closely to Plato's "best city in speech" in his *Republic.* Similarly, Zeno's theory of natural law represents an attempted improvement over Plato's teaching on natural justice in the *Republic.* Finally, I argue that the institutional arrangements of Zeno's best regime are best explained as a deliberate response to Plato's paradox of the rule of the philosopher-kings.

The next two chapters explore the sources and motivation of Arcesilaus' claim to find in Socrates' dialectical practice the warrant for his own skepticism and suspension of judgment, or ἐποχή. In Chapter 12, Julia Annas examines the plausibility of Arcesilaus' interpretation of the skeptical Socrates as portrayed in Plato's dialogues and shows how he could have met the most obvious apparent obstacles to this interpretation—Socrates' quest for truth, his use of shared premises in argumentation, and his firm moral convictions. Annas then turns to the skeptical Academy's interpretation of the project of Plato's dialogues as entirely consistent with skepticism and offers a sympathetic account of the plausibility of this reading of Plato.

Chapter 13 also is concerned with Arcesilaus' relation to the Platonic Socrates but arrives at rather different conclusions. Defending the unorthodox view that Arcesilaus was committed to *epochē* in his own name and not merely as a conclusion drawn solely from his interlocutors' premises and canons of logic, Christopher Shields attempts to clarify how Arcesilaus could have considered this view of *epochē* consistent with the dialectical practice of Socrates. He suggests several differences between the two—most importantly, Arcesilaus' commitment to a much more general form of skeptical argumentation with stronger modal commitments than we find in the Platonic Socrates.

In the final chapter of the volume, Voula Tsouna McKirahan offers a reassessment of the philosophical work of Antisthenes and Aristippus and of their relation to the Cynic and Cyrenaic schools of the early Hellenistic period. Beginning with the stance each Socratic adopts on pleasure and its relation to virtue, she argues that Antisthenes cannot reasonably be characterized as a crude antihedonist nor Aristippus as a hedonist, concluding that their positions are more nuanced and less opposed than generally assumed. She then focuses on their doctrines concerning political participation, exploring the way each develops certain strands in Socrates' attitude toward political participation as portrayed by Plato and Xenophon. She concludes by defending the plausibility of the ancient view that Antisthenes and Aristippus were in an important sense founders of the Cynic and Cyrenaic schools respectively.

Although the other contributors should not be assumed to share the editor's opinions as expressed in this Introduction, this volume reflects a collective consensus that study of the Socratic revolution in philosophy would benefit from a renewed investigation of the portrayal of Socrates outside the Platonic tradition. A collective effort on the part of fourteen scholars of different persuasions will necessarily betray a greater degree of accident in the choice of topics than a similar work from a single hand. Certainly there are subjects here absent that could enrich our investigations. But we hope that the volume will stimulate a renewed interest in the Socratics and will thus foster further investigation of other neglected aspects of the Socratic movement.[43]

[43]I would like to thank Diskin Clay, Michael Gillespie, and Gisela Striker for helpful advice on this Introduction.

PART I

Socrates in the *Sōkratikoi Logoi*

[1]

The Origins of the
Socratic Dialogue

Diskin Clay

1. *Sōkratikoi*

Socrates—Socratic, Pythagoras—Pythagorean, Plato—Platonic, Epicurus—Epicurean: some philosophers have a way of becoming adjectives, and their followers substantives. In their transformation first into adjectives and then into substantives these philosophers are usually transformed into a philosophy or a school; only rarely are they transformed into a way of life.[1] But none (so far as I know), except Socrates, has lent his name to a genre of literature that is the mimesis of a philosophical life.

The first attestation of the adjective Σωκρατικός appears not in the writings of the "Socratics" but in Aristotle, who refers to the Σωκρατικοὶ λόγοι along with the mimes of Sophron and Xenarchus as a recognizable yet nameless genre of Greek "poetry" (*Poet.* 2, 1447b11). Aristotle's difficulty is that Greek failed to recognize the generic term crucial to the philosopher and critic of poetry. If mimesis, and not meter, is the critical concept that grounds a description of both the poetic and the prose forms that imitate humans in action, then some prose works are the proper subject of a larger theory of mimesis, which would include both the μῖμοι of Sophron and the genre Aristotle identifies as that of the *Sōkratikoi logoi;* and these would be included along

---

[1] As in the case of the Pythagorean mode of life (βίος) described by Plato in *Republic* 10, 600b.

with music, dance, and painting in a vastly extended theory of ποι-
ητική as mimesis. Greek was inadequate to Aristotle's theory because it
did not recognize the mimes of Sophron and Xenarchus or the *Sōkratikoi logoi* as "poetic," that is, mimetic. Like Sophron, the authors of
Sōkratikoi logoi were ἠθοποιοί.

But what precisely does the adjective "Socratic" mean? Were these
logoi Socratic in that they resembled the kind of discourse Socrates gave
his name to—that is, the heuristic method of question by someone who
professes to be asking more than rhetorical questions, and answers by
someone who might or might not be able to produce a satisfactory response? This was indeed a feature of some of the *Sōkratikoi logoi,* but
Aristotle's conception of poetry as mimesis and the term *mimoi* suggest
a larger interpretation of the adjective: just as the mimes of Sophron
represented the different sexes and the variety of human types engaged in their characteristic pursuits, the authors of *Sōkratikoi logoi* imitated the character of Socrates as he engaged in his characteristic
manner of conversation and interrogation.

But Aristotle's association of the Sicilian mime with the imitations of
the conversations of Socrates seems to suggest even more, and at the
same time to create a problem for an assessment of the literary character of the *Sōkratikoi logoi*. The fragments of the mimes of Sophron
(and the scant testimonia for the mimes of Xenarchus) leave absolutely
no doubt that his representations of men and women were of lower-
class men and women, speaking in a Doric dialect of great interest to
later grammarians, and, in Greek terms, fundamentally comic characters. They can be said to represent a low representation of low characters, or, in the words of the "Tractatus Coislinianus," "the imitation of
an action that is laughable and without any grandeur."[2] Presumably,
the mimesis of Socrates and his conversations by the writers of the
Sōkratikoi logoi was on a higher level both in the object of its imitation
and in its language. But in search of the origins of the Socratic dialogue
it is well to keep in mind Aristotle's significant pairing of the Sophronic
mime and the Socratic dialogue, for this is the beginning of the tradition that associates Plato with the Sicilian mime of Sophron.

There were Socratics and Socratics. I am interested in Plato and the
associates of Socrates who composed *Sōkratikoi logoi,* or the Attic mimes

---

[2]κωμῳδία ἐστὶ μίμησις πράξεως γελοίας καὶ ἀμοίρου μεγέθους, 3.1, in the edition of
R. Janko, *Aristotle on Comedy: Towards a Reconstruction of Poetics 2* (Berkeley and Los Angeles, 1984), p. 23. Mimes are one category of dramatic or "practical" mimesis for the
"Tractatus," and diminutives such as Σωκρατίδιον (3.2.1) are a source of laughter. In *Poetics* 1449a31–32, Aristotle speaks of comedy as the representation of men of the meaner
sort but a representation that does not encompass every kind of vice (μίμησις
φαυλοτέρων, οὐ μέντοι κατὰ πᾶσαν κακίαν). For an exploration of Aristotle's opinion of
the
low character of the comedian that matched the object of his imitation, G. F. Held,
"Σπουδαῖος and Teleology in the *Poetics,*" *TAPA* 114 (1984): 159–76.

of Socrates' life and conversations. There were other "Socratics" who imitated him in another medium—that of their dress, manners, and conversation. Well before Aristotle applied the adjective Socratic to the Socratic dialogues a comic poet coined the verb "to Socratize" (σωκρατεῖν) for the followers of Socrates: they "aped the manners of Sparta, let their hair grow long, went hungry, refused to wash, 'Socratized,' and carried walking sticks."[3] Such a Socratic was Chaerephon, and Apollodorus of the *Symposium* (cf. 173d) was his fellow; Menedemus of Eretria and Epictetus and Lucian's Demonax of Athens number among their distant descendants. All of these were faithful imitators of Socrates in that they left no record of their thought in the written word, something that distinguishes them from the other Socratics with whom we are now engaged.[4]

Most of the other Socratics, both great and small, associated with Socrates during his lifetime and left memorials of his life after his death and, if we are to trust anecdotes, even when he was alive.[5] How faithful these Socratics were in their literary imitation of Socrates and his conversations is an open question, but not even the most avid biographer of biography in antiquity can make them out as Boswells to Socrates' Dr. Johnson. And we are entitled to ask if these Socratics were genuine Socratics in even their non-Socratic writings. Were Xenophon's *Anabasis* or *Cyropaedia* and Antisthenes' *Cyrus* or *Heracles* Socratic writings? Socrates appears in none of these quasi-philosophical writings (except by indirection in Xenophon's *Cyropaedia*),[6] but does his absence disqualify these writings as Socratic? Aristotle would surely have answered that it does, for the simple reason that Socrates did not figure as an object of imitation in those writers whose thought he might have influenced.

[3]πρὶν μὲν γὰρ οἰκίσαι σε τήνδε τὴν πόλιν / ἐλακωνάμανουν ἅπαντες ἄνθρωποι τότε, / ἐκόμων ἐπείνων ἐρρύπων ἐσωκράτουν / σκυτάλι᾽ ἐφόρουν, A. *Av.* 1280–83 (on Athens before Peisthetairos' foundation of Nephelokokygyia). There is also the word σωκρατίζειν, which Koerte restored in a papyrus fragment from Eupolis' *Demoi*, but in Colin Austin's new text it no longer yields these letters; cf. Eupolis fr. 99.114–17 *PCG* 5:351. For the lost participle, see Koerte in "Fragment einer Handschrift der Demen," *Hermes* 47 (1912): 291 and *SSR* 1.a.11.5 (1:5).

[4]Some of the Socratics who imitated Socrates in his manner and dress and, most important, in his decision to leave no written record of his thought are presented by Klaus Döring in *Exemplum Socratis: Studien zur Sokratesnachwirkung in der kynisch-stoischen Popularphilosophie der frühen Kaiserzeit und im frühen Christentum*, Hermes Einzelschriften 42 (Wiesbaden, 1979). Epictetus was perhaps the most impressive of these (Döring, pp. 43–79). As a consequence of his decision not to convey his thought in writing, Arrian can imitate Xenophon, one of the most important of the literary Socratics, in recording his conversations.

[5]The anecdote concerning Socrates' reaction to Plato's *Lysis* is part of the genre of anecdote in which the living character criticizes his memorialist; cf. D.L. 3.35 and A. S. Reginos, *Platonica: The Anecdotes Concerning the Life and Writings of Plato*, Columbia Studies in the Classical Tradition 3 (Leiden 1976), anecdote 17, p. 55.

[6]3.3.1.10–14 and 38–40, where he appears in the guise of an Armenian sophist.

2. Plato, The Minor Socratic

How many Socratics were there, and how many of these wrote *Sōkratikoi logoi*? In the second, enlarged edition of Gabriele Giannantoni's *Socratis et Socraticorum Reliquiae* there are now entries for some seventy Socratics. It is not surprising that Plato and Xenophon are missing from this collection. Two of the other "major" Socratics (cf. οἱ κορυφαιότατοι in D.L. 2.47), Antisthenes and Aeschines, are now represented. (Aeschines was missing from the first edition, entitled *Socraticorum Reliquiae*.) No one would have looked for the comic poets of fifth-century Athens in a *Socraticorum Reliquiae*, but in the enlarged *Socratis et Socraticorum Reliquiae* they appear along with the dramatic dialogues of Lucian in which Socrates and his companions return to the stage, as do the minor fifth-century Socratics now represented in volume 2. There are also the followers of Phaedo of Elis, Menedemus of Eretria, and Aristippus of Cyrene, who do not have separate entries.

We encounter one of the first groupings of the companions of Socrates in Plato,[7] but before he achieved his lasting fame as the most brilliant exponent of the Socratic dialogue, Plato figures as a minor Socratic. At the moment of Socrates' death and for a generation later, he was by no means the best known of the Socratics. But Plato was a presence during Socrates' life. He was evidently present in court when Socrates was tried for impiety; Socrates could point to him as one of the young Athenians he had not corrupted (*Ap.* 34a). Plato, who was twenty-eight when Socrates stood trial, is named with three other young Athenians (Theodotus, Theages, and Apollodorus) and accorded no pride of place even by his own reckoning. He is conspicuously absent from the group of faithful companions who gathered in prison for a last time on the day of Socrates' execution: Phaedo of Elis, Apollodorus, Crito and his son Critoboulus, Hermogenes, Epigenes, Aeschines, and Antisthenes. To this list Phaedo adds: "Also there were Ctesippus of the deme of Paeania and Menexenus and other Athenians. Plato, I think, was sick" (Pl. *Phd.* 59b). Counting Simmias, Cebes, and Phaedonides from Thebes, Eucleides and Terpsion from Megara, and Aristippus and Cleombrotus, who were detained on Aegina, Plato is simply one in a large group of Socratics, seventeen of whom are named by Phaedo in his narrative as being present on Socrates' last day. But Phaedo's "Plato, I think, was sick" makes it clear that he could be reasonably expected among the close companions of Socrates.

---

[7]In *SSR* 1.h.1–3 (1:343–44), Giannantoni gives some other groupings of the Socratics, but he does not include *Apology* 34a. Still another grouping is given in *SSR* 1.h.5 (D.L. 2.47).

Years after Socrates' death, when Xenophon composed his second apology for Socrates in *Memorabilia* 1.1–2, Plato does not even figure in Xenophon's list of Socrates' associates (ὁμιληταί, *Mem.* 1.2.48), which includes Crito, Chaerephon, Chaerecrates, Hermogenes, Simmias, Cebes, and Phaedonides but excludes Antisthenes and Aeschines as well as Plato and Xenophon himself—the four major literary Socratics. Plato seems to reciprocate for this glaring omission. Xenophon is never named in his dialogues, and in the *Phaedo* it is not said that "Xenophon, I believe, was with the army of Cyrus in Asia Minor." Plato, on the other hand, is mentioned once in the writings of Xenophon. In *Memorabilia* 2.6.1 he is named in passing as the brother of Glaucon, a young man in whom Socrates had taken an interest. But Xenophon also makes it clear that Socrates was interested in Glaucon for the sake of Plato. The virtually total silence of Xenophon regarding Plato and Plato's total silence regarding Xenophon are answered by the titles of some of Xenophon's Socratic dialogues that are clearly meant to rival the homonymous dialogues of Plato, such as the *Symposium* and the *Apology.*[8]

In the changing circles of the Socratics, the name of Plato does not stand out conspicuously—even in his own modest presentation of himself in dialogues where he never speaks. Plato was a Socratic and at the moment of Socrates' death a minor Socratic: he was certainly younger than one of the four Socratics who came to stand out among the Socratics later in antiquity, Antisthenes. Aeschines' dates are not fixed, but an argument can be made that he began to write Socratic dialogues before Plato or at least that he elaborated a representation of Socratic eros before Plato.[9] And we shall see that Plato does not figure in the tradition of the "first discoverer" of the dramatic rather than the narrative representation of Socrates' conversations. Simon the shoemaker, the mysterious Alexamenus of Teos, and even Xenophon all had claims

---

[8]The long tradition of the rivalry between Plato and Xenophon was inspired in part by their virtually total silence on one another and in part by the titles of Xenophon's Socratic writings that challenge comparison with Plato. Herodicus in his vituperation of Plato makes strong claims for such a rivalry (cf. Ath. 11.505c), and Diogenes Laertius devotes a paragraph to the topic in his life of Plato (D.L. 3.34; cf. 2.57). Ingemar Düring has presented Herodicus' hostile account of the relations between Plato and Xenophon in *Herodicus the Cratetean* (Stockholm, 1941), pp. 24–26. In an appendix to *SSR* (i.h. [1:358–73]), Giannantoni gives a long catalogue of the passages in the Platonic dialogues that have been spotted (by Karl Joël especially) as allusions to other Socratics. Of these, Antisthenes is clearly the most popular phantom, but Xenophon does not figure even in Giannantoni's catalogue.

[9]And it has been made persuasively by Barbara Ehlers in *Eine vorplatonische Deutung des sokratischen Eros: Der Dialog Aspasia des Sokratikers Aischines*, Zetemata 41 (Munich, 1966), and the consequences are persuasively exploited by Charles Kahn in Chapter 3 of this volume.

on the honor of inventing the type of dialogue in which Socrates' conversations are directly and "mimetically" represented; and it is quite
apparent from Aeschines' *Alcibiades* and Aristippus' mysterious *Herostrophus* that Plato was not the first to write a "narrative" dialogue.

It is also clear from the mere titles of the works of his three greatest
rivals in the genre of the Socratic dialogue that Plato's literary ambitions were limited to the dialogue form and for the most part to the
Socratic dialogue or, to speak with needed caution, the dialogues in
which Socrates is the main speaker. From the fragments of Antisthenes
alone it is very difficult to see that Socrates played a great part in the
dialogues that were the most significant portion of his vast literary production, and it would seem that Antisthenes' ethical models were not
Socrates but Odysseus, Cyrus the Great, and Heracles. Despite the an-
tique praise of his devotion to the "Socratic genre,"[10] it is not absolutely
clear that Socrates played a role in all of Aeschines' seven dialogues.
Xenophon wrote in many other genres than the dialogue or the
Socratic dialogue.

In a later age, Plato came to be considered as one of the four "major"
Socratics and the greatest of these, even as Socrates had become Platonic and was known as a philosopher mainly from the Platonic dialogues. But if we exert an effort of imagination and return to the
moment when Plato began to write, whenever that was, we realize that
the Socratic dialogue was already a recognized genre. Many of the
companions who gathered together in Socrates' prison on the day of
his execution were credited with dialogues, and some of these dialogues were Socratic dialogues in that they were—or purported to be—
records of Socrates' conversation. But it is difficult to assess how many
of these Socratics wrote *Sōkratikoi logoi* in the strict sense given this term
in Aristotle's *Poetics*—that is, dramatic representations of Socrates in
conversation and in action. Of the eighteen Socratics named by Phaedo
of Elis in Plato's *Phaedo,* nine imitated Socrates in not writing Socratic
dialogues; nine imitated Socrates in writing Socratic dialogues.

In the time of Diogenes Laertius and in the mind of Diogenes Laertius the mark of being a literary Socratic was to write dialogues. To review the nine literary Socratics we know first from Plato's *Phaedo* and
then from Diogenes in roughly Phaedo's order we can reconstruct a
late tradition of what it meant to be a literary Socratic. First, Phaedo
himself, Plato's memorialist for what was said and done during
Socrates' last day (cf. *Phd.* 58c), is given two "genuine" dialogues by Diogenes Laertius (2.105 = *SSR* 3.a.8), the *Zopyrus* and *Simon*. His *Nicias*
was disputed, as were still others. Like the great majority of Plato's
Socratic dialogues, the dialogues of Phaedo are identified by the name

---

[10]τὸ . . . ἰδίως καλούμενον εἶδος Σωκρατικόν, ps.-Demetr. *Eloc.* 297.

of Socrates' interlocutor rather than by the subject of their conversation. Aulus Gellius knew of readers of his dialogues and might have read some himself. He certainly knew that they involved Socrates ("sermones eius de Socrate admodum elegantes legunter," *NA* 2.18 = *SSR* 3.a.3). The only dialogue ever identified by a quotation is Phaedo's *Zopyrus*.[11] It begins with a dramatic address of Socrates: "Socrates, people say that the youngest son of the king gave a lion cub as a gift to a friend" (*SSR* 3.a.11). It clearly reflects a theme common among the first generation of the Socratics—a fascination with Persia and its empire.

Phaedo names ten Athenians (ἐπιχώριοι) as present at Socrates' death, and there were still others he does not name. Three of those Phaedo names wrote Socratic dialogues: Crito, Aeschines, and Antisthenes. Plato, who was ill, makes eleven and four. For Crito we have no fragments, only titles. Diogenes Laertius speaks of a single volume containing seventeen dialogues. Only one has a personal name as a title. This is *Protagoras: or, The Statesman* (D.L. 2.121 = *SSR* 6.b.42). There is also the curious detail in the Suda concerning Crito, "The philosopher": ἔγραψε Σωκράτους ἀπολογίαν, "He wrote a defense of Socrates" (*SSR* 6.b.43). Since there is no definite article, this must mean that Crito was thought to have written an apology for Socrates. If this is the case, we might have an explanation for the perplexing plural in the opening of Xenophon's *Apology*: γεγράφασι μὲν οὖν . . . καὶ ἄλλοι, "Others have written [a defense] as well" (1). Plato's *Crito* is the only dialogue that can qualify as Crito's apology for Socrates, since Crito was the only Socratic present at this conversation in which Socrates justified his decision to stay in prison. If this is the case and if the notice that Crito wrote an "apology" for Socrates is based on the conjecture that Plato derived his knowledge of Crito's conversation with Socrates from Crito, the plural "others" in Xenophon remains a mystery unless it was intended to deflect attention from Plato. In any case, the devoted Crito can now teach us nothing about the origins of Socratic dialogue.

We will return to Aeschines, who, after Plato, Xenophon—and Aristophanes—is the only author of Socratic dialogues whose writings can offer us a glimpse of his talents. It is enough to commemorate now some of his titles: *Callias* (the wealthy Athenian in whose house Plato's *Protagoras* is set), *Aspasia* (the companion and mistress of Pericles, who inspired both Plato's *Menexenus* and Antisthenes' *Aspasia*), and *Alcibiades*—another favorite of the literary Socratics.[12] Antisthenes is a more

---

[11] *SSR* 3.a.9–11. Seneca quotes a striking sentence from a dialogue of Phaedo's in which Phaedo artfully compared the insensible effect of the words and very presence of the wise to the bite of an insect that is not felt and is recognized only when a welt appears (*Ep.* 94.41 = *SSR* 3.a.12).

[12] Other than Aeschines' *Alcibiades*, we have an *Alcibiades* from Antisthenes (*SSR* 5.a.198–202; cf. 5.a.141) and an *Alcibiades* from Eucliedes (*SSR* 3.a.10) and Phaedo (*SSR*

difficult case. Despite the evidence of proper names as titles for his dialogues (an *Aspasia*, an *Alcibiades*, and a *Menexenus*), Socrates' name is hardly mentioned in later accounts of his dialogues; but we do have his *Sathon*—or *The Pecker*—a dialogue whose title is an obscene pun on the name Plato and the unique Socratic dialogue in which Plato might have played a role.

From this point in Phaedo's listing we lose titles but gain in the number of books attributed to Socrates' companions. For Simmias of Thebes we have twenty-three dialogues in a single roll, all on various topics and none with a personal name as its title (D.L. 2.123). His fellow countryman, Cebes, gives us only three (D.L. 2.125). We then travel west to Megara, where we encounter Eucliedes, who is given six dialogues by Diogenes (2.108 = *SSR* 2.a.10), three or four of which seem at home— if only as titles—among the dialogues of the first generation of the Socratics: an *Aeschines*, a *Crito*, an *Alcibiades*, and an *Eroticus*, but in our fragments the only voice we hear is that of Eucliedes.

We then cross the Saronic Gulf to Aegina, where we find Aristippus, who was later reviled for being there and not in Athens and in Socrates' prison on the day of his death. Most of his writings are now no more than titles indicating an interest in a great variety of philosophical topics addressed to a variety of persons, including Socrates.[13] He is credited with some twenty-five dialogues, written in both Attic and Doric. His dialogues in Doric are surely ancient inventions,[14] but the dialect does connect with the tradition linking Sophron with the *Sōkratikoi logoi*. Among his titles there are very few proper names: a *Hermeias*, an *Artabazus*, and a *Philomelus*. One anecdote is revealing for his credit in antiquity as a writer of *Sōkratikoi logoi;* Dionysios the Elder was said to have kept him under house arrest because he had become an expert in Socratic conversations.[15]

3.a.8). There are the two dialogues of that title in the Platonic corpus, and if either one or both are spurious, we have still more Socratic dialogues either by Plato and an anonymous hand or by anonymous hands. Alcibiades looms large in Plato's *Symposium* (212b–223a), where his award of a crown to Socrates seems to represent Plato's version of Socrates' award of a trophy to Alcibiades in Antisthenes' *Alcibiades*. The treatment of Alcibiades among the Socratics has been explored by Heinrich Dittmar in *Aischines von Sphettos: Studien zur Literaturgeschichte der Sokratiker, Untersuchungen und Fragmente,* Philologische Untersuchungen 21 (Berlin, 1912), pp. 65–177.

[13]Listed in D.L. 2.84–85 = *SSR* 6.a.144.

[14]The single example of a writing with some Doric forms is *SSR* 6.a.225 = Socratic Epistle 16 Orelli (= 16 in L. Köhler, *Die Briefe des Sokrates und der Sokratiker,* Philologus Supplementband 20.2 [Leipzig, 1928]).

[15]λόγων ἐπιμελητὴν τῶν Σωκρατικῶν, *SSR* 4.a.222. The term *epimelētēs* is the correct one for such a Socratic; it describes Apollodorus at the beginning of Plato's *Symposium* (172a, c). It does not mean, of course, that he wrote these conversations down, any more than did Apollodorus.

One of his fragments, from a Syriac source, represents a dialogue between Socrates and an otherwise unknown interlocutor by the name of Herostrophus.[16] Frigid is perhaps too warm a word to describe the literary style of the exchange between Herostrophus and Socrates, but we must judge Aristippus' style at two removes, as the beginning of this dialogue has been translated from Greek into Syriac, and from Syriac into Italian. Even so, the form of this dialogue and its hypothesis are of some interest. Herostrophus has apparently been brought to Athens by Socrates' reputation, as was Aristippus himself (cf. D.L. 2.65: ἀφιγμένος δ' 'Αθήναζε . . . κατὰ κλέος Σωκράτους). The dialogue is a dialogue with only two participants and is narrative in form. We must have its opening words: "Socrates says: 'Herostrophus, what is the occasion that has brought you to me?'" The present tense is odd for a narrative dialogue; I know of no other examples. Herostrophus replies that it is Socrates' fame as a philosopher. It is very unlikely that the *Herostrophus* is actually the work of Aristippus, but our Syriac dialogue gives us still another bit of evidence for the fascination the Socratic dialogue held for ancient writers and rhetoricians.[17]

We have scarcely any evidence for reported conversation from the other fragments of Aristippus. In some of the fragments of his *On the Sensuality of Our Ancestors* (Περὶ παλαιᾶς τρυφῆς) a sentence of Xenophon is reported directly, but we do not know in what context.[18] All that can be concluded from our very meager evidence for Aristippus as an author of *Sōkratikoi logoi* is that the form of his twenty-five dialogues was so indistinct that it was lost in transmission and that his *Herostrophus* (for which we have no evidence beyond its Syriac translation) does not lay a claim on the title as the first dramatic rendition of Socrates' conversations. Indeed, it is likely to be a production from much later in antiquity.

We return to Athens and Plato, "who was ill," Xenophon, who was with the Greek mercenaries in the defeated army of Cyrus in Asia Mi-

---

[16]*SSR* 4.a.159. The fragment was first edited by P. A. Lagarde, *Analecta Syriaca* (Leipzig, 1858), pp. 158–67. There is a German translation of this dialogue by V. Ryssel, "Der pseudosokratische Dialog über die Seele," *RhM* 48 (1893): 175–95. In his commentary on the Greek original implied by the Syriac, Ryssel makes it abundantly clear why this fiction must be post-Aristotelian. His full version of the Syriac original also makes it clear that there are three more narrative intrusions after the introduction (all in the past tense); cf. pp. 186, 187, and 195. Giannantoni first published a partial Italian translation in *I Cirenaici* (Florence, 1958), pp. 265–69.

[17]A very recent entry in the catalogue of pseudepigraphic Socratic dialogues is Köln papyrus 205, edited by M. Gronewald in *Kölner Papyri* 5 (1985): 33–53. Gronewald dates the script of this papyrus to the third century B.C., its language to the fourth. We have here an apparently dramatic dialogue between Socrates and a single companion set in the period between Socrates' condemnation and execution. The conversation centers on the fear of death. Gronewald suggests that it might originate in one of the Cyrenaics— possibly Hegesias "Peisithanatos" (p. 50 n.4).

[18]D.L. 2.49 = *SSR* 4.a.154.

nor, and, finally, Simon, who, if he was not dead, was working at his last in Athens. This Simon seems to have had a shop in the agora of ancient Athens. The shop has been excavated, and Simon has been identified as its proprietor, but we do not have a single word from any of his dialogues.[19] He seems to have recorded Socrates' conversations in a book of dialogues that he—or others—called *Cobbler's Talk* (or perhaps *Conversations at the Cobbler's Shop*). Plato's Socrates is notorious for his interest in cobblers, but none of his dialogues and none of the *Sōkratikoi logoi* (except Xenophon's *Memorabilia* 4.2.1) have their setting at a cobbler's shop.

Diogenes Laertius tells us virtually all we know of Simon and preserves the learned tradition that he was first to record Socrates' conversations in the form of a dramatic dialogue (if this is the meaning of the curious expression πρῶτος διελέχθη in 2.123). His thirty-three dialogues were contained in a single roll, and they must have been short. Like the works of many other Socratics, and like the conversations recorded in Xenophon's *Memorabilia,* his dialogues were more easily described by the subject of the conversation recorded. As the true inventor of the Socratic dialogue in its purely mimetic and dramatic form, he seems to have preferred the immediacy of the spoken word to the editorial presentation of a conversation that has to be recalled either by another or by Socrates himself.

3. The "Invention" of the Socratic Dialogue

There was, of course, a contest over the title of the inventor of the Socratic dialogue as a literary genre. Diogenes Laertius recognizes the claims of four contestants. Three of these are Socratics. The fourth is a

---

[19]The archaeological evidence has created quite a stir among archaeologists, but not yet among students of ancient philosophy. There are a number of fragments of evidence pointing to the activity of a fifth-century cobbler by the name of Simon just outside the Agora: the base of a black-glazed cylix identified by a graffito as the property of Simon; a number of hobnails and eyelets of bone for fastening boots discovered in a shop in a triangular complex near the Tholos. But the connection between this drinking cup, these hobnails, and the Simon associated with Socrates is made at best out of a gossamer web of hope. This material is illustrated in M. Lang, *Socrates in the Agora* (Excavations of the Athenian Agora, Picture Book no. 17 (Princeton, 1978), fig. 13; and J. M. Camp, *The Athenian Agora: Excavations in the Heart of Classical Athens* (London, 1986), pp. 145–47. The finds are reported by H. A. Thompson, "Excavations in the Athenian Agora: 1953," *Hesperia* 23 (1954): 51–54, and "Excavations in the Athenian Agora: 1954," *Hesperia* 24 (1955): 54, and *The Athenian Agora*[2] (Athens, 1962), p. 112. The cylix base is on display in case 38 of the Agora Museum (p22998). Only recently has a student of ancient philosophy hailed this distant evidence; cf. R. S. Brumbaugh, "Simon and Socrates," *AP* 11 (1991): 151–52. Ronald F. Hock, writing in 1976, could dispense with the archaeological evidence and concentrate on the Cynic appropriation of Simon in the Socratic letters:

mystery. One claim is that of the cobbler Simon, as we have just seen: "He was the first, it is related, to record Socrates' conversations in pure dialogue form" (οὗτος, φασί, πρῶτος διελέχθη τοὺς λόγους τοὺς Σωκρατικούς (D.L. 2.123 = SSR 6.b.87). This tradition seems to recognize tacitly the claim of some anonymous writer to be the first to write narratives of Socratic conversations. The second claimant recognized by Diogenes is Alexamenus of Teos: "They say that Zeno of Elea was first to write dialogues. But Aristotle in the first book of his *On Poets* says that it was Alexamenus of Styra or Teos. My authority is Favorinus in his *Memorabilia*. But in my view Plato ought to be awarded the prize of priority both for discovery and for the beauty of the genre, since he brought it to its perfection" (D.L. 3.48).[20] Athenaeus is an indirect witness to this same tradition, and he produces a quotation from Aristotle's dialogue *On Poets* to make a point against Plato.[21] His text is difficult, but its sense is that Alexamenus of Teos was the first to write Socratic dialogues and that these were a form of mimesis in prose—like the mimes of Sophron. We now have the claim confirmed and disputed by a literary treatise from Oxyrhynchus, where we read that [Plato] imitated Sophron the μιμογράφος in the dramatic character of his dialogues, and are warned against the malicious claim of Aristotle (in the first book of his "Poetics") that before Plato dramatic dialogues were composed by Alexamenus—of Teos. The terms of this discussion of mimesis derive ultimately from Socrates' discussion of the style of poetic narrative in book 3 of the *Republic* (392d), and they will claim our attention later. The last claimant is Xenophon, whose *Memorabilia* Diogenes took to be the first publication of the transcripts of Socrates' conversations (2.48).

4. Syracusan Mimes and Sicilian Comedy

But the fundamental question posed by the genre of the *Sōkratikoi logoi* is not who claims the honor of having first invented it, for we learn nothing from the answer Alexamenus of Teos or Simon the cobbler. We should ask rather what genre of Greek literature the *Sōkratikoi logoi* were modeled on. In the case of Plato's Socratic dialogues, the answer

---

"Simon the Shoemaker as an Ideal Cynic," *GRBS* 17 (1976): 41–54. Interestingly, the tradition of simple Simon the copyist of philosophical conversations held in his own shop is reproduced in the case of Homer the copyist of anecdotes in the shop of a leatherworker in the Herodotean life of Homer; cf. T. W. Allen, ed., *Homeri Opera* (Oxford, 1912), 5:197.114–16.

[20] It seems to have been the tendency of the biographers to make the innovator in a genre its "inventor"; cf. J. A. Fairweather, "Fiction in the Biographies of Ancient Writers," *Ancient Society* 5 (1974): 264–65.

[21] Fr. 205 Rose.

of the ancient critics who asked this question was clearly Sophron. Aristotle had made the connection between the *Sōkratikoi logoi* and the Syracusan mimes of Sophron and his son Xenarchus long before the anecdotal tradition connecting Plato and Sophron had come to life, both in the *Poetics* (1, 1447b9) and in his early dialogue *On Poets*, where we find a statement of one of the interlocutors (preserved for better or worse in Athenaeus) who draws the following inference: "Should we not then deny that the so-called *Mimes* of Sophron, which are not even in meter, are conversations and that the imitations [μιμήσεις] of Alexamenus of Teos, which are the first Socratic conversations that have been written down, are conversations?"[22] The connection between Plato and Sophron seems to have been first drawn by Duris of Samos, who studied with Theophrastus. In one of his derisory remarks about Plato he claims that the great philosopher had Sophron's mimes constantly in his hands.[23] The contrast between Plato the philosopher and the low mimes of Sophron is obviously meant to humble Plato by bringing him ignominiously to earth. The anecdote is retold by a number of authors, and it gains a number of vivid details as it grows. In one version, Plato kept the mimes of Sophron under his pillow even in the last year of his life.[24]

But the accretion that attracts attention is the statement that Plato used the mimes of Sophron as the literary model for the dramatic character portrayal in his own dialogues—καὶ ἠθοποιῆσαι πρὸς αὐτῶν.[25] These fables present in the emblematic form of ancient anecdotes a judgment on the literary character of the Platonic dialogue. The Platonic dialogues can be described as imitations of human characters in

---

[22]οὐκοῦν οὐδὲ ἐμμέτρους τοὺς καλουμένους Σώφρονος μίμους μὴ φῶμεν εἶναι λόγους καὶ μιμήσεις, ἢ τοὺς Ἀλεξαμενοῦ τοῦ Τηΐου τοὺς πρώτους γραφέντας τῶν Σωκρατικῶν διαλόγων; Ath. 11.505a = Aris. fr. 72 Rose. Michael Haslam discusses the many difficulties of this text (which are not at bottom textual) in "Plato, Sophron, and the Dramatic Dialogue," *BICS* 19 (1972): 17–18. Since Aristotle's dialogue *On Poets* is itself dramatic, Otto Jahn's emendation of οὐκοῦν in a question for ὄκουν in a statement helps recover the sense of the passage; cf. J. D. Denniston, *The Greek Particles*[2] (Oxford, 1959), pp. 430–35. The pairing of *mimous/logous* (Sophron) and *mimēseis/logous* (Alexamenus) reveals Aristotle's early engagement with the critical habit of restricting mimesis to poetry. If there can be conversations that are mimetic and mimes that are conversational, mimesis cannot be restricted to poetry; cf. *Poet.* 1, 1447b13: οἱ ἄνθρωποί γε συνάπτοντες τῷ μέτρῳ τὸ ποιεῖν. The restriction of poetry to meter seems to be the position of the interlocutor in Aristotle's *On Poets*.

[23]Ath. 11.504b = *FGrHist* 11.a.76.

[24]Where, perhaps, they kept company with the writing tablet containing a number of versions of the beginning of the *Republic;* cf. Quint. *Inst.* 1.10.17. The full tradition is set out by Hermann Reich in *Der Mimus: Ein litterarentwickelungsgeschichtlicher Versuch* (Berlin, 1903), pp. 381–82, as in Reginos (above, note 5), pp. 174–76.

[25]D.L. 3.18, repeated in Tzetz. *Chil.* 10.809 and 11.8–10, in the edition of P. A. M. Leone (Naples, 1968).

prose that are not narrative but are articulated in question and an-swer—or dialogue. Where, then, the ancient critic asked, did Plato dis-cover the model for them? He found his answer in the mimes of Sophron, which are dramatic imitations of a variety of human charac-ter types. This genealogy of the literary form of the Platonic dialogue is reinforced by the historical connection of Plato with Syracuse and the court of Dionysius I and II.[26] But this connection presents a curious historical problem. Plato first visited Sicily and Syracuse in ca. 390–387. His return to Athens in 387 would be the date of his introduction of the indigenous mimes of Sophron to an Athenian audience.[27] But if this is the case, he would have gone without a model for any of the dra-matic dialogues he wrote during the twelve years after Socrates' death. The anecdotes of Plato and Sophron make pretty reading and difficult literary history. They have a hostile beginning in Duris of Samos, but as literary criticism these anecdotes neglect much more than they ex-plain. If the Sicilian mimes of Sophron provide a model for Plato's dra-matic dialogues, they also make 387 a terminus post quem for dramatic dialogues such as the *Lysis*. And this literary history neglects the fact that Aeschines had already been writing dramatic dialogues.

Anecdotal criticism also disregards the fact that Sophron imitated not contemporaries but humble, and therefore, comic, types. His mimes divide into two natural categories: male and female; and their titles are perhaps as revealing of their character as the fragments col-lected under them. We have evidence for the following: *Sorceress* (or *Healer*), *Mother-in-law*, *Women at the Isthmian Games*, *The Tuna Fishers*, and *The Fisher and the Farmer*. These Sicilian mimes stand a world apart from the world captured and recalled in the *Sōkratikoi logoi*, some of which are named after the contemporaries of Socrates who figure as his interlocutors.

There are, indeed, proper names in Sophron, and more of women than of men: Rongka (no. 3, p. 67), Mormolyka (no. 7, p. 77), Koikoa (no. 23, p. 89), and Physka (no. 31, p. 92); Kothonias, the drunkard (no. 55, p. 101), and Boulias, the orator (no. 117, p. 125), are names for men, as is Trellon (no. 137, p. 131). It has been thought that Myrilla (no. 134) was a nickname for the architect Demokopos, but this is cer-

---

[26]The word *form* translates the ἰδέα or εἶδος of the ancient critics; cf. D.L. 3.37 and 48; Ath. 11.505c (Herodicus); and p.s.-Demetr. *Eloc.* 297.

[27]By this anecdotal tradition, Plato brought up the books of Sophron when they had fallen out of fashion in Sicily and was the first to introduce them to Athens; cf. D.L. 3.18; Tzetz. *Chil.* 11.1–10 and 37–41. For the other books Plato shipped to Athens from Sicily (Philoaus, a collection of Pythagorean writings, and Timaeus), cf. Reginos (above, note 5), pp. 169–74 and 179.

tainly not the case.[28] The names in Sophron are the names of types in his commedia dell'arte.

Very little consecutive text survives from his mimes. Their dialect interested later grammarians, and their gastronomy provided a philological delicatessen for Athenaeus. So we are left with the word ψίν (no. 101, p. 120), proverbs, and words for fish (such as βάτις, no. 72, p. 111). Of the fragments from both the female and the male mimes, only two show dialogue (no. 31, p. 92 and no. 73, p. 112), and in these the speaking parts are distributed as A and B. Only one of these (no. 31) involves question and answer.

The literary judgment conveyed by the anecdotes connecting the Platonic dialogue and the Sicilian mimes of Sophron and Xenarchus sheds no light on the literary character of either the Platonic dialogue in particular or the *Sōkratikoi logoi* in general, but it does reveal what a difficult task it was for ancient critics to discover the literary ancestor of the *Sōkratikoi logoi*.

There was also the tradition taking the Platonic dialogue back to the comedies of the Syracusan Epicharmus. It seems to derive from Alkimus of Sicily, and Diogenes Laertius produces a number of passages of Epicharmus that illustrate the doctrinal dependence of the Athenian philosopher on the Sicilian comic poet.[29] Here the question of literary genre does not arise; Alkimus was interested only in Plato's plagiarism. What we know of both Epicharmus and the later forgeries that went under his name makes him an implausible model for the Platonic dialogue or for the *Sōkratikoi logoi*. He is a comic poet, and like all comic poets he is mimetic and dramatic in his style, but he is metrical and Doric. He is also generic, and some of his comedies have mythological plots.[30]

There is, as one would expect, some question and answer, and for this reason Epicharmus figures in Rudolf Hirzel's *Der Dialog*,[31] but, as in the case of Sophron, questions and answers must be divided anonymously between A and B. Plato clearly knew Epicharmus, and he re-

---

[28]Cf. A. Olivieri, *Frammenti della commedia greca e del mimo nella Sicilia e nella Magna Grecia*[2], Colanna di studi greci 5 (Naples, 1946), 2:130–31.

[29]D.L. 3.9–17 = *FGrHist* 560.F.6 (and Fr. 23 B 1–6 DK). For Alkimus, we have the study of K. Gaiser, "Die Platonreferate des Alkimos bei Diogenes Laërtios (3.3–17)," in *Zetesis: Album amicorum door vrienden en collegas aangeboden aan Prof. Dr. E. de Strycker* (Antwerp and Utrecht, 1973), pp. 61–79; and H. Dörrie, *Der Platonismus in der Antike* (Stuttgart-Bad Cannstatt, 1987), 1:308–18. M. Gigante, "Epicarmo, Pseudo-Epicarmo e Platone," *PP* 8 (1953): 161–75, has provided a valuable study of Plato's knowledge of Epicharmus.

[30]As does his "Odysseus, the Deserter," in D. L. Page, *Select Papyri*, vol. 3, *Literary Papyri* (Cambridge, Mass. and London, 1941), no. 37, pp. 194–95 = no. 50 Olivieri (1: 36–39) and "Pyrrha and Prometheus," nos. 61–69 Olivieri (1: 42–45).

[31]*Ein literarhistorischer Versuch* (Leipzig, 1895), vol. 1: 20–26.

fers to him by name (as in *Theaetetus* 152d–e and *Gorgias* 505e); he also clearly knew Sophron, and he refers to him by allusion (as in *Republic* 5, 451c and possibly in 10, 606c). For our limited purposes his references to Epicharmus are of no great interest. Plato knew and appreciated the comic poet. But his allusions to Sophron are worth attention. His first allusion to Sophron in the *Republic* is indicative of Plato's conception of the character of his own dramatic dialogue. As Socrates moves from the topic of the training of the male guardians to the topic of the training of the female guardians he describes his project in terms of the division of the Sophronic mime: τάχα δὲ οὕτως ἂν ὀρθῶς ἔχοι, μετὰ ἀνδρεῖον δρᾶμα παντελῶς διαπερανθὲν τὸ γυναικεῖον αὖ περαίνειν, "Perhaps this would be the best course: to go through with the female drama, once we have concluded the male" (5, 451c). His language not only recognizes the distinction between the male and female mimes of Sophron; it reminds us that it is possible to see the proposals and the very style of the *Republic* itself as comic and dramatic.[32]

5. Attic Mimes of Socrates

The only genre of poetry known to me that offers us a clear model for the *Sōkratikoi logoi* and the mimesis of the conversations of a contemporary historical character like Socrates is Attic comedy. I will offer a specimen from "a certain comic poet." Socrates is addressing a pupil, and a part of the comic incongruity of this exchange must come from the fact that Socrates' pupil is an older man, not one of the young and wealthy Athenians with whom Socrates liked to associate:

Soc. Now I want to ask you a few short questions, to see if you have a good memory.
Pupil. In the name of Zeus, I have a good memory when it comes to one thing: when someone owes me money, I never forget. But just the opposite happens when I am in trouble and owe money. Then my mind's a sieve.
Soc. Tell me now: do you have any talents as a speaker?
Pupil. No talent there, but I'm brilliant as a thief.
Soc. But how will you manage to learn anything?
Pupil. No problem, I'd do brilliantly.
(Ar. *Nub.* 482–88)

[32]As Socrates recognizes as he anticipates one of the three waves of laughter that threaten to swamp his proposals, and as the plot of Aristophanes' *Ecclesiazusae* (of 392) makes manifest. Arlene W. Saxonhouse offers an excellent analysis of one of the facets of the comedy of Socrates' proposals in her "Comedy in Callipolis: Animal Imagery in the *Republic*," *APSR* 72 (1978): 888–901.

Here we have what must be our first example of the imitation of *Sōkratikoi logoi*. It comes from Aristophanes' *Clouds*, which was produced in the Greater Dionysia of 423, when Socrates was about forty-five, but which we know from its second production and second edition, for which we have no date. The character of Aristophanes' representation of Socratic questioning coheres with what we know of the character of his conversations rendered by the Socratics who wrote later. Socrates operates by question and answer rather than by long epideictic speeches; he prefers βραχυλογία and is concerned with the quickness to learn and the memories of his would-be associates.³³

Question and answer is a mode of discourse that continues throughout the *Clouds*. Socrates is not always cast in the dominant role of questioner. In *Clouds* 373–411 it is Strepsiades who questions Socrates about the divinity of the clouds, and in the rest of the dialogue there are two later scenes that involve Socrates and his pupil Strepsiades in question and answer.³⁴ One of the striking features of our first exhibit of the *Sōkratikoi logoi* on the comic stage (*Nub.* 482–88) is that this interrogation involves not only question and answer but a trial of character. In posing his questions to Strepsiades, Socrates is more concerned with coming to an understanding of Strepsaides' character than he is with finding answers to questions that genuinely perplex him. Indeed, his questions do not involve any issue larger than Strepsiades' memory and verbal abilities. In asking these questions, he is following the instructions of the clouds, who ask him to stir his intellectuals and test his character: διακίνει τὸν νοῦν αὐτοῦ καὶ τῆς γνώμης ἀποπειρῶ (477). Kenneth Dover has aptly called this Socrates' "tutorial" method.³⁵ The term *apopeirasthai* does not seem to occur in just this sense in the other

---

³³Socrates' preference for a dialogue in which he asks the questions and his interlocutor is maneuvered into a position of answering them is the "customary procedure" of Socrates in Plato's *Apology* (19c), and it is illustrated in the *Apology* itself by Socrates' interrogations of Callias, Apollo, and Meletus (20a–c; 21b; cf. 23b and 24c–27e), as well as by the "conversation" Socrates has with the members of the jury who had voted to acquit him (39e). This manner is illustrated most vividly in Plato's Socratic dialogues. I would call attention to *Symposium* 194d and Socrates' interrogatory of Agathon (199c–201c) and Diotima's very similar interrogatory of Socrates (201d–208b). The choice of question and answer over a long and uninterrupted epideictic display is offered in *Protagoras* 329b and 337a–338a, *Gorgias* 448d and 449c, and *Republic* 1, 337a. Quickness to learn and the capacity to retain what is learned are the main requirements of the philosophical nature; cf. *Chrm.* 159e; *Meno* 88b; *Rep.* 6,486c–487a and 494b (as well as *Leg.* 4, 709e); and Xen. *Mem.* 4.1.2.

³⁴These come in 635–99, where Socrates examines Strepsiades on crucial distinctions such as that between the genders cock and hen—a lesson Strepsiades actually remembers and applies in his Socratic interrogation of Pasias at the end of the dialogue (1246–51); and in 723–90, where Socrates asks Strepsiades for his thoughts after their indoor session offstage in the φροντιστήριον.

³⁵In his edition of Aristophanes' *Clouds* (Oxford, 1968), p. 34.

Socratics, although there are passages in Aeschines and Xenophon that obviously show Socrates interrogating his interlocutor's character rather than his knowledge. In Plato, though, who would have known the *Clouds* only as a text (or possibly in its second production), the term occurs in exactly the sense of *Clouds* 477. In the *Theaetetus*, the young Theaetetus responds to Socrates' questioning by saying that he feels that Socrates is trying to test him; and in the *Protagoras*, the young Socrates responds to the older Protagoras in much the same way.[36]

In the *Clouds*, Socrates does not appear alone. In his *phrontistērion* are to be found Chaerephon and their pupils. Socrates and Chaerephon do not appear again in the comedies of Aristophanes, but they are spoken of in his later comedies. We have noticed already the characterization of Socrates' disciples in *Birds* 1280–84.[37] Later in the *Birds* an unwashed Socrates is to be espied in a marsh near the land of the Skiapodes, where he calls souls up from Hades in the infernal company of Chaerephon, "the bat" (1553–55 and 1564). There is no mention of Socratic dialogue here, but in the *Frogs*, of nearly a decade later (405), Socratic dialogue is recalled for perhaps the last time in Aristophanes:

> χαρίεν οὖν μὴ Σωκράτει   1491
> παρακαθήμενον λαλεῖν,
> ἀποβαλόντα μουσικὴν
> τά τε μέγιστα παραλιπόντα
> τῆς τραγῳδικῆς τέχνης.   1495
> τὸ δ' ἐπὶ σεμνοῖσιν λόγοισι
> καὶ σκαριφησμοῖσι λήρων
> διατριβὴν ἀργὸν ποιεῖσθαι,
> παραφρονοῦντος ἀνδρός.

Life is bliss when you are not seated next to Socrates,
running off at the mouth; when you have cast away Music and Culture;
when you have left behind the grand speeches and attire of the
Tragic Art. But it is the life of a lunatic to spend your time
doing nothing but mouthing high faluting words and picking at lint.

The chorus sing these lyrics immediately after Dionysus has declared Aeschylus victor in the tragic contest in the society of dead poets. They connect Socrates with Euripides in an association that is both long-

---

[36]Cf. *Th.* 154e and 157c; and *Pr.* 331b and 349c, where it is the "young" Socrates who realizes that his mettle is being tested. This test of character, which is a preliminary to a test of a student's capacity for philosophy, is illustrated by Socrates' questioning of Alcibiades in Aeschines' *Alcibiades* frs. 7 and 9 (Dittmar = *SSR* 6.a.48 and 50) and by Socrates' test of Euthydemus in Xenophon's *Memorabilia* (4.2).

[37]This passage from the *Birds* now figures as a witness for Socrates in *SSR* 1.a.4.

standing and significant. The picture of Socrates, seated on a bench, perhaps in a gymnasium,[38] speaking to a single companion, is a familiar one. The ludicrous subjects of Socrates' conversation are vaguely suggested: he has thrown over the great and weighty matters of Aeschylean tragedy and of old Athenian culture in general and has turned to idle and indolent conversation. The phrase by which Aristophanes conveys the nature of his conversation is *skariphēsmoisi lērōn* (1497). *Lēros* and *lērein* are terms familiar from the *Clouds* and congenial as descriptions of Socrates' talk;[39] the other term, obviously a comic inversion of *semnoisin logoisi* (1496), is difficult to decipher, but it might mean "chicken scratching" or, as W. B. Stanford would have it, "verbal scratchifications."[40]

An illustration of the kind of twaddle Socrates engaged in—as his conversations were represented by a comic poet—comes from an earlier scene from the *Frogs*, when Euripides begins to defend his claim on Dionysus' consideration as a tragic poet (971–79). He had brought his Athenian audience to expose their everyday life to shrewd and penetrating questions. Λογισμός and σκέψις are his contributions to the tragic art; before it had not been philosophical. Aeschylus has no difficulty in putting these contributions into comic terms:

> Where oh where are my pitchers gone?
> Where is the maid who hath betrayed
> My heads of fish to the garbage trade?
> Where are the pots of yesteryear?
> Where the garlic of yesterday?
>   (*Ran.* 978–79)[41]

Still other comic poets were aware of the rich potential Socrates provided for a burlesque of intellectual life in Athens of the 420s. These poets produced their plays in the decade when the first writers of *Sōkratikoi logoi* were old enough to attend the dramatic festivals of Athens. Almost all of our fragments from the plays in which Socrates either appeared on stage or was spoken of by actors on stage come from

---

[38]The *Alcibiades* of Aeschines begins with Socrates narrating to an audience unknown his conversation with Alcibiades: ἐκαθήμεθα μὲν ἐπὶ τῶν θάκων ἐν Λυκείῳ, οὗ οἱ ἀθλοθέται τὸν ἀγῶνα διατιθέασιν, p.s.-Demet. *Eloc.* 205 = fr. 1 Dittmar = *SSR* 6.a.43. Parallels are to be found in Plato *Lysis* 203a–b; *Euthydemus* 271a and 303b, imitated in *Axiochus* 366e and *Eryxias* 397c.

[39]Cf. *Nub.* 359; *Ran.* 809 and 1005 (of Euripides' twaddle); and Pl. *Chm.* 176a and *Th.* 176d (for Socrates' description of the impression his conversation might make on his younger interlocutors).

[40]In his edition of Aristophanes' *Frogs* (London, 1958), p. 198.

[41]Lines 981–91, represented in part by the perfect translation of Richmond Lattimore, *Aristophanes: The Frogs* (Ann Arbor, 1962), p. 63.

Diogenes Laertius, who evidently had in hand a work devoted to the topic of Socrates κωμῳδοποιούμενος.

Socrates *kōmōidopoioumenos* is, I would argue, significant for the history of the *Sōkratikoi logoi* as they are to be placed in the context of ancient literary genres. The Attic comic poets of the 420s produced low and ludicrous imitations of Socrates made ridiculous; and, as Plato knew, they did manage to capture the cruder and most apparent features of his complex physiognomy. There is an anecdote in Aelian that Socrates stood up silently in the Theater of Dionysus during a production of the *Clouds* as if to proclaim: "I, this man standing before you in the audience, am Socrates—not that buffoon on stage in the comedy of Aristophanes" (*SSR* 1.a.29). But in the play it seems that Aristophanes did not need to fashion a portrait mask for Socrates; he already had ready the mask of silene. Antisthenes, Aeschines, Xenophon, and Plato were all Athenians, and before any of these—the greatest exponents of the *Sōkratikoi logoi* in the fourth century—wrote their dialogues, they had seen—or could read—the Attic forerunners of their own imitations of Socrates in conversation and in action. It is significant that in the later biographical tradition a cobbler claimed the honor of creating a mime out of Socratic conversations and that the one influence claimed for Plato in his *Sōkratikoi logoi* was the low-life mime of Sophron. In his appearance, as in his conversations, there was something fundamentally comic about Socrates. But we tend to forget that there was not only a Plato who was a comic poet and the contemporary of Socrates; there is something comic about the Platonic dialogues themselves. Plato, who was credited with writing comedy and with sleeping in a very crowded bed with copies of Aristophanes' plays under his pillow, was well aware of the comic potential of the outlandish object of his imitation. His style and the style of other literary Socratics can be properly compared to the colloquial grace of the Attic comic poets and their elegant humor. Cicero appreciated this: he speaks of a playful genre of rhetoric that ancient comedy and the Socratics shared "iocandi genus . . . elegans, urbanum, ingeniosum, facetum, quo genere non modum Plautus noster et Atticorum antiqua comoedia, sed etiam philosophorum Socraticorum libri referti sunt," "A mode of eloquence . . . [that is] elegant, urbane, fanciful, and witty, a mode that informs not only our Roman Plautus and the Old Comedy of Attica, but which fills the books of the Socratic philosophers" (*Off* 1.29.104 = *SSR* 1.h.21).

6. History and Tragedy

When assessing the writings of the literary Socratics and in attempting to recognize the distinguishing characteristics of the genre which they created and in which they wrote, the overwhelming temptation is to disregard questions of literary models or priority of discovery and to concentrate on Socrates and the immediacy of his conversations and confrontations with his contemporaries. In the dramatic dialogues of Plato in particular, we find ourselves seated at a drama that develops immediately and spontaneously before our eyes. The illusion this drama creates was articulated in the symbolic form of literary anecdotes in antiquity: Simon the cobbler took notes on Socrates' conversations at his shop, not as a stenographer but soon after they had ended (D.L. 2.122 = SSR 6.b.87); Aeschines obtained copies of at least some of Socrates' conversations from his widow, Xanthippe, and passed these off as his own (D.L. 2.60 = SSR 6.a.22). Xenophon was the first of the Socratics to take notes upon and publish Socrates' conversations (D.L. 2.48). The literary judgment these tales convey is that of conversation recorded either by a member of their audience or by one of their participants. This is precisely the impression we get from the four frame dialogues of the Platonic corpus: the *Phaedo*, the *Symposium*, the *Theaetetus*, and the *Parmenides*.[42] The formulas that introduce the short dialogues reported in Xenophon's *Memorabilia* seem to reinforce this impression: τούτων δὴ γράψω ὅποσα ἂν διαμνημονεύσω (1.3.1).[43]

Yet none of the literary Socratics were intent on simply preserving Socrates' conversations for their own pleasure or on recalling them for posterity. One can justly say that "the Socratics experimented in biography, and the experiments were directed towards capturing the potentialities of individual lives."[44] Of Aeschines, and Xenophon, it is fair to say that they did not evince a concern for providing their Socratic dialogues with a historical setting. Aeschines prepared for much that we will find in the Platonic dialogues. In his *Alcibiades* we find Socrates

[42]I attempt an analysis of the meaning and function of these frame dialogues in "Plato's First Words," in *Beginnings in Greek Literature*, ed. F. M. Dunn and T. Cole, Yale Classical Studies 29 (Cambridge, 1992), pp. 120–25.

[43]Xenophon's statements concerning his role in the conversations he reports have made him seem a reliable and virtually stenographic witness, especially when he introduces a report by a phrase such as Ἤκουσα δέ ποτε αὐτοῦ καὶ περὶ φίλων διαλεγομένου, "once I heard him speaking on the topic of friends as well" (2.4.1; cf. 2.5.1 and 4.3.1). But he also says that he "knows of" a Socratic conversation, and his manner of expressing himself does not mean that he was himself present: Οἶδά ποτε αὐτὸν τοιάδε διαλεχθέντα (3.3.1; cf. 4.5.2). But on the single occasion in the *Memorabilia* when he records a conversation he had with Socrates he speaks not in the first person but of a Xenophon, as he had spoken of himself in the *Anabasis* (3.4–10). He claims that he once heard the conversation Socrates has with Critoboulus on household management, but he was not in Athens in the short period between the death of Cyrus the Younger in 401 and Socrates' execution in 399; cf. *Oec.* 1 and 4.18–19 (where Cyrus is referred to as having died) and *Ap.* 1.

[44]A. Momigliano, *The Development of Greek Biography* (Cambridge, Mass., 1971), p. 46.

narrating his conversation with Alcibiades to an unnamed audience, and he is careful to give the setting of this dialogue in place if not in time: "We were sitting on the benches of the Lyceum where the officials stage the contests" (fr. 2 Dittmar = *SSR* 6.a.43). Socrates, therefore, as narrator of one of his conversations is not new with Plato, nor is the setting of a dialogue in place or the dramatization of a dialogue by the introduction of a gesture such as Alcibiades putting his head on his knees and weeping out of frustration (fr. 10 Dittmar = *SSR* 6.a.51). Our evidence does not allow us to determine whether the Socratics also developed the purely dramatic dialogue before Plato, but the example of Aeschines' *Alcibiades* makes it certain that at least one of them did. And the speculations about the origins of the distinctively Socratic dialogue in mimesis and not narrative (διήγησις) and the inventions of Simon and Alexamenus, as well as that of Xenophon, would lose their motivation if there had not been a prevailing sense in antiquity that the narrative dialogue preceded the dramatic dialogue.

What then did Plato add to a literary form he found already well developed? The setting of the *Charmides* gives us one answer: he seems to have invented the historical setting for some of his dialogues—which allows him as an author and his reader as his audience the ironies of the tragic dramatist. The *Charmides* opens with Socrates narrating one of his conversations to an unknown companion:

> The evening before we had arrived from the campaign at Potidaea. And with joy in my heart after so long an absence I returned to my familiar haunts. I entered the wrestling school of Taureas, the one just opposite the precinct of the Queen, and there I came upon a considerable crowd. Some were strangers to me, but most of the people there were my acquaintances. And when they saw me make my unexpected appearance they all sprang up from where they were seated to greet me. And Chaerephon, being the impulsive person he is, leapt up from the crowd and raced up to me and, taking me by the hand, he asked me: "Socrates, how did you escape from the battle with your life?" (153a)

The setting of the *Charmides* and its cast of characters reveal the dramatist's concern for creating a context of which his actors can have no awareness and in which their unwitting words and actions possess a larger significance. It is meaningful that Socrates has returned from battle to discuss self-restraint, or σωφροσύνη, with two Athenians who had remained in Athens and are to be found in a wrestling school; they grow up to be two of the Thirty Tyrants of 404, and their vague threat of force at the very end of the dialogue (176c) points to the violent end of their oligarchy in 403.

Alcibiades was murdered by agents of the Thirty in 404. We do not know when Antisthenes, Aeschines, Eucleides, Phaedo, and Plato wrote their dialogues with his name as their title. It is true that Athenaeus claims (on the authority of Satyrus) that Antisthenes said that he had firsthand experience of Alcibiades' character and appearance,[45] but this claim does not give us a date for his *Alcibiades*. What can be claimed, however, is that any *Alcibiades* written after 404 (or even 415) would be a potentially different dialogue than one written before his profanation of the mysteries or after his demonic career came to its brutal end. The same claim can be made for the *Sōkratikoi logoi* in general. If he wrote before Socrates' execution in 399, the author of a Socratic dialogue could not exploit the dramatic irony of contemporary Attic tragedy; if after, he could.

More than any of the literary Socratics who came before him or followed him, Plato exploited the ironies of the tragic poet in his dramatizations of Socrates' conversations. Like the tragic poet, he worked with a myth well known to his contemporaries in the fourth century— the myth of Socrates' life. To exploit the potentialities of tragic irony, Plato was careful to provide his Socratic dialogues with a setting in time, as well as place. He was censured in antiquity for the anachronisms of these settings,[46] but these very criticisms point to one of the features of the Socratic dialogues of Plato that distinguishes them from the work of the other Socratics. Plato is careful to give his dialogues a setting in place and in time, when this serves his purpose.

His *Alcibiades* 1 (whose authenticity is disputed) is clearly set in a time when Pericles is still alive and Alcibiades is not yet twenty (cf. 188c and 135d). At this time, Alcibiades' fate was still in doubt, and Socrates can utter a dark prophecy. In response to Alcibiades' youthful promise "From this day on I will pursue justice" Socrates replies: "If I could have my wish, you would end your life in this pursuit. But I have a dreadful premonition—not because I do not have confidence in your character, but because I fear the might of the city—that this might well overwhelm both me and you" (135e). Socrates might indeed have had such a premonition, but it was Plato who could conclude the dialogue with this prophecy *post eventum*. To the Platonist who doubts the Platonic authorship of *Alcibiades* 1, there are other examples of this same tragic irony in other Platonic dialogues. There is Socrates' description

---

[45] *Ath.* 12.534c = *SSR* 5.a.198.

[46] Again, most of these criticisms are retailed in Athenaeus; they are collected by Düring (above, note 8), pp. 20–24. Interestingly enough, they also apply to Xenophon and the historical setting he provided for his *Symposium*, in imitation of the historical setting Plato provided for his *Symposium*.

of Alcibiades' career in *Republic* 6, 494a–495c (which ironically includes a description of Plato's career as well), and there are the many instances when, in well-defined contexts, Socrates predicts his own fate.

Socrates was overcome by the might of Athens in 399. From that point, the author of *Sōkratikoi logoi* could discover a model for his dialogues in tragedy, for Socrates was no longer a contemporary figure, pilloried on the comic stage, he was a tragic figure from the past, stalking the stage of tragedy. The myth of his life and death were well known. In Plato, a dark form of irony hovers over the bright irony of Socrates himself. Plato is not the only Socratic who recognizes Socrates as a prophet; in Xenophon's *Apology*, in the face of his own death, Socrates predicts the fate of the son of Anytus, one of his accusers (29–31). And Xenophon confirms the truth of this prophecy. But it is only in the Socratic dialogues of Plato that Socrates' words apply to himself and possess a significance that he himself could not have been aware of.

In Plato, the shadow of Socrates' trial and execution is cast over the varied scenes in which he acts and speaks. We glimpse intimations of his mortality and the fate of the philosopher in the democratic polis in the *Gorgias*, the *Meno*, the *Theaetetus*, the *Republic*, and even in a late dialogue like the *Statesman*—a dialogue in which Socrates stands as a silent presence.[47] Perhaps the most perfect and poignant example of Plato's tragic irony is to be found in the seventh book of the *Republic*, when Socrates has nearly completed his parable of the cave and asks Glaucon a question: What would happen to the prisoner who had, by some divine providence, been freed from the cave, should he be forced to return to its darkness? "And if the prisoners could lay their hands on the person who tried to release them from their bonds and lead them upward, would they not put him to death?" "They would, indeed" (Σφόδρα γ', ἔφη, 517a).

The Socratic dialogues of Plato allow us to realize that if the comic poets of Athens offered models for the literary Socratics while Socrates was alive,[48] the tragic poets of Athens offered models for the dramatic representation of Socrates once he was dead. In dealing with history, the literary Socratics who wrote after Socrates' death could exploit a

---

[47]Cf. *G.* 484c–d, 508c, and 527a; *Meno* 94e; *Th.* 173d–3e; *Rep.* 7, 517a; *Plt.* 299b–300c (where the visitor from Velia addresses the young Socrates in the silent presence of the older Socrates, 299d).

[48]The evidence for *Sōkratikoi logoi* recalled orally or written down during Socrates' lifetime is gathered and assessed by Livio Rossetti in "*Logoi Sokratikoi* anteriori al 399 A.C.," *Logos e logoi* 9 (1990): 21–40; David Sider assesses the anecdotal evidence in "Did Plato Write Dialogues before the Death of Socrates?" *Apeiron* 14 (1980): 15–18, and favors the inference that he did.

resource available to both the tragedian and the historian; the actors in the events they narrate or dramatize were unaware of the full implications of their words and actions. This is particularly true of Thucydides and the Melian dialogue, which is often seen as a fifth-century prototype of the Socratic dialogue.[49]

More than any of the literary Socratics of the fourth century, Plato took care to provide some of his Socratic dialogues with a significant historical setting, and it can properly be asked whether Plato wrote Socratic dialogues of the kind we know from Antisthenes, Aeschines, Aristippus, and Xenophon of the *Memorabilia*.[50] Plato also parts company with the other literary Socratics in reflecting within his Socratic dialogues on the established literary genres in terms of which his dialogues were to be understood and against which they were to stand in contrast. This is the meaning, I believe, of the riddle posed by Socrates at the end of the *Symposium:* "Is it possible for one and the same poet to compose both tragedy and comedy?" Neither Agathon nor Aristophanes grasped the answer to this riddle at once, and it is an answer Socrates could not have grasped himself. Plato is the tragic and comic poet of the *Symposium,* and the object of his imitation is Socrates, who moves between the sublime and the ridiculous.[51] Plato also draws attention to the literary character of his Socratic dialogues when he has Socrates offer Adeimantus a lesson in literary criticism in book 3 of the *Republic.* Socrates has discussed the subject matter of poetry (*logos*), and he moves on to discuss its style (λέξις, *Rep.* 3, 392c). There are three possible styles of narrative (*diēgēsis*): simple, mimetic, and mixed. Homer works in the mixed style and both speaks as the narrator (αὐτὸς ὁ ποιητής, 393a) and impersonates one of his characters. For the ethical purposes of education, the mimetic or dramatic style is potentially the most dangerous, for the student of poetry risks becoming like the character whose role he takes (395c–396a). Adeimantus immediately grasps the application of the purely mimetic style to tragedy; it is Socrates who reminds him that it also applies to comedy (394b). It is paradoxical, in light of these distinctions, that Socrates and Adeiman-

---

[49]A connection expertly drawn by C. Macleod, "Form and Meaning in the Melian Dialogue," *Historia* 23 (1974): 385–400, reprinted in *Collected Essays* (Oxford, 1983), pp. 52–67. In considering the historical function of the speeches in Thucydides, Macleod reminds us: "The speeches . . . invite the reader's critical scrutiny, the result of which may be not only a sense of enlightenment, but of tragedy. For they move the reader by their fallibility no less than they illumine him by their penetration" (p. 386).

[50]As does Charles H. Kahn in "Did Plato Write Socratic Dialogues?" *CQ* n.s. 31 (1981): 305–20.

[51]As I argue in "The Tragic and Comic Poet of the *Symposium*," *Arion* n.s. 2 (1975): 238–61, reprinted in *Essays in Ancient Greek Philosophy,* ed. J. P. Anton and A. Preus (Albany, 1983), 2:176–202.

tus should finally declare a preference for the "pure imitator," but this preference depends on the object of the poet's imitation (τὸν τοῦ ἐπιεικοῦς μιμητὴν ἄκρατον, 397d).

Socrates' lesson in distinctions of style has a long history in Greek literary criticism, and a practical result. The Platonic dialogues themselves came to be described as either narrative, dramatic (or "mimetic"), or mixed. Proclus, when he classified the *Republic* itself as a mixed dialogue, did not register the fact that, properly described, it is entirely dramatic, since Plato's reader, if he reads aloud and dramatically, takes the part of Socrates, its narrator.[52] These distinctions are deployed in the tradition of the "first inventor" of the *Sōkratikoi logoi*, and the category of the dramatic or mimetic seems to represent the essential form of this genre. We are reminded finally that Plato's *Sōkratikoi logoi* are Attic mimes and that Plato, like his Sicilian master, Sophron, is an *ēthopoios*. The object of his imitation is not an easy thing to comprehend, "especially for the motley crowd in a festival or gathered in theaters." "This is the character that acts with deliberation and calm and is always very much like itself" (τὸ ... φρόνιμόν τε καὶ ἡσύχιον ἦθος, παραπλήσιον ὂν ἀεὶ αὐτὸ αὑτῷ, Rep. 10, 604e).[53]

---

[52]Cf. Proclus *In Platonis Rem Publicam*, ed. W. Kroll (Leipzig, 1901), pp. 14.15–16.25; D.L. 3.50; and Haslam (above, note 22).

[53]I thank the editor of this volume for the invitation to write this essay and for advice as it was being written, and Charles Kahn for both the inspiration of his own unpublished work on my theme and his comments on two earlier versions of what I present here. He also has done much to temper my youthful enthusiasm for the discovery of the Socratic Simon in the Athenian agora.

[2]

Socrates in the Clouds

Paul A. Vander Waerdt

According to a well-established ancient tradition, Socrates effected a revolution in the orientation of philosophy: whereas it previously had dealt with such questions as numbers, motion, the origins of all things, and celestial phenomena, Socrates, who had learned of these subjects from his teacher Archelaus, "first called philosophy down from heaven, set her in the cities, introduced her into men's home, and compelled her to investigate life and customs, good and evil."[1] So reads Cicero's assessment of the Socratic revolution, widely paralleled in Hellenistic philosophical polemic[2] and in ancient doxography[3] as well as in mod-

---

[1]Cic. *Tusc* 5.10–11; cf. 3.4.8; *Acad.* 1.1.3, 1.4.15; *Rep.* 3.5; *De or.* 1.4.2; *Off.* 3.9.77.

[2]The most striking formulation of which is Timon's description of Socrates in his *Silloi* as a "people-chiseling custom-chatterer" who turned away from the study of nature (fr. 799 in H. Lloyd-Jones and P. J. Parsons, *Supplementum Hellenisticum* [Berlin, 1983] =D.L. 2.19). For the interpretation of this passage as a rejection of φυσιολογία in favor of an exclusive concentration on ethics, see Clem. Al. *Strom.* 1.14.63.3 and esp. Sext. Emp. *Math.* 7.8–10, who notes that Timon censured Plato for unwillingness to allow Socrates to remain ἠθολόγος. For the manner in which Socrates' followers—Cebes, Phaedo, Aristippus, and Aeschines of Sphttus—kept philosophical discussion "within the boundaries" of good and evil, household and city, see Them. 34.5, with Euseb. *Praep. evang.* 15.62.7ff.; for the Cyrenaic claim to follow Socrates in rejecting enquiry into scientific causation: Sext. Emp. *Math.* 7.190.1; Apul. *De deo Soc.*, prol. 2, p. 2.11ff.; for the claim that Plato attributed his own doctrines to Socrates: Cic. *Rep.* 1.15–16; D.L. 2.45.

[3]The doxographical tradition relies principally on Xenophon *Memorabilia* 1.1.11–16: see esp. ps.-Galen *Hist. philos.* in *DG* 597.1–17, a rewriting of this text in Hellenistic terminology; Sext. Emp. *Math.* 7.8 and D.L. 2.45, both quoting Xenophon: the latter cites Socrates' conversations about divine providence (e.g., *Mem.* 1.4) as evidence that he was also interested in physics despite Xenophon's claim (according to Diogenes) that Socrates

ern handbooks.[4] If we turn to the Socratic source on which this assessment of Socrates' philosophical achievement is based, we find the claim explained as follows: Socrates first made *physiologia* instrumental to enquiry into the human soul, rendering the pre-Socratic approach to the study of nature obsolete by insisting that *physiologia* become ethically useful.[5]

When we enquire what considerations motivated Socrates to advance this position, however, we find our ancient sources remarkably reticent. The obvious place to look, Socrates' "intellectual autobiography" in Plato's *Phaedo* (96a–99d), offers an account of the difficulties in the pre-Socratic approach to causation that led Socrates to adopt the method of hypothesis in his "second sailing," but does not explain why Socrates' conversion entailed the instrumentality of natural philosophy to human happiness.[6] Indeed, Plato treats Socrates' pre-Socratic career as an enthusiastic natural philosopher with such apologetic delicacy that he appears at times to deny that Socrates ever had a pre-Socratic past. Thus Plato has his Socrates, charged with impiety and corruption of the youth (D.L. 2.40; Xen, *Mem.* 1.1.1–2; *Ap.* 10; Pl. *Ap.* 18b–c, 19b–d, 24b), appear to deny at his trial that he has ever engaged in the study of nature—to the popular prejudice against which he attributes the

concerned himself only with ethics; Cic. *Acad.* 1.4.15, whose claim that Socrates regarded celestial phenomena as beyond human comprehension relies upon *Memorabilia* 1.1.13 and 4.7.6. The importance of Xenophon in forming the Hellenistic portrait of Socrates' exclusive interest in ethics is noted by A. A. Long, "Socrates in Hellenistic Philosophy," *CQ* n.s. 38 (1988): 150–71 at pp. 151, 153.

[4]E.g., W. K. C. Guthrie, *Socrates* (Cambridge, 1971), pp. 97–105; G. S. Kirk, J. E. Raven, and M. Schofield, *The Presocratic Philosophers*[2] (Cambridge, 1983), p. 452; G. Vlastos, *Socrates: Ironist and Moral Philosopher* (Ithaca, N.Y., 1991), pp. 160–62.

[5]For the interpretation of Xenophon's testimony, on which Cicero's assessment relies, see section 4 below. There were of course alternative traditions concerning the foundation of ethics, but our own histories of philosophy tend to presuppose the assessment of Socrates' philosophical achievement advanced by his fourth-century apologists.

[6]In his portrayal of Socrates' intellectual biography Plato separates his account in the *Phaedo* of the considerations that led Socrates to reject pre-Socratic *physiologia* from his account in the *Apology* of Socrates' attempted *elenchus* of the Delphic oracle, to which he traces his preoccupation with ethical questions. Plato nowhere indicates how to connect these two episodes in Socrates' philosophical development and thus does not provide explicit support for the traditional interpretation (deriving from Xenophon *Memorabilia* 1.1.11–16), which sees in the motivation of Socrates' disavowal of *physiologia* the source of his mature preoccupation with ethics. Aristotle's account is similarly reticent: he tells us in *Metaphysics* 987b1–2 (cf. 1087b17) that "Socrates concerned himself with ethical questions and not at all with nature as a whole," and in *De partibus animalium* 642a28 that in Socrates' time the study of nature was given up as philosophers turned their attention to practical philosophy. These testimonia are consistent with *Memorabilia* 1.1.11–16, but their source is uncertain. In his *On Philosophy* Aristotle traced the origin of Socrates' ζήτησις to the Delphic command "Know yourself" (fr. 1 Ross = Plut. *Adv. Col.* 1118c), where Aristotle clearly is following Plato (*Ap.* 21b–29c) rather than Xenophon (*Ap.* 14–17), who rejects the role Plato assigns to the oracle in Socrates' philosophical development.

charges against him (*Ap.* 19b–d; cf. 18b–c);[7] only when on the verge of execution does the Platonic Socrates detail his pre-Socratic past (96a–99d).[8] The apologetic purpose of Plato's Σωκρατικοὶ λόγοι, intended as they are to vindicate Socrates against the judgment of his Athenian jury in 399 B.C., has obscured in certain respects our understanding of the Socratic revolution by placing a veil over Socrates' own development from a pre-Socratic to a Socratic philosopher.[9] For, if we wish to understand this philosophical revolution, the obvious place to begin is Socrates' own motivation in repudiating *physiologia* as he had come to practice it in his own time and place.

If we are to make any progress in reconstructing Socrates' philosophical development and in assessing the Socratic revolution, we need to examine two sources rarely accorded serious consideration in Socratic studies today. The first, antedating Socrates' death, cannot be said to suffer from the apologetic bias of the *Sōkratikoi logoi*. Aristophanes' comic portrayal of Socrates as a natural philosopher in the *Clouds* is in fact the sole document we possess that dates from Socrates' own lifetime,[10] and the neglect of it in contemporary Socratic studies has, I suggest, deprived us of what has justly been called "one of the most

[7]The Platonic Socrates' defense against Aristophanes on this point is more ambiguous than usually noted: Socrates does not flatly deny having engaged in such enquiries, but in disclaiming knowledge of natural philosophy states (in contrast to Xenophon *Memorabilia* 1.1.11–16) that he does not dishonor those who possess it; he then invites his jurors to bear witness that none has heard him conversing about it (*Ap.* 19b–c). Xenophon in contrast suppresses all reference to Socrates' first accusers in his *Apology* (14–15), though he accords them a prominent place in the dramatic setting of the *Oeconomicus* (for reasons I have tried to explain in "Socratic Justice and Self-Sufficiency: The Story of the Delphic Oracle in Xenophon's *Apology of Socrates*," *OSAP* 11 [1993]: 1–48.)

[8]Xenophon adopts a similar strategy: when defending Socrates from the same charges in *Memorabilia* 1.1, he states flatly that Socrates "did not even make enquiry concerning the nature of the cosmos" (1.1.11); only in the penultimate chapter of the *Memorabilia* (4.7), just before he recounts Socrates' noble conduct during the thirty days after his condemnation, does Xenophon admit that Socrates was "not inexperienced" (οὐκ·ἄπειρος) in the study of geometry and "not ignorant" (οὐδὲ ἀνήκοος) of astronomy, both being ancillary disciplines of natural philosophy that Socrates taught his associates to learn in order to become free and self-sufficient καλοικἀγαθοί: see section 4 below. For Socrates' appeal to a natural teleology in his account of piety in *Memorabilia* 1.4 see the analysis by Joseph DeFilippo and Phillip Mitsis in Chapter 10.

[9]Socrates' pre-Socratism is usually treated, on the strength of *Phaedo* 96a, as a youthful flirtation. But the evidence of the *Clouds* (supported by Xenophon's response at *Symposium* 6.6–8, 7.3–4, the dramatic date of which is 421 B.C.) suggests that it may have extended well into the middle of his life. Socrates was forty-six in 423 B.C., when the *Clouds* was produced for the first and only time. If we accept that Socrates' "conversion" could not have taken place by that date, on the grounds that it would render Aristophanes' portrayal of Socrates' enthusiasm for *physiologia* dramatically ineffective (see below, note 59), then the pre-Socratic stage in Socrates' intellectual development must have extended well beyond his youth; J. Ferguson, "On the Date of Socrates' Conversion," *Eranos* 62 (1964): 70–73, proposes 421 B.C.

[10]Apart from the formal indictment against him preserved in the Metroon, if the document to which Favorinus refers is genuine (D.L. 2.40).

precious of all documents for the study of the development of Greek philosophical thought."[11] The hazards of relying upon a comic parody for information on which to reconstruct Socrates' philosophical biography should not be underestimated.[12] Nonetheless, I shall argue that the *Clouds,* when read with proper care and caution, illuminates the pre-Socratic stage in Socrates' philosophical development that corresponds closely to the account of his "first sailing" as described in Plato's *Phaedo* and so provides important evidence to augment our meager sources for Socrates' intellectual biography.[13] The close and precise correspondences between these two texts enable us to place Socrates' pre-Socratic interests in natural philosophy in the context of contemporary *physiologia* and so to set the stage for consideration of the arguments that led him to repudiate this phase in his philosophical development and to advocate the study of nature only to the extent that it is ethically useful.

For this development in Socrates' philosophical biography we must have recourse to Xenophon's unjustly neglected account of Socratic ethics, which has recently been undergoing a rehabilitation in certain circles. His detailed report of Socrates' criticism of pre-Socratic natural philosophy in *Memorabilia* 1.1.11–16 is both the principal source of the traditional assessment of the Socratic revolution and our fullest account of the considerations that motivated Socrates to insist that *physiologia* become ethically useful. This account, I shall argue, reflects Xenophon's distinctive interpretation of Socratic ethics: hence if we are to understand the traditional assessment of the Socratic revolution, we need to consider Socrates' arguments as set forth in *Memorabilia* 1.1.11–16 in light of that interpretation.[14] Moreover, Xenophon portrays the influence of the *Clouds* on Socrates' intellectual autobiography quite differently than Plato does, representing the play—perhaps

[11]This is the judgment of A. E. Taylor, "The *Phrontisterion*," in his *Varia Socratica,* St. Andrews University Publications no. 9 (Oxford, 1911), pp. 129–77 at p. 129 (this important contribution came to my attention only as I was preparing the final version of this chapter, and I am delighted to be able to adduce Taylor's agreement on the points signaled below).

[12]We face a similar situation in attempting to reconstruct Pyrrho's skepticism, for it was the satirist Timon who first established, probably in polemic against the skeptical Academy, the tradition that Pyrrho was an epistemological skeptic (see J. Brunschwig, "Aristocles on Timon on Pyrrho Once Again," in his *Kleine Schriften* [Cambridge, forthcoming]): hence any interpretation of Pyrrho's skepticism presupposes a view of the accuracy of Timon's satires.

[13]Among earlier discussions of the Aristophanic Socrates as a natural philosopher I have found the most useful J. Burnet, *Plato's Phaedo* (Oxford, 1911), pp. xxxviii–xlii, and Taylor (above, note 11).

[14]It is ironic that scholars who do not hesitate to denigrate Xenophon's account of Socratic ethics nonetheless regularly accept the assessment of Socrates' philosophical achievement that derives from him. Perhaps that provides sufficient justification for a renewed and more sympathetic consideration of his testimony.

ironically—as marking the crucial stage in Socrates' philosophical development in which his mature preoccupation with *kalokagathia* first emerges. Thus if we are to understand how Aristophanes' play helped to shape the portrayal of Socrates' philosophy by his fourth-century philosophical heirs, we need to consider the portrait of Socrates' development that emerges from Xenophon's *Sōkratikoi logoi*. In this essay I propose to reconstruct the picture of the Socratic revolution that emerges if we give these two neglected sources the serious consideration they deserve.[15]

1. The Aristophanic Socrates

Aristophanes' *Clouds* placed third in the competition at the City Dionysia in 423 B.C., but his comic portrayal of Socrates exercised a formative influence on Socratic literature well into the fourth century. Attic comedy may have provided a model for the genre of literature known to Aristotle (*Poet.* 1447b11) as the *Sōkratikoi logoi,* as Diskin Clay has argued in Chapter 1. And while Socrates became a familiar figure on the comic stage, it was Aristophanes' portrayal that engaged the attention of later Socratics.[16] The two authors on whom we rely for first-hand accounts of Socrates and his philosophy offer elaborate replies to Aristophanes' charges of corruption and impiety in their attempts to vindicate his memory. In Plato's *Apology* (18b–23e), Socrates traces the present charges against him to the performed version of Aristophanes' play, some twenty-four years before; and numerous Platonic texts undertake to answer his comic indictment of the moral and political consequences of Socrates' enquiries into nature.[17] Xenophon too rep-

---

[15]See also my remarks in the Introduction concerning the representation of Socrates as a natural philosopher in our three principal sources.

[16]Socrates figured also in Ameipsias' *Connus* (fr. 9 *PCG*), which was named after Socrates' music teacher (cf. Pl. *Euthphr.* 272c, 295d; *Menex.* 235e) and which placed second in 423 B.C., and later in plays of Callias (fr. 15 *PCG*), Eupolis (fr. 386 *PCG*), and Telekeides (frs. 41–42 *PCG*); see also the evidence for *Clouds* I collected at *PCG* 3.2: 214–19; *Av.* 1282, 1553–64; *Ran.* 1491; and the survey of comic evidence in Guthrie (above, note 4), pp. 39–57. While the loss of Ameipsias' play has deprived us of comparative material that would have been most useful in assessing Aristophanes' portrayal of Socrates, the close parallels between that portrayal and Eupolis', for example (see next note), suggest that Aristophanes constituted the figure of the comic Socrates in the genre of comedy as well as in the *Sōkratikoi logoi:* if that is so, then the loss of these later comic parallels is less of an impediment to interpretation of the *Clouds* than if Aristophanes wrote in an established tradition of comic parody.

[17]Cf., for instance, the expulsion of the comic poets from Plato's second-best regime in *Laws* 935d–936a (with 816d–817a); the comic reversal of the *Ecclesiazusae* in *Republic* 5 (on which see now M. F. Burnyeat, "The Practicability of Plato's Ideally Just City," in *On Justice,* ed. K. Boudouris [Athens, 1989], pp. 95–104 at pp. 98–101); the response to

resents Aristophanes' charges in the *Clouds* as marking a turning point in Socrates' intellectual biography: in the *Oeconomicus*, Socrates recounts to Critoboulos how he undertook to recover from his Aristophanic reputation as an idle chatterer with his head in the air (*Oec.* 11.3: ὧν ἀνὴρ ὅς ἀδολεσχεῖν τε δοκῶ καὶ ἀερομετρεῖν; cf. *Nub.* 225, 1479–85) by seeking instruction in *kalokagathia*, or moral nobility, from Ischomachus—renowned by everyone as the perfect *kaloskagathos*.[18] Since it is the Xenophontic Socrates' preoccupation with *kalokagathia*— that is, his concern to answer the questions knowledge of which would render one a *kaloskagathos* (*Mem.* 1.1.16)—that distinguishes his mature philosophical perspective, Xenophon appears by the dramatic setting of the *Oeconomicus* to suggest that it was the charges set forth in the

---

Socrates' ἀδολεσχία (*Nub.* 225, 1479–85), adapted by Eupolis (fr. 386 *PCG*) in parody of Socrates (cf. fr. 388 *PCG*); *Rep.* 488e–489c; *Phd.* 70b–c; *Prm.* 135d; *Plt.* 299b–c; *Tht.* 195b; *Phdr.* 269e–270a; see also *Cra.* 401b; *Phd.* 99b; *Euthd.* 277d–e, 285c–d, with H. Tarrant, "*Clouds I*: Steps towards Reconstruction," *Arctos* 25 (1991): 157–81 at pp. 162–66, who assembles further evidence of the numerous allusions to the *Clouds* in the *Euthydemus;* also L. Cooper, *An Aristotelian Theory of Comedy* (New York, 1922), pp. 38–39, 104–6. Note also the rich rebuttal to Aristophanes' charge of corruption in the setting and action of Plato's *Theages*: see T. L. Pangle, "Socrates on the Problem of Political Science Education," *Political Theory* 13 (1985): 112–37, reprinted in his *Roots of Political Philosophy: Ten Forgotten Socratic Dialogues* (Ithaca, N.Y., 1987), pp. 147–74. The biographical tradition attests that Plato took a great interest in Aristophanes: thus when Dionysus of Syracuse wanted to study "the πολιτεία of the Athenians," Plato sent him Aristophanes' plays (Arist. *Vit.* 42–45 in *PCG*). The preoccupation of the Platonic Socrates with Aristophanes is particularly noteworthy in view of the fact, emphasized by T. G. West, *Plato's Apology of Socrates* (Ithaca, N.Y., 1979), pp. 81–133, that this section of the *Apology* does not answer the formal indictment against him.

[18]When Ischomachus undertakes to teach Socrates about *kalokagathia* in *Oeconomicus* 11, he uses a quotation from the *Clouds* to set up a careful rejoinder to its dramatic action (*Nub.* 32 with *Oec.* 11.18, 3; 3.7–10; cf. *Nub.* 112–18, 893–95 with *Oec.* 11.25), as L. Strauss pointed out in *Xenophon's Socratic Discourse* (Ithaca, N.Y., 1970), pp. 159, 163–65 (see further next note). In Xenophon's *Symposium*, whose dramatic date is two years after the performance of the *Clouds*, we find a similarly revealing rejoinder to Aristophanes: here (6.6–7.4) the Syracusan entertainer, jealous of the attention Socrates is receiving, abuses him as a φροντιστής, or thinker, one who investigates the most unbeneficial subject, the heavenly things, and who employs geometry to measure distances in flea's feet. Socrates responds to these charges by turning them back against the Syracusan: he answers the imputation of impiety implicit in the characterization of him as a "thinker on heavenly things" by asking whether the Syracusan knows anything more heavenly than the gods; and he answers the claim that he is concerned for "the most unbeneficial things" with an elaborate joke on how the gods benefit human beings by rain and light (cf. *Mem.* 1.4, 4.3; contrast *Nub.* 366–97). This response measures the distance between the Xenophontic Socrates and his Aristophanic namesake: the latter's enquiries into the material causes of natural phenomena, which entail the denial of Zeus's existence and have no beneficial effect on human beings, illustrate for the former the divine providence whereby the natural order is constituted for mankind's benefit. For the echoes of Aristophanes in Socrates' further reply in 7.3–4, see below, note 67. His rejoinder wins Socrates' approval (7.4), and in this case Aristophanes' portrayal is just grist for Socrates' irony.

Clouds that first led Socrates to raise the questions that characterize his mature philosophical outlook. Now there is good reason to suppose that the dramatic setting of the *Oeconomicus* is ironical, that Socrates in fact casts doubt upon Ischomachus' conception of *kalokagathia* even as he purports to be learning from him.[19] Nonetheless, the fact that Xenophon depicts Socrates as developing his mature philosophical position in response to Aristophanes' charges well illustrates the extent to which the *Clouds* succeeded in setting the agenda for later Socratics who wished to vindicate Socrates against the judgment of his Athenian jury in 399 B.C. Aristophanes' charges of impiety and corruption of the youth in fact motivate the very different philosophical biographies that Plato and Xenophon develop in their attempts to provide a publicly respectable defense of Socratic philosophy. Since both Plato and Xenophon would have been young boys when the *Clouds* was performed for the first and only time,[20] they must have known the play from its written text as well as from its performance in 423 B.C. It is clear that they found Aristophanes' attack on Socrates a specifically individuated one, which raised such troubling issues as to merit detailed response decades later.

This judgment by Socrates' philosophical heirs of the importance of Aristophanes' portrayal has found little favor in recent decades among scholars of ancient comedy and philosophy, for whom it has become the fashion to doubt whether the Socrates parodied in the *Clouds* bears any relation at all to his eponymous historical father. They view the Aristophanic Socrates as a "typical sophist," a composite character on whom Aristophanes has foisted all the objectionable characteristics of contemporary sophists: in the words of Kenneth Dover, author of the standard Greek edition of the play, "most of the elements in Aristophanes' portrayal of Socrates can be identified either as general characteristics of the sophists or as conspicuous characteristics of

[19]Even Ischomachus suggests that Socrates is joking (*Oec.* 11.7). Arguments in favor of an ironical reading of the dramatic setting of the *Oeconomicus* are set out by John Stevens in Chapter 8.

[20]Our text of the *Clouds* is clearly an extensive (but probably incomplete) revision, which dates from several years after its initial performance: Hypothesis VI = I Dover summarizes the main differences between the two plays (see further *PCG* 3.2: 214–16); for discussion: K. J. Dover, *Aristophanes' Clouds* (Oxford, 1968), pp. lxxx–xcviii; and now the insightful recent work of T. K. Hubbard, "Parabatic Self-Criticism and the Two Versions of Aristophanes' *Clouds*," *CA* 5 (1986): 182–97, *The Mask of Comedy: Aristophanes and the Intertextual Parabasis*, Cornell Studies in Classical Philology 51 (Ithaca, N.Y., 1991), pp. 88–113; and of H. Tarrant, "Alcibiades in *Clouds* I and II," *Ancient History: Resources for Teachers* 19 (1989): 13–20, and his learned essay on *Clouds* I (above, note 17). Tarrant adduces evidence that suggests that Plato knew *Clouds* I rather than II: certainly it could have been the former rather than the latter that was responsible for turning public opinion against Socrates, though the evidence seems to me insufficient to determine whether Plato also know *Clouds* II.

some contemporary intellectuals."[21] The effect of this view, unsurprisingly, has been to remove the *Clouds* from serious consideration as a possible source of information about Socrates' philosophy and intellectual biography.[22]

This consequence might lead one to question the premises of this influential interpretation. If we dismiss the evidence of the *Clouds,* we lose the sole text we possess that dates from Socrates' own lifetime, and the precious illumination that it could throw on Socrates' intellectual biography. It is true, of course, that comedy transforms its historical figures in the service of comic wisdom, but it is less often remarked that the other genres that preserve information about Socrates—particularly the *apologia* and the *Sōkratikoi logoi*—present a Socrates similarly transformed by authorial interpretation. Plato and Xenophon portray Socrates with such systematic differences of philosophical orientation, even when reporting the same episode in his life, that it is difficult to resist the conclusion that in each case the reporter's philosophical agenda has decisively shaped his portrayal of Socrates.[23] Arnaldo Mo-

---

[21]Dover (above, note 20), pp. xxxii–lvi at p. xl (in accordance with this interpretation he largely banishes from his commentary the *comparanda* provided by Xenophon and Plato—contrast the edition of Starkie cited below—so suppressing the information necessary to test that interpretation). Dover's remarks have been reprinted as "Socrates in the *Clouds,*" in *The Philosophy of Socrates,* ed. G. Vlastos (New York, 1971), pp. 50–77, and have been widely followed (e.g., T. Gelzer, "Aristophanes," *RE* Suppl. 12 [Stuttgart, 1970], cols. 1441–44). Vlastos (above, note 4), p. 12, describes Dover's discussion as a "masterly essay," though it can hardly be said to answer the eloquent anticipatory refutation by Taylor (above, note 11), pp. 129–30, of the notion (already "commonly" held in 1911) that Aristophanes' Socrates is "no real individual man, but a composite photograph in which all the leading peripatetic professors are ingeniously blended." For Kierkegaard's argument that Aristophanes does not identify Socrates with the sophists, see *The Concept of Irony, with Continual Reference to Socrates* [1841], ed. and trans. E. V. and E. H. Hogg (Princeton, 1989), pp. 146–49. Dover's position, which of course is not original (see, for example, G. Grote, *A History of Greece*² [London, 1862], 6: 136–38; W. J. M. Starkie, *The Clouds of Aristophanes* [London, 1911], pp. xxx–xxxvii; P. Pucci, "Saggio sulle Nuvole," *Maia* 12 [1960]: 120), has been repeatedly rejected in the past (e.g, R. Philippson, "Socrates' Dialektik in Aristophanes' Wolken," *RhM* 81 [1932]: 30–38; W. Schmid, "Das Sokratesbild der Wolken," *Philologus* 97 [1948]: 209–28; L. Strauss, *Socrates and Aristophanes* [Chicago, 1966], pp. 3–53; and the further literature cited by Hubbard 1991 [above, note 20], pp. 88–89 n. 4–5) and more recently (e.g., E. A. Havelock, "The Socratic Self As It Is Parodied in Aristophanes' Clouds," *YCS* 22 [1968]: 1–18; M. Nussbaum, "Aristophanes and Socrates on Learning Practical Wisdom," *YCS* 26 [1980]: 43–97; K. Kleve, "Anti-Dover or Socrates in the Clouds," *SO* 58 [1983]: 23–37; L. Edmunds, "Aristophanes' Socrates," *PBACAP* 1 [1985]: 209–30).

[22]To take an extreme and therefore especially revealing example, T. H. Irwin writes that Aristophanes "aimed (with incomplete success) to be funny; he did not try to be accurate, and he betrays malice as well as misunderstanding" (*Classical Thought* [Oxford, 1989], pp. 68–70, 232 n. 1). These claims are not supported by argument, but presumably Irwin considers none necessary. If, as he claims, Aristophanes presents Socrates as the "typical sophist" in his "crude and malicious attack on sophists in the *Clouds,*" there is no reason to study his play as evidence for Socrates' life or philosophy.

[23]As I have tried to show in one particular case (above, note 7).

migliano has drawn a similar conclusion about the Socratic memorial literature in general.[24] If, as he argues, the Socratics' portraits of Socrates guide us through *terra incognita* rather than through the terrain Socrates traveled in his own life, we can approach his philosophy only through the mediation of thinkers none of whom sought to offer a memorial of merely historical interest. Hence the "historical Socrates," even assuming that he is the Socrates who ultimately interests us, is accessible only through the portraits of specific authors who sought to appropriate his authority or notoriety for their own purposes. Seen from this perspective, the Socrates of the *Clouds* arguably presents difficulties of interpretation no more perplexing than the Socrates of Aeschines, Plato, or Xenophon. And if we take seriously the high claims Aristophanes makes on behalf of comedy as a vehicle of civic education,[25] epitomized in his coinage of the word τρυγῳδία to rival tragedy's claims to make the citizens better (cf. *Ran.* 1009–10),[26] the *Clouds* may be seen to raise questions no less worthy of serious investigation than those raised by Socrates' philosophical heirs.

The widespread consensus among modern scholars that the figure of Socrates in the *Clouds* is that of a typical sophist does not constitute an argument in favor of this interpretation. And this modern interpretation sits poorly with the extensive philosophical attention that Xenophon and Plato devote to refuting Aristophanes' portrait. It does not of course follow from the central role Aristophanes' charges play in shaping their presentation of Socrates that they regarded this portrait as a parody of his philosophical position at a certain stage in his intellectual biography. That conclusion can emerge only on the basis of the detailed comparison developed in section 2 below between the Platonic

---

[24]*The Development of Greek Biography* (Cambridge, Mass., 1971), p. 46: "Biography acquired a new meaning when the Socratics moved into that zone between truth and fiction which is so bewildering to the professional historian. . . . With a man like Plato, . . . this is a consciously chosen ambiguity. The Socratics experimented in biography, and the experiments were directed towards capturing the potentialities rather than the realities of individual lives. Socrates, the main subject of their considerations . . . ,was not so much the real Socrates as the potential Socrates. He was not a dead man whose life can be recounted. He was a guide to territories yet unexplored."

[25]For the poet's claims to serve as teacher: *Ach.* 628, 656–58; *Pax* 738; *Av.* 912; fr. 348.3 *PCG*.

[26]See esp. *Ach.* 496–501 (with 315–18 for context), where Dicaeopolis says: "Do not be indignant with me, members of the audience, if I—though a beggar—speak before the Athenians about the city, making a *trugoidia*. For *trugoidia* also [καί] knows the just: I shall say shrewd things, but just." For the construction of these lines and other evidence that Aristophanes has coined *trugoidia* to rival τραγῳδία, see O. Taplin, "Tragedy and Trugedy," *CQ* n.s. 33 (1983): 331–33; and, for Dicaeopolis' elaborations of the educative power of *trugoidia*, see esp. *Ach.* 628–58, with the Persian king's judgment at 650–51 that, as between the Athenians and Lacedaimonians, those who have been most abused by the comic poet "have been made much better human beings and will win the war by much, having this one as adviser." Note also the joke at *Wasps* 650–51.

Socrates' account of his pre-Socratism and the Aristophanic Socrates' natural philosophy. But if Socrates' heirs regarded this portrait as simply crude and malicious,[27] it was open to them to dismiss it as a parody of the typical sophist with whom Socrates himself shared little or nothing. At the least, their sustained preoccupation with the *Clouds*—noteworthy not least because they probably saw its performance as young boys and their responses provide our sole contemporary guide to its interpretation—strongly suggests that they did not construe the Aristophanic Socrates as the composite figure of the sophist but rather as a comic parody that raised philosophical issues of the utmost seriousness.

More generally, the hypothesis that Socrates would have been chosen to fill the role of a typical sophist, had Aristophanes been looking for one, is intrinsically implausible.[28] For Socrates was a notoriously atypical figure who stood out from his sophistic rivals because of his distinctive personal mannerisms, his refusal to accept fees for teaching, and his preference for dialectic rather than rhetoric—all features to which Aristophanes, as we shall see shortly, draws attention in the *Clouds*. Thus Socrates does not serve as a plausible figure if Aristophanes' target is the sophists in general.

Nor is it plausible, if we take seriously Aristophanes' high claims for comedy as a vehicle of civic education, that he would attach sophistic traits at will to a composite figure if he wished to illustrate the corrupting effects of a particular kind of philosophical activity: parody must be plausibly specific to serve its function as social criticism.[29] That Aristophanes himself was not hostile to philosophy in general is made abundantly clear by the fact that he claims for himself some of Socrates' most distinctive intellectual traits in the parabasis of the *Clouds* (see section 3 below). Hence Aristophanes' attack is not directed against philosophy or sophistry as such but rather at the particular version of it practiced by Socrates (with the qualification introduced below in our discussion of the φροντιστήριον). And if Aristophanes is to succeed in exposing the corrosive political effects of Socrates' philosophical activ-

[27]Plato's portrayal of the relationship between Aristophanes and Socrates in the *Symposium*, whose dramatic date is seven years after the *Clouds*, does not lend credence to such a view: to the contrary, Plato represents Socrates as being on such friendly terms with Aristophanes that he is able to persuade him that the good comic poet will also be a good tragic poet; see D. Clay, "The Tragic and Comic Poet of the *Symposium*," *Arion* n.s. 2 (1975): 238–61, reprinted in *Studies in Ancient Greek Philosophy*, ed. J. P. Anton and A. Preus (Albany, 1983), 2:176–202.

[28]A more plausible choice for the "typical sophist" might have been found among the chorus of sophists whom Ameipsias put on stage in his *Connus* (*ap.* Ath. 218c).

[29]For a similar argument to the effect that "baseless misrepresentation . . . must be fatal to the popular success of a caricature," see Taylor (above, note 11), p. 131.

ity, he must portray it in a plausibly specific manner.[30] Put differently, his parody of Socrates must be firmly enough grounded in fact that later Socratics could not simply dismiss it, as they manifestly did not, by denying that the figure depicted was Socrates.[31]

Such general considerations by themselves do not of course demonstrate that the Aristophanic Socrates is a specifically individuated portrait of Socrates set at a certain stage in his philosophical development rather than a composite figure of the typical sophist. Let us turn then to the text of the *Clouds*. I shall argue that Aristophanes takes great care to individuate Socrates, and to call our attention to his main differences from the sophists.

First, his physical appearance: Socrates was notorious for going around shoeless, unwashed, and apparently malnourished—characteristics that Antiphon claims make him a teacher of κακοδαιμονία.[32] These characteristics are all parodied by Aristophanes.[33] Similarly, when the chorus of clouds explain that they listen to Socrates "because you swagger in the streets and cast your eyes from side to side, and shoeless you endure many evils and put on a solemn face for us" (362–63), they are presumably caricaturing Socrates' personal mannerisms, because Alcibiades (hardly a hostile witness) adapts these lines in speaking to Aristophanes in Plato *Symposium* 221b.

Second, his poverty: whereas many sophists, such as those gathered at Callias' house in Plato's *Protagoras*, had become quite wealthy by teaching for a fee, the Aristophanic Socrates lives in utter poverty (175), a fact that provides eloquent testimony to his complete lack of interest

---

[30]On the serious function of Aristophanic comedy, see especially J. Henderson, "The *Demos* and the Comic Competition," in *Nothing to Do with Dionysus? Athenian Drama in Its Social Context*, ed. J. J. Winkler and F. I. Zeitlin (Princeton, 1990), pp. 271–313, and now Hubbard 1991 (above, note 20), esp. pp. 1–8, developing Plato's account (*Phlb.* 48c–49c) of the relation between comedy and self-knowledge. The position I am rejecting is that taken by A. W. Gomme, "Aristophanes and Politics," in *Aristophanes und die alte Komödie*, ed. H.-J. Newinger (Darmstadt, 1975), pp. 75–98.

[31]The parallel case of the *Frogs* illustrates this point well: in the contest staged by Dionysus in Hades to find the poet best able to save Athens, Aristophanes bases his portraits of Aeschylus and Euripides directly on their own plays, using their distinctive styles of meter, diction, prologue construction, and so forth as the starting point for a parody intended to expose their capacity to engender virtue among the citizen body. For Aristophanes to succeed in his stated agenda of guiding the Athenians to a successful and peaceful settlement of their war against Sparta, he must construct his contest for the Chair of Tragedy in such a way as to expose the fundamental political alternatives posed by each contestant. Hence no one, I trust, would be prepared to argue that Aeschylus or Euripides in the *Frogs* represents a composite portrayal of the "typical tragic poet."

[32]Xen. *Mem.* 1.6.3; cf. 1.2.1, 3.5, 6.2; Pl. *Symp.* 174a, 220b.

[33]Shoeless: *Nub.* 103, 363; unwashed: *Av.* 1282, 1554–55; *Nub.* 837; hungry: *Nub.* 175, 185–86, 416, 441; Ameipsias fr. 9 *PCG*.

in money.[34] Contrary to a common assumption, Socrates does not accept payment for his teaching in the *Clouds*.[35] Strepsiades thinks that Socrates teaches for pay (98), but he is so ignorant of the thinkery that he cannot even name who dwells there (100). In fact, Socrates takes no interest in Strepsiades' offer of a fee (244–45; for the theft of Strepsiades' cloak, see section 3 below); he says that Hyperbolus learned oratory for a talent (876), but there is no evidence that it was Socrates who taught him; and the unspecified gift Strepsiades offers at 1146–47 is nowhere contracted and seems just to result from his opinion that "one ought somehow to show admiration for the teacher."[36]

Third, his philosophical method: Aristophanes frequently parodies Socratic methods of enquiry known to us from Plato and Xenophon.[37] Thus Socrates employs a kind of proto-elenchus in explaining the crash of thunder on the basis of Strepsiades' experience with digestive disorders at the Panathenaea (385–93). "I shall teach you from yourself" (385) captures one crucial feature of Socrates' elenctic method as portrayed by Xenophon and Plato,[38] while his insistence on learning Strepsiades' character (his τρόπος, 478–80) before teaching him,[39] and his demand that Strepsiades form his own φροντίδες before Socrates examines them,[40] capture others. The method of division and collection recommended at 740–42 may represent another reminiscence of Socratic dialectical practice,[41] while 137–40 have often been taken as a reference to Socratic midwifery as expounded in the *Theaetetus*.[42] Cer-

[34]Contra: Edmunds (above, note 21), p. 209, for example. For a survey of the evidence, see D. L. Blank, "Socrates and the Sophists on Accepting Payment for Teaching," *CA* 4 (1984): 1–49.

[35]So, for instance, Dover (above, note 20), pp. xxxiv, xlvi; an exception is Taylor (above, note 11), pp. 158 n. 2, 177.

[36]For speculations about the identity of the gift, see Dover (above, note 20) ad loc.

[37]Dover (above, note 20), pp. xlii–xliv, attempts to discredit evidence such as that presented below, but not persuasively in my opinion.

[38]Similarly, Unjust Speech, who seems to dwell on the premises of the thinkery and whose argumentative technique owes something to Socratic method, boasts that "from whatever things [his opponent] says," he will shoot him down with novel thoughts (941–44). The elenchus represents a distinctively Socratic contribution to dialectical practice: see, for example, the account of N. Gulley, *The Philosophy of Socrates* (London, 1968), pp. 29–62, which reviews sophistic antecedents to the elenchus.

[39]Cf. Pl. *Prt.* 352a; *Chrm.* 1156b–c.

[40]See the material collected by Taylor (above, note 11), p. 172.

[41]Taylor (above, note 11), p. 171 n. 1, compares Xenophon *Memorabilia* 4.5.11, 12, on διαλέγοντας κατὰ γένη τὰ πράγματα. Cf. Epicrates' parody of the practice of διαίρεσις in Plato's school.

[42]E.g., Taylor (above, note 11), pp. 148–51; J. Tomin, "Socratic Midwifery," *CQ* n.s. 37 (1987): 97–102; but H. Tarrant, "Midwifery and the *Clouds*," *CQ* n.s. 38 (1988): 116–22, expresses doubts.

tainly the Aristophanic Socrates is unlike the typical sophist in avoiding rhetorical set pieces, and in preferring to argue dialectically on the basis of his interlocutor's premises.[43]

Thus Aristophanes appears to have taken the care to delineate a plausibly specific portrait of Socrates and to distinguish him from the "typical sophist." The main reason that Dover's view has found such ready acceptance is that scholars have been prepared to attribute to Socrates himself views ascribed generally to those dwelling in the thinkery.[44] The thinkery is first introduced to us by Strepsiades, who offers the following ill-formed description:

> ψυχῶν σοφῶν τοῦτ' ἐστὶ φροντιστήριον.
> ἐνταῦθ' ἐνοικοῦσ' ἄνδρες οἳ τὸν οὐρανὸν
> λέγοντες ἀναπείθουσιν ὡς ἔστιν πνιγεύς,
> κἄστιν περὶ ἡμᾶς οὗτος, ἡμεῖς δ' ἄνθρακες.
> οὗτοι διδάσκουσ', ἀργύριον ἤν τις διδῷ,
> λέγοντα νικᾶν καὶ δίκαια κἄδικα.

> That is a thinkery of wise souls.
> In there dwell men who by speaking
> persuade one that the heaven is a stove
> And that it is around us, and we are charcoals.
> If someone gives them money, they teach him
> how to win both just and unjust causes by speaking.
> (94–99)

If taken to apply to Socrates himself, these five lines arguably contain four basic misrepresentations and well illustrate the hazards of attributing to him the characteristics ascribed to him by so hopeless a candidate for initiation into the mysteries of the thinkery as Strepsiades: (1) Hippon apparently *compared* the heaven to a stove (*pnigeus*, a hemispherical cover used in baking bread) but did not say that it *is* a stove;[45] (2) Heraclitus similarly *compared* men to glowing charcoals in his ac-

---

[43]Consider also the possible allusion to the Socratic doctrine that no one willingly does wrong at *Birds* 603–5, with R. Stark, "Sokratisches in den 'Vogeln' des Aristophanes," *RhM* 96 (1953): 77–89 at pp. 86–89.

[44]The objection that this distinction would have been lost on Aristophanes' audience does not impress me. Comedy, like other serious literature, may be written on many levels, and an attempt to reduce interpretation of the *Clouds* to the most vulgar possible denomination is especially inappropriate, for Aristophanes goes out of his way in the parabasis to emphasize that this play was undertaken for the σοφοί among his audience (525–26; contrast the concessions to public taste in the *Wasps* [65–66, 1048–50], a play presented in 422 B.C., with the interpretation of Hubbard 1991 [above, note 20], pp. 116–19).

[45]For the evidence, see Dover (above, note 20) ad loc.

count of the "divine λόγος" (fr. 22 A16 DK); (3) these doctrines are nowhere attributed to *Socrates* elsewhere in the play, nor are they implied by views he does hold; and (4) the notion that Socrates teaches for pay, as we have seen, is incompatible with his poverty and is not borne out in the course of the play itself. When Socrates does undertake to test Strepsiades' suitability as a pupil, after the latter has affirmed his desire to know clearly the divine things and to commune with the clouds (250–53), he refuses Strepsiades' repeated requests to teach him the unjust speech; and when Strepsiades returns with his son Pheidippides, Socrates leaves the stage, showing no interest in the debate between Just and Unjust Speech that follows. Socrates' indifference to the outcome of this debate might be supposed to render him guilty, in dramatic terms, of corrupting the youth, but we must not confuse this problem with that of identifying his own philosophical position. Strepsiades' misunderstandings of Socrates,[46] and the differences between the latter's view and those of Just and Unjust Speech (see section 3 below), show that we cannot necessarily attribute to Socrates himself the doctrines held by his companions in the thinkery.

If we focus carefully on the doctrines the Aristophanic Socrates advocates in his own name, on the other hand, we will find that he professes a consistent, and historically plausible, philosophical position quite different from that of the typical sophist. The Socrates of the *Clouds* is an enthusiastic proponent of the explanation of all natural phenomena in terms of their material constituents, and in this respect he resembles the later Ionian φυσικοί who were his contemporaries. But the similarity, I shall argue, runs deeper: Socrates is consistently represented in the *Clouds* as an adherent of the views of Diogenes of Apollonia, who flourished in the 430s, traditionally being recognized as the last of the *physikoi*.[47] Diogenes exercised an influence in popular thought unparalleled among pre-Socratic philosophers, as is witnessed in tragedy by Euripides' numerous allusions,[48] in Middle Comedy by Philemon's portrayal of Air as an omniscient spectator—also known as Zeus—of all that god or human being may do (fr. 95 *PCG*), in medical theory by

---

[46]For several examples of the humorous misunderstandings that arise from the confrontation of popular thought with Socratic doctrine in Strepsiades' education, see L. Woodbury, "Strepsiades' Understanding," *Phoenix* 34 (1980): 108–27.

[47]This is on the basis of Theophrastus' description of Diogenes (*ap.* Simpl. *In phys.* 25.a = fr. 64A5 DK) as "almost the youngest" of those concerned with the study of nature. For a critical review of scholarship on Diogenes' place in the history of pre-Socratic philosophy, see A. Laks, *Diogenes d'Apollonie*, Cahiers de philologie 9 (Lille, 1983), pp. xix–xl.

[48]See esp. frs. 836, 869, 903, 911, 935, 1007 *TGF*; Eur. *Tro.* 884–89; *Hec.* 884–88, with E. E. Beers, *Euripides and Later Greek Thought* (Chicago, 1914), pp. 4–9, 72–75; R. Scodel, *The Trojan Trilogy of Euripides*, Hypomnemata 60 (Göttingen, 1980), pp. 93–95.

the extensive adaptation of his physiological doctrine by Hippocratic writers[49] and by Aristotle's long quotation of his doctrine on φλέβες (fr. B6 DK = *Hist. an.* 511b31ff.), in natural philosophy by Xenophon's adaptation of his argument from the design of nature in reporting Socrates' doctrine of divine providence,[50] and in literary criticism by the Deverni papyrus' use of him as a major source.[51]

Such widespread influence may seem surprising in the case of a thinker often said to have been among the least as well as the last of the pre-Socratics.[52] But I think that Diogenes' philosophical project merits a far more sympathetic assessment, one that recognizes him as a major figure entirely worthy of his influence on the philosophical enquiries of the young Socrates.

In his *On Nature* Diogenes develops a comprehensive natural philosophy that aims to show how, accepting the Eleatic argument against the generation of anything out of what it is not,[53] one can still account for

---

[49]See, among others, F. Willerding, *Studia Hippocratica* (Göttingen, 1914), pp. 18–24; W. A. Heidel, *Hippocratic Medicine* (New York, 1941), pp. 51–53; H. W. Miller, "A Medical Theory of Cognition," *TAPA* 79 (1948): 168–83, and "The Concept of the Divine in *De Morbo Sacro*," *TAPA* 84 (1953): 1–15; F. Solmsen, "Greek Philosophy and the Discovery of the Nerves," *MH* 18 (1961): 153–57; J. Jouanna, "Rapports entre Melissos de Samos et Diogène d'Apollonie, à la lumière du traité hippocratique de natura hominis," *REA* 67 (1965): 306–23, esp. pp. 307–14.

[50]Diogenes' argument from the design of nature in fr. B3 DK appears to be the first instance of an argument that features prominently in later discussions of teleology: see esp. *Mem.* 1.4, 4.3, whose close verbal parallels with Diogenes fr. 3 are emphasized by W. Theiler, *Zur Geschichte der teleologischen Naturbetrachtung bis auf Aristoteles* (Zurich, 1925), pp. 9–36, and W. Jaeger, *The Theology of the Early Greek Philosophers* (Oxford, 1947), pp. 189–95; the withering criticism Laks (above, note 47), pp. xxvii–xxviii, 250–57, levels against their reconstruction does not provide an impartial assessment of the evidence that suggests that Diogenes significantly influenced Socratic teleology, though he is certainly right to point out that Xenophon's Socrates goes beyond Diogenes in seeing nature as a whole constituted for the benefit of mankind. See below, note 81 for the implications of Diogenes' apparent influence on the Xenophontic Socrates.

[51]The text has been published by R. Merkelbach as an appendix to *ZPE* 47 (1982); for the commentator's use of Diogenes, see W. Burkert, "Orpheus und die Vorsokratiker," *A&A* 14 (1968): 93–114.

[52]J. Barnes, *The Presocratic Philosophers* (London, 1979), 2:265, quoting E. Hussey, *The Presocratics* (London, 1972), p. 141, offers this patronizing assessment: "By common scholarly consent, he was at least as well as last: he worked eclectically rather than creatively, and 'does not seem to have attempted original thought'; indeed, he represents a positive regression, for his 'general level of philosophical awareness suggests the age of Anaximines, not that of Anaxagoras and the sophists.' " On the next page (p. 266) Barnes describes Diogenes as "an essentially second-rate man" and implies that he is a "bore"; by the end of the chapter (p. 281) he has become "a judicious eclectic and a bold synthesizer." Diogenes' interest and originality become clearer as one's knowledge of the text deepens.

[53]While it is sometimes claimed that Diogenes took no account of the Eleatic challenge (thus, for example, H. Cherniss, "The Characteristics and Effects of Pre-Socratic Philosophy," *JHI* 12 [1951]: 344, reprinted in *Selected Papers*, ed. L. Tarán [Leiden, 1977], p. 87, maintains that he wrote "as if Parmenides had never lived," likening his project to

change and plurality in the cosmos. Diogenes' strategy is to postulate that all things originate from a single source, thereby accepting Parmenides' ban on the generation of something from nothing, and to identify this source as "intelligence [νόησις], what is called air by human beings, and by it all human beings are steered, and it has power over everything."[54] Diogenes undertakes to demonstrate the workings of nature's intelligent design from the orderly succession of the seasons down to the internal workings of the human body.[55] In elaborating this theory, Diogenes freely appropriates and adapts what he found best in the previous tradition of *physiologia,* such as Anaxagoras' theory of νοῦς and Empedocles' theory of pores; but he consistently does so not in an "eclectic" manner—if that be understood in its usual rather patronizing sense[56]—but rather to serve his original strategy in answering the Eleatic challenge. His wide influence may be explained in part by the likelihood that his *On Nature* provided the best summation of the pre-Socratic approach to the study of nature available in Athens during the final quarter of the fifth century B.C.

In what follows, I argue that Aristophanes consistently represents Socrates as an adherent of Diogenes' natural philosophy, parodying not only the claim that air is the material principle of all natural phenomena, but also a variety of other views distinctively held by Diogenes. The fact that the Aristophanic Socrates is represented as holding a variety of views attested for Diogenes seems to me to provide strong evidence against the variant of Dover's interpretation that would see Aristophanes as simply foisting on Socrates a philosophical doctrine that especially lent itself to parody. Since the "intellectual autobiography" of Plato's *Phaedo* shows that Socrates, at a certain stage in

---

"the last meaningless twitches of a broken habit, uncoordinated repetitions of a pattern of past meaning"). I have been persuaded by M. F. Burnyeat in an oral presentation on Diogenes fr. B2 DK that this text turns the strategy of Melissus frs. B7–8 DK against the Eleatics as an argument for pluralism. I would argue that the argument from design in fr. B3 DK, as developed in the later parts of *On Nature,* is intended to support this Eleatic rejoinder in fr. 2 by showing how plurality is possible if we can derive all things from the same source structured by intelligence in the noblest possible way.

[54]καί μοι δοκεῖ τὸ τὴν νόησιν ἔχον εἶναι ὁ ἀὴρ καλούμενος ὑπὸ τῶν ἀνθρώπων, καὶ ὑπὸ τούτου πάντας καὶ κυβερνᾶσθαι καὶ πάντων κρατεῖν· αὐτὸ γάρ μοι τοῦτο θεὸς δοκεῖ εἶναι καὶ ἐπὶ πᾶν ἀφῖχθαι καὶ πάντα διατιθέναι καὶ ἐν παντὶ ἐνεῖναι. καὶ ἔστιν οὐδὲ ἓν ὅ τι μὴ μετέχει τούτου· μετέχει δὲ οὐδὲ ἓν ὁμοίως τὸ ἕτερον τῷ ἑτέρῳ, ἀλλὰ πολλοὶ τρόποι καὶ αὐτοῦ τοῦ ἀέρος καὶ τῆς νοήσιός εἰσιν· ἔστι γὰρ πολύτροπος. . . , fr. B5 DK.

[55]The interpretation of Diogenes' project outlined here will receive detailed defense in a paper I am preparing on Diogenes' account of human physiology as reported by Theophrastus in *De sensu* 39–48 and in the Hippocratic *De morbo sacro.*

[56]As evident, for instance, in the remarks of Barnes quoted in note 52 above or in the section heading in Kirk, Raven, and Schofield (above, note 4), p. 436, entitled "The Eclectic, But Not Valueless, Nature of Diogenes' Thought."

his philosophical development, was an eager proponent of the explanation of natural phenomena in terms of their material constituents (*Phd.* 96a–99d),[57] it is perfectly plausible that the historical Socrates might at some point have fallen under Diogenes' sway during the 430s or 420s.[58] The fact that Aristophanes caricatures a Socrates who advocates a single, consistent philosophical position in line with contemporary Ionian *physiologia* thus provides a reasonable historical link between Diogenes and the pre-Socratic Socrates.[59]

[57]Cf. also Socrates' praise of the writings of "the most wise men" on nature and the universe at *Lysis* 214b; and his reference to the *sophoi* who call the universe κόσμος at *Gorgias* 507e–508a.

[58]There is no reason on chronological grounds why Diogenes could not have exercised a significant influence on Socrates: while exact dates are lacking, Socrates is usually said to have been a pupil of Archelaus, himself a pupil of Anaxagoras (D.L. 2.16, 23), and Diogenes was a famous contemporary of Anaxagoras (D.L. 9.57). Given his interest in Anaxagoras' account of the role of *nous* in the explanation of natural phenomena as attested in *Phaedo* 97b–98b, Socrates might have taken especial interest in the modifications Diogenes introduces into the Anaxagorean theory in his own account of the role of intelligence in ordering air in the noblest possible way according to the design of nature.

[59]If we ask, however, not whether the Aristophanic Socrates' philosophical position is historically plausible, as it manifestly is, but whether we are entitled to conclude that Socrates actually was an adherent of Diogenes when the *Clouds* was performed in 423 B.C., caution is in order. The close correspondences between the evidence of Plato and of Aristophanes discussed below in section 3 appear to me to rule out the possibility that the latter's portrayal is simple invention. The Platonic Socrates reports that in his youth he considered a wide variety of pre-Socratic explanations, and there is no reason why he could not have undergone a stage in which he explored Diogenes' theory that air is the material principle of all natural phenomena.

Yet it is difficult to assess the extent of dramatic anachronism possibly at play in Aristophanes' portrayal. On the one hand, Socrates must have been known as a proponent of material explanations of natural phenomena for Aristophanes' play to appear credible as a parody of a specific philosophical position. This consideration provides one indication of relative chronology in Socrates' intellectual biography: Aristophanes' portrayal must precede the story of the Delphic oracle as recounted by Plato, for that portrayal would hardly have seemed plausible if Socrates were already known in 423 B.C. for preoccupation with ethical questions of the kind that, according to Plato, occupied Socrates subsequent to his attempted elenchus of the Delphic oracle. This consideration would appear to rule out the speculation sometimes advanced that Socrates became a target of comic parody starting in 423 B.C. because the story of the Delphic oracle had then come to public attention. If this were so, it is surely astonishing that Aristophanes makes no reference to it. The outbursts on the part of Socrates' jury, in the versions both of Plato and of Xenophon, when he mentions the oracle also suggest that the story was not popularly known. The Platonic account of the oracle thus provides some constraint on the possibility of dramatic anachronism in Aristophanes' portrayal of Socrates (Xenophon denies any link between the oracle and Socrates' philosophical mission in *Apology* 14–15: see Vander Waerdt [above, note 7]), though of course one must bear in mind the possibility that Plato's story of the oracle is a literary fiction.

On the other hand, if we take the Aristophanic Socrates as a comic representation of the historical Socrates' position in 423, the question arises whether it is plausible that by this late date Socrates still had not read Anaxagoras' book, whose influence on his intellectual development is described in *Phaedo* 97b–99d, since Anaxagoras is reported to have died in Lampsacus in 428/427 B.C. (D.L. 2.7); for Anaxagoras' chronology, see Kirk, Raven, and Schofield (above, note 4), pp. 352–55; D. Sider, *The Fragments of Anaxagoras*

Natural philosophy is not, to be sure, the Aristophanic Socrates' sole interest: he is also concerned with meter, rhythm, and the correct explanation of names,[60] but the study of these subjects as propaedeutic to dialectic is perfectly compatible with his central interest in the material causes of natural phenomena. It is clear, moreover, that the Aristophanic Socrates takes little or no interest in the ethical questions (e.g., whether law is founded in nature or convention, the relative merits of Old and New Education) favored by contemporary sophists, questions that Aristophanes treats in the debate between Socrates' fellow dwellers in the thinkery, Just and Unjust Speech. While Socrates is commonly assumed to be responsible for Unjust Speech's teachings, their views in fact diverge in fundamental ways, and there is no reason to assign to Socrates himself the positions advocated by his companions in the *phrontistērion*, or thinkery.[61] The thinkery itself poses an important related problem, since there is no evidence that Socrates himself ever ran any kind of school.[62] I suggest that Aristophanes has invented the thinkery as a dramatic device precisely in order to introduce certain sophistic themes in which Socrates himself, being principally concerned with the study of nature, took little or no interest.[63] In general, Aristophanes is much more careful than has been recognized to distinguish the doctrines Socrates holds from those of his associates, on whom he allegedly exercised a pernicious influence.

My argument is structured as follows. First, I try to show that the portrayal of Socrates as a natural philosopher in the *Clouds* corresponds to his "first sailing" as described in his intellectual autobiography in the *Phaedo*. Next I explore the affinities of this portrayal with earlier pre-Socratic thought, arriving at the conclusion that the Aris-

---

(Meisenheim an Glan, 1981), pp. 1–11. This difficulty disappears if one recognizes that the *Phaedo* telescopes chronology from the perspective of Socrates' "second sailing": Plato does not give a clear enough indication of how long the fourth phase in Socrates' development lasted to settle such a precise question of chronology (see section 2 and notes 76 and 81 below).

[60]For the Prodicean and Protagorean background of Socrates' interest in linguistic matters, see A. Sommerstein's note *ad* 659 in *Aristophanes: Clouds* (Warminster, 1982), p. 196.

[61]Aristophanes indicates as much by use of stage directions to distance Socrates from the teaching of his fellow inhabitants in the thinkery: note, for example, the latter's departure from stage during the contest between Just and Unjust Speech.

[62]The closest indication of group study is Xenophon's reference to Socrates' exploration of the "treasures of the wise men of old" (*Mem.* 1.6.14) in the company of his friends. There appears to be no adequate parallel among the sophists at this period for a formal school of the kind envisaged by Aristophanes.

[63]Reformulated in Dover's terms, Aristophanes parodies "general characteristics of the sophists" by associating Socrates with a *phrontistērion* that, unlike Socrates himself, takes an interest in the ethical questions that concerned contemporary sophists.

tophanic Socrates' philosophical hero is Diogenes of Apollonia. Then I turn to Aristophanes' criticism of Socratic enquiry into nature, which remarkably parallels the mature Socrates' view, as represented by Xenophon, and discuss the latter's account of the considerations that led Socrates to reject the pre-Socratic approach to the study of nature but to advocate study of the ancillary disciplines of natural philosophy insofar as they are necessary to develop human freedom and self-sufficiency.

2. Socrates as a Natural Philosopher

If we are to understand why Socrates turned away from his early interest in the study of nature, we need to grasp as clearly as possible its original character. Our strategy will be to look for correspondences between the text that records the Platonic Socrates' criticism of pre-Socratic natural philosophy, *Phaedo* 96a–99d, and what is attributed to Socrates in the *Clouds*. My claim is that the Aristophanic Socrates, who attempts to explain all natural phenomena in terms of their material constituents, displays the same philosophical orientation as does the young Socrates, whose break with his pre-Socratism is motivated in part by dissatisfaction with this approach.[64]

What then are the central characteristics of this orientation? In the *Phaedo,* Socrates distinguishes several stages in his "first sailing." The initial stage is marked by great eagerness for enquiry into nature, coupled with an attempt to explain all natural phenomena as reducible to certain material constituents (96a–d). In the second stage, reflection on the problem of unity led Socrates to become dissatisfied with his attempt to account for the causes of things in material terms (96d–97b); but, in the stage that followed, Anaxagoras' view that *nous* arranges and causes all things seemed for a time to offer a way out of these difficulties (97b–98b); until, in the next stage, Socrates realized that Anaxagoras too reduces the causes of things to material constituents such as air, ether, and water, failing entirely to explain the true causes of things—namely, why it is *best* for them to be as they are (98b–99d). Socrates' dissatisfaction with Anaxagoras leads him to abandon

---

[64]The sole argument that Dover (above, note 20), p. xlix, offers against the interpretive strategy I adopt (which he would characterize as "the only recourse of those who believe that because Aristophanes and Plato are both admirable writers they must also be just, accurate and truthful") is that the "metaphysical curiosity" in *Phaedo* 96a–99d "is separated by a very wide gulf from Aristophanes' portrayal of a Socrates who professes to teach scientific doctrine in mechanistic terms." In this section I argue that there is little or no gulf between the Aristophanic Socrates and the youthful Socrates' enquiries into *physiologia* as set out at *Phaedo* 96a–b.

the pre-Socratic approach to nature altogether, and to embark finally on his "second sailing," wherein he seeks to investigate the truth of beings through *logoi* (99e), that is, through the method of hypothesis.[65] The Aristophanic Socrates, I suggest, corresponds to the initial stage of Socrates' first sailing.

Socrates undertakes to narrate his youthful experiences (τὰ πάθη) with the causes of generation and destruction in order to answer Cebes' concern that the soul, even if it undergoes reincarnation repeatedly, may prove to be not immortal but merely long-lasting. He begins as follows:

ἐγὼ γάρ, ἔφη, ὦ Κέβης, νέος ὢν θαυμαστῶς ὡς ἐπεθύμησα ταύτης τῆς σοφίας ἣν δὴ καλοῦσι περὶ φύσεως ἱστορίαν· ὑπερήφανος γάρ μοι ἐδόκει εἶναι, εἰδέναι τὰς αἰτίας ἑκάστου, διὰ τί γίγνεται ἕκαστον καὶ διὰ τί ἀπόλλυται καὶ διὰ τί ἔστι. καὶ πολλάκις ἐμαυτὸν ἄνω κάτω μετέβαλλον σκοπῶν πρῶτον τὰ τοιάδε. "Ἆρ' ἐπειδὰν τὸ θερμὸν καὶ τὸ ψυχρὸν σηπεδόνα τινὰ λάβῃ, ὥς τινες ἔλεγον, τότε δὴ τὰ ζῷα συντρέφεται; καὶ πότερον τὸ αἷμά ἐστιν ᾧ φρονοῦμεν, ἢ ὁ ἀὴρ ἢ τὸ πῦρ; ἢ τούτων καὶ μὲν οὐδέν, ὁ δ' ἐγκέφαλός ἐστιν ὁ τὰς αἰσθήσεις παρέχων τοῦ ἀκούειν καὶ ὁρᾶν καὶ ὀσφραίνεσθαι, ἐκ τούτων δὲ γίγνοιτο μνήμη καὶ δόξα, ἐκ δὲ μνήμης καὶ δόξης λαβούσης τὸ ἠρεμεῖν, κατὰ ταῦτα γίγνεσθαι ἐπιστήμην; καὶ αὖ τούτων τὰς φθορὰς σκοπῶν, καὶ τὰ περὶ τὸν οὐρανόν τε καὶ τὴν γῆν πάθη, τελευτῶν οὕτως ἐμαυτῷ ἔδοξα πρὸς ταύτην τὴν σκέψιν ἀφυὴς εἶναι ὡς οὐδὲν χρῆμα.

When I was young, Cebes, I was marvelously eager for this wisdom, which they call enquiry into nature. For it seemed to me glorious, to know the causes [*tas aitias*] of each thing, why each thing comes into being, why it perishes, and why it is; and many times I unsettled myself, investigating first such questions as these: (1) Is it when hot and cold give rise to putrefaction, as some say, that living beings are nourished? (2) And is it blood by which we think, or air or fire, or by none of these, but the brain that provides sensations of hearing and seeing and smelling, whence comes memory and opinion, and does knowledge come from memory and opinion in a state of rest according to these things? (3) And again, investigating the destruction of these things, the phenomena [*ta pathē*] of heaven and earth, I came at last to decide that I was by nature not fit at all for this investigation. (96a–b)

[65]On which see now D. L. Blank, "Socrates' Instructions to Cebes: Plato, *Phaedo* 101d–e," *Hermes* 114 (1986): 146–63. For the place of this account within the argument of the *Phaedo*, see the stimulating essay by M. Davis, "Socrates' Pre-Socratism: Some Remarks on the Structure of Plato's *Phaedo*," *RevMeta* 32 (1980): 559–77. D. W. Graham, "Socrates, the Craft Analogy, and Science," *Apeiron* 24 (1991): 1–24, has now argued that the demand for teleological explanation set forth in this passage is motivated by the moral requirements of Socratic ethics. See below, note 81 for the suggestion that Diogenes of Apollonia's argument from design in fr. 3 provides an important antecedent to the Platonic Socrates' demand for teleological explanation.

This account of the young Socrates' eager enquiry into the material causes of the generation and destruction of natural phenomena seems to characterize perfectly the activities of the Aristophanic Socrates, who likewise takes a comprehensive interest in the study of nature. Before Socrates even appears on stage he has been identified as a new Thales (cf. 180; *Av.* 1009), renowned for his enquiry into the heavenly things.[66] Socrates himself is reported to investigate such subjects as the number of its own feet a flea can jump (145), the physiology of the gnat (156–65), and the courses and revolutions of the moon (171–72).[67] When we first catch sight of his students, upon Strepsiades' entry into the thinkery, some are busily engaged in investigation of "the things under the earth" (188), while others stoop down so far as to delve into Erebus under Tartarus (192), while the πρωκτός looks up to heaven so that it, "itself by itself" (a clear parody of Socratic language), may learn astronomy (193–95; cf. 201). Geometry (177–79, 202–3),[68] geology (187–88), and geography (202–16) fill out the school's curriculum.[69] These and other examples testify to a comprehensive interest in the explanation of natural phenomena, both animate and inanimate, stretching from the heavens down to the deepest reaches of Tartarus.

Now the Aristophanic Socrates seeks to account for these phenomena in terms of their material causes, that is, in terms of the "necessity" that causes them to be constituted as they are. This corresponds to Socrates' attempt, in his pre-Socratic phase as described in the *Phaedo*, to look for the *aitia* of each thing (96a), by which he means the material constituent that is responsible for its physical constitution. The *aitia* for which the pre-Socratic Socrates seeks thus corresponds to the "necessity" that the Aristophanic Socrates offers in explanation of the material constituents of natural phenomena. This approach leads him to reject any explanation of these phenomena that appeals to divine will rather than material necessity. A good example is provided by Socrates' account of thunder, which Strepsiades challenges him to explain in view of his denial of the existence of Zeus:

---

[66]Cf. Hdt. 1.74.2 for Thales' prediction of the solar eclipse of 585 B.C.

[67]That Socrates, at least at a certain stage in his life, had an interest in questions of this general kind is confirmed by Xenophon *Symposium* 7.4 (which forms part of Socrates' rejoinder to the Aristophanic φθόνος of the Syracusan entertainer in 6.6–7.5), where he mentions as "marvels" immediately at hand the questions of why a lamp because of its bright flame gives light, but a bright bronze mirror does not produce light by reflections; and why olive oil, although wet, increases the flame, but water, because it is wet, puts the fire out.

[68]See further Taylor (above, note 11), pp. 154–56, for parodies of mathematical terminology in this opening scene.

[69]From Socrates' later instruction of Pheidippides it appears that the study of meter (638ff.) and grammar (658ff.) are propaedeutic disciplines that the initiate must master in order to enter the school.

ὅταν ἐμπλησθῶσ᾽ ὕδατος πολλοῦ κἀναγκασθῶσι φέρεσθαι
κατακρμνάμεναι πλήρεις ὄμβρου δι᾽ ἀνάγκην, εἶτα βαρεῖαι
εἰς ἀλλήλας ἐμπίπτουσαι ῥήγνυνται καὶ παταγοῦσιν.

When they are filled up with much water and are compelled
to be borne along by necessity, hanging down full of rain, then
they heavily fall into each other, bursting and clapping.

(376–79)

Socrates' account here relies solely on the material constituents of the
clouds: when they become filled with much water, they are borne along
by "necessity" until they collide with one another, and produce thunder
by their bursting and clapping.[70] This search for material causes is paralleled in other cases.[71]

Thus the Aristophanic Socrates seeks to explain all natural phenomena in terms of their material causes, just as described in the *Phaedo*.
But does he also investigate the specific subjects that the mature Socrates there offers as examples of the application of his search for material causes? Two of the three sentences marked in the passage from
the *Phaedo* translated above are clearly attested for the *Clouds*, and the
third is a doctrine held by Socrates' teacher.

To begin with the last, (1) is a clear allusion to the zoogony of Archelaus, Socrates' teacher.[72] Archelaus follows Anaxagoras in holding
that there is a material mixture and in adopting the same first principles, but he modifies his doctrine of *nous* by holding that there is a certain mixture in it, and that motion originated in the separation of hot
and cold (Hippol. *Haer.* 1.9.5).[73] The doctrine to which Plato alludes is
put by Hippolytus as follows in his account of Archelaus' zoogony:
when "the hot and the cold were mingled, many animals began to appear, including human beings, all with the same manner of life and all
deriving their nourishment from the slime."[74] It is likely that Socrates
encountered this doctrine in the course of his study with Archelaus.
Aristophanes' silence about it may not be significant: for it is evident
from *Phaedo* 96c–d that Socrates' enquiries into the origin of living be-

---

[70]Socrates' explanation of βροντή in terms of the moisture in the clouds may well derive from Diogenes (see *Placita* 3.3.8 in *DG*).

[71]So, for example, in the case of the thunderbolt (403–7).

[72]This is on the authority of Theophrastus, as Simplicius (*In phys.* 27.23) indicates; cf.
the Suda, s.v. "Archelaus"; Porph. *Hist. philos.* fr. 12; D.L. 2.16, 23.

[73]Cf. Burnet *ad* Pl. *Phd.* 96b3; Kirk, Raven, and Schofield (above, note 4), pp. 385–89.

[74]περὶ δὲ ξῴων φησίν, ὅτι θερμαινομένης τῆς γῆς τὸ πρῶτον ἐν τῷ κάτω μέρει, ὅπου τὸ
θερμὸν καὶ τὸ ψυχρὸν ἐμίσγετο ἀνεφαίνετο τά τε ἄλλα ξῷα πολλὰ καὶ οἱ ἄνθρωποι,
ἅπαντα τὴν αὐτὴν δίαιταν ἔχοντα ἐκ τῆς ἰλύος τρεφόμενα (ἦν δὲ ὀλιγοχρόνια), ὕστερον
δὲ αὐτοῖς ἡ ἐξ ἀλλήλων γένεσις συνέτη (Hippol. *Haer.* 1.9.5). The language of this passage explains *syntrephetai* in (1) marked in *Phaedo* 96a–b as translated above.

ings form part of his attempt to explain the generation and passing away of all natural phenomena in terms of their material causes, and we have already seen that this is a central concern of the Aristophanic Socrates.

Socrates' interest in the material causes of thinking, signaled in (2), is clearly attested for the Aristophanic Socrates in *Clouds* 227–34, where he adopts the physiology of cognition advocated by Diogenes of Apollonia. We may infer that the Aristophanic Socrates adheres to Diogenes' theory in detail and does not just allude to it in passing, for he refers to two distinct features of it in this passage: Diogenes' explanation of thinking in terms of air, and his claim that moisture impedes *nous*. His position that air is the material cause of all natural phenomena, as we shall see shortly, is repeatedly parodied in the *Clouds*. If we are right to infer that the Aristophanic Socrates is an adherent of Diogenes, we need not worry that he does not dwell on the physiology of memory and sensation.[75] Of course, Diogenes' is only one of the theories of cognition considered by Socrates in the course of his "first sailing" (others include Empedocles' doctrine that blood is the organ of thought [fr. B105 DK], and Heraclitus' that it is fire), but it is the stage in Socrates' philosophical development Aristophanes has chosen for parody.

Socrates' final example of the kind of enquiries in which he engaged, (3) the phenomena of heaven and earth, is abundantly attested for the Aristophanic Socrates. As we have already noted, his students, when they first appear on stage, are investigating "the things beneath the earth" (187–92), as well as the heaven (194); they learn how to use the equipment of astronomy and geometry (202–4); and Socrates himself first appears suspended aloft in a basket, claiming that he could not otherwise discover the heavenly things (τὰ μετέωρα πράγματα) correctly (216–28). He later says that his patrons, the clouds, nourish most of the sophists, who are "imposters about the heavenly things [μετεω-ροφένακας]" (331–33; cf. 360, 1284).

The Aristophanic Socrates thus investigates the same questions, from the same philosophical perspective, as does the young Socrates of Plato's *Phaedo*. The latter account, written as it is from the perspective of Socrates' "second sailing," suggests that Socrates considered over the years a broader range of pre-Socratic explanations than is attested in the *Clouds*, where he is represented as adhering to the views of Diogenes of Apollonia. This difference in perspective between the two ac-

---

[75] A full account may be found in Theophrastus' *De sensu* 39–44 (= 64A19 DK) and in *De morbo sacro* 19 (= 64C3a DK).

counts may well be responsible for their minor differences of emphasis and detail.[76]

So far, then, we have seen that the Aristophanic Socrates seeks to explain all natural phenomena by identifying the "necessity" that accounts for their material constitution. How does this philosophical orientation relate to contemporary pre-Socratic thought of the 420s? Is it plausible to suppose that Socrates might have engaged in the kind of study of nature as depicted in the *Clouds* at this time?

Let me begin by justifying further my suggestion that the Aristophanic Socrates is represented as an adherent of Diogenes of Apollonia. This is not a novel view,[77] but the evidence that supports it has been considerably underestimated. When he first appears on stage, suspended aloft in a basket, Socrates at once appeals to Diogenes' doctrines to explain why he cannot investigate the heavenly things from the ground. Here is his dialogue with Strepsiades:

Σω.   τί με καλεῖς, ὦ 'φήμερε;
Στ.   πρῶτον μὲν ὅτι δρᾷς, ἀντιβολῶ, κάτειπέ μοι.
Σω.   ἀεροβατῶ καὶ περιφρονῶ τὸν ἥλιον.
Στ.   ἔπειτ' ἀπὸ ταρροῦ τοὺς θεοὺς ὑπερφρονεῖς,
         ἀλλ' οὐκ ἀπὸ τῆς γῆς, εἴπερ;
Σω.   οὐ γὰρ ἄν ποτε
         ἐξηῦρον ὀρθῶς τὰ μετέωρα πράγματα
         εἰ μὴ κρεμάσας τὸ νόημα καὶ τὴν φροντίδα,
         λεπτὴν καταμείξας εἰς τὸν ὅμοιον ἀέρα.

---

[76]John Ackrill has drawn to my attention a possible difficulty in reconciling the chronology of *Phaedo* 96a–b with the reconstruction here developed. Are we to suppose that Socrates went through a period in which he explored Diogenes' position before the third stage of his intellectual autobiography, in which he examined Anaxagoras' account of *nous* as a possible answer to the problems he found in accounting for natural phenomena in material terms? This chronology might seem unlikely, especially since Diogenes' doctrine of *nous* appears to be a revised version of Anaxagoras', which, I suggest in note 81 below, is not vulnerable to the same objections leveled against Anaxagoras at *Phaedo* 98b–99d. Once again our evidence seems insufficient to settle so precise a question of chronology, which the *Phaedo* telescopes from the perspective of Socrates' "second sailing" without relating it to other episodes in Socrates' biography. Socrates might well have retained an interest in Diogenes' thought throughout the first four stages of his development; and while the detailed parallels between Aristophanes and Plato assembled in this section certainly attest that interest for the first stage, other evidence of Socrates' association with Diogenes suggests that the *Phaedo* may take some liberties with chronology in Socrates' repudiation of *physiologia* (see below, note 81).

[77]The best statement of it is that of Burnet (above, note 13), pp. xxxix–xlii. The identification of Diogenes as Aristophanes' source in the lines that follow goes back to H. Diels, "Über Leukipp und Demokrit," *Verhandlungen den 35.Versammlung deutscher Philologen und Schulmänner v.27–30.9 1880* (Stuttgart, 1881), pp. 96–109 at pp. 105–8, reprinted in *Kleine Schriften zur Geschichte der antiken Philosophie*, ed. W. Burkert (Darmstadt, 1969), pp. 184–98 at pp. 194–97.

εἰ δ᾽ ὢν χαμαὶ τἄνω κάτωθεν ἐσκόπουν,
οὐκ ἄν ποθ᾽ ηὗρον· οὐ γὰρ ἀλλ᾽ ἡ γῆ βίᾳ
ἕλκει πρὸς αὑτὴν τὴν ἰκμάδα τῆς φροντίδος.
πάσχει δὲ ταὐτὸ τοῦτο καὶ τὰ κάρδαμα.

Soc. Why are you calling me, ephemeral one?
Strep. First, I beseech you, tell me what you're doing.
Soc. I tread on air and contemplate the sun.
Strep. Then you look down on the gods from a perch
  and not from the earth—if that's what you're doing?
Soc. I would never
discover the matters aloft correctly
except by suspending mind and subtle thought
and mixing them with their like, the air.
If I considered the things above from below on the ground,
I would never discover them. For the earth forcefully
pulls to itself the moisture from the thought.
The same thing happens also to the water cress.

(223–34)

That Socrates is relying specifically on Diogenes in lines 229–30 is beyond doubt. Diogenes holds that air is the single source from which all other things come into being (fr. B2 DK = Simpl. *In phys.* 25.1–9); and he defends the position that all existing things are alterations of air by a novel application of the Parmenidean ban against the generation of anything out of that which it is not: he maintains that if anything were different in its nature and were not simply an alteration of air, it could not mix with anything else, and hence there could be no generation. It follows then that human beings depend upon this material principle of air for their life and thought:

ἄνθρωποι γὰρ καὶ τὰ ἄλλα ζῷα ἀναπνέοτα ξώει τῷ ἀέρι. καὶ τοῦτο αὐτοῖς καὶ ψυχή ἐστι καὶ νοήσις, ὡς δεδηλώσεται ἐν τῇδε τῇ συγγραφῇ ἐμφανῶς, καὶ ἐὰν τοῦτο ἀπαλλαχθῇ ἀποθνῇσκει καὶ ἡ νόησις ἐπιλείπει.

Humans and other animals, inasmuch as they breathe, live by the air. And this is for them both soul and intelligence, as will have been shown clearly in this treatise; and if this departs, they die and their intelligence is lost. (Fr. B4 DK)

This then is the doctrine that underlies Socrates' reference to mixing thought with its "like," air; and since no other pre-Socratic philosopher held this position, we can be sure that Diogenes is the source. This conclusion is supported by Socrates' joke in lines 232–34 (cf. 762), where he draws upon Diogenes' position that moisture inhibits or destroys the mind (hence animals that breathe air from the earth are feebler in intellect)[78] to explain why he could not discover the heavenly things from the ground.

This elaborate parody clearly identifies Socrates, in his first appearance on stage, as an adherent of Diogenes. This is by no means the only evidence linking the two. In fact, I suggest that the clouds, who are Socrates' divine patrons in this play, represent a comic parody of Diogenes' position that "that which possesses intelligence [*noēsis*] is called air by human beings, and by it all human beings are steered, and it has power over everything. For it is this that seems to me to be god and to have reached everything and to arrange everything and to be in everything" (fr. B5 DK). If Socrates considered the clouds to represent air, which is divine, in a condensed form, it would explain why he invokes the clouds as goddesses,[79] who rule over mortals' affairs. It would also explain why Socrates invokes his goddesses by such inconsistent designations: he calls them air, ether, and clouds (263–66; cf. 570 with Dover ad loc.); chaos, clouds, and tongue (423); respiration, chaos, and air (627); Strepsiades also swears "by the mist" (814). Yet we know that the clouds alone are divine (365). An explanation lies ready at hand if we suppose that ether, chaos, respiration, tongue, and the clouds are just alterations of the same material principle, air, which takes these different forms as it condenses and rarefies. If one wonders how respiration or tongue could be counted as a form of air, our hypothesis that Aristophanes is developing an elaborate parody of Diogenes' theory provides a ready answer: according to Diogenes, air *becomes* intelligence when humans breathe it through respiration (frs. B4–5 DK; cf. Arist. *De an.* 404a9–10; Heraclitus 22A16 DK = Sext. Emp. *Math.* 7.129). It is for this reason, I suggest, that the Aristophanic Socrates attributes the powers of thought to the clouds:

> ἥκιστ', ἀλλ' οὐράνιαι Νεφέλαι, μεγάλαι θεαὶ ἀνδράσιν ἀργοῖς,
> αἵπερ γνώμην καὶ διάλεξιν καὶ νοῦν ἡμῖν παρέχουσιν
> καὶ τερατείαν καὶ περίλεξιν καὶ κροῦσιν καὶ κατάληψιν.

> They're heavenly Clouds, great goddesses for idle men,
> who provide us with notions and dialectic and mind,
> and marvel telling and circumlocution and striking and seizing.
> (316–18)

---

[78]See Theophr. *Sens.* 43–45; *De morbo sacro* 19. For a Heraclitean antecedent of Diogenes' position, see frs. B117, 36, 77 DK.

[79]E.g., 263–72, a passage that alludes to Diogenes' view on the position of the earth (cf. Dover [above, note 20] *ad* 272).

My suggestion, then, is that we explain Socrates' conception of the clouds and their powers in terms of Diogenes' theory of air as the material principle of all things. This suggestion has the dual advantage of accounting very neatly for some central peculiarities in Socrates' conception of the clouds and of attributing to him, so far as is consistent with comic parody, a single philosophical position.[80]

In thus portraying Socrates as an adherent of Diogenes of Apollonia, Aristophanes attributes to him a single philosophical orientation that is entirely consistent with the state of contemporary philosophical activity. Nor is this the only evidence connecting the two, for in *Memorabilia* 1.4 and 4.3 Xenophon attributes to Socrates a natural teleology that appears to draw upon the argument from the design of nature first put forward in fragment 3 of Diogenes, although Xenophon in suggesting that the gods have created the entire natural order in such a way as to benefit human beings goes well beyond Diogenes' own claim.[81] There seems accordingly no cogent reason to doubt the possibility that Socrates once engaged in the study of nature along the lines caricatured in the *Clouds*. Plato himself provides decisive evidence that Socrates, at a certain point in his life, was an enthusiastic proponent of the explanation of natural phenomena in terms of their material causes. The fact that Socrates is not elsewhere named as an adherent of Diogenes may have no significance, given the paucity of

[80]Further evidence that the Aristophanic Socrates is an adherent of Diogenes may be found in (1) the reference to his views about the flooding of the Nile (272, with Dover [above, note 20] ad loc.); (2) Socrates' view that the material principle of air is "boundless" (262, 392), to which only Diogenes among the pre-Socratics subscribed; (3) Socrates' interest in the physiology of the gnat (156–68), which may represent a parody of Diogenes fr. B8 DK; (4) Socrates' appeal to μεγάλοις σημείοις in 369, which is a characteristic feature of Diogenes' argumentative style in *On Nature* (cf. μεγάλα σημεῖα in fr. B4 DK); and (5) references in 762 and 1276 that appear to recall Diogenes' physiology of sensation.

[81]See above, note 50. Diogenes' apparent influence on the Xenophontic Socrates is important for two principal reasons. First, if Xenophon's Socrates borrowed the teleological argument from design from Diogenes, then we have evidence independent of Aristophanes' *Clouds* that at a certain stage of his philosophical development Socrates was in some sense an adherent of Diogenes. Second, such influence, if established, would place Socrates' demand for teleological explanations in the *Phaedo* in a different light: he there represents this demand as entailing a rejection of the whole pre-Socratic approach to the study of nature, appearing to imply that no material explanation of natural phenomena is available that also explains how these phenomena are structured in the best possible way. Yet a central purpose of Diogenes' *On Nature* is to show that one can explain the organization and functioning of all natural phenomena—from the orderly progression of the seasons down to the internal workings of the human body—in terms of a single process, which, itself being intelligent, arranges them all in the noblest possible way. This account, which explains in material terms how all natural phenomena are structured in accordance with a natural teleology, provides the only possible pre-Socratic source for Socrates' own argument that god has ordered the natural world in the best possible way. Socrates thus may have been inspired by Diogenes' *On Nature* to develop the argument that he represents in the *Phaedo* as one of the dividing lines between pre-Socratic and Socratic philosophy.

our information about his intellectual biography. And Aristophanes' portrayal is fitting in another respect. Diogenes was recognized in antiquity, as early as Theophrastus, as the last of the *physikoi,* and this designation is particularly apt if one of his adherents was responsible for turning philosophy in a new direction. For as tradition would have it, it was Socrates who called philosophy down from the heavens.

3. Aristophanes and Socrates

We may now turn to consider Aristophanes' judgment on Socrates and his enquiries into nature. Aristophanes conveys this judgment in two ways: first, through what he says in his own name in the parabasis of the *Clouds* (518–62); and second, through the action of the play itself. More specifically, Aristophanes conveys his criticism of Socrates through actions that his characters take or advocate as a direct result of views they have come to hold through their association with Socrates: these include denial of the existence of Zeus, refusal to repay debts backed by oaths sworn in Zeus's name, father-beating, and the advocacy of incest and of mother-beating. In the final scene of the *Clouds,* Aristophanes portrays the burning-down of the thinkery by an irate father who seeks to punish Socrates for his own corruption and that of his son, and whose arson receives divine sanction through Hermes' appearance—which provides a visible refutation, as it were, of Socrates' denial of the existence of the Olympian gods. Surely, we may suppose, the conclusion of the *Clouds* conveys a negative judgment on Socrates.

Yet we must be cautious. The chorus of clouds themselves suggest that Strepsiades is responsible for what has transpired (1454–55), because he twisted himself into villainous affairs; and they claim credit for throwing him into evil "so that he may know dread of the gods" (1461).[82] Strepsiades' corruption and his impiety thus precede his introduction to Socrates: at most, if we follow the chorus' interpretation of the action of the play, Socrates is responsible for providing instruction in dialectic to an imprudent student who avowedly wishes to put it to unjust ends. Does Socrates deserve destruction for this, given that the debate between Just and Unjust Speech, held on the premises of the thinkery, shows that mastery of the weaker speech leads to the triumph of injustice? On what grounds is Socrates' punishment justified?

In the parabasis of the *Clouds,* Aristophanes comes out to speak on his own behalf. He does not mention Socrates by name, but if we com-

---

[82]There are many important parallels between Strepsiades and the figure of Bdelycleon in the *Wasps;* see David Konstan, "The Politics of Aristophanes' *Wasps,*" *TAPA* 115 (1985): 27–46.

pare what he claims for this, "the wisest of my comedies" (καὶ ταύτην σοφώτατ' ἔχειν τῶν ἐμῶν κωμῳδιῶν, 522), with the characteristics he ascribes to Socrates in the play, we may infer his judgment on Socrates.[83] In enumerating why his "shrewd spectators" (θεατὰς δεξίους, 521; cf. 527) should grant the *Clouds* the prize it failed to attain in its first performance, Aristophanes claims that "I always sophisticate by bringing in novel ideas not at all like one another—and all shrewd" (547–48; cf. 561–62; *Vesp.* 65–66, 1043–53; *Ach.* 501). He thus seems to appropriate for himself Socrates' chief characteristics.[84] In pandering to his shrewd spectators with shrewd ideas, Aristophanes recalls Socrates' own enquiries into nature, which are described as "most shrewd" (148; cf. 757, 834, 852), as well as the clouds' promises to Strepsiades (418, 428); in boasting that he introduces novel ideas, he claims an affinity with Unjust Speech, whose wisdom and capacity for victory in argumentation consist in discovering new thoughts (895; cf. 937, 943, 1032), and with Pheidippides, who, urged by his father to recite something new (1370), chooses a passage from Euripides' *Aeolus* about a brother's incest with his sister. These parallels suggest that Aristophanes can hardly mean to censure Socrates simply for introducing novel ideas. On the other hand, Aristophanes surely means to distance himself from the use to which Unjust Speech and Pheidippides put Socrates' novel ideas, given that their actions lead, in the final scene of the play, to Socrates' punishment at the hands of the gods. These considerations suggest that Aristophanes does not oppose the search for shrewd and novel ideas per se but the particular use to which they are put by Socrates' associates.[85]

If we look through the parabasis for further hints as to how Aristophanes distinguishes himself from Socrates, we find one significant indication: this is Aristophanes' claim that his play is "moderate by nature" (σώφρων: 529, 537). Neither Socrates nor his students ever even refer to moderation; the only advocate of moderation in the *Clouds,* in fact, is Just Speech, whom Aristophanes represents as being decisively defeated by Unjust Speech through his use of Socratic argumentative techniques. What leads Just Speech to desert to his rival's cause? The answer in part must consist in his inability to offer a satis-

---

[83]See now the careful analysis by Hubbard 1991 (above, note 20), pp. 88–112, who well brings out the multiple levels of irony and self-reference in this text and who notices (pp. 94–95) the close parallels between the *sophia* of Socrates and of Aristophanes.

[84]This consideration alone suffices to refute the claim of Dover (above, note 20), p. lii, that "in order to understand *Nu.* we must make an imaginative effort to adopt . . . the position of someone to whom all philosophical and scientific speculation, all disinterested intellectual curiosity, is boring and silly."

[85]Cf. the parabasis of the *Acharnians* at 497–501, where Dicaeopolis promises to instruct the city with "things shrewd but just" (ἐγὼ δὲ λέξω δεινὰ μὲν δίκαια δέ).

factory account of the rewards of moderation (1060–82): when challenged to give an example by Unjust Speech, he offers that of Peleus, who was given the goddess Thetis in marriage on account of his moderation; but the example backfires, as Unjust Speech points out that she left him, being neither hubristic nor pleasant to spend the night with. Just Speech, not unlike other early conventionalist thinkers of his day,[86] conceives the reward of moderation to consist in pleasure, ultimately in sexual pleasure. Since Unjust Speech can openly advocate gratification of the "necessities of nature" (1075), it is hardly surprising that Just Speech proves unable to sustain his case for moderation.

How then are we to assess Aristophanes' own position as he presents it in the *Clouds*? In accounting his own play moderate, Aristophanes sides with Just Speech, who advocates the ancient education of Marathon days, equipped as it was with justice and *sōphrosynē* (961–62). But he also shows that Just Speech's advocacy of moderation cannot withstand the onslaught of Unjust Speech and his new sophistry. To restore the ancient life of moderation for which Just Speech expresses nostalgia, one would have to master the study of nature, and all the techniques of persuasion and refutation it offers. Like Socrates, Aristophanes pronounces himself a sophisticate who is always ready to introduce novel ideas; unlike Socrates, he offers these novel ideas in the cause of moderation.[87] In support of this line of interpretation, I turn to Aristophanes' portrayal of the moral and political dilemmas to which Socrates' study of nature leads.

Socrates himself is wholly absorbed in the study of nature. In contrast to Just and Unjust Speech alike, he evinces no interest in the "necessitates of nature"; and his poverty provides sufficient evidence of his indifference to money and worldly goods. Hence Socrates lacks the motivation of a Strepsiades to engage in injustice for personal gain. Yet even Socrates requires certain minimal resources to maintain his ascetic way of life. As Aristophanes portrays him, he is prepared to use his knowledge of nature, and the superior skills of persuasion it provides him, to engage in injustice. Put more bluntly, Aristophanes represents Socrates as a petty thief. When Strepsiades comes to the thinkery, one of its students explains how Socrates contrived the previous day to provide them with dinner: under the guise of doing geometry, he made away with the cloak from the wrestling school

---

[86]See L. Strauss, *Natural Right and History* (Chicago, 1953), pp. 97–115.

[87]I am pleased to be able to cite in support the similar conclusion, reached independently, by Hubbard 1991 (above, note 20), p. 95: "Aristophanes differs from Socrates in that there is a moral dimension to his *sophia*; his comedy is not only *sophos* but also *sophron* (vv. 529, 537), and not only 'clever' but also 'prudent.' "

(177–79).[88] Nor is this his only misdeed involving cloaks: when Strepsiades undertakes to burn the thinkery down in the last scene of the play, he identifies himself to a student as "the one whose cloak you took" (1498). When we recall that Socrates himself insisted that Strepsiades take off his cloak before entering the thinkery (497), and that Strepsiades later tells his son that he did not lose but "thought away" the cloak and lost his sandals for "something needful," recalling a famous episode of bribery by Pericles (856–59), we surmise that members of the thinkery are not above taking advantage of initiates. Such acts of petty theft would be unnecessary, of course, if Socrates accepted pay for his teaching, as Strepsiades offers at the outset (245–46); but Socrates is so indifferent to worldly goods that he makes no provision either for himself or for his students.

If Socrates himself does not exploit his knowledge of nature and his dialectical skill for personal gain, his students certainly do. And Socrates is perfectly willing to teach them how to exploit their knowledge of nature for unjust gain. When Strepsiades exclaims that he wants to learn "the most unjust speech" (657), not about meters and rhythms, Socrates tells him that he must learn other things first, such as what quadrupeds are correctly called males. The results of this instruction are evident in Strepsiades' treatment of the two creditors who come demanding repayment of his debt to them. It is quite clear that Strepsiades believes that this knowledge of nature discharges him from any obligation to honor these debts. When his creditor swears by Zeus that Strepsiades will not get away with his refusal to pay, Strepsiades responds "swearing by Zeus is laughable to those who know" (1241); and when the creditor calls a panette a "pan," Strepsiades responds that he would not give such a man even an obol (1250–51). When the second creditor arrives, the following exchange ensues:

> Στ.   κάτειπέ νυν·
> πότερα νομίζεις καινὸν αἰεὶ τὸν Δία
> ὕειν ὕδωρ ἑκάστοτ', ἢ τὸν ἥλιον
> ἕλκειν κάτωθεν ταὐτὸ τοῦθ' ὕδωρ πάλιν;
> Χρ. οὐκ οἶδ' ἔγωγ' ὁπότερον, οὐδέ μοι μέλει.
> Στ. πῶς οὖν ἀπολαβεῖν τἀργύριον δίκαιος εἶ,
> εἰ μηδὲν οἶσθα τῶν μετεώρων πραγμάτων;

> *Strep.*   Tell me now,
> do you believe that Zeus always rains fresh
> water on each occasion, or does the sun

---

[88]Cf. Strauss (above, note 21), p. 14. Ameipsias appears to have made a similar joke in his *Connus*, also performed in 423 B.C., having the chorus leader ask Socrates how he would procure a cloak (fr. 9 *PCG*). The scholium to *Clouds* 179e cites Socrates' theft as a parallel to Eupolis fr. 395 *PCG*.

draw the same water back up from below?
Cred. I don't know which, nor do I care.
Strep. How then is it just for you to get your money back
if you know nothing of the heavenly things?

(1278–84)

Strepsiades' argument appears to rely upon the well-known Socratic principle that knowledge alone confers title of ownership (see, for example, Xen. *Oec.* 1.1–2.18). Strepsiades clearly presupposes that those who possess knowledge, more specifically the knowledge of nature that encompasses the heavenly things, have no obligations or bonds of justice to those who lack it. He apparently thinks that the contracts into which he freely entered are rendered invalid by his superior knowledge, that he has no need to honor oaths sworn in Zeus's name once he learns that Zeus does not exist. Like Socrates, he exploits the dialectical skills this knowledge gives him for unjust purposes. It is unclear whether either Socrates or Strepsiades believes that bonds of justice obtain between those who equally share in knowledge of nature, as is perhaps suggested by Pheidippides' refusal, in the final scene, to do injustice to his teachers (1467). But it is clear that neither acknowledges the conventional bonds on which political communities must rely.

Thus the Aristophanic Socrates is a figure who takes no interest in the community on which his thinkery relies for its subsistence. He makes no provision for his own survival or that of his students but exploits his superior knowledge and dialectical skill to purloin what he needs. His enquiries span the whole range of natural phenomena, but they do not include the human things. The Aristophanic Socrates takes no interest in such subjects as justice, piety, or the family. Hence whenever he or his students come into contact with the community in which they dwell, the results are predictably disastrous.

It is well known that the mature Socrates, as he is portrayed by his fourth-century heirs, differs from his pre-Socratic counterpart in almost every respect: he is the most just and pious of all men, and all of his philosophical enquiries are devoted to the understanding of the human things. What then is the source of Socrates' conversion? What considerations led him to abandon his search for material explanations of natural phenomena and to call philosophy down from the heavens by making the study of nature instrumental to human happiness?

4. The Ethical Purpose of Socratic Enquiry into Nature

The reticence with which Socrates' philosophical apologists treat his intellectual biography, as I remarked at the outset, complicates any assessment of this problem. Yet they could hardly avoid accounting for the obvious differences between their portrayal of Socrates and Aristophanes'. Plato has his Socrates appear to deny in court that he ever engaged in *physiologia* of the kind caricatured by Aristophanes. The intellectual autobiography that Socrates expounds in the *Phaedo* after his trial and condemnation has given us reason to doubt this denial, but Plato offers no account here or elsewhere in the dialogues why Socrates' rejection of pre-Socratic *physiologia* entailed a particular emphasis on ethical questions.[89] Hence if we wish to understand the traditional assessment of Socrates' philosophical achievement, we must consider Xenophon's account of the relation between Socrates' disavowal of the pre-Socratic approach to *physiologia* and his own mature preoccupation with human *kalokagathia*.

In the course of his defense of Socrates against the charge of impiety leveled against him at his trial, Xenophon undertakes to explain how Socrates' enquiries differed from those of the "sophists" who concerned themselves with investigation of the causes of celestial phenomena. Socrates himself, Xenophon tells us, concerned himself exclusively with "the human things" and characterized his philosophical opponents as "madmen." Socrates' criticism of pre-Socratic natural philosophy in *Memorabilia* 1.1.11–16 is the principal source of the traditional assessment of Socrates' philosophical achievement:

> (11) No one ever saw or heard Socrates doing or saying anything impious or unholy. In fact, he did not enquire in the same way as most of the others concerning the nature of the universe, how the cosmos—so called by the sophists—was born, and by what causes [τίσιν ἀνάγκαις] each of the heavenly things comes into being; but he even considered those who worry about such things foolish. (12) In the first place, he would enquire of them whether they proceed to worry about such things, considering their knowledge of the human things sufficient, or whether they consider that they are doing what is fitting in neglecting the human things but enquiring into the divine [τὰ δαιμόνια]. (13) Moreover, he wondered if it were not clear to them that it is not possible for human beings to discover these things, since even those who think most of themselves for their speech about these things do not agree with one another but are disposed toward one another like madmen. (14) For of madmen some do not fear fearful things, while others fear things not frightening; some do not believe it shameful to say or do anything whatever in a crowd, while others believe one ought not even go out among human beings; some honor neither temple nor altar nor any other divine thing, while others worship stones, chance wooden objects, and beasts. And of those who worry about the nature of the universe, some think that being is one only, others that

[89]See above, note 6.

it is infinite in number; some that everything is always in motion, others that nothing can ever be moved; some that everything both comes into being and perishes, others that nothing ever could come into being or perish. (15) He used also to make the following enquiry about [the sophists]. Just as those who learn about the human things consider that whatever they learn they will be able to put to use for themselves and anyone else they wish, do those who investigate divine things think that when they know by what causes each comes into being, they will make winds, waters, seasons, and whatever else of such things they need whenever they wish, or do they not even hope for this, but it suffices for them only to know how each of these things comes into being?

(16) Such then was his speech concerning those who busy themselves with these things. He himself always enquired into the human things, what is piety, what is impiety, what is noble, what is shameful, what is just, what is unjust, what is moderation, what is madness, what is courage, what is cowardice, what is a state [πόλις], what is a statesman, what is rule over human beings, what is a ruler over human beings, and concerning other things of which those knowledgeable he considered *kaloikagathoi*, while those ignorant could justly be called slavish.

This passage identifies three objections that Socrates brought against the sophists' enquiry into the causes of celestial phenomena. These objections are formulated as questions to which Socrates presumably supposed they could not provide adequate answers, though the second question at 1.1.13 contains an assertion of the impossibility of discovering the causes of celestial phenomena that provides our best indication of the argumentative underpinning of Socrates' criticism of *physiologia* here. In seeking to expose the sophists' rationale for enquiry into the divine at the expense of human things this criticism not only presupposes Socrates' own mature preoccupation with human *kalokagathia* but also relies for its argumentative force upon his own philosophical position.[90] In what follows, I shall attempt to clarify how Socrates' criticism of pre-Socratic philosophy here is rooted in Xenophon's own distinctive interpretation of Socratic ethics. The status of this passage as the source of the traditional assessment of Socrates'

---

[90]In view of this fact, it is possible that the criticism of pre-Socratic natural philosophy presented in *Memorabilia* 1.1.11–15 may not be identical with the considerations that first led Socrates to disavow *physiologia* except insofar as it elucidates the human things. In other words, this passage, no less than the autobiography of the *Phaedo*, may be written from the perspective of a "second sailing." On the other hand, the dramatic setting of the *Oeconomicus*—even if ironical—indicates clearly that in Xenophon's understanding Socrates undertook to escape from his Aristophanic reputation as an idle chatterer with his head in the air (*Oec.* 11.3; cf. 6.12–17; 2.16) through enquiry into human *kalokagathia*: hence the objections set out in *Memorabilia* 1.1.11–15 are certainly consistent with Socrates' "conversion" as Xenophon understands it.

philosophical achievement makes it especially important to understand the precise sense in which Socrates disavows *physiologia* here.

Socrates' first objection aims to clarify how the sophists themselves understand the relation between their enquiry into divine and into human things. Do they investigate celestial phenomena because they consider that they have attained sufficient knowledge of the latter, or rather because they consider investigation of the former fitting? Leaving to one side in this context the possibility that the sophists might claim already to possess a sufficient understanding of the human things, Socrates introduces another objection apparently intended to refute those sophists who would defend the second alternative. He asserts: "It is not possible for human beings to discover these things."[91] On the basis of this assertion, Socrates ridicules proponents of the second alternative as "madmen" who fail to recognize the limitations of human knowledge. He characterizes the sophists' philosophical madness in terms of an elaborate comparison between three pairs of "madmen" and three examples of disagreement concerning the nature of the universe.[92]

Why does Socrates think that his examples of disagreement between Eleatics and Atomists justify his conclusion that those who investigate the nature of the cosmos in the sophists' manner are conceited madmen?[93] The logic of this argument appears to rely on Socrates' assertion at 1.1.13 that discovery of the causes of celestial phenomena is in some sense impossible for human beings. Yet this claim admits of different interpretations: Socrates may hold (i) that *physiologia* as practiced by the sophists is impossible because knowledge of nature is entirely beyond human capacity, in which case his rejection of the sophists' approach would amount to rejection of the study of nature per se; alternatively, Socrates may believe (ii) that some knowledge of

---

[91]Cf. the parallel criticism of Anaxagoras at *Memorabilia* 4.7.6: κινδυνεῦσαι δ' ἂν ἔφη καὶ παραφρονῆσαι τὸν ταῦτα μεριμνῶντα οὐδὲν ἧττον ἢ 'Αναξαγόρας παρεφρόνησεν ὁ μέγιστον φρονήσας ἐπὶ τῷ τὰς τῶν θεῶν μηχανὰς ἐξηγεῖσθαι. Note Xenophon's allusion here to Aristophanes in appropriating his coinage μεριμνοφροντισταί—Strepsiades' characterization of the inhabitants of the thinkery whom he cannot name (*Nub.* 100)—to parody sophistic investigation into the nature of the universe.

[92]L. Berns, "Socratic and Non-Socratic Philosophy: A Note on Xenophon's *Memorabilia* 1.1.13 and 14," *RevMeta* 28 (1974): 85–88, points out the parallel and suggests that the Xenophontic Socrates believes that a particular form of madness corresponds to each of the pre-Socratic positions contrasted.

[93]Socrates appears to cite the sophists' disagreement with one another as support for his assertion that their objects of enquiry are not discoverable by human beings. This puzzling line of argument may rely in part on Socrates' position that philosophical argument must proceed by steps that gain general assent (a strategy at which Socrates himself excelled: *Mem.* 4.6.15). The fact of systematic disagreement among the pre-Socratics may, according to this view, suffice to discredit their enquiry, even to justify the imputation of madness to them.

nature may be attained by human beings, but not the causes of celestial phenomena that the sophists aim to acquire. If the second interpretation is correct, Socrates in rejecting pre-Socratic *physiologia* may not mean to disavow study of nature per se; to the contrary, he may regard some knowledge of it both possible and necessary for his own enquiries into human *kalokagathia*. Since Xenophon does not explicitly decide between these alternatives in *Memorabilia* 1.1.11–16, we must turn to consider the broader argument in which Xenophon situates this passage. While most readers seem to have adopted the first interpretation,[94] I shall argue in what follows that the second is correct.

In defending Socrates' piety in the immediately preceding context (*Mem.* 1.1.7–9), Xenophon draws attention to a distinction between divine and human knowledge on which Socrates relies in giving moral advice to his associates. This distinction represents a central point of difference between Socrates and his sophistic opponents, and I suggest that it informs both his position on the possibility of knowledge of nature and his characterization of his opponents as madmen. According to Xenophon, Socrates thinks that knowledge of the crafts—from carpentry and farming through household management and generalship—is attainable by human beings, but "he said that the gods reserved to themselves the greatest of these things" (1.1.7). More specifically, Socrates holds that the gods have so ordained the natural order as to reserve knowledge of certain things, most notably in this context how the appreciation of human craft knowledge will turn out in particular circumstances ("it is not clear to you who plant a field finely who will harvest it"), for themselves. Accordingly, while human beings should pursue the knowledge available to them through the practice of the crafts, they should also recognize that knowledge of the outcome of their activities is accessible to them only through the signs the gods offer through divination (1.1.9).[95] Socrates characterizes those who fail to recognize this limitation, who believe that all things fall within human judgment, as not rational [δαιμονᾶν, 1.1.9), though it is also irrational to resort to divination in the case of those matters that the gods have given to human beings to learn by their application of craft knowledge. For Socrates the paradigm of such a failure to appreciate the limitations of human knowledge is Anaxagoras, whose attempts to explain the gods' celestial machinery Socrates characterizes as insane (4.7.6–7, partly quoted in note 91). Thus Socrates' assertion at 1.1.13 that the sophists fail to recognize that knowledge of the causes of celestial phenomena and his characterization of them as madmen

---

[94]See above, notes 2–4.
[95]See David O'Connor's discussion in Chapter 6.

both rely upon the distinction between divine and human knowledge that Xenophon explains at 1.1.7–9.

Let us return then to the question of whether Socrates differs from the sophists simply in holding that their enquiries into the causes of celestial phenomena fall beyond the reach of human judgment. Our discussion so far might seem to support the first interpretation, that Socrates asserts that the gods have entirely reserved knowledge of celestial phenomena for themselves, and so rules out the study of nature per se. Indeed Xenophon appears to say as much in summary in 4.7.6, holding that "he generally discouraged thought [*phrontistēs*] concerning he heavenly things, how god contrives each thing: for he considered that these things are not discoverable by human beings."

Yet it is clear that Xenophon did not understand Socrates' rejection of the sophists' *physiologia* as entailing a rejection of the study of nature per se. When he explains in *Memorabilia* 4.7 how Socrates attempted to make his associates self-sufficient (αὐτάρκεις) in the actions appropriate to a *kaloskagathos*, Xenophon reports at some length that Socrates encouraged them to acquire as much knowledge of the technical disciplines of natural philosophy, such as geometry, astronomy, and arithmetic, as would prove practically beneficial. In the case of geometry, his first example, one should pursue its study to the point at which one is capable of measuring a parcel of land or performing some calculation related to its acquisition or management; in the case of astronomy, one should learn enough to discern the time of night, month, and year, to use as guidance on a journey.

> But he strongly discouraged learning astronomy to the point of including knowledge of bodies that are not revolving in the same courses, and of planets and comets, and wearing oneself out by enquiry into their distance from earth, their revolutions, and the causes of these things. For he said that he saw no benefit in these enquiries, although he himself was not ignorant [*anēkoos*] of them; but he said that these were sufficient to occupy a human being's life and to prevent him from enquiring into many other beneficial things. (4.7.4–5)

This account of the mature Socrates' attitude toward natural philosophy makes it clear that study even of its more technical disciplines should be pursued insofar as the knowledge in question confers some practical benefit upon its possessor, though knowledge is not to be pursued for its own sake, and "vain pursuit" (μάταιον πραγματεία, 4.7.8) of unbeneficial knowledge is to be avoided. Thus Socrates, so far from rejecting the study of nature per se, regards some knowledge of it as essential for one to be free and self-sufficient, or a *kaloskagathos*. Moreover, it is clear that Socrates does not see some knowledge of nature as essential simply on account of the practical benefit here mentioned. For although Xenophon does not offer a thematic account of Socrates' own philosophy of nature, there can be no doubt that he relies on a very definite conception of the cosmos and mankind's place in it in formulating his own substantive moral doctrines. So, to take an example discussed in detail in Chapter 10 of this volume, Socrates appeals to a teleologically and providentially ordered cosmos in *Memorabilia* 1.4 and 4.3 to elaborate and defend his particular conception of piety. Learning that Aristodemus "the dwarf" went so far as to mock divination, which Socrates identifies in 1.1.7–9 as the craft that may enable human beings to transcend the limitations of human knowledge, Socrates undertakes an *elenchus* in which he argues from the design of human intelligence to the design of the cosmos itself and then uses this account as the basis for a conception of piety that accords with the gods' omniscient and purposive character. While some of the premises in Socrates' argument in this chapter are supplied by Aristodemus, the central arguments themselves are advanced by Socrates in his own name, and Xenophon—who never suggests that Socrates professed ignorance—gives us no reason to think that Socrates subscribes to them merely for ad hominem purposes in this dialectical encounter. Thus there is good reason to suppose that the Xenophontic Socrates, so far from restricting the study of nature in a rather prosaic way for purposes of practical benefit, instead relies upon a very specific natural philosophy in developing his own substantive moral doctrines.[96]

In sum, then, Socrates in rejecting pre-Socratic *physiologia* cannot mean to hold that all knowledge of celestial phenomena falls beyond the realm of human knowledge, as the first interpretation of *Memorabilia* 1.1.13 considered above would suggest. What he rejects as beyond human knowledge are the particular questions the sophists' enquiries into nature seek to answer, that is, their attempts to identify the causes of celestial phenomena.

In his third objection Socrates returns to the uselessness of pre-Socratic philosophy for human *kalokagathia:* even if the sophists could attain the knowledge for which they strive, it would confer no benefit upon them. Socrates asks, Do the sophists, like investigators of the human things, believe that their knowledge will confer some benefit

---

[96]In keeping with the apologetic character of his *Sōkratikoi logoi*, Xenophon does not emphasize this aspect of Socrates' philosophical activity, since it might leave Socrates open to charges of believing in gods other than those of the city; but nonetheless Xenophon does provide his readers with clear indications in 1.4 and 4.3 that Socrates' enquiries into "the human things" in fact presuppose a certain conception of nature and the divine.

upon them, such that when they have learned the causes of things they will be able to produce winds, rains, seasons, and so forth, as they desire? In keeping with his characteristic reticence concerning Socrates' deeper pursuits, Xenophon leaves this question unanswered. But his account of Socrates' positive interest in natural philosophy leaves little doubt that only knowledge that confers benefit upon its possessor is worthy of pursuit, and that failure to respect the distinction between knowledge that the gods have given human beings for their use and that which they have left obscure can only result in a form of philosophical madness destructive of human *kalokagathia*. Thus the question that the mature Socrates, according to Xenophon, brought to the subject of his youthful enquiries was this: What knowledge of nature must one have to live as a free and self-sufficient human being? That is the question that led Socrates to call philosophy down from the heavens, and guided his enquiries to his dying day.[97]

[97]This essay was originally prepared for the panel "Socrates and Literary Criticism" at the Society for Ancient Greek Philosophy meeting in New York City, October 1989, and I thank my commentator on that occasion, David Konstan, for much stimulating discussion. My thinking on this subject profited greatly from further discussion with him and with Harold Tarrant during a very memorable visit to the University of Sydney during the antipodean winter of 1990. A seminar on Diogenes of Apollonia held in Cambridge during Easter term 1992 helped me to clarify my understanding of the philosophical background of the Aristophanic Socrates' natural philosophy. I have presented earlier versions of this essay to meetings at the University of Sydney in August 1990 and at the University of Auckland, Victoria University of Wellington, and the University of Canterbury, Christchurch, in September 1990, as well as to the Philosophy Faculties of the University of Oxford and of the University of Warwick in May 1992. I am grateful to these audiences for their valuable comments. Special thanks are due to Peter Burian, Thomas Hubbard, Phillip Mitsis, Dirk Obbink, A. E. Raubitschek, Bernd Seidensticker, Christopher Taylor, and Graham Zanker.

[3]

Aeschines on Socratic Eros

Charles H. Kahn

Aeschines is the only Socratic, other than Plato and Xenophon, for whom we have substantial literary remains.[1] His Socratic dialogues were widely read in antiquity, down to the time of Plutarch, Lucian, and beyond, and the extant fragments from his *Alcibiades* and *Aspasia* are extensive enough for us to form a relatively full picture of these two dialogues. In the literary form of the Socratic dialogue Aeschines was clearly an innovator, above all for his portrait of Socratic eros. In fact, from the point of view of literary history, Aeschines can be regarded as the originator of the notion of Socratic eros. Of course there must have been some historical basis for this notion in the personality of Socrates himself. But the literary presentation of Socratic eros, in Aeschines' *Alcibiades* and *Aspasia* as in Plato's *Lysis*, *Charmides*, and *Symposium*, refers in every case to a period in Socrates' life of which neither Aeschines nor Plato can have had any personal knowledge.[2] Since the question of historicity eludes us, we may most profitably pursue this topic as a theme in the philosophical literature of the early fourth century. For this development the two dialogues of Aeschines are documents of the first

---

[1]His fragments are quoted here from the edition of H. Dittmar, *Aischines von Sphettos: Studien zur Literaturgeschichte der Sokratiker, Untersuchungen und Fragmente*, Philologische Untersuchungen 21 (Berlin, 1912); among more recent work, see especially B. Ehlers, *Eine vorplatonische Deutung des sokratischen Eros: Der Dialog Aspasia des Sokratikors Aischines*, Zetemata 41 (Munich, 1966); and below, note 17.

[2]For an attempt to show how Plato's treatment of Socratic eros responds to earlier literary accounts, see my essay "Plato as a Socratic," in *Hommage à Henri Joly, Recherches sur la philosophie et le langage* 12 (Grenoble, 1990), pp. 287–301.

importance. They have been the object of intensive study in German scholarship but have largely been ignored in English.[3] We will find, I think, that they repay a closer look.

Important as an author, as a personality Aeschines is a kind of poor relation among the Socratics. His place as a member of the inner circle is guaranteed by Plato's references to him in the *Apology* (33e) and the *Phaedo* (59b), but his life in Diogenes Laertius is extremely meager.[4] We know nothing of when he was born or when he died. The reference in the *Apology* to his father as present in court suggests that he may have been younger than the others, and one anecdote definitely represents him as junior to Aristippus (D.L. 2.83). He was a poor man and gave lectures for pay (D.L. 2.62), apparently after Aristippus had already begun to do so, since the latter is said to have been the *first* to charge for his teaching (D.L. 2.65). According to one tradition it was Aeschines who urged Socrates to escape from prison; Plato transferred this role to Crito "because Aeschines was too friendly with Aristippus" (D.L. 2.60).[5] His poverty drove him to write speeches for the law court and perhaps to teach rhetoric (D.L. 2.62–63). He is reported to have spent time at the court of Dionysius, where Plato ignored him but Aristippus introduced him to the tyrant (D.L. 2.61). He is said to have returned to Athens only after the expulsion of Dionysus II in 356.[6] Unlike Antis-

---

[3]W. K. C. Guthrie, in his *History of Greek Philosophy* (Cambridge, 1969), 3:395, does quote, and misinterpret, one important fragment; but for details he refers to G. C. Field's *Plato and His Contemporaries* (London, 1930). Field translates the longer fragments from our two dialogues (pp. 148–151) but gives no general picture of these works: he is reluctant to make use of Dittmar's pioneering study because he distrusts Dittmar's "fondness for unproved hypotheses" (p. 146n). In a work as rich and suggestive as Dittmar's, there are certainly some statements that are too bold and even uncritical (for some relevant criticism, see I. Düring, *Herodicus the Cratetean* [Stockholm, 1941], pp. 69–70), but many of the basic judgments are sound, and the collection of material is indispensable. The only serious attempt in English to make use of Dittmar's material is A. E. Taylor's interesting but largely neglected essay "Aeschines of Sphettus," in his *Philosophical Studies* (London, 1934), pp. 1–27. (I ignore A.-H. Chroust, *Socrates, Man and Myth* [London, 1957] as too irresponsible to do more than cast discredit on any attempt to deal with lost Socratic writings.) Taylor is above all interested in finding in Aeschines support for his own extreme view of the historicity of Plato's account of Socrates. But he gives an excellent account of the *Alcibiades* (with full translation of the fragments) and a good discussion of the *Telauges*. His treatment of the *Aspasia* goes beyond Dittmar but falls short of the new insights in Ehlers' monograph. E. G. Berry, "The Oxyrhynchus Fragments of Aeschines of Sphettus," *TAPA* 81 (1950): 1–8, has a brief discussion of the Oxyrhynchus fragments of Aeschines' *Alcibiades*. He proposes to bring Apollodorus into the conversation with Alcibiades, but the text is too scanty to give any assurance on this point.

[4]D.L. 2.60–64; among the Socratics, the only shorter life is that of Phaedo.

[5]D.L. 2.60 and 3.36, from Idomeneus of Lampsacus (*FGrHist* 338F17).

[6]D.L. 2.63. In the statement at 2.62 that upon his return to Athens (in 356) he did not dare to teach philosophy (σοφιστεύειν) "because of the prestige of those around Plato and Aristippus," the name Aristippus must be a mistake for Speusippus (according to the convincing suggestion of Zeller cited by G. Giannantoni, *Socraticorum Reliquiae* [Naples, 1983–85], 3:126).

thenes and Aristippus, Aeschines never appears in person in the pages of Xenophon's *Memorabilia*, although his literary influence can be detected there.[7]

It is above all for his dialogues that Aeschines was remembered; they were admired for their lifelike portrayal of Socrates' character and personality. Many ancient critics praise these works for natural style and purity of diction, and some authors prefer them to Plato's.[8] We know the names of seven dialogues, and there may have been more. I limit the discussion here to the two dialogues that can be reconstructed in some detail.

1. The *Alcibiades*

The *Alcibiades* was a narrated dialogue, in which Socrates reports to an unidentified audience a conversation he has had with Alcibiades. The dialogue's external form is thus the same as in Plato's *Charmides* and *Lysis*. The internal form is simpler here, since in the reported conversation Socrates has only one interlocutor, whereas in the *Charmides* he has two (and one more in the prologue) and in the *Lysis* he has four. On the other hand, the form of Aeschines' dialogue is more complex than the *Alcibiades* of Antisthenes, which apparently had the mime structure of a direct conversation, without any narrative frame.[9] We probably have the opening words of Aeschines' dialogue in the sentence "We were seated on the benches in the Lyceum, where the judges organize the games."[10] The gymnasium setting reminds us of the *Lysis*,

[7]See the references to Aspasia as Socrates' mentor in matchmaking (*Mem.* 2.6.36) and the erotic atmosphere of Socrates' visit to the courtesan Theodote (*Mem.* 3.11).

[8]"There are seven dialogues of Aeschines that have captured the ἦθος of Socrates" (D.L. 2.61). For other literary judgments see Dittmar (above, note 1), pp. 261–65.

[9]Antisthenes *Alcibiades* fr. 3 Dittmar = fr. 33 Caizzi = SSR 200. The mime form is attested only to the extent that this brief dialogue quotation is typical of the whole work. That would not prove that Antisthenes' dialogue was earlier (though it probably was), only that it was artistically less complex, as we might expect. But another possibility is worth considering. If, as Giannantoni assumes, αὐτόπτης in his fr. 198 (= fr. 30 Caizzi) and the dialogue in fr. 200 (= fr. 33 Caizzi) come from the same work, Antisthenes must have introduced this conversation between Alcibiades and the stranger by a narrative in the first person, like the "I was present when . . ." passages in Xenophon's *Memorabilia*. Artistically speaking, Antisthenes' works may have been more like Xenophon's, Aeschines' more like Plato's.

[10]Aeschin. fr. 2 Dittmar. The form of the quotation does not guarantee that it is from the *Alcibiades*, and Dittmar (above, note 1), p. 182, later thought of assigning it to the *Miltiades*. But there is no evidence for that, and some for a connection with the *Alcibiades* (see Dittmar [above, note 1], p. 117). Furthermore, Demetrius' quotation of fr. 2 as "Aeschines says," without title, parallels his quotation of the first sentence of the *Republic* as "Plato says," also without title. Such a parallel certainly suggests that fr. 2 is the beginning of a work so familiar that the title is unnecessary. The *Alcibiades* was apparently Aeschines' best-known dialogue, as we can see from the many later echoes and quota-

where Socrates is initially heading for the Lyceum until he is stopped by Hippothales.[11]

Aeschines' readers may have been familiar with a dialogue in which Antisthenes described (from personal experience, αὐτόπης γεγονώς) the extraordinary physical strength, courage, and beauty of Alcibiades, which was such that "if Achilles did not look like this, he was not really handsome."[12] Some such picture was either presented or presupposed by Aeschines. Alcibiades appears here as so proud of his talents, his wealth, and his family connections that "he might easily have found fault with the twelve Olympian gods" (fr. 5), and he regards his Athenian competitors as beneath contempt. Socrates undertakes to expose to him the folly of his self-conceit and the need for some serious moral and political training for a political career.[13] Thus the situation is structurally the same as in the pseudo-Platonic *Alcibiades* 1, where Socrates says to him: "You are in the depths of ignorance [ἀμαθία], and so you rush into politics before being trained" (118b). In both dialogues the task of Socrates is to bring Alcibiades to a more realistic view of himself and hence to a desire for improvement. But the situation is more artfully handled in Aeschines than in the pseudo-Platonic parallel. The first part of the conversation is partially preserved on a papyrus published in 1919 (and hence not available to Dittmar).[14] The papyrus fragments begin with a comparison to Themistocles: "Would you have wanted to treat your parents as he did?" "Hush, Socrates," says Alcibiades. "Do you think it is necessary for men to be untrained in music [ἄμουσοι] before they are trained [μουσικοί], and untrained in riding before they are trained?" Alcibiades agrees that is necessary. Here the first fragment breaks off, but Socrates is presumably making the point

---

tions. The *Miltiades*, by contrast, is reported to have been his first and least successful composition (D.L. 2.61). It would most likely have been in the simple mime form we know from other early Socratic dialogues: Plato's *Crito, Ion,* and *Hippias minor,* and perhaps Antisthenes' *Alcibiades* (above, note 9). If so, there would have been no place for the narrative frame of fr. 2 in the *Miltiades.* Taylor (above, note 3), p. 8, points out that fr. 47 shows that the *Telauges* was also narrated (or included a narration?), and he wishes to generalize this form for most if not all of Aeschines' dialogues. But he is mistaken in regard to the *Aspasia* and has no textual evidence for the form of the other dialogues.
[11]See *Lysis* 203a–b. The parallel would be much more striking if the agon in fr. 2 were for the Hermaia, as Hermann suggested. See C. Fr. Hermann, *Disputatio de Aeschinis Socratici Reliquiis* (Progr. Göttingen, 1850), p. 29 n. 93. For the cult of Hermes in gymnasia see L. R. Farnell, *The Cults of the Greek States* (Oxford, 1986–1909), 5:28–29 with notes; and compare *Lysis* 206d2 etc.
[12]Frs. 30 and 32a–b Caizzi = SSR 198–99.
[13]See also Xenophon's account in *Memorabilia* 3.6 of how Socrates undertook to show Glaucon, for Plato's sake, that he lacked the knowledge necessary for the political career to which he aspired.
[14]*P. Oxy.* 13.6 (1919), no. 1608, pp. 88–94.

that excellence did not come naturally to Themistocles but required training. His bad relations with his parents are cited as proof that he did not start well: he was publicly disowned by his father, as the next papyrus fragment shows. Then there is another gap, and we come to the section preserved in the literary tradition. "I noticed that he was jealous of Themistocles" (fr. 7 Dittmar). So Socrates develops, in a long and eloquent speech that is fully preserved, the intellectual achievements of Themistocles first in organizing the Greek victory over Xerxes and then in securing Xerxes' favor, so that when he was later exiled from Athens he was able to enjoy great esteem and power among the Persians (fr. 8 Dittmar). The missing sections must have referred to the effort of self-improvement or "care for himself" (ἐπιμέλεια ἑαυτοῦ) that led to this success, since the preserved text emphasizes that his achievements were due to his superiority in ἀρετή, his skill in deliberation (βουλεύεσθαι), his intelligent planning (φρονεῖν)—in short, to his knowledge (ἐπιστήμη).[15] But even such intellectual mastery was not sufficient to prevent Themistocles' failure in Athens and his exile in disgrace (fr. 8.49–51).

The effect of this speech upon Alcibiades is overwhelming. He burst into tears and, "weeping, laid his head upon my knees in despair" (fr. 9), as a sign of supplication, begging Socrates to rid him of his depraved condition and help him to gain *aretē* (fr. 10). Alcibiades had come to see that so far from being Themistocles' equal he was, in his ignorance and lack of education, no better than the meanest laborer in the city (fr. 6 with Dittmar, pp. 99–100). As far as we can tell, this was the end of the reported conversation with Alcibiades. The dialogue closes with a return to the narrative frame, where Socrates reflects upon the reasons for his success with Alcibiades and upon the limits of his powers. The final section (fr. 11) is important enough to quote in full:

If I thought that it was by some art [τέχνη] that I was able to benefit him, I would find myself guilty of great folly.[16] But in fact I thought that it was by divine dispensation [θεία μοῖρα] that this was given to me in the case of Alcibiades, and that it was nothing to be wondered at.

For many sick people are made well by human art, but some by divine dispensation. The former are cured by doctors; for the latter it is their own

[15]See fr. 8.21, 24, 38, 49, 52, 56 Dittmar. Besides the characteristic Socratic "care of oneself" note the curious identification of virtue with knowledge. In view of Themistocles' bad beginning and worse end, there must be a point of irony here that is not included in the impact on Alcibiades but is left to the reflective reader. As Taylor sees (above, note 3), p. 16, the cunning of Themistocles is not really to be taken for Socratic wisdom. A similar point is made independently by Döring (see below, note 19).

[16]Presumably the folly of believing that he could teach *aretē*.

desire [ἐπιθυμία] that leads them to recover. They have an urge to vomit when it is in their interest to do so, and they desire to go hunting when it is good for them to have exercise.

Because of the love [ἔρως] that I have for Alcibiades, I have the same experience as the bacchantes. For when the bacchantes are possessed [ἔνθεοι], they draw milk and honey from wells where others cannot even draw water. And so although I know no science or skill [μάθημα] that I could teach to anyone to benefit him, nevertheless I thought that in keeping company with Alcibiades I could by the power of love [διὰ τὸ ἐρᾶν] make him better.

This text raises many fascinating questions, both in itself and in its relationship to the preceding dialogue. First of all, what exactly is the knowledge or virtue that Themistocles lacked? What is the significance of Alcibiades' sudden breakdown in response to Socrates' story? In what sense is Socrates going to make him better (βελτίων)? And how does eros play a role? I shall here summarize the results of recent discussion by Barbara Ehlers, Konrad Gaiser, and Klaus Döring, with a few comments of my own.[17]

In the Socrates of fragment 11, who denies that he had any *technē* to make men better by teaching them something, we immediately recognize the Socrates of Plato's *Apology*, who speaks with ambiguous admiration of the art of educating people (παιδεῦσαι ἀνθρώπους) in the virtue of man and citizen but who also firmly denies that he possesses any such art (19e–20c). We may plausibly count this as a well-documented contrast between the position of the historical Socrates and that of the sophists as professional teachers.[18] Aeschines' own attitude to such sophistic training seems to be less negative then Plato's, but the text is not complete enough for a definite conclusion on this point. In any case, the *aretē* in which Themistocles excelled is precisely what young men of Alcibiades' generation flocked to the sophists to learn. Instead, we find Alcibiades in the company of Socrates. Will Socrates teach him political *aretē* in Themistocles' sense? Certainly not. Will he teach him, or rather will he help him to release within himself the desire to acquire the kind of knowledge and excellence in which Themistocles was *deficient*? Perhaps so. At least the first step has been taken. Alcibiades has come to recognize his own ignorance, his nullity

---

[17]Besides the detailed analysis in Ehlers (above, note 1), pp. 10–25, see K. Gaiser, *Protreptik und Paranëse bei Platon* (Tübingen, 1959), pp. 77ff., esp. pp. 92–95, and above all his review of Ehlers in *AGP* 51 (1969): 200–209; K. Döring, "Der Sokrates des Aischines von Sphettos und die Frage nach dem historischen Sokrates," *Hermes* 112 (1984): 16–30.

[18]On this contrast, see D. L. Blank, "Socrates and the Sophists on Accepting Payment for Teaching," *CA* 4 (1984): 1–49.

as far as the excellence of man and citizen is concerned. To that extent he has already been made "better." But what is the *next* step? It has been strongly implied that true excellence will somehow depend upon knowledge. And it has been explicitly claimed that the result so far is due to eros. How are eros and knowledge related to one another? And how is eros related to the kind of wisdom that Themistocles lacked, according to Aeschines, or to the wisdom that, according to Plato, Socrates vainly sought among the politicians, the poets, and the artisans?

The answers to these tantalizing questions are not clear from the preserved sections of the *Alcibiades,* and since we have both the climax to the conversation with Alcibiades and what looks like the theoretical conclusion to the whole work, it seems unlikely that the lost sections would have made the answers much clearer. We can learn more about Aeschines' view of Socratic eros by turning in a moment to his *Aspasia,* but both dialogues leave many questions unanswered.[19] This seems to be an essential part of Aeschines' art: to stimulate the reader to think further about the issues raised,[20] in particular about the pursuit of excellence and wisdom and about the impact of Socrates upon his associates. The one thing that is unmistakable is the important role assigned to eros in this connection. In the concluding passage of the *Alcibiades,* eros is presented as a kind of divine gift, like Philoctetes' bow, an almost irrational power by contrast both with the worldly wisdom of Themistocles and with the technical training, or *mathēmata,* of the arts and crafts.

As far as we know, no one before Aeschines proposed to understand the protreptic and educational influence of Socrates in terms of eros. We can only speculate whether it was this conception that led him to write about Alcibiades in the first place, or whether it was reflection on the Alcibiades theme (as treated perhaps earlier by Antisthenes) that led Aeschines to his view of Socratic eros.[21] There must have been historical grounds, in fact or at least in gossip, for both Aeschines and

[19]For example, does Aeschines' use of Themistocles as a model for Alcibiades imply unqualified approval? Probably not. Döring (above, note 17), pp. 20–21 n. 11, points out that the charge against Themistocles was Medism. So Aeschines' reference to the power and honor he achieved at the Persian court silently calls attention to his moral failure: a greater concern for his personal advantage than for the public good.

[20]So Gaiser 1969 (above, note 17), pp. 202–3, 205–6, on the subject of irony in Aeschines. In this connection Gaiser suggests an interpretation of Themistocles' exile in terms of a failure on his part to generate enough love and trust on the part of his fellow citizens; he compares Xenophon, *Memorabilia* 2.6.13, where the success of Pericles and Themistocles is described in terms of love charms that made the city love them (φιλεῖν).

[21]The second line of thought was proposed by O. Gigon: the theme of Socratic eros would originally have been connected only with the Socrates-Alcibiades relationship and later generalized (*Sokrates* [Bern, 1947], p. 310, cited by Ehlers [above, note 1], p. 11 n. 1).

Plato to represent Socrates as the lover (ἐραστής) of Alcibiades. Of course Alcibiades' speech in the *Symposium* has the ring of truth about it, but that is simply the extraordinarily deceptive power of Plato's art. The events in question, when Alcibiades was in his "bloom," belong before the time of Plato's birth, and Aeschines was probably even younger.[22] Plato was in no position to know the truth about this relationship, and in the elaborate narrative structure of the *Symposium* he has gone to considerable lengths to disclaim any direct knowledge of the facts. As far as history is concerned, we may accept Plato's account as the most likely story available to us; but as far as the literary development of this theme is concerned there is good reason to think that Aeschines was the initiator.[23] He does not tell us how he understood the relationship. But perhaps Aeschines is saying in his simpler way, through the ambiguous syntax of *dia to eran* in the last words of the dialogue (which seems to mean "because of my love for Alcibiades" but might also mean the converse), what Plato indicates more explicitly in Alcibiades' speech in the *Symposium:* that what looked to the world like Socrates' flirtatious interest in handsome young men was in fact his way of focusing upon them the magnetic power of his own personality and thus drawing them to him "through the power of love," instilling in them a desire to imitate in their own lives the philosophical pursuit of *aretē* that they saw embodied in his. If this was not what Aeschines intended to say in comparing Alcibiades' impulse to the *epithymia* that leads a sick man to spontaneous recovery, that is at any rate what Plato understood when, following Aeschines' lead, he came to give his own literary portrayal of Socratic eros in the *Charmides*, the *Lysis*, and the *Symposium*.

2. The *Aspasia*

We can form a much clearer picture of this dialogue as a result of Ehlers' 1966 monograph. Whereas earlier scholars, following Dittmar, had seen the *Aspasia* as focused on the problem of women and the relation between the sexes, Ehlers has conclusively shown that the theme

---

[22]By contrast Antisthenes was old enough to know Alcibiades personally; in fact, if he was born ca. 445 B.C., he was only a few years his junior. So he could describe Alcibiades from firsthand knowledge. But there is no mention of the erotic theme in extant references to Antisthenes' *Alcibiades;* and any positive development of that theme would be very surprising, given Antisthenes' views on eros.

[23]Here again Aeschines' innovation may have been stimulated by Antisthenes' very different treatment of the Alcibiades theme. For what little we know about Antisthenes' *Alcibiades* see F. Decleva Caizzi, *Antisthenis Fragmenta* (Milan, 1966), pp. 97–98; Giannantoni (above, note 6), 3:317–19.

of the *Aspasia* is the power of love and its connection with the pursuit
or possession of *aretē*.

Unfortunately there are fewer verbatim quotations here than from
the *Alcibiades*, the longest being a Latin translation by Cicero. As a result, the external form of the dialogue is not so definitely known; but
there is no evidence of a narrative frame. We seem to have the simple
mime form of a direct dialogue between Socrates and Callias. (Callias'
son may be thought of as present, since the conversation concerns his
education, but there is nothing to suggest that he had a speaking part.)
The internal structure is more complex. Socrates makes several long
speeches, including the full report of a conversation in which Aspasia,
playing the part of Socrates, cross-examines Xenophon and his wife.
Thus the literary form is like that of Plato's *Menexenus* but even more
variegated, since the dialogue contains at least one play-within-the-
play, namely, the Aspasia-Xenophon conversation enclosed within the
Socrates-Callias dialogue.

Callias begins by asking Socrates to recommend a teacher for his son.
This is a typical situation with many parallels in Plato and Xenophon,
but Callias is no typical father. He is the fabulously wealthy man who
has spent a fortune on the sophists, "more money than all the rest put
together" (*Ap.* 20a5), and who is represented in the *Protagoras* as having
three famous sophists living in his house at once.[24] In the *Apology* Callias is the father cited by Socrates as the one to whom this very question
might be addressed: "Whom would you select to train your sons in
aretē?" (20b). If, as seems likely, the *Apology* came first, this may have
suggested to Aeschines the starting point for his own dialogue, but with
the ironical twist that this time it is Socrates who must answer
questions.[25] In any case we may be surprised to find that this man, with
such a vast educational experience, should be turning to Socrates for
advice on a question of this kind. Even more surprising, however, is
Socrates' answer: Send your son to Aspasia (fr. 17 Dittmar).

As Pericles' semilegal wife, Aspasia was the most famous woman in
Athens and the butt of a thousand jokes, above all in comedy. Her image is, on the one hand, that of the hetaira, or courtesan, and, on the
other hand, that of the dominating female who has Pericles under her
thumb. Aristophanes has her getting Pericles to start the Peloponne-
sian war in order to take revenge on the Megarians for kidnapping two
of her prostitutes (*Ach.* 526–39). Since Callias was said to have dissi-
pated a part of his fortune on pleasures of this kind, the proposal of

---

[24] In Xenophon's *Symposium*, where Callias is host, the name of Gorgias is added to the
list of sophists he has subsidized (1.5).

[25] On this reversal of the usual situation, see Ehlers (above, note 1), p. 43. Note that in
Plato's *Apology* Callias actually recommends a teacher, namely, Evenos of Paros.

Aspasia will have seemed unusually provocative as addressed to him.[26] And if the reader is familiar with an earlier dialogue by Antisthenes in which Aspasia is presented as a personification of the life of sensual indulgence, then the philosophical provocation in recommending her as a teacher of virtue will also be unmistakable.[27] Callias must have reacted with shock and disbelief. What! Send a man to study with a woman? And with *such* a woman! It is probably from Callias' response that we have the isolated quotation "All those women from Ionia are adultresses and gold diggers" (fr. 20).[28] Can Socrates be serious?

Socrates stands his ground. He himself regards Aspasia as his teacher; he goes to her for instruction on matters on which she is expert (fr. 19). We do not have the actual words in which Socrates describes Aspasia as his teacher. Later authors who have read Aeschines say that Socrates went to Aspasia "for philosophy" or more specifically for instruction in τὰ ἐρωτικά, "matters of love."[29] That Aspasia was Socrates' teacher in matters erotic may or may not have been explicit in Aeschines' text; given Aspasia's reputation, it was most certainly implied. As far as we can tell, the rest of the dialogue consists of three different kinds of examples introduced by Socrates in defense and explanation of his claim that Aspasia is the best teacher of *aretē*, and all three sets involve the power of love. The examples are as follows:

1. Two other outstanding women: Rhodogyne and Thargelia
2. Aspasia as a teacher of political excellence: Pericles and Lysicles
3. Aspasia as a teacher of moral excellence: Xenophon and his wife

(1) In answer to the objection that a man cannot be taught virtue by a woman, Socrates demonstrates that an exceptional woman can have all the qualities of an exceptional man. To prove his point he cites the military successes and unflinching devotion to royal duty displayed by the (fictitious) Persian queen Rhodogyne, a kind of Amazon type like the more famous Semiramis.[30] In answer to the charge that, whatever may be true of Persian queens, Ionian courtesans are not in this class, Socrates invokes his second example, the Milesian hetaira Thargelia, who, because of her beauty, married a Thessalian prince and, after

---

[26]Ehlers (above, note 1), p. 40.

[27]For the earlier date of Antisthenes' *Aspasia* and the likelihood that Aeschines is responding to it, see Ehlers (above, note 1), pp. 30–34.

[28]Ehlers places this response later, between the Rhodogyne and Thargelia episodes.

[29]See the passages listed as fr. 29 by Dittmar (above, note 1), pp. 280–81.

[30]See fr. 18 and Ehlers (above, note 1), pp. 44–51. Unlike Semiramis, Rhodogyne is not amorously inclined and hence has no plebeian lovers who need to be murdered.

his death, ruled over the Thessalians for thirty years and entertained Xerxes on his campaign into Greece.[31]

The example of Thargelia prepares us for the transition to Aspasia, another Milesian courtesan turned queen: she rules Pericles, and Pericles rules Athens. Ehlers (following Dittmar and others) suggests that Aeschines may have managed the transition from Thargelia to Aspasia even more skillfully by presenting the Thargelia story *in a speech composed by Aspasia* that Socrates recites from memory.[32] This hypothesis cannot be definitely established, but there is some evidence in its favor,[33] and it would nicely explain why the one literal quotation that we have from the Thargelia episode is in extreme Gorgianic style (fr. 22); for, as we shall see, Aspasia is presented by Aeschines as a master of rhetoric in the manner of Gorgias. Even if Thargelia's speech was not presented as a composition by Aspasia, it anticipates another Platonic virtuoso trick, namely, the speech of Agathon in the *Symposium;* for Aeschines here (in fr. 22), as Plato there, has produced an imitation of Gorgias' diction exaggerated to the point of caricature.

(2) Aspasia is then praised for her role in Pericles' political career. She was not only the source of wise political advice; she also taught him rhetoric. She thus made Pericles into a powerful political orator by "sharpening his tongue on Gorgias" (fr. 24). The idea of Aspasia as Pericles' teacher in public speaking may just possibly have surfaced as a joke in fifth-century comedy.[34] But even if Aeschines did not invent this story, he was the first to take it seriously. Just how seriously he took it is another matter; fragment 24, just quoted, certainly has a comic tone. But Aeschines developed the idea systematically, just as Plato was to do in the *Menexenus.* Aspasia not only made Pericles into an effective

[31]Thargelia is a figure in between history and folktale who was mentioned by Hippias the sophist as having been so beautiful and wise that she was married to fourteen men (Dittmar [above, note 1], p. 30 = 86 B4 DK). Aeschines seems to have married her only to Antiochus, the "ruler" of Thessaly (frs. 21–22). The attempt of Ehlers (above, note 1), pp. 52ff., to reconstruct the historical facts behind this fantastic tale seems to me unconvincing and unnecessary.

[32]Here again Aeschines would provide the model for Plato's *Menexenus.*

[33]Plutarch (*Per.* 24 = fr. 21 Dittmar) implies that Aspasia had compared herself to Thargelia. This would be easier to fit into the dialogue if Aspasia is supposed to be the author of the Thargelia speech (see Ehlers [above, note 1], pp. 58–60).

[34]The scholium to Plato's *Menexenus* that reports that Aspasia made Pericles into a public speaker "according to Aeschines in the dialogue *Aspasia*" (fr. 23) adds "and Callias likewise in the [comedy] *Pedetai*" (fr. 14 Kock). This brief and ambiguous bit of information is the only basis, so far as I can see, for the view (e.g., in Ehlers [above, note 1], pp. 29–72) that the picture of Aspasia as a master of oratory, which we find in Aeschines' *Aspasia* and Plato's *Menexenus,* actually goes back to a fifth-century comedian. In the absence of any comic quotations to this effect, it seems more likely that this was an invention of Aeschines.

speaker; she repeated the performance with Lysicles the sheep merchant (fr. 26).

Lysicles must be the Athenian general who died in Caria in 428, scarcely a year after Pericles' death (Thuc. 3.19.1). His fame lived longer, above all in comedy, where he serves as a model for jokes about vulgar tradesmen with successful political careers. So in Aristophanes' *Knights*, produced in 424, the oracle that announces Cleon's imminent overthrow by the sausage seller mentions as precedents a rope seller overthrown by a sheep seller (Lysicles) who is in turn overthrown by a leather seller (Cleon).[35] But the story of Lysicles' connection with Aspasia, which we read in Plutarch and a few scholia, must come from Aeschines and is not likely to be historical.[36] Thus Plutarch reports as follows: "Aeschines says that Lysicles the sheep merchant, of humble birth and undistinguished talent, became first among the Athenians by living with Aspasia after Pericles' death" (*Per.* 24 = fr. 26). The function of the story in the dialogue has been fully clarified by Ehlers' use of a Syriac parallel. In response to Socrates' praise of Aspasia for her influence on Pericles, Callias must have objected that Pericles' talent, training, and family background were quite sufficient to explain his success.[37] The Syriac version makes explicit what we might have

[35]See *Eq.* 132 with scholium; Lysicles is mentioned by name at 765.

[36]The story is taken at face value by Kahrstedt in *RE* 13 (1927), cols. 2550–51, s.v. "Lysikles," who has him married to Aspasia. Gomme (note on Thuc. 3.19.1) is more cautious. The story must have been invented at a time when the date of Lysicles' death had been long forgotten, but his lowly occupation still remembered (from Aristophanes no doubt). It is extraordinary that such a story, with such a chronology, should come to pass for history. Scholars are reluctant to recognize Aeschines' originality, which consists in part in a total disregard for historical verisimilitude. As far as I can see, not one of the five episodes (Rhodogyne, Thargelia, Pericles, Lysicles, Xenophon and wife) cited by Socrates in the *Aspasia* is historically accurate or even historically plausible. (It is as easy for Aeschines' Socrates to make up exotic stories as it is for Plato's Socrates in the *Phaedrus,* 275b.) Pericles' undignified behavior at Aspasia's trial might just possibly be historical (though if it were, we would rather expect to find it cited by Antisthenes, not Aeschines). Pericles learning Gorgianic rhetoric from Aspasia is chronologically absurd. And does any historian believe that Socrates visited Aspasia for instruction—and took his friends' wives along (fr. 30, from Plutarch)? Writing forty or fifty years later, Aeschines is as indifferent to the historicity of his Athenian stories as he is when describing the exploits of an imaginary Persian queen. Even Ehlers, who recognizes that Aeschines is our only source for the Aspasia-Lysicles story, believes that Aeschines must respect historical possibilities. (She mentions the date of Lysicles' death [above, note 1], p. 73 n. 137, but draws no conclusions.) The Thargelia story, which begins with Antiochus and ends with Xerxes, is also a chronological fantasy, and politically dubious to say the least (cf. Ehlers [above, note 1], p. 52, for the problem of dating Antiochus). In Rhodogyne's case, even the name is fictitious.

[37]The Syriac version goes as follows: "The Athenians said it was not Aspasia who made Pericles wise, but he was a man of clear intelligence who became a skillful orator by his own effort and training. When she heard this, Aspasia wanted to expose the falsehood; so she went to live with a sheep merchant and educated him, so that he became a skillful orator and an admired general." (This is my paraphrase of Ehlers' translation

guessed from the Greek fragments, namely, that Aeschines then introduced the example of Lysicles as a case where the decisive influence of
Aspasia was undeniable, since she had raised him from humble origins
to the height of power and made a man of no talent and training into
"a skillful orator and an admired general,"[38] just like Pericles. This
comparison must have sounded strange to anyone who remembered
Lysicles' image in Aristophanes, or the disastrous campaign recorded
by Thucydides, which ended in Lysicles' death. But in the absence of
the original text it is hard for us to estimate the degree of seriousness
or mock seriousness in Socrates' argument. What we can say is that
Aeschines has taken the figures of Aspasia and Lysicles from comedy,
Thargelia from Hippias, and Rhodogyne apparently from his own
imagination, as the final episode with Xenophon and his wife is certainly imaginary; and that he has combined these fantastic elements in
a neat and meaningful plan.

It is part of the plan that, both in the story of Pericles and in that of
Lysicles, Aspasia's role as teacher and inspirer of excellence is (like the
political career of Thargelia before her) directly dependent upon her
status as hetaira, that is, her role as an attractive woman capable of
arousing sexual passion in a man. Unfortunately the preserved texts do
not indicate how Aeschines developed this connection. We do have
some quotations that show how devoted Pericles was to her and how,
when she was on trial for impiety, he pleaded her case in tears, begging
the judges for her acquittal and weeping more on her behalf than when
his own life and property were at stake (fr. 25). This story casts Pericles
in a rather undignified role; it is easy to see how Antisthenes might
have used it to illustrate the demoralizing power of eros. In the context
of Aeschines' dialogue it must have served to make a quite different
point. Since Socrates' goal is to praise Aspasia, he must have told this
story to show how great a passion she inspired in Pericles. They were,
after all, "the two most famous lovers of their time."[39] Pericles is also

---

from the Syriac [above, note 1], pp. 75–77.) It is obvious that the Aspasia-Lysicles story
from Aeschines (frs. 26–27) has been preserved here in a free-floating form, without its
context in the dialogue. Hence the skeptical reaction of Callias, which motivates the story
and so cannot be omitted, is reassigned to Athenian public opinion.

[38]See the Syriac version in note 37. The scholiast to Plato has ῥήτωρ δεινότατος (fr. 26
Dittmar).

[39]Ehlers (above, note 1), p. 66. Note that Ἀσπασίᾳ συνόντα in Plutarch's version of fr.
26 may have the double sense of cohabiting with Aspasia and frequenting her as a
teacher. As Ehlers, p. 79 with n. 164, points out, there is nothing in the texts to suggest
love on Aspasia's part: unlike the typical Athenian wife, she is presented only as beloved,
not as loving. And this contrasts also with Socrates' role in the *Alcibiades*. Pericles' un-
Socratic behavior at Aspasia's trial may have been introduced (even invented?) to suggest
that he, like Themistocles, did not after all possess true excellence.

the most famous statesman and orator. Aeschines can take these facts for granted; what is altogether new and surprising is to derive the latter fact from the former, to explain Pericles' *aretē* by his love for Aspasia. In his case, as again in the case of Lysicles, the power to spur a man on to excellence is essentially connected with the power of love. In this respect Aeschines' theme is the same here as in the concluding speech of the *Alcibiades,* although the form that eros takes is quite different. In these examples the love is felt by the persons who are to be improved. That will again be true, but in a quite different way, in Socrates' last illustration.

(3) The concluding episode is the only one that directly answers Callias' misgivings about Aspasia's qualifications as a teacher of virtue for his young son. Since her achievements with Pericles and Lysicles depend upon her role as sexual partner, that is scarcely a recommendation for Callias, who is not looking for a mistress for his son.[40] We end, then, with an example where Aspasia's role is entirely respectable and the eros in question is love between husband and wife. The structure of the example is such that any more or less conventional loving couple might serve. The couple chosen by Aeschines is surprisingly familiar: it is our old friend Xenophon and his wife. Since Aspasia must have died before Xenophon was old enough to be married, the encounter is wonderfully implausible. But that, as we have seen, is true of all the examples cited by Socrates.[41]

The Xenophon episode is preserved in full in Cicero's translation (fr. 31 Dittmar = *Inv. rhet.* 1.31.51–52). The literary form is complex, since what we have is first a conversation between Aspasia and Xenophon's wife (presumably the source of the story that Socrates brought his disciples *with their wives* to visit his "teacher"; cf. fr. 30), and then one between Aspasia and Xenophon himself, the whole of which is *narrated by Socrates.* Cicero's translation does not make this point clear, but Socrates must be reporting this conversation to Callias in support of his recommendation. So we have a genuine (reported) dialogue-within-a-dialogue. This is a literary experiment of some audacity, to which there seems no exact parallel in Plato. The closest thing is the reported conversation with Diotima in *Symposium* 201dff. And Diotima is in many ways Plato's response to Aeschines' Aspasia.[42] But there is a significant

---

[40]Cf. Ehlers (above, note 1), p. 85.

[41]See above, note 36.

[42]Gigon asks: "Has anyone ever pointed out that Plato conceived the Diotima of his *Symposium* as the successful rival and counterpart [als überwindendes Gegenbild]—in more than one sense—to the Aspasia of Aeschines?" (*Kommentar* on Xen. *Mem.* 2.6.36, cited by Ehlers [above, note 1], p. 136 n. 81; similarly Gaiser 1969 [above, note 17], p. 208). The answer to Gigon's question is yes. The parallel between Aspasia and Diotima

formal difference, since Socrates is there narrating a conversation in which he himself was a participant, which makes the report more natural. In this respect, as in the overall form of the reported dialogue as we found it in the *Alcibiades,* and also in the parody of the Gorgianic style, Aeschines seems to be the innovator, but Plato the perfecter of each technical advance.

The passage has the form of a Socratic ἐπαγωγή or, as Cicero rightly says, an *inductio.* So Aspasia figures here as "a female Socrates."[43] She first asks Xenophon's wife whether if her neighbor possessed finer gold jewelry, she would prefer her neighbor's gold to her own, and next whether if her neighbor had more precious clothes and ornament, she would prefer her neighbor's clothes to her own. In both cases the wife answers that she would prefer her neighbor's portion. The third question is "If she had a better man as husband than you have, would you prefer hers or yours?" At this point the wife blushes, and Aspasia begins to question Xenophon. When asked concerning a better horse and a better estate, Xenophon answers as expected, like his wife, that he would prefer the better share. And then comes the third question: "What if the neighbor had a better wife than you, would you prefer yours or his?" And here too Xenophon falls silent. Then Aspasia speaks: "Since neither of you answered the question I wanted most to hear answered, I will say what each of you was thinking. You, the wife, want to have the best husband, and you, Xenophon, want to have the most excellent wife. Hence unless you bring it about that there is no better man and no more excellent woman on earth, you will both be lacking in what you regard as most desirable [*optimum*], namely, that you have married the best possible wife and she the best possible husband."

Here end the quotations from Aeschines' *Aspasia.* We do not know how far Socrates' final remarks will have elaborated the point of this little conversation and of the whole dialogue. But it seems clear that Aspasia is appealing to the love that Xenophon and his wife have for one another in order to urge them on to a mutual effort of self-improvement. Thus Aspasia in her "Socratic" role serves to generalize the principle that Socrates embodies at the end of the *Alcibiades:* to make someone better *dia to eran,* through the power of love. In that passage it was not clear whether Socrates' love for Alcibiades was

---

was noted by C. Fr. Hermann in 1850 (above, note 11), p. 19: "Socrates, quae eam [sc. Aspasiam] disserentem audivisset, eodem fere exemplo quo Diotimae praecepta in Platonis Convivio, alteri narraverit"; and it is taken for granted in several ancient authors. See the quotations from Maximus of Tyre, Theodoretus, and Lucian in fr. 29, Dittmar (above, note 1), pp. 280–81; and cf. Ehlers (above, note 1), pp. 97–100.

[43]Hirzel's apt phrase, quoted by Dittmar (above, note 1), p. 51.

thought of as provoking eros in Alcibiades as well. But in this dialogue there is no doubt: it is by inciting or appealing to eros in others that Aspasia is able to act as moral guide and lead Xenophon and his wife to *aretē*, as she had previously led Pericles and Lysicles.[44] In their case the arena of excellence was public life; here it is private and domestic. There she functioned as courtesan and mate; here she is the wise woman, the female sage, who can use her rare knowledge of *ta erōtika* to stimulate a passion for self-improvement in others without herself being personally involved. We thus have several different versions of that deep, somewhat mysterious link between sexual eros and the urge to *aretē* that was brought out in the conclusion of the *Alcibiades*.

In the absence of a complete text for either dialogue, it is impossible to see precisely how Aeschines meant this link to be understood. The three long quotations from the *Alcibiades* and the *Aspasia* give the impression that the dialogues of Aeschines were composed like an artful short story, written with deceptive simplicity in a gently mocking tone, but revealing an emotional and intellectual landscape with several different perspectives, a strange mixture of truth and fantasy, seriousness and spoof, where the reader is left to a large extent free to work out his or her own interpretation. In the case of the *Aspasia*, the dosage of the comic and fantastic is unusually strong. I conclude this discussion by referring to two previous attempts to carry Ehlers' cautious analysis one step farther. Döring has called attention to an interesting parallel between the chastening of Alcibiades and the elenchus of Xenophon and his wife. In both cases an internal conflict is provoked in the interlocutors of Socrates/Aspasia, and the conflict finds expression in external symptoms: weeping, blushing, silence. In both cases the procedure is designed to induce the interlocutors to look critically at themselves, to recognize their deficiencies, and to see the need for improvement. In Aeschines' eyes, Socrates' "erotic art and his elenctic art are two sides of the same coin."[45] From a somewhat different point of view, Gaiser has suggested that Aeschines may have seen in eros "not only a means for the attainment of *aretē* but a component of *aretē* itself."

---

[44]This is the line of interpretation proposed by Ehlers (above, note 1), pp. 88ff., and accepted with variants by Gaiser 1969 (above, note 17), pp. 202ff., and Döring (above, note 17), pp. 16–30. Earlier commentators misread the *Aspasia* as a contribution to the "debates on the question of women in ancient Athens"; Aeschines was thought to be drawing the full consequences of "the Socratic view of the moral equality of women" (Dittmar [above, note 1], p. 52). These issues may be germane, but Aspasia is scarcely a typical representative of Athenian womanhood; she is, after all, not even an Athenian.

[45]Döring (above, note 17), p. 25, who cites evidence for a similar pattern of self-discovery with physical expression in the *Callias*, the *Telauges*, and the unspecified dialogue that reported the conversation of Aristippus at Olympia (*ap.* Plut. *De curios.* 2, 516c = *SSR* 4.a.2; cf. Ehlers [above, note 1], p. 293).

Perhaps Aeschines located virtue in a form of knowledge that cannot exist without love (ἔρως) or friendship (φιλία) and that can form the basis for community life. But Gaiser rightly emphasizes the half-playful tone of the *Aspasia*, the tone set from the beginning by the strange recommendation of the courtesan as moral guide. Apparently Aeschines does not believe that the nature of Socratic eros can be grasped by a direct approach; in both of these dialogues "it is left to the reader to form his own conception of the *aretē* that Socrates intends."[46]

Appendix: On the Chronology of Aeschines' *Aspasia* and *Alcibiades*

There is an obvious connection between Aeschines' *Aspasia* and Plato's use of Aspasia in the *Menexenus*, where she is said to be the author of the funeral oration that Socrates recites and that he claims she composed from the leftovers from the speech she wrote for Pericles. I think there is no doubt that in this case Plato is the debtor and that it is from Aeschines that he has taken the motif of Aspasia as teacher of rhetoric for Pericles and Socrates. That the borrowing goes in this direction and not conversely is indicated first of all by the fact that Plato can simply take for granted the point that Aeschines is at pains to establish, namely, that Aspasia "has produced many good orators, including the finest in Greece, Pericles son of Xanthippus" (235e). And Plato carries this motif one step farther. In Aeschines Aspasia teaches rhetoric to Pericles; in Plato she writes his speeches, including the famous Funeral Oration. At the same time Plato is careful to avoid the more obvious role for Aspasia as a specialist in love. Socratic eros is not mentioned, not even alluded to, in the *Menexenus*. The reason for this is clear. Plato has no intention of allowing this topic to be sullied by contact with Aspasia. His Socrates will learn about love from a priestess, not from a courtesan. So the resemblances and differences between the two dialogues are fully intelligible on the assumption that Plato is selectively adapting a theme first explored by Aeschines. (There is no insightful line of explanation going in the other direction. For instance, it is the absence of the erotic element in the *Menexenus* that needs to be accounted for, not its presence in the *Aspasia*.) So it is as certain as anything can be on the basis of internal evidence alone that the *Aspasia* was written before the *Menexenus*.

Now in the case of the *Menexenus* we have that very rare thing, an absolute date. Because of the nature of its reference to the King's Peace

---

[46]Gaiser 1969 (above, note 17), p. 206; cf. pp. 203ff.

of 386 (at 245b–e), the *Menexenus* must have been written in the same year or immediately thereafter.[47] So Aeschines' *Aspasia* will have been composed before 386, but perhaps not by much. We can provisionally situate it in the early 380s.[48] And if (as we have inferred, following Ehlers) Aeschines in turn is reacting to Antisthenes' *Aspasia,* he will probably have done so while that work was still fresh. So we get ca. 390 as a plausible date for Antisthenes' *Aspasia,* and 389–387 for Aeschines' dialogue. We cannot actually rule out an earlier date for either dialogue, but there seems to be no evidence in *favor* of an earlier date.

A terminus ante quem for Aeschines' *Alcibiades* is not so clearly indicated. I assume that it predates Plato's treatment of the Alcibiades theme in the *Symposium.* So far as I know, no scholar has doubted that priority.[49] But if we follow K. J. Dover in dating the *Symposium* between 384 and 379,[50] the date is too late to be of much use in this connection. (We will find evidence below, from Lysias, to show that much of Aeschines' major work must have been done before 380.) However, if (as I propose to do) we follow Ehlers in interpreting the *Aspasia* as a kind of sequel to the *Alcibiades,* then we see that the latter must also fall before 386.

Can we establish a terminus post quem? Some scholars, including Ehlers, have thought that Aeschines' *Alcibiades* contains a backward reference to Plato's *Gorgias.* But that claim is not soundly based, and it has been rightly rejected.[51] Hence Gaiser concludes that we lack any fixed post quem reference for Aeschines' two dialogues; but he has overlooked a point noted by Ehlers and others. There is a striking verbal parallel, too close to be accidental, between the bacchantes drawing milk and honey when possessed in Aeschines' *Alcibiades* (fr. 11c) and in Plato's *Ion* (534a). Since the imagery of possession is deeply imbedded in the *Ion* context but somewhat surprising in Aeschines (where Socrates does not seem to be possessed), it is natural to suppose that in this case Aeschines is echoing Plato.[52] Now the *Ion* is plausibly dated in or shortly after 394.[53] So we have the following coherent picture:

[47]The King's Peace is much more than a terminus post quem, if I am right in seeing the *Menexenus* as a kind of political protest against the terms of that peace; see "Plato's Funeral Oration" *CP* 58 (1963): 220–34.

[48]A date in the late 390s is also possible, but Plato's use of the Aspasia motif is not likely to have been separated so very far in time from its inspiration in Aeschines' dialogue.

[49]Thus Gaiser 1969 (above, note 17), p. 208, accepts Ehlers' claim that in Aeschines we have a "pre-Platonic interpretation of Socratic eros."

[50]See K. J. Dover, "The Date of Plato's *Symposium*," *Phronesis* 10 (1965): 2–20.

[51]By Gaiser 1969 (above, note 17), p. 208, and by Döring (above, note 17), p. 21 n. 11.

[52]So Ehlers (above, note 1), p. 22, following H. Flashar, *Der Dialog Ion als Zeugnis platonischer Philosophie* (Berlin, 1958), p. 21.

[53]Flashar (above, note 52), pp. 101–2.

Plato's *Ion,* ca. 394–392
Aeschines' *Alcibiades*
Aeschines' *Aspasia*
Plato's *Menexenus,* 386–385

I do not attempt to locate Antisthenes' *Alcibiades* and *Aspasia* here, although I conjecture that both of them belong before the corresponding dialogues of Aeschines. Their remains, however, are too scanty for any real confidence, and I see no basis, even conjectural, for dating them in relation to the *Ion.*

My proposed chronology is a tissue of probabilities, and it depends crucially on the assumption that the *Aspasia* postdates the *Alcibiades.* (Otherwise we have a terminus post quem for the *Alcibiades* but not for the *Aspasia,* and vice versa in the case of a terminus ante quem.) But this assumption is not ad hoc; it was proposed independently by Ehlers, and it is a reasonable inference from the further development of the theme of eros in the *Aspasia.* In addition, my construction involves no other hypothesis that seems to me intrinsically dubious. Granted that first-order certainty is not to be had concerning this chronology, we do get a certain kind of second-order or epistemic certainty: it is certainly more reasonable to accept the proposed sequence (as probable) than to deny that we have any credible information about the chronology of these dialogues.

Furthermore, my proposed dating for Aeschines' dialogues receives a kind of confirmation from an entirely independent piece of evidence, Lysias' attack on Aeschines cited by Athenaeus (13.612b).[54] Lysias describes Aeschines as "a pupil [μαθητής] of Socrates and the author of many solemn discourses on virtue and justice." Lysias' activity cannot be traced beyond 380, and hence he is usually thought to have died soon after that date. If so, the passage just quoted shows that Aeschines' work must have been well known a good deal earlier.[55]

One more point on chronology. It is often said that the entire Socratic literature on Alcibiades is a response to Polycrates' *Accusation* (κατηγορία), which we know attacked Socrates as a teacher of Alcibiades and Critias, and which is generally dated to 393–392.[56] But the frequent repetition of this claim does not suffice to make it convincing. I do not see how the emphasis on Socrates' love for Alcibiades in Aeschines' dialogue, or the playful treatment of the same theme in the prologue to Plato's *Protagoras,* can possibly be regarded as apologetic in the

[54]See Dittmar (above, note 1), p. 257.
[55]As Gigon (above, note 21), p. 308, pointed out.
[56]So, for example, Giannantoni (above, note 6), 3:319.

way we would expect if either Aeschines or Plato were seriously concerned to answer Polycrates' charge.[57]

There is also a question about the date of Polycrates' *Accusation*. Although it must be later than 394, how much later is not clear.[58] The latest discussion of this question, on the basis of Isocrates' reference to Polycrates in the *Busiris*, dates the work after 390 and anywhere in the early or middle 380s.[59] In view of the indifference of Plato and Aeschines, it seems more likely that (as has occasionally been suggested) Polycrates' anti-Socratic display piece was provoked by the Socratic literature on Alcibiades rather than vice versa. Perhaps no close associate of Socrates would have felt that Polycrates' rhetorical tract deserved an answer. As Gigon has pointed out for Lysias,[60] and as we can add for Isocrates, the orators who did answer Polycrates were less interested in defending Socrates than in attacking their rival. Among authors of Socratic literature only Xenophon, the last and least Socratic, is actively concerned to respond to Polycrates. And he has a different motive for doing so: it gives him a literary pretext for organizing and publishing his recollections. There is no similar motive that might have induced Antisthenes, Aeschines, or Plato to take Polycrates seriously, and no real evidence that they did so. In rhetorical circles this pamphlet obviously caused quite a stir. But I suspect that its importance for the Socratics has been grossly exaggerated by scholars in search of literary infighting between fourth-century authors.[61]

---

[57]Even less apologetic is Plato's depiction of the conversation between Socrates and Critias in the *Charmides*, for there really was no need for Plato to choose *these* interlocutors.

[58]P. Treves's reasons for dating it "mit Sicherheit" in 393–392 (in *RE* 21.2 [1952], col. 1740) are the same as those of M. Pohlenz, which are rightly rejected by E. R. Dodds, *Plato's Gorgias* (Oxford, 1959), p. 29 n. 2.

[59]C. Eucken, *Isokrates* (Berlin, 1983), p. 174.

[60]Gigon (above, note 21), p. 23.

[61]This essay is extracted from a forthcoming book entitled *Plato and the Socratic Dialogue*, to be published by Cambridge University Press.

[4]

The *Hippias Major* and
Socratic Theories of Pleasure

Harold A. S. Tarrant

In Hellenistic times there were two schools tracing their origins to
Socrates that espoused extreme positions on the desirability of pleasure. The Cynics, more important for their social than for their philosophic role, took an antihedonistic stance, emphasizing the role of toil
in promoting the good life; and the Cyrenaics, of little social importance but of potentially greater philosophic interest, embraced a number of hedonistic sects for whom the pleasures of Epicurus were
insufficiently down-to-earth.

Lucian represents Diogenes of Sinope, who is for him the archetypal Cynic just as Chrysippus is the archetypal Stoic, as one who conducted a quasi-military campaign against pleasures; the philosophy of
Aristippus,[1] however, is summed up as "to despise everything, make
use of everything, and derive a contribution to one's pleasure from every source." He is the "sophist of pleasant sensations."[2] It is unfortunate that his inebriated condition prevents him from actually speaking
in Lucian's sketch. However, it is clear that for Lucian and his popular
but surprisingly sophisticated audiences, the Cyrenaic philosophy is
the hedonistic philosophy par excellence, while the Cynic philosophy is
the antihedonistic philosophy par excellence.

That two such diametrically opposed moral philosophies should both
trace their origins to Socrates is in some respects surprising. Certainly

---

[1]That Aristippus the Elder, pupil of Socrates, is intended is clear from the notion that
Epicurus derived his philosophy from the Laughing Creed (= Democritus) and the
Drunken Creed (= Aristippus).

[2]Lucian *Vit. auct.* 8 (Diogenes), 12 (Aristippus).

Socrates was a man with questions rather than answers and consequently became "all things to all men" more easily than most. But was there no coherence or consistency either in his own views or in the views that his leadership fostered in others? That would be a difficult thesis to defend; fortunately we do not have to subscribe to it.

Lucian, we noted, takes as his representative of the Cynic school Diogenes of Sinope, not his Socratic teacher Antisthenes. He had good dramatic reasons for doing this, but it may very well have been Diogenes who had most influenced the subsequent character of the Cynic movement. Likewise there is a significant problem as to the real founder of the Cyrenaics: was it Aristippus the Elder, or was it rather his grandson, Aristippus the Mother-taught? And how far did Cyrenaic doctrine remain constant in any case?[3] How far, indeed, did its acknowledgment of a debt to Socrates endure?

A primary source of our knowledge of Cyrenaic ethics, the summary of general Cyrenaic doctrine given by Diogenes Laertius (2.86–93), is such that their differences from the Epicureans are constantly brought to our attention. Whether this is due to the desire of others to bring out the contrasts, or whether the ultimate Cyrenaic source was itself late enough to be responding to Epicurean dogma is unclear, and not of immediate importance. In either case it is not a reliable source for the doctrines of Aristippus the Elder, and thus not evidence for an original Socratic tradition. If we seek the extent to which Socrates' own teaching could have inspired different views, we ought surely to confine ourselves to what can reliably be attributed to the Socratic disciples who inspired the two schools: to Antisthenes in the one case, and to Aristippus the Elder in the other.

Even here a sharp difference in attitude to pleasure may be detected, leading one to ask whether both could possibly have derived their moral inspiration from a single teacher. Taking an early witness for the views of Aristippus, we find Xenophon drawing attention to his pursuit of ease and of pleasuring.[4] Antisthenes, on the other hand, is reported to have said frequently: "I would go mad rather than feel pleasure."[5] Contradictions among the pupils of Socrates over the question of pleasure's role here seem to reach their peak, though we shall find in due

---

[3]There is a particular problem in relation to this school, since Diogenes treats separately the doctrines of three Cyrenaic splinter groups: those following Hegesias, Anniceris, and Theodorus the atheist. That may mean that the general summary of doctrine has a special claim to be viewed as orthodox, but if the orthodoxy was determined by Aristippus the Younger, then it tells us little about the original Socratic traditions on pleasure.

[4]*Mem.* 2.1.9.

[5]D.L. 6.3 (and cf. Gell. *NA* 9.5.3, who interprets it to mean that pleasure is the worst of evils!) = fr. 108 Caizzi = *SSR* 122: ἔλεγέ τε συνεχές, Μανείην μᾶλλον ἢ ἡσθείην.

course that the evidence for Antisthenes and Aristippus is not so clear-cut. There are times when the internal evidence for individual followers of Socrates is very difficult to reconcile. One can receive very different impressions of the Socratic view of pleasure's worth from reading two different passages of Xenophon, or two different passages of Plato. How is the evidence to be reconciled? Can we believe that Socrates did not think out the question of pleasure's value?

In some ways it would be extraordinary if he had not done so. Pleasure and pain are a principal topic of moral philosophy from early Plato on. The value of pleasure is a subject that no moral philosophy could thereafter ignore. Aristotle himself had declared that "pleasure and pain follow every experience and every act, and on this account [moral] virtue has to do with pleasures and pains,"[6] and we have two substantial contributions of his to the subject of pleasure at *Nicomachean Ethics* 7.11–14 and 10.1–5. Had Socrates no inkling of the importance that this topic was about to assume? I cannot here tackle all evidence for Socratic views on pleasure. Rather I wish to focus our attention upon one Platonic work, which, when correctly understood, can help us to clear up some of the difficulties.

1. Interpreting the *Hippias Major*

The *Hippias major* presents considerable problems for those who would wish to use it as evidence for Socrates. To begin with there is the authorship question. Is it by Plato, or is it not? Even today there are those who do not regard the work as authentic Plato, however much it may follow in the Platonic tradition.[7] Perhaps the emphasis in the debate has shifted from whether the work can be Platonic in philosophical content, for there is now no great obstacle to the belief that it somehow reflects his general metaphysical position just prior to the enunciation of the Theory of Ideas in the middle period works.[8] But there is a lingering feeling that much of the language and the general compositional technique cannot be matched in the rest of the corpus, and that some of it is better explained by the postulation of a later date than those who would accept Platonic authorship would care to postulate.[9]

The authorship question, however, may in fact be a secondary problem. If not Plato himself, then whoever the author is, he is still much

[6]*Eth. Nic.* 2, 1104b14–16.
[7]E.g., H. Thesleff, "The Date of the Pseudo-Platonic *Hippias Major*," Arctos 10 (1976): 105–17; C. Kahn, "The Beautiful and the Genuine," *OSAP* 3 (1985): 261–87.
[8]Plato, *Hippias major*, trans. with comm. and essay by P. Woodruff (Oxford, 1982), pp. 161–80.
[9]See particularly Thesleff (above, note 7).

influenced by Plato's early dialogues of definition, by Platonic metaphysics, and by a recognizably Platonic view of Socratic inquiry; it is less
because of concerns about authorship that I believe the work deserves
a special place in an examination of the Socratic tradition than because
it presents us, on the face of it, with two Socrates characters. The famous alter ego is not just Socrates' double: he is far more forthright,
aggressive, intolerant, and committed to searching for the truth than is
what we may call the surface Socrates of the work. The device is without parallel in the Platonic corpus, and it is of considerable importance
to know how it is to be interpreted.

It may strike one as purely a device for enabling a conversation to
take place between Socrates and a self-admirer such as Hippias, who
has no time for Socratic small talk and would not tolerate being openly
refuted and "put down" by Socrates.[10] Paul Woodruff believes that
the device is so necessary that it is not merely Socrates who has to
pretend that the questioning and dissatisfaction come from a third
party—eventually identified as "the son of Sophroniscus" (= Socrates,
298b–c); Hippias too needs to maintain the pretense.[11] I doubt if this
can be right. Irony would not suit so outspoken a person as Hippias; it
too is beneath him. How is it that he twice inquires as to the questioner's identity (288d1 and 298b10)? How is it that he seems so surprised
that the questioner might give Socrates a beating in a seemingly just
city (292a–b)? How is it, moreover, that the reader could feel that Hippias had been beaten if he had successfully managed to maintain this
pretense throughout the conversation, until finally delivering a strong
condemnation of Socrates' methods (304a–b). This interpretation
makes Hippias one of the most perceptive of Socrates' sophistic interlocutors, not, as we feel in the *Protagoras* and *Hippias minor,* one of the
least sensitive.

There is a further point that arises here. The writer was under no
compulsion to choose Hippias as interlocutor. If he had wished to enable Socrates to deliver a stinging criticism of the explanation of "the
fine" being proposed, he could simply have chosen an interlocutor who
would stand up to the criticism: one committed to the task of pursuing
a definition of the elusive quality under consideration. There would
then have been no need for dishonesty or dissimulation on Socrates'
part, and consequently no need for an alter ego. Why has Hippias been
chosen? It is partly because he is the epitome of "the fine" himself, so
that the writer follows all too consciously the good Platonic practice

---

[10]The word for "small talk" is σμικρολογία, a term employed by others who wish to be
involved in public life rather than in nonproductive speculation: cf. *Tht.* 175a.

[11]Woodruff (above, note 8), pp. 123–35.

of making the initial interlocutor one who has claims to the quality under discussion; but partly for the sake of humor, humor deriving from his pompousness and insensitivity, which are wide open to Socratic exploitation. If the reader was to imagine Hippias in control all along, deliberately avoiding the kind of answer that Socrates wants and participating in the irony of the occasion, then we should not be laughing at him.

Both for these reasons and because the alter ego is persisted with even after the conversation has broken down (304d–e), one has to look for another explanation of this second Socrates, one that would see it as an intentional and meaningful element in the work, not as a mere device for overcoming compositional problems; one, perhaps, that sees some real duality in the familiar figures. To deny that this duality is intended by the author is to accept that the Socrates of this work is a blatant deceiver, ironically inventing a twin brother behind whose mask he can hide.[12] The Socrates of the *Charmides* tells lies in a constructive cause (155bff.); the Socrates of the *Hippias major* would be telling them rather for the sake of making Hippias seem more ridiculous. A vivid picture of the alter ego emerges in the course of the work, partly through Socrates' descriptions of him and partly through Hippias' reactions: He asks the most disrespectful questions (293a); he is ignorant and boorish (288d–289e); he is rude and given to mocking laughter (291e–292c); he inclines toward violence (292a), though he sometimes takes pity on Socrates and helps him along (293d). Most significantly though, he will not leave things unexamined (298b–c). In this respect he is the old familiar Socrates.[13] In other respects he has an almost Cynic appearance, particularly insofar as he is ready to use his staff to back up his disrespect and mocking contempt for the values of civilized society and its most prestigious representatives. Is he in fact too scornful to be a participant in Plato's ideal sort of dialectical investigation?

I ask this question because the closest parallel to the alter ego is to be found in a work acutely conscious of the right and the wrong types of questioner: the *Theaetetus*. In a famous passage Socrates demands, on Protagoras' behalf, that he himself should not be unfair in argument and should keep the competitive spirit out of his discussions. He should not be trying to trip his opponent up but should rather endeavor to help him up when he has fallen (167e–168a). Proper conduct will result in the gratitude of his interlocutors, who will blame their confusion on themselves rather than on him. He should avoid arguments that de-

---

[12]It is therefore not easy to reconcile this explanation with Vlastos' view of Socratic irony as expounded in "Socratic Irony," *CQ* n.s. 37 (1987): 79–96.

[13]For the worthlessness of the unexamined life see *Ap.* 38a; for Socrates' inability to allow falsehoods to pass unchallenged see *Tht.* 151c–d.

pend merely upon the way we use words (168a–c). We in fact see a kind of expurgated Socrates in the *Theaetetus,* one less likely to be led by his enthusiasm for knowledge into trying merely to expose an opponent's weaknesses and into the more antagonistic forms of irony. The kind of problem that Socrates had just been producing for Theaetetus had in fact been characterized as "antilogical" and disputatious (164c) and had been connected there too with wordplay.

The apparent self-criticism shows that Plato was conscious now of the need to distance Socrates from certain kinds of argument that he would associate rather with more sophistic opponents. He had just introduced a line of questioning at 163d with the words "If someone were to ask. . ." Now he will continue to distance himself from this type of questioning. At 165b he states the "most formidable question," an "inescapable question" asked by "a man who can't be unsettled"; this character, a rather more brazen Socratic type than "Socrates" here appears, is then further described as a "light-armed combatant lying in ambush" and a "wage earner in argument" (165d) who pursues his questions relentlessly. Somewhat earlier (158b5) he had introduced a dispute (ἀμφισβήτημα, b5, c8, d1) about whether one might really be dreaming rather than waking, and whether one should credit one condition rather than another. Socrates distances himself from the idea by suggesting that Theaetetus may often have heard this kind of thing, though there seems no prima facie reason why he could not make these suggestions himself. Unlike the rest of the work up to that point, the passage is clearly marked as late by the presence of the late period response formulae ὀρθῶς and παντάπασι μὲν οὖν at 158d7 and d10.[14]

Later in the dialogue, during the digression on false opinion, Plato resorts to a similar technique. First there is a hint that some unnamed person may have been partly responsible for Socrates' perplexity about false opinion (187d2); then an anonymous questioner is introduced at 188d to challenge whether it is possible to "think what is not." He returns at 195c–e so as to introduce the embarrassing case of numbers and mockingly challenge Socrates' wax-tablet explanation of false opinion. Then at 197a there is a suggestion that an "antilogical" person would require Socrates to converse without terms of cognition until such time as he discovers what knowledge is. Finally there is a reference back, presumably to these passages, to "that refutative fellow," who mockingly produces severe difficulties for Socrates' final attempt to ex-

---

[14]On these response formulae see Thesleff's table 3 in *Studies in Platonic Chronology* (Helsinki, 1982), p. 79. The only earlier case of a characteristically late-period response formula is the τί μήν at 145e5, where I suspect that e2–5 is a late addition springing from the desire to clarify the theory of the identity of knowledge and wisdom. At e2 τὸ ποῖον; seems rather a slow response from the quick-minded Theaetetus.

plain false opinion, based (like certain sophisms in the *Euthydemus*) upon a rigid dichotomy between knowledge and ignorance.

When we look at the section on false opinion we may very well suspect that it is raising difficulties anonymously in order to save Plato from the charge of mystifying us in matters where he had already developed solutions. The *Sophist*'s long and careful solution to the problem of false statement incorporates an explanation of false opinion too (264a). This may not extend to the understanding of the physical or psychological aspect of false opinion's development, but it at least removes the difficulties raised at *Theaetetus* 188d over "opining what is not." I do not make the improbable claim that the *Sophist* was penned before the *Theaetetus*, but *Euthydemus* 284c already shows Plato en route to his solution. Plato has answers and is therefore engineering aporia in the *Theaetetus*, no doubt because he realizes its value for arousing curiosity and getting others to think for themselves (155c–d). But he does not want to be raising spurious and contentious objections directly, even though the early works would have happily allowed Socrates to present such difficulties.

The language that Plato uses in the *Theaetetus* to describe the kind of approach he is at pains to avoid is that of dispute, refutation, and antilogic.[15] Such terms are easily applied to the alter ego of the *Hippias major*. Similarly one can say that the attitudes suggested by these terms are not openly displayed by the surface Socrates, who is at pains to explain to Hippias carefully the defects of his answers. If merged, the two faces of Socrates begin to look like the Socrates of the early dialogues: when they are kept separate we are confronted with something new in both cases. Neither figure is very attractive, the surface Socrates having neither the urgent desire for truth nor the guts to ask tricky questions for himself, and the alter ego being all too hostile in his interrogations. The surface Socrates is Socrates the over-helpful comrade and ironic flatterer, as was evident during the introductory conversation; the other Socrates is the impatient exposer of ignorance, a formidable and persistent opponent, ever ready to ask seemingly boorish questions on the road to exposing the inconsistencies of his interlocutors' beliefs. I see in this segregation of the two sides of the earlier Socrates an ironic comment upon the tendency, visible in the *Theaetetus*, to distance Socrates from contentious lines of questioning.[16]

---

[15]ἀμφισβ-, ἐλεγκτ-, ἀντιλογ-.

[16]Thesleff, "Platonic Chronology," *Phronesis* 34 (1989): 23 n. 89, has more to say on the dichotomy of Socrates, as has Tuija Jatakari, "Der jüngere Sokrates," *Arctos* 24 (1990): 29–46, who concentrates on the "young Socrates" of the *Theaetetus*, the *Sophist*, and the *Statesman*. Chronological considerations may suggest to some that parallels in these works are of limited use for our interpretation of the *Hippias major*; this is not so.

When we proceed to the *philosophy* of the *Hippias major* we see very little difference between the two Socratic characters until the final episode—the one involving the suggestion that "the fine" may be what is pleasant to the sight and to the hearing. At this point we temporarily see the surface Socrates, who has supplied the definition out of the blue himself, partnering Hippias in resisting pressure from the alter ego.[17] The following questions are asked of him at 298d–e:

> Why have you separated off things that are pleasant in this way, and denied the term "fine" to food, drink, sex, and all the rest?

> Don't you recognize such things as "pleasant" or as "pleasures," nor anything else unless it be seen or heard?

> Given that they are no less pleasant, why do you deprive them of the description "fine"?

The alter ego immediately homes in on the *qualification* that has been applied to the notion that "the fine" is explained in terms of its pleasantness. He seems to be suggesting that this qualification is somehow misguided. He seems to be asking: "What's wrong with the other pleasures?" The answer that he receives from the surface Socrates is singularly unconvincing in terms of Socratic philosophy, for it makes appeal to the ἔνδοξον: to leave the term "pleasant" unqualified would be "utterly ridiculous," says Socrates, and "As for sex, everyone would contend that. . ."[18] Here we have that great champion of the views of the one expert against those of the multitude uncharacteristically appealing to the majority view.[19] The alter ego is suitably scathing: "I too can see why you have an ingrained distaste for calling these pleasures fine, because people don't think they are. But I was asking you what *is* fine, not what is commonly held to be fine." The weight of the majority opinion means nothing to the alter ego (which is another reason for

---

Thesleff (pp. 22–23) maintains his argument for dating the work around 360 B.C. In my view he has excellent reasons for supposing the finally published work dates from this period, but I tend to assume that the work was an attempt to prepare an earlier Platonic sketch for publication, and to do so according to Plato's latest requirements.

[17]Or in fact from anybody who would ask the same questions, 298d5–6: the flexible identity of the questioner is reminiscent of the *Theaetetus.*

[18]Translations in this sentence and in the second sentence below are Waterfield's, in the Penguin *Plato: Early Socratic Dialogues,* ed. T. J. Saunders (London, 1987).

[19]That this is atypical is clear from such a consciously Socratic passage as *Crito* 47aff., where there is the clear motive of justifying Socrates' refusal to escape in terms of uncontroversially Socratic doctrine. Similarly one may appeal to *Gorgias* 471eff. For the inappropriateness of appeals to the *endoxon* in Socratic argument see Vlastos in his now famous article "The Socratic Eleuchus," *OSAP* 1 (1983): 27–58.

seeing him as somehow more Socratic than his counterpart): he is interested only in realities, not in appearances. There seems to be a suggestion that the majority opinion *is just an appearance,* though like a good Socratic the alter ego refrains from making any statement to that effect. He leaves the matter for Socrates to consider, but all that Socrates can do is to restate his position without any justification, and to invite the questioner to refute it if he can. Socrates fails to look deeply into the realities of the matter, as the alter ego was inviting and as dialectic requires; instead he takes his stance.

Naturally the questioner obliges with an attack. It is of course the qualification to the idea that what's fine is pleasant that is attacked, and attacked through the interesting argument that what's fine isn't fine because it's pleasant or because it's seen or because it's heard or because it's seen and heard.[20] It is attacked on rather technical grounds, without the slightest hint that there is anything wrong with the use of pleasure in explaining "the fine." This is of course analogous to the typical ending of dialogue concerned with the definition of a virtue: the notion that the virtue concerned is some kind of ἐπιστήμη is not attacked in the *Euthyphro* or the *Laches* or the *Charmides.* What is attacked is the particular attempt(s) to qualify the term *epistēmē.* The qualifications are attacked because Socratic philosophy resists the suggestion that the virtues are separable (when looked at as a moral force within man that secures right conduct).[21] Does that mean that here in the *Hippias major* the qualifications to the equation of "the fine" and the pleasant are likewise resisted because Socratic philosophy resists the separation of those notions—at least when examined in a particular way?

In view of the general impression that the alter ego dislikes the qualification and regards the surface Socrates as being rather timid in his adoption of it, it is surely necessary to consider whether the reader is not being invited to reflect further on the hedonistic premise that "the fine" and "the pleasant" are properly identical. Certainly that is not how the commentators view the passage. Take Robin Waterfield, for example: "Since this is presumably meant to be the most plausible attempt at defining fineness in aesthetic terms, and since it is rejected, it tells us not to limit fineness to the aesthetic and sensible."[22] One cannot stop at observing that a definition is rejected; one must observe also

---

[20]The argument at one point bears an obvious similarity to *Theaetetus* 185a–b.

[21]The virtue terms can also of course be applied to the conduct that arises from such a moral force.

[22]In Saunders (above, note 18), p. 225. Woodruff (above, note 8), p. 77, remarks that " 'Socrates' record elsewhere suggests that he would not take the Questioner's radical hint at 298de, and define the fine simply as what produces pleasure." Perhaps Woodruff might agree that it is vital to determine here which "Socrates" is truer to Socrates himself.

why it is rejected. Its rejection has nothing to do with its limiting "the fine" to the sensible realm qua realm of pleasure, for pleasure belongs also to the intellectual realm, as numerous Platonic passages testify. Only the restriction that the pleasure be visual or auditory causes problems. Waterfield's assumption that this ought to be the most plausible definition of its kind seems to imply that the aporetic dialogues all do their best to be other than aporetic, something that we should be better advised to doubt.

Yet Waterfield's view is typical. The prevailing view is to assume that the latter pages of the work are somewhat antihedonistic. There is no other reason for this, I believe, than the general supposition that Plato's Socrates tended toward antihedonism. That supposition is fraught with problems, not least the necessity of seeing the apparent hedonism of the *Protagoras* not merely as neutral theory to which Socrates fails to subscribe but even as something that our truth-loving Socrates, so anxious to set himself apart from the sophists who don't care what they argue for,[23] has fundamental objections to. There is no space here for tackling the labyrinth of the *Protagoras*, but let it suffice to say that if Socrates and/or Plato (at the time of writing) had regarded this hedonism as a dangerous theory upon which to found one's life, that theory would never have been presented in such a way that Socrates could be assumed by many readers to be advocating it.

2. Hedonism Elsewhere in Plato

Protagoras 351ff. is not the only passage in Plato's allegedly Socratic works to be founded upon an ultimately hedonistic ethic. Of far greater importance when dealing with the *Hippias major* is *Gorgias* 474dff., where Socrates discusses the nature of "the fine" with Polus. The passage is closely linked with our work insofar as it utilizes very much the same categories of fine things: bodies, shapes, colors, and sounds; laws and practices (ἐπιτηδεύματα), coupled also at *Hippias major* 298d1; learning (475a1; cf. *Hp.ma.* 296a5: σοφία). The *Gorgias* explains "the fine" as that which is either pleasure-giving or useful/beneficial.[24] It is evident that the terms "useful" and "beneficial" are being used in a manner similar to that of *Hippias major* 295c–297d, where the former means "suitable for achieving a desired end," the lat-

---

[23]Cf. *Euthd.* 288a–b.

[24]It is left to Polus to equate what is useful or beneficial with what is good (475a3), thus apparently indicating that "good" is here used in a contributory rather than a final sense; it is presumably this restriction of the term "good" that underlies Polus' refusal to follow Socrates in identifying the good with "the fine." Socrates is then able to use bad as the opposite of useful/beneficial.

ter "suitable for achieving a good end." That is to say that the *Gorgias*, in explaining "the fine" in terms of that which is either pleasant or beneficial, is attributing two senses to it, one relating to its contribution to some unspecified good end, the other relating to its contribution to the balance of pleasure over pain.

Now first it should be clear that all pleasures qua pleasant are going to be "fine" according to this theory. The only circumstances in which a pleasure can be denied to be "fine" are those in which it is so linked with αἰσχρά—either "pains" or "harmful effects"—that these latter outweigh the immediate pleasant effects. Second, it should be observed that if the further goal to which what is "fine" qua beneficial contributes is itself καλόν (and how could it not be in Socratic theory?), then that further goal must be either beneficial or pleasant. If beneficial, then it must contribute to a further goal either beneficial or pleasant, and so on. *Either* there is an infinite regress *or* else the argument used against Polus rests on theory that makes pleasure the ultimate explanation of all *kala*. It is certainly not the pleasure of the moment, that is, pleasure contemporary with the experience, that allows an experience to be designated *kalon*, but that does not alter the fact that Socrates is employing an ultimately hedonistic method of evaluation, very similar to that which he employs in the *Protagoras*.

This claim would seem particularly strange in the light of the fact that the *Gorgias* is the very work of Plato's by which scholars judge Socrates to have been an antihedonist. First, the very denial of the status of τέχνη to rhetoric had been based on a division between true arts aimed at the good and "flatteries" aimed rather at pleasure.[25] Can it be possible for the whole thrust of the work to be based upon this fundamental distinction if that which is best and that which is ultimately pleasantest are identical? To this I can confidently answer yes. Plato's flatterers are not aiming at what is ultimately pleasantest, but at what is pleasantest in the short term. Flatteries are also distinguished from arts by their inability to *calculate* their effects (501a7) and to give an explanation for what they are doing.[26] To aim at the good would still require a calculus or the knowledge of certain explanatory laws by which present conduct was linked to future success; to aim at immediate pleasure requires only experience of what tends to generate it. The theory of the *Protagoras* would be a perfectly sound basis for a distinction between arts and flatteries along these lines.

Next of course one has to cope with the fact that Socrates seems personally committed to disproving the identification of pleasure and the good that Callicles espouses at 495a. Though it is abundantly evident

[25]*Grg.* 464c–465a, 500d–501a.
[26]465a, 501a, c.

that the term "pleasant" is here being applied only to what given pleasure at a given moment, with the arguments relying upon this temporal factor, I do not want to argue that the tenor of this passage is compatible with the *Protagoras,* as J. C. B. Gosling and C. C. W. Taylor do.[27] Plato is writing with a mission at this point, and his mission appears to be to undermine the hedonistic ethic altogether. However, I am prepared to argue that this very commitment of "Socrates," like the new Pythagorean element, is an indication that the arguments with Callicles bid farewell to any Socratic stage in Plato's thought. This I have argued before, and I see no reason to change my mind.[28]

At very least one should be prepared to allow *Gorgias* 474dff. to speak for itself, without feeling constrained to read it in the light of the arguments with Callicles. We should be alert to the fact that this passage tends to reduce ultimately to hedonism, but we should also bear in mind that Plato has not brought that fact to the fore. There is certainly no intention on his part of converting us to hedonism: to judge from both the *Protagoras* and the *Laws* (e.g., 5,732eff.) he thought man's nature needs no converting. But he is willing to allow important theory to be based upon ultimately hedonistic premises. It may be that scholars will prefer to regard the argument against Polus, like that with Protagoras, as ad hominem. But they would have to be prepared to show how these arguments can be ad hominem in a way that other arguments in the "Socratic" dialogues are not.

3. The *Kalon* of the *Hippias Major*

It is time that we returned to the *Hippias major.* What I hope to do now is to show how logically the work develops, bearing in mind the various aspects of the *Gorgias's* treatment of "the fine." The initial at-

[27]J. C. B. Gosling and C. C. W. Taylor, *The Greeks on Pleasure* (Oxford, 1982), pp. 69–78, manage to reconcile the overall position even of the arguments with Callicles with the enlightened hedonism of Plato's *Protagoras.* It is the amazing difference in attitude that strikes me: the fact that Socrates is totally at ease with a hedonistic ethic in one work and unusually keen to expose it in another.

[28]See my "Composition of Plato's *Gorgias,*" *Prudentia* 14 (1983): 3–22. I am much indebted to the *TLG* computer-readable texts, which enabled me to discover that every single one of the thirty-nine cases of the verbal forms in -τέος and so on in the *Gorgias* occurs after Polus has spoken his last word (i.e., from 480e on). The arguments with Gorgias and Polus resemble the early *Hippias minor* in being free of such forms, in spite of the frequent occurrence of alternatives such as δεῖ and χρή. Another significant difference is that Plato has now acquired a physical theory of pleasure that seems not to treat pleasure and pain as strict opposites (always implied in the argument with Polus): pleasure is akin to a process of filling, pain to a condition of emptiness rather than an emptying, and hence the two are contemporaneous.

tempts by Hippias to say what "the fine" is need not detain us long. That there are three attempts to offer a preeminent example of the quality concerned rather than the usual one might be attributed either to the obtuseness of Hippias or to his cunning escape from offering Socrates a straight answer or to his desire to raise the conversation to the heights to which he aspires; but one reason is surely the multifaceted nature of the term "fine," to which the author wishes to draw attention early. The term is applied by Hippias first to the beauty of the human body (the fine-looking girl, 287e), then by Socrates to other animals and artifacts; thus it acquires an aesthetic sense that can be applied to bodily things in general. Hippias is now able to offer something preeminently fine that can be attached to any body at all (gold, 289e). The objections to this effort of Hippias do two separate things: first, still in the realm of aesthetics, they introduce the concept of what is fitting or appropriate, which will be needed shortly. Second, they introduce cases where the fineness and appropriateness of an object are determined by its utility (what we *do* with it) rather than by its pleasant appearance. This in turn leads Hippias to look into the world of human endeavor, the realm of those fine νόμοι and *epitēdeumata* to which the *Symposium* has us turn after we have experienced physical beauty in general (210c, 211c). He explains "the fine" in terms of the archetypally desirable human life according to Greek tradition. We have a glimpse of that which is "fine" not merely because of its delightful appearance or its utility, but of something that is fine qua end: the final object of striving for any ordinary Greek.

By the time that Socrates had disposed of this explanation too, the reader is aware of all the major classes of "fine" things in Plato (fine learning having been squeezed in 292d) and has been introduced to three senses in which things may be fine: qua pleasant, qua useful for some desirable end, and qua desirable in their own right. This is of course all going to have be taken into consideration. It is notorious that Socratic writings seek single, unified definitions even for words that seem to be applied to diverse things in diverse senses, and the initial task of the writer is to give some indication of the extension that he wishes the term to have.

The work now proceeds in a very logical manner, with Socrates being the one to take each successive forward step. First he reverts to the concept of "the fine" as what's fitting or appropriate. That term had been applied already both to things aesthetically pleasant and to things well adapted to their use; but it tended to suggest the immediate impact of the object concerned, and consequently tended to be associated with appearance rather than underlying reality. In many cases, perhaps, there would be no gulf between them, but there might be where something had long-term detrimental effects. Socrates therefore rejects it as being as quality that causes things to seem fine rather than to be fine.

When one considers long-term effects in relation to how "fine" anything may be, one is thinking of its usefulness or harmfulness. Thus Socrates now suggests an equation of what's "fine" and what's useful (295c) and manages to apply it with some success to all classes of "fine" things. However, the term "useful" focuses upon the means without specifying that the end be desirable; things used merely for bad ends can hardly be fine, so the term "beneficial" is substituted for "useful." This term applies to anything that tends to contribute to an eventual good outcome. The problem now is that to restrict "the fine" to that which contributes to some good end means that it cannot be applied to anything that is viewed as a good purely in its own right. To put it bluntly, nothing that does not have consequences can be "fine."

Such a notion was counterintuitive and is soon rejected. Any definition of "the fine" as Socrates is well aware in the *Gorgias,* must apply both to things that contribute to a good end and to things viewed as good in themselves: to the fine kitchen tool, for instance, and to the fine-looking girl. Awareness that the term "beneficial" cannot cover things that are enjoyed purely for what they are, not for what they produce, ought now to lead to a definition that covers things enjoyed for what they are.

What could the writer possibly offer here? What is there that is fine in itself but is never pursued for some desirable consequence? There is happiness, of course, but such an answer begs the question; one has to be able to explain what happiness consists in. It is presumably composed of other things that are good in themselves. What can such things be if not pleasures? What can they be valued for if not for the pleasure itself? Aristotle seems unaware of any genuine alternative (*Eth. Nic.* 10.2). More important, what alternative did Plato offer? Knowledge is suggested as an alternative end in the *Republic,* but what knowledge other than knowledge of the Good (505b–c)? And do we really want it for its own sake, or for the sake of the Good? The mature Plato may have had answers, but Socrates, ever reliant on the thought patterns of the ordinary educated Greek, is unlikely to have been so esoteric. That which was desired for its own sake and which was not felt to be in need of desirable consequences was pleasure. The argument with Polus had virtually acknowledged that, and it is predictable that Socrates would now try to relate "the fine" to pleasure in some way.

Thus the attempted definition in terms of what is pleasant to sight and hearing is a logical step after the observation that the beneficial covers fine means but not fine ends. The rejection of this definition in no way entails the rejection of pleasure as a possible explanation of a thing's being fine. Indeed it leads to an attempt to explain further what it is that makes these pleasures superior to others (303e). They are, it seems, the most harmless pleasures. To anybody familiar with the theory of the *Protagoras* that would signify that there are no long-term pains that counterbalance the pleasures. We are on the point of a solution to the problem of defining "the fine."

This kind of definition dialogue, however, is not wont to end in solutions. One can scarcely imagine Socrates thanking Hippias for his enormous help in finding the answers that will satisfy the alter ego. The reintroduction of the kind of consequences that certain pleasures have has given the alter ego a new weapon; for to distinguish between pleasures in respect of their good or bad consequences again raises the issue of what will be beneficial and what will be harmful. Without an explicit statement to the effect that pleasures are good *unless* counterbalanced by harmful (hence painful) consequences, it inevitably seems that it was the benefits rather than the pleasure that made beneficial pleasures "fine." Again the definition leads to what is productive of good rather than to what is good in itself. And with that the search has gone round in its Daedalian circle (cf. *Euthphr.* 15b).

4. Socratic Pleasures

Our examination of the *Hippias major* has helped us to see that it is one of a number of Platonic texts that suggest that Socrates may have founded his ethics on ultimately hedonistic principles: the others being *Gorgias* 474dff. and *Protagoras* 351bff. Certainly no Platonic texts suggest that Socrates would have espoused a life of uncritical pleasuring, and there is no doubt that he advocated the traditional Greek caution in the pursuit of the pleasures of the body. The openly antihedonistic passages in the Platonic corpus, however, seem later and less acceptably Socratic because of an infusion of Pythagorizing material.

When one comes to Plato's main rival in the depiction of Socrates as an ethical philosopher, Xenophon,[29] one finds a variety of passages that either treat pleasures (or what is pleasant) or give some hint as to how they are viewed. The *Oeconomicus* is quite consistent in regarding pleasure as *at least one* criterion for assessing the desirability of types of

[29]Aristophanes, of course, had either no knowledge of Socratic ethics in 423 B.C. or no comic interest in them. It is, however, difficult to imagine either that Aristophanes could not have found amusing ways of satirizing Socrates' ethics and politics or that if Socrates already had well-developed moral views, Aristophanes did not know them. See the essay by Paul A. Vander Waerdt (Chapter 2).

conduct.[30] The *Memorabilia* and the *Symposium* also have a number of such passages,[31] and the *Apology* perhaps two (5–6, 18). Of these the former values Socrates' just and holy life all the more because of the supreme pleasure that his knowledge of his impeccable conduct brings him; and he justifies willingness to die on the grounds that he could not live pleasantly if he knew that his sensory and intellectual powers were declining. The latter shows Socrates valuing his ability to live more pleasantly than others without the expense of providing for luxuries. In the *Memorabilia* and the *Symposium* alike one finds passages that suggest that one might easily be misled in the pursuit of pleasure, and the *Memorabilia* also contains passages that dwell on the dangers of particular pleasures. Among these is the passage at *Memorabilia* 2.1.1.ff. where Socrates tackles his follower Aristippus; the pleasures of the adulterer, for instance (2.1.5), and the pleasures of the moment generally (2.1.20); but the remarkable thing is that Socrates is quite ready to argue on the assumption that it is the life that is ultimately pleasanter that should be chosen (e.g., 2.1.10), without so much as a hint that there is anything particularly wrong with this thesis. Never is pleasure as a whole treated as something to be scorned.

Xenophon thus presents Socrates as one who choose his pleasures carefully but chooses pleasure nevertheless. There is a clear connection between the goodness of an action or practice and the pleasure that it ultimately yields. Xenophon is not sufficiently keen on theory to want to inquire too closely into the nature of this connection: into whether it is because goodness is to be judged purely in terms of pleasure anyway, or whether pleasure naturally follows from our choosing the life of goodness. There are, however, two passages that might suggest that the relation of pleasure to goodness is one that is built into the framework of a rationally governed universe. This universe is organized in accordance with what is pleasant for the universal wisdom (*Mem.* 1.4.17), a clear indication that pleasure itself is a noble thing when it is pleasure *in what is good*. God takes pleasure in the rational workings of his world, and we should be able to take pleasure in our own good works too. Then again at *Memorabilia* 4.3.11 we find that man's possession of sense organs for the enjoyment of what is good, and of that reasoning by means of which we may pursue the good and shun the bad, is attributed to divine design. We are so structured as to take pleasure in good things and pursue their pleasures.

---

[30]This work gets around the problem of those pleasures normally regarded as inferior owing to their unpleasant consequences by maintaining that "as time goes on they are revealed even to those whom they have deceived as pains wrapped up in pleasures, which come to dominate and prevent them from undertaking useful tasks" (1.20).

[31]E.g., *Symp.* 2.25.

Now one may doubt whether such passages as introduce a rational god to plan for the universe accurately represent Socrates' views. Such a device, however, is entirely in agreement with the account of Socrates' enthusiasm for Anaxagoras' intelligent creative power in Plato's *Phaedo* (97b–98b), and it provides a suitable explanation for Socrates' thesis that the good life was also the pleasantest, which is one aspect of his thesis at *Protagoras* 351bff. that endures even until the *Republic*,[32] where the life of the just man is found to be 729 times pleasanter than that of the tyrant. The identity of the good life with the pleasant life can hardly be seen as a matter of chance by Socrates, for there would then be no reason why *my* good life should also turn out to be pleasantest. But a divinity organizing the universe in accordance with what is best would surely arrange for men to derive most pleasure (in the long run) when progressing toward good ends, even though it might involve short-term toils. Pleasure would then be an incentive for us to cooperate with that power's aims.

Does that make Socrates a hedonist? Does he advocate the pursuit of long-term pleasures for pleasure's sake, or for morality's sake? *We* pursue pleasure at the human level perhaps, but the divinity may have us pursue pleasure for the sake of what's morally best. One might, however, ask whether God has us pursue what's morally best *because it's best* or *because it pleases him!* This is the kind of theoretical question that Xenophon would have us believe was foreign to Socrates' agenda (*Mem.* 4.7). What matters is that Socrates was prepared to defend the same kind of life on a variety of criteria. In 1985 a papyrus was published that contained fragments of an unknown Socratic dialogue;[33] in it Socrates defends his willingness to die on a variety of criteria, moving (in col. 3) from a hedonistic defense to one based on the assumption that the honorable life is best. Is this not the Socrates with whom we are familiar, equating all kinds of goodness and arguing that it is the same individual who attains them all?

Whatever else emerges from Xenophon, it is the respectability of pleasure; it is its improper pursuit that is frowned upon. Thus Gosling and Taylor are able to say: "On the whole, Xenophon's Socrates stands for moderate hedonism."[34] This is a rather crude way of describing

---

[32]The conclusion at 587d–e is prepared by a fascinating (though problematic) discussion taking up much of book 9. We ought perhaps to acknowledge that both the later pages of the *Gorgias* and the *Phaedo* have temporarily abandoned the equation of the best with the pleasantest life (pace Gosling and Taylor [above, note 27], p. 87), but they employ after lives to redress the balance. Thus if "pleasant" is used for "productive of pleasure" (without a time limit), then the good life is to that extent pleasantest even in these works.

[33]*Kölner Papyri* 5 (1985): 22–53, no. 205.

[34]Gosling and Taylor (above, note 27), p. 38.

Socrates' stance, as if it were sufficient to place thinkers on some sliding scale between sybaritic hedonism (which they attribute to Aristippus) and out-and-out antihedonism (which they attribute to Antisthenes), but it has a certain validity. What it misses is the historical truth behind Xenophon's rather less crude picture: Socrates' ability to play the hedonist or the moralist as it suited either him or his friends.

Finally we return to Aristippus and Antisthenes. For the former one would like to show that he attended to Socrates sufficiently to exercise some caution in his choice of pleasures. A few fragments may be sufficient to show that this was so:

> The one to master pleasure is not he who abstains but he who employs it without being carried away by it. (Stob. *Ecl.* 3.17.17)[35]

> It is not going in [to the brothel] that is a problem, but not being able to come out. (D.L. 2.69).[36]

> Aristippus, while clothed in purple and anointed with perfumes, was not less temperate than Diogenes; for just as if somebody had equipped his body with the ability to be untouched by fire, he would be of good cheer even if he entrusted his person to Etna, so too anybody who has equipped himself well for pleasure will neither, when engulfed in it, get hot nor burn nor melt. (Max. Tyr. 1.9)[37]

Aristippus approached pleasure with the firm intention of not being overcome by it, and hence presumably of not being subjected to any unpleasant consequences. There was no intention to avoid any of the experiences normally designated pleasures; the intention was rather to avoid that feeling of being swept away by pleasure, which is the very aspect of a pleasure that many might think most deserved the name "pleasure." Such persons might very well accuse Aristippus of rejecting the pleasure in pleasures, and being left with nothing but a pleasant physical sensation. And what then of the young sybarite with whom Socrates converses at *Memorabilia* 2.1? One should surely remember that Xenophon is here trying to show an Aristippus who currently indulges himself too much being taught to get a grip on himself by Socrates (2.1.1). This is no portrait of Aristippus qua follower of Socrates; it is Aristippus as Socrates had found him. The strong implication is that the mature Aristippus did in fact master himself and did so under the influence of Socrates.

[35]Fr. 55 Mannebach = *SSR* 98.
[36]Fr. 59 Mannebach = *SSR* 87.
[37]Fr. 56 Mannebach = *SSR* 58.

We now come to the alleged out-and-out antihedonist. How do Antisthenes' views on pleasure fit into the Socratic tradition, particularly if Socrates was as agreeable to the cause of pleasure as I have suggested? Did Antisthenes not frequently say that he would go mad rather than feel pleasure? In saying this he certainly did not mean that he would never be pleased, for in that case he would never feel pleasure in virtue or the like. It matters crucially what one takes pleasure in, as Aristotle (*Eth. Nic.* 2.3, 1104b 11–12) and Plato (*Leg.* 659d–e) recognize when claiming that it is a key part of education to ensure that young men take pleasure in the right things. He might have said in all sorts of situations that he would go mad rather than feel pleasure, but it need mean no more than an insistence on taking pleasure only in cases when pleasure is the appropriate response.

Other fragments of Antisthenes might be used to argue that his views too were compatible with enlightened hedonism. What is good is "pleasure that one does not repent of" or "pleasure that follows toil, not that which precedes it."[38] These are not the words of somebody who is an antihedonist in theory, though they do suggest an attitude of intense suspicion of pleasure. That suspicion is shown in Xenophon's *Symposium* (4.38–41), where Antisthenes is happy to accept that he has a very pleasant life, and has reservations that it may be a little more pleasant than is expedient for him. He is worried, perhaps, by that same dominating tendency of pleasure that Aristippus was wary of. But he is no killjoy in this work and is far more at home in a jovial setting than the Stoics and Platonists at the symposium described in Lucian's *Lapiths*. Aristippus may indulge, but Antisthenes can hardly be said to abstain. This is most evident in the case of his sexual desires; for he is happy to have intercourse with any woman who will appreciate it,[39] sees no merit in abstaining from adultery, and generally regards nothing as being foreign to, or impracticable for, the wise man.[40] In general, Antisthenes derives his pleasant life from ensuring that he can enjoy whatever is on offer, while Aristippus derives his in the more orthodox fashion, from enjoying the most luxurious things on offer. They are not poles apart.

It is worth quoting H. D. Rankin at this point: "Antisthenes' attitude to pleasure, and in particular, sexual pleasure, could be designated deliberately cool."[41]

[38]Ath. 12.513a and Stob. *Ecl.* 3.29.65 = *SSR* 126–27 = frs. 110, 113 Caizzi.
[39]Xen. *Symp.* 4.38.
[40]Frs. 116, 81 Caizzi = *SSR* 59, 134.
[41]*Antisthenes Sokratikos* (Amsterdam, 1986), p. 134.

The message of the fragment of Aristippus in Maximus Tyrius, quoted above, is precisely that one should remain cool when experiencing pleasures. That coolness is not specifically Socratic but is implied by the Greek concept of σωφροσύνη, the virtue particularly concerned with self-control and self-awareness.[42]

This study set out to try to reconcile the seemingly disparate Socratic traditions on the question of the value of pleasure. While it was inevitable that different attitudes toward pleasure would be taken by the very different individuals whom Socrates attracted to his circle, it must be said that there is little sign that these attitudes were accompanied by vastly different theoretical positions. The extremes of hedonistic and antihedonistic theory are not, I suggest, represented among Socrates' followers. Hence it is to Eudoxus and Speusippus that Aristotle looks for elucidation of hedonistic and antihedonistic theory respectively (*Eth. Nic.* 10.2, 7.12), not to the Socratic schools. As for Socrates himself, he probably had a complex position that was neither that of a sybarite nor that of the ascetic. To call such a position Epicurean hardly does justice to the totally different views on the organization of the universe and indeed of morality that Socrates and Epicurus adopted;[43] but to call it mild hedonism would do Socrates no justice either. The historical Socrates was not more mild than was his alter ego in the *Hippias major.*

[42]On this, see J. Annas, "Self-Knowledge in Early Plato," in *Platonic Investigations*, ed. D. O'Meara (Washington, D.C., 1985).

[43]See T. H. Irwin, "Socrates the Epicurean," *ICS* 11 (1986): 85–112, esp. pp. 103–4.

[5]

Socrates in the Context of Xenophon's Political Writings

Thomas L. Pangle

In the past two generations we have rediscovered what Yvon Garland calls the "intellectual audacity" of Xenophontic political theory.[1] This voyage of liberation from the prejudices dominating Xenophon scholarship for most of the nineteenth and twentieth centuries has depended heavily for its orientation on the authoritative guidance of Machiavelli (and, in the case of Garland, Marx). Even a casual survey of Machiavelli's most famous works indicates that the Florentine wizard ranks Xenophon well above Plato, Aristotle, Cicero, Polybius, and indeed all other previous political theorists. The Xenophontic writings that prompt Machiavelli's accolades are *Hiero; or, On Tyranny* and the accounts of "Cyrus"—above all the *Cyropaedia*. The fictional Cyrus portrayed in "the life of Cyrus written by Xenophon" is a preeminent "hero" of Machiavelli's *Prince*, serving as *the* exemplary "armed prophet."[2] Machiavelli has helped us to recognize that in order to begin to appreciate the radicalism of Xenophon as a political theorist one

---

[1] Y. Garland, *Slavery in Ancient Greece*, revised and expanded English edition, trans. J. Lloyd (Ithaca, N.Y., 1988), p. 176. For some high points in the literature, see L. Strauss, "The Spirit of Sparta or the Taste of Xenophon," *Social Research* 6 (1939): 502–36, and *On Tyranny*[2] (Glencoe, Ill., 1963); W. Newell, "Tyranny and the Science of Ruling in Xenophon's 'Education of Cyrus,' " *Journal of Politics* 45 (1983): 889–906; G. Proietti, *Xenophon's Sparta* (Leiden, 1987).

[2] "Cyrus" in the works of Xenophon is ambiguous, as the name may refer to either the younger or the older Cyrus, or to an amalgam of the two (as in *Oec.* 4). For Machiavelli's discussions of Xenophon and Cyrus, see *Il principe*, chaps. 6, 14, 16, 26; *Discorsi sopra la prima deca di Tito Livio* 2.13, 3.20–21.

need only read the *Cyropaedia* without prejudice, for the *Cyropaedia* lays
out searching and comprehensive challenges to what would otherwise
appear to be fundamental theses, not to say givens, of "classical political theory." To mention the most obvious foreground: the work questions the superiority of the Greek *polis* to "mass society" wisely ruled by
morally and intellectually superior Orientals ("barbarians"),[3] it questions the preferability of republicanism (in any of its forms) to central-
ized bureaucratic administration under an absolute monarchy, and it
questions the dependence of civic or moral virtue (at its peak) on republican virtue or citizenship.

Yet our rediscovery of Xenophon's originality as a theorist of politics
remains truncated so long as it is not accompanied by a recognition and
understanding of Xenophon's more fundamental concern, a concern
largely disregarded by Machiavelli. I refer to Xenophon's presentation
of Socrates, as the epitome of the most self-conscious philosophic way
of life. Only when we have integrated our renewed appreciation of Xenophon's political theory, centered on the figure of Cyrus, into his account of the philosophic life, centered on Socrates, will we be in a
position truly to comprehend Xenophon's whole account of the human
situation.[4]

Given the manifold difficulties that attend any attempt to take the
measure of Socrates, it is neither surprising nor inappropriate that this
dimension of Xenophon's thought remains in greater obscurity than
Xenophon's political theory strictly defined. But I would like to try to
offer some assistance to readers who have begun to sense, with some
natural bewilderment, the complexity and the playfulness of Xenophon's treatment of this highest theme of his thought and writing.

The overall suggestion that underlies my discussion may be stated as
follows. Xenophon's teaching on the Socratic, philosophic way of life is
best approached by imaginative and questioning reflection on the political and personal drama through which that teaching is conveyed.
Above all, we ought to reflect on the juxtapositions and contrasts Xenophon constructs between Socrates and key representatives of respectable, alternative (i.e., subphilosophic) ways of life. These richly
revealing comparisons come to sight not only within the Socratic writings but also when those writings are set beside the nonSocratic writings. By allowing or prompting us to make these comparisons,
Xenophon permits us to see how far the Socratic life stands from other
eligible or respectable ways of life, while he simultaneously introduces

---

[3] See J. J. Farber, "The *Cyropaedia* and Hellenistic Kingship," *AJP* 100 (1979): 514.
[4] The best introduction to Xenophon's philosophy as a whole is C. Bruell, "Xenophon," in *History of Political Philosophy,*[3] ed. L. Strauss and J. Cropsey (Chicago, 1987), pp.
89–117.

us to the question of why or in what sense the life of Socratic philosophy can reasonably claim superiority to those other ways of life.

1. The Rhetorical Defensiveness of Xenophon's Portrait of Socrates

The most massive feature of the political context in which Socrates is to be viewed is of course his execution as a criminal, condemned to death for the very serious crimes of impiety and corrupting the young. Accordingly, Xenophon's account of Socrates is emphatically defensive. This primary characteristic of the Xenophontic presentation appears not only in the *Apology of Socrates to the Jury* and the *Memorabilia* but also in the somewhat less directly apologetic *Oeconomicus* and *Symposium*. To mention only the most striking indication: in each of these latter two works, emphatic reference is made to the great Aristophanic satire (the *Clouds*) that made Socrates notorious as one who impiously investigated the the things on high (*Symp.* 6.6–10; *Oec.* 11.3).

In thus offering a primarily defensive account, Xenophon follows the example, as it were, of his Socrates: in Xenophon's Socrates we see a man who himself was preoccupied, for much if not all of his mature life, with his own defense. As Xenophon twice tells us (*Mem.* 4.8.4; cf. *Ap.* 3), after Socrates was indicted for impiety and corrupting the young, Hermogenes told him, or asked him whether he didn't think, he "ought to consider, what he intended to say in defense"; to which Socrates replies: "Don't I seem to you to have spent my life preparing for this?" The preparation consisted in "going through life doing nothing else except examining the just things and the unjust things, doing the just and refraining from the unjust."

Xenophon's Socrates was a man passionately concerned with doing what is right; but to a degree unsurpassed by any other citizen or philosopher, Socrates recognized the need first to *understand* what is right in order to be able truly to act in the right way. This is to say that he was arrested by the initial recognition of his own, and of others', *ignorance* of what exactly is right. The need to *learn* what justice is was thus intimately interwoven, in Socrates' self-understanding, with the need to defend or justify himself. It was the peculiar intensity of these twin concerns that set Socrates apart as a philosopher; it is this that allows us to speak of him in retrospect as the first political philosopher.[5] On the

---

[5]Cf. *Mem.* 1.1.11–16, with Cic. *Tusc.* 5.10–11 and *Acad.* 1.4.15; see the discussion of these passages and their relationship in W. K. C. Guthrie, *Socrates* (Cambridge, 1971), pp. 97–105, esp. p. 100.

other hand, it was the unique intensity and character of these twin concerns that set Socrates apart as a citizen: to borrow for a moment the Platonic characterization, it was this that allowed Socrates to speak of himself as the only citizen who practiced "the true political art" (see *Grg.* 521d).

Xenophon makes Socrates' distinctiveness as a citizen most visible in the *Oeconomicus*, where we find Socrates in dramatic juxtaposition with Ischomachus. Ischomachus, according to Socrates' description of him in the *Oeconomicus*, is a man who is universally recognized as the paradigmatic good citizen or perfect gentlemen (καλός τε κἀγαθός). In order to understand this remarkable work, which presents the single most important juxtaposition in all of Xenophon, one must always bear in mind its comic and rather complex dramatic situation and structure. The *Oeconomicus* is a fictional story told by Xenophon of a conversation between Socrates and Critoboulus, the young son of Crito, in the presence of Xenophon. Socrates' ostensible purpose in the drama is to try to convince the ne'er-do-well Critoboulus (who spends too much time in boyish fun, and especially in attending comedies, sometimes in the company of Socrates—*Oec.* 2.7, 3.7–9) to take seriously his duties as a gentleman farmer and household manager. In order to effect this improbable end, Socrates not only exhorts Critoboulus and sketches some of the elements of the art of farming or household management; he also tells a fictional story of a conversation that he (Socrates) supposedly once had with the perfect gentleman farmer Ischomachus. Socrates tells the story as if it were the account of the conversation that was the turning point in his life. He does not specify exactly when in his life the conversation is supposed to have taken place, but he portrays himself, at the start of the conversation, in these terms: as a mature man in ill repute on account of his poverty and his Aristophanic, comic reputation as a natural scientist and idle talker; as a man who has become acutely conscious of the fact that he has not yet begun to practice what is generally respected as "virtue"; as a man who has decided to enquire, for the very first time, into the nature of virtue, so as to be able to begin to practice it; and as a man who is ludicrously ignorant of the ordinary-language signification of the word καλόν—"noble" or "fine" or "beautiful" (*Oec.* 8.13–17, 7.1–3, 11.3–6). This self-portrait is explicitly a "joke" (*Oec.* 11.7), and it becomes apparent in the course of the conversation that Socrates is not so much intent on learning from Ischomachus as he is on confirming certain critical judgments he has already formed regarding conventional virtue. More important, the fictional narration is a way of teaching Xenophon, and, through Xenophon, Xenophon's readers, the difference between Socratic and orthodox gentlemanliness or virtue.

To confirm and illustrate what we have been saying about the peculiarly defensive character of the Socratic concern with justice, let us begin by considering the contrast between Socrates' concern to defend himself and the similar concern exhibited in the portrait of the paradigmatic gentleman Ischomachus (*Oec.* 11.21–24). Socrates reports that Ischomachus remarked to him that despite or because of his immense public services in peace and war he was slandered by many false accusers. This prompted Socrates to ask the gentleman whether he was concerned to practice giving an account of himself or securing such an account from another. Ischomachus assured Socrates that he devoted himself to practicing his defense or "apology," and that this defense consisted in his doing no one injustice, but rather benefiting many, as much as he could. Furthermore, Ischomachus added, he practiced lodging accusations against persons he discovered doing injustice to many in private and to the city, while benefiting no one; he never ceased practicing, in the course of ruling his slaves, speeches concerned with cross-examination and judging in domestic judicial processes; he practiced speeches concerned with praising and blaming and reconciling friends; during military exercises he blamed and defended and accused fellow soldiers and engaged in deliberations about what ought to be done, praising what seemed desirable and blaming what seemed undesirable; but, Ischomachus concluded, he had never been able to employ guileful rhetoric.

As E. C. Marchant notes,[6] there is an evident parallel between this passage and the passage we earlier cited from the *Memorabilia* (4.8.4), in which Socrates describes his own lifelong preoccupation with defending or giving an account of himself. The contrasts are numerous and remarkable. Most striking of all is the fact that Socrates has been throughout his life primarily concerned to investigate what justice is and what injustice is: for the philosopher, the nature of justice is (to begin with, at any rate) a great problem, a major puzzle. Ischomachus' concern with justice and injustice presupposes that he knows what justice is, without lengthy investigation, and that the serious question is how to apply the moral principles—in praising and blaming, in judicial proceedings and especially accusations, and in policy deliberations.

To be sure, in the *Memorabilia* Socrates says he has also been concerned to do the just things and to refrain from the unjust things, thus implying that he is far from being in total ignorance as to the nature of justice. But the deeds dictated by justice insofar as Socrates under-

[6]E. C. Marchant, *Xenophon in Seven Volumes* (London, 1968), 4:461. Cf. L. Strauss, *Xenophon's Socratic Discourse: An Interpretation of the Oeconomicus* (Ithaca, N.Y., 1970), pp. 165–66.

stands justice are very different from the deeds the perfect gentleman assumes are dictated by justice. It is precisely Socrates' knowledge of the problematic nature of justice, or of the difficulties encountered in an investigation into justice, that makes him lead a more restricted civic life than that of Ischomachus (see also *Mem.* 1.6.15).

2. Xenophon's Socrates as Upholder of Obedience to Law

Yet lest we misinterpret or overstress the difference between the Socratic and the ordinary gentlemanly or civic virtues, we should keep always in the foreground the immense Socratic respect for law. The Socratic respect for law is a direct result of the Socratic conception of justice and is therefore so far from being contradicted by Socrates' criminal execution that it is in a sense vindicated by that sad and troubling event. It may seem paradoxical that an intense concern for justice, and respect for law, could contribute to a philosopher's getting into trouble with the law. The paradox diminishes when we remind ourselves that men of principled justice are sometimes found to be severely at odds with conventionally respectable opinion and even with the positive law.

Xenophon certainly demonstrates that the Socratic concern for justice has something important in common with the concern to do what is right that characterizes the gentleman, or *kaloskagathos,* who, as a good citizen of the republican polis, is determined at all costs to be faithful to the law—even or above all when everyone else seeks to ignore or bend the law. In the *Hellenica* (1.7, esp. secs. 12 and 15) Xenophon provides a famous and vivid example of Socrates acting as such a citizen, in the affair of the trial of the generals from the battle at the Arginusae. There we see Socrates standing like a nobly isolated gentleman in the face of the democratic majoritarian claim that "it is a terrible thing if the people are not allowed to do what they wish": "so the Presidents were frightened and all agreed to put it to a vote except Socrates the son of Sophroniscus; this man said he would not but would do everything according to law."

Yet this incident is singular, rather than representative of Socrates' life or even of the sort of behavior that got him into trouble. Xenophon indicates this with his characteristically light touch: apart from his account of this heroic act, he does not breathe a word of Socrates in the work entitled *Greek Matters.* Socrates *as philosopher* was not "Greek" in Xenophon's eyes, and his life and characteristic words and deeds and, above all, his thoughts do not belong in a work such as the *Hellenica*.[7] The "Greek historian's" narration of the heroism of the *citizen* Socrates, "the son of Sophroniscus," does not take us to the heart of the *philosopher* Socrates' concern for justice, and hence to the heart of his—and Xenophon's—defensiveness.

It is true that in the *Memorabilia*'s thematic discussion of Socrates' justice (*Mem.* 4.4) Xenophon again stresses the philosopher's obedience to law and exemplifies that obedience by adducing actions that include the stand Socrates took at the affair of the generals. But the *Memorabilia* focuses on Socrates' more philosophic deed, his refutation of the sophist Hippias. In that elenchus, Xenophon presents Socrates successfully maintaining that the lawful is the just. But the arguments Xenophon puts into Socrates' mouth, and even his thesis about the relation between justice and legality, are stated most ambiguously. Moreover, as Marchant observes,[8] Socrates' apparent thesis, to the effect that the laws are the embodiment of justice, is "not wholly consistent with what Socrates says in other parts of the *Memorabilia*." Marchant concludes that the refutation of Hippias "is really unconvincing as an exposition of Socrates' views on Justice," and suggests that Xenophon was governed here by the conviction that it was incumbent on him to rebut in crushing fashion the alarming charge that Socrates was a despiser of the established laws (see *Mem.* 1.2.9).

In other words, Marchant directs us to bear in mind the likely rhetorical character of Xenophon's defensive portrait of his convicted and executed former teacher. I regard this as a most sound and illuminating suggestion. I would add that insofar as Xenophon employed rhetorical arguments to reconcile the Socratic way of life to common opinion, he would have again been following the example set by his Socrates. A decisive clue to understanding all of the Xenophontic Socrates' words—and thereby all of Xenophon's words about his

---

[7]The prevailing scholarly view of the treatment of Socrates in the *Hellenica*, indeed the prevailing scholarly view of the work as a whole, is based on a failure to recognize the artistic character of the work and its place in what Shaftesbury called the "system" of Xenophon's writings (*Characteristics of Men, Manners, Opinions, Times* 6.5.1). See W. P. Henry's critical summary of the scholarly consensus in *Greek Historical Writing: An Historiographical Essay Based on Xenophon's Hellenica* (Chicago, 1966), p. 194. Henry does not seem, however, to have been altogether successful in liberating himself from the conventional view he rightly criticizes: see Leo Strauss's review of Henry's book, "Greek Historians," *Rev Meta* 21 (1968): 656–66. A recent path-breaking revision of the conventional approaches to the *Hellenica*, laying great stress on the work's unique "literary" character and place within the Xenophontic corpus, is Proietti (above, note 1). Given his central theme, Proietti does not discuss what he terms the "apparent digression" of *Hellenica* 1.7 (p. 21).

[8]Marchant (above, note 6), 4: xix–xx.

Socrates—would seem to be provided by Xenophon's account of Socrates' manner of arguing, communication, and teaching (*Mem.* 4.6: Xenophon gives this account shortly after his account of Socrates' justice, the account centered on the refutation of Hippias to which we have referred). Socrates, Xenophon reports, spoke and argued in two radically different ways with two radically different sorts of interlocutor. In so doing, Socrates explicitly patterned his mode of communication after that of Homer's wily Odysseus (see also *Mem.* 1.2.58).

When someone challenged Socrates by disagreeing, but without presenting a demonstration, Socrates would lead the entire argument back to the fundamental principle through step-by-step dialectic. In this way he arrived at truth, evident to the interlocutor as well as to Socrates, because the interlocutor had been allowed and impelled to question and answer along with Socrates.

But most of the time, when he was not interrupted by challenges but instead allowed to go through an argument by himself, Socrates proceeded in the manner that he said was the only "safe" way to speak: by way of generally accepted notions, imitating the Homeric Odysseus, who as a "safe rhetorician" did not depart from the prejudices of the general run of human beings. In this way Socrates arrived at "agreement" as opposed to "truth," and succeeded in doing so to a degree unmatched in Xenophon's experience.

In the light of what Xenophon repeatedly shows throughout the *Memorabilia,* we are justified in adding that Socrates (and Xenophon by way of his character Socrates) is eminently capable of carrying on these two different modes of communication at one and the same time. While leading his docile interlocutors to "agreement," Xenophon's character Socrates is able to provoke in his more intransigent hearers the questions they ought to be asking, and to indicate the path toward answers. A beautiful example is afforded by his deliciously ironic dialogue with Hippias about justice and law.

The question to which we need to attend, however, is this: Precisely what moral and legal duties dictate, and explain, this adoption of guileful Odyssean rhetoric as the proper mode of public philosophic communication? A partial answer is suggested by Socrates' famous knowledge of his ignorance. The Xenophontic Socrates found himself led to a severe doubt of the grounds for central features of all conventionally respectable notions of nobility, justice, the common good, and piety, or the nature of the gods. *But* such knowledge as he believed he did have, of the true nature of the divine and of the true common good and truly just and noble for human beings, was not of such a character as to allow him to suppose that he could offer an alternative, or substitute, grounding for *civic* morality and piety. Socrates was therefore obliged to proceed in a way that would not undermine conventional piety and morality, even or especially when he sought to make some occasional contributions, in some individual cases, to improving or at least making less problematic that piety and morality. Xenophon himself, as a writer and to that extent a more public communicator than his teacher, was a fortiori required to present the Socratic teaching on nobility, justice, and piety in a responsible, Odyssean, or allusive manner—in a manner that always conciliated the most decent religious and moral prejudices generally held among human beings.

As Marchant observes in the passage previously quoted, Xenophon's Socrates "of course insisted on obedience to the laws"; but the question, as Marchant insists, remains: What understanding of justice underlies or entails this practical teaching and conclusion? When Xenophon presents Hippias complaining that in fact Socrates never offers in public his own account of what justice is, Xenophon has Socrates reply: "If not in word, then in deed I display my opinion of justice" (*Mem.* 4.4.9–10). This statement, especially when taken in context, has the artful effect of hiding while revealing the fact that deeds by themselves cannot possibly indicate their principled basis. Besides, Socrates' deeds cannot help but provoke wonder. Everyone can see that Socrates obeyed the laws and taught others to respect and obey the laws; but everyone can also see that Socrates lived a life that, however lawful, was highly unorthodox. Everyone can easily become aware that the Xenophontic Socrates did not live the life of a respectable gentleman in the ordinary sense. But what principled conception of life and of the noble and the just and the pious underlies this puzzling combination of conformity and nonconformity?

3. The Socratic and the Orthodox Attitude toward Property

By making the proper posture toward material wealth a principal theme of the *Oeconomicus*, Xenophon alerts us to the need to begin our reflections from this point. What then emerges from the dialogue as to the difference between the philosopher Socrates and the "perfect gentleman" Ischomachus in this crucial respect?

The perfect gentleman Ischomachus is very seriously devoted to maintaining and enlarging a prosperous farm. From the farm income he secures not only economic independence for himself and his family, but also the "leisure" and wherewithal to become an accomplished member of the civil cavalry; in addition, the farm is large enough to provide Ischomachus the surplus that allows him to bestow generous and magnificent gifts that relieve his fellow citizens and beautifully adorn the city as a whole, including the city's gods. Ischomachus says he takes pleasure in this exercise of the moral virtues of public-spirited courage, justice, prudence, generosity, and magnificence, despite the fact that, as we have already noted, he is exposed to slanderous prosecutions as a result, despite the fact that he is regularly called upon to make greater financial contributions to the city than he would wish, or believes himself able to afford, and despite the fact that he has very little if any true leisure from his busy preoccupation with managing the farm, engaging in civic affairs, and practicing horsemanship (*Oec.* 7.1–3; and 11 entire).

Socrates, by contrast, depends on the generosity of others for support and thereby lives a life of freedom from business. His practice of justice and generosity, as exemplified in the action of the *Oeconomicus*, consists in giving private advice to some fellow citizens and in sharing his quest for understanding himself and the human situation with a few close friends, especially among the young who long for nobility. In other words, Socrates' lengthy conversation with a man who is the perfect gentleman in the eyes of the city, on the day Socrates began his enquiry into the virtue he knew he lacked, did not lead to his being convinced to embrace that virtue or that gentlemanliness.[9]

This indeed is the basis of the subtle comedy that runs throughout the *Oeconomicus*. The ostensible purpose of the dialogue is to convince the ne'er-do-well son of Crito to become serious about household management, and above all the management of his own farm. The report of the conversation with Ischomachus is supposed to illustrate the essential superiority and attractiveness of the life of the gentleman farmer. The unobtrusive but risible difficulty is, Socrates has himself never for one moment followed the model he so vividly portrays and claims enthusiastically to endorse (see esp. *Oec.* 2). Even the somewhat ponderous Ischomachus realized, Socrates reports, that Socrates was "joking" when Socrates told him that he was intending to imitate,

---

[9]In particular, we find little sign that the Xenophontic Socrates ever had much to do with military affairs. Given the erroneous notion abroad among scholars that Xenophon's writings reveal him to have been attracted to Socrates mainly because of the latter's military prowess, it is worth stressing, as does Strauss (above, note 6), p. 88, that "all we know of Socrates as a soldier from the primary sources we know through Plato and in no way through Xenophon. . . . Xenophon speaks only once of Socrates' noble conduct as a soldier; he says that Socrates showed his justice (not his manliness) 'both in civil life and on campaigns' [*Mem.* 4.4.1–4]; but while he adduces four instances of his justice as shown in civil life, he does not adduce a single instance of his justice as shown in war." Strauss is criticizing J. Burnet, *Greek Philosophy* (London, 1928), p. 137 n. 2; see also Burnet, *Plato's Phaedo* (Oxford, 1911), pp. xvii–xviii, and, as a chief example of the continuing power of this notion of the basis for Xenophon's attraction to Socrates, Guthrie (above, note 5), p. 15.

within his economic means, and insofar as he could understand, the life of the perfect gentleman, after having learned what the gentleman does (*Oec.* 7). Socrates' failure to make good on his prospective imitation of the *kaloskagathos* cannot be explained, then, by the fact that Socrates was never granted the opportunity to own a farm; in the one place where Socrates suggests some such excuse (*Oec.* 2.12–13), he is manifestly trying to avoid having to take responsibility for Critoboulus' finances, and in the immediately preceding context he makes it perfectly clear that he regards himself as "sufficiently wealthy" precisely insofar as he does *not* own or have to manage much property and does *not* have to worry about great sacrifices to the gods, magnificent hospitality, and magnificent adornment of his city (*Oec.* 2.2–8).

Still, in his report of his conversation with Ischomachus Socrates presents himself as being so deferential and docile that one might, on a superficial reading at least, wonder whether Socrates' failure to follow the authority of the perfect gentleman is not due to an awareness of his own ignorance in some important regard: could Socrates not be in the position of being unable to decide whether or not Ischomachus' virtue is true virtue? Could it not be that Socrates suspects that the perfect gentleman's life and virtue depend on some sort of "divine dispensation" that Socrates senses he lacks and does not even understand well (cf. the end of Plato's *Meno*)? After all, the *Oeconomicus* ends with Socrates' report of a beautiful oration of the perfect gentleman, in which that gentleman declared that ruling over willing subordinates, which is the supreme component of household management as well as of politics, and which is therefore the peak of the gentleman's business and life, is "not altogether a human matter, but divine": that "it is given to those who are truly initiated into the holy mysteries of moderation" (*Oec.* 21.12).

It is Socrates' public and private speech as reported by Hermogenes in the *Apology of Socrates to the Jury,* and in a softened version in the *Memorabilia* (4.8), that rules out any such possibility that Socrates remained uncertain of the relative rank of his life and the life of a purportedly perfect gentleman such as Ischomachus. Through the eyes and ears and report of Hermogenes, Xenophon allows his readers to discern a key feature of Socrates' self-understanding that Xenophon otherwise keeps partially hidden: Socrates' extraordinary self-esteem, which manifests itself, in the report of Hermogenes, as something akin to pride or greatness of soul. Among other things, Socrates is reported to have told Hermogenes in private:

I would refuse to concede that any human being has lived a better life than I have up until this point; for to me belongs what is the most pleasant thing, the knowledge that I have lived my whole life piously and justly. As a result, I strongly admire myself, and I have discovered that those who regularly consort with me have the same understanding of my life. (*Ap.* 5–6)

Reporting the same conversation in the *Memorabilia* (4.8.7), Xenophon has Socrates telling Hermogenes that his favorable opinion of himself arose in part from his "studying himself in comparison with the rest of humanity": a key example, perhaps *the* key example, is the comparative study whose confirmation Socrates showed to Xenophon by narrating the dialogue with the paradigmatic gentleman Ischomachus.

We see then that Xenophon presents Socrates as saying he devoted his entire life to thinking about his defense in a context—the conversation near the end of his life with Hermogenes—in which Socrates makes it abundantly clear that the defense is not simply a rebuttal of charges of injustice. The defense is rather a vindication of the Socratic way of life as the best, the most just, and the most pious life of any human life of which Socrates had knowledge.

Once the full dimension of Socrates' self-defense becomes apparent, we are compelled to look back to see exactly what decisive flaws in the life of the man reputed to be a perfect gentleman were uncovered in the conversation Socrates retold or invented in the *Oeconomicus*. The guiding clue is to be found by reflection on what we have seen to be the greatest difference between the life and excellence of the reputed gentleman and that of the philosopher Socrates. The reputed gentleman devotes most of his private waking life to working his farm so that he may remain independently wealthy and therefore capable of just and magnificent acts of public service and generosity to gods and men. His life culminates in what Socrates characterizes as "noble" deeds: deeds of justice or of contribution to the common good of his city and his friends (*Oec.* 11.9–10). But does Ischomachus have a clear conception of what this—or any—"common good" consists in? Has he given adequate thought to the relation between his own good, the good of his own soul, and the good of others, human beings and gods, which he nobly devotes so much of his time and energy to serving or preparing to serve? Does he have a clear and convincing conception of the relation between the individual and the community, at the various levels and dimensions of "community"?

4. The Understanding of the Noble, the Just, and the Common Good

These fundamental questions about the moral foundation of the conventionally respectable gentleman, and of the "commonsense" moral world that honors and looks to such a gentleman as a model, emerge indirectly but emphatically by way of the first major topic on which Ischomachus enlightens Socrates. At Socrates' urging,[10] Ischomachus relates to Socrates the moral education that his young and almost completely innocent or untutored wife received from him. At the core of that moral education was an education as to the nature of the common good that unites husband and wife in one home or household community. In presenting to the young Xenophon and other young friends a perfect gentleman's account of how he taught his nearest and dearest the nature of the marital bond, Xenophon's Socrates may be said to be shown inviting his young students to reflect on a mature moral man's understanding of the most basic, intimate, and undeniable form of human community.

Ischomachus, as a prudent gentleman, does not pretend to be altogether confident of the unassisted persuasive or educative strength of his teaching on his and his wife's unquestionably noble duties: he was careful (he passionately affirms with an oath by Zeus) to sacrifice something of value to the gods and to pray for divine help before commencing the moral education of his young wife. More precisely (and Socrates' report is very precise in this respect), the pious gentleman says he sought the gods' help to insure that his teaching, and his wife's learning, might be of that which was best (and not merely noblest) for both of them. In addition, Socrates' question draws out, the pious gentleman saw to it that his young wife not only shared in both the sacrifice and the prayers but, what is more, that she solemnly promised before the gods that she would become the sort of person she ought to become; this most solemn promise of course preceded any learning, any hearing of the arguments explaining and justifying, what she ought to become (*Oec.* 7.7–8). The perfect gentleman's moral principles and moral teaching are decisively dependent on piety centered on the belief in a divinity that supports noble duty by making its performance ultimately in the interest of the nobly dutiful—at least when the divinity has been invoked in the proper way, especially through sacrifices, honors, and oaths.

Of course, duty would cease to be duty, it would cease to be noble, it would cease to move us as it does, it would cease to be deserving of our and of the gods' recompense and honor, if it were immediately pleasant or good; or if it were in itself our natural fulfillment and happiness, or the clear means and direct path to our happiness and natural fulfillment. Hence noble and lawful community requires solemn promises, whose solemnity reminds us that their fulfillment, at the noblest—that

---

[10]As Strauss (above, note 6), p. 132, says, "On no other occasion does Socrates in the *Oeconomicus* express his eagerness to learn in such strong terms."

is, the toughest—moments, will not be easy or pleasant or wholly ful-
filling. Yet the promises are before gods who sanction the promises and
who thus make it in the interest of the promiser to keep the promises.
As Ischomachus taught his wife, there is a close-to-perfect congruence
between the good and the noble, or between divinely ordered nature
and lawfully praised nobility.

But the congruence cannot be perfect, or else the noble would dis-
appear into the good and prudential; the distinctiveness of the noble
would evaporate. So the congruence or correlation between the noble
and the good or beneficial must be imperfect; surely it must be rather
imperfectly evident. This appears most simply in the fact that the noble, the just, and the lawful are—as Ischomachus stresses—praiseworthy. Praise is accorded not to those who are enjoying or are about to
receive benefits and pleasures (such we congratulate, we do not praise)
but rather to those who are forgoing them or giving them to others.
Hence the praiseworthy is also the deserving: the deserving of something beyond the praiseworthy itself—the deserving, at the least, of the
reward of praise. As the deserving, the praiseworthy points strongly
beyond itself, to a redemptive good or consoling fulfillment bestowed
by the gods, whose limits—and hence whose hope-inducing powers—
are not easy to define. The noble and just must somehow lead to the
good, and it is the divinity that guarantees this—for otherwise, what
would constitute the moral relevance of the divinity? What would make
the divinity serious (σπουδαῖος), or the object of reverence, as opposed
to mere dread? But this divine guarantee of the goodness of the noble
and the just, this divine sanction that makes congruent and correlative
the noble and the beneficial, has to be manifest if the guarantee is not
to be merely a hope or a wish.[11]

Ischomachus reveals in several ways his awareness of the uneasy and
perplexing fit between the noble or just, on the one hand, and the
good, on the other hand, or between law, even the highest unwritten
law, and nature, even divine nature. He does not ascribe the law, the

---

[11]Compare *Oeconomicus* 9.13–17 with the rich ambiguity of Aristotle *Rhetorica* 9.3–17:
"The noble then is that which being choiceworthy for its own sake would be praiseworthy; or that which being good would be pleasant. If this is the noble, virtue is necessarily
noble: for, being good, it is praiseworthy. And virtue is a capacity, as it is opined, of procuring and guarding good things, and a capacity of doing many and great goods, and all
goods concerning all things. . . . But the greatest virtues are necessarily those that are the
most useful for others. This is why they especially praise the just and the courageous
men: for the one in war, and the other in peace, is useful to others. . . . And as many
things as have for their reward honor are noble. And as many things as have honor
rather than money. And as many of the choiceworthy things as someone does not do for
himself. And the things that are good simply, as many as one does for the fatherland
while neglecting oneself. And the things that are by nature good, and not good for oneself—for those are done for one's own sake."

unwritten and universal moral law of ladies and gentlemen—the law
that forbids adultery or the violation of marriage vows, for instance—
to the divine or to nature. When his wife asks him what things she can
do to help the household, Ischomachus replies: "By Zeus! The things
that the gods made you by nature capable of and that the law in addition praises" (*Oed.* 7.16). A little later, after summarizing the wonderful
if somewhat obscure way divine nature has divided the labor appropriate to male and female so as to make them complementary in the
household, he makes more specific why or with a view to what the law
praises, whereas god or nature simply directs: "The law in addition
praises these things, yoking together man and woman. And just as the
god made them partners in offspring, so also the law establishes them
as partners in the household. And the law shows to be noble those
things that the god makes each by nature more capable of (*Oec.* 7.30).
In other words: by nature the two sexes procreate, and for this they are
not praised for being noble; by law they are yoked in marriage and restrict their procreation to the lawful spouse, and for this they are of
course praised for acting nobly; for the law does not receive unambiguous support from the god: "If someone goes against what the god
made natural, perhaps, in causing some disorder, he does not escape
the notice of the gods and pays a penalty" (*Oec.* 7.31). Moreover,
Ischomachus interrupts his narrative of his teaching of his wife the nature of order to tell Socrates about a visit he once made to a large non-
Hellenic ship: there, the pious gentleman says, he saw an amazing
example of order and learned from the barbarian boatswain why human sailors are so meticulous, so nobly meticulous, in their concern
for order:

> There is no time, when the god raises a storm at sea, to look for what is
> needed or to give something that is awkwardly stowed. For the god threat-
> ens and punishes those who are slack. It is wonderful if he just doesn't
> destroy those who have done nothing wrong; but if in addition he saves
> those who serve him very nobly, much gratitude is due to the gods. (8.16)

Ischomachus prudently refrained from including an account of his
instructive visit to the barbarian ship in the long discourse on the nature of order that he delivered to his wife. What Xenophon or his
Socrates prompts us to ponder here is not simply or even principally
the difficulty of perceiving divine providence in the world; we are
prompted to ponder, because we witness in the drama, the precise
character and source of the moral gentleman's suppressed awareness
of, and wrestling with, the troubling relation between the good, the noble, and the pious. From this we begin to share in the Socratic under-

standing of gentlemanliness and its conception of the noble, the good, and the pious.

Ischomachus' report of his conversation with the foreign boatswain shows that he is aware that the empirical evidence for the divinity required by his principles and his teaching is not in itself conclusive (see also *Oec.* 5.7, 12–16; 17.4). He is or could be made aware, we may surmise, that the most powerful testimony to the existence of this divinity is the experience of his own soul, centered on his moral experience. It is then essential that the moral experience and its attendant hopes be made intelligible; and this is what we see Ischomachus struggling to do as he reports to Socrates his attempts to teach that moral experience or its principles to his nearest and dearest partner in community.

Teaching requires learning, and learning requires thought or questioning. This is especially true of dialectical (conversational) learning, which can sometimes resemble a contest. In the case of the perfect gentleman and his young wife, of course, the two conversational partners seem so unevenly matched that we might expect little in the way of a contest. Yet Socrates says he will enjoy hearing of Ischomachus' education of his wife more than he would enjoy hearing of the noblest wrestling match or horse race.

Ischomachus' young wife is prompted to raise her most telling questions when Ischomachus introduces the analogy of the beehive as an appropriate analogy for the human community, or for the aspiration to community he believes in and seeks to teach. Ischomachus of course does not mean that human beings are communal in the way bees are: humans are rational, and their community depends therefore on choices and deliberations made by each of the free members. Young bees do not require speeches and conversations on the moral principles that ought to guide their deliberation and choice in order to become good members of their natural community. Young humans do; the highest such governing principle of deliberation and choice within the human community is the good, the common good. But community requires leadership or hierarchy, as the analogy with the beehive limns: how exactly is the question of ultimate authority settled in the human hive? When Ischomachus suggests that his young wife should regard herself as equivalent to the "leader of the hive," she understandably expresses some perplexity, and that perplexity understandably grows as Ischomachus rather unsuccessfully attempts to explain the hierarchy within the household, a hierarchy that culminates in the wife who is animated by the "gentlemanly" desire to be cherished and honored more than her husband by all the members of the household, and who therefore does a greater share of the generous deeds and winds up turning her husband into her servant (*Oec.* 7.17, 32–end), "for," as

Ischomachus says he said in concluding this first and most important part of his moral teaching, "the gentlemanly things [*ta kala te kagatha:* literally, "the noble and the good things"] increase for human beings not through youthful bloom but rather through the exercise of the virtues in life."[12] In a subsequent didactic conversation with his wife (*Oec.* 9.16ff.), Ischomachus reports, he told her that she had no just right to complain if he imposed on her more duties than he did on the servants with regard to the household property, since, as he went on to "demonstrate" to her, the "master" receives by far the greatest benefit from his property.

Socrates at this point voices acute curiosity as to how the young wife reacted to this part of the teaching. Ischomachus rather proudly reports that his wife informed him that he did not know her, inasmuch as he supposed that she regarded it as a burden to care for the property, since just as it seems to be according to nature more pleasant for a sensible woman to care for her own offspring rather than to neglect them, so with regard to the property that is pleasing because it is her own it is more pleasant for a sensible woman to care for her own than to neglect it. In response, Socrates declares, with an oath by that docile divine wife Hera: "Ischomachus, you display the manliness of your wife's understanding!"

5. Is Socratic Virtue Teachable?

Socrates' very strong interest in learning how a gentleman teaches his wife the principles of life cannot help but make us think of the contrast between the gentleman's relation to his discretely nameless wife and Socrates' relation to the notoriously tempestuous Xanthippe—a relation made famous above all through the pages of Xenophon. In the *Symposium*, the deep impression a talented dancing girl makes on Socrates induces him to remark that "the nature of woman happens to be in nothing inferior to that of man, except in judgment and strength, and so if any of you has a wife, let him take heart and teach her whatever he wishes her to know in order to make use of her" (2.9).[13] Upon saying this, Socrates is challenged by Antisthenes to explain why he has not educated Xanthippe, who is "the most difficult of women in the present, and I believe the past and future times" (2.10). Socrates replies

---

[12]This crucial asseveration leaves unclear the precise relation between the virtues and the gentlemanly things; compare the penultimate sentences of the *Memorabilia*, where Xenophon distinguishes ἀρετή and καλοκἀγαθία. See also above, note 11.

[13]François Ollier, *Xenophon: Banquet, Apologie de Socrate*, 2d and rev. ed. (Paris, 1972), p. 44, comments ad loc.: "en imitant l'Ischomaque de l'*Economique* VII–X."

by first drawing an analogy to those who wish to become skilled horsemen and therefore seek out the most spirited (θυμοειδεῖς) horses; he then explains that he views his relations with Xanthippe as a kind of test case for his relations with mankind in general. A few moments later, Socrates remarks to general laughter that he is in the habit of dancing alone, in a room with seven empty couches. As Leo Strauss remarks in concluding his study of Ischomachus' education of his wife, "If Socrates failed to educate Xanthippe, he was superior to Ischomachus by having no delusions in this regard or by being aware of his ignorance of the art of managing one's wife."[14]

Ischomachus, as the mature Socrates presents him in narrating that long-ago conversation with the younger Socrates, was not deeply troubled by the problems or contradictions in his moral teaching, problems of which he was somehow aware; indeed, he was wonderfully confident that his wife and he would live together in fidelity, harmony, and prosperity (*Oec.* 10.13). Yet that he could have been made much more troubled seems suggested by the remark with which he begins his response to Socrates' request that he cease describing his education of his wife and start describing his own deeds as a gentleman: Ischomachus says that it will greatly please him to do so because Socrates may "correct" him if he seems to Socrates to be doing anything that is not noble (*Oec.* 11.2). The perfect gentleman, as a "serious" man (*spoudaios*), or like any serious human being, recognizes the power of the distinction between what seems to be right or noble and what truly is right or noble; he knows it is his duty to discover and do the latter; he recognizes the compelling power of the truth, or of the knowledge that one lacks the truth.

But Socrates' purpose in narrating the conversation with the perfect gentleman is not to show Xenophon and his other young students how he engaged in the quixotic project of upsetting and correcting reputable gentleman. His purpose is rather to show his young interlocutors how and that he *could* have upset and begun to correct such gentlemen, and thereby to demonstrate why or in what sense he did not accept the standard set by such gentlemanliness, and insisted on a higher, because truer, standard. That standard is stated in the *Memorabilia*, although the full import of the statement is barely visible unless and until we have come back to it and considered it in light of the dramatic encounter narrated in the *Oeconomicus:*

> He for his part always carried on dialogues about the human things, enquiring what is pious, what is impious, what is noble, what is base, what is

---

[14]Strauss (above, note 6), p. 158; cf. L. Strauss, *Xenophon's Socrates* (Ithaca, N.Y., 1972), pp. 145–48.

just, what is unjust, what is moderation, what is madness, what is courage, what is cowardice, what is a city, what is a statesman, what is rule of human beings, what is a man skilled in ruling human beings, and about the other matters: with regard to which he considered those who were knowers to be gentlemen [*kalouskagathous*], and those who were ignorant to be justly called slaves. (*Mem.* 1.1.16)

According to Socrates, virtue depends on knowledge, or the knowledgeable quest for knowledge, of the human things (piety, nobility, justice, moderation, courage, the city, the statesman, etc.); and vice is the product of the corresponding ignorance, or ignorance of ignorance. Though Socrates could state, he could not easily teach this standard to a man like Ischomachus. To see why, it helps to observe how Socrates does go about trying to teach it to Euthydemus, the youth of exceptional beauty and very modest promise whom Xenophon introduces us to as the comic example of the young men longing for the noble art of rule on whom Socrates exercised his protreptic. What Socrates says and does to Euthydemus in book 4 of the *Memorabilia* is obviously not the sort of thing he could get away with saying and doing to the serious, mature pillars of the community. Especially noteworthy, as a confirmation of what we have observed about the key problem revealed in Ischomachus' view of life, is Socrates' proof to Euthydemus that the youth does not know what justice is, because he does not know the relation between the commonsense principles of justice and what is good. Socrates follows this up by introducing his own standard of gentlemanliness (which we quoted a moment ago), and the conception of freedom implied in this standard. Then there is this exchange:

Tell me, Euthydemus, have you ever been to Delphi?

Twice, by Zeus!

Then did you notice inscribed somewhere on the temple the "Know thyself"?

I did.

Was the inscription then of no concern to you, or did you attend to it and try to examine yourself, to see who you might be?

By Zeus, I didn't! For I thought I certainly knew this, at least; because I could hardly know anything else if I didn't know myself! (*Mem.* 4.2.24)

Indeed: the last phrase contains the wisest words Euthydemus is ever heard to utter. The discovery of the knowledge of one's own ignorance is the foundation for the construction of a true inner strength, self-admiration, and capacity for wise and overflowing benevolence; but initially, the discovery, if it is a real discovery and not a mere mouthing, is humiliating, perhaps frightening, and even paralyzing. To bear it requires a resilience and a grace that are rare even in youth.

By confining his serious teaching to carefully selected young people, Socrates did not avoid one major source of trouble. A gentleman like Ischomachus, or, as is more likely, inferior to Ischomachus in reasonableness, may well father a son like Euthydemus, or superior to Euthydemus. The effect of the successful Socratic awakening of such a youth was that "he understood that there was no way he would become a worthwhile man except by spending as much time as possible with Socrates; he stayed with Socrates as much as possible; and in some respects he imitated his practices" (*Mem.* 4.2.40). How will a gentleman take to the fact that Socrates has made his son admire Socrates more than his own father? In the *Cyropaedia* (3.1.38–39), Xenophon tells of such a father, and of how he killed "Socrates."

Yet Xenophon's *Symposium* shows, with exquisite grace, how urbanely Socrates could accommodate himself, and even a certain playful measure of his philosophizing, to the company of a reputable gentleman in his playful hours. In the *Symposium* we see Socrates drinking and laughing with Lycon and his beautiful son Autolycus. Particularly illuminating is an exchange that takes place at the beginning of the evening's discussion and drinking, just prior to the remarks about educating wives that we have discussed above. With the dinner concluded, the host Callias proposes the introduction of perfumes; but Socrates protests at such an unmanly pleasure: real men enjoy smelling of the olive oil used in the gymnasium. He adds the observation that it takes many years of toiling at the tasks of a free man to acquire the peculiarly sweet smell of the truly free man's sweat. At this, the phlegmatic gentleman Lycon perks up:

All well and good for the younger fellows, but what are we who are too old for the gymnasia to smell of?

Gentlemanliness, by Zeus!

And where does one procure this anointment?

Theognis says: "You will learn nobility from noble men; but if you mix with bad, you will destroy your intelligence [*nous*]."

Say, are you listening to this, Son?

He certainly is, by Zeus! And he puts it into practice. . . . He will enquire together with you, who it is that seems to him most sufficient in this way of life, and he will have intercourse with him.

At this many people spoke up, Xenophon reports. One asked: "Where will he find a teacher of this?" Another said that it wasn't teachable. Another, that if anything ought to be learned, this should be. Socrates then said: "Since this is a debatable question, let's postpone it to another occasion" (*Symp.* 2.4–7).

An impressive performance on Socrates' part. All the more impressive is the fact that, in later years, Lycon joined Meletus and Anytus as one of the three chief accusers of Socrates. The Xenophontic Socrates' inability to educate Xanthippe is the comic mirror of his inability to avoid eventually antagonizing a gentleman like Lycon.

6. Cyrus as the Alternative to Socrates

Once we begin to understand how very limited the Socratic capacity to reform republican life is, we are led back with renewed interest to Cyrus, the rival moral axis within the Xenophontic corpus. The portrait of Cyrus in the *Cyropaedia* is the portrait of the statesman and founder at his peak. According to Xenophon, the statesman-founder properly understood must be seen to be animated not only by intense spiritedness and love of glory but above all by philanthropic love. Cyrus is consumed by the passionate desire to be the benefactor or source of good for all mankind; at the same time he seeks to win, in return, the affection of all mankind.

In order to bring to light all that is implied in this amazing impulse when it animates a man of superior moral and intellectual capacity, Xenophon presents such a man as he emerges from and transforms the best possible republican regime. Cyrus was born and remains the legitimate heir to the throne of Old Persia, a limited monarchy of the Spartan type and a regime dedicated to virtue and education in virtue. The best regime, so conceived, is dominated by men similar to, though not identical with, Ischomachus. (The leading lights of the best republic do not live the same life as Ischomachus because, instead of dwelling as somewhat embattled gentlemen in a relatively permissive democracy, they dwell in a city where they constitute the ruling class; many important secondary features of their lives and characters are accordingly affected.)

Cyrus' distinctive nature is allowed to discover itself because he spends the crucial formative years of his adolescence away from Persia, in the opulent court of the Median despot who is his mother's father. There he learns more than the arts of hunting and war; he experiences the neediness of human beings and becomes aware of his own capacity for satisfying or alleviating that neediness. He experiences in rich measure the joy of making others feel and express uncoerced and spontaneous gratitude (see especially *Cyr.* 1.4.1–4, 12–14, 26).

Young Cyrus returns to Old Persia and easily fits once again into the manly regime, but at the cost of submerging, to a considerable extent, those longings that truly set him apart (*Cyr.* 1.5.1); for Old Persia is not very hospitable to φιλανθρωπία. Just as for Plato and Aristotle, so for Xenophon the best regime is an intensely fraternal, closed, and even isolationist polis: most duties end at the borders (*Cyr.* 1.6.28; cf. Pl. *Rep.* 423a; Arist. *Pol.* 1325b15–31). The best regime's disdain for commerce and acquisitiveness insures its poverty and necessarily entails the consequences that the vast majority of the inhabitants are in fact unable to participate in the civic education and full political life: the best regime is a noncommercial oligarchic class society (*Cyr.* 1.2.15; 8.3.37; cf. Pl. *Leg.* 846d–850c; Arist. *Pol.* 1330a24–33). Last but not least, the civic virtue cultivated by Xenophon's best regime is almost as austere as that cultivated by Plato's *Republic:* dedication to such virtue entails the suppression or severe restriction of most of the spontaneous outpourings of human emotion, even among fellow members of the elite. This virtue demands, moreover, that citizens conform to communal mores; it does not allow individuals to diversify according to their unequal geniuses. The revealing keynote of the education in virtue is struck by Xenophon's description of the law on education to justice and to gratitude (understood as a subdivision of justice). The boys learn justice, Xenophon explains, by indicting and convicting one another on many charges but especially on that charge for which "humans hate one another the most but indict one another the least, ingratitude; and whomever they know to be capable of returning a favor but not doing so, they punish severely" (*Cyr.* 1.2.7). Old Persian moral education thus guarantees that almost everyone practices "gratitude," and almost no one ever experiences gratitude.

Cyrus begins the "liberation" of himself and his fellow Persians by seizing the opportunity offered by a foreign war. With astounding ease his oratory convinces the Persian elite who are to staff the expeditionary force that in practicing virtue for its own sake they and their forefathers have failed to understand or act upon virtue's power to procure prosperity, happiness, and honor (*Cyr.* 1.5.8). Cyrus subsequently hoodwinks the same elite into allowing him to transform the army by opening up equality of opportunity for all—rich and poor, non-Persians as well as Persians. He proceeds to use the new meritocratic

military machine to liberate the whole of Asia, to bring it under effi-
cient administration, and to achieve prosperity, lawful order, and peace
for the vast, ethnically heterogeneous masses he rules.

The story Xenophon weaves of Cyrus' magnificent adventure in
founding his empire is exhilarating and enchanting, not least because
of the remarkable personal qualities of Cyrus himself: his guileful but
benevolent charm, his versatile intelligence and capacity to listen and
learn, his penetrating and manipulative knowledge of men, his consummate trickiness, his manly but graceful self-control, his capacity for
decisiveness and, when necessary, ruthless action. Cyrus uplifts the
downtrodden, avenges the outraged, sweeps aside the incompetent
and venal, reconciles age-old enemies, forgives his contrite antago-
nists, and distributes rewards of honor and wealth with an astute and
godlike hand.

So skillfully does Xenophon make us participants in the enthusiasm
of empire building that we naturally react with surprise and even shock
to the searing criticism of Cyrus' legacy with which Xenophon concludes the book. But when, prompted by the rude awakening, we return to a more careful and thoughtful review of the *Cyropaedia*, we are
in a position to appreciate the spiritual hollowness that is at the core of
Cyrus' project from its inception. That hollowness becomes fully evident as the great project reaches its culmination in the final chapter of
book 7. Cyrus and his minion Chrysantas proclaim the continued and
indeed increased importance of Persian virtue; but the virtue that the
new Persians practice is a grotesque counterfeit of the old Persian virtue. Even at its best, the new Persian virtue substitutes courtiership for
citizenship. More generally, in the place of obedience to law, and the
mature self-discipline and brotherhood of independently wealthy citizens equal under the law, is substituted a childlike dependence on a distant, paternalistic despot whose authority rests on lavish gift giving
combined with the abolition of property rights, and on the institution
of a ubiquitous secret police, bewitching religious rites, an enormous
praetorian guard, a personal bodyguard of eunuchs, and a bureaucratic administration fueled by anxious and endless competition for favor among all subordinates.

But worst of all is the fate of Cyrus himself in the order he has established. This man who in his youth had a heart so generous, a mind
so keen, and a spiritedness so invincible spends his mature years as a
public figure parading before the masses in effeminate makeup and
engaged in contemptible theatrics, while in private he schemes to keep
his "friends" insecure and antagonistic toward one another. He marries
a grim woman who provides him with sons he cannot trust, and typically takes his evening meal in an empty palace alone or in the com-

pany of a sycophantic eunuch. He does occasionally preside over a banquet, one notable example of which Xenophon describes for us (*Cyr.* 8.4). The banquet of Cyrus obviously bears comparison with the banquet described in the *Symposium,* to which Callias invited his Athenian fellow gentlemen, including Socrates. Seen in the light of that contrast, Cyrus' "big night" is leaden, not to say chilling.

Cyrus, as one of his closest companions remarks at the banquet, is "a cold king." In expending his life on cultivating his love for humanity, Cyrus has had to extinguish or allow to wither any possibility of love for another individual or even for himself. In order to make himself the source of all other men's welfare, Cyrus has had to abandon or forget the good of his own soul.

By sweeping us up into the dramatic promise of Cyrus' dynamism—the growth, the victory, the liberation, the prosperity of the new order—and then compelling us to experience the emptiness of the outcome, Xenophon teaches an unforgettable lesson about the temptations of political life. He thus shows us the necessity of resigning ourselves to the limits of republican life. The exploration of political ambition and excellence in its fullest manifestation imaginable would seem then to be a negative proof of the superiority of the alternative, Socratic life of political philosophy.

[6]

The Erotic Self-Sufficiency of Socrates: A Reading of Xenophon's *Memorabilia*

David K. O'Connor

In the *Memorabilia*, Xenophon presents a Socrates who inspired his associates with a passionate desire to imitate him: "He made [his associates] desire virtue and gave them hope that if they took care for themselves, they would become gentlemen [καλοικἀγαθοί].[1] And though he never professed to be a teacher [of how to be *kaloskagathos*], he made his associates hope by imitating him to become so, since he was himself manifestly of this sort" (1.2.2–3).[2] Among these admiring imitators of Socrates were Alcibiades, burning with political ambition; Aristippus, founder of the Cyrenaics and an apolitical hedonist; Aristodemus, a quirky little agnostic; and Euthydemus, a talented, smug bibliophile. What was there about Socrates that attracted lovers of such diverse characters and ambitions? I will argue that Xenophon traces much of this admiring imitation to a single source: all these many admiring lovers are more or less imperfect imitators of Socrates' self-sufficiency (αὐτάρκεια). The *Memorabilia* ends with a detailed account of how Socrates "took care that his associates be self-sufficient in the actions appropriate to them" (4.7.1), and this care was possible be-

---

[1]"Gentleman" and its derivatives are used throughout this paper simply as convenient one-word English versions of *kaloskagathos* and its derivatives. The disadvantages of the rather quaint and snobbish ring of "gentleman" are outweighed by the advantage of preserving consistency, since the nature of and criteria for *kalokagathia* (gentlemanliness) are central concerns of Xenophon, in the Socratic works and elsewhere.

[2]Xenophon often mentions that Socrates influenced his associates by the example of his actions as well as by his speech; for examples, see *Mem.* 1.2.17–18, 1.3.1, and 1.5.6.

cause, as the peroration of the *Memorabilia* points out (4.8.11), Socrates was "so intelligent he never erred in judging the better and the worse but rather, without need of anyone else, was self-sufficient with regard to knowledge of these things." Our first task, then, will be to understand better the nature of Socrates' own self-sufficiency so that we can better appreciate his influence on so many different kinds of people. Why was Socrates attractive to his lovers?

But as we try to understand Xenophon's emphasis on Socrates' self-sufficiency, we will be forced to confront a second question: Why were these lovers attractive to Socrates? If Socrates was a paradigm of self-sufficiency, why was so much of his philosophical activity bound up with relationships to other people? Here one might focus on Socrates' epistemological reasons for caring about other people, emphasizing the importance of dialectic and elenchus to his conception of philosophical understanding.[3] Xenophon shares to some extent this dialectical conception of Socrates' "method"; for example, he characterizes Socrates less by a distinctive set of doctrines than by a distinctive set of questions (see *Mem.* 1.1.16). But he focuses on the special sort of erotic satisfaction that Socrates found in philosophizing with his friends, and we will follow him in trying to understand the connection between Socrates' self-sufficiency and his erotic relationships. Socrates appears to be the first figure in the history of philosophy who makes such top-

---

[3]This emphasis is characteristic of Gregory Vlastos' discussions of Socrates' interest in other people. His Socrates (drawn exclusively from Plato's earlier dialogues) is strikingly unerotic, whether as lover or beloved. The "spiritualized egocentrism" of Vlastos' Socrates requires that "in the last analysis Socrates has just one reason for moral conduct [including forming and maintaining friendships]: the perfection of his soul" ("The Individual as an Object of Love in Plato," in *Platonic Studies*[2] [Princeton, 1981], p. 30 and n. 90). Vlastos later grounded this egocentric view of Socrates' relationships more firmly in epistemological considerations when he argued, against Grote and his own earlier view, that Socrates needs the elenchus not only to refute the errors of his interlocutors but to "find positive support for those strong doctrines of his on whose truth he based his life" ("The Socratic Elenchus," *OSAP* 1 [1983]: 46). It comes as no surprise that on Vlastos' final view, leaving aside any pious duties of general benevolence, "what Socrates wants is partners in elenctic argument" who can be "fellow-seekers after moral truth" (*Socrates: Ironist and Moral Philosopher* [Ithaca, N.Y., 1991], p. 177). One can see why Vlastos was tempted to think that the relationships of such a Socrates betrayed a "failure of love" (p. 44 n. 82): his only interest in his associates seems to come from the epistemological gains he makes from them. Socratic eros, which Vlastos contrasted on this point to Platonic eros, means no more than that "physical beauty gives a special relish to [Socrates'] affectionate encounters with [his associates'] minds" (p. 41). Xenophon directly contradicts this stark portrait of a Socrates for whom the erotic is a superficial relish, overwhelmed in "the dynamics of his psyche . . . [by] an incomparably mightier drive" (p. 40). This should, I believe, undermine the assumptions behind Vlastos' exclusion of Plato's *Symposium* and *Phaedrus* from the "Socratic" dialogues, that is, from the dialogues most relevant for reconstructing the historical Socrates. Plato's Socrates is much closer to Xenophon's than to Vlastos', as long as we do not exclude arbitrarily evidence from the two great erotic dialogues.

ics central problems for reflection. Of course earlier wise men must have had friends and disciples, and Plato even suggests that Parmenides and Zeno were lovers. But deciding how to treat associates and live with them was not, I think, a theme of earlier philosophizing. But for Socrates, his relations to his associates are not external or incidental to his understanding of what the philosophical life is. Plato's interests in these issues, especially in the three erotic dialogues—*Lysis, Symposium,* and *Phaedrus*—are of course well known. But Xenophon's Socratic writings perhaps give the issues even more prominence. Particularly in the *Memorabilia,* Xenophon maintains a constant focus on the nature of Socrates' relations to his associates.

My interpretation of Xenophon's treatment of this theme is built on two guiding principles. The first concerns how Xenophon goes about presenting his account of Socrates in the *Memorabilia.* Xenophon's presentation of Socrates' self-sufficiency is indirect. He does not simply tell us his own interpretation of Socrates' virtue. Instead, he presents us with an extremely diverse *collection* of interpretations, both from Socrates' admirers and from his detractors. Perhaps because he proceeds in this way, Xenophon is sometimes charged with lacking a distinctive interpretation of his own, and with having been too dull and practical-minded to understand the "real" Socrates. The diversity of the views present in his work also tempts scholars to treat Xenophon merely as a source for this or that other figure, as if his value is on a par with, say, Diogenes Laertius. I believe both these tendencies are to be resisted. I suggest that Xenophon presents a diversity of interpretations of Socrates to force us to triangulate, as it were, from the mistaken or partial interpretations to the authentic interpretation. Through reflection on the imperfect imitations of Socrates' admirers, and the misplaced criticisms of his detractors, the reader approaches the "true" Socrates, as Xenophon saw him.

My second guiding principle concerns the criterion of success for an account of this "true" Socrates. One might be guided by the idea that to understand the "true" Socrates is primarily to reconstruct from Socrates' paradoxical and ironic speeches a single, coherent theory that underlies them. Gregory Vlastos' attempt to, as he put it, "crack the puzzle" of the historical Socrates by resolving Socrates' "complex ironies" is a splendid example of an approach guided by the assumption that Socrates had such an underlying theory. But I do not think this was Xenophon's criterion for a successful interpretation of the "true" Socrates. His indirect mode of presentation is, of course, compatible with this criterion; he could have believed a unified account of Socrates' self-sufficiency could be given, so that the partial views that he selects and presents would all converge on one focal point. If this were Xenophon's intention, then after we correct for the distortions of admirers and detractors, we would be able to put together an account that removes the seemingly paradoxical or contradictory character of Socrates. But Xenophon's indirect presentation fits better with the view that Xenophon did not intend a unified Socrates to emerge at all. Perhaps Xenophon was more concerned to limn unresolved and unresolvable tensions in Socrates' attractions, and so to show him as an unlimited source of provocations, than to give a stable and delimiting account of Socrates. Part of *Xenophon's* attraction, I think, is precisely that he, even more than Plato, preserves the tensions between the various sides of Socrates. He sees in Socrates not so much a puzzle to be solved as a mystery to be pondered. And the criterion for more deeply appreciating a mystery or a paradox is different from the criterion for successfully solving a puzzle. Xenophon's Socrates is not simply the founder of a research program, whose pioneering insights can then be taken up and refined by his successors; for he cannot be appropriated and controlled, built upon and then relegated to the brilliant but naive beginnings of a maturing enquiry. Rather than a mere defender of one position among many about the nature and value of self-sufficiency, he is himself the matrix that produces and defines the set of possibilities. This Socrates overshadows any particular "development" of his views and remains a living provocation rather than becoming an honored but dead ancestor.[4] Perhaps the "true" Socrates as Xenophon perceived him is more a locus of dispersion for a discourse (to use Michel Foucault's phrase) than a stable and unified focal point.

My aim, then, is not to reconstruct a "Socratic" theory from the *Memorabilia* that would reveal a hidden consistency behind the Xenophontic Socrates' various arguments and positions. It is to show how Xenophon deepens our appreciation of the paradoxical complexity of Socrates' self-sufficiency by revealing it through the partial and distorting views of his disparate admirers and detractors. We begin with three admirers who are attracted by, and imperfectly try to imitate, his self-sufficiency. The first is the notorious Alcibiades. Alcibiades was consumed by ambition for political leadership, and this ambition seemed to his critics, and to some of Socrates' critics, to move him toward tyranny. Xenophon tries to show how this crudely political aspiration to complete control is a distorted reflection of Socrates' own self-sufficiency. But in distancing Socrates from Alcibiades, one can be tempted to go too far

[4]In distinguishing between Socrates as the (surpassable) founder of a research program and as a permanently relevant provocation, I have been influenced by Michel Foucault's distinction between founders of sciences and initiators of discursive practices, in the essay "What Is an Author?" in *Language, Counter-Memory, Practice,* trans. D. F. Bouchard (Ithaca, N.Y., 1977), p. 131.

by denying that Socrates was in any essential way a political man himself. The second passage addresses this distortion, presenting Socrates' critique of Aristippus' apolitical understanding of self-sufficiency. It turns out that neither Alcibiades' political ambition nor Aristippus' political indifference is an authentic imitation of the "true" Socrates. But then Socratic self-sufficiency seems to be a paradox, combining the desire for control, which Alcibiades sees but Aristippus ignores, with the rejection of the usual political means of satisfying that desire, as Aristippus but not Alcibiades can see. The third passage elucidates without resolving this paradox. It presents Socrates' attempt to teach his follower Aristodemus a proper concern for and dependence on the divine.[5] As we will see, the passage highlights the special contribution made to Socrates' self-sufficiency by his famous daimonion, the "divine sign" that was his unique mantic endowment.

In the final two sections, I will try to give a more positive account of Socrates' self-sufficiency and its connection to his erotic relationships. First I will follow up Xenophon's emphasis on Socrates' mantic knowledge by considering the account at the end of the *Memorabilia* of the difference between the type of knowledge required by the self-sufficiency Socrates promoted in his associates and the type required by Socrates' own self-sufficiency. Finally, I will conclude with Xenophon's account of Socrates' erotic nature. Here my interpretation will hinge on two passages, the first with a detractor, the second with an admirer: Socrates' defense of his self-sufficiency and erotic relations against the attack of Antiphon, and his "seduction" of the noble youth Euthydemus.

1. Alcibiades: Self-Sufficiency as Tyranny

Socrates was charged with undermining his associates' respect for the established political democracy, thereby catering to their tyrannical ambitions (*Mem.* 1.2.9). The most spectacular associate about whom this form of the corruption charge was plausible is of course Alcibiades. Besides being attracted to Socrates, this promising young man became "of all in the democracy the most licentious, the most outrageous, and the most violent" (*Mem.* 1.2.12). How could such a man ever have

---

[5]Xenophon's indirect presentation of Socrates' self-sufficiency fits into his overall scheme in *Memorabilia* 1 of alternating passages defending Socrates against the two official charges at his trial. Xenophon's distancing of Socrates from the tyrannical ambition of Alcibiades and the political indifference of Aristippus is part of the refutation of the charge that Socrates did injustice by corrupting the youth; his distancing Socrates from Aristodemus' neglect of the gods is directed at the impiety charge.

found Socrates attractive? Xenophon suggests that, along with Critias, Alcibiades was driven by the ambition "to do everything for himself [πάντα δι' ἑαυτῶν πράττεσθαι] and become more famous than anyone" (*Mem.* 1.2.14). This is the political man's understanding of self-sufficiency, and it was to satisfy this ambition for self-sufficiency that Alcibiades associated with Socrates. He saw reflected in Socrates' self-sufficiency (*autarkeia*), self-control, and power in speech (*Mem.* 1.2.14) an image of the capacity for speech and action to which he aspired (*Mem.* 1.2.15).

Xenophon does not simply dismiss this tyrannical appropriation of Socrates, nor does he answer the charge as thoroughly and unambiguously as we might expect. In the first place, he leaves the reader with a lingering doubt whether Socrates himself did much to mitigate Alcibiades' contempt for law and his tendency toward violence and outrage. Three features of the *Memorabilia*'s account contribute to this doubt. First, Xenophon provides a long, detailed account of how Socrates tried to chasten and undermine the tyrannical excesses of Critias (*Mem.* 1.2.29–37) without providing any examples at all of any chastening of Alcibiades. Since Xenophon treats Socrates' relationships to Critias and Alcibiades together as part of a single accusation (*Mem.* 1.2.12), this silence is surprising. Second, Xenophon reports the accusation that Socrates incited his associates to the use of violence by making intelligence rather than selection by lot the title to rule, and by calling democratic practices "stupid" (μῶρον) and productive of irrational mistakes that would never be tolerated in helmsmen, builders, or flautists (*Mem.* 1.2.9). Very uncharacteristically, Xenophon does not answer this charge by citing some Socratic maxim against violence or by replacing the sinister reading of Socrates' critique of democracy with a more benign interpretation.[6] Instead, he offers *on his own authority* an argument to the effect that intelligent people would use persuasion rather than violence, since violence tends to produce hatred, while persuasion produces living allies (*Mem.* 1.2.10–11).[7] This argument that

[6]For more characteristic responses to accusations against particular sayings of Socrates, where Xenophon offers benign interpretations of the offending sayings, see, for example, *Mem.* 1.2.49–50 (Socrates' comparison of ignorance to madness did not imply that sons should fetter their ignorant fathers); 1.2.51–55 (Socrates' argument that unintelligent friends and relatives are worthless was not intended to alienate affections); and 1.2.56–57 (Socrates' use of Hesiod's tag "No work is dishonorable" did not imply that even unjust or shameful "work" could be justified).

[7]Xenophon makes a philosophical argument on his own authority rather than on Socrates' in only one other place in the *Memorabilia*: 1.2.19–28, where against "many who call themselves philosophers" he argues that someone who has learned to be virtuous can later reverse and become vicious. This rather un-Socratic-sounding thesis is part of Xenophon's explanation of why it is no reflection on Socrates that Alcibiades and Critias

persuasion rather than violence is the best policy would already sound suspicious to a democrat who charged Socrates with encouraging Alcibiades' tendency toward tyranny, since it is purely prudential. But Xenophon's marked and uncharacteristic dependence on his own authority for the argument raises an additional question in the reader's mind about what Socrates himself did or said about Alcibiades' violent tendencies. Finally, Xenophon records a conversation between the teenaged Alcibiades and Pericles, who was his legal guardian, that does not put Socrates' influence in a very good light (*Mem.* 1.2.39–46). In a dialectical exchange that certainly appears to owe something to his association with Socrates, Alcibiades quizzes Pericles about the nature of law and concludes by questioning the legitimacy of the laws of the democracy. Xenophon reports this suspicious conversation as evidence of Alcibiades' early and enduring political ambition, but he does nothing to remove the impression that Socrates did indeed promote that skill in speech of which Alcibiades later made such dubious use.

On top of this rather compromising defense against the charge that Socrates abetted Alcibiades' violent contempt for the established political order, Xenophon also makes it clear that Socrates was some sort of defender of kingship, a position that someone with Alcibiades' ambitions might find hard to distinguish from a defense of tyranny.[8] For example, a passage that follows closely the account of Socrates' relations with Alcibiades and Critias addresses the charge that Socrates "selected passages from famous poets . . . to use as evidence in teaching his associates to be unscrupulous and tyrannical" (*Mem.* 1.2.56). Xenophon argues that Socrates' use of the poets did not tend to this result, and he discusses a specific passage from Homer (*Il.* 2.188–206) to refute the allegation that it was used by Socrates to encourage his associates to abuse the common people. The references to kingship in the passage are striking, especially if we restore Xenophon's curious omissions (Xenophon leaves the italicized passages out of his quotation);

Whenever [Odysseus] encountered some king, or man of influence,
he would stand beside him and with soft words try to restrain him:
"Excellency! It does not become you to be frightened like any

---

turned out so badly despite their long association with him. Like Xenophon's own argument against the prudence of violence, this argument leaves the reader wondering whether Socrates himself would have accepted it.

[8]A fuller treatment of the possibility of Xenophon's philosophical tolerance for tyranny would need to consider the *Hiero*, where Xenophon reports the "wise" recommendations of Simonides for reforming Hiero's tyrannical rule. Note as well that the only person whom Xenophon shows Socrates actively encouraging into politics is Charmides (*Mem.* 3.7), who became one of the Ten in the Piraeus during the rule of the Thirty Tyrants. A most ambiguous defense!

coward. Rather hold fast and check the rest of the people.
You do not yet clearly understand the purpose of Atreides.
Now he makes trial, but soon will bear hard on the sons of the Achaians.
Did we not all hear what he was saying in council?
May he not in anger do some harm to the sons of the Achaians!
For the anger of god-supported kings is a big matter,
to whom honour and love are given from Zeus of the counsels."
When he saw some man of the people who was shouting,
he would strike at him with his staff, and reprove him also:
"Excellency! Sit still and listen to what others tell you,
to those who are better men than you, you skulker and coward
and thing of no account whatever in battle or council.
Surely not all of us Achaians can be as kings here.
Lordship for many is no good thing. Let there be one ruler,
one king, to whom the son of devious-devising Kronos
gives the sceptre and right of judgment, to watch over his people."

(Il. 2.188–206, trans. Lattimore)

That Xenophon concedes that this passage was in fact a favorite of Socrates' is revealing, for its praise of kingship is clear, even though Xenophon elides the most explicit lines in his response to the charge.[9]

But of course the tyrannical imitation of Socratic self-sufficiency *is* a distortion. Whatever ambiguous sympathy Socrates may have had for kingship, and in whatever contempt he held the established democracy, his self-sufficiency was fundamentally different from that to which Alcibiades aspired. The root of the difference is the contrast between Socrates' consummate control of his passions and Alcibiades' utter abandonment to them (*Mem.* 1.2.24–25). There was no place in Alcibiades' and Critias' tyrannical imitation for Socrates' own asceticism, for his moderation (σωφροσύνη). As Xenophon says, "I believe that if a god had granted them the choice between living their whole life as they saw Socrates living or being dead, they would have chosen to be dead" (*Mem.* 1.2.16). Still, at least the tyrannical appropriation of Socrates respects his essential concern with moral and political life. That Socrates was in some way a political man seems to have been easy for some of his less political associates to overlook. Xenophon presents us with an especially striking misinterpretation of this sort in Aristippus, to whom we now turn.

---

[9]Socrates' explicit praise of kingship in his polemic with Aristippus is an even clearer case, which we will examine in the following section. (What is being praised there and in the other passages I will discuss is kingship for the individual, that is, the *life* of being a king, not the political system of kingship.)

2. Aristippus: Self-Sufficiency as Alienation

Aristippus was the first follower of Socrates to accept payment from students, and he founded the Cyrenaic school of philosophy, whose central doctrine was a special form of hedonism. Xenophon's long report of Socrates' examination of Aristippus (*Mem.* 2.1) accordingly takes hedonism as a target and concludes with Prodicus' fable of Heracles' choice of Virtue, a sober and modest lady, over Vice, a debauched and forward tart. More precisely, the passage shows how Socrates exhorted his associates to the practice of self-control (*Mem.* 2.1.1). This exhortation to asceticism and critique of sensualism has a notably political emphasis. "Noticing that one of his associates was rather licentious with regard to [sensual pleasures]," reports Xenophon, "[Socrates] spoke: 'Tell me, Aristippus, if you needed to educate two youths who had been handed over to you, one so that he would be capable of ruling, the other so that he would not even think of trying to rule, how would you educate each of them?' " (*Mem.* 2.1.1).[10] The entire conversation between Socrates and Aristippus is governed by this opening question.

What we have in this conversation, then, is a critique of hedonism and an exhortation to self-control set in a very special rhetorical context. Xenophon is at least as interested in Socrates' specially *political* approach to attracting his associates to self-control as in the critique of hedonism in itself.[11] Given this interest, we would interpret the passage too narrowly if we focused exclusively on the contrast between the ascetic Socrates and the hedonistic Aristippus. The rhetorical context instead invites us to contrast Socrates' praise of the capacity for political rule, which in this passage is at the root of his exhortation to self-control, with Aristippus' indifference to political involvement, which complements his hedonism. By emphasizing this contrast between the political Socrates and the apolitical Aristippus, Xenophon focuses on a feature of Aristippus' life no less characteristic than his hedonism; for

[10]We need not assume that the associate whose licentiousness Socrates noticed was Aristippus himself, for there are other examples in the *Memorabilia* of Socrates conversing with one person for the benefit of someone in the audience; for example, 1.3.8–13 (Socrates talks to Xenophon to get at Critias) and 4.2.2 (Socrates talks to unnamed companions to stir up Euthydemus). Since Xenophon presumably intended the passage to be an example of *effective* exhortation, we should probably understand the unnamed licentious associate to have had considerably more political ambition than the strikingly apolitical Aristippus. Otherwise Socrates' exhortation is rather inept.

[11]*Memorabilia* 4.5.1–11 also shows Socrates promoting the self-control of his associates, but there Socrates' exhortation, while it still makes a point of the political importance of self-control, does not appeal to the ambition to rule in anything like the way the present passage does.

as Diogenes Laertius reports, "When [Aristippus] was asked what he had gotten out of philosophy, he replied: 'The ability to associate comfortably with anyone. . . . If all the laws are done away with, we [philosophers] will go on living the same way.' "[12] This aloofness from political entanglements is at the heart of Aristippus' mistaken imitation of Socrates' self-sufficiency.

Socrates begins his examination of Aristippus by going through a list of sensual temptations (food, drink, sleep, sex, avoiding hard work) and secures agreement that in each case people capable of resisting such temptations will be better suited for rule than people of the contrary type (*Mem.* 2.1.1–7). Socrates concludes this part of the argument by asking Aristippus, "Have you ever considered into which of these categories you would rightly put yourself?" Someone with any political ambitions would be squirming at this question, especially if he were "rather licentious with regard to sensual pleasures." But Aristippus is ready with an answer that shows he rejects the very political ambition to which Socrates has tried to appeal: "I have considered it, and I would not at all put myself into the category of those who want to rule. For it seems to me that only an unintelligent human being would not be satisfied with making provision for his own needs—which is a big enough job—but would add to this the further job of supplying what his fellow citizens need" (*Mem.* 2.1.8; see also 2.1.17 on the burdens of political rule). On this view, political involvement is simply a useless burden. It undermines a person's ability to satisfy his own needs and exposes him to the censure of the community without providing any compensating benefits.

At this point, Socrates must reverse his tactics. So far he has been supporting self-control and attacking hedonism by appealing to the political ambition to rule. In light of Aristippus' rejection of political ambition, this argument has come to a dead end. Now Socrates must directly defend the desirability of rule by showing that its burdens are worth bearing, despite the alternatives to rule that Aristippus will present. Socrates begins this line of argument with an appeal to hedonism: "Then should we consider this too," he replies to Aristippus, "which lives more pleasantly, the rulers or the ruled?" (*Mem.* 2.1.10). Socrates' willingness to shift the argument to this question shows that Aristippus' indifference to politics rather than his hedonism is Socrates' primary target in this conversation. The rest of the discussion revolves around Aristippus' claim that there is a third alternative to being

[12]D.L. 2.8.68. See also 2.8.66: "[Aristippus] was capable of fitting in with every place and time and person, and of fittingly playing a part in any circumstance." He showed this chameleonlike adaptability especially by staying in the good graces of Dionysius, tyrant of Syracuse.

either a ruler or a subject, a master or a slave, and Socrates' insistence that Aristippus' apolitical path is untenable.

Socrates first asks Aristippus to compare the pleasantness of the lives of nations that are politically dominant (for example, Persia) and nations that are dominated (for example, Lydia). Aristippus refuses to play along and announces his intention to avoid the burdens of either dominating or being dominated: "I certainly do not put myself into the category of slavery [instead of mastery]. I believe there is a middle path between these two, on which I try to walk, which goes through neither rule nor slavery but rather through freedom, which is just the path that leads best to happiness" (*Mem.* 2.1.11). Socrates responds that unless Aristippus' "path" also avoids going through not just rule and slavery but human life altogether (δι' ἀνθρώπων), this strategy of avoiding political entanglement is doomed, since the stronger always threaten to plunder and enslave the weaker (*Mem.* 2.1.12–13). If one won't play the hammer, one must play the anvil. Aristippus' "freedom" is a sham, since it requires a transcendence of the inescapably political context of human life. If you live among human beings, suggests Socrates, you have only three choices: rule yourself, be ruled, or be willing to serve the rulers. Whatever the burdens of ruling oneself, they are less oppressive than being a slave or (perhaps even worse) a flatterer of the powers that be.[13]

At this point Aristippus plays his trump card: "But to avoid just these sufferings, I do not close myself into any political community; instead, I am everywhere an alien [ξένος]" (*Mem.* 2.1.13). This is the most radical statement of Aristippus' strategy for transcending the bonds of political entanglement. The freedom he tries to achieve is not within politics but from politics. Socrates argues that the alien's life is too exposed to provide this freedom, since without the support of laws and publicly enforced punishment, human beings cannot protect themselves against thieves and other malefactors (*Mem.* 2.1.14–15). The solitary outcast, according to Socrates, has even less chance of achieving happiness than the oppressed citizen or servile courtier. In light of Socrates' constant emphasis in this entire conversation on political rule (rather than merely on citizenship), it comes as no surprise that Aristippus finally exclaims, "Socrates, you seem to hold that the art of kingship [βασιλικὴ τέχνη] is happiness' (*Mem.* 2.1.17). Socrates does not question the inference. Political rule, though encumbered with all the burdens Aristippus has mentioned, appears to be a necessity for achieving whatever happiness is possible within the limitations of hu-

[13]D.L. 2.8.66 and 78 report anecdotes that show that some of Diogenes' sources considered Aristippus a flatterer of Dionysius.

man life. Kingship, whatever its hardships, is the only human access to the stable control over one's own success that Aristippus' strategy of alienation cannot provide. So at least this argument seems to conclude.

Aristippus' celebration of alienation represents the opposite pole in defining a self-sufficient life from Alcibiades' tyrannical immersion in leadership. Can Xenophon's Socrates both insist on the necessity of political involvement against Aristippus and deny the attraction of tyranny against Alcibiades, while still defending the centrality of self-sufficiency? Aristotle addresses this same tension between tyrannical and alienated self-sufficiency in the *Politics,* and his approach provides an interesting contrast to Xenophon's. Aristotle argues that the proper view of the place of political concern in a human life falls between two extreme views. On one extreme view, the best life is the life of political mastery and tyranny, since it gives the most scope for and control over the greatest and finest actions (*Pol.* 7.3, 1325a34–36; also 7.2, 1324b1–3). This is the Alcibiades position. On the other extreme view, the best life cannot be a political life at all, since, on the one hand, despotism is unjust and degrading, while, on the other, beneficent political rule, "though it does not involve anything unjust, is an impediment to one's own well-being" (*Pol.* 7.2, 1324a35–38). People who hold this view "believe the life of the free person is different from that of the political person [ὁ πολιτικός] and is the most choiceworthy," and defend "the life of alienation and separation from political community [ὁ ξενικὸς βίος καὶ τῆς πολιτικῆς κοινωνίας ἀπολελυμένος]" (*Pol.* 7.3, 1325a19–20; 7.2, 1324a16–17). This is the Aristippus position. The mean between these extremes seems to be a special kind of theoretical life: it must be political insofar as it is regulative of actions outside of itself (*Pol.* 7.3, 1325b21–23), yet still be "separate [*apolelumenos*] from everything external to itself" (*Pol.* 7.2, 1324a27–28) insofar as it is "complete in itself" (αὐτοτσλεῖς) and for its own sake rather than for the sake of actions that follow from it (*Pol.* 7.3, 1325b18–21). In other words, Aristotle tries to combine Alcibiades' aspiration to self-sufficiency through political leadership with Aristippus' aspiration to self-sufficiency through apolitical separation, integrating both into a theoretical life that is politically concerned and practically useful even though it separates the thinker from direct involvement in the business of political ruling. Perhaps the *Politics* itself is an example of the kind of thinking that Aristotle proposed in order to combine political and philosophical aspiration.

Aristotle tries to preserve as much as he can of the claims for political involvement, but his solution to the tension still seems to lean toward philosophical transcendence. Xenophon's Socrates has a different way out of the dilemma. On the face of it, he seems in his conversation with

Aristippus simply to accept the view of the partisans of political life. To be sure, in the end he praises kingship rather than tyranny, but still the emphasis on rule and mastery is unmistakable. But in this conversation with Aristippus, I suggest, Xenophon's Socrates exaggerates the power of the art of kingship to guarantee happiness. The fact that Socrates is exhorting his associates to self-control by appealing to its importance for political rule explains this exaggeration: the more important he shows the art of ruling to be, the more he increases their attachment to virtue. Recall that throughout this section of the *Memorabilia*, Xenophon is interested primarily in showing Socrates' good influence, not in simply presenting Socrates' views. In fact, Socrates has here assigned to the kingly art, the *basilikē technē*, an importance that no merely human power can have, and that as we will see in the next section, is elsewhere assigned to divination (μαντική). Only a power divine or daimonic can play the role here assigned to kingship. To this extent, Xenophon agrees with Aristotle in moving away from the political view toward a kind of transcendence. But he does not locate this transcendence in self-sufficient philosophical thinking, complete in itself and separated from external things. Instead, he locates it in human access to divine guidance, the theme to which we now turn.

3. Aristodemus: Self-Sufficiency as Atheism

Aristodemus (know as Shorty) was an ardent follower of Socrates and is presented by Plato as Apollodorus' source for the report of the erotic evening of the *Symposium*. In *Memorabilia* 1.4, Xenophon presents a long conversation between Aristodemus and Socrates intended to counter the charge that while Socrates could exhort people to virtue, he could not initiate them into it.[14] The primary virtue that Socrates promotes in this conversation is piety.[15] Aristodemus, reports Xenophon, "did not sacrifice to the gods or make use of divination [*mantikē*] but even laughed at those who did" (*Mem.* 1.4.2). This distancing of the gods, I suggest, can be seen as in part a strategy for achieving self-sufficiency, since the removal from human life of divine concern and intervention greatly increases the scope of human direction and con-

---

[14]*Mem.* 1.4.1. This objection to Socrates is the theme of the Platonic *Cleitophon*, where Cleitophon argues that Thrasymachus is superior to Socrates as an educator because he actually tells people what to do to be virtuous, rather than merely inspiring them with a desire to be virtuous.

[15]At the same time, Socrates is also promoting the *justice* of his companions by teaching them always to be mindful of the ever-watchful gods (*Mem.* 1.4.19); compare the similar account in *Memorabilia* 1.1.19 of how Socrates' own justice is supported by his pious belief in divine concern.

trol. By finding sacrifice and divination laughable, Aristodemus is able to take himself all the more seriously. Xenophon shows Socrates undermining this impious version of self-sufficiency in a way that highlights Socrates' own special relationship to divination and the divine.

This connection between divination and self-sufficiency will be clearer if we consider Xenophon's various accounts of the need for and benefits of divination. He reports that Socrates counseled his associates to concern themselves with divination "if any of them wanted to prosper beyond the limits of human wisdom [ἀνθρωπίνη σοφία]" (*Mem.* 4.7.10). Divination completes a deficiency in merely human rational powers. Human wisdom can of course take us far, and Socrates declared any reliance on divination in matters appropriate for human discernment to be impious and deranged (or more literally, "god-obsessed": δαιμονᾶν) (*Mem.* 1.1.9). But the most important matters are hidden from human discernment (ἄδηλα), and so are not under human control through art or calculation (*Mem.* 1.1.6, 8). These great and hidden things concern especially whether or not we will *benefit* from exercising or developing various human powers. Divination is necessary because without divine guidance we do not know what will contribute to our secure possession of happiness.[16]

Xenophon makes an explicit link between this view of the limits of human wisdom and Socrates' understanding of the value of rule. He reports that Socrates claimed that "people who are going to govern households and cities well" cannot rely solely on becoming skilled in ruling human beings, in running a household, in being a general, or in practicing any other art under the control of human judgment (ἀνθρωπίνη γνώμη). To find out whether or not you will benefit from employing any of these merely human kinds of knowledge, you need divination as well (*Mem.* 1.1.7–8).[17] Socrates goes on to list some examples of the uncertain benefit of human undertakings: "It is not clear

---

[16]For a similar point about prayer and the hiddenness of the beneficial, see *Mem.* 1.3.2: "[Socrates] believed that people who pray to get gold or silver or tyrannical power or anything else of this sort would be no different if they prayed for a chance to roll dice or for a fight or for anything else the result of which is manifestly hidden [*adēla*]." In *Memorabilia* 4.2.36, after Socrates has refuted all of Euthydemus' views about what would be beneficial for him, the frustrated young man exclaims: "I concede I don't even know what I should pray for!" I will discuss this passage in the concluding section.

[17]There is a similar account in *Memorabilia* 4.2.31–36 of the uncertain benefit of human goods and powers, but there self-knowledge rather than divination guarantees success. I will treat this passage in the final section. Xenophon's report of Socrates' use of the story of Circe turning Odysseus' men into pigs (see *Od.* 10) also illustrates the necessity of both human judgment and divine advice in a successful life: "[Socrates] said playfully that it was through the advice of Hermes, as well as through his own self-control, . . . that Odysseus avoided being turned into a pig" (*Mem.* 1.3.7).

[*dēlon*] to one who cultivates [φυτευσάμενος] a field well who will have its fruits,[18] nor to one who builds a house well who will live in it, nor to one skilled in generalship if he will benefit from being a general, nor to one skilled in politics [*politikos*] if he will benefit from leading the city" (*Mem.* 1.1.8). Now we can see how much Socrates exaggerated the connection between mere kingship and happiness in his conversation with Aristippus, since there he spoke as if there were no great and hidden things beyond human control. Divination rather than kingship proves the indispensable means of gaining control over one's own happiness.

Under Socrates' questioning, Aristodemus reveals what is at the root of his contempt for sacrifice and divination: he denies that "the gods have any concern [φροντίζειν] for human beings" (*Mem.* 1.4.11). Socrates tries to wean Aristodemus from this neglect of the divine by arguing for the existence of general providence (*Mem.* 1.4.2–14), with a particular emphasis on the design of human bodily and psychic capacities. Socrates concludes this part of his argument with a rhetorical question: "When will what the gods do convince you that they are concerned [*phrontizein*] with you?" Aristodemus responds: "When they send, as you say they send, counselors about what I should and should not do" (*Mem.* 1.4.15). This pointed reply gives the argument a new twist. Aristodemus appears to have in mind Socrates' notorious daimonion, and to be telling Socrates that without the sort of special providence that the daimonion offers there are no persuasive reasons to believe that the divine is mindful of human beings, and thus no reason for humans to be mindful of the divine. But Socrates deflects the personal focus of Aristodemus' response. Sarcastically, he asks Aristodemus whether he takes himself to be the only human being, in Athens, in Greece, or in the whole world, denied the gods' communication through consultation of oracles and interpretation of preternatural signs. Surely, suggests Socrates, such publicly available oracles and signs are sufficient proof that Aristodemus' refusal to depend on the divine is neither prudent nor pious. Though this answer fits with Xenophon's own assimilation of Socrates' daimonion to publicly recognized divination (see *Mem.* 1.1.2–4), it evades Aristodemus' point, if he is in fact referring to Socrates' unique access to divine guidance through the daimonion. Unlike a dependence on the vagaries and im-

---

[18]This is reminiscent of one of the harms of rejecting political rule that Socrates uses in his argument against Aristippus: "Haven't you noticed people who cut down the crops and trees that others have planted and cultivated [*phuteusantes*], and attack in all kinds of ways those who are weaker and unwilling to serve them, until the weaker are persuaded to choose slavery rather than fighting with the stronger?" (*Mem.* 2.1.13). Rule or kingship plays the role in this passage that divination plays in *Memorabilia* 1.1.8.

precision of mantic interpretation of the flights of birds, the shapes of entrails, or the riddles of the Pythia, Socrates' reliance on the daimonion does not diminish his self-sufficient control over his own happiness.[19]

Aristodemus' reply *could* be taken to mean only that Socrates claims that the gods send counselors to human beings generally, rather than as a reference specifically to the daimonion. But in the closely parallel passage of *Memorabilia* 4.3, where Xenophon reports a conversation between Socrates and his young follower Euthydemus, the reference is fully explicit. The conversation is meant to illustrate how Socrates "tried to make his associates respectful toward the gods" (*Mem.* 4.3.2), and he again rehearses the design arguments for general divine concern before turning to the special concern shown by the usefulness of divination (*mantikē*), upon which Euthydemus replies, "Toward you, Socrates, the gods seem to behave even more lovingly than toward other people, if in fact, without even being asked by you, they give you a sign of what you should and should not do" (*Mem.* 4.3.12). In this passage too Socrates does not comment directly on his own special relationship to the divine and perhaps even plays it down by telling Euthydemus to be satisfied with indirect evidence of special providence: "That what I say [about the concern of the gods manifested through divination] is true you too will recognize if you do not wait on an appearance of the gods in visible form but rather are satisfied to revere and honor the gods on seeing their works" (*Mem.* 4.3.13).

With both Aristodemus and Euthydemus, then, Xenophon seems to present Socrates as encouraging a dependence on the divine in his associates that his own particular privileged position as a mantic does not require. Socrates' personal mantic art contributes much to his approach to that divine needlessness that (reports Xenophon) he saw at the heart of happiness: "To need nothing is divine; and as the divine is best, what is closest to the divine is closest to the best" (*Mem.* 1.6.10, discussed in the next section). The daimonion is an essential albeit puzzling aspect of Socrates' imitation of the divine.

To tyrannical imitators like Alcibiades and Critias, Xenophon opposes Socrates' asceticism; to alienated imitators like Aristippus, his

---

[19]As Mary R. Lefkowitz points out very nicely (in her comment on Vlastos' "Socratic Piety," *PBACAP* [1991]:245, "It was revolutionary (and dangerous) [of Socrates] to claim that the gods spoke directly to him and told him what was right" (p. 239); for "in saying that the god sends him frequent, but private negative signs that no one else hears or sees, Socrates implies that he has a closer relationship to the gods than even the sons of the gods and goddesses in traditional myth." It is no wonder that Aristodemus and (as I will show shortly) Euthydemus were both very interested by this aspect of Socrates, and perhaps also not surprising that Socrates tries to deflect their interest into more traditionally pious channels.

praise of the kingly art; and to practical atheists like Aristodemus, Socrates' daimonic nature. Three very different ways of aspiring to self-sufficiency, all undermined in the example of Socrates. How can Socrates be both an inspiration to and the refutation of so many different aspirations? What allows Socrates to contain in one life what his admirers fragment into competing ways of life? Or to put the question another way, Why instead of founding a Socratic school did he launch a Socratic movement? In the concluding two sections I will try to address these questions. In the next section, we must try to sharpen our understanding of the contrast between Socrates' own self-sufficiency and the self-sufficiency of his associates. Then we will turn to the final difficult question of how the various aspects of Socrates' peculiar self-sufficiency are held in balance within his erotic life.

4. The Daimonic: Between the Sophist and the Gentleman

We have seen that Socrates' daimonion is not merely a personal quirk or an amusing curiosity in Xenophon's presentation. In the peroration of the *Memorabilia*, Xenophon makes a particular point of this mantic self-sufficiency: "For my part, I have described [Socrates] just as he was: so pious he did nothing without the judgment [*gnōmē*] of the gods, . . . so intelligent he never erred in judging the better and the worse, but rather, without need of anyone else, was self-sufficient [*autarkēs*] with regard to knowledge [γνῶσις] of these things" (*Mem.* 4.8.11). In other human beings, this juxtaposition of unshakable piety and unerring intelligence would be an impossibility. It would require us to become deranged ("god-obsessed": *daimonan*) by reducing the great things hidden by the divine (daimonion), which transcend our control, to the level of what is under merely human judgment (*anthrō-pinē gnōmē*) (see *Mem.* 1.1.9). But Socrates' daimonion, his mantic nature, allows the reconciliation in one human being of the seeming tension between pious reliance on divine *gnōmē* and self-sufficient reliance on one's own *gnōsis*.

The *Memorabilia*'s concluding celebration of Socrates' daimonic self-sufficiency in judging the better and the worse is part of a much broader exploration in the entire last section (from *Mem.* 4.7 on) of how Socrates' self-sufficiency was different from the self-sufficiency of his associates (see *Mem.* 4.7.1). Only the latter part of this section (*Mem.* 4.7.10–4.8.10) focuses directly on Socrates' daimonion. After reporting that Socrates recommended to his associates that they should concern themselves with divination "if any of them wanted to prosper beyond the limits of human wisdom" (*Mem.* 4.7.10, quoted earlier), Xenophon immediately turns to a discussion of Socrates' trial and execution. This section is not an intrusion or a disconnected anecdote. It brings out directly the difference between the associates' lives, which must be dependent on the external support provided by divination, and Socrates' life under the sure direction of the daimonion. Socrates claimed the daimonion had stopped him when he thought about how to defend himself before the jury (*Mem.* 4.8.5). Xenophon realizes some people believe that Socrates' subsequent condemnation refuted his claim to have special access to divine guidance (*Mem.* 4.8.1). But throughout the whole passage, Xenophon tries to show that this view is wrong, and to demonstrate that death was actually a benefit for Socrates. Insofar as he succeeds, he has indeed shown that the daimonion allowed Socrates "to prosper beyond the limits of human wisdom." Thus the report of Socrates' condemnation and the defense of the rationality of his death is an indispensable part of Xenophon's defense of his daimonic self-sufficiency.

But the broader treatment of Socrates' self-sufficiency comes in the earlier part of this concluding section (*Mem.* 4.7.1–8), which distinguishes the role that knowledge (in general, not just mantic knowledge) played in Socrates' life from the role it played in his associates' lives.[20] This presentation also allows Xenophon to comment on the difference between Socrates' transcendence of human limitations and the counterfeit transcendence of the natural philosophers (whom Xenophon terms sophists). Xenophon focuses on how Socrates "took care that his associates be self-sufficient [*autarkeis*] in the actions appropriate to them [αἱ προσήκουσαι πράξεις]" by providing them with whatever knowledge was "appropriate for a gentleman" (*Mem.* 4.7.1). It becomes clear in this discussion that Socrates' own self-sufficiency was of a different character from the self-sufficiency of his gentlemanly associates. Socrates "taught them up to what point the properly educated gentleman should be familiar with any particular subject" (*Mem.* 4.7.2), but his own knowledge often exceeded this limit. For example, Socrates

---

[20]*Memorabilia* 4.7.9, a short discussion of health, seems at first glance out of place in the entire section from 4.7 on, which contrasts Socrates' knowledge (of geometry, astronomy, celestial science, arithmetic, and divination) with the knowledge he promoted in his associates. But note the passage's emphasis on knowledge, and particularly self-knowledge: "[Socrates] vigorously exhorted his associates to care for their health, both by their learning whatever they could from knowledgeable people and by one's paying close attention during all of one's life to how particular things affect oneself. . . . For it is the accomplishment of the person who pays close attention to himself in this way, to discover, better even than a doctor who considers it closely, what is beneficial for one's health." (The shift from plural to singular in the first sentence is in the original.) The next section will consider the links between the kingly art, divination, and self-knowledge in Xenophon's account of Socrates' "seduction" of Euthydemus.

recommended that his associates learn enough geometry and astronomy for practical uses like land measurement and night navigation, but discouraged them from pursuing the more abstruse and speculative parts of these sciences. Xenophon has Socrates explain this limitation twice in virtually identical words, once for geometry and once for astronomy (*Mem.* 4.7.3 and 5): "Such studies are capable of using up an entire human life and preventing many other useful kinds of learning." But in both cases Xenophon also tells the reader that despite this advice Socrates himself *was* familiar with the more theoretical parts of the sciences.[21] Similarly, Socrates turned his associates away from imitating Anaxagoras and becoming concerned (*phrontistēs*) with heavenly phenomena (*Mem.* 4.7.6), yet the immediately following critique of Anaxagorean theories shows that Socrates himself *was* quite familiar with speculation on such subjects (*Mem.* 4.7.7). Socrates' self-sufficiency allowed, perhaps required, a theoretical interest that transcended the practical interest of his gentlemanly associates.

Even though such theoretical studies would merely "use up" a gentlemanly life and would therefore make no contribution to the self-sufficiency of Socrates' associates, they did not waste Socrates' life. His concern was not limited to ethical and political affairs in the narrow sense that the concern of his gentlemanly friends was so limited. Yet when Socrates went beyond the limits of the gentleman, he did not become simply another "sophist" indulging in speculation about the "so-called cosmos" (*Mem.* 1.1.11). Though he transcended the limits of gentlemanly knowledge, he did not, like the naturalists, leave behind the gentleman's interests in virtue and ordinary human, political life. Xenophon reports Socrates' demonstration that people who concern themselves (*phrontizontes*) with "the nature of all things" are foolish worriers (μωραίνοντες, μεριμνῶντες) who "think so highly of themselves [μέγιστον φρονοῦντες] that they resemble madmen in their ill-grounded convictions" (*Mem.* 1.1.11, 13–14). A person who worries [*merimnon*] about such things runs the risk of becoming utterly thoughtless [παραφρονῆσαι], like Anaxagoras, who thought highly of himself (*megiston phronēsas*) on the basis of his interpretation of the cosmological machinery of the gods (*Mem.* 4.7.6).[22] Socrates suggests two

---

[21]Geometry: "Though indeed he himself was not unfamiliar [ἄπειρος] with [the more abstruse parts of geometry]" (*Mem.* 4.7.3); astronomy: "Though indeed of [the more abstruse parts of astronomy] he himself was not uninformed [ἀνήκοος]" (*Mem.* 4.7.5). The near repetition in these two passages emphasizes the distinction between Socrates and his associates about the proper limits of knowledge.

[22]Xenophon seems in these passages to be alluding to Aristophanes' *Clouds*, where Socrates is presented as deserving the very critique Xenophon has him level against the cosmologists. Note especially the repeated use of *phrontizō* (to be concerned about, to think about) and *merimnaō* (to worry about); Aristophanes coined *merimnophrontistēs* (anx-

explanations of this impious pride of the natural philosophers (*Mem.* 1.1.12): they may believe they already understand human matters (*ta anthrōpina*) well enough, so they move on to these other matters; or they transcend human matters altogether and think they are engaging in the actions appropriate to themselves (*ta prosēkonta*) only when they investigate "daimonic" or divine matters (*ta daimonia*).

This view of which actions are "appropriate" clearly separates the naturalists from the view of self-sufficiency that Socrates promoted in his gentlemanly associates. Indeed, to a certain extent it puts the naturalists closer to Socrates than to his gentlemen friends. Like Socrates, they claim to transcend human limits by access to the divine realm, to *ta daimonia*. But their appeal from the human to the divine is an imperfect imitation of Socrates' daimonic self-sufficiency. It is an imitation because Socrates could seem every bit as arrogant and dismissive of ordinary canons of human judgment as any naturalist. As Xenophon reports, he "accused people of stupidity [μωρίαν κατηγόρει]" if they acted to avoid ill repute among human beings rather than following "the signs of the gods," while "he himself despised [ὑπερεώρα] all human matters in comparison to counsel from the gods" (*Mem.* 1.3.4).[23] But the imitation is imperfect because in another sense Socrates concerned himself with exactly those questions about political and moral life of most interest to gentlemen, questions the naturalists despised as beneath them: "He was always conversing about human matters [*ta anthrōpina*] and investigating . . . whatever he thought would make gentlemen of those who knew about them" (*Mem.* 1.1.16).[24] Xenophon presents Socrates as a kind of mean between the gentlemanly acceptance of human limitation by the divine and the sophistical rebellion against it. He shares the gentleman's interests, and so rejects the sophist's contempt for the merely human; but he transcends the

---

ious brooder) as a comic word for Socrates. Leo Strauss has pointed out Xenophon's allusions in the *Oeconomicus* to the *Clouds* in his *Xenophon's Socratic Discourse* (Ithaca, N.Y., 1970), pp. 91, 112, 159, 163–64, 166.

[23]There may be a verbal reminiscence here (indicated by italicized words) of an earlier passage: "The *accuser [katēgoros]* said that [Socrates] made his associates *despise [hyperoran]* the established laws by telling them that it was *stupid [mōros]* to choose the city's rulers by lot" (*Mem.* 1.2.9). The appeal from *ta anthrōpina* to *ta daimonia*, whether the claimed transcendence is cosmological (like that of the naturalists) or ethical (like that of Socrates), can look suspicious to a partisan of the current standards of political and moral judgment.

[24]Xenophon gives in this passage a list of seven pairs of topics central to Socrates' discussions: the pious and the impious, the noble and the base, the just and the unjust, sound-mindedness (*sōphrosynē*) and madness, courage and cowardice, the city and the politician, and rule and the ruler of human beings. The central pair, contrasting sound-mindedness and madness, seems to be especially relevant to the present passage. The madness of the naturalists' transcendence of human concerns contrasts with Socrates' sound and respectful acceptance of them.

gentleman's limits, partly because he has a wider horizon, acquired by familiarity with "theoretical" subjects that the "mere" gentleman will suspect of being sophistical, and partly because his unique mantic endowment transcends the gentleman's dependence on the divine.

Because Socrates preserves an interest in human matters even while escaping the limits of human matters, he can have his virtue and transcend it too. His approach to divine needlessness is unimpeded by his attachment to humanity. The naturalists, on the other hand, do not have Socrates' daimonion. Their self-sufficiency is blocked when it comes to the pressing human concerns embedded in moral and political life. In this respect they are no better off, no more divine, than the humble gentlemen. They suffer, however, from a transcendental illusion: instead of humbly accepting the dependence of their happiness on divination about human matters, they contemptuously reject the importance of human matters altogether. Socrates playfully suggests that perhaps the naturalists fantasize that their knowledge of divine things will enable them to control the winds and rains and seasons, the way knowledge of human matters can be used for benefit. But in the end it seems that the naturalists' contempt is based on the claim that knowledge (*gnōsis*) of the divine order is sufficient in itself for their happiness (*Mem.* 1.1.15). Socrates denies both that such knowledge is available and that if it were, it would be enough. Knowledge, no matter how daimonic, how transcendent, must serve our most pressing interest in human virtue, human vice, and political rule. In light of this difference, the naturalists' appropriation of divine transcendence makes them more akin to Aristippus and Aristodemus than to Socrates. Like Aristippus, they unjustly separate themselves from the political and ethical concerns of the conventional gentleman. Like Aristodemus, they impiously lay claim to access to or control over what rightfully belongs to the divine alone. Only Socrates, with the peculiar "ethical" transcendence afforded by his daimonion, can lay claim to self-sufficient control over his happiness while preserving his piety and justice.

5. Antiphon and Euthydemus: Self-Sufficiency and the Erotic

Antiphon was a sophist who, reports Xenophon, once tried to attract away Socrates' associates. He criticized Socrates' own happiness and his effect on his associates and imitators on three related grounds: (1) Socrates' way of life is mired in abject poverty, primarily because Socrates obtains no money from his associates (*Mem.* 1.6.2–3); (2) since

Socrates accepts no money for his intercourse (συνουσία) with his associates, he must know nothing of any real value (*Mem.* 1.6.11–12); and (3) even if Socrates did understand political affairs, he would not be able to make others adept at politics, since he does not himself engage in politics (*Mem.* 1.6.15). Socrates' response to Antiphon's attack brings into play all three aspects of his self-sufficiency on which we have focused: his asceticism (in contrast to Alcibiades' tyrannical ambition), his political orientation (in contrast to the counterfeit transcendence of human political concerns by Aristippus and the naturalists), and his mantic divinity (in contrast to Aristodemus' practical atheism and the pious limitation of his gentlemanly associates). But because Antiphon's challenge focuses directly on the attachment between Socrates and his associates, Socrates is forced in this passage to justify his ascetic, political, and mantic aspirations in light of some account of the nature and benefits of his relationships. Xenophon has him do this by emphasizing their erotic character. In the end, the special pleasures of Socrates' eroticism explain his ascetic refusal of money, his interest in politics despite his avoidance of political engagement, and the attractiveness of his mantic divinity.

Socrates' refusal (or is it inability?) to get money from his way of life is the point that most directly inspires Antiphon to doubt Socrates' happiness. After ridiculing Socrates for the cheap quality of his food, drink, and clothing, Antiphon goes on to say, "You also get no money, which is enjoyable to receive, and which makes those who possess it live in greater financial independence [ἐλευθεριώτερον] and more pleasantly" (*Mem.* 1.6.3). Furthermore, Antiphon argues that Socrates' refusal to take money for letting people have intercourse (*sunousia*) with him makes sense only because Socrates knows nothing of any value (*Mem.* 1.6.12). How can a man who lives in wretched poverty, and who does not have enough confidence in the value of what he teaches to charge a fee for it, be a worthy object of imitation to his associates? As Socrates says, "You seem to me, Antiphon, to think I live so wretchedly that I am persuaded you would choose to die rather than to live as I do" (*Mem.* 1.6.4). This is exactly the sentiment that Xenophon ascribes to the licentious Critias and Alcibiades: "I believe that if a god had granted them the choice between living as they saw Socrates live or being dead, they would rather choose to be dead" (*Mem.* 1.2.16). Antiphon shares with Alcibiades' tyrannical appropriation of Socratic self-sufficiency a blindness to any pleasures or benefits beyond the crassly political ones of wealth and power. Like Plato's Callicles, Antiphon can see nothing but a despicable slavishness in Socrates' asceticism (see *Mem.* 1.6.2). What are the pleasures that Socrates' ascetic life can set against the claims of Antiphon and Alcibiades?

Socrates' response to this attack culminates in his claim to approximate the self-sufficiency of the divine: "You seem to think, Antiphon, that happiness is luxury and extravagance. But I believe that to need nothing is divine, and to need as little as possible is closest to the divine; and as the divine is best, what is closest to the divine is closest to the best" (*Mem.* 1.6.10). Socrates supports this claim in two quite different ways. Part of his defense seems exclusively concerned with his own *personal* pleasures (*Mem.* 1.6.5–8). He argues first that his self-control, far from denying him pleasures that luxurious indulgence would provide, actually heightens his enjoyment of material pleasures (food, drink, clothing, shoes), since overindulgence has not desensitized him to them. Furthermore, Socrates argues that training in endurance has made him capable of obtaining pleasures superior to these material pleasures, especially the psychic pleasures of successful action: "People who think they are not acting successfully have no enjoyment, while people who believe they are advancing themselves, whether in farming or shipping or in something else they are trying to accomplish, have enjoyment because they think they are acting successfully" (*Mem.* 1.6.8). With both material and psychic pleasures, Socrates' self-control proves a personal boon.

On its own, this defense of the divine needlessness of Socratic self-sufficiency makes Socrates look rather snobbish and narcissistic.[25] But his defense of his ascetic refusal to take money shows that this approximation to divine self-sufficiency also depends directly on the nature of his relationships.[26] The pleasures of successful action to which he makes claim come in and through his peculiarly erotic relationships. Socrates begins by pointing out that teachers who take payment from students are obligated to have intercourse with whoever pays the fee,

[25]As he looks to Gregory Vlastos and Martha Nussbaum. Vlastos (above, note 3), pp. 176–77, attributed this to the "egocentricity that is endemic in Socratic eudaimonism, as in all eudaimonism," and argued that this selfishness was mitigated only by Socrates' independent belief in our duty to serve a benevolent god, whose service required general benevolence from humans. This appeal to an externally motivated interest in others is another symptom of the unerotic character of Vlastos' Socrates (see also note 3 above). Nussbaum's view is more interesting, since she takes the tension between Socrates' self-sufficiency and his eroticism to be central to our understanding of him (see "The Speech of Alcibiades: A Reading of the *Symposium*," in *The Fragility of Goodness* [Cambridge, 1986], esp. pp. 197–99; and her recent review of Vlastos: "The Chill of Virtue," *New Republic* 205:12–13 [16 and 23 September 1991]: 34–40). Her claim that Socrates' self-sufficiency (as portrayed in Plato's *Symposium*) makes him incapable of being a lover (though not a beloved) of individual human beings disagrees with Xenophon's account of how erotic relationships permit and even empower the other aspects of Socrates' self-sufficiency; but a discussion of these points is beyond the scope of this essay.

[26]When Socrates explains to Hermogenes his refusal to prepare a defense speech, his description of the happiness of his life combines these same two elements of personal accomplishment and relationship to friends (*Mem.* 4.8.6–7).

while he preserves his freedom (*eleutheria*) to converse with whomever he wants (*Mem.* 1.6.5; see also 1.3.5). The importance of this independence in the choice of companions is clarified when Socrates goes on to contrast explicitly the erotic character of his own relationships with the mercenary nature of the relationships of sophists, "prostituters of wisdom" (*Mem.* 1.6.13). The erotic attachment that Socrates aims at between himself and his associates is inconsistent with the sophist/client relationship. Because his relationships are erotic rather than sophistical, Socrates preserves a kind of self-sufficiency that distinguishes a well-bred lover from a prostitute, deeper than the mere financial independence so prized by Antiphon. Far from being the oppression by grinding poverty that Antiphon takes it to be, Socrates' asceticism is the necessary condition for his erotic freedom from entanglement in mercenary relationships. Free love is more important than hard cash for approximating divinity.

Socrates replaces, then, the crass political pleasures of Antiphon and Alcibiades with the more precious enjoyment of erotic friendship. His eroticism justifies his asceticism. But Socrates' turn to love does not replace the public pursuit of political pleasures with a private pursuit of erotic pleasures, devoid of political relevance;[27] this would be simply to repeat the mistaken aspiration to transcend politics that Xenophon exposes in Aristippus and the naturalists. Socrates claims that he "takes care to make as many people as he can capable of acting in political affairs" (*Mem.* 1.6.15). This is possible because his greatest erotic satisfactions require not only his personal advancement in successful action but also the improvement of his friends: "There is no greater pleasure from [success in any activity] than to think that one is becoming better oneself and obtaining friends who are better" (*Mem.* 1.6.9; see also 1.2.7–8). Socrates focuses his erotic pleasure in improving his friends on exactly that gentlemanly excellence (*kalokagathia*) that he promoted in his associates' self-sufficiency: "We believe that a man who notices someone else's good natural endowments and tries to make that person his friend by teaching him whatever good he can is doing exactly what is appropriate for a gentlemanly citizen" (*Mem.* 1.6.13–14). In other words, Socrates' erotic pleasures are politically responsible. They require the cultivation in his associates of just those virtues that make human beings adept at taking care of their city.

---

[27]As Callicles charges in Plato's *Gorgias* 485d3–e2: "A human being [who pursues philosophy throughout his life] . . . becomes unmanned; he flees from the city's center and the marketplace, where the poet says men win distinction, and slinks away to live his whole life in some corner, whispering with three or four boys, never uttering anything free or great or powerful."

It is helpful to recall here the difference between Socrates' political interest and Aristippus' political alienation. Besides being a hedonist and a flatterer of tyrants, Aristippus was the first of Socrates' associates to charge for his intercourse. We earlier saw how Xenophon shows Aristippus' preference for alienation to involve a false sense of self-sufficient independence from the demands of political life. We can now see that his political indifference fits well with unerotic, mercenary relationships. Without the erotic interest in his associates' improvement that drives Socrates' relationships and makes them of political benefit, Aristippus simply caters to the tastes of his clients. His indifference to politics not only provides him with a false model of personal self-sufficiency but also shows itself in his unerotic and prostituted relationships with his associates. This politically indifferent relationship to others is the opposite pole from Alcibiades' politically obsessed relationship. Socrates' erotic (and thus ascetic) independence supports a more intimate and principled interest in his associates than either alienation or obsession can. The ascetic and the political are reconciled in the erotic.

The Antiphon passage indicates *that* Socrates' eroticism has this political importance, but it offers only a slight indication of the *how*, that is, of what Socrates' erotic and unpurchasable intercourse was like. Xenophon has Socrates describe his activity with his associates this way: "The treasures [θησαυροί] that the wise men of the past have left written in their books I open and go through in common with my friends; and if we see anything good, we pick it out, and we believe it a great profit if we prove useful to one another" (*Mem.* 1.6.14). To find out more about these "treasures" and Socrates' erotic activity, we must turn to the fourth book of the *Memorabilia,* where Xenophon gives an extended account of Socrates' "seduction" of one particularly talented youth named Euthydemus. As we will see, Xenophon here provides the third link between Socrates' self-sufficiency and his smitten imitators, by showing the essential role that the mantic plays in Socrates' erotic relationships.

Socrates "often said he was in love [ἐρᾶν] with someone, though he obviously was attracted to good natural dispositions of souls toward virtue, not of bodies toward youthful good looks" (*Mem.* 4.1.2). Xenophon enumerates Socrates' criteria of "the good natures": "easily learning what one studies, easily remembering what one has learned, and desiring to learn everything through which one governs well a household or city, or generally makes good use of human beings and human affairs [*ta anthrōpina*]." Acuity, memory, and a love of all learning concerned with governing human beings are what Socrates looks for in his erotic partners.[28] But people with these fine natural endowments fall prey to typical prejudices about themselves and their powers, so that Socrates' erotic intercourse with them consists especially in exposing their ignorance and making them receptive to improvement, especially to improvement in self-knowledge. It is the shame of discovering one's false sense of oneself, coupled with the expectation one can advance in self-knowledge through intercourse with Socrates, that Xenophon presents as the heart of Socrates' erotic attractiveness.[29]

Part of Socrates' erotic art was his ability to adapt his "seduction" of a promising youth to the particular type of prejudice by which that youth's self-knowledge was obstructed (*Mem.* 4.1.3). Xenophon discusses three typical ways that "the good natures" become conceited and overlook the deficiency of their self-knowledge. For the first two types he gives only a brief account of Socrates' approach, while to illustrate the third he relates in detail the way that Socrates won over Euthydemus.[30] The first type thinks that because of their natural endowments they can be good by nature, that is, spontaneously; such people hold learning in contempt (*Mem.* 4.1.3–4). Socrates overturned their conceit by demonstrating to them that with humans as with horses those with the most natural vigor and capacity are most thoroughly corrupted by want of training. Without direction, this greater power may simply be squandered in base and harmful actions. The second type thinks that they can accomplish whatever they want through their wealth, so that they have no further need of education (*Mem.* 4.1.5). These Socrates attacked for not realizing that without learning, their wealth is no guarantee of successful action, since they are ignorant of the beneficial and the harmful. With both types, then, Socrates' erotic intercourse undermines the naturally talented person's false sense of confidence in his capacity for successful action, a false confidence grounded in exactly those sorts of goods that in other places Socrates calls "unclear" (*adēla*). Natural vigor and spirit, access to political power, wealth: these are the very sorts of goods that, as we have seen,

[28]Compare *Republic* 485b–486d, where Socrates enumerates among the characteristics of the true *philosopher* acuity (486c), memory (486c), and a love of all learning *concerned with true being* (485b).

[29]Compare Alcibiades' drunken account of his attraction to Socrates (in Plato's *Symposium* 215d6–216c3), where Alcibiades' shame, his enchantment by Socrates, and his ignorance of himself are connected.

[30]Commenting on this section of the *Memorabilia*, Leo Strauss points out that, strictly speaking, none of the three conceited types fulfills the criteria for being a "good nature," so that Xenophon never shows Socrates conversing with someone of the highest type (*Xenophon's Socrates* [Ithaca, N.Y., 1972], p. 94). He is right that all three types Xenophon discusses have some characteristic prejudice that limits their love of all learning concerned with governing human beings well, and so to this extent they are not "good natures"; but this will not affect my argument.

can tempt human beings to deny the humbling dependence of their success and happiness on the divine. The political ambition of "the good natures" leads them to overrate their power to control their happiness in something like the way Socrates himself in his conversation with the politically indifferent Aristippus exaggerated the capacity of kingship to guarantee happiness. Socrates' erotic love for those with good natural endowments is based, from his point of view, on improving them by making them aware of this humbling dependence; and Socrates' erotic attractiveness to his associates is based, from their point of view, on the peculiar pleasure of realizing, and perhaps of mitigating, one's shameful lack of self-knowledge. These sublime erotic pleasures are the complete answer to Antiphon's challenge.

Xenophon chooses to illustrate most fully this integration of the ascetic, political, and mantic within Socrates' eroticism with the handsome young man Euthydemus, an instance of the third type of "good nature." Persons of this type are characterized by the belief that "they have obtained the best education," which leads them to "think highly of themselves on the basis of wisdom [*sophia*]." Euthydemus' conceited sense of his own wisdom depends especially on his collection of books by "poets and sophists of high repute" (*Mem.* 4.2.1). With the misplaced confidence this bookish learning has produced, Euthydemus "aspires to that virtue through which human beings become adept at politics and household management, capable of rule, and beneficial to both other human beings and themselves"; in short, he "aspires to the finest virtue and the greatest art, . . . namely, kingship" (*Mem.* 4.2.11). Out of his erotic interest in the young man, Socrates endeavors to undermine this confidence and to replace it with a fuller awareness of what sort of wisdom would really be required to fulfill these "kingly" aspirations. In the end, Euthydemus became ashamed of his pretensions to wisdom and humbly began to imitate Socrates (*Mem.* 4.2.40).

Socrates begins his seduction by complimenting Euthydemus on his collection of the books of "the so-called wise men of the past": "I admire you, since you do not choose to possess treasures [*thēsauroi*] of silver and gold over those of wisdom" (*Mem.* 4.2.8–9). Xenophon implicitly reminds us here of the Antiphon passage, where Socrates reported that his erotic intercourse with his associates involved picking out the treasures (*thēsauroi*) from the books of the wise men of the past (*Mem.* 1.6.14).[31] His further intercourse with Euthydemus shows him replacing the counterfeit treasures of poetry and sophistry, which Euthydemus could have purchased from the likes of Antiphon or Aris-

---

[31]The word *thēsauroi* (treasures) appears in the *Memorabilia* only in these two passages.

tippus, with the true and priceless treasures available only in Socrates' erotic relationships.

The most important of these erotic treasures is a concern with self-knowledge as the necessary condition for any successful action, including the "kingly" actions to which Euthydemus aspires. After he realizes his inability to answer Socrates' enquiries about which sorts of acts are just and unjust (*Mem.* 4.2.14–20), Euthydemus exclaims: "By the gods, I had always thought I was engaging in philosophy [in my study of my books], through which I believed I had been educated in the things appropriate [*ta prosēkonta*] to a man aiming at gentlemanliness [*kalokagathia*]" (*Mem.* 4.2.23). Now that he sees he has failed to learn "the things appropriate for gentlemanliness," Socrates suggests to him that his failure can be traced to his lack of self-knowledge (*Mem.* 4.2.24–29). Euthydemus, it seems, will be in no position to exercise the kingly art with any guarantee of profit until he can recognize "what is expedient for himself and what he can and cannot do" (*Mem.* 4.2.26).

Socrates goes on to convince Euthydemus of just how problematic this sort of knowledge of "the good and the bad" really is (*Mem.* 4.2.31–35). He argues that the goodness of even such apparent blessings as health, wisdom, and prosperity is disputable (ἀμφίλογον), since they can sometimes turn out to be disadvantageous. For example, health may permit someone to make an unsuccessful military campaign or sea voyage that sickness would prevent; or wisdom may make one the object of desire by a tyrant, or envy by a rival. This argument is similar to Socrates' arguments for the necessity of mantic insight: "the hidden things" (*ta adēla*)—namely, whether we will benefit from exercising or developing some human power—are beyond human discernment, and so require divine signs. Given this parallelism between the disputable (*amphilogon*) and self-knowledge, and the hidden (*adēla*) and divination, one of Socrates' examples of how wisdom can be disputable is especially striking: Palamedes being killed by Odysseus out of envy for his wisdom (*Mem.* 4.2.33). Socrates uses the same example after his trial (Xen. *Ap.* 26) to illustrate the injustice of his own conviction, in a context that emphasizes Socrates' mantic justification for courting death (see *Ap.* 4-5, 22).

This connection between Euthydemus' lack of self-knowledge and Socrates' mantic self-sufficiency is driven home by Euthydemus' reaction to discovering that all he thought unquestionably good is in fact disputable. At first he is despondent and exclaims: "I concede that I don't even know what I should pray for!" (*Mem.* 4.2.36). The mention of prayer reinforces the connection between "the disputable things," which reveal Euthydemus' ignorance, and "the hidden things," which are the objects of divination.[32] He goes away, "holding himself in contempt" for his ignorance and "believing that he is in fact slavish" (*Mem.* 4.2.39; see also 4.2.21–22). But unlike some who refused ever again to associate with Socrates after being reduced to this state, Euthydemus became deeply attached to him; and for his part, Socrates from that time "explained directly and clearly what he thought one should know and what one would be best to do" (*Mem.* 4.2.40). The first thing Xenophon shows Socrates explaining in this clear and direct way is a proper respect (*sōphrosynē*) for the divine, in a conversation that culminates (as we saw in the previous section) in a contrast between Socrates' mantic self-sufficiency and Euthydemus' and other humans' dependence on the mantic art (*Mem.* 4.3).

Euthydemus begins with a false confidence in his own wisdom and a strong ambition to master the art of kingship. He ends with a pious acceptance of human dependence on the divine and an erotic attachment to Socrates. This attachment was initiated by his shame at his own need for self-knowledge to live up to his political aspirations and maintained by his conviction that Socrates could fulfill this need. But his intercourse with Socrates reveals, to him and to us, that Socrates will not fulfill his need as he originally understood it. In the end, it seems that only Socrates' unique daimonic endowment gives him access to the sort of self-knowledge required to fulfill political aspirations like those of Euthydemus. The self-knowledge Socrates provided to his gentlemanly friends is primarily a pious acknowledgment of human limitation in the face of the divine, rather than the empowering kingly art they so coveted at the beginning of their intercourse with him. Such transmutations of political ambition into pious humility, mediated by the shame of acknowledging one's ignorance of oneself, are at the heart of Socrates' erotic attraction.

What then is this "true" Socrates, resisting every appropriation—an ascetic to tyrants, a politician to the alienated, a mantic to agnostics, a lover to them all? When we correct for the imperfections in these imitations of Socrates' self-sufficiency and triangulate back to their source, we do not solve the puzzle but only deepen the mystery. Xenophon's Socrates is erotically *attractive* to his associates because he alone has the daimonic insight that (he shames them into seeing) they need to fulfill their aspirations, whether political or not, to self-sufficiency. He is erotically *attracted* by his associated because he enjoys improving them through bringing them to acknowledge their ignorance. These

---

[32]See especially above, note 16.

[180]   *David K. O'Connor*

aspects of Socrates' self-sufficiency do not somehow add up to a teaching or doctrine, as if Socrates (like Epicurus or Epictetus, for example) could be the exemplar of a successful life to which we should all aspire, at least insofar as we are wise. We do not know how to copy him; for without his daimonic gift, the erotic tie that binds together the ascetic and the political must come undone, so that every imitation is bound to tilt toward one pole or the other. In the end, Xenophon teaches us that we learn our deepest lessons from Socrates, not simply by trying to imitate him but by acknowledging and accepting the humbling limits to our imitation, limits only the erotic self-sufficiency of Socrates could transcend, limits we see most clearly and feel most keenly when we remember him.[33]

[33]Preliminary work on this essay was supported by a Fellowship for University Teachers from the National Endowment for the Humanities in 1988–89 and by a summer grant from the University of Notre Dame's Institute for Scholarship in the Liberal Arts. Some of its ideas were first presented at the conference "The Socratic Movement" at Duke University in 1990, and I thank the other conference participants, particularly Michael Gillespie, for their comments. I also thank Alasdair MacIntyre, Alven Neiman, Patrick Powers, and especially Paul A. Vander Waerdt for their support and encouragement.

[7]

Xenophon's Socrates as Teacher

Donald R. Morrison

Plato and Xenophon, along with many of their contemporaries, were intensely interested in the moral character of Socrates. Insofar as Socrates has served, and continues to serve, in our tradition as providing a certain paradigm for a human life, we too must be interested in these questions: What kind of man was Socrates? Was he praiseworthy or not? Should he be emulated? Was he justly or unjustly condemned? These questions are not abstract enough to be, strictly speaking, philosophical questions. But, as Plato and Xenophon each surely believed, the example of Socrates can be an important test case for moral theory.

Xenophon's goal in the *Memorabilia* is to defend Socrates against the charges leveled against him at the trial.[1] In particular, Xenophon defends Socrates against the charge of corrupting the young by means of a thoroughgoing defense of his moral character generally. By showing that Socrates was beneficial to those around him, not just in one respect but in many ways, Xenophon aims to convince the reader that Socrates was beneficial to his young associates, hence that he did not corrupt them and was therefore unjustly condemned.

Both Plato's and Xenophon's testimony make clear that the most important test cases for the charge of Socrates' corruption of the young

---

[1] *Memorabilia* 1.1–2 directly treats the trial. The apologetic purpose of the rest of the work is signaled at 1.3.1 and 1.4.1.

were Alcibiades and Critias.[2] These extremely gifted and ambitious men were for a time associates of Socrates yet later went on to commit what Athenian society saw as serious evil deeds.[3] No one supposed that Socrates himself was in favor of such deeds, or exerted evil influence on these men by instilling in them the values of ambition and greed from which their later behavior sprang. Rather, the thought was either that Socrates' probing, critical spirit had a kind of nihilistic influence on the young, relaxing the hold that traditional values might have on them and thus allowing the baser human impulses to take over, or that quite apart from the question of moral influence, Socrates gave his young associates a mental training that amounted to a powerful tool or weapon that they could then use for the good or ill of the society around them. If Socrates were to hand out this weapon indiscriminately, that is without regard to the character of the recipient, Socrates himself would be a danger to society. Giving such mental training to Alcibiades would be tantamount to putting a sword in the hands of a madman.

Xenophon defends Socrates against both parts of this charge. He argues that Socrates not only encouraged positive moral values in his young associates, but took care that they learned prudence *before* learning the mechanics of rhetoric and affairs (*Mem.* 4.3.1). He also argues that Socrates was choosy about the moral character as well as the intellectual gifts of his young companions. His explicit discussion of the Alcibiades case comes in *Memorabilia* 1. But the most detailed account we possess of how Socrates conducted himself in selecting—and also

---

[2]Although Critias and Alcibiades are not mentioned in either Plato's or Xenophon's *Apology*, Xenophon indicates that they were cited by Polycrates in his speech against Socrates (*Mem.* 1.2.12). (They may be alluded to in Plato's *Apology* at 33a4–5.) I will not comment here on the complicated matter of how the details of Polycrates' arguments might be influencing Xenophon's defense. For a survey of this question, see A.-H. Chroust, *Socrates, Man and Myth* (London, 1957).

[3]Given their early intellectual curiosity and interest in the sophists, it is reasonable to suppose that both Alcibiades and Critias began to associate with Socrates while still in their teens. Their association with Socrates continued well into adulthood, however. Since Critias was only ten to fifteen years younger than Socrates, and much older than Plato and Xenophon, both authors naturally tend to treat him more as a contemporary of Socrates than as a student. (See, for example, *Mem.* 1.2.29, where Critias is criticized for trying to seduce a young member of the Socratic circle, Euthydemus.) Of course, the basic moral issue is whether Socrates' influence on his companions is beneficial or harmful, regardless of their age. His effect on his *young* associates gets special attention from Xenophon for two reasons. First, they are more impressionable, and consequently Socrates specially seeks them out. Second, the charge at the trial is that he corrupts the *young*. The word for "young" in the charge is νέοι, which is broad enough in meaning that it can be used (or, at least, allowably stretched—see *Mem.* 1.2.35) to cover men as old as thirty. Perhaps this word was chosen deliberately by the accusers to leave no doubt that Critias and Alcibiades and Charmides are included.

intellectually seducing—his young associates is given to us in *Memorabilia* 4.2.1ff., the story of Euthydemus. The subtle and complex structure of this account puts the lie to anyone who would claim that Xenophon was too dull to understand Socrates.[4]

1. The Stages of Socratic Education

Why did Xenophon choose Euthydemus as his example of how Socrates selected and educated his associates step-by-step? The answer to this question affects our view of how widely we can generalize from his example, for Xenophon tells us that Socrates adopted different strategies, depending on the soul of the interlocutor (*Mem.* 4.1.3). Important evidence that will help us to answer this question is given in the first chapter of book 4, in which Xenophon sets the stage for the story of Euthydemus which follows.

In the opening line of the book, Xenophon asserts that nothing was more beneficial (ὠφέλιμον) than to be with Socrates and spend time with him, no matter what the circumstances or where. But Socrates, Xenophon implies, did not desire to spend time with just anyone. He would often say: "I love so-and-so," but the people he desired were not the ones with beautiful bodies, but rather those with souls well disposed toward virtue. He used three traits as signs of such souls: (1) the ability to learn quickly; (2) the ability to remember what has been learned; and (3) a desire for every kind of knowledge by which they could manage the household and the city, and could deal comfortably with men and their affairs. Notice that the first two traits differ from the third in being less amenable to education. Although the abilities to learn and to remember can be developed, they are basically a natural gift. Determining whether a young person has either of these traits will therefore be relatively easy. The desire for knowledge, however, is something that can be awakened in a person who originally lacks it. Here, too, the person's nature matters: even after education, the strength and durability of the desire for knowledge varies from soul to soul; and some sluggish souls will resist every effort to arouse in them a desire for knowledge.

Xenophon goes on to tell us that Socrates did not approach everybody in the same way. He illustrates this by describing Socrates' different approach to each of three types: (1) those who thought that nature

<hr/>

[4]See H. R. Breitenbach, *Xenophon von Athen* (Stuttgart, 1966), col. 1825; O. Gigon, "Antike Erzählungen über die Berufung zur Philosophie," *MH* 3 (1946): 10.

had made them good, and therefore scorned his teaching;[5] (2) those
who considered that wealth would make them good; and (3) those who
believed that they had the finest education and were conceited because
of their wisdom. Socrates approaches Euthydemus as an illustration of
the third type.

The relationship between these personality types and the "marks of
lovability" is important. Presumably, all the young men whom Socrates
approached were ones he was interested in—else why approach them?
Thus we may assume that Socrates believed that the young men had at
least the potential to be objects of his love. This implies that he had
reason to think that these young men had the two "easily discoverable"
marks of lovability: the ability to learn quickly and the ability to retain
what has been learned. If Socrates were to discover that a young man
lacked these abilities, he would lose interest and leave off his approach.
What about the third mark—a desire for every kind of knowledge useful for the conduct of life? Neither of the first two personality types has
that trait! Neither those who think that they are by nature good, nor
those who think that wealth is sufficient, desire knowledge. Socrates'
approach to these two types is designed to provoke in them a desire for
knowledge. His strategy is to show them, via argument, that neither native talent (in the first case) nor wealth (in the second) is sufficient for
a successful life. Depending on whether these arguments succeed in
awakening a durable desire for knowledge in the person or not, Socrates will either come to "love" the person, or else lose interest.

By contrast, those of the third type already have the desire for every
kind of knowledge when Socrates meets them. (The problem with this
group is not that they do not desire knowledge, but that they mistakenly think that they already have the knowledge they desire!) This
group has a special attraction for Socrates. Members of the other two
groups might become lovable if a desire for knowledge can be awakened in them; but Socrates will find members of the third group lovable from the start. Euthydemus belongs to this third group. Perhaps
the reason Xenophon chose Euthydemus to illustrate Socrates' approach is that Socrates found Euthydemus especially lovable, and therefore an especially promising prospect.[6]

Given that Euthydemus is introduced as representing only one of
three personality types, how widely can we generalize from his example? To answer this question I must anticipate a little. According to the
interpretation that follows, the process by which Euthydemus becomes a

[5]Xenophon's remarks at *Memorabilia* 1.2.24 suggest that he would put Alcibiades in
the first group.

[6]On the attractiveness of Euthydemus and on Socrates' effort to protect him from un-
wholesome suitors, see *Mem.* 1.2.29–30.

close associate of Socrates has seven stages. Stages 1-3 constitute the initial approach, stage 4 is the crucial elenchus, stages 5 and 6 are further testing, and at stage 7 Euthydemus is accepted as a close associate of Socrates. When Xenophon presents Socrates' "approach" to the first two personality types (*Mem.* 4.1.3–5), what he provides corresponds to stage 4. We may assume that for these people, too, there would be preliminary stages analogous to stages 1-3 in the Euthydemus story. Since individual personalities differ, the content or these stages is likely to differ considerably from person to person. Stages 5 and 6 in the Euthydemus story are evidence that Socrates cares about the strength and durability of the desire for knowledge, and not merely its minimal presence. Since his reasons for caring about these traits apply equally to everyone, we are entitled to infer that he would put everyone through the testing stages (5 and 6). Furthermore, although the duration may vary, the basic character of these stages will be the same for all.

2. The Testing of Euthydemus

Socrates hears that Euthydemus "the beautiful," although very young, has acquired a large collection of the writings of the poets and the wise. He prides himself on being wiser than others of his age, and he is ambitious. Now such a young man is just the sort to interest Socrates:[7] beautiful, intelligent, ambitious, and with a demonstrated serious interest in acquiring wisdom. One may suppose that this same description at one time applied to Alcibiades.[8]

Socrates seeks the young man out. With some other young companions he goes to a leatherworker's shop that Euthydemus is known to

---

[7]Leo Strauss claims that Euthydemus is not a "good nature" on the grounds that Euthydemus thought he knew it all and that his earlier desire for learning had been "perverse" (*Xenophon's Socrates* [Ithaca, N.Y., 1972], pp. 94, 100). Against this, I would argue that Euthydemus' mistaken opinions are typical of what a young, untutored "good nature" might naturally fall into on his own, prior to encountering Socrates.

[8]Parallels between Socrates' discussion with Euthydemus in *Memorabilia* 4.2 and his discussion with Alcibiades in Aeschines' *Alcibiades* are detailed in H. Dittmar, *Aischines von Sphettos: Studien zur Literaturgeschichte der Sokratiker, Untersuchungen und Fragmente*, Philologische Untersuchungen 21 (Berlin, 1912), pp. 125–28. However, Dittmar's claim that these parallels prove that Xenophon borrowed much of this material from Aeschines is exaggerated. For example, Dittmar notes that the level of emotional excitement in the *Alcibiades* continues to rise, whereas in Xenophon it levels off and stays even. "This proves," says Dittmar, "that Xenophon inherited his motif rather than invented it." It proves no such thing: as Dittmar himself notes, the difference in the development of the two tales results from the difference in the character of the interlocutors.

The report in Diogenes Laertius 2.48 of Xenophon's first encounter with Socrates suggests that Xenophon may have modeled the Euthydemus story, at least in part, on his own youthful experience. (Alternatively, of course, it may be Diogenes or his source who models his account on the Euthydemus story.)

frequent. But Socrates' approach is subtle. He does not address Euthydemus directly, but instead addresses to another young man words intended to move Euthydemus. What he says—to this other young man—is that since teachers are needed for the lesser arts, surely skill in the greatest of the arts, that of governing a city, does not come automatically to men. This initial "softening up" is stage 1.

Stage 2 of the process by which Euthydemus becomes a closer associate of Socrates happens sometime later. Euthydemus is present, but hangs back from the group and is careful not to give the appearance that he is impressed with Socrates' wisdom. This time Socrates mentions Euthydemus by name, though he still does not address him directly. I suppose, he says, that when Euthydemus is grown and offers advice to the assembly, he will begin his speech by bragging that he has never learned anything from anyone. He has never had a teacher, has in fact completely avoided learning anything from anyone; yet he will give the assembly whatever advice happens to fall into his head. At this, everyone present laughs. Euthydemus has been made fun of; he has been "stung"; from now on, Xenophon tells us, Socrates has Euthydemus' attention. But note Socrates' timing. If he had made fun of Euthydemus in this way on their first meeting, quite likely the boy would have been put off and would have avoided Socrates from them on.

Socrates now has Euthydemus' attention. But Euthydemus will not answer Socrates. He remains reluctant to say anything, thinking that he will appear more prudent by keeping silent. Further public teasing might drive the boy away. So at stage 3 Socrates reverts to his previous technique, making general comments about how it is important for aspiring politicians to find eminent teachers and to study long and hard. But at this stage it will be clear to Euthydemus that Socrates' remarks are meant to apply to him. Xenophon implies that this stage continued for some time, though how long he does not say.

When Socrates notices that Euthydemus is more inclined to endure his conversation, and more eager to listen, he moves on to stage 4. Socrates has it in mind to refute the young man for the first time: to bring him, by means of elenchus, face-to-face with his own ignorance. But Euthydemus is proud, and his sensibilities are tender. To save him public embarrassment, and thus make the refutation easier for him to accept, Socrates goes along to the leatherworker's shop and talks with Euthydemus privately. At first he flatters Euthydemus by praising his collection of books and his evident desire for wisdom. Xenophon says: "And Euthydemus was pleased to hear this, for he thought that Socrates believed he was heading in the right direction toward wisdom. Socrates, well aware that Euthydemus was pleased with this praise" (*Mem.* 4.2.9), then begins his elenchus.

The elenchus is of the classic type familiar from Plato. Socrates establishes that Euthydemus seeks the noblest and greatest art, the art of ruling, and that one who has the art of ruling necessarily also has the virtue of justice. Euthydemus claims to be as just as any man. But justice has its product, just like any other craft. It is characteristic of craftsmen that they can discriminate the objects of their craft from other things. (Here the refutation is logically more powerful than those we are familiar with from Plato, because it depends on a weaker assumption. It is not claimed that craftsmen can explain their craft [*Ap.* 22b–d; cf. *Grg.* 465a, 501a]—a doubtful requirement—but merely that they can discriminate products of their craft from other things, which is surely an appropriate minimal condition of craftsmanship.) Socrates makes two columns, one for the just and the other for the unjust acts, and proceeds to demonstrate that Euthydemus does not know under which column various kinds of act should be classed. Lying, enslaving, doing mischief—all of these seem to Euthydemus to be unjust, but Socrates leads him to acknowledge that under certain circumstances they are also just.

Socrates brings the refutation home in language also familiar from Plato:[9] "Now then, if someone wants to tell the truth but never says the same things about the same things; if when he shows you the road, he tells you first that it runs east, then that it runs west, and when he makes a single calculation produces first a larger result and then a smaller one; what would you think of such a person?" Euthydemus: "Clearly, by god, that he does not know what he thought he knew" (*Mem.* 4.2.21). Euthydemus admits that such ignorance is slavish, and that one must make every effort to avoid being a slave.

But Euthydemus is in aporia: "Socrates, how discouraged do you think I am, knowing that in spite of my pains I am not able to answer a question about the things it is most necessary to know, and have no other way through which I might improve?" (4.2.23) We have reached stage 5, which is the turning point. Euthydemus recognizes his ignorance and the inadequacy of his previous method of searching for wisdom. But he is helpless; he has no other method. To break out of this state of blockage and discouragement, he is dependent on Socrates' help and guidance. Socrates responds to Euthydemus' plea with a speech in praise of the Delphic maxim "Know thyself." That is *not* what Euthydemus needs.[10] "Have no doubt, Socrates," he says, "that I

---

[9]Cf. *Euthphr.* 15b; *Lysis* 222d; *Chrm.* 174b; *Prt.* 361b.

[10]Dittmar (above, note 8), p. 125, gives the speech a more positive function: "This passage is a resting place for Euthydemus, gives him something positive, restores him [*baut auf*]." Dittmar's interpretation and mine are compatible, in a way that enhances the subtlety of Socrates' approach. The speech both encourages Euthydemus, through a con-

value self-knowledge very highly. But where should one begin the process of examining oneself?" This is what I look to you for, if you are willing to tell me" (4.2.30).

Socrates responds to Euthydemus' plea for guidance with another elenchus, demonstrating that Euthydemus does not know what things are good and bad (4.2.31–36), and that he doesn't know what democracy is (4.2.36–39). That is, Socrates refuses to give Euthydemus the guidance he asks for. The process until now has been one of Socrates seducing Euthydemus, which has required careful handling and some kindness. At this stage, however, Socrates wishes to test Euthydemus, and that requires toughness. No guidance, no encouragement, just refutation and aporia.

Stages 4 and 5 show that Xenophon considers subjecting people to the elenchus to be an essential part of the Socratic method. In this he agrees with Plato, even if he does not put as much literary emphasis on it as Plato does. In Xenophon, the function of the elenchus is twofold: (1) to awaken a desire for wisdom, for every kind of knowledge relevant to the conduct of life; and (2) to test the strength and durability of this desire, by seeing if it withstands the frustration of repeated and unmitigated elenchus. Here, too, Xenophon's view is compatible with Plato's.

Now that Socrates has refuted him again and again, Euthydemus leaves completely discouraged, despising himself and thinking that he truly is a slave (4.2.39). Xenophon's next words indicate that what Euthydemus is going through is nothing unusual, but is part of Socrates' regular procedure: "Many of those put into this condition by Socrates never came near him again, and he thought these people to be blockheads."

But Euthydemus understood—without being expressly told!—that he would not become worthy of repute (ἀξιόλογος) unless he spent as much time with Socrates as possible. This is stage 6. Euthydemus hangs out with Socrates as much as he can, and even begins to imitate some of Socrates' practices—that is, his life-style, habits, and character.

Presumably this stage lasted a good while. Here, as elsewhere in the *Memorabilia*, Xenophon compresses time for the sake of economy of presentation. When Socrates eventually recognizes that Euthydemus really does have the right sort of character, Socrates changes his behavior once more. No more savagery, no more throwing him into the sea

---

structive protreptic, and frustrates him, by refusing to give him what he asked for. Dittmar errs only in calling the speech a resting place. By frustrating Euthydemus, Socrates intentionally keeps up the pressure.

of aporia without a lifeline. Here at stage 7, Euthydemus is a confirmed and close associate of Socrates.

In stages 1 through 6 Xenophon describes a process, not only of seduction, but of rigorous selection. The rigor of the process is important to Xenophon as a means of defending Socrates against the charge of handing out intellectual tools indiscriminately to those who will misuse them. Xenophon wishes to show that Socrates was careful to admit into his inner circle only those whose habits and moral values—including but not limited to a commitment to the examined life and the search for wisdom—are similar to his own. One question that arises, but Xenophon does not address in book 4, is, How successful was Socrates' procedure in ensuring him the right sort of companions? This question may be divided into two others: (1) How successful is the procedure in weeding out pretenders—those who seem to have the right values but do not? (2) How successful is the procedure in weeding out unstable characters—those who, having reached stage 7, might later fall out of sympathy with Socrates and go on to commit evil deeds?

These questions bring us back to the cases of Critias and Alcibiades. These men were well known to have consorted with Socrates, yet they turned out bad. Xenophon has three alternatives for explaining these cases. He could claim either (1) that Critias and Alcibiades never progressed beyond stage 6, which involved spending a lot of time with Socrates, but without intimacy, or (2) that Critias and Alcibiades reached stage 7 through subterfuge, pretending to be in sympathy with Socrates when they were not, or (3) that Critias and Alcibiades reached stage 7 fairly and were admitted to intimacy with Socrates, but their characters were unstable, so that they fell away again. For Xenophon's apologetic purpose, the most satisfactory explanation of Critias and Alcibiades would the first, that they never really *belonged* to Socrates' circle at all. However, Xenophon does not go that route.[11] In *Memorabilia* 1.2.12–24 he admits that Socrates included Critias and Alcibiades among his companions. Xenophon's explanation is the third, that Critias and Alcibiades met Socrates' standards for admission to stage 7, but that their characters were unstable, so they fell away again.

According to Xenophon's portrayal, when Critias and Alcibiades first met Socrates they are like Euthydemus in two ways, being talented and ambitious. But whereas Euthydemus wants the whole of wisdom, the ambitions of Critias and Alcibiades are narrower: they want honor, power, and prominence. Euthydemus mistakenly thinks he has the wisdom he wants; by contrast, Critias and Alcibiades recognize that Socrates has something they lack but believe they need: namely, debating

---

[11]Pace Chroust (above, note 2), p. 179.

skills. Thus, whereas shy Euthydemus needed seducing, Critias and Alcibiades—clearly more forceful characters—probably did not. Xenophon stresses that Critias' and Alcibiades' values were at the outset hostile to Socrates. Their attitude was: rather than live the simple independent life of Socrates, I would prefer to die (*Mem.* 1.2.16). But under Socrates' influence, their attitudes and behavior changed. Xenophon claims that so long as Critias and Alcibiades were with Socrates, they acted temperately, not because they were afraid of being penalized or beaten by Socrates, but because, at the time, they thought that this sort of conduct was best (1.2.18). In *Memorabilia* 1.2 this is stated as an isolated fact; but from the Euthydemus story we can infer its significance. Before Critias and Alcibiades could become regular companions of Socrates, their attitudes and behavior would have to have changed. Stages 5 and 6 of the process are designed to ensure just that.

On the other hand, according to Xenophon the Socratic transformation of Critias' and Alcibiades' characters was not complete. Underneath their virtuous actions and beliefs, their political ambitions and base desires remained. So long as Critias and Alcibiades stayed with Socrates, they were able, with his help, to master these desires (1.2.24). But when they left him, they fell into bad company, and the baser side of their natures reemerged.[12]

What are the lessons of this story? Xenophon's express purpose in this section of the *Memorabilia* is to argue that Socrates did not corrupt Critias and Alcibiades, but on the contrary was a good influence so long as they were with him. Moreover, putting this story together with the story of Euthydemus, we can see that Socrates exercised due diligence, taking on as companions only those who came to share his values and life-style. But the story of Critias and Alcibiades supplements the Euthydemus story by showing that this process, however diligent, is fallible. Critias and Alcibiades came to Socrates, met his tests, and learned reasoning and dialectical skills from him, as well as temperance. Later when they parted from Socrates their temperance left them; but the reasoning and dialectical skills they learned from him presumably remained, to be put to evil ends (cf. *Mem.* 4.3.1).

---

[12]Xenophon was no intellectualist. His explanation requires that Alcibiades could believe that temperance is best, while having contrary (though repressed) desires (ἐπιθυμίαι). Thus Xenophon, unlike the Socrates of Plato's early dialogues, believes that beliefs and desires can conflict. Although Xenophon does not make the connection explicit, presumably he can use this belief to explain how, in cases like those of Critias and Alcibiades, virtuous habits can be lost. Under changed circumstances, the suppressed part emerges to cause trouble. As explained by Xenophon, Alcibiades' case resembles that of an adolescent guardian in Plato's *Republic* who wanders off while on patrol, meets up with some barbarians, and is seduced by the glory and excitement of their way of life into staying with them forever (compare *Rep.* 538–39 and *Tht.* 150e).

Once Euthydemus reached stage 7, Xenophon says that Socrates "avoided disturbing or confusing him but rather explained most simply and clearly the things he thought it most necessary to know and best to practice" (4.2.40). With these words those inclined to think that Xenophon is a bore, and that he passed on this quality to his character Socrates, might think their suspicions confirmed. Xenophon's Socrates reveals a certain roughness and irony in relation to those who are not his close companions—such as the professional sophists and young men whom he wants to impress—but to his close companions he reveals his true self, namely a fatuous giver of conventional moral advice. However, this reaction would be a mistake. Clearly Xenophon's Socrates does give advice. But it is not entirely, or even mainly, conventional moral advice. What Xenophon's Socrates gives, in passage after passage throughout the *Memorabilia* and elsewhere, is Socratic moral advice: with all the emphasis on care of the soul and disdain for material well-being that one has learned to expect from Plato's Socrates. Moreover, Xenophon's Socrates is quite willing to back up earnest, avuncular advice with biting cross-examination, as in his discussion between Xenophon and Critoboulus at *Memorabilia* 1.3.8–13.

3. Socratic Moral Advice

Furthermore, Plato's Socrates must also give moral advice to his students. (By "giving moral advice" I mean "asserting to someone that they ought to do [or not do or aim for or avoid] something.") Notice that I do not say: Plato also shows Socrates giving moral advice to his students. Plato does not show Socrates giving moral advice to his students. This has given some scholars the impression that Plato's Socrates is not the sort of person to give moral advice.[13] But that is a wrong conclusion, because—as we'll see in a moment—the character of Plato's Socrates will lead him to give moral advice, in certain situations. Why did Plato choose not to depict these situations in his dialogues? Maybe because he thought that Socrates' advice giving was not a very important aspect of his character. If so, Plato was wrong about this, and Xenophon right. More likely is the hypothesis that Plato wished deliberately to downplay this side of Socrates' character. One reasonable motive Plato might have had for suppressing scenes of Socratic advice giving is that they might leave the (in Plato's eyes, mistaken) impression that Socrates was a teacher. In any case, Xenophon's Socrates is, on this point, both more true to life than Plato's and more complete.

[13]See most recently A. Nehamas, "Meno's Paradox and Socrates as a Teacher," *OSAP* 3 (1985): 1–30.

To see that Plato's Socrates is the sort of person to give moral advice, consider the *Crito*. In the *Crito*, Socrates does not give moral advice, but he does give philosophical argument resolutely in favor of a particular practical decision. The only reason that his activity is not a case of giving practical advice is that the actor in question is not one of his associates, but himself.[14] Now suppose the practical situation were reversed: the person condemned and considering whether to break out of jail is Plato or Phaedo or Crito, and Socrates is party to the discussion. Would he not take hold of the discussion and lead it similarly to the way he does in the *Crito*? I cannot think of any plausible reason to deny that he would.[15] And conducting a discussion in this way, announcing: "I think Phaedo ought not to escape [or ought to, depending on the nature of the case] and here are the reasons why. Let us cross-examine them and see if they are sound" is just to give Socratic moral advice. The density of philosophical argument in the *Crito* should not mislead us. Philosophical argument is an equally essential part of the moral advice given by Xenophon's Socrates. In both Plato and Xenophon, the way that Socrates explains to his students that such-and-such a course of action is right, or that so-and-so is the correct goal to have, is by showing that this course of action or goal has the strongest arguments in its favor.[16] True, Plato's Socrates has more brilliant arguments. But his emphasis on the brilliance of the arguments should not blind us to a fact that Xenophon rightly stresses, and the evidence in Plato supports, namely that Socrates and his students con-

---

[14]Objection: another reason is that in *Crito* Socrates is not deliberating about what to do, but rather justifying to others a decision already—firmly—made. Reply: Socrates' commitment to following where the argument leads invalidates, in the case of actions not yet taken, the distinction between deliberation and justification. If Crito had managed to marshall conclusive arguments in favor of escape, then (despite the rhetoric of *Crito* 54d), Socrates would have changed his mind and fled.

[15]One reason that has been suggested to me is this: perhaps Socrates believes that giving advice is the wrong way to help, that what is needed is for his associates to find out the needful thing for themselves. But this is implausible. Socrates probably did think that merely giving people advice on what to do, without the reasons that explain why the advice is good advice, is cheap and does not do lasting good to the advisee. But Socratic advice is different: it is accompanied by argument and reasons. The *Crito* shows Socrates guiding his associates to the conclusion that Socrates should not escape. So he cannot think that his associates must be left to figure out everything by themselves. And if one of these young men were about to commit a grievous wrong, in the false belief that the action is right, would not Socrates come to his young friend's aid by convincing him of its wrongness? Remember, Socrates loves his young friends. If he is faced with a choice between seeing his young friend commit a great wrong and convincing him beforehand of its wrongness, surely Socrates' benevolence would lead him to choose the latter course.

[16]Even when Xenophon's Socrates gives straight advice, without accompanying argument, the assumption is that his advice is reasoned advice and that he has arguments to give should they be called for. For example, Socrates' famous advice to Xenophon to consult the oracle (*An.* 3.1.5) is supported by the arguments on when to consult the gods at *Memorabilia* 1.4.1–18 and 4.6.10.

stituted a community set off from the rest of the society by distinctive values. It is wholly unrealistic to suppose that such a community would have been brought into being by a Socrates whose sole dialectical activity was the fruitless search for definitions. No, despite Socrates' lack of success in searching for definitions, he thought he had convincing arguments in favor of a certain set of values. Positive moral arguments such as we find in the *Apology*,[17] *Crito*, *Phaedo*, and *Memorabilia* must have been part of Socrates' daily activity, and they are crucial to our evaluation of him as a philosopher and as a moral being.

Against this it might be objected that even if Socrates did give advice, this activity was not very important to him. According to Plato, Socrates saw it as his mission to deflate people who thought they knew so that they would be ripe for undertaking enquiry; his mission was not to advise those who were aware that they did not know. If that is so, the advice giving was probably a very marginal Socratic activity. Given his mission, it seems probable that he talked most often with, and sought out, people who would prefer to give advice rather than receive it.[18]

In view of the meager evidence, no one cay say with confidence how much time Socrates spent on which activity. But the objection seems to me psychologically improbable. Socrates had a circle of friends and admirers. He *loved* these people. How could he not desire to spend time with them, and to give them what help he was able—including advice?

The moral importance of Socrates' advice giving is part of a larger point. There is an "intellectualizing" current of Socrates interpretation which holds that what is morally important about Socrates is his *intellectual* activity, that is, dialectic. The persistently *negative* results of Socratic dialectic lead some intellectualizing interpreters to the view that Socrates' beneficial influence on those around him consists in his dialectical refutations of their views, and their consequent recognition of ignorance. The intellectualizing interpretation of Socrates is suggested by some things Plato says, and surely Plato places greater emphasis on this aspect of Socrates than Xenophon does. But it should be clear that the intellectualizing interpretation of Socrates is not Plato's own.

Plato recognizes the importance of Socrates' moral example, and of the influence his approval and disapproval has on his young associates.

---

[17]See esp. *Ap.* 30a–b, d; 36c; and 41a.

[18]Advice giving was the role of Socrates' daimonion. This might tempt someone to suggest that Socrates' daimonion "took over" the advice-giving role, so that Socrates himself never gave advice, either to himself or to others, but always "projected" that role onto the daimonion. This suggestion, however, gives the daimonion far too great a scope. Socrates' daimonion is a difficult and mysterious topic; but surely the daimonion intervened only in matters beyond human foresight, and only (or usually) negatively. The scope of appropriate advice giving in normal human affairs is much wider than this.

The evidence for this is scattered throughout the dialogues, but Alcibiades—famously—puts it best: "Socrates is the only man in the world who can make me feel ashamed" (*Symp.* 216b). Both silently, by his example, and verbally, through both ridicule *and* refutation, Socrates makes people feel ashamed.

In both Plato's and Xenophon's portrayals, Socrates induces this sense of shame not only, or even primarily, by intellectual means. Instead, as Alcibiades knew, he induced shame in his companions by means of his mastery of erotics: his ability to make himself so attractive to the young people around him that they yearned to follow his example and to earn his approval and became despondent and ashamed of themselves when they failed. His mastery of erotics is obviously an essential feature of Socrates the teacher. To this theme I shall return.

4. Socrates as Moral Educator

The portraits that Plato and Xenophon paint of Socrates are less incompatible than they might seem. Even though Plato does not actually show Socrates doing it, he does give testimony that Socrates gave a certain kind of practical advice, namely, advice about what to study and with whom. Xenophon's Socrates also showed concern with (*Mem.* 4.7) and claimed expertise in (*Ap.* 20–21) these educational matters.

At the beginning of the *Laches,* Laches praises Socrates' abilities as an adviser for the education of the young, since "he is always spending his time wherever there is a fine field of study or occupation for the young of the sort that you [Lysimachus and Milesias] are looking for" (180c). Then Nicias adds his support: Socrates has recently introduced to him a music teacher for his son, a man who not only is a skilled musician, but who "in every other respect you might wish is a worthy companion for young men of that age." In this dialogue, of course, Socrates declines to give such practical advice. It suits Plato's purpose to have him direct the discussion toward more abstract topics. But the words of Laches and Nicias testify that Socrates was regarded as a good adviser about the education of the young quite generally—not just about philosophy in the narrow sense—and that he did give such advice.

Similarly, in the *Theages* Demodocus comes to Socrates for advice about placing his son with a sophist (122a). Socrates puts him off a little, saying: "This is a most divine matter"; and he expresses wonder that Demodocus would have thought Socrates better than Demodocus himself at advising the son. But even so, and whether or not the *Theages* is actually by Plato, it does give evidence that Socrates was regarded as the sort of man one goes to for advice about the education of the young.

The beginning of the *Protagoras* reinforces this impression. The advice Socrates gives to young Hippocrates about the dangers of spending time with a sophist could come only from a man who has thought long and carefully about education. That Hippocrates would come to Socrates for an introduction to Protagoras at all suggests that Socrates not infrequently took on the middleman's role.[19]

Socratic advice about what to study and whom to study with is *practical* advice about what to *do*, not *theoretical* advice about, for instance, which moral principles to *believe in*. The two kinds of advice are importantly different. But Plato and Xenophon present Socrates as a kind of moral expert. The model of expertise for Socratic advice about moral principles is something like "older colleague" or "more advanced student." If you are one of his intimates, he will state plainly what principles he believes in, and commend them to you.[20] But the commendation is based on his assumption—rooted in extensive dialectical experience—that if you investigated the question with him for a while, you would come to see the truth of this principle for yourself. And in both Plato and Xenophon, Socrates does not want his associates to believe the principles merely on his say-so. He wants them to go through the arguments with him, proofing them at every step, so that their belief will be based on understanding, and in hopes that he might learn something new.

Some practical decisions in life hinge mainly on a question of moral principle. Thus Socrates' decision about whether or not to escape from jail hinges mainly (though not entirely) on the question of whether such an action would be just or not. Therefore, it is appropriate for Socrates in the *Crito* to direct the conversation toward a discussion of moral principles. However, not all practical decisions are of this sort. In particular, decisions concerning what to study and whom to study with are not like that. To know what a particular young person ought to study, and with whom, one needs to be, as Socrates says in the *Laches*, "an expert in the care of souls" (185d). To possess this expertise in its complete form presumably requires knowledge of important and difficult

[19]A further example in the Socratic literature occurs in Aeschines' *Aspasia*, where Callicles asks Socrates to recommend a teacher for his son, and Socrates recommends Aspasia (fr. 17 Dittmar). In Xenophon's *Oeconomicus* 3.6, Socrates recommends that Critoboulus study with Aspasia. Since Critoboulus is a middle-aged aristocrat, this incident proves what one would anyway have guessed: that Socratic advice giving, like his elenchus, is in principle available to everyone, regardless of age or social status.

[20]Socrates can also be frank about his principles to nonintimates, as, for example, in his confrontation with Callicles in the *Gorgias* and to the Athenian crowd during his defense speech. But Socrates will be *consistently* frank with intimates in a way he is not with strangers, to whom he is often ironical, evasive, and negatively dialectical instead.

moral principles—such as what the best life is for a human being, if there is such a thing. But it also requires an understanding of particulars—above all, of particular souls. The expert in the care of souls must be able to judge accurately what the condition of a particular soul is, what its strengths and weaknesses are, and where its potentialities lie. Moreover, an understanding of how various influences affect various souls is also required. In regard to the question—With whom should this young person study?—this understanding also involves the ability to judge accurately the characters of the prospective teachers.

When Socrates gives positive educational advice to young boys, he often cannot hope to bring them to see for themselves its correctness through his usual elenctic demonstration. (The negative task of showing the boy that his own ideas about his education are ill founded is, by contrast, ideally suited for elenchus.) In the first place, for psychological reasons that have become notorious since Freud, people have special difficulties obtaining an accurate view of their own characters. In the second place, the boys simply lack the experience that would enable them to understand (a point much stressed by Aristotle). Socrates' ability to give educational advice is a moral expertise, but its model is not that of "older colleague" or "more advanced student." Of the standard models of expertise in Athenian culture, the best one for this purpose is, I believe, the "trainer." A trainer's judgments about what to eat, how and when to practice, and, for example, which other trainers to seek out to learn specific skills are based on long experience as well as an understanding of certain basic principles. Because of the experiential element, the trainer cannot always justify his judgments. Sometimes he just *tells* the trainee what it would be best for him to do, and the trainee must just accept it. The trainee's acceptance need not rest on blind faith. It may be based on a *general* confidence in the trainer's expertise, which in turn is based on the extent of the trainer's experience, the reputation of the trainer's own teachers, and the trainer's own past record of success—both in practicing the art itself, perhaps, and in training others.[21] Socrates acts directly as a "trainer" in influencing the characters of his young associates.[22] In his role as educational expert, Socrates is a kind of "master trainer": he is the trainer one goes to for

---

[21]For Socrates' own list of criteria, see *Lach.* 185b–186c.

[22]For Socrates as trainer, see M. Foucault, *The Use of Pleasure: The History of Sexuality,* vol. 2 (New York, 1985), p. 1, chap. 3, pp. 72–73. Foucault wisely rejects intellectualizing interpretations of Socrates, calling the recognition that "*mathesis* alone is not sufficient; it has to be backed up by a training, an *askesis,*" . . . "one of the great Socratic lessons" (p. 72).

advice concerning which trainers to choose. In that role, Socrates must give advice that he cannot fully justify to the recipient.[23]

The difference between Xenophon's Socrates and Plato's is also mitigated by the fact that Plato's Socrates is not always as savage as he is with Gorgias, Polus, Thrasymachus, Euthyphro, and the Athenian crowd. Indeed, careful analysis will reveal significant differences in Socrates' attitude and conduct toward these people. But more important for us are the gross differences between Socrates' relative hostility toward these people—persons outside his moral community, who, he is confident, will remain outside it regardless of how the conversation goes—and his kind, gentle, and appreciative attitude toward his own associates—Glaucon and Adeimantus in the *Republic,* Crito in the *Crito,* Simmias and Cebes in the *Phaedo.* Plato and Xenophon agree in showing Socrates displaying a vastly different manner to those inside his circle, and to those firmly outside of it. Neither of these groups, however, is the most interesting for us. The group into which Euthydemus falls at the beginning of the discussion in *Memorabilia* 4 is a third, very important group: those who are *potential* intimates of Socrates. By my count, Plato shows Socrates in discussion with only four "potential intimates": Cleinias, Lysis, Menexenus, and Charmides.[24] From these four portraits we learn a little about Socrates' approach to this group, but not much. In the *Euthydemus* Socrates employs open protreptic, praising philosophy to the young Cleinias. Perhaps one reason why Plato lets him do this is that the sophists Euthydemus and Dionysidorus had already accomplished the task of elenchus.[25] Neither the *Lysis* nor the *Charmides* gives us even that much data. In the *Lysis,* Menexenus, the older and more experienced boy, gives up rather quickly in the face of refutation, and Lysis, the new boy, takes over. But Lysis undergoes no character development in the dialogue, and Socrates does not vary

[23]Thus Nehamas is wrong to argue that moral experts are worthy of obedience only if we can understand and approve of their reasons ("Socratic Intellectualism," *PBACAP* 2 [1986]: 302–3). Justified belief that certain people are moral experts can be gotten simply from observing their track record. And if these people can give us convincing reasons that they are in a position to know or adequately appreciate reasons that we ourselves are not able to know or appreciate, we may reasonably conclude that, in the areas governed by these reasons, we ought to accept their authority.

[24]Hippocrates in the *Protagoras* might be added as a fifth (see esp. *Prt.* 311b–314c). Note that the bystanders in Socratic dialogues often include "potential intimates." A full exploration of this problem would have to analyze, case by case through the dialogues, Socrates' "indirect communication"—the intended effect of his words (and of the entire discussion that he steers) upon those who are present but to whom he is not directly talking.

[25]Whether Cleinias is really a beginner is cast into doubt later in the dialogue (290c–291a), when Socrates, the narrator, admits that Cleinias had been represented as giving answers to Socrates' questions that no neophyte would be likely to give.

his approach. We learn something more about Menexenus in the dialogue named after him, when Socrates supposes that Menexenus is going in for politics, having finished with education and philosophy. Menexenus says that he will seek office "if Socrates allows and advises it." This is a curious remark, since it implies that Menexenus still considers himself one of Socrates' circle, and that Socrates' followers expected, and presumably received, such advice. But Socrates' supposition, and his sarcasm later in the dialogue, reveal that Menexenus is not now, if he ever was, regarded by Socrates as one of his associates. Finally, in the dialogue named after him, Charmides shows himself to be a charming and intrinsically promising boy, whose later turn to tyranny is implicitly explained by the strong influence of his intemperate guardian Cleinias. All in all, there is not much in Plato to compare with Xenophon's account of Socrates' conquest of Euthydemus.

5. Socrates as Master of Erotics

The grand theme of Socrates as the master of erotics, common to Plato and Xenophon, is the most important (if also very difficult) piece of evidence that Socrates took an interest in all aspects of the education of the young. The theme is significant, because unless Socrates has knowledge of erotics, his avid pursuit of talented young people is unjustified and wrong.

In Plato's *Symposium* Socrates says that erotics is the one thing he knows (177d); in the *Lysis* (211e) and in the *Theages* (128b) fundamentally the same claim recurs.[26] In Xenophon's *Symposium* Socrates presents a version of this claim that connects it directly with education.[27] Socrates says that he prides himself most on being a "procurer" at 3.10, where the word used has sexual connotation. Later, at 4.57, Socrates explains what he means. The procurer is one who can make a person attractive to his or her associates. Thus, the best procurer is one who can make a person attractive to the whole city (4.60). (Notice that Socrates the procurer, condemned to death by a popular court, was thus a failure as a procurer, namely at applying his art to himself. To suppose that this consequence was not noticed by Xenophon would be to make a serious error. Sometimes Xenophon's irony is even stronger than Plato's, because it is carried out more quietly.)

---

[26]See also the dialogue with Critoboulus on friendship, where Socrates is giving advice on the choice of friends (which includes the choice of teachers), and explicitly erotic imagery is used (*Mem.* 2.6.28–29). See also *Cyr.* 8.4.17–19 and *Mem.* 4.1.2.

[27]For Socrates' claim to educational expertise, see Xen. *Ap.* 20–21.

In what follows, Socrates ascribes to Antisthenes the trade not only of procurer, but also of go-between, a trade which he says "follows on" procuring. Being a go-between follows on procuring in the sense of perfecting it. The go-between not only makes people attractive to each other, makes them desire each other, but also is able to recognize those who are useful to each other—and, by implication, those who are not (4.64). Now procuring alone is no virtue—whether being made attractive to a particular person is a good thing or not depends on whether that person's company is beneficial. But the trade of go-between is a virtue in the strict Socratic sense. With it, as Socrates says, a person can arrange valuable friendships, not only among individuals but also between states. Moreover, the role of educational expert, the ability to know with whom a particular young person should study and associate, is but one branch of the art of the go-between.

The art of the go-between is especially useful because it can be applied reflexively: if a person has mastered the art of the go-between, he can recognize those whose company will be beneficial to him, and those to whom his company will be beneficial; and he can make himself attractive to such people. If Socrates were to possess this art, he would know which young people are suited to his company, and he would be able to attract them.

Socrates ascribes to Antisthenes the art of the go-between. Although I think he chose Antisthenes for a reason,[28] I also think that his choice was a humorous and well-bred way of describing the art upon which he prides himself.[29] Let me put it this way: unless Socrates does possess the art of the go-between, at least in educational matters, he has no business seducing the young as energetically and as selectively as he does. For if Socrates does not possess this art, then he cannot know whether or not he is harming these youngsters: some by his associating with them, others, perhaps, by driving them away. That is, unless Socrates possesses the art of the go-between, he cannot know whether he is guilty of corrupting the young. And if he does not know that, then he has no business taking the risk.

This risk should not be underestimated. In fact, the moral dangerousness of Socrates' situation in cultivating the company of bright, impressionable young men is parallel to Euthyphro's in the Platonic dialogue. Euthyphro's action in prosecuting his father is morally controversial, and its potential consequences are grave. In the dialogue, Socrates makes clear his attitude that under such circumstances one had better know what one is doing (*Euthphr.* 4e). Anyone who would run

---

[28]See also *Mem.* 3.4–4.
[29]See also *Oec.* 3.14–16.

such risks had better be sure of his expertise. Similarly, if Socrates does not know whether he is corrupting the young, he had better not run the risk of associating with them.

In the *Laches* Plato shows Socrates to be extremely aware of the moral gravity of decisions concerning education. Melesias and Lysimachus are looking for a teacher for a young man, and Socrates says to them: "Or do you think it a slight matter that you and Lysimachus have now at stake, and not that which is really your greatest possession? For I take it that according as the sons turn out well or the opposite will the whole like of their father's house be affected, depending for better or worse on their character" (185a; see also 186b). But, unfortunately, in the *Laches* Plato has Socrates disclaim the very skill that he must have if he is to defend his practice of seeking out and selecting young associates. The skill required is the art of caring for souls (185c). This enables one to know what particular things a particular young person needs to learn (*Lach.* 185e–186e). *This* art Socrates explicitly disclaims: "Now I, Lysimachus and Melesias, am the first to avow that I have had no teacher in this respect, . . . and to this moment I remain powerless to discover the art myself" (185c).[30]

Socrates, an intensely charismatic man who is fully aware of his charisma, actively cultivates the company of talented young men. If he is as ignorant of the "art of caring for souls" as he admits in the *Laches,* then he does not know whether associating with him is good for these young men or bad for them. The Socrates of the *Laches* does not know whether he is guilty of corrupting the young. And if Socrates does not know that, then he—like Euthyphro—has no business taking the risk.[31]

In the *Theaetetus,* however, Socrates claims a related ability. In the famous "midwife" passage, Socrates says about those unfortunate young men whose minds are not pregnant that "with the best will in the world I undertake the business of matchmaking; and I think I am good enough at guessing [πάνυ ἱκανῶς τοπάζω]—God willing—with whom they might profitably keep company. Many of them I have given

---

[30]To be precise, Socrates does not need the whole of this art in order to defend himself, but only enough of it to be able to make correct decisions concerning his own case. However, neither here nor elsewhere does Plato defend the view that Socrates has even this much of the art.

[31]In the *Apology,* Socrates defends himself against Meletus' charge by claiming that he does not *intentionally* corrupt the young. While this is an effective defense against Meletus, it does not help him here. If Socrates does not know whether he is corrupting the young or not, he is running an awful risk, and he ought to stop. (Of course, if Socrates is right about the ignorance of his compatriots, then they are in no better position than he is.)

away to Prodicus; and a great number also to other wise and inspired persons" (151b).

This passage confirms the other testimony from Plato and Xenophon that Socrates gave young people advice about what and with whom to study. Here Socrates does claim reliable judgment in what Xenophon's *Symposium* calls "the trade of the go-between."[32] But Socrates stops short of claiming either *knowledge* of what is best for these young men or the *art* (τέχνη) of caring for souls. What he claims is, in the language of the *Gorgias*, a certain knack: he is *good at guessing* what is good for them, God willing.[33] This raises several questions. Is guessing correctly good enough? (Compare the discussion of true belief later in the *Theaetetus*.) What are Socrates' grounds for believing that his guesses are correct? The advice Socrates gives has a decisive impact on these young mens' lives. Therefore, it is morally crucial that Socrates' confidence in his judgments be well grounded. But in the *Theaetetus*, Socrates' confidence concerning this matter is left unexplained and undefended. One suspects that the Socrates of the *Laches* would claim that the only person who is justified in being confident of his judgments about educational matters is the person who possesses the art of caring for souls.[34]

In his judgments about infertile souls, Socrates can only "guess." By contrast, for dealing with intellectually pregnant young men, Socrates

---

[32]Objection: the final sentence of this passage drips with irony. Socrates does not think that Prodicus will benefit young people, nor that these "other persons" are truly wise and inspired. Since the people Socrates is sending the young people to will not benefit them, and Socrates knows this, the claim that he engages in matchmaking is not meant straight, but only ironically. Reply: Socrates did think that learning to make distinctions, which Prodicus taught, was useful, even if Prodicus carried it to extremes. Further, the objector must decide how much to take ironically: Socrates' claim to send young people to others or only his claim that those he sends them to benefit them. If only the second claim is meant ironically, then Socrates is knowingly sending young people to those who will not benefit them, and so he is pandering, not matchmaking. Taking the first claim ironically runs afoul of all the other testimony that Socrates gave educational advice. This text and the others I cite confirm each other on this point.

For a reading of the passage as ironical, see M. F. Burnyeat, "Socratic Midwifery, Platonic Inspiration," *BICS* 24 (1977): 7–13. Burnyeat's reading works best if the verb ὀνίνημι at 151b5 is taken to mean "please" rather than "benefit." But if Socrates sends young people to those who merely please them, he is a panderer. Those who are tempted to find Vlastovian "complex irony" at work in this passage might consult my objections to this notion in "On Professor Vlastos' Xenophon," *AP* 7 (1987): 9–22 at pp. 11–14.

[33]Just how good does Socrates think his ability is? It is hard to tell precisely: πάνυ ἱκανῶς is a rare phrase in fourth-century Greek prose. Presumably it means "well enough for one's purposes, but not infallibly." Socrates' awareness of the importance of acting as a go-between is shown by the phrase "God willing" (σὺν θεῷ εἰπεῖν), which is a conventional expression used to ward off the penalties for hubris.

[34]Clearly, this passage in the *Theaetetus* raises—but does not help resolve—the notorious problem in Socratic epistemology of how one is justified in relying on particular judgments if one lacks knowledge of the matter at hand.

claims to possess a *technē*—the art of midwifery. The "highest power" of this art of his is the ability to test whether a young man's ideas are false or fertile (150c). In this passage Socrates assumes that undergoing his midwifery is beneficial to the young people who undergo it. This assumption is implied by his calling it midwifery, the true art, rather than pandering. But of course, this assumption is controversial and needs defense. The thesis, put in terms of Plato's metaphor, that Socrates' activity is midwifery rather than pandering, is precisely the point denied in more ordinary language by Socrates' accusers in their charge that he corrupts the young. In the *Theaetetus* Plato creates a rich and lovely image that rhetorically suggests Socrates' innocence: Socrates is a midwife, and how could midwifery *not* be beneficial? But in the *Theaetetus*, Plato uses this image to avoid, rather than address, that issue.

Recently C. D. C. Reeve has faced up to the problem of whether Socrates' elenctic activity could be shown not to corrupt the young, and he has admitted that he cannot find a solution.[35] He notes the remarkable fact that the question of whether the elenchus tended to corrupt the young is not much discussed by recent writers. Sensibly, he then observes that one would have to know quite a bit about the psychological effects of the elenchus in order to settle the question with authority.

Thomas Brickhouse and Nicholas Smith, on the other hand, offer a solution to the problem. They propose that Socrates can claim to know that he is not corrupting the young, on the basis of two other facts: he has been commanded by the gods to associate with the young in the way he does (Pl. *Ap.* 33c); and the god is wise, and hence infallibly beneficent.[36]

This is a good argument: if Socrates did know the premises, he would be entitled to know the conclusion that he does not corrupt the young. But does Socrates know the premises? Xenophon's Socrates provides arguments for the second premise at *Memorabilia* 1.4; while Plato's Socrates, as Brickhouse and Smith acknowledge, merely assumes it.[37] Xenophon's account lacks the story of Socrates' divine mission that Plato gives,[38] so his Socrates does not know the first premise. The Socrates of Plato's *Apology* seems utterly convinced of his divine mission. But does he know the first premise? Surely not; for, first, if all he knows is his ignorance (and he does not know anything "fine"), then

[35]C. D. C. Reeve, *Socrates in the Apology* (Indianapolis, 1989), pp. 166–69.

[36]T. Brickhouse and N. Smith, *Socrates on Trial* (Princeton, 1989), pp. 199–200. This conception of Socrates' divine mission is shared by G. Vlastos: "Piety is doing god's work to benefit human beings" (*Socrates: Ironist and Moral Philosopher* [Ithaca, N.Y., 1991], p. 176).

[37]They call it an "article of faith": Brickhouse and Smith (above, note 36), p. 120.

[38]See P. A. Vander Waerdt, "Socratic Justice and Self-Sufficiency: The Story of the Delphic Oracle in Xenophon's *Apology of Socrates*," *OSAP* 11 (1993): 1–48.

he does not know that he is carrying out the will of the god. Second, and perhaps more important, interpreting the Delphic oracle is a notoriously risky business. In order to know that his activities are approved by the god, Socrates must know not only that the oracle is the accurate expression of the god's judgment but also that he has interpreted the oracle correctly, and that he is carrying out the instructions competently and accurately. In all fairness, the interpretation of the oracle and the execution of the instructions are complicated and inherently controversial matters, which Plato's Socrates is not in a position to claim to know.[39]

Our earlier discussion has shown that the performance of the god's instructions is a more complicated matter than interpreters of Plato's Socrates have tended to realize. If we set aside the implausible view that elenchus is beneficial always and everywhere and however conducted, then Plato's Socrates faces the questions about his execution of the divine mission to which Xenophon responds with the story of Euthydemus. Is Socrates choosing the right people to refute? The right moment? Is he effectively mixing in other approaches—flattery, encouragement, sarcasm, indirect communication—so that the elenchus, when it comes, will be maximally effective? For Plato's Socrates to know that he is correctly carrying out the god's mission (and therefore benefiting his compatriots) he would need to know the answers to these questions. This is more than his profession of ignorance will allow him to claim.

6. Was Socrates a Teacher of Virtue?

Socrates' relation to Euthydemus and to the other young men around him raises the famous question of whether Socrates was a teacher of virtue. Socrates himself denied that he was a teacher of virtue—on this point both Plato and Xenophon agree.[40] But in both Plato and Xenophon, Socrates does claim to be beneficial to his compatriots.[41] And this means claiming that he can make them better persons, that is, more virtuous. How, then, can Socrates disclaim being a teacher of virtue?

Plato and Xenophon offer different answers to this question. Plato's Socrates denies that he is a teacher of virtue on the grounds that he is

---

[39]One might claim that Socrates can justify his claim properly to perform the god's instructions by appeal to the god's foresight: if Apollo had foreseen that Socrates would foul it up, he would have had the prudence not to have given him the mission in the first place. But the Delphic oracle typically gives its recipients plenty of room to go wrong.

[40]Xen. *Mem.* 1.2.3, 1.2.8; but cf. *Mem.* 1.6.13,14. See also *Mem.* 4.4.5; Pl. *Ap.* 19e, 20c.

[41]See esp. Pl. *Ap.* 31b, 36c; Xen. *Ap.* 32; *Mem.* 1.2.8; 1.4.1; 1.6.13, 14.

not a teacher (*Ap.* 19e, 20c). Xenophon's Socrates, by contrast, does claim to teach, but not virtue. Xenophon's Socrates disclaims the title of teacher of virtue, because he has not mastered the art. There are two reasons for this. First, a master craftsman can promise his customer a high-quality product of his craft. But Socrates cannot promise to make someone virtuous (*Mem.* 1.2.3). For one thing, only a few people are suited to become his students. Of course, every craftsman requires good materials. A more distinctive difficulty for the craft of moral education is that it requires the active cooperation of the "raw materials." Becoming virtuous requires continual effort and cooperation on the part of the learner.[42] Socrates can make the sort of careful tests that we see in the Euthydemus story, but he cannot guarantee the young man's stamina, or that other, less beneficial influences will not seduce him away.

Second, Socrates does not know everything there is to know about virtue. There is much he has not figured out yet. Xenophon's Socrates knows some things about virtue, and he is willing to teach his companions whatever good he can (*Mem.* 1.6.13–14; 4.7.1). But this falls short of the complete art of virtue.[43]

Plato's Socrates gives a different reason. Plato's Socrates denies that he is a teacher of virtue on the grounds that he does not teach at all (*Ap.* 19e, 20c). Does Xenophon's Socrates deny that he is a teacher? Answering this question turns out to be a little complicated. Xenophon claims at *Memorabilia* 4.7.1 that "everything it is fitting for a good man [καλὸς κἀγαθὸς ἀνήρ] to know, Socrates eagerly taught [ἐδίδασκεν], so far as he himself knew it." Strictly speaking, Xenophon's claim is compatible with Socrates' teaching nothing, if there is nothing that he knows. But rhetorically and in the context, it is clear that Xenophon means to imply that Socrates knows quite a few things that the good man needs to know, and that he taught them.

Xenophon makes this claim about Socrates. Does he show Socrates making this claim about himself? Yes, but indirectly. Socrates tells Antiphon that "we think that whoever makes a friend of one whom he recognizes as having a good nature, and teaches him what good he can, does what a good man and citizen ought" (*Mem.* 1.6.13). Since Socrates aimed at being a good man, we may safely suppose that he would apply

---

[42]See the emphasis on Socrates' companions' efforts at self-improvement at *Memorabilia* 1.2.3.

[43]In his *Alcibiades* Aeschines gives a third reason why Socrates is not a teacher of virtue, one that would prevent Socrates from being a teacher of virtue in the ordinary sense; namely, that he was able to help Alcibiades only due to a "divine dispensation" (θεία μοῖρα), that is, "because of love" (frs. 11a–c Dittmar). If Socrates really depended on something as uncertain as a divine dispensation to guarantee the suitability of his young associates to benefit from his company, then he was a dangerously reckless man.

this principle to himself. By claiming that the good man teaches his good-natured friends what good he can, Socrates is implicitly acknowledging that he himself will "teach his friends what good he can."

Xenophon's Socrates thinks that his claim to benefit those around him is based primarily on the influence of his moral example,[44] secondarily on the truth of the moral beliefs for which he argues in discussion with his students,[45] and (implicitly—this is never said in so many words) only thirdly on the training in philosophy and dialectic that he gives them. Which, if any, of these activities count as "teaching"?

In the *Memorabilia*, Xenophon's Socrates does not make explicit whether providing a moral example counts as teaching. He certainly thinks that being influenced by a moral example counts as learning: he twice quotes with approval Theognis' line "From the good you shall learn good things."[46] But it does not follow from this that providing the example counts as teaching.

The context of the claims that Socrates "teaches what good he can" makes clear that Xenophon and Xenophon's Socrates count his dialectical activity as teaching and consider the many propositions of which he convinces his interlocutors to be "knowledge taught." Scholars have recently argued that Plato's Socrates does not "teach," in part because his elenchus is based upon beliefs that the interlocutor already has, and because one cannot teach a person what they already ("in a sense") know.[47]

Xenophon was aware of this line of argument. His *Oeconomicus* resembles Plato's *Parmenides* in that another character, in this case the gentleman Ischomachus, takes over the "Socratic" role of leading the discussion, and Socrates himself has the lesser role of interlocutor. Ischomachus claims to teach (*didaskein*), not the whole of virtue, but a certain type of justice;[48] and he claims to be a teacher, with Socrates his pupil (*Oec.* 17.6). Yet Ischomachus uses the question-and-answer method, and he repeatedly draws attention to its reliance on the interlocutor's antecedent knowledge. He says to Socrates: "I believe that you

---

[44]*Mem.*1.2.3; 4.4.10.

[45]*Mem.*1.2.8; 1.2.3; 4.7.1.

[46]*Mem.*1.2.20; *Symp.* 2.5.

[47]Nehamas (above, note 13). See also Reeve (above, note 3), pp. 160–68. Reeve claims that Socrates' disclaimer of teaching applies only to the elenchus, and that Socrates denies that "*elengchein* is *didaskein*" (p. 163). But Socrates' disclaimer of teaching applies to more than the elenchus, since he claims that he never teaches the young, and his activity in their presence includes more than refutation. Among other things, it includes setting a moral example, and it includes giving advice. (Pace Reeve, the lesson to learn from Plato *Apology* 21b1–2 is simply that Socrates contradicts himself.)

[48]Note the verb of promising (ὑποδύειν), and contrast this with the denial of ὑπάρχειν at *Memorabilia* 1.2.3.

know a great deal about [farming] yourself, without being aware of the fact" (*Oec.* 15.10). Moreover, Ischomachus implies that Socrates knows beforehand as much as he, the teacher, does, about each of the subjects discussed (18.1, 3, 5). Ischomachus even suggests that Socrates' readily elicited antecedent knowledge extends so far that he is capable of teaching the subject himself![49] Socrates responds with a revealing comment: "I really wasn't aware that I understood these things; and so I have been thinking for some time whether my knowledge extends to smelting gold, playing the flute, and painting pictures. For I have never been taught these things any more than I have been taught farming; but I have watched men working at these arts, just as I have watched them farming" (*Oec.* 18.9).

In the *Meno* and the *Phaedo* the antecedent knowledge that enables one to respond correctly to certain dialectical questions was obtained in a prior, disembodied existence. In the *Oeconomicus* Xenophon points out that Plato's picture is, at best, incomplete: we acquire our implicit knowledge of many arts from ordinary experience. In some cases, we do not even need to practice the art itself: having watched skilled craftsmen at work is sufficient.

As regards farming and painting pictures, Plato's Socrates and Xenophon's Socrates may not disagree. But Xenophon's Socrates applies this analysis to the art of living, or virtue, in a way that diverges from Plato. Just as having observed skilled farmers at their work is a necessary condition for being able to correctly answer dialectical questions about farming, so correctly answering dialectical questions about virtue requires exposure to virtuous people. Plato's Socrates gives the impression that all of the knowledge required for a successful dialectical examination of virtue is innate. Xenophon's Socrates recognizes that this is not so, and that Euthydemus when he first meets Socrates is less able to answer dialectical questions about virtue than he will be after long association with Socrates, in part for other reasons, but in part because he will learn a great deal about virtue from observing Socrates.

In the quotation above, Socrates says that "no one taught him" farming. This implies that providing a model for observation does not count as teaching. Socrates' own activity of self-consciously providing a model of virtue for his young associates does not count, for him, as "teaching" them anything. (But it does count as beneficence, and as helping them to learn.) Ischomachus implies at *Oeconomicus* 17.6 that his activity of dialectically examining Socrates about farming is "teaching."[50] Though the inference from what Ischomachus says

[49]*Oec.* 18.9; cf. 15.10.
[50]Note the participle *didaskonti*.

to what Socrates would say is not uniformly valid, in this case it seems safe to say that Xenophon's Socrates, who, unlike Plato's, does claim to teach, would follow Ischomachus in claiming to teach through dialectic.

But in teaching through dialectic, what exactly is it that one teaches? The obvious answer is that one teaches the propositions that survive dialectical examination. But if the learner already knew these propositions, there is an equally obvious problem: How can you teach someone something that he or she already knows? Xenophon's Socrates says about the art of sowing: "I know it, but I had forgotten that I know it" (*Oec.* 18.10). What the dialectical teacher does is teach the pupil various propositions about the subject by reminding him of what he knows, by removing forgetfulness (λήθη). Plato's Socrates, with his theory of recollection, has a similar description of the process but declines to call it "teaching."

Is the disagreement between Plato's Socrates and Xenophon's Socrates on whether dialectic constitutes "teaching" therefore merely verbal? I do not think so. By calling dialectic teaching, Xenophon's Socrates acknowledges his superior position. Socrates is the one who is aware of what the learner has forgotten he knows; and Socrates leads the discussion. By denying that dialectic is teaching, Plato's Socrates emphasizes that the origin of the views arrived at is within the interlocutor himself; and he deflects responsibility for the outcome from himself onto the pupil. This deflection of responsibility is useful for escaping the corruption charge; but it is disingenuous. Socrates was a sufficiently skilled dialectician that he would have been able, had he wanted, to draw on other, perhaps mistaken, beliefs of his interlocutors in order to generate false and even vicious conclusions. By accepting the designation "teacher," Xenophon's Socrates—quite properly— accepts responsibility for the moral consequences of his dialectical conversations.[51]

Socrates is the patron saint of philosophy; and scholarly writing about Socrates often bears an uncomfortable resemblance to hagiography. Scholars do disagree about Socrates' life and character. But that he was a saint; that he was a hero; and that he was innocent of corrupting the young is unquestioned or treated as unquestionable. Plato and Xenophon thought that Socrates was a hero, and that he was the best man of his time. But I believe that both Plato and Xenophon had a much sharper sense of the moral dangerousness of Socrates' activity

---

[51]Behind this disagreement there may also be a political motivation. When Plato denies that Socrates was a teacher at all, he differentiates Socrates sharply from the sophists. By allowing that Socrates was a teacher, Xenophon softens the contrast but does not eliminate it.

than most modern writers do. Although they thought that Socrates was innocent of the charge of corrupting the young, they did not believe that he was *obviously* innocent. Various recent scholars have written as if it were obvious that the effect of Socratic elenchus is always beneficial. But Plato and Xenophon knew better. After all, the free philosophizing of Plato's Socrates is forbidden under the rules of Plato's *Republic* (537e–539e). In the Euthydemus story, Xenophon shows Socrates being very careful about what he says, and to whom, so as to minimize the clear danger of corruption.

Xenophon stresses more than Plato does the importance of Socrates' moral character and its influence for our overall evaluation of the man. Here Xenophon's portrayal provides an important supplement and corrective to Plato's account. Historically, what is most important about Socrates is his contribution to philosophy in the narrow sense—to the awakening of wonder, to philosophical method, and to the development of certain philosophical problems. But the historical importance of a person is for the most part independent of his moral worth. What makes Socrates morally admirable are his remarkable character and the substantive moral opinions that he held. Plato and Xenophon agree that central to Socrates' moral being is a certain kind of intellectuality: his commitment to the examined life and to the reasoned search for wisdom. But this commitment by itself is not enough. If Socrates had been just as clever a philosopher, and just as convinced of his own ignorance, but greedy, lecherous, and power-hungry, neither Xenophon nor Plato would have thought him a good man.[52]

[52]Thanks are due to David Calhoun, Michael Frede, Cynthia Freeland, Paul Vander Waerdt, Gregory Vlastos, Roslyn Weiss, Stephen White, Paul Woodruff, and Harvey Yunis for their helpful comments on earlier drafts. The Alexander von Humboldt Foundation generously supported my initial work on this essay, and a Summer Seminar on Socrates sponsored by the National Endowment for the Humanities gave me both leisure and a remarkably collegial environment in which to expand and revise it.

[8]

Friendship and Profit in Xenophon's *Oeconomicus*

John A. Stevens

The art of managing an estate, οἰκονομία, is not a subject one generally associates with Socrates. Yet Xenophon provides some clues that demonstrate why he considered the subject important: the Xenophontic Socrates twice compares the knowledge of how to rule a city to the knowledge of how to rule a single household, inasmuch as to rule a city is to rule ten thousand households (*Mem.* 3.4.12, 3.6.14, 3.9.10–11; *Oec.* 21.2), and thereby accepts the argument that one who knows the kingly art of ruling, the βασιλικὴ τέχνη, rules all things well.[1] Aristippus says that Socrates seems to identify this art with happiness (*Mem.* 2.1.17), and Socrates suggests, in response, that happiness begins with a certain sort of self-sufficiency, which is gained by ruling over one's desires (*Mem.* 2.1.18–34; 1.6.1–10).[2] This self-control is the origin of gentlemanly virtue (*Mem.* 1.2.1–2), which Socrates defines as a knowledge about human concerns, such as what is holy and what impious, what is noble and what shameful, what is just and what unjust, and so on (*Mem.* 1.1.16). Since the skilled manager of an estate must understand these things to run it well, the seemingly narrow topic of estate management inevitably raises fundamental political and ethical ques-

---

[1]Hdt. 3.80–82, 5.29; Pl. *Plt.* 258e–259c; *Prt.* 318e; *Leg.* 690a; Arist. *Pol.* 1252a1–16.
[2]It is not clear whether ἐγκράτεια, self-sufficiency, is sufficient for happiness. It is clearly the first step to happiness, because one cannot rule anything well without first ruling oneself. Yet the Xenophontic Socrates seems to leave open the possibility that ruling others is connected with and perhaps even necessary for happiness (*Mem.* 2.1.10–16).

tions, which the Xenophontic Socrates undertakes to clarify in the *Oeconomicus.*[3]

The *Oeconomicus* touches on all of these issues, because Socrates' interlocutor, Critoboulus, stands in need of instruction in (1) the ruling art, for he appears unable to rule his household (*Oec.* 3.10–13) or to run his estate profitably (*Oec.* 1.16–17; 2.5–14; 6.1); (2) self-sufficiency, for he cannot govern his impulses (*Oec.* 1.18–23; 2.7); and (3) gentlemanly virtue, for he does not know how to become a gentleman (*Oec.* 4.1; 6.12). Socrates attempts to show how pitiful (οἰκτρός, *Oec.* 2.4, 7, 9) he is, by arguing that the liturgies for which he must pay to maintain his reputation as well as his pursuit of boys are liable to bankrupt him (*Oec.* 2.4–8). Indeed, Critoboulus' erotic impulses are his defining feature in Xenophon's other Socratic writings, and he is *the* figure with whom Xenophon's Socrates discusses φιλία, friendship (*Mem.* 2.6).[4] In the course of their conversation, Socrates undertakes to tame Critoboulus' impulses by instructing him about estate management through the narration of a conversation he once had with a man reputed to be a gentleman, Ischomachus. This story occupies the last two-thirds of the *Oeconomicus,* and Socrates never returns to tell Critoboulus (or the reader) what to make of the story.

Many commentators take the views of Ischomachus to be those of Xenophon himself, in that he, like Xenophon (*An.* 5.3.7–13 and *Cyn.*), is a master of the art of estate management.[5] Philodemus, in his polemic against Socrates, says that Socrates was an ironic figure, an ἐρῶν, who denied that he knew anything and attributed whatever wisdom he

---

[3]The principal works on the *Oeconomicus* are H. R. Breitenbach in *RE* 9A, 2 (1967), cols. 1837–71; E. Delebecque, "Sur la date et l'objet de l' 'Économique,' " *REG* 64 (1951): 21–58; L. Strauss, *Xenophon's Socratic Discourse* (Ithaca, N.Y., 1970). Sarah Pomeroy's forthcoming commentary (Oxford University Press); and for the agricultural content of the work, see Kl. Meyer, *Xenophon's "Oikonomikos"* (Westerburg, 1976). See also P. Chantraine, *L'Économique* (Paris, 1949); J. Luccioni, *Xénophon et le Socratisme* (Paris, 1953), pp. 112–19. Cicero translated the *Oeconomicus* into Latin, for which see V. Lundström "Ciceros öfversätning af Xenophons Oikonomikos," *Eranos* 12 (1912): 1–31; L. Alfonsi, "La traduzione Ciceroniana dell' 'Economico' di Senofonte," *Ciceroniana* 3–6 (1961–64): 7–17, argues that Cicero was not merely translating, nor engaged in as a stylistic exercise, but that he took an interest in the philosophy of the Xenophontic Socrates.

[4]See also *Mem.* 1.3.8–10, 13; *Symp.* 2.3, 3.7, 4.10–28, 5.1–6.1, 8.2.

[5]The view that Ischomachus expresses the sentiments of Xenophon is widely held, although stated with varying degrees of certainty. Delebecque (above, note 3), p. 58, calls the *Oeconomicus* "peut-être son œuvre la plus personnelle." E. C. Marchant, *Xenophon* (Cambridge, 1923), pp. xxvi, says: "But Ischomachus is Xenophon, and the little lady is . . . Xenophon's wife Philesia." R. Waterfield, *Conversations of Socrates* (New York, 1990), pp. 273, 285–87, although taking ample note of the arguments against the identification, perpetuates the stereotype when he says: "Xenophon's attitude, through the mouth of Ischomachus, is that of the amateur farmer" (p. 285).

possessed to others.[6] Socrates, by this argument, may have chosen to present his own views in the mouth of Ischomachus.[7] Leo Strauss has sufficiently dispelled the first assumption.[8] As for the intimations of Philodemus, I suggest that there are several reasons to suppose that Socrates does not endorse the views of Ischomachus.

First, because Critoboulus is preoccupied with affairs of the heart, Socrates tries to lead him to see that *oikonomia* has applications to human relationships. He suggests that friends and enemies are properly part of one's estate, if one considers an estate to be the sum of all one "possesses" (*Oec.* 1.7, 14–15). One must know how to "use friends well" and how to "benefit" from them in order to count them as assets (*Oec.* 1.7–10). Ischomachus benefits from his wife and bailiffs in that they look after his financial interests and make his real estate more valuable. His relations with them are warm but governed by utility. Xenophon's Socrates, however, says that while others may value a good horse or dog or bird, he takes pleasure even more in good friends and devotes his

[6]When Socrates appears in Philodemus' discussion of the character of an *eirōn* (*De vit.*, cols. 21.37–23.37) he is said to attribute his knowledge, for example, to Aspasia and [ ]αχωι (col. 22.32–35). Ischomachus is the name restored in C. Jensen's text (Leipzig, 1911), and since Philodemus studied Xenophon's *Oeconomicus* and since Aspasia and Ischomachus are the two experts to whom Socrates says he will take Critoboulus (*Oec.* 3.14, 6.12–17), the restoration seems sound.

[7]Philodemus suggests (Περὶ οἰκονομίας, col. 2. 19ff.) that Socrates' line of argument is inconsistent and contradicted by his use of other speakers like Ischomachus and Aspasia, as though Socrates was himself the source of their views. Because of the Epicurean tradition of hostility to Socrates as an ironist (εἴρων) and an imposter (ἀλαζών) one cannot expect to find a sympathetic reading of Xenophon's *Oeconomicus* in Philodemus. See P. A. Vander Waerdt, "Colotes and the Epicurean Refutation of Skepticism," *GRBS* 30 (1989): 225–67 at pp. 253–59; K. Kleve, "*Scurra Atticus:* The Epicurean View of Socrates," in *Syzetesis: Studi sull' epicureismo greco e romano offerti a Marcello Gigante*, ed. G. Macchiaroli (Naples, 1983), pp. 227–53; and M. Riley, "The Epicurean Criticism of Socrates," *Phoenix* 34 (1980): 60–64. For the Περὶ οἰκονομίας, see C. Jensen's edition (Leipzig, 1907); R. Laurenti's commentary, *Filodemo e il pensiero economico degli Epicurei* (Milan, 1973), esp. pp. 21–53; and see A. Angeli, "La critica filodemea all' 'Economico' di Senofonte," *CErc* 20 (1990): 39–51.

[8]Strauss (above, note 3), p. 90, suggests that Xenophon resembles Critoboulus rather more than Ischomachus: "Xenophon is the only interlocutor of the Socratic Xenophon who is ever called by his urbane master, 'you wretch' and 'you fool.'" Socrates says these words to him when they are discussing how Critoboulus once kissed Cleinias (*Mem.* 1.3.8–13). Xenophon provokes these outbursts when he says that if kissing Cleinias is dangerous, he might throw caution to the wind himself. The identification of Xenophon and Critoboulus gets curious confirmation from Diogenes Laertius (2.49), quoting Aristippus, who is said to have remarked in the fourth book of his Περὶ παλαιᾶς τρυφῆς that Xenophon was madly in love with Cleinias. But Xenophon's expression of desire is quoted word for word from Critoboulus' longing for Cleinias in Xenophon's *Symposium* (4.12). At any rate, Xenophon is expressly mentioned as being present on the occasion of the *Oeconomicus* along with other friends of Socrates (*Oec.* 1.1; 3.1, 12), and he seems to portray himself more as a young man with the same problems as Critoboulus than as the older gentleman, Ischomachus.

life to benefiting them (*Mem.* 1.6.14). While Ischomachus values human beings for their contribution to his material prosperity, Socrates values them for their friendship.

The second cause for doubt is that Socrates never claims that he met a real gentleman, but a man who really deserved to be "called" a gentleman. If one examines *Oeconomicus* 6.12 carefully, it becomes clear that Socrates underlines the difference between appearances and reality.[9] He does so with a purpose, moreover, because Critoboulus longs for the reputation of being a gentleman but does not yet understand how very far away he is from attaining gentlemanly virtue, καλοκἀγαθία (*Oec.* 6.12; cf. 1.16–2.1).[10] Thomas Pangle argues (see Chapter 5 in this volume) that Xenophon's Socrates does not endorse the kind of *kalokagathia* practiced by Ischomachus, that is, the virtue commonly praised by the city. In his conclusion, Pangle suggests that Xenophon's *Cyropaedia* reveals what an Ischomachus might do if unfettered by the limitations of republicanism, and he implies that Xenophon's indictment of the society Cyrus creates would be an indictment of Ischomachus' way of life as well. It seems to me that Pangle's argument on the political implications of the difference between Socratic virtue and "commonsense" virtue is confirmed by Socrates' manipulation of appearance and reality in his introduction to the topic of *kalokagathia*.

Third, there is historical information concerning Ischomachus and his wife which would have been familiar to Xenophon's audience. The woman whom Ischomachus trains so well in *Oeconomicus* 7–10 and whom E. C. Marchant charmingly calls "that long-suffering little saint" is, in all probability, the same woman with whom Callias was involved in a most notorious scandal.[11] In section I of this chapter, I shall argue that widespread public knowledge of this scandal would have cast serious doubt upon the teaching Ischomachus relates to Socrates, just as

[9]The text, with language denoting appearance and reality in italics, is as follows: "What if I go through for you, from the beginning, how I was once with a man who *seemed* to me to be *in reality* one of those men to whom the *name* that *is called* a beautiful and good man [gentleman] is rightly given. [ὃς ἐμοὶ ἐδόκει εἶναι τῷ ὄντι τούτων τῶν ἀνδρῶν ἐφ' οἷς τοῦτο τὸ ὄνομα δικαίως ἐστίν, ὃ καλεῖται καλός τε κἀγαθὸς ἀνήρ.]" Socrates creates some doubt about whether he will show Critoboulus someone who *is* a gentleman, or who only *has the name* of gentleman, when he refers to the man as someone—to whom the name of gentleman is rightly given. The very fact that Socrates has loaded his statement with sophistic language suggests the latter. One can compare *Symposium* 8.43, where Socrates uses very similar language to suggest that Callias will fail in politics unless people can see that he cares for virtue "not in appearance but in reality."

[10]The response of Critoboulus displays how his erotic desires dominate his nature: ἐρῶ τούτου τοῦ ὀνόματος ἄξιος γενέσθαι, "I long to become worthy of the consideration of that name." Notice that this concern for reputation and his erotic urges go hand in hand.

[11]Marchant (above, note 5), p. xxvi.

Socrates' reference to this scandal in his conversation with Callias in Plato's *Apology* (20a–c) casts doubt on his use of that conversation in a defense against the charge of corrupting the youth.[12] For all of these reasons, it seems prima facie unlikely that Socrates agrees entirely with Ischomachus' views.

By relating the story of his encounter with Ischomachus to Critoboulus, Socrates appears to show what he could become if he learns the gentleman's art of ruling. But if Socrates' purpose in relating this story to Critoboulus is ironic, one wonders what Xenophon's intention is.[13] Part of the explanation may be found in the place Xenophon assigns to Socrates' encounter with Ischomachus in the former's intellectual biography. When Socrates describes how he comes to meet Ischomachus, he says that he was unable to find "the beautiful and the good" in searching for it among the good builders, smiths, painters, and sculptors. He found, likewise, that although the good and the beautiful go together, beautiful people were not necessarily good; hence he turned to a man who was reputed to be both "good" and "beautiful," a gentleman (*Oec.* 6.13–17).

This account clearly represents Xenophon's rejoinder to Socrates' attempted elenchus of the Delphic oracle in Plato's *Apology* (20e–23c).[14] Socrates' encounter with Ischomachus comes at the juncture in Socrates' career when he has been cast into ill repute by the accusations of Aristophanes (*Oec.* 11.3, 25; see Chapter 2 in this volume). These references to the *Clouds* occupy the middle chapter of the *Oeconomicus*, where Socrates asks Ischomachus to teach him what human virtue is (*Oec.* 11.4–6). Xenophon seems to be suggesting, however comically, that Socrates' reaction to the *Clouds* was to take Aristophanes' advice and to inquire into the value of *kalokagathia* conventionally understood. Since Socrates, however, does not go on to become a gentleman farmer, it is fair to suppose that he does not accept Ischomachus' view of *kalokagathia*, or of the best form of life.

Xenophon offers not a simple but a complex reply to the *Clouds* in the *Oeconomicus*. Socrates, in his later life, exposes his young student, Critoboulus, to a conventionally impeccable moral education by exposing him to the ideal citizen, Ischomachus. But Socrates offers the lesson ironically in an attempt to bring Critoboulus to realize the limitations

[12] See T. G. West, *Plato's Apology of Socrates* (Ithaca, N.Y., 1979), pp. 98–103.

[13] Xenophon's capacity to employ irony is deprecated by G. Vlastos, "The Paradox of Socrates," in *The Philosophy of Socrates*, ed. G. Vlastos (New York, 1971), pp. 1–21, but see D. Morrison's reply, "On Professor Vlastos' Xenophon," *AP* 7 (1987): 9–22. The varieties of Socratic irony are further considered in G. Vlastos, "Socratic Irony," *CQ* n.s. 37 (1987): 79–96.

[14] Cf. Strauss (above, note 3), p. 164, and now P. A. Vander Waerdt, "Socratic Justice and Self-sufficiency," *OSAP* 11 (1993): 1–48.

of Ischomachus' way of life. By portraying Socrates in this way, Xenophon has the rhetorical advantage of being able to defend Socrates against the charge of corrupting the young, while intimating that Socrates rejects the conventional definition of *kalokagathia* for a higher one. It is left for Critoboulus to decide for himself whether the benefit that human beings confer upon one another is to be measured by the businessman's profit and loss or by friendship, as the philosopher and true gentleman measures it.

1. The Characters and the Literary Tradition

The temptation to see the *Oeconomicus* as a simple treatise on the management of an estate is undercut by the fact that Critoboulus, as portrayed in Xenophon's other Socratic writings, is a figure whose erotic desires pose special difficulties for Socrates. The best place to begin to interpret the *Oeconomicus*, in my view, is to consider what Socrates must prove to Critoboulus in order to achieve his stated objectives.

Critoboulus' two conversations with Socrates outside of the *Oeconomicus*, take place at *Symposium* 4.10–28 and 5.1–6.1 and *Memorabilia* 2.6.[15] In the *Symposium*, the subject proposed for discussion is "what each one considers to be the most valuable thing he knows" (ὄ τι ἕκαστος ἡγεῖται πλείστου ἄξιον ἐπίστασθαι 3.3). Callias focuses the question by saying that he is able "to make men better" (3.4). From that point on, the standard of what makes men best is applied to each participant's answer. Critoboulus says that his beauty is able to make men better, and he makes it plain that this is his only possession (3.7). What he means by this emerges from the first passage in *Symposium* 4.10–28.

Critoboulus says that he is more just than Callias, who makes men better by giving them money, because he is able to lead men "to every virtue" (πρὸς πᾶσαν ἀρετὴν, 4.15) by his beauty. He claims that beautiful people make others ἐλευθεριωτέρους εἰς χρήματα, φιλοπονωτέρους, φιλοκαλωτέρους, αἰδημονεστέρους, and ἐγκρατεστέρους, "freer with their money, lovers more of toil and nobility, more reverent and more

---

[15]The other mentions of Critoboulus are passing allusions derived from the more detailed discussions in these two passages. *Memorabilia* 1.3.8–13 is concerned with Critoboulus' love of Cleinias and the harmful effects of kisses, a theme treated at length in *Symposium* 4. *Symposium* 2.3 refers to his wife as young, an important theme for the *Oeconomicus*. *Symposium* 3.7 introduces 4.10–28. *Symposium* 8.2 shows Critoboulus emerging from his role as an object of others' affection to become an active seeker of the love of others, a topic that seems to be taken up by *Memorabilia* 2.6.

self-controlled." These tall claims take on added significance when they are compared with Callias' claim that his ability to make men better with his money by teaching them justice is identical with teaching them "gentlemanly virtue," *kalokagathia* (3.4). It is clear, then, that if Critoboulus is more just than Callias, he must also teach *kalokagathia* better than Callias. Herein lies the wit of Xenophon's portrayal of Critoboulus: because he is καλός, handsome, and takes pride in his κάλλος, beauty, he claims to be able to make another καλὸς κἀγαθός, a gentleman.

But in his final words Critoboulus reveals the sham of his claims to teach virtue, when he says that he is able to use his beauty to take pleasure from whomever he wishes, for he is far more able to persuade others to kiss him without even saying a word than Socrates speaking wisely and at great length (4.18). This provokes the beauty contest between Socrates and Critoboulus that occupies the central chapter of the *Symposium*, in which Socrates clearly wins every argument, but Critoboulus is unanimously declared the victor (5.1–6.1). It is left to Socrates to show that using beauty to extract favors from lovers produces a relationship that is purely mercenary and that has no bond of affection in it (8.21).

In his second dialogue with Socrates, Critoboulus shows that despite a lengthy and moving speech by Socrates on the superior friendship of the gentleman (*Mem.* 2.6.21–29), he desires to use this knowledge, ἐπιστήμη, of making friends, to acquire friends with beautiful bodies (2.6.30). Critoboulus still finds beauty, *kallos*, to be more important than gentlemanly virtue, *kalokagathia*. Indeed, when Socrates agrees to help Critoboulus form the right sort of friendships, Critoboulus expects him to tell others how noble he is even if he is not (2.6.36–37). Socrates concludes by telling him that he will never have gentlemen for friends unless he first becomes a gentleman himself. Socrates shows him that not only is his beauty insufficient to make others gentlemen but that he is doomed to have base friends who only want his body unless he first learns *kalokagathia* himself. This is a subject that the *Oeconomicus* takes up, but Critoboulus shows a great reluctance to learn this lesson, because his beauty allows him to pursue an effortless life of pleasure. Since Socrates was unable to teach Critoboulus *kalokagathia* either by jovial conversation in the *Symposium* or by direct dialogue in the *Memorabilia*, clearly more sophisticated and persuasive measures are necessary.[16]

---

[16]Donald Morrison's essay in Chapter 7 on Socrates as a teacher sets out the stages of Socratic education and how Socrates deals with various types of students.

Critoboulus also figures in the Platonic tradition and the portrayal of him in the *Oeconomicus* takes up issues not only from Xenophon's other dialogues but from Plato's dialogues as well. Critoboulus' father was Crito, the man to whom Socrates entrusted his immortality in his last words (*Phd.* 118a).[17] Crito was a farmer (*Euthd.* 292d), so estate management is an appropriate subject for his son to master. When Crito is contemplating how to educate Critoboulus at the end of Plato's *Euthydemus*, however, he does not desire that his son be taught farming but philosophy, and he expresses despair that those who teach it are sophists:

ἐγὼ μὲν οὖν ὅταν σοὶ συγγένωμαι, οὕτω διατίθεμαι ὥστ᾽ ἐμοὶ δοκεῖ μανίαν εἶναι τὸ ἕνεκα τῶν παίδων ἄλλων μὲν πολλῶν σπουδὴν τοι-αύτην ἐσχηκέναι, καὶ περὶ τοῦ γάμου ὅπως ἐκ γενναιοτάτης ἔσονται μητρός, καὶ περὶ τῶν χρημάτων ὅπως ὡς πλουσιώτατοι, αὐτῶν δὲ περὶ παιδείας ἀμελῆσαι· ὅταν δὲ εἴς τινα ἀποβλέψω τῶν φασκόντων ἂν παιδεῦσαι ἀνθρώπους, ἐκπέπληγμαι καί μοι δοκεῖ εἷς ἕκαστος αὐτῶν σκοποῦντι πάνυ ἀλλόκοτος εἶναι, ὥς γε πρὸς σὲ τἀληθῆ εἰρῆσθαι· ὥστε οὐκ ἔχω ὅπως προτρέπω τὸ μειράκιον ἐπὶ φιλοσοφίαν.

Whenever I am with you I am so disposed that it seems to me that it is madness to be so greatly concerned about all those irrelevant things for the sake of our sons: we are concerned about marriage so that they will be born of the noblest mother possible; concerned about money so that they may be as rich as possible; but we are unconcerned about their education. Yet whenever I look to one of those who claim to educate people, I am dumbstruck, and it seems to me when I examine them that every one of them is completely out of his mind to tell you the truth. And so I don't know how I can persuade my boy [Critoboulus] to study philosophy. (306d–e)

Crito finds an excessive concern about wives and money to be the mark of an inadequate education, but these are precisely the subjects that Socrates teaches Critoboulus at length in the *Oeconomicus.* Xenophon seems to be replying playfully to the Platonic characterization of the problem of how to educate the young. Crito sets out what he perceives to be the shortcomings of both parents and teachers. Parents tend to be concerned too little with the "moral" improvement of their children and concerned too much with their reputations and financial well-

---

[17]Socrates' last words are "We owe a cock to Aesclepius. See that it is paid." The cock is the symbol of a new day, a new existence, and Aesclepius is the god who can bring back the dead to life. He is also the son of Apollo, in service to whom Socrates has spent his life. Socrates makes this request of Crito to suggest that this life of service to the god will be rewarded in his new life of the soul.

being. Teachers of philosophy, at least those unlike Socrates, are all sophists, whose version of "moral" education seems to be nothing more than an education in unscrupulous rhetoric. Xenophon's Socrates teaches the things of which parents approve, how to pick a wife and how to run a farm. But Crito does not want Critoboulus to learn these things; he wants him to learn philosophy from someone who is not a sophist.

Xenophon's Socrates promises that he will show Critoboulus what a gentleman is, by teaching him about wives and farming. But this is Xenophon's playful way of showing that Socrates both is and is not a sophist. He can be sophistical in that he teaches one thing in order to accomplish another: Critoboulus' education about wives and farming should really teach him about philosophy. On the other hand, he is not a sophist, because his teaching will truly improve Critoboulus, although indirectly, for Xenophon's Socrates never claims to teach virtue. His students must become gentlemen on their own (*Mem.* 1.2.3). The education that Xenophon's Socrates gives Critoboulus will be sophistical in its speech but not in its content.

This brings us to the subject of who Ischomachus and his wife are. The first and longest section of Socrates' discussion with Ischomachus deals with the education of the latter's wife (*Oec.* 7–10). Ischomachus is concerned to make her as "beneficial" as possible to himself by educating her. His teaching stresses that the duty of a wife is to work to increase the value of the household they share (7.15), which she may best accomplish by working constantly herself and by supervising others (10.10). The financial and marital concerns of Ischomachus seem to coincide in his interpretation of how to rule his household, *oikonomia.*

The wife of Ischomachus, however, was one of the most famous women in Athens, and so the quality of her education is colored by what we know of her. Andocides reports in the *De mysteriis* (124–27) that Callias married the daughter of an Ischomachus.[18] While he was priest of the cult of the Mother and Daughter, he took the girl's mother as his mistress less than a year after his marriage. In due course the daughter tried to kill herself and eventually fled the house, and the mother became pregnant with Callias' second child. Callias drove the mother out but later took her back and acknowledged the child as his own.

---

[18]The standard text of the *De mysteriis* is D. M. MacDowell, *Andokides on the Mysteries* (Oxford, 1962). See also W. E. Thompson, "Notes on Andocides," *Acta classica* 13 (1970): 141–48; A. D. J. Makkink, *Andokides' Eerste Rede* (Amsterdam, 1932); and E. C. Marchant's Loeb edition, *Andocides, De mysteriis and De reditu* (London, 1889).

Scholars have admitted the possibility that the Ischomachus in Andocides is the same as in the *Oeconomicus*, but no one has advanced an
interpretation of the work as a whole that accepts and explains this.[19]
J. K. Davies has argued persuasively that the father-in-law of the Callias story is the same person as Xenophon's Ischomachus.[20] He main-

---

[19]Strauss (above, note 3), pp. 157–58; H. Dittmar, *Aischines von Sphettos: Studien zur literaturgeschichte der Sokratiker, Untersuchungen und Fragmente, Philologische Untersuchungen*
21 (Berlin, 1912), pp. 60–62; Breitenbach (above, note 3), cols. 1848–49; MacDowell (above,
note 18), pp. 151–52; Waterfield (above, note 5), pp. 285–87. Two short notes propose
that the two Ischomachuses are one and the same: F. D. Harvey, "The Wicked Wife of
Ischomachus," *EMC* 28 (1984): 68–70; and D. C. Mackenzie's refutation of Harvey's conclusions. "The Wicked Wife of Ischomachus—Again," *EMC* 29 (1985): 95–96.

[20]*Athenian Propertied Families* (Oxford, 1971), pp. 263–69, no. 7286 XI–XIV; pp. 296–
98, no. 8429 IV. There are several very complicated problems concerning marriages of
Callias that cannot be resolved, and there are some inconsistencies in Davies' line of argument. Although these inconsistencies do not materially affect the claim that the
Ischomachus in Andocides is Xenophon's Ischomachus, they ought to be noted. Andocides reveals, in the story of the scandal, that Callias was married first to the daughter
of Glaucon, by whom he had his first son, Hipponicus (3). He was then married to the
daughter of Chrysilla and Ischomachus. West (above, note 12), p. 99, says that he had a
child by the daughter, but there is no evidence to substantiate this, and Andocides would
not have failed to mention anything to make Callias' behavior sound more outrageous.
Callias did, however, have a child (whose name is unknown to us) by his wife's mother,
Chrysilla. When Plato says that Callias has two sons (*Ap.* 20a), he must mean Hipponicus
and this one. West must be confused by the story of two quick marriages and the two
children in the Plato passage. At issue between Andocides and Callias is the daughter of
Epylicus, who died intestate. The date of the *De mysteriis* is put at 400 by MacDowell
(above, note 18), p. 205; during this trial, the dispute over Epylicus' daughters is not yet
decided. Andocides says that if Callias were to win custody of the girl, and presumably
marry her (although we cannot know), then in addition to Callias' previous outrage,
where mother drove out daughter, now granddaughter would drive out grandmother
(128). That is, the daughter of Epylicus is the granddaughter of Chrysilla. This means
that the wife of Epylicus, Chrysilla's daughter, was either Callias' second wife herself or
her sister. Davies proposes that Callias married the widow of Epylicus when he died in
Sicily. The first problem arises with Davies' dating of the death of Epilycus to the Sicilian
expedition in 415–413. He wants the date to be in this period so that he can date the
marriage of Callias to Epylicus' widow ca. 413 and that to her mother in the next year.
This would mean that Ischomachus would have died somewhat after 413, when Chrysilla
would have become available. He needs to have some period of years between the death
of Epylicus and the trial in 400 in order to give Callias time to marry Epylicus' widow,
and then her mother, and have a son who was already registered with the Ceryces in 400,
(mentioned by Andocides at 127). This means, however, that the case of Epylicus' daughters goes undecided from 413 to 400, and, a fact that Davies seems to overlook, that Callias has already been their stepfather once and thrown them out with their mother for
Chrysilla. Andocides would surely have used this as ammunition against Callias in his
claim for the daughter now. MacDowell suggests that Epylicus died in 401 or 400 (p. 145)
and that Callias did not marry Epylicus' widow but her sister (p. 207); this is a much
simpler solution. Davies rejects MacDowell's version of events (p. 298), but he would have
to explain what happened to Chrysilla's daughter, and the daughters of Epylicus' when
Callias divorced her. For thirteen years, they would have had no known relationship with
a male to control the estate. The last problem with Davies' analysis is that Andocides says
that Callias put in a claim for the daughter of Epylicus, not for himself but for his son,
and Davies takes this to mean Hipponicus. This is most unlikely because in the opening
words of *De mysteriis* 124, Andocides introduces the scandal of the mother and the daugh-

tains that a consistent portrait of a single individual emerges from the following sources other than Andocides and Xenophon. First, the comic poet Cratinos remarks on the closefistedness of an Ischomachus ca. 420 (*CAF* 328 = Ath. 1.8a) In the *Oeconomicus*, Ischomachus teaches his wife that she would appear more pleasing to him if she put color in her cheeks with hard work rather than with expensive cosmetics (10.2–13). Second, Lysias mentions two sons of an Ischomachus worth over seventy talents who inherit only ten talents each, and he says that this story dates well before the time of the speech, which is ca. 388 (Lys. 19.45–46). This coincides with the portrait of Ischomachus as a very wealthy real-estate tycoon in the *Oeconomicus* (20.23–29). Third, Lysias' speech Πρὸς Διογένην ὑπὲρ Ἀρχεστράτου περὶ χωρίου seems to have dealt with the estate of the sons of an Ischomachus that was controlled by a Callias. Finally, Ischomachus was asked by Aristippus at Olympia about Socrates (Aeschin. fr. 49 Dittmar = Plut. *De curios.* 2, 516c).

Davies proposes that Ischomachus was a wealthy landowner who had three children, the daughter mentioned in Andocides and the two sons mentioned in Lysias. The sons would have been minors at his death, so that the estate mentioned in Lysias' two speeches would fall into the hands of Callias, who married the mother in order to control the landholdings more directly. Ischomachus, therefore, would have died shortly after the marriage of his daughter to Callias, with whom Chrysilla, the wife mentioned in Andocides, would have taken up promptly. Callias, Davies argues, hoped to take full advantage of Ischomachus' massive real-estate holdings, but the Spartan garrison at Decelea prevented that.[21] The effects of war upon the farmland and

---

ter to show that the unnamed but famous (τοῦτον) son of Callias is unfit to be awarded the girl. The son of the scandal, that is, the son of Chrysilla, is the one in whose name Callias made his claim, and MacDowell and Waterfield (above, note 5), pp. 285–87, do not even consider that Hipponicus could be the claimant, because Andocides seems clearly to say that it is his second son. This raises two final concerns. The first is that the date of the scandal and the death of Ischomachus must be moved back to at least 418 in order to allow the son of Chrysilla and Callias to be an adult by 400. The second is more worrisome. Callias' first son, Hipponicus, was related (on his mother's side) to Epylicus and could make a claim for his daughter, although he was not so closely related to him as Andocides. Callias' second son does not seem to have been related to Epylicus and would have no claim to his daughter. MacDowell, p. 207, and W. E. Thompson, "Leagros," *Athenaeum* n.s. 49 (1971): 328–35, and (above, note 18) p. 141, following Makkink (above, note 18), p. 301, have tried to find a way to make Callias' second son related to Epylicus through Callias' line, but without conclusive results.

[21]Davies argues that Callias suffered serious financial losses when the Laureion mines could not be worked after 413. But his use (above, note 20), of this fact to explain Callias' behavior depends on a date for the marriage of Callias and Chrysilla in the period after the Sicilian expedition (p. 265), and this is probably wrong if Callias' second son is eighteen in 400. This does not necessarily undermine the thesis that Callias was interested in

Callias' plundering of the estate for capital explain why the estate was worth so much less by the time the sons of Ischomachus came of age. The strength of Davies' hypothesis lies in the consistent picture of a very wealthy but frugal man that emerges from the reports of Cratinos, Lysias, and Xenophon and in the possibility that Callias had financial reasons for behaving so outrageously.

Davies' hypothesis is strengthened further by the portrayal of Callias in philosophical writings, including Plato's *Protagoras*, Xenophon's *Symposium*, and Aeschines' *Aspasia*. In these three works, Callias is depicted as a fantastically rich man who spent his wealth on sophists and lived a dissolute life. In Plato's *Apology*, Socrates is able to allude to the infamous scandal of the mother and daughter merely by using the dual of Callias' *two* sons, the second son being the product of the scandal:[22]

ἐστὸν γὰρ αὐτῷ δύο υἱέε, ὦ Καλλία, ἦν δ' ἐγώ, εἰ μέν σου τὼ υἱέε
πώλω ἢ μόσχω ἐγενέσθην, εἴχομεν ἂν αὐτοῖν ἐπιστάτην λαβεῖν καὶ
μισθώσασθαι, ὃς ἔμελλεν αὐτὼ καλώ τε κἀγαθὼ ποιήσειν τὴν προσή-
κουσαν ἀρετήν· ἦν δ' ἂν οὗτος ἢ τῶν ἱππικῶν τις ἢ τῶν γεωργικῶν·
νῦν δ' ἐπειδὴ ἀνθρώπω ἐστόν, τίνα αὐτοῖν ἐν νῷ ἔχεις ἐπιστάτην
λαβεῖν; τίς τῆς τοιαύτης ἀρετῆς, τῆς ἀνθρωπίνης τε καὶ πολιτικῆς,
ἐπιστήμων ἐστίν;

You have two sons, Callias, I said; if your sons were colts or calves, we could find and hire a trainer for them who would see to making them *kalos te kagathos* with respect to their appropriate virtue. This man would be one of the horse trainers or farmers. But as it is, since you have human beings, what trainer do you intend to find for them? Who is knowledgeable about this kind of human and political virtue? (20a–b)

When Socrates describes the proper training of a colt, he says that its overseer would be a farmer or a groom. The notion that a farmer might make a human being *kalos te kagathos* is considered impossible by Plato's Socrates, yet, in a certain way, that is whom Xenophon's Socrates has chosen to teach Critoboulus. Once again, Xenophon seems to be responding to a philosophical tradition in an unusual way. Callias' response to Socrates' question is "Evenos of Paros, five minae." Callias supposes that the proper educator of a human being is a soph-

---

additional landholdings before the war, because he was already using them, as collateral for loans in the 420s (Davies, p. 261, citing Cratinos, *CAF* 333; J. V. A. Fine, *Horoi: Studies in Mortgage, Real Security and Land Tenure in Ancient Athens*, Hesperia Suppl. Vol. 9 [Baltimore, 1951], p. 171). In other words, it may be that Callias was not in dire straits until the war, and that he was motivated by greed rather than need, as Davies suggests. In any event, the motive was money. Davies' explanation of what happened to Callias during the war might explain, however, part of his motive to take Chrysilla back after some years, when the son was a few years old, if he decided that he then needed her landholdings.

[22]See West (above, note 12), pp. 98–100, but also the caveat in note 20 above.

ist. Xenophon responds playfully to this passage in Plato with an even more absurd answer, "Ischomachus, the farmer." Xenophon reveals in two places that he is responding to the Platonic Socrates' comparison of educating horses to educating human beings. When Socrates is speaking with Critoboulus about the latter's fondness for comedies, he asks Critoboulus whether he should not learn the art of managing horses, since he spends so much time dealing with them (*Oec.* 3.9). Critoboulus does not quite understand what Socrates is implying, so Socrates says that horses, like human beings, reach a point where they become useful and capable of improvement (3.10). The Socratic comedy of the *Oeconomicus* is the education of the young knight, Critoboulus, and somehow the encounter with a farmer, Ischomachus, will educate not a horse but Critoboulus. The second passage that shows how Xenophon is setting out the problem of educating human beings has to do with Ischomachus' training of his bailiffs. Ischomachus says that colts learn to obey when they get something sweet for obedience, and something unpleasant for disobedience. Men can be trained in the same way with various rewards and punishments (*Oec.* 13.6–14.10). Ischomachus, the farmer, educates men the same way he does colts. Xenophon responds to the dialogue with Callias from Plato's *Apology*, which set out the problem of Socrates as an educator, by playfully suggesting that his own Socrates used the events surrounding the life of Callias to educate his students in a most unconventional way. Xenophon's Socrates speaks not with Callias but with his father-in-law, who actually believes that men can be trained like horses.

In the *Aspasia* Aeschines, the Socratic, reverses the scene in Plato's *Apology* and has Callias ask Socrates to recommend a teacher for his sons.[23] Socrates is probably alluding to this same scandal by proposing Aspasia as their teacher, inasmuch as Aspasia's special skill was counseling husbands and wives in the ἐρωτικὴ τέχνη, the erotic art.[24] In the course of the dialogue, Socrates probably defended his choice of Aspasia by giving examples of her teaching skills, the last of which is her counseling of Xenophon and his wife, which is preserved in Cicero's *De inventione rhetorica* (31.51–52 = fr. 31 Dittmar). Aspasia first questioned them one at a time, asking whether each would prefer the possessions of another if they were better or more valuable, to which they said they would. When she asked them if they would prefer the husband or wife of another if they were better, each fell silent:

[23]Fr. 17 Dittmar = Max. Tyr. 38.4. For Aeschines' *Aspasia*, see Charles Kahn's discussion in Chapter 3; also, for a general survey of the writings of Aeschines, see A. E. Taylor, "Aeschines of Sphettos," in *Philosophical Studies* (London, 1934), pp. 1–27.

[24]Fr. 30 Dittmar = Plut. 24. See B. Ehlers, *Eine vorplatonische Deutung des sokratischen Eros: Der Dialog Aspasia des Soleratikeis Aischines*, Zetemata 41 (Munich, 1966), pp. 35–43.

Post Aspasia: Quoniam uterque vestrum, inquit, id mihi solum non re-
spondit, quod ego solum audire volueram, egomet dicam, quid uterque
cogitet. Nam et tu, mulier, optimum virum vis habere et tu, Xenophon,
uxorem habere lectissimam maxime vis. Quare, nisi hoc perfeceritis, ut
neque vir melior neque femina lectior in terris sit, profecto semper id,
quod optimum putabitis esse, multo maxime requiretis, ut et tu maritus
sis quam optimae et haec quam optimo viro nupta sit.

Then Aspasia said, "Since each of you did not tell me the one thing I
wanted to hear, I'll tell you what each is thinking. You, his wife, want to
have the best husband there is, and you, Xenophon, want especially to
have the most desirable wife there is. Therefore, unless you see to it that
there is no better husband and no more desirable wife in the world,
clearly that which you will consider best you will always lack most especially, namely, that you be husband to the best wife there is and that she be
wife to the best husband there is. (31.51–52)

Xenophon makes a passing allusion to his role in the *Aspasia* of Aeschines by his reference to Aspasia in the *Oeconomicus*. Socrates and
Critoboulus are discussing the need for husbands to educate their
wives. When Critoboulus asks whether husbands train them themselves, Socrates replies: "I shall introduce Aspasia to you, who will reveal all to you with much more knowledge than I" (συστήσω δέ σοι ἐγὼ
καὶ ᾿Ασπασίαν, ἣ ἐπιστημονέστερον ἐμοῦ σοι ταῦτα πάντα ἐπιδείξει,
Oec. 3.14). The answer to Critoboulus' question is yes and no. Husbands take their wives to Aspasia, but Aspasia tells them to make one
another "as good as possible," which implies that they should teach one
another. When Socrates continues speaking, however, he says that the
goodness of a wife lies in the way she manages the household finances.
The economic definition of a good wife to which Socrates alludes must
have some connection to the erotic and moral definition suggested by
Aeschines' *Aspasia*.[25] This subject will be taken up in section 3 of this
chapter.

From these passages it is clear that the scandalous story of Callias
and Ischomachus' daughter and wife played a central role in several

[25]Concerning the comparative teachings of Aspasia and Ischomachus, there are those
who would argue that against the background of a highly repressive society such as Athens, Ischomachus' view of his wife's capacities is relatively enlightened: e.g., S. Pomeroy,
"The Persian King and the Queen Bee," *AJAH* 9 (1984 [pub. 1990]): 103–5; S. Mur-
naghan, "How a Woman Can Be More Like a Man: The Dialogue between Ischomachus
and His Wife in Xenophon's *Oeconomicus*," *Helios* 14 (1988): 9–22. A much less flattering
view of Ischomachus may be found in S. Vilatte, "La femme, l' esclave, le cheval, et le
chien: Les emblèmes du kalos kagathos Ischomaque," *DHA* 12 (1986): 271–94. Aeschines' *Aspasia*, however, presents a more enlightened view still than Ischomachus' in
that women have the same capacity for moral virtue as men. In comparison with Aspasia's teaching, Ischomachus limits the possibilities of women.

philosophical dialogues of this period. Xenophon has taken the subject of the education of wives in which he himself figured in Aeschines and removed it to the previous generation in order to discuss the education of the famous wife of Ischomachus. The fact that Xenophon mentions Aspasia in the *Oeconomicus* and in *Memorabilia* 2.6.36, where marriage is discussed between Socrates and Critoboulus, lends support to the thesis that Xenophon is replying to Aeschines. Moreover, the fact that his *Symposium* is hosted by Callias and that Callias' half brother Hermogenes is the source of his *Apology* demonstrates the central place of Callias in Xenophon's philosophical writings.

For all these reasons there should be little doubt that Xenophon's Ischomachus is the father-in-law of Callias and that the education of his wife must be interpreted accordingly. If the education that Ischomachus gave to his wife prepared her for the kind of outrage she committed with Callias, and if this is what one would call a training in conventional moral virtue, then the greatest threat to the religious conventions of society would turn out to be the education of which society most approves. That there is a need for Socrates to show the limitations and failings of the conventional definition of *kalokagathia* was shown by Critoboulus' unshakable confidence in the power of his beauty to obtain whatever he wished without cultivating virtue. Xenophon has created a tension between the conventional education Socrates appears to give and the unconventional education that Critoboulus needs, and for this reason, his defense of Socrates as a teacher responds to the indictment of Socrates by Aristophanes.

2. Xenophon's Response to Aristophanes: Socrates as a Teacher

The broad outlines of the *Oeconomicus* recall Aristophanes' *Clouds*. A young knight, obsessed with the aristocratic good life and horses, comes to Socrates for help with his deteriorating financial situation.[26] In the *Clouds*, the father sends his son; in the *Oeconomicus*, Critoboulus has to be persuaded that he has money problems. In the *Clouds*, the father wants his son to learn dishonest means of eluding creditors, while in the *Oeconomicus* Critoboulus wants to learn only noble arts.[27] Yet the educational problem calls for the same solution. Pheidippides, the son of Strepsiades, gets the dishonest education his father wants. He is taught how to thwart convention and the laws. Critoboulus is

[26]Compare *Nub.* 25–32, 83, 108–9, 119–25 and *Oec.* 2.6, 3.8–10.
[27]*Nub.* 239–46, 429–30, 433–34, 1105–12; *Oec.* 2.1–9, 4.1.

given the appropriate education. He is taught how to make his farm profitable and thus avoid ruin.

Three overt references to the *Clouds* in the *Oeconomicus* demonstrate that Xenophon himself intended to reply to Aristophanes' charges of corruption by having Socrates give his student the right education.[28] All three references occur in the central chapter where Socrates and Ischomachus are discussing the activities of the gentleman. First, Socrates deprecates himself by saying that he "seems to babble sense-lessly and to have his head in the clouds" (*Oec.* 11.3). He points to Aristophanes' characterization not only with the words he chooses (cf. *Nub.* 225 and 1480) but also by emphasizing that he "seems" or "is reputed" (δοκῶ) to be this way. In the second reference Ischomachus describes his daily activities, saying that after a good ride he has his groom "give his horse a roll" (*Oec.* 11.18). The *Clouds* begins with the young Pheidippides dreaming about horses, and when his father tries to wake him, the boy tells his father "to give his horse a roll" (*Nub.* 32). In the third instance, although Ischomachus devotes himself assiduously to rhetorical exercise, he cannot win arguments with his wife. Socrates suggests that his problem is that "he cannot make the weaker argument the stronger one" (*Oec.* 11.25). In the *Clouds*, Strepsiades sends his son to Socrates expressly to learn how to argue this way (*Nub.* 112–18), and the boy is shown a debate between two kinds of speakers in which the one who can "make the weaker argument the stronger" wins (*Nub.* 893–95).

Socrates hosts this debate between δικαῖος λόγος and ἄδικος λόγος, Just and Unjust Speech. Just Speech advocates a traditional education consisting of musical training in patriotic songs (964–72), with emphasis on modesty and chastity, σωφροσύνη (961–63, 973–83, 991–99), and athletic competition (1005–8). He teaches civic virtue of an aristocratic bent that is purely conventional. He cannot give a reasoned justification, λόγος, for believing his education superior. It is simply that of which society approves by custom, νόμος. Unjust Speech advocates a vulgar hedonism that emphasizes luxury (1071–73), sexual license (1068–70, 1079–82), and the practice of sophistic rhetoric (1055–59). He teaches that there is no justice (900–901) and that since none of society's conventions have a rational defense, man might as well yield to the nature, φύσις, that prompts him to pleasure (1075).[29] This debate pits a *kaloskagathos* against a sophist.

---

[28]Cf. Breitenbach (above, note 3), col. 1855; Strauss (above, note 3), pp. 159, 163–64.
[29]See L. Strauss, *Socrates and Aristophanes* (Chicago, 1966), pp. 3–53; M. Nussbaum, "Aristophanes and Socrates on Learning Practical Wisdom," *YCS* 26 (1980): 43–97, esp. pp. 54–56, 62, and 70.

Xenophon's portrait of Ischomachus and Socrates differs in some respects from Aristophanes' depiction of an encounter between a gentleman and a sophist. In the *Clouds,* Unjust Speech refutes Just Speech on the basis of premises admitted by him. Socrates performs no such elenchus on Ischomachus. It is precisely this fact that makes the encounter between a philosopher and a gentleman possible. It is as though Socrates were able to have a conversation with one of those grand figures like Cephalus who flee at the first sign of an elenchus (Pl. *Rep.* 331c).[30]

If Socrates is diplomatic with Ischomachus, his behavior stands in sharp contrast to his elenchus of Critoboulus. The two parts of the *Oeconomicus* follow two different patterns. If the encounter between Socrates and Ischomachus shows the dialogue of a philosopher and a gentleman, the dialogue between Socrates and Critoboulus shows a sophist forcing a young knight into self-refutation. In the first two chapters, Socrates confounds his student with three paradoxes. He convinces Critoboulus that human beings can be considered possessions (1.6); that he himself, though one hundred times poorer, is really wealthier than Critoboulus (2.1–9); and that although he is wealthier, he himself cannot teach Critoboulus anything about the science of *oikonomia* (2.21–14). Socrates repeatedly refutes Critoboulus with the very definitions he accepts.[31] After asserting that he cannot help Critoboulus personally, he says that he will take him to those who can.

In chapter 3, Socrates makes a series of promises to Critoboulus that reveal his paradoxical attitude toward *oikonomia* (3.1–6). He will show him some men who build expensive useless houses, and others who build useful ones for less; some who have many valuable movables but cannot find them to use, and others who have less but ready to hand;

[30]There are certain indications that the encounter between Socrates and Ischomachus is modeled on that of the wise man and the tyrant. Xenophon's *Hiero* begins with the statement that Simonides and Hiero, the tyrant, met "when there was leisure [σχόλη]" (1.1). Socrates and Ischomachus also are able to meet only because of Ischomachus' unexpected leisure (*Oec.* 7.1–2; see Strauss [above, note 31], p. 131). Socrates listens patiently and does not interrupt the extended speeches of his opponent, much as Simonides allows Hiero to speak without interruption for several chapters (*Hiero* 2.3–6.8). Unlike the wise man, however, who refuses to praise the tyrant, Socrates is rather free with praise, albeit ironic praise. Cf. Solon and Croesus: Hdt. 1.30.2–32.9; *Xen. Oec.* 10.1; 11.10, 19–21; 12.2; 21.1. Xenophon's *Hiero* treats this subject with great complexity. Simonides praises tyranny but does not praise Hiero, who is an unhappy tyrant. See V. J. Gray, "Xenophon's *Hiero* and the Meeting of the Wise Man and Tyrant in Greek Literature," *CQ* 36 (1986): 115–23; L. Strauss, *On Tyranny* (New York, 1963), esp. pp. 40–45. On Strauss's general view of the relationship of the *Oeconomicus* to the *Hiero*, see pp. 30–34, and Strauss (above, note 3), pp. 208–9.

[31]Philodemus notes the improper use of language involved in the paradoxes he creates: fr. 1, line 19; col. 5, lines 3–4, p. 14; col. 6, lines 11ff., pp. 16ff; see Laurenti (above, note 7), pp. 26–27.

some who keep slaves bound and anxious to escape, and others who put them under no restraint and make them willing to work and remain; and last, some who say that they are destroyed by farming, and others who have what they need in abundance.

Strauss claims that Socrates keeps only the second half of each promise.[32] Actually, he keeps neither half of any of these promises. As for the first two, Ischomachus has a big house with so many things in it that his wife cannot find what he requests until he trains her (8.2). He openly tells Socrates that he enjoys wealth and plentiful possessions and their attendant problems (11.9). Ischomachus has neither a big useless house nor a small practical one. He seems to have a big practical estate, for, as Socrates observes, his farm is not only self-sufficient but produces enough wealth for Ischomachus to adorn the city (11.10). Third, the Draconian law by which he rules his slaves says that anyone caught stealing shall be "bound" and "executed" (14.5). Next, Ischomachus probably cannot be described by either half of the fourth promise, for Socrates has been portraying the positive example in each promise as someone with a simple operation. Ischomachus is not impoverished, nor does he have a simple operation that meets its "needs." Ischomachus is a real-estate tycoon (20.22–29).

The puzzling promises of Socrates cannot be said to be fulfilled in any ordinary way. Socrates as much as announces that his discourse on *oikonomia* with Ischomachus will require some unconventional interpretation. After Socrates has made these promises, he asks Critoboulus to watch and learn. When Critoboulus says that he will if he can, Socrates says: "Well then, you must cross-examine yourself as you watch and ask yourself whether you are understanding what you see" (οὐκοῦν χρὴ θεώμενον σαυτοῦ ἀποπειρᾶσθαι εἰ γνώσῃ, 3.7). Socrates compares the education he is about to give Critoboulus to a comedy, noting that Critoboulus is always dragging him to comedies, but that this is the first time he ever invited Socrates to teach him something. When Critoboulus watches this comedy, however, Socrates says that he must not be passive and watch for pleasure as he usually does; he must be active and critical of himself if he is to understand the message (3.7–10).

---

[32]Strauss (above, note 3), pp. 107–12. Strauss suggests first that Socrates is showing Critoboulus only the successful farmer, Ischomachus, and that "the *Oeconomicus* would be deliberately incomplete," but then he adds that "Socrates might be the always present model of the bad practice of the economic art or at least of some of its parts" (p. 109). Strauss's division of good economist/bad economist does not work, for Socrates cannot be the bad economist with the big, unprofitable, disorganized estate, nor can Ischomachus be the good economist with the small, profitable, organized estate.

This passage is a guide to the interpretation of the *Oeconomicus*. What we are about to see is a comedy, but not one that is designed to delight. It is a comedy of education and an educating comedy. Socrates will speak in a way that Critoboulus will misunderstand unless he "puts himself to the test," "acts as his own dialectical opponent" (*sautou apopeirasthai, Oec.* 3.7).[33] Critoboulus has been given a hint that Socrates will be saying things, the meaning of which will not be self-evident—that is, he will be saying things that do not mean quite what they appear to mean. When, in chapters 4 and 5, Socrates begins the test of Critoboulus, he appears to be deliberately sophistical, a portrait whose best parallel is the dissembling *adikos logos* of Aristophanes' *Clouds*.

After hearing Socrates' promises, Critoboulus asks to be taught those branches of knowledge that "seem to be the most noble" (αἳ δοκοῦσι κάλλισται τῶν ἐπιστημῶν, 4.1). Critoboulus is concerned to acquire an education that has the appearance of nobility. Socrates proposes that they pass over the manual trades because they make men bad citizens.[34] What remain are the arts of war and farming, and these must have something to do with being a gentleman, for at *Symposium* 3.4, Antisthenes says that the manual trades are the opposite of *kalokagathia*.

Socrates proposes to examine these arts by using the King of Persia as their model: "Socrates said, "We shall not be ashamed to imitate the King of the Persians, shall we?" (Ἆρα, ἔφη ὁ Σωκράτης, μὴ αἰσχυνθῶμεν τὸν Περσῶν βασιλέα μιμήσασθαι, 4.4). The form of his question not only seeks a negative answer but may also indicate fear at what the answer may be (H. W. Smyth, *Greek Grammar* [Cambridge, 1956] 598–99). Critoboulus is shocked by the suggestion that the King of Persia actually cares about farming (4.5). One can imagine that Callias was equally shocked in Aeschines' *Aspasia*, but whereas an expert on marriage might be the most appropriate teacher for members of Callias' family, there is no indication that the Great King, as the wealthiest landowner in the world, would be the best teacher for Critoboulus;[35] for Crito-

---

[33]LSJ s.v. gives this sense of *apopeiraomai*, adducing as evidence Plato *Portagoras* 311b, 349c. Cf. Ar. *Nub.* 477, where the chorus tell Socrates to "make trial of" or "refute" (*upopeirō*) the beliefs of Strepsiades.

[34]Socrates' slight of the βαναυσικαὶ τέχναι, the "illiberal" arts, ought to be taken, with Strauss (above, note 3), p. 115, as a biased remark playing on the prejudices of Critoboulus. The philosophical implications of the remark, however, lie in Socrates' use of the word καταλυμαίνονται, which is a recurrent theme in the *Oeconomicus*. In the instances where it occurs, it implies that one may "harm" an instrument if one does not know how to use it (2.13, 3.10). If, therefore, the manual arts spoil the bodies of those who practice them, they must not fulfill the highest function of a human being, which is the general purport of the passage.

[35]Strauss (above, note 3), p. 113.

boulus problems are related not to money but to his careless pursuit of lovers (*Oec.* 2.7).

In the speech that follows, Socrates advocates imitation of the King of Persia and farming in particular. He emphasizes the "pleasant," ἡδύς, and the "beautiful" or "noble," καλός, aspects of the life of the Great King in chapter 4 and of the farming life per se in chapter 5. Socrates notes that the Great King's personal farms are paradises, full of good and "beautiful" things. When Lysander sees the gardens at Sardis, Cyrus is dressed in unusually "beautiful" clothes of which Lysander takes special note (*Oec.* 4.23). Lysander remarks on the "beauty" of the gardens, which "pleases" Cyrus greatly (4.21–22). Yet after seeing how elaborately dressed the king is, Lysander refuses to call him a *kaloskagathos* and, withholding the *kalos*, calls him only *agathos* (4.25).[36]

When Socrates describes farming, he calls it a luxury, ἡδυπάθεια, a word that denotes debauchery in the *Memorabilia* (2.6.24) and *Symposium* (4.9, 41). The earth is said to provide decoration for altars along with the most "pleasant" smells and sights (*Oec.* 5.3).[37] He asks: "What art is more 'pleasant' than farming, inviting all comers to take what they will? What art more generous for entertaining guests?" (5.7). (The obligation to entertain guests is one of Critoboulus' problems at *Oeconomicus* 2.5). The farming life provides warm baths in winter, is "pleasant" for wives, and desired by children (5.10). He again emphasizes the "pleasantness" of farming by saying that no possession is more "pleasant," ἥδιον (5.11). The earth is said to teach justice, but her definition of justice is that she allows the most hardworking (5.4), the strongest (5.7), and the most manly to benefit from her the most. This definition based on the survival of the fittest describes the justice of nature, *physis*, not of man. The entire passage is very similar to the position advocated by Unjust Speech in the *Clouds.*[38]

The same sort of parallels exist between Ischomachus and the *dikaios logos*. Just Speech is older (*Nub.* 915), is plainly dressed, and disdains

---

[36]Strauss (above, note 3), p. 119. We also know that Lysander wanted money from Cyrus for his navy, a fact that might suggest that even Lysander's limited praise is prompted by need (Xen. *Hell.* 1.5.1–9; Plut. *Lys.* 4).

[37]κόσμος and κοσμέω are used throughout chapters 4 and 5 to emphasize the appearance and luxury of Cyrus: 4.8, 23; 5.3.

[38]The emphasis on pleasure recalls Unjust Speech's hedonistic τέλος (*Nub.* 1074). The portrayal of Cyrus in all of his torques and fine robes recalls the appearance of Unjust Speech when he enters the stage (920). All three issues with which Unjust Speech refutes Just Speech are advocated by Socrates in chapters 4 and 5. Socrates praises warm baths, as does Unjust Speech (1044–54). The justice that the earth teaches has its parallel in the argument by Unjust Speech that rhetorical skill should be used to the advantage of the best speaker (1055–59). Last, the entire basis of Socrates' panegyric on the farming life is its pleasure, an argument from *physis* used by Unjust Speech (1075).

the ornate decoration of his opponent (920); he rejects makeup (977), warm baths (991, 1045), and those who linger in the agora practicing rhetoric (1003–4); he approves of modesty and chastity, τὸ σωφρονεῖν (1061–69), and he is slandered by an unchaste audience of citizens (1085–1104); he is manly and advocates vigorous exercise to give the skin that desirable glow (1009–18). Ischomachus is clearly the older of him and Socrates; he disdains ornate dress (*Oec.* 10.3) and makeup (10.5) and uses a strigil to clean himself in the manly fashion rather than baths (11.18); he takes note of the idlers in the agora who do harm to others and the city (11.22); he believes in *to sōphronein*, which he defines not as chastity but as "making one's possessions as good as possible and increasing them by just and noble means" (7.15); he too is slandered by the city (11.21); he advocates work for his wife (10.11) and exercise for himself (11.12) to produce that healthy glow.[39] Last, Just Speech loses the debate because he cannot use rhetoric and argument to defend his position.[40] Ischomachus loses arguments with his wife because he cannot "make the weaker argument the stronger" (11.25).

Socrates continues to use "pleasant" and "beautiful" throughout his dialogue with Ischomachus.[41] Xenophon portrays his own version of the debate between Unjust and Just Speech in the dialogue of Socrates and Ischomachus. In Xenophon's version, however, Socrates need not refute his adversary, because the ultimate refutation of Ischomachus' teaching is already known. (Just as Socrates' school is burned to the ground in the *Clouds*, Ischomachus' family is brought to shame and infamy by the public outrage his wife commits.) Rather, Socrates is able to let Critoboulus judge the merit of Ischomachus' discourse for himself. The task that remains is to discern whether Xenophon was indicting Socrates as Aristophanes did, or whether there is some higher purpose to Xenophon's response to the *Clouds*. One must ask whether Socrates actually corrupts the young Critoboulus, as Unjust Speech did Pheidippides, or whether some positive teaching emerges from his suspect method.

3. Eros and Economics

In his long speech at the end of the *Symposium*, Socrates attempts to persuade Callias with ironic praise not to make improper advances on

---

[39]Cf. εὐχροωτέραν at *Oec.* 10.11 and χροιὰν λαμπράν at *Nub.* 1012, and see *Oec.* 10.1 for the manly training of Ischomachus' wife.

[40]Nussbaum (above, note 29), pp. 62–63; Strauss (above, note 29), pp. 31–33.

[41]*Oec.* 7.9; 10.1; 11.10–11, 13; 15.13; 16.9.

his beloved, Autolycus (8.12). He argues that one should use neither force nor persuasion to attain what one wants from a lover:

ὁ μὲν γὰρ βιαζόμενος ἑαυτὸν πονηρὸν ἀποδεικνύει, ὁ δὲ πείθων τὴν τοῦ ἀναπειθομένου ψυχὴν διαφθείρει. ἀλλὰ μὴν καὶ ὁ χρημάτων γε ἀπεμπολῶν τὴν ὥραν τί μᾶλλον στέρξει τὸν πριάμενον ἢ ὁ ἐν ἀγορᾷ πωλῶνκαὶ ἀποδιδόμενος;

For the man who uses force reveals himself as a lecher, but one who uses persuasion corrupts the soul of the one he persuades. By the same token, why in the world would one who sells his youth for money have more affection for the one who buys it than would a businessman who sells and delivers his wares in the market? (8.20–21)

After portraying the problem of treating lovers casually, as things that can be bought, sold, forced, or won over, Socrates attempts to describe the difference between Heavenly Love and Vulgar Love.[42]

καὶ γὰρ δὴ δοκεῖ μοι ὁ μὲν τῷ εἴδει τὸν νοῦν προσέχων μεμισθωμένῳ χώρον ἐοικέναι. οὐ γὰρ ὅπως πλείονος ἄξιος γένηται ἐπιμελεῖται, ἀλλ’ ὅπως αὐτὸς ὅτι πλεῖστα ὡραῖα καρπώσεται. ὁ δὲ τῆς φιλίας ἐφιέμενος μᾶλλον ἔοικε τῷ τὸν οἰκεῖον ἀγρὸν κεκτημένῳ· πάντοθεν γοῦν φέρων ὅ τι ἂν δύνηται πλείονος ἄξιον ποιεῖ τὸν ἐρώμενον.

For truly, one who pays attention to his lover's appearance alone seems to me to be like someone who has leased a plot of land. For he will not take pains that it become more valuable, but only that he himself reap as great a harvest as possible. But one who longs for friendship is more like someone who has acquired his very own field. By bringing whatever he can from wherever he can get it, he makes that which he loves more valuable. (8.25)

These passages help to explain the Xenophontic Socrates' conception of the relationship of *oikonomia* and of the *basilikē technē* to *philia*.

The goal of the estate management in this passage is to increase the "value" of the estate but not to make the estate as productive as possible at the expense of its "value." The long-term good of the estate is more important than its short-term profitability. When he speaks of friendship, Socrates implies that either one can attempt to reap a momentary profit of pleasure from a friend or one can invest in a long-term relationship "by bringing whatever one can get from wherever one can get it" in order to make the friend better. Since Socratic education is aimed at the "improvement" of a human being, one might conclude that education grows out of friendship and that both are

---

[42]Cf. the speech of Pausanias in Plato *Symposium* 180d–185c.

founded on Socrates' understanding of *oikonomia*. When this concept of management is applied to political rule, it implies that one rules not for one's own sake but for the sake of the governed. Socrates and Thrasymachus argue this same point in the *Republic,* where the art of making money, chrematistics, has to be separated from the art of ruling (341c–344c).[43] Thrasymachus supposes that the purpose of ruling is to reap a profit; Socrates argues that its purpose is to make the governed better. When Socrates discusses *philia* in Xenophon's *Symposium,* the chrematistic view becomes Vulgar Love and the true art of ruling becomes Heavenly Love.

The subtlety with which Xenophon treats these issues should not go unnoticed. The precise wording of Socrates' summary of Ischomachus' view is masterfully obfuscating: Νὴ Δία, ἐγὼ δέ γέ σοι, ἔφην, ὦ Ἰσχόμαχε, ἐπομόσας λέγω ἦ μὴν πιστεύειν σοι φύσει φιλεῖν ταῦτα πάντας, ἀφ' ὧν ἂν ὠφελεῖσθαι νομίζωσιν, "By Zeus, I said, I say to you, Ischomachus, with a solemn oath, that I believe you that all men love by nature those things by which they may think they are benefited" (*Oec.* 20.29). Socrates uses the word *phileō* to allude to the difference between the two different conceptions of "love," and he masks his position by the ambiguous use of *ōpheleō.* "Beneficial" is a neutral term that can apply to things or to people. When it is used to describe how one benefits from a thing, it refers to profit, and when it is used of benefit from people, to good service. The definition of *oikonomia* as the knowledge of how to make that which one possesses "beneficial" can suit either chrematistics or the true art of ruling. In order to show how Socrates intends for Critobulus to apply the art of ruling to his goal of becoming a gentleman and making friends with gentlemen, it is useful to examine how Ischomachus conceives of the application of the "beneficial" to his relationships with people.

The process of making people "beneficial" is a kind of education. Xenophon introduces the subject of education in chapter 3, where he and Critoboulus discuss the need to train wives. Socrates says that young men, like young horses, reach an age where they become useful and "continue to become better" (3.10). Plato's Protagoras promises that anyone who studies with him becomes better and every day "continues to become better" (*Prt.* 318a). Aeschines' Aspasia tells Xenophon and his wife that they must make each other as good as possible (Cic. *Inv. rhet.* 31.52). The implication in the *Protagoras* and in the *Aspasia* is that improvement comes about through an education in moral virtue. Xe-

---

[43]See Breitenbach (above, note 3), cols. 1869–70; Strauss (above, note 3), pp. 200–204. This section attempts to disprove Strauss's position (p. 202) that Socrates is recommending chrematistics to Critobulus.

nophon conceives of improvement in the same way in the *Memorabilia*, where Socrates associates "becoming better" with moral education.[44] Education enables people to know and do what is "beneficial" (*Mem.* 4.1.5).

There is no hint of Ischomachus giving either his wife or his servants moral education. Ischomachus first teaches his wife that *sophrosyne* is the practice of making one's property as good as possible and of increasing it by noble and just means (7.15). She is to accomplish this by overseeing the interior needs of the house: keeping the inventory (7.25), rousing the workers to the fields (7.33), presiding over the loom (7.34), and the like. She is taught organization (8.10) and administrative control over the servants (9.14). Last, she is taught to avoid makeup and to make herself pleasing by working (10.9–10).[45] Each part of her education will make her more "profitable" to Ischomachus, but no part will give her insight into the nature of virtue.

When Ischomachus trains his bailiffs, he teaches them the following: loyalty by giving them a share of the profits (12.6–7); concern for the welfare of the estate by gifts and praise (12.15–16); the art of ruling by teaching them to punish slaves when they disobey and to reward them when they obey (13.4–12); and justice, that is, not to steal, by treating them just as he told them to treat the slaves with punishments from the laws of Draco and Solon and rewards from the laws of the King of Persia (14.3–10). The basis of his entire training is financial reward for obedience and punishment for disobedience. He holds a high esteem of his training and claims that he treats his loyal servants "*just like* free men" (ὥσπερ ἐλευθέροις) by enriching them and by honoring them "*like* gentlemen" (ὡς καλούς τε κἀγαθούς, 14.9). This should not obscure the fact that Ischomachus uses money and praise to win the "willing" obedience of those who are not free to choose to disobey. Xenophon's use of *ōsper*, "just as," indicates that Ischomachus gives "the

---

[44]*Mem.* 1.2.61; 1.6.9; 2.2.4, 6; 2.3.17; 3.3.2; 4.2.23; esp. 4.8.6–11.

[45]The observation of Strauss (above, note 3), pp. 147–50, that her education on the subject of order, for instance, is a model for the method by which Socrates himself teaches is well taken. I disagree with his interpretation of Xenophon's intentions, however, when he suggests that Socrates learned how to be a philosopher from Ischomachus (p. 148). I would state the case differently. Socrates is showing Critobulus a model of pure chrematistics that so alienated Socrates in his youth that he turned to human investigations. Strauss's interpretation of Ischomachus' teachings as a model of the Socratic enterprise implies that Critoboulus should imitate him. Strauss fails to define whether Critoboulus should imitate him exactly or by some enlightened interpretation, and so I would see the philosophical applications of Ischomachus' teachings as an indication that he is a sort of anti-Socrates, as Just and Unjust Speech are opposites of one another, although sharing some common attributes.

appearance" of being free and "the appearance" of being gentlemen to men who are "in reality" neither.[46]

Socrates expresses dissatisfaction with the training both of Ischomachus' wife and of his bailiffs. While listening patiently to Ischomachus' discourse with his wife, Socrates expresses his surprise at the way he teaches and asks whether it works (8.1; 9.1, 18; 10.9). When Ischomachus describes how he teaches servants, Socrates expresses the same surprise (12.6, 10; 13.5; 15.3) and continually asks whether the servants "need [to learn] something more" (13.1, 3; 14.1; 15.1). The source of his dissatisfaction appears to lie in Ischomachus' failure to appreciate the potential of human beings for some higher kind of improvement. Ischomachus even compares his training to the way one trains colts (13.7), an apparent allusion to the Callias passage in Plato's *Apology* (20a–b; cf. *Oec.* 3.10).

Throughout Ischomachus' discourse on his relations with human beings, Socrates is largely silent or dubious and questioning, with one exception. In the central chapter of the *Oeconomicus*, where Ischomachus describes what a *kaloskagathos* does, Socrates engages Ischomachus. He has a special interest in understanding what a gentleman is and does. When Ischomachus says that Socrates might be able to correct him if he speaks out of turn, Socrates deprecates himself by alluding to his characterization by Aristophanes. He says that this slander would have disheartened him entirely if he had not learned that money was not necessary to acquire virtue. He says that when he saw a crowd admiring the horse of Nicias the foreigner, he asked whether the horse had a lot of money. When he was met with puzzled looks, he realized that money was not a condition for virtue, and he now asks Ischomachus to teach him virtue. Ischomachus responds: "You're a kidder, Socrates" (11.3–7). This passage demonstrates that Socrates indeed desires to separate chrematistics from virtue. Moreover, his humorous reference to the horse emphasizes rather pathetically that a human being cannot be educated like an animal.

When Socrates and Ischomachus pass to a discussion of farming per se, a dramatic shift takes place. Socrates expresses renewed interest in the views of Ischomachus. They speak freely, and Ischomachus leads Socrates through dialectic to an understanding of farming. The reason

---

[46]There are two forces of *ōsper:* to indicate a close comparison, "like as, even as"; and to limit or modify an assertion or apologize for a metaphor, "as it were, so to speak" (LSJ s.v. I and II). I submit that while Ischomachus may flatter himself by thinking that he treats them "just as free men," the latter meaning, "free men, as it were," gives the appropriate pathetic ring to what Xenophon intends.

for this sudden change is that Ischomachus is no longer talking about the education of human beings, where his limited view of human "benefit" left Socrates dissatisfied. When he speaks of the land, his desire to make it as good as possible seems to fit Socrates' simile of Heavenly Love until the very end, when Socrates discovers that here too chrematistics is more important to Ischomachus than his love of farming.

In the course of their dialogue, Ischomachus speaks about farming in a way that is consistent with Socrates' description of farming in his simile from the *Symposium*. Ischomachus' words have certain applications to moral education. They first discuss the nature of the soil (16.1–2). As a teacher, Socrates had first to consider the nature of his students (*Mem.* 4.1.3).[47] When they discuss the sowing of seed, Socrates asks whether soil is like draught animals in that the more one puts in them, the more one gets out (*Oec.* 17.9). Ischomachus again says that Socrates is "kidding around" and replies that weak soil needs less seed (17.10–11). Although Ischomachus trains men like animals, he recognizes that land must be treated differently, case by case, and whereas he teaches his servants justice only by rewarding the hardest workers, he treats land according to its own particular nature, *physis*. Socrates focuses attention on his interest in the philosophical applications of this discussion by calling himself a philosopher (16.9). When Ischomachus compares weeds to useless drones in a beehive, Socrates reacts very eagerly (17.14–15). The mention of drones recalls to Socrates the need to "cut out" like weeds that which is "unbeneficial" in one's life: vice (*Cyr.* 2.2.25; *Mem.* 1.2.54–55). Finally, they consider the planting of fruit trees (*Oec.* 19.1). Socrates compares the cultivation of friends to the cultivation of fruit trees in *Memorabilia* 2.4.7.

In the end, Socrates learns that Ischomachus buys run-down farms and improves them (*Oec.* 20.22–23), just as he himself improves those who need education. But while Ischomachus does so for profit (20.24–28), Socrates improves human beings for their own sake. In the *Memorabilia* Socrates reveals that his purpose in educating others is not money but friendship:

ἐθαύμαζε δ', εἴ τις ἀρετὴν ἐπαγγελλόμενος ἀργύριον πράττοιτο καὶ μὴ νομίζοι τὸ μέγιστον κέρδος ἕξειν φίλον ἀγαθὸν κτησάμενος, ἀλλὰ φοβοῖτο, μὴ ὁ γενόμενος καλὸς κἀγαθὸς τῷ τὰ μέγιστα εὐεργετήσαντι μὴ τὴν μεγίστην χάριν ἔξοι.

He was amazed that anyone would take money for introducing others to virtue and that anyone would not consider that he would have the greatest

---

[47]David O'Connor's essay treats the kind of students Socrates seeks and the significance of the requirement that they have "good natures" (see Chapter 6, section 5).

gain from acquiring a good friend and would instead fear that anyone who had become a gentleman would not have the greatest affection for the one who had given him the greatest benefaction. (1.2.7)

In order to interpret how Socrates' promises in chapter 3 are fulfilled, one must understand that Socrates has a higher or even "ironic" definition of *oikonomia*. Socrates is using the topic of estate management to teach Critoboulus about friendship. For Socrates, the worth of a household must be measured in human terms. An increase in the value of a household can be accomplished only by making those who use it better educated and thus more beneficial to one another. Ischomachus possesses great material wealth, but his knowledge of how to make money does not make human beings more "beneficial" to others, only more "profitable" to him. Socrates, on the other hand, possesses very little material wealth and yet has an abundance of friends who are a source of "benefit" to him and to others. The true possessor of the kingly art and the true gentleman knows how to benefit human beings and treats friends as his most valuable possession.

The question of why Socrates would teach this lesson so paradoxically and of why Xenophon would compare this lesson for Critoboulus to the debate between Just and Unjust Speech is best explained by the profoundly ironic final words of Ischomachus: "[The gods] give tyrannical rule over unwilling subjects, as it seems to me, to whomever they consider to be worthy to live just like Tantalus is said to live in Hades: spending all eternity in fear of dying a second time" (τὸ δὲ ἀκόντων τυραννεῖν διδόασιν, ὡς ἐμοὶ δοκεῖ, οὓς ἂν ἡγῶνται ἀξίους εἶναι βιοτεύειν ὥσπερ ὁ Τάνταλος ἐν Ἅιδου λέγεται τὸν ἀεὶ χρόνον διατρίβειν φοβούμενος, μὴ δὶς ἀποθάνῃ, *Oec.* 21.12). The irony of the reference of Tantalus is twofold. Ischomachus, like Tantalus, has wealth beyond measure, the source of which is land.[48] They share a love of both money and land. There is some doubt, moreover, that Ischomachus rules over willing subjects. His wife is bound to him by marriage, and his bailiffs and slaves are bound to him by ownership and ruled by the laws of Draco and Solon. His system of rewards for fidelity is nothing more than an attempt to buy willingness with money. Socrates argues in the *Symposium* that while one who uses force on a lover exposes his own baseness, one who uses persuasive means corrupts the soul of the one he persuades (8.20–21). There are good grounds to suspect that

---

[48]Aes. *Niobe* frs. 158–59 = Plut. *De exil.* 603a–b and *Max.cum princ.* 778b–c. Interestingly enough, Plutarch refers to Xenophon both times he cites fr. 158. He portrays Tantalus as a large landholder and uses the metaphor of farming for friendship (cf. *Max. cum princ.* 776d). Plato also considers Tantalus' wealth prodigious (*Euthd.* 11d; *Prt.* 315d).

Ischomachus is very much like Tantalus and that the destruction to which his family comes is like the punishment of Tantalus.

These words also express the nature of Socrates' practice of the kingly art as a teacher. He can lead his students to virtue only if they themselves wish to be led. Xenophon makes much of the fact that Critias and Alcibiades did not become true followers of Socrates because they were "unwilling" to be refuted (*Mem.* 1.2.47). Socrates teaches his students what they want to learn. When they, like Critoboulus, desire only wealth and reputation and sexual license, Socrates shows them that the ultimate outcome of their desires will be ruinous. Just as Aristophanes taught Socrates the necessity of examining the human things, so too Socrates prompts Critoboulus to consider the human things by a comedy of his own.

I have argued in this essay that the *Oeconomicus* is a Socratic dialogue, not a treatise expressing Xenophon's views on farming. The problems that Critoboulus is shown to have in Xenophon's other writings must affect how one understands Socrates' purpose in this dialogue. Socrates must be attempting to teach Critoboulus the difference between real friendships and the hedonistic trysts he currently pursues. Socrates gives Critoboulus a subtle warning that he will not understand the story of his encounter with Ischomachus unless he "cross-examines" himself as he listens. He must ask himself whether what he is hearing about *oikonomia* has some applications to his own favorite topic of *philia*.

The identity of Ischomachus should create substantial doubts in the mind of Critoboulus about emulating this "reputed gentleman." Moreover, the sophisticated use of parallels between Socrates and Ischomachus and Unjust and Just Speech from Aristophanes' *Clouds* should confirm these doubts. Socrates puts on a comedy for Critoboulus where he stars as Unjust Speech and Ischomachus stars as Just Speech. Critoboulus knows that just as Socrates' school burned to the ground in Aristophanes' *Clouds,* in this real-life comedy Ischomachus' family comes into the most hideous ill repute. The closing reference to the punishment of Tantalus would only confirm his fears. Socrates shows him how appealing the life of a "reputed gentleman" can be with his constant references to the "sweetness" and "beauty" of the farming life. But Critoboulus should also beware that "the sweet life" has a price. The kind of "willing subjects" Ischomachus has is not the kind Critoboulus wants. Socrates has tried to show Critoboulus that his usurious kind of love is a misapplication of the kingly art of ruling: Critoboulus has been tyrannical with his beauty, using it to buy and sell lovers for pleasure the way Ischomachus uses people and property for his own profit.

There is another way to treat people, and this is suggested by the example of Socrates himself, who does not imitate Ischomachus. Socrates went on to find a higher definition of "a ruler of willing subjects" in his investigation of the human things. He cannot force this definition upon his students against their will, as that would contradict the definition itself. He shows those who are willing to do so how to evaluate themselves by what one might rightly call an "ironic" method of telling stories that have an apparent meaning and a higher and truer meaning. This method suggests not only that Socrates does not approve of the conventional definition of a gentleman but that he regards this life as having only the appearance of virtue without the necessary substance. The life that uses wealth as the basis of human relationships ignores the paradoxical truth that Socratic poverty makes possible friendship, which is the truest form of wealth and the basis of the best way of life.

PART II

The Hellenistic Heirs
of Socrates

[9]

Plato's Socrates and the Stoics

Gisela Striker

It is no novelty to say that the Stoics saw themselves as followers of Socrates. According to Diogenes Laertius (7.2), Zeno turned to philosophy after reading the second book of Xenophon's *Memorabilia*. The Socratic descent of the Stoics was canonized into a school genealogy by the Hellenistic historians, who constructed the "succession" Socrates-Antisthenes-Diogenes-Crates-Zeno. As far as this suggests that each of the older philosophers was in some formal sense a teacher of the next, this is probably an exaggeration.[1] However, it is easy to find typically "Socratic" doctrines in Stoic ethics—such as, for example, the conception of virtue as a kind of knowledge, with its corollary, the denial of ἀκρασία; the thesis of the unity of the virtues; and also, at least on one common ancient interpretation of Socrates, the notorious thesis that virtue is identical with happiness. But the genealogy also seems to indicate that the Stoics' Socrates was not, or not primarily, Plato's Socrates, but rather the Socrates of Antisthenes and the Cynics, or possibly Xenophon's.[2] And indeed the Stoic system looks at first sight so different from what we seem to find in Plato's early dialogues that one might be inclined to think that the Stoic version of Socratic doctrine had very little to do with the Socrates of those dialogues. This may be the reason why recent studies of Stoic philosophy have tended, in the

[1]Cf. G. Giannantoni, *Socraticorum Reliquiae* (Naples, 1983–85), 3:706–11.
[2]For Xenophon's Socrates as a possible source of reflection for the early Stoics, see the essay of Joseph DeFilippo and Phillip Mitsis in Chapter 10 of this volume.

absence of extant texts by the major Cynics, to concentrate on the influence of Aristotle rather than Plato as a philosophical predecessor
of Stoicism.[3]

This picture has of course been radically challenged by F. H.
Sandbach;[4] but whether or not the Stoics read Aristotle at all, we might
take Sandbach's monograph as a salutary reminder that proximity in
time need not mean proximity in thought. By contrast with Aristotle,
there seems to be good evidence that the Stoics read Plato. Zeno is
said to have written against the *Republic* (Plut. *De Stoic. repugn.* 1043e),
and Plutarch also mentions several times a book by Chrysippus entitled *Against Plato on Justice* (*De Stoic. repugn.* 1040a; cf. 1040d, 1041c–
d; *De comm. not.* 1070f), in which Chrysippus too seems to have mainly
criticized the *Republic*.[5] Zeno also is said to have been a pupil of Xenocrates and Polemon, but no Peripatetic is mentioned among his teachers. So apparently Zeno went to the Academy, not the Lyceum. The
assumption that he must have known and studied Aristotle's writings seems mainly based on the tradition according to which Theophrastus was the most popular teacher of philosophy at the time Zeno
came to Athens.

If the Stoics knew at least some of Plato's books rather well but also,
as is evident, did not agree with most of his ethics, we should assume
that they could hardly have ignored what Plato had to say about those
Socratic doctrines that they themselves had adopted. That is to say, we
should expect them to have sought a way out of the difficulties Plato
had pointed out, so as to show that they were not open to the same
objections. I think indeed that this is what they did—they tried to construct a Socratic ethics that would be immune to Plato's criticisms, and
they attacked Plato in turn where they thought he had left Socratic
ground, thereby producing an alternative version of certain doctrines
that were developed by Plato (and, as it happens, Aristotle) in a different direction. Thus I think Socrates' influence on the Stoics was not
limited to some attractive theses the Stoics undertook to argue on independent grounds. To some extent their Socrates was also Plato's, and
their version of Socratic doctrine might even be illuminating in places
where Plato apparently took an objection to be conclusive and tried a
different line.

---

[3]Cf. J. M. Rist, *Stoic Philosophy* (Cambridge, 1969), p. 1: "The phrase 'post-Aristotelian
philosophy' is gradually being taken to refer to philosophy largely governed by Aristotle
rather than to philosophy posterior to Aristotle but largely unrelated to him." See also B.
Inwood, *Ethics and Human Action in Early Stoicism* (Oxford, 1985), pp. 9–17, with my discussion, *Canadian Journal of Philosophy* 19 (1989): 91–100 at pp. 93–96.

[4]*Aristotle and the Stoics*, Proceedings of the Cambridge Philological Society 10 (Cambridge, 1985); for some reservations, see B. Inwood, *PR* 95 (1986): 470–73.

[5]For discussion, see P. A. Vander Waerdt's essay in Chapter 11.

I try to illustrate this general picture by two connected examples: first, the thesis that virtue is sufficient for happiness,[6] and second, the doctrine that virtue is a kind of knowledge or a craft, namely, knowledge of good and evil. Both were abandoned by Plato in his mature dialogues, and both were defended by the Stoics.

1. The Sufficiency of Virtue for Happiness

The *Gorgias* contains probably the most explicit statements of Socrates' thesis that virtue (or justice) is all that is needed for happiness. At 471e, Socrates declares: "I say that the admirable [καλός] and good person, man or woman, is happy, but that the one who is unjust and bad is miserable."[7] In the *Gorgias,* this claim is defended first by an indirect argument to show that injustice is the greatest evil and hence incompatible with happiness; then, after the refutation of Callicles, by arguments purporting to show that even on Callicles' view, justice, being the good of the soul, will be needed for a happy life. Socrates concludes his argument at 507c by stating that "the good man does well and admirably whatever he does, and the man who does well is blessed and happy, while the corrupt man, the one who does badly, is miserable." As far as I can see, Socrates' arguments in this dialogue do not really support the claim that virtue or justice is not only necessary but sufficient for happiness—one has the impression that Socrates is overstating his case (and that Plato is aware of this—see the reactions of Callicles).

A different line of support for Socrates' thesis comes up in the *Euthydemus* (278e–282e and 289e–292e). There Socrates argues that the "kingly craft," easily recognizable as the "knowledge of good and evil" identified with virtue in other early dialogues, is the only good, strictly speaking. This is said to be so because all other so-called goods, things like health, beauty, wealth, and power, will be useful to those who have them only if used in the right way—and the kingly craft is what tells us how to use them. Therefore, as Socrates says (281d), "in all these things we said at first were good, the question is not how they are in themselves good by nature, but this is the point, it seems: if ignorance leads them, they are greater evils than their opposites, inasmuch as they are

---

[6]For this as a Socratic thesis, see, for example, G. Vlastos, "Happiness and Virtue in Socrates' Moral Theory," *PCPS* 30 (1984): 181–213; T. Brickhouse and N. Smith, "Socrates on Goods, Virtue, and Happiness," *OSAP* 5 (1987): 1–27.

[7]In this essay I have borrowed translations (sometimes modified) of the *Gorgias* from D. Zeyl, of the *Republic* from G. Grube, of the *Euthydemus* from L. Cooper, and of the *Philebus* from R. Hackforth.

more able to serve the leader who is bad; but if intelligence [φρόνησις] leads them, and wisdom, they are greater goods, while in themselves neither kind is worth anything at all." In this passage of the *Euthydemus,* Socrates asserts repeatedly that the user's craft alone (μόνον) will make us happy (cf. 232c, e; 292c1). Whether or not the conception of virtue as a user's craft is a good support for Socrates' apparent thesis, it must have been the one that most interested the Stoics, since they defended the theory that virtue is indeed such a craft.

I think that the *Euthydemus* already shows, on closer inspection, that the support provided by the theory of a "ruling craft" is not unambiguous. When Socrates says that "this craft alone will make us happy," does he mean it will make us happy all by itself, or only that it is indispensable for happiness? The statement that the ruling craft is the only real good might be taken to support the stronger claim; the fact that the conventional goods—health, wealth, and so on—are called goods after all, albeit only if used in the right way, might point to the weaker interpretation. I do not think that the text of the *Euthydemus* by itself is clear enough to settle the question. In fact, as I will now try to show, the craft model can be developed in two different ways to support one or the other view.

Let us suppose that virtue consists in making the right use of available resources. Then one might argue that, far from virtue being the only real good, and sufficient for happiness, a happy life requires both virtue and the nonmoral goods. It may be true that all other so-called goods besides virtue can be misused and will turn out harmful and dangerous in the absence of virtue, while virtue itself can bring no harm. But then it seems also true that the skill of using these "conditional goods" (Gregory Vlastos' term) would not help us much unless there was something upon which it could be exercised. A piano is no use without the pianist's skill, but neither is the skill worth much without an instrument. We seem to value both the skill and the instrument because we value the music, for which we need both.

Furthermore, it is clear that the quality and quantity of resources will make a difference to the result. While a good violinist might be able to play well even on a poor instrument, the music will certainly sound better if she has a Stradivari.[8] Similarly, the exercise of virtue is to some extent dependent upon available means. As Aristotle remarks (*Pol.* 2.5, 1263b13–14), in order to act generously, one needs some funds; so where there is no property, there is no largesse. For Aristotle as for the Stoics, the "goods of fortune" are the materials and instruments of virtuous activity. But according to Aristotle, if happiness consists in virtu-

---

[8]For this line of argument, cf. Alex. Aphr. *De anima* 2.160.31–161.3.

ous activity, it will not be complete without the "external" or "bodily" goods that permit us to exercise our virtue to the fullest degree.

Taken in this way, the craft model will still support the claim that virtue, and virtue alone, is necessary for happiness. Presumably one does not need each and every one of the nonmoral goods; they are to some extent interchangeable. All one needs is a fair amount of some of them, while nothing will turn out good if one lacks virtue. But at the same time the model surely undermines the claim that virtue is sufficient for happiness. The Stoics, I think, saw this point. But they wanted to defend both the craft model and the claim that virtue is sufficient for happiness, taking both of these, of course, to be Socratic doctrine. Hence they adopted a different way of evaluating performances and exercises of skill.

I assumed before that a violinist's performance was valued in terms of the music one hears. But of course one could also evaluate a performance as good or bad in terms of virtuosity alone. A good performer will be able to make the best of any given resources, and it is quite conceivable that an excellent violinist will do better on a mediocre instrument than a poor musician on a good one. It is also possible that a mediocre performer will sound better with a superb instrument than a superb musician on a bad instrument, but we might still recognize that the second performance was better, in one sense, than the first. This is certainly so with respect to virtue—notoriously, a small donation from a poor person may show greater generosity than a much larger gift from a millionaire, although the millionaire might benefit more people. Thus if we evaluate performances in terms of degree of skill, it will appear that materials or instruments are unimportant. All that counts is how well one plays, not how the music sounds. In order to maintain that virtue is the only good, one should interpret the craft model in this second way—and that is, I suggest, what the Stoics did. According to their theory, acting well is strictly a matter of skill, not of success. They maintained that the nonmoral goods were totally indifferent, neither good nor bad. For this they could, for example, find support in Socrates' repeated statements in the *Euthydemus* that the conventional goods are neither good nor bad. Hence they could also say that the quantity and quality of these things is irrelevant for the good life. They did not deny that a wise person would prefer health and wealth to their opposites, poverty and illness, but they insisted that the value of an action, and indeed the value of a life, does not depend on its success or results, so that the humble potter's life could in principle be just as good as the aristocratic politician's, provided they were equally good people. I would suspect that this interpretation of the craft model might have been more in line with the intuitions of the historical

Socrates than the more elitist and perfectionist conception of Aristotle. But the doctrine of virtue as a craft, as I have tried to show, is open to both interpretations. If one puts the stress on the results achieved by the craft, one will arrive at Aristotle's view. If one keeps in mind that virtue is to be the only thing that counts, one will prefer the Stoic perspective. As far as Socrates is concerned, I think what this suggests is that he may well have been an "unsystematic" philosopher, so that we should not try to decide which way *he* would have wanted to go. That is, after all, what one should expect from a man who refused to put anything in writing and practiced philosophy only by questioning his fellow citizens. To be sure, he had deep moral convictions; but I am not sure that they amounted to anything like a theory. Consistency is all that is required or guaranteed by Socrates' favorite technique, the elenchus—and the sufficiency of virtue for happiness is certainly consistent with the view that virtue is a craft, but it does not simply follow from that doctrine.

2. Virtue as Knowledge of Good and Evil

My second example is a little more complicated: Plato's criticism of the doctrine that virtue is knowledge of good and evil, and the Stoic response to it. The Stoics, like Plato and Socrates and unlike Aristotle, do not seem to have drawn a clear line between craft and knowledge,[9] and so "virtue as a craft" and "virtue as knowledge" are used to refer to the same thesis here. Plato's objections are stated at *Cleitophon* 409a–410a, *Euthydemus* 292a–e, and briefly again at *Republic* 505b–c. There seem to be two connected points.

In the *Cleitophon*, Socrates' disciples are asked to name the function or product (ἔργον) of the craft that is supposed to be justice. Clitophon insists, on the basis of examples, that for every craft there must be a product that is distinct from the craft itself. It is only when we know what the product is that we can understand what craft we are talking about, and in what way it could be useful. Apparently neither Socrates' disciples nor Socrates himself is capable of giving a satisfactory answer. The anonymous disciples first try answers like "the useful" or "the advantageous," which are rejected as being too general. As Clitophon points out, any craft should produce something useful; but still for each specific craft we should be able to say which specific useful result it produces.

[9]See M. Isnardi-Parente, *Techne* (Milan, 1966), p. 287.

The request for a distinct product of a craft has its parallel in the requirement of naming a distinct object for each specific branch of knowledge. Hence the initially promising suggestion that justice produces friendship in cities leads into the same difficulty as before when it turns out that the kind of civic friendship involved should be defined as ὁμόνοια, or agreement in knowledge; for then the question will be, Knowledge of what? which brings us back to where we were.

That the questions about the product of a craft and about the object of a branch of knowledge are treated as parallel comes out, for example, in the *Charmides* (165e–166b). Where there is no external product, as in the case of calculating, there will at least be a distinct object, namely, "the odd and even." I think the point is a conceptual one, which happens to hold for knowledge and craft alike: both branches of knowledge and crafts must be "of" something (τινος), where the genitive can cover different relations, such as knowledge—object (mathematics), craft—product (house building), or skill—performance (flute playing). The parallelism may have been suggested by the fact that where there is a product, the respective technical skill can be described alternatively as knowledge of X or as a craft of X, such as knowledge or craft of house building. Where the object of knowledge is something that can be made or brought about, Socrates assumes that the person who has the knowledge can also produce the object.

Plato's readers would probably remember from earlier dialogues that a Socratic answer to the question about justice might be that it is knowledge of (the) good. This is not even mentioned in the *Cleitophon*, presumably because it would fall under the same verdict as such answers as "advantageous" or "useful": every craft produces some good, but what we want to know is what specific good is produced by the craft that is justice.

One reason for the apparent difficulty in Socrates' position comes out in the *Euthydemus*. Socrates has argued that the only real good is some kind of knowledge, understood as the craft that knows how to use all the various things people tend to consider as goods—health, strength, wealth, and so forth (281d–282a). When he later raises the question about the product of this kingly craft, it turns out that the interlocutors can find no illuminating answer, because, on the one hand, wisdom is said to be the craft that will make us good and happy, and, on the other hand, the good that it produces seems to be wisdom itself:

> What about the kingly craft, ruling over everything that it rules? What does it produce? Perhaps you cannot say exactly.

> No indeed, Socrates.

Nor could we, my dear Crito. But I know this much, that if it is the craft we are seeking, it must be useful.

Certainly.

Then surely it must provide some good for us?

Necessarily so, Socrates.

But good, as Clinias and I agreed together, is nothing but some kind of knowledge. (292a–b)

The problem, then, seems to arise from the fact that Socrates wants to hold both that wisdom is knowledge of good and that wisdom itself is the good that is its product. So the description of wisdom as knowledge of good turns out to be uninformative, because "good" is defined in terms of knowledge of good; and it also offends against the requirement that the object or product should be distinct from the knowledge or craft.

The same difficulties are briefly summarized again at *Republic* 505b–c, just before Socrates sets out to describe the Form of the good. Plato mentions two current but unacceptable answers to the question of what the good is: pleasure and wisdom or knowledge (*phronēsis*). The second candidate is disqualified by the remark that when the advocates of knowledge are asked what their knowledge is (knowledge) "of," they have no other answer than knowledge of the good. This is in itself ridiculous (505b11), presumably because *phronēsis* is said to be its own object; and it is also unilluminating because the good is defined in terms of the good itself. These people, though just acknowledged to be more sophisticated than the many who believe in pleasure, "blame us for not knowing the good and then again . . . talk to us as if we did know the good" (505c1–4).

It seems evident from the doxographical sources that the Stoics held both of the two theses that lead to the impasse in Socrates' theory: that virtue is knowledge of good (and evil), and that virtue is the only (human) good.[10] Consequently, Plutarch claims (*De comm. not.* 1072b) that they fall to Plato's objection: when asked what is the good, they will reply: "wisdom"; when asked what wisdom is, they will say: "knowledge of the good." But should we really assume that the Stoics simply ignored Plato's criticism? Since they certainly knew the *Republic*, and

---

[10]See, for example, Plut. *De Stoic. repugn.* 1034c–d; *De virt. mor.* 441a; Stob. *Ecl.* 2.101.5–6 Wachsmuth; Alex. Aphr. *De fato* 199.12 Bruns.

probably the *Cleitophon* and the *Euthydemus* as well,[11] this is rather un-likely. In any case, I think it can be shown that their theory avoids Pla-to's objections, and one might actually suspect that they found their solution by reflecting upon Plato's doctrine, though this cannot of course be proved.

After mentioning and rejecting pleasure and knowledge as candi-dates for the good, Plato in the *Republic* proceeds to describe what ap-pears to be his own candidate—the Form of the good. He seems to tell us that "what every soul pursues" is the object of knowledge, not the knowledge itself. Obviously, we cannot reach that object except by way of philosophy, and so perfect virtue will still include knowledge, but this is not itself the good. But this Platonic move, as Aristotle rightly insisted, was a mistake. The great achievement of the theory of Forms, I take it, is the distinction between subjects and properties, or, if you will, particulars and universals, not the discovery of some splendid and eternal objects of desire, whatever Plato may have thought in the *Sym-posium*. The Form of the good is not another candidate for the human good; it is rather what accounts for the goodness of all good things, including a good life or happiness—it is goodness itself, not the good for man. The human good must be such that we can do or acquire it (cf. Arist. *Eth. Nic.* 1, 1096b34). Plato, I think, had quietly corrected this error by the time he came to write the *Philebus*, where he explicitly distinguishes between the good life and the goodness inherent in it: "Then if we cannot hunt down the good under a single form, let us secure it by the conjunction of three—beauty, proportion, and truth—and then, regarding these three as one, let us assert that that may most properly be held to determine the mixture [i.e., the best life], and that because that is good, the mixture itself has become so" (65a). But once one sees that the Form of the good, or goodness, should not be placed on the same level as pleasure or knowledge, it also becomes apparent that it—or rather the distinction between goodness itself and the good life—might offer a solution to the problem of virtue as knowledge of the good; for when the object of this knowledge is construed, not as the human good, but as goodness, one can say that virtue is the *human* good, without thereby postulating a kind of knowledge that is its own object.

The Stoics, I think, noticed this point. At any rate, the Stoic sage's knowledge of the good does not seem to be simply describable as knowledge of the human good. The wise man will have grasped the

---

[11] For the *Cleitophon*, see H. Cherniss' note (a) to Plut. *De Stoic. repugn.* 1039d in his *Moralia XIII*, pt. 2 (Cambridge, Mass., 1976).

notion of the good; he will understand "what really deserves to be called good" (Cic. *Fin.* 3.21)—namely, rational order and harmony; and hence he will also realize that a human life will be good if it agrees with the order and harmony of nature. His knowledge of what is good or bad for human beings derives from this insight. His knowledge comprises, but is not limited to, knowledge of the human good. The difficulty in the *Euthydemus* seemed in part to arise from taking "knowledge of the good" to mean "knowledge of the human good"—certainly the most plausible interpretation of this phrase in the Socratic dialogues. If we interpret "knowledge of the good" as primarily knowledge of goodness, part of the problem raised for Socrates' doctrine disappears, since we can now distinguish between the sage's knowledge and its object. But we seem still to be left with a craft that is its own product—virtue was, after all, supposed to be the "art of living that produces happiness," according to the Stoics (Alex. Aphr. *De anima* 2.159.34). But here the Stoics could and certainly did use the distinction between a disposition or skill and its exercise. Strictly speaking, happiness consists in living virtuously, not in virtue itself, and living virtuously can be distinguished from virtue as the skill of a flute player can be distinguished from flute playing. So even if they took virtue to be knowledge of the human good, they would not be forced to admit that it was identical with its own object or product.

But this would not yet solve Plato's second problem, namely, that the human good is apparently defined in terms of the good itself. The Stoics still needed a definition that would explain what the goodness of a human life consists in. Notoriously, they did offer such a definition: they held that goodness consists in the rational order and harmony displayed most conspicuously by the order of the universe. Hence their official definition of the end for man as "living consistently" or "living in agreement with Nature" (see, for instance, D. L. 7.85–88). And there is also some evidence that they were aware of the fact that this definition can avoid the difficulty pointed out by Plato in the *Euthydemus* and the *Republic*. Plutarch reports that Chrysippus attacked Ariston of Chios—who was perhaps a more naive Socratic than Chrysippus himself—for defining virtue as "indifference toward what is neither good nor evil," and then the good in terms of virtue itself. Chrysippus insisted, I think, that if virtue was defined in terms of good and evil, then good and evil would have to be explained in some other way.[12] Ariston apparently refused to provide such an explanation. He may well have thought he was closer to Socrates than other Stoics when he

[12]For Chrysippus' argument against Ariston, see my "Following Nature: A Study in Stoic Ethics," *OSAP* 9 (1991): 1–73 at pp. 14–24.

refused to consider "physics" as a useful part of philosophy—and therefore also rejected the definition of the good that provides a non-circular explanation of virtue as knowledge of the good. But Chrysippus could hardly have criticized Ariston in this way if he had been subject to the same objection—pace Plutarch, who maintains just that.

Given the distinction between skill and performance, and the definition of the good in terms of rational order and harmony, both of Plato's objections to Socrates' doctrine could be disarmed. But in finding their solution the Stoics had to go beyond Socrates' own doctrine—and in a direction that seems to me remarkably similar to what Plato suggested in the *Philebus*. It is tempting to think that the Stoics not only noticed Plato's objections but also used him to find their solution. If Plato himself did not return to Socrates' theories after he had found ways of solving those puzzles, it will have been because he had come to doubt other parts of Socratic doctrine—for example, the underlying psychology, and indeed the thesis that virtue is sufficient for happiness.

[10]

Socrates and Stoic Natural Law

Joseph G. DeFilippo and Phillip T. Mitsis

It is widely acknowledged that Socrates was an important model for the Stoics. Not only do they cite him as a philosophical authority, but they frequently reflect on his arguments and his actions when developing their own doctrines.[1] In key respects, however, the Stoics' claim to be following in Socrates' footsteps might seem disingenuous. For instance, their self-conscious formulation of a unified philosophical system comprising logic, natural philosophy, and ethics does not look typically Socratic. Indeed, if one accepts the common portrait of a Socrates who rejects natural philosophy to concentrate exclusively on ethics, it is hard to avoid the conclusion that, given such sharply contrasting general outlooks, the Stoics' wish to be seen as "Socratics" is in fact rather odd.[2] Moreover, despite undeniable similarities in their respective ethical doctrines—for instance, an overall commitment to intellectualism and the unity of virtue—Socrates also served as a model for philosophers with widely divergent views, such as the Cyrenaics, the Cynics, and the Academic skeptics. Thus one might reasonably wonder how the Stoics could take themselves, or hope to present themselves to others, as Socrates' special heirs.

This question comes into sharper focus when one compares the Stoics to other ancient philosophical schools claiming descent from a great

---

[1]See A. A. Long, "Socrates in Hellenistic Philosophy," *CQ* n.s. 38 (1988): 150–71; M. Schofield, "Ariston of Chios and the Unity of Virtue," *AP* 4 (1984): 83–96; and Gisela Striker's essay, Chapter 9.

[2]For a typical example of the Stoics' claim to be "Socratics" see Philod. *De Stoic.*, cols. 12–13, in the edition of T. Dorandi, *Erc* 12 (1982): 91–132.

forerunner. No one today would suggest, for example, that Plato had Neoplatonist metaphysics in mind when writing the *Republic*. But even apart from Plotinus' explicit claims about his debts to Plato, it is obvious that Plato's writings are the direct inspiration for Neoplatonism. Plotinus does exegesis of Platonic texts and draws out their philosophical implications; the system he constructs, despite some obvious differences, is recognizably derived from Plato.

At first glance, it is not readily apparent how the Stoics could have derived elements of their theory of natural law from Socrates in a comparable manner. Whereas the separation of ethics from natural philosophy is often taken to be Socrates' most characteristic contribution to the history of philosophy, a hallmark of the Stoic theory is the conviction that one can derive principles of morality from laws governing the natural world. Thus, for example, Chrysippus claims that the most appropriate way to do ethics is from the perspective of natural philosophy:

πάλιν ἐν ταῖς 'Φυσικαῖς Θέσεσιν "οὐ γὰρ ἔστιν ἄλλως οὐδ' οἰκειότερον ἐπελθεῖν ἐπὶ τὸν τῶν ἀγαθῶν καὶ κακῶν λόγον οὐδ' ἐπὶ τὰς ἀρετὰς οὐδ' ἐπ' εὐδαιμονίαν, ἀλλ' <ἢ> ἀπὸ τῆς κοινῆς φύσεως καὶ ἀπὸ τῆς τοῦ κό-σμου διοικήσεως." προελθὼν δ' αὖθις· "δεῖ γὰρ τούτοις συνάψαι τὸν περὶ ἀγαθῶν καὶ κακῶν λόγον, οὐκ οὔσης ἄλλης ἀρχῆς αὐτῶν ἀμείνονος οὐδ' ἀναφορᾶς, οὐδ' ἄλλου τινὸς ἕνεκεν τῆς φυσικῆς θεωρίας παραληπτῆς οὔσης ἢ πρὸς τὴν περὶ ἀγαθῶν ἢ κακῶν διάστασιν."

Again in his *Physical Propositions* he [Chrysippus] says: "For there is no other or more suitable way of approaching the theory of good and evil or the virtues or happiness than from the universal nature [*koinēs phuseōs*] and from the dispensation of the universe." And further on once more: "For the theory of good and evil must be connected with these, since good and evil have no better beginning or point of reference, and physical speculation is to be undertaken for no other purpose, than for the discrimination of good and evil." (Plut. *De Stoic. Repugn.* 1035c = *SVF* 3.68, trans. Cherniss)

The Stoic view, moreover, is not simply that natural philosophy is necessary for achieving ethical understanding but that moral principles are in fact natural principles that reflect the rational order of the cosmos. These principles are not purely descriptive laws of nature, since they consist of moral commands issued by nature to rational beings.[3] A succinct formulation of this tenet of Stoicism is given by Chrysippus in the exordium to his Περὶ νόμου (*On Law*):

[3]Thus, unlike purely physical laws of the cosmos, the commands of natural law can be transgressed. For the Stoics, however, this fact does not vitiate their status as universal laws. The Stoics appealed to the inexorable adverse consequences of any violations— violations that, in a sense, mar one's functioning as a rational being (see below).

ὁ νόμος πάντων ἐστὶ βασιλεὺς θείων τε καὶ ἀνθρωπίνων πραγμάτων· δεῖ δὲ αὐτὸν προστάτην τε εἶναι τῶν καλῶν καὶ τῶν αἰσχρῶν καὶ ἄρχοντα καὶ ἡγεμόνα, καὶ κατὰ τοῦτο κανόνα τε εἶναι δικαίων καὶ ἀδίκων καὶ τῶν φύσει πολιτικῶν ζῴων προστακτικὸν μὲν ὧν ποιητέον, ἀπαγορευτικὸν δὲ ὧν οὐ ποιητέον.

Law is king of all things divine[4] and human. It must preside over what is honorable and base, both as ruler and as guide, and in virtue of this it must be the standard [*kanōn*] of justice and injustice, prescribing to animals whose nature is political what they should do, and prohibiting what they should not do. (Marcian *Inst.* 1 = *SVF* 3.314, trans. Long and Sedley 67R [adapted])

These two passages exhibit the basic contours of the Stoic theory of natural law. Human actions are taken to be governed by a universal moral law—a law that itself is thought to be identical with the rational order and administration of nature.[5] A virtuous and hence happy life depends, accordingly, on an understanding of that natural order and an ability to follow its dictates.

One might suppose, then, that only an arbitrary or self-deceptive mode of interpretation could have allowed the Stoics to view themselves as Socrates' heirs on the question of nature's rationality and morality. Such a supposition is further encouraged, no doubt, by the long-standing tradition concerning Socrates' rejection of natural philosophy. As Aristotle famously says in the *Metaphysics*, Socrates was concerned with ethics and "not at all with nature as a whole" (987b1–2). Aristotle's remark, when conjoined, for example, with the rejection of natural philosophy attributed to Socrates by Plato (*Ap.* 18b–23e; *Phd.* 96a–99d), suggests that Socrates would be hostile to the kind of nature-based ethics one finds in Stoicism.[6] Indeed, it is on this very point that Gisela Striker, writing on the origins of natural law theory, locates the Stoics' divergence from Socrates:

[According to the Stoics] knowledge of the good thus turns out to be, more precisely, knowledge of the rational order of nature. And since this order was assumed to have been created by divine reason, its rules could also be conceived of as laws given by a divine legislator.

[4]"Divine things" (τὰ θεῖα) almost certainly means here the heavenly bodies and their motions and thus stands for the natural world as a whole.
[5]Cf. Cleanthes *Hymn to Zeus* = *SVF* 1.537; Cic. *Nat. d.* 1.36: "Zeno autem . . . naturalem legem divinam esse censet, eamque vim obtinere recta imperantem prohibentemque contraria."
[6]Gregory Vlastos, for instance, argues that Socrates is no "dabbler in teleological cosmology. . . . Given his obsessive concentration on ethics, a *natural theology* he could not have produced" (*Socrates: Ironist and Moral Philosopher* [Ithaca, N.Y., 1991], p. 162).

Now of course this theory of nature as a rationally organised whole goes beyond anything Socrates ever said.[7]

We want to suggest, however, that on this particular question the Stoics took themselves to be well within the limits of what they thought Socrates himself had said; indeed, they were able to appeal to authoritative texts from Xenophon and Plato to establish a Socratic lineage for the chief elements of their theory. Our argument proceeds in two stages. First, we show how *Memorabilia* 1.4 was instrumental in the Stoics' adoption of Socrates as an authority for their conception of the divinely ordered rationality of nature. Xenophon's account provided the Stoics with a Socratic warrant for their natural theology, while giving them an authoritative source to rely on in rejecting the tradition that Socrates was in no way concerned with nature as a whole.[8] Second, we consider texts that would have suggested to the Stoics that Socrates held moral laws to be legislated by a rational deity. *Memorabilia* 4.4 explicitly sets out such a view; moreover, Plato's depiction of Socrates' calm and rational acceptance of death became a Stoic paradigm of how one should live in accordance with nature's divine laws. For the Stoics, Socrates' moral choices as he faced death exemplified not just those of a preeminently virtuous citizen of Athens; rather, they came to be seen as embodying the very principles that divine reason legislates for nature as a whole.

Of course, this is not to suggest that the Socrates we find in Xenophon and Plato, much less the historical Socrates, ever explicitly formulates a theory of natural law. But the presence in Socratic texts of the basic components of such a theory enabled the Stoics to construct their own account on a recognizably Socratic foundation. Indeed, it is likely that they considered themselves to be Socrates' heirs just insofar as they based their ethical principles on a conception of nature as a rationally ordered whole.

1. Socrates and the Rationality of Nature

In the first book of the *Memorabilia*,[9] Xenophon recounts a conversation between Socrates and Aristodemus, a notorious atheist (1.4.2).

---

[7]"Origins of the Concept of Natural Law," *PBACAP* 2 (1986): 79–94 at pp. 90–91.

[8]Here we are indebted to Long's observations (above, note 1), p. 163, about the importance of Xenophon for Zeno's adoption of Socrates as a source for "doctrines fundamental to Stoicism—thoroughgoing teleology, divine providence, the god's special concern for man, and the cosmic underpinnings for law and society."

[9]For general discussion of the *Memorabilia* see L. Robin, "Les 'Memorables' de Xenophon et notre connaissance de la philosophie de Socrate," *L'année philosophique* 12 (1910):

Socrates' overall goal is to demonstrate to Aristodemus the necessity of piety for happiness;[10] but to do so, he must first convince him that the gods actually exist. The basic strategy of Socrates' argument is to demonstrate that one can infer rationality in the natural world from human rationality; he then takes the presence of a rational order in nature to create a strong presumption in favor of the existence of god. It is worth considering these arguments in some detail, since they were to prove important for the Stoics' view of Socrates and for the development of their own philosophical theology.

Socrates begins his argument by attempting to show that living beings are products of rational design. At the outset, he gets Aristodemus to concede the general claim that if something is clearly useful for a purpose, then it must be the product of reason. Offering the sense organs as an initial example of things that are well designed to perform their functions, Socrates argues that they are paradigms of the purposiveness inherent in natural organisms. He then quickly extends his argument to include the appetites, emotions, and the general arrangement of the body. Socrates does not address the question of whether human beings have an overall purpose, but he takes himself to have established that since humans are the products of design, there must be a craftsmanlike cause of this design.

Socrates next turns to human reason (νοῦς) to show more directly that there is a rational power in the cosmos (1.4.8). The argument here is not that our reason is evidently the product of a rational designer. Instead, Socrates frames an analogy between *nous* and the material elements. He claims that if the small portions of earth, water, and other elements making up our bodies are drawn from vast stores of these elements in nature, the same must hold for the small portion of reason in each human being. On the basis of this analogy, he concludes that there must be reason at work in nature as a whole:

Ἄλλοθι δὲ οὐδαμοῦ οὐδὲν οἴει φρόνιμον εἶναι; καὶ ταῦτα εἰδὼς ὅτι γῆς τε μικρὸν μέρος ἐν τῷ σώματι πολλῆς οὔσης ἔχεις καὶ ὑγροῦ βραχὺ πολλοῦ ὄντος, καὶ τῶν ἄλλων δήπου μεγάλων ὄντων ἑκάστου μικρὸν μέρος λαβόντι τὸ σῶμα συνήρμοσταί σοι; νοῦν δὲ μόνον ἄρα οὐδαμοῦ ὄντα σε εὐτυχῶς πως δοκεῖς συναρπάσαι, καὶ τάδε τὰ ὑπερμεγέθη καὶ πλῆθος ἄπειρα δι' ἀφροσύνην τινὰ οὕτως οἴει εὐτάκτως ἔχειν;

Do you really believe that there is nothing intelligent [*phronimon*] anywhere else, especially since you know that you have in your body only a

---

1–47. For an extremely negative view of Xenophon as a source for the historical Socrates see H. Maier, *Sokrates, sein Werk und seine geschichtliche Stellung* (Tübingen, 1913).

[10]In Chapter 6 of this volume David O'Connor discusses other dimensions of Socrates' attack on Aristodemus' atheism.

small portion of all the earth that exists, and only a tiny bit of the vast
quantity of water, and that the portion of each of the other things comprising your body is minute in comparison to the whole? Do you suppose
that by some lucky chance you have snatched away and carried off for
yourself [*sunharpasai*] reason, though it alone exists nowhere else, and do
you thus believe that these huge and infinite masses are in such a well-
ordered state despite a lack of intelligence? (1.4.8–9)

Aristodemus initially resists this line of argument by claiming that he
can perceive no rational force governing the world (cf. *Mem.* 4.3.14).
However, by pointing out that the human soul governs the body,
Socrates forces him to concede that there is nothing paradoxical in the
existence of an explanatory entity that cannot be perceived.

Xenophon thus attributes to Socrates a teleological outlook that
extends both locally and globally. Local teleology is established by a
design argument that shows how both the parts and the overall structure of small-scale entities, that is, animal bodies, exhibit purpose. The
large-scale teleology of nature is defended by an analogy between reason and matter. Just as human bodies are composed of material stuffs
that are bits of larger masses, so too is each individual instance of rationality a portion of reason in the world at large. It is worth noting,
however, that Socrates offers no justification for treating reason as similar to matter in the relevant respects. His argument perhaps relies on
the causal principle that something cannot come from nothing, that is,
individual instances of reason must have some source or other. Or he
might be relying on the more specific version of this principle, what
Jonathan Barnes has called the "synonymy principle of causation,"
namely, if A brings it about that B is F, then A is F.[11] Either explanation, however, requires further defense, for Socrates has not shown that
reason cannot arise in humans from combinations of nonrational elements. Consequently, his argument is incomplete as it stands. We shall
see later that Zeno attempts to insulate his own conception of cosmic
reason from this type of attack, in part because of his reflections on
this gap in Socrates' argument.

The final section of *Memorabilia* 1.4 addresses Aristodemus' objection that even if the gods exist, they neither need service (θεραπεία)
from humans nor care about them at all (1.4.10). To counter this objection, Socrates first appeals to the benefits that gods have conferred
on men in virtue of the way they have designed them. This design—
including upright posture, hands, and the power of speech, as well as
intellect—is what distinguishes human beings on the *scala naturae* and

[11]See J. Barnes, *The Presocratic Philosophers* (London, 1979), 1: 119.

affords them a degree of happiness unattainable by other creatures. A crowning element of this happiness, Socrates concludes, is man's ability to perceive the existence of the divine in the beauty and order of the world (1.4.13).

The general tendency of these arguments in Xenophon conflicts with the familiar portrait of a Socrates who rejects natural philosophy as useless for making individuals virtuous and happy. Xenophon's Socrates proposes arguments that make explicit use of facts about the natural world and about man as part of nature's order. To be sure, he does not recommend a fine-grained analysis of the composition of living bodies in the style of certain pre-Socratics. To this extent, at least, he can be said to reject the goals of these natural philosophers. Nevertheless, he relies on a particular conception of the natural world and man's place in it as a natural organism. His arguments imply that, far from being useless, philosophizing about nature is necessary for establishing the nature and existence of the gods, and hence man's proper relationship to them. Ethical arguments on their own would therefore fail to encompass elements that he takes to be fundamental for understanding the nature of human happiness.

Xenophon's account of Socrates' attitude toward natural philosophy becomes clearer if we examine the foregoing claims in conjunction with *Memorabilia* 1.1. There Xenophon describes Socrates as eschewing the study of "the whole of nature" (τῆς τῶν πάντων φύσεως), and as deflating the pretensions of those who investigate the origin of the cosmos and the causes (ἀνάγκαι) of heavenly phenomena (1.1.11). Socrates does so by asking the φυσικοί whether they thought that they were doing the right thing by neglecting human affairs (τἀνθρώπινα) in favor of the divine (τὰ δαιμόνια, 1.1.12).[12] From the physicists' disagreements about *ta daimonia*, moreover, he draws the conclusion that knowledge about the detailed workings of nature is not even possible for humans (1.1.13). Socrates does not maintain a genuinely skeptical position, however, since he allows that the gods possess knowledge; his doubts extend to the possibility and usefulness of human knowledge about such divine matters.

It is evident from this passage that Socrates places his primary emphasis on ethical knowledge (cf. 1.1.16). Yet it might appear that in having Socrates claim to eschew the study of nature as a whole, Xenophon is guilty of inconsistency. In *Memorabilia* 1.4, we have seen, Socrates is

---

[12]Interestingly, *ta daimonia* is used here to characterize the natural world as an object of scientific study. The reason for this particular use of the word becomes clear from the larger context of *Memorabilia* 1.1.6. Human knowledge does not allow one to predict how future events will turn out, because the gods keep some causes hidden and available only

committed to a particular conception of natural philosophy. How, then, can this commitment be compatible with those claims in *Memorabilia* 1.1?[13] The inconsistency begins to dissolve when one recognizes that in *Memorabilia* 1.1 Xenophon qualifies the claim that Socrates eschews the study of nature as a whole. He makes it clear that Socrates is not committed to rejecting the study of natural philosophy *tout court*. Rather, Socrates' criticism is directed solely at the sort of detailed enquiry into physical causes that is so prevalent in pre-Socratic thought. That this is his target is suggested first by Xenophon's reference to such questions as the generation of the cosmos and the mechanisms (*anankai*, literally "necessities") of the natural world. This impression is strengthened at *Memorabilia* 1.1.14, where Socrates argues for a skeptical attitude toward the theories of the Eleatics and Atomists. His rejection of these sorts of detailed physical explanations, however, does not count as a whole-cloth dismissal of the value of natural philosophy.[14] What he objects to is concentrating on the study of *ta daimonia* at the expense of *tanthrōpina* (1.1.12). Socrates' own conversation, Xenophon tells us, always concentrated on human things (περὶ τῶν ἀνθρωπίνων), and he included in his enquiries such questions as What is piety? (*Mem.* 1.1.16). But as we have seen in *Memorabilia* 1.4, Socrates advances arguments for the teleology of the natural world in order to defend the importance of piety for human happiness, and he connects his teleology of nature to a particular conception of human nature and conduct. Far from ruling out natural philosophy, therefore, he uses it to establish the existence of the divine and a link between piety and happiness. What distinguishes Socrates from his pre-Socratic predecessors, therefore, is not a lack of interest in nature as such but his doubts about the possibility and worth of detailed accounts of the hidden workings of natural phenomena (cf. 1.1.15). He thinks that disagreements among the *physikoi* should engender skepticism about the possibility of our learning these hidden workings, and consequently that such enquiries have no ethical value. Moreover, if they in-

---

to themselves. It is these hidden causes that the pre-Socratics were trying to discover, that is, they were trying to learn things that are appropriate only to the gods, hence the term *ta daimonia* for the (hidden) workings of nature.

[13]K. Lincke, "Xenophon und die Stoa," *Neue Jahrbücher für das klassische Altertum, Geschichte und deutsche Literatur* 17 (1906): 673–91, and Gregory Vlastos (above, note 6), pp. 161–62, both take the view of natural philosophy in 1.4 to be foreign to the historical Socrates. Lincke argues that 1.4 must be an interpolation because he thinks that Xenophon is a good Socratic (pp. 680–81). Vlastos assumes that the passage is authentic and infers, therefore, that Xenophon is not a good Socratic. The Stoics hold with Lincke that Xenophon is a good Socratic and with Vlastos that the passage is genuine.

[14]Cf. *Mem.* 4.7 for the claim that Socrates recommended gaining a working familiarity with astronomy and geometry.

volve meddling in matters that the gods wish to keep hidden, they may turn out to be impious, and therefore pernicious (cf. 1.1.8).

These arguments reveal an attitude toward natural philosophy that is less cut-and-dried than the position attributed to Socrates by Aristotle and Plato. Xenophon's Socrates does not reject the study of nature outright; he opposes enquiries into nature that bypass or exclude its providential teleology. Moreover, since he believes that the correct teleological view of nature (*ta daimonia*) is tied to a belief in the existence of the divine, he holds that fundamental parts of ethics (*ta anthrōpina*) such as piety will require correct views about nature.

The teleological picture of nature that emerges from Xenophon was well suited to Stoic interests. Indeed, there is good evidence that Socrates' arguments in *Memorabilia* 1.4 had a substantial impact on Stoic thinking on the question of the rationality of nature. Cicero and Sextus, for instance, refer explicitly to *Memorabilia* 1.4 in setting out early Stoic arguments for the existence and providence of god.[15] Their reports suggest that the Stoics took up Socrates' arguments for nature's rationality and used them as a point of departure in further defending and developing their own doctrine. Thus for what is arguably the most crucial element in the development of their thinking on natural law— the divine rationality and order of nature—the Stoics were in a position to appeal to the authority of Socrates himself.

At *De natura deorum* 2.5.13–8.22, Balbus, Cicero's Stoic interlocutor, recounts arguments of Zeno, Cleanthes, and Chrysippus for the existence of god. In the course of this discussion Balbus quotes directly from *Memorabilia* 1.4.8, translating *sunharpazein* with "arripuit":

Et tamen ex ipsa hominum sollertia esse aliquam mentem et eam quidem acriorem et divinam existimare debemus. Unde enim hanc homo "arripuit," ut ait apud Xenophontem Socrates? Quin et umorem et calorem qui est fusus in corpore, et terrenam ipsam viscerum soliditatem, animum denique illum spirabilem si quis quaerat unde habeamus, apparet quod aliud a terra sumpsimus, aliud ab umore, aliud ab igni, aliud ab aere eo quem spiritum dicimus.

Yet even man's intelligence must lead us to infer the existence of a mind [in the universe], and that a mind of surpassing ability and in fact divine. Otherwise, whence did man "pick up" [*arripuit*] (as Socrates says in Xe-

---

[15]It is difficult to ascertain from Cicero's presentation in *De natura deorum* whether these arguments are being ascribed to Zeno or to Chrysippus. Sextus attributes them directly to Zeno. For a discussion of the doxographical problems involved in these attributions see M. Dragona-Monachou, *The Stoic Arguments for the Existence and Providence of the Gods* (Athens, 1976), p. 50; P. Boyancé, "Les preuves stoïciennes de l'existence des dieux d'après Cicéron," *Hermes* 90 (1962): 46–71.

nophon) the intelligence that he possesses? If anyone asks the question, whence do we get the moisture and the heat diffused throughout the body, and the actual earthy substance of the flesh, and lastly the breath of life, within us, it is manifest that we have derived the one from earth, the other from water, and the other from the air which we inhale in breathing. (*Nat. d.* 2.6.18, trans. Rackham)

The form and strategy of this argument are essentially that of *Memorabilia* 1.4.8. As in Xenophon, the argument's purpose is to establish the rationality of the cosmos by an appeal to human rationality, and it does so by relying on the same analogy between reason and the material elements. Moreover, the direct quotation indicates that the correspondences with Socrates' argument in the *Memorabilia* are deliberate. One might question, perhaps, whether the explicit reference to Xenophon in this passage should be attributed to the early Stoa. However unlikely, it may be that the quotation is only a learned parenthesis of Cicero's;[16] even so, it still would be significant that someone as deeply imbued in Stoicism as Cicero could see Socrates as an intellectual precursor of Stoic natural teleology. As we shall see, however, there is good evidence for thinking that the appeal to *Memorabilia* 1.4.8 originated in the early Stoa.

A passage in Sextus allows us to trace the connections between *Memorabilia* 1.4.8 and the early Stoic conception of nature more precisely. At *Against the Professors* 9.92, Sextus offers a paraphrase of Socrates' argument and goes on to claim that Zeno took it as the starting point (τὴν ἀφορμὴν λαβών, 9.101) for his own doctrine of seminal reason. In Xenophon, Socrates had argued that our rationality, on analogy with our material components, must come from a larger supply of rationality in the cosmos. As we noted, this analogy is not explicitly justified, even though it is the crux of the argument. Not surprisingly, a series of objections arose that fastened on this lack of justification. It will be helpful to turn to Sextus' report of these criticisms, since they posed a challenge to the Stoics' adoption of Socrates' argument.

Critics of Socrates' analogy argued that if everything that exists must come from an independent supply of that same stuff in the world at large, then it must also be the case that the gall, blood, and phlegm of individual bodies come from larger supplies of those stuffs in the

---

[16]It is unlikely that the appeal to Socrates in this context is Cicero's own contribution rather than that of his Stoic sources. Cicero views Socrates' characteristic contribution to be a move away from natural philosophy to ethics (cf. T. B. DeGraff, "Plato in Cicero," *CP* 35 [1940]: 143–53). Cotta's response in book 3, moreover, suggests that this link between Xenophon and the early Stoics was taken for granted in the Academy (see below, note 18).

cosmos.[17] This conclusion is supposed to illustrate the absurd consequences that follow from the analogy.[18] It would not be absurd of
course to claim that the cosmos produces gall, since after all gall exists
in human bodies. The point of the objection, therefore, should be seen
in the light of the Socratic argument about reason, which assumes that
our reason must be "snatched away and carried off" directly from an
independently existing supply of reason in the world. If gall and blood
are not snatched directly from the world, these critics argue, why should
we suppose that reason is?

As it stands, this attack on the Socratic analogy fails. As defenders
were quick to point out (*Math.* 9.97), it is meant to apply only to simples
such as the four elements, not to compounds like gall and blood. Thus,
for a Stoic wishing to defend Socrates' argument against these critics,
the challenge is to demonstrate how reason is not something that
emerges from the combination of more primary elements, but is itself
a simple entity relevantly like them.

According to Sextus, Zeno took up the challenge of defending
Socrates' analogy in *Memorabilia* 1.4.8 and in the process developed his
own doctrine of seminal reason. In Xenophon, Socrates' analogy between reason and matter is open to the objection that individual reason
and its cosmic sources are different in kind. Consequently, at jeopardy
in Socrates' argument is the very attempt to show that individual reason is part of a cosmic reason. Zeno attempts to ward off this kind of
attack by positing a part-whole connection between individual and cosmic reason and then bolstering it with an analysis of the causal con-

[17]For a discussion see M. Schofield, "The Syllogisms of Zeno of Citium," *Phronesis* 28
(1983): 31–58. He suggests that the strategy employed in these criticisms can be traced
back to Alexinus (pp. 44–49).

[18]The same strategy is employed by Cotta in his skeptical attack in *De natura deorum* 3
on the Stoics' appeal to *Memorabilia* 1.4.8: "At enim quaerit apud Xenophontem Socrates
unde animum arripuerimus si nullus fuerit in mundo. Et ego quaero unde orationem
unde numeros unde cantus. . . . Naturae ista sunt, Balbe, naturae non artificiòse ambu-
lantis ut ait Zeno, quod quidem quale sit, iam videbimus, sed omnia cientis et agitantis
motibus et mutationibus suis." ("But then you tell me that Socrates in Xenophon asks the
question, if the world contains no rational soul, where did we pick up ours? And I too ask
the question, where did we get the faculty of speech, the knowledge of numbers, the art
of music? . . . These faculties, Balbus, are the gifts of nature—not nature 'walking in a
craftsman-like manner' as Zeno says [and what this means we will consider in a moment],
but nature by its own motions and mutations imparting motion and activity to all things,"
Nat.d. 3.27–28, trans. Rackham). Moreover, Cotta opposes the Zenonian conception of
nature *artificiose ambulans* to a mechanistic one, according to which all things are the
product of motions that are not divine *because* they are natural (3.28). In many ways, the
opposition of mechanism to teleology corresponds to Socrates' distinction in *Memorabilia*
1 between himself and the pre-Socratics. As a skeptic Cotta would naturally oppose the
Stoic doctrine by defending a position that the Stoics, following Socrates, originally
meant to reject. This suggests, perhaps, that *Memorabilia* 1.4.8 commonly figured in Stoic
and skeptic disputes about natural teleology.

nections between parts and wholes. The doctrine of seminal reason furnishes a way of understanding how cosmic and individual reason can be the same in kind by hypothesizing a mechanism for the transmission of reason from cosmic whole to individual part. The causal relations that underlie this transmission, Zeno argues, require that individual and cosmic reason not differ in kind.

Zeno's argument begins with the following syllogism:

τὸ προϊέμενον σπέρμα λογικὸν καὶ αὐτὸ λογικόν ἐστιν· ὁ δὲ κόσμος προίεται σπέρμα λογικόν· λογικὸν ἄρα ἐστὶν ὁ κόσμος.

That which projects the seed of the rational is itself rational; but the universe projects the seed of the rational; therefore, the universe is rational. (Sext. Emp. *Math.* 9.101, trans. Bury)

This argument is valid, but what it needs in order to be convincing is a proper explanation of the major and minor premises—that is, what does Zeno mean by "projecting the seed of the rational," and how exactly does this idea apply to the universe?

Sextus reports a Stoic defense of this syllogism that focuses on the causal relations between parts and wholes. It takes the form of an argument concerning the origin of motion in the soul. Every motion proceeds from the ruling part of the soul, and it is in virtue of this ruling part (τὸ ἡγεμονικόν) that the entire soul has the power of motion.[19] Accordingly, no part has a power that is not possessed by the whole. As Sextus puts it,

What the part is in point of power, that the whole must certainly be first. (*Math.* 9.102, trans. Bury)

This conclusion supports the syllogism by providing independent reason for believing that the rationality displayed by parts of the cosmos has its causal origin in the cosmos as a whole, and specifically in whatever functions in the role of *to hēgemonikon*. Zeno's doctrine of seminal reason then buttresses this claim by providing a vehicle for the transmission of rationality from the universe to its parts. In the *Memorabilia*, Socrates asks: "From where do we snatch and carry off our reason?"

[19]Cf. Cic. *Nat. d.* 1.39 for the Stoic claim that god is the *hēgemonikon* of the world. See A. A. Long, "Scepticism about Gods in Hellenistic Philosophy," in *Cabinet of the Muses*, ed. M. Griffith and D. J. Mastronarde (Chico, Calif., 1990), pp. 281–88, for a discussion of skeptical challenges to Stoic assertions of the sentience, appetition, and morality of the cosmos.

The implicit answer is supposed to be "From the world." The doctrine of seminal reason then provides a causal framework for understanding the mechanism by which individuals get reason from the world.

By the same token, Zeno attempted to disarm the objection that the rationality exhibited by individuals may arise simply from their composition and not from the rationality of the cosmos, with the following distinction:

> καὶ διὰ τοῦτο εἰ προίεται λογικοῦ ζώου σπέρμα ὁ κόσμος, οὐχ ὡς τὸν ἄνθρωπον κατὰ ἀποβρασμόν, ἀλλὰ καθὸ περιέχει σπέρματα λογικῶν ζώων· περιέχει <δὲ> [το πᾶν], οὐχ ὡς ἂν εἴπομεν τὴν ἄμπελον γιγάρτων εἶναι περιεκτικήν, τουτέστι κατὰ περιγραφήν, ἀλλ᾽ ὅτι λόγοι σπερματικοὶ λογικῶν ζώων ἐν αὐτῷ περιέχονται. ὥστε εἶναι τοιοῦτο τὸ λεγόμενον "ὁ δέ γε κόσμος περιέχει σπερματικοὺς λόγους λογικῶν ζώων· λογικὸς ἄρα ἐστὶν ὁ κόσμος."

Consequently, if the universe projects the seed of a rational animal, it does not do so like man, by frothy emission, but as containing the seeds of rational animals; but it does not contain them in the same way as we might speak of the vine "containing" its grapes,—that is, by way of inclusion,—but because the "seminal reasons" of rational animals are contained in it. So that the argument is this—"The universe contains the seminal reasons of rational animals; therefore the universe is rational." (Sext. Emp. *Math.* 9.103, trans. Bury)

Zeno's argument employs a distinction between two senses of "containing," hence two kinds of causal relations.[20] Grapes, though causally dependent on their vine, are different from it in kind, since vines and grapes exhibit different essential properties. On the other hand, rational animals have their rationality, Zeno argues, as an individual manifestation of the larger rationality of the cosmos. Reason does not arise from the combination of more simple nonrational elements, nor is it a complex of more primary elements in the way that grapes are. Grapes arise from combinations of simple elements that subsist in the vine and are transmitted from it in the right proportions. Reason, on the other hand, has its causal source in reason alone, and the mechanism of its transmission from cosmos to individual ensures that it does not differ in kind. This attempt to defend the isomophism between individual and cosmic reason fills a gap in the original argument in Xenophon. At the same time, however, both the framework and overall goals of Zeno's argument remain recognizably Socratic.

---

[20]Cf. Alex. Aphr. *Mixt.*, p. 216, 4 Bruns = *SVF* 2.473.

We have good reason to suppose, therefore, that Socrates' argument in *Memorabilia* 1.4.8 exerted a significant influence on Stoic views about the rationality of nature. Clearly, it allowed the Stoics to see the divinely ordered rationality of the natural world as a Socratic doctrine. This tenet of Socrates, however, was not merely adopted by Stoics because they were seeking to pin their views on an ancient authority. As Sextus indicates, Zeno's reflection on Socrates' argument for the rationality of the cosmos influenced the formation of the doctrine of seminal reason. In this case, then, Socrates seems to have occupied a position for the Stoics similar to that occupied by Plato for many later Platonists. They not only appeal to Socrates' views for authority, but they attempt to articulate them more precisely and defend them from attack. As a result, they come to develop new doctrines, which at the same time bear clear marks of their origins in Socrates.

2. Socrates and Divine Moral Principles

We have seen how a text in Xenophon enabled the Stoics to attribute to Socrates a conception of nature as a rationally ordered whole. The Stoic theory of natural law, however, assumes additionally that the divine order of nature legislates a system of moral laws that provides a normative structure for human conduct. This characteristic feature of the Stoic theory is exemplified in the passage from Chrysippus' Περὶ νόμου quoted above in the introduction to this essay. Chrysippus there asserts the authority of law over all things, including the divine, by which he clearly means nature as a whole. Moreover, he claims that the law that governs nature makes prescriptions that have the status of moral principles, and hence that it serves as a guide for human conduct. He thus envisions the strongest possible formal links between nature and the laws of morality.[21]

As we have seen, in the first book of the *Memorabilia*, Socrates advances a conception of the rationality of nature and draws from it certain ethical implications, especially with respect to piety. Lacking in this discussion, however, is any notion that nature provides guidance to individuals in the form of moral laws or rules. Thus we must now consider whether the Stoics had a Socratic precedent for this aspect of their theory of natural law as well.

At first glance, it may again appear that Socrates would be an unlikely figure on whom to hang a positive conception of moral rules.

---

[21]For an illuminating discussion of this aspect of Stoic morality see G. Striker, "Following Nature: A Study in Stoic Ethics," *OSAP* 9 (1991): 1–73.

Socrates has often been viewed as the founder of a type of virtue ethics in which 'being' is promoted over 'doing';[22] thus the goal of his moral enquiries is taken to be the delineation of individual qualities of soul rather than the discovery and defense of moral rules. But there is evidence to suggest that the Stoics were able to find authoritative Socratic texts for their conception of moral rules and of the role played by such rules in action.

Plato's *Phaedo* and *Crito* played a critical role in this aspect of Stoic thinking about natural law. However, it will be helpful, once again, to begin with a passage in Xenophon. In *Memorabilia* 4.4, Socrates and Hippias take up the question of divinely legislated laws. After they have agreed that the lawful (νόμιμον) and the just (δίκαιον) are the same (4.4.18), Socrates advances a conception of unwritten laws:

"'Αγράφους δέ τινας οἶσθα," ἔφη, "ὦ Ἱππία, νόμους;" "Τούς γ᾽ ἐν πάσῃ," ἔφη, "χώρᾳ κατὰ ταὐτὰ νομιζομένους." "Ἔχοις ἂν οὖν εἰπεῖν," ἔφη, "ὅτι οἱ ἄνθρωποι αὐτοὺς ἔθεντο;" "Καὶ πῶς ἄν," ἔφη, "οἵ γε οὔτε συνελθεῖν ἅπαντες ἂν δυνηθεῖεν οὔτε ὁμόφωνοί εἰσι;" "Τίνας οὖν," ἔφη, "νομίζεις τεθεικέναι τοὺς νόμους τούτους;" "Ἐγὼ μέν,"ἔφη, "θεοὺς οἶμαι τοὺς νόμους τούτους τοῖς ἀνθρώποις θεῖναι· καὶ γὰρ παρὰ πᾶσιν ἀνθρώποις πρῶτον νομίζεται θεοὺς σέβειν." "Οὐκοῦν καὶ γονέας τιμᾶν πανταχοῦ νομίζεται;" "Καὶ τοῦτο," ἔφη. "Οὐκοῦν καὶ μήτε γονέας παισὶ μείγνυσθαι μήτε παῖδας γονεῦσιν;" "Οὐκέτι μοι δοκεῖ," ἔφη, "ὦ Σώκρατες, οὗτος θεοῦ νόμος εἶναι." "Τί δή;" ἔφη. "Ὅτι," ἔφη, "αἰσθάνομαί τινας παραβαίνοντας αὐτόν." "Καὶ γὰρ ἄλλα πολλά," ἔφη, "παρανομοῦσιν· ἀλλὰ δίκην γέ τοι διδόασιν οἱ παραβαίνοντες τοὺς ὑπὸ τῶν θεῶν κειμένους νόμους, ἣν οὐδενὶ τρόπῳ δυνατὸν ἀνθρώπῳ διαφυγεῖν."

"Hippias, do you think," Socrates said, "that there are some laws that are unwritten?"
"Those, at least, that are observed in every country on the same points," he replied.
"Would you be prepared to say that men established them?" he asked.
"How could they? They could not all come together, nor do all they speak the same language."
"Who, then, do you think established these laws?" he asked.
"I think that the gods established these laws for men; for among all men, the primary law is to honor the gods," he replied.

---

[22]Cf. M. F. Burnyeat, "Virtues in Action," in *The Philosophy of Socrates*, ed. G. Vlastos (Garden City, N. Y., 1971), pp. 209–34. For a recent defense of the claim that Socrates' search for definitions relies on the view that knowledge (hence moral requirements) can be reduced to context-free rules see H. Dreyfus, "The Socratic and Platonic Basis of Cognitivism," *Artificial Intelligence and Society* 2 (1988): 99–112. This is challenged by W. I. Matson and A. Leite in "Socrates' Critique of Cognitivism," *Philosophy* 66 (1991): 145–67.

"So, then, is it also a law everywhere to honor one's parents?"

"Yes," he replied.

"And therefore neither for parents to have sex with their children nor children with their parents."

"In this instance, Socrates," he said, "this does not seem to be a law of god."

"Why?" he asked.

"Because I notice that there are some who transgress it," he replied.

"Indeed, they violate many other laws as well. But those who transgress the laws founded by the gods have paid a penalty that it is utterly impossible for men to escape." (4.4.19–21)

This passage contains many elements that Stoics could view as their own. At a general level, the claim that the gods establish moral laws that are in force everywhere could hardly sound more Stoic.[23] In *De republica* 3.33, for example, Cicero virtually reproduces Xenophon's description of unwritten laws in his own Stoicizing account of the true law as "right reason in accord with nature." In the course of responding to Phlius' report of Carneades' infamous defense of injustice, Laelius describes several features of nature's law, among which are the following:

1. Universal application among all peoples at all times ("Nor will there be one law [*lex*] at Rome, another at Athens, one law now, another in the future.")
2. God as legislator ("God will be the one common ruler and commander of all, the founder [*inventor*], judge, and promulgator of this law.")
3. Transgression of divine law brings its own punishment ("Whoever disobeys will be fleeing from himself and . . . will suffer the greatest punishments, even if he succeeds in escaping what is commonly taken to be punishment.")

Though certainly striking, these correspondences on their own do not establish a direct link between Xenophon and the Stoics, since there is no ancient testimony tying the Stoic conception of divinely legislated moral laws to *Memorabilia* 4.4. It is hardly out of the question, of course, especially in light of the well-attested influence of the *Memorabilia* on Zeno,[24] that Xenophon's Socrates influenced Stoic views on

---

[23]Even the specific claim in this passage about honoring one's parents has a Stoic analogue. Honoring one's parents is a star example of a Stoic determinate moral rule or a "proper function that admits of no exception" (ἀεὶ καθῆκον); see D. L. 7.108–9 = *SVF* 3.495, with the discussion of A. A. Long and D. N. Sedley, *The Hellenistic Philosophers* (Cambridge, 1987), 1: 365–66.

[24]Cf. D. L. 7.1 = *SVF* 1.1 for anecdotal evidence about the effect on Zeno of Xenophon's portrait of Socrates.

this score.[25] But without any direct testimony, it is perhaps best not to press these connections too hard.

Additional evidence for understanding how the Stoics came to associate Socrates with divine moral laws has been provided by David Sedley in a paper focusing on Stoic interpretations of Plato.[26] As is well known, the death of Socrates remained a topic of interest throughout the history of the Stoa.[27] Sedley demonstrates how Plato's depiction in the *Phaedo* and *Crito* of Socrates' calm acceptance of his death provided the Stoics with a model of the sage's affirmation of the rational and providential order of nature. One need only think, for example, of representations of Seneca's death to see how thoroughly this Socratic exemplum impressed itself on Stoic thinking.[28] By the same token, it is also clear that for the Stoics, Socrates' equanimity in the face of death exhibited his understanding and affirmation of Zeus's rational order.

The question that presents itself now is whether the Stoics believed that Socrates' actions were motivated by moral principles that themselves were expressions of Zeus's cosmic order. If so, we can see how they might naturally have come to believe that Socrates governed his actions in accordance with the prescriptions of the κοινὸς νόμος.

In the first book of Cicero's *De divinatione*, the Stoic interlocutor, Quintus, recounts the story of Socrates' dream in Plato's *Crito* (1.52). The dream, it will be recalled, correctly predicts that Socrates will not die for another three days. Sedley observes that "To a Stoic, it will have seemed Socrates' decision to stay and die was to a large extent guided by the revelation that he was bound in any case to die on that day—a divine indication that it was morally preferable for him to do so willingly."[29] Nor should we underestimate the extent to which the Stoic argument moves in the other direction—that is, inferring divine sanction from performances of morally correct actions.

Because of the Stoics' interest in Socrates' death, Plato's *Phaedo* and *Crito* became central texts for them. As it happens, the *Crito* is also the text where Socrates enunciates a moral principle that he insists over-

---

[25]The dialectical context of these arguments and the fact that Hippias makes many of the requisite claims about divine legislation may have made it harder for the Stoics to appropriate these as obviously Socratic doctrines.

[26]"Chrysippus on Psychophysical Causality," in *Passions and Perceptions*, ed. J. Brunschwig and M. C. Nussbaum (Cambridge, 1993) pp. 313–31.

[27]See K. Döring, *Exemplum Socratis: Studien zur Sokratesnachwirkung in der kynisch-stoischen Popularphilosophie der frühen Kaiserzeit und im frühen Christentum*, Hermes Einzelschriften 42 (Weisbaden, 1979), pp. 25–31, 49–55, 130–35, 142–49.

[28]For a comprehensive discussion see M. Griffin, "Philosophy, Cato, and Roman Suicide," *Greece and Rome* 33 (1986): 67–77, 192–202.

[29]Sedley (above note 26), p. 316.

rides all other claims—a principle that Gregory Vlastos describes as taking us "to the deepest stratum" of Socrates' ethical theory.[30] In setting out the principle (ἀρχή) underwriting his decision to remain in jail (48e), Socrates asserts that we should under no circumstances commit an injustice (οὐδαμῶς ἄρα δεῖ ἀδικεῖν, 49b), even in return for an injustice suffered (49c). Socrates' most basic principle, from which his rejection of the *lex talionis* is derived, is that we should never commit an injustice. As the *Crito* unfolds, we see that it is Socrates' commitment to this moral principle that leads him to choose to obey the law and die rather than to continue his life by escaping from prison.[31] This is because he thinks that were he to flout the laws of the city, he would be returning injustice for injustice (οὕτως αἰσχρῶς ἀντιδηκήσας, 54c).

In the *Crito*, the overall structure of Socrates' moral deliberations as well as his final decision can plausibly be taken to conform to a familiar pattern of rule-governed activity. Socrates isolates a fixed moral principle that overrides all others and then proceeds to apply it to his own particular circumstances. Such a picture could hardly have been more congenial to the Stoics.[32] Epictetus, for instance, extracts precisely this moral from Socrates' actions in the *Crito*.[33] At *Dissertationes* 4.1.159–69,[34] he paraphrases the *Crito* and recounts several well-

---

[30]Vlastos (above, note 6), p. 199.

[31]For an account of how the principle that one should never commit injustice generates a moral obligation to obey the law under Socrates' present circumstances but not under all circumstances see J. G. DeFilippo, "Justice and Obedience in the *Crito*," *AP* 11 (1991): 249–63, esp. p. 261.

[32]For a general discussion of the role of moral rules in Stoic morality see P. Mitsis, "Seneca on Reason, Rules, and Moral Development," in *Passions and Perceptions*, ed. J. Brunschwig and M. C. Nussbaum (Cambridge, 1993), pp. 285–312.

[33]As Sedley (above, note 26) suggests, we can be fairly confident in tracing back to the early Stoa the view that Socrates' actions exhibit the convergence of divine causality and moral principle. Epictetus gives a more detailed interpretation of Socrates' actions in the *Crito* that fleshes out the nature of these convergences. Although it is not certain that every detail of his account can be traced back to the early Stoa, the evidence from Epictetus shows that such a reading of the *Crito* would have been both attractive and possible for the early Stoics (especially since so many closely related elements of their theory of natural and moral principles are traceable to their engagement with Socratic texts). Moreover, as Adolf Bonhoffer has plausibly argued in *Epiktet und die Stoa* (Stuttgart, 1890), Epictetus often relies on early Stoic writings in a very direct way. For a summary of scholarship on Epictetus' attitude toward Socrates see J. P. Hershbell, "The Stoicism of Epictetus: Twentieth Century Perspectives," *ANRW* II.36.3 (Berlin, 1989), pp. 2153–55.

[34]*Dissertationes* 2.17 takes up the corresponding epistemological problem of how we are to apply the general principles (θεωρήματα) of philosophers, or our preconceptions of right action, to our individual circumstances (cf. Long and Sedley [above, note 23] 40S = *Diss.* 1.22.1–3.9–10, with their comments, 1: 253). At *Dissertationes* 1.4.18–27, Epictetus examines this issue in the context of moral progress (προκοπή). In discussing how we are to put our guiding principles into action no matter what subject is at hand (ἐπὶ τῆς ἀεὶ παραπιπτούσης ὕλης τὰ προηγούμενα ἐκπονῶν, 1.4.20), he again invokes the example of Socrates in the *Crito*. Quoting from *Crito* 43d7–8 (ὦ φίλε Κρίτων, εἰ ταύτῃ τοῖς θεοῖς φίλον, ταύτῃ γινέσθω, 1.4.24), he argues that Socrates' calm acceptance of his fate stems

known incidents in Socrates' life in order to demonstrate that Socrates is preeminently free. This freedom depends, Epictetus insists, on Socrates' unwavering commitment to principles of justice and on his understanding and acceptance of Zeus's rational order. So precisely do Socrates' moral principles conform to divine command, in fact, that his actions can be taken as paradigmatic for a life of complete freedom.

Readers of the *Crito*, even while admiring Socrates' commitment to justice, often question whether he might somehow have made a mistake in applying his principles. One might reasonably wonder, for instance, whether Socrates is wrong in thinking that by escaping he will be destroying the city and its laws.[35] What such an objection points to, of course, is a standard problem for rule-based theories of morality, the problem of misapplying rules in particular circumstances. The Stoics, however, have the means of addressing this problem—at least in the case of Socrates' choice—in an extremely interesting way. We have seen that they believe that Socrates was given a divine indication that his death was fated. The presence of a divine sign, therefore, confirms for the Stoics that Socrates' decision to remain in prison and die accords with the rational and moral order of the universe. Consequently, the divine sign furnishes an actual verification of the morality of his action and hence of his correct application of a fundamental moral principle. That is, the Stoics' doctrine of providential determinism helps them to pick out and assess the correct applications of moral rules. On the other hand, Socrates' recognition and unwavering adherence to a basic principle of morality gives an analogous indication that his action is in accord with the divine and moral order of nature. In Socrates' decision and action in the *Crito*, therefore, we see what would have been for the Stoics the mutual implication, indeed the absolute convergence, of moral principle and nature's divinely rational plan. It is for this reason that Socrates functions as a Stoic paradigm for the sage whose attitudes and actions most precisely embody the dictates of the *koinos nomos*.

In his *Outlines of the History of Ethics*, Henry Sidgwick argues that the Stoics provide a transition between what he calls ancient and modern conceptions of ethics. Modern ethics, he claims, characteristically "connects itself in a new way with theology, so far as the rules of duty are regarded as a code of divine legislation . . . , [and] has a close affinity to

---

from his ability to put his principles into practice. The *Encheiridion* concludes as well with an exhortation to remember on every occasion these same words of Socrates (in both instances Epictetus not surprisingly drops the phrase τύχη ἀγαθή from the Platonic original).

[35] A. D. Woozley, *Law and Obedience: The Arguments of Plato's "Crito"* (Chapel Hill, N.C., 1979), chap. 6, provides a good discussion of the philosophical merits of the *Crito*'s "arguments from destruction."

abstract jurisprudence, so far as this is conceived to treat of rules of Law cognisable by reason as naturally and universally valid."[36] Sidgwick believes that the Stoics are the initiators of the movement toward "modern" ethics and ethical theory. Certainly, there is a sense in which he is correct, since they are the first philosophers to formulate explicitly an ethics grounded in the rationality and morality of nature's law. But such a view of the history of moral philosophy fails to account for the degree to which the Stoics' views were developed by reflecting on the arguments and actions of Socrates.[37] Here, as in most areas of the history of ancient ethics, one overlooks the power and reach of Socrates at one's peril. Of course, the Stoics' Socrates, with his commitments to cosmic rationality and to leading a life governed by divinely legislated moral rules, is only one among many competing images of Socrates in antiquity. But it is an image that has had some of the most fundamental and pervasive effects on the methods and goals of subsequent moral philosophy. Indeed, it is hardly an exaggeration to place the origins of natural law theory, and hence the characteristic style of "modern" ethics, firmly within the framework of the Socratic movement.[38]

[36]*Outlines of the History of Ethics* (London, 1886), pp. 6–7.

[37]This is not to claim, of course, that Socrates was the sole influence on Stoic thinking about natural law. See Chapter 11 in this volume for some suggestions about the role of Plato's *Republic* in the formation of the Stoic theory; and for Heraclitean influences see M. Schofield, *The Stoic Idea of the City* (Cambridge, 1991), pp. 74–84.

[38]We would like to thank Steven Strange and the editor of this volume for helpful comments.

[11]

Zeno's *Republic* and the
Origins of Natural Law

Paul A. Vander Waerdt

The origins of natural law theory pose a curious problem. In its traditional meaning, the term *natural law* (νόμος φύσεως, *lex naturalis*) des-
ignates a law, discernible by reason, which determines what is right and
wrong by nature, and which therefore holds valid everywhere, always,
and for everyone, independently of circumstance and local custom. It is
not difficult to find evidence to support the commonly held assumption that the early Stoic scholarchs first advanced the theory of natural
law.[1] Thus when Cicero defines natural law in *De legibus* 1, the fullest
account of the theory to survive from antiquity, he employs a formula
whose Stoic paternity is well attested: "Law is the highest reason, im-
planted in nature, which commands what ought to be done, and forbids the opposite. This reason, when firmly fixed and perfected in the
human mind, is law."[2] This definition clearly recalls the early Stoic

---

[1]So, for example, G. Striker, "Origins of the Concept of Natural Law," *PBACAP* 2
(1986): 79–94 (with a reply by B. Inwood on pp. 95–101), now supplemented by "Following Nature: A Study in Stoic Ethics," *OSAP* 9 (1991): 1–73 at pp. 35–50. I have offered a very different reconstruction of the original theory of natural law and of its
development in antiquity in my forthcoming book, *The Theory of Natural Law in Antiquity*
(Ithaca, N.Y.), where I provide a detailed defense of the interpretation summarized in
this section. For the most cogent defense of the traditional interpretation of Stoic natural
law as being constituted by a code of moral rules, see P. Mitsis, "Natural Law and Natural
Right in Post-Aristotelian Philosophy: The Stoics and Their Critics," *ANRW* II.36.7 (Berlin, 1994), pp. 4812–50, whose criticism of my position is answered in my book.

[2]*Leg.* 1.18: "igitur doctissimis viris proficisci placuit a lege, haud scio an recte, si modo,
ut idem definiunt, lex est ratio summa insita in natura, quae iubet ea, quae facienda sunt,
prohibetque contraria. eadem ratio cum est in hominis mente confirmata et perfecta

position that man's end (τέλος) as a rational animal consists in living according to nature, refraining from every action prohibited by the common law (κοινὸς νόμος), which is identified with the sage's right reason (ὀρθὸς λόγος), and patterning his conduct on the divine order and harmony evident in the rational order of the cosmos.[3] We have clear evidence that the founder of the Stoa, Zeno of Citium, first advanced this theory, in its most radical and controversial form, in his *Republic*,[4] and that his two successors as scholarch subsequently defended and elaborated it—Cleanthes in his *Hymn to Zeus* (Stob. *Ecl.* 1.1.12 = *SVF* 1.537), and Chrysippus in his *On Law*.[5] Thus we can be confident that the early Stoics first originated the theory that had come by Cicero's time to be identified as the theory of natural law.

Yet as soon as we begin to enquire how the early Stoics themselves understand their formula that law is right reason as applied to conduct, it becomes clear that they construe it quite differently than the later natural law tradition does. In Aquinas' formulation in his treatise on law in *Summa theologiae* I.ii, natural law has a very generous scope, encompassing everything to which man is rationally inclined by nature, including all of the virtues (q. 94 a. 3) as well as the principles of the decalogue (q. 100 aa. 3, 11), and indeed all activities that practical reason apprehends as man's good (q. 92 a. 2). Aquinas details an elaborate code of precepts based upon God's *lex aeterna* by distinguishing (q. 92 a. 2) a single primary precept from three classes of secondary precepts, each of which is ranked according to the order of man's natural inclinations.[6] Traditionally it has been assumed that the early Stoics too

---

[Vahlens; confecta ABH], lex est." Cf. *Leg.* 1.23, 42; 2.10; *Rep.* 3.33; *Nat. d.* 1.36 (citing Zeno); *Inv. rhet.* 2.65–68, 160–62; *Top.* 90.

[3] This formula appears in a variety of early Stoic texts, including Zeno's *On the Nature of Man* and Chrysippus' *On Ends* (D. L. 7.87–89), as well as the exordium of Chrysippus' *On Law* (Marcian *Inst.* 1 = *SVF* 3.314), which treat *koinos nomos* and *orthos logos* as equivalent ways of referring to the canon or standard that human beings follow in living according to nature. Cf. also Arius Didymus *ap.* Stob. *Ecl.* 2.96.10–12, 102.5–6 Wachsmuth; Alex. Aphr. *De fato* 35 = *SVF* 2.1003.30–34 on p. 295; Philo *De Joseph.* = *SVF* 3.323; Clem. Al. *Strom.* 2.420 = *SVF* 3.332.

[4] See Plut. *De virt. Alex.* 329a–b, discussed below in section 1; Cicero *De natura deorum* 1.36 confirms the attribution of the theory to Zeno.

[5] We possess only its exordium and Plutarch's criticism of its account of the moral conduct prescribed by *nomos*: Marcian *Inst.* 1 = *SVF* 3.314; Plut. *De Stoic. repugn.* 1037c–1038a = *SVF* 3.520.

[6] For guidance with Aquinas' theory, see, for instance, G. Grisez, "The First Principle of Practical Reason: A Commentary on the *Summa Theologiae*, 1–2, Question 94, Article 2," *Natural Law Forum* 10 (1965): 168–96, reprinted in *Aquinas: A Collection of Critical Essays*, ed. A. Kenny (London, 1970), pp. 340–82; D. J. O'Connor, *Aquinas and the Natural Law* (London, 1968), pp. 57–79; and, for the complex problem of the derivation of secondary from primary precepts, R. A. Armstrong, *Primary and Secondary Precepts in Thomistic Natural Law Teaching* (The Hague, 1966), esp. pp. 58–85.

adhered to a rule-following model of natural law, the moral conduct prescribed by which could be specified by a set of moral rules corresponding to the natural hierarchy of man's impulses.[7] Yet there are strong reasons to resist this assumption.

In the first place, the early Stoics never even use the term *nomos physeōs* to refer to their theory,[8] nor do they recognize any "natural laws," in the sense of immutable rules of conduct not subject to exception, at all. In particular, in his account of the content of the moral conduct prescribed by law or right reason, Chrysippus denies that there is any class of actions (καθήκοντα, in technical Stoic terminology) which invariably accords with nature,[9] recognizing only one exception:[10] the particular class of actions designated "perfect *kathēkonta*" or κατορθ-ώματα, the perfectly virtuous actions which only one who acts out of the sage's unique rational disposition is able to perform.[11] The "canon of justice and injustice" which Chrysippus undertakes to provide in his account of *nomos* (*SVF* 3.314) thus prescribes *katorthōmata*, while it proscribes all actions which fall short of this morally infallible standard.[12]

---

[7]See above, note 1.

[8]The closest examples are Cicero *De natura deorum* 1.36 ("Zeno naturalem legem divinam esse censet eamque vim obtinere recta imperantem prohibentemque contraria"; but this probably translates an original *orthos logos* rather than *nomos physeōs*: see H. Koester, "The Concept of Natural Law in Greek Thought," in *Religions in Antiquity*, ed. J. Neusner [Leiden, 1968], pp. 521–41 at p. 529); Arius Didymus' account in his epitome of Stoic ethics (Euseb. *Praep. evang.* 15.15 = *SVF* 2.528.23–29) of the community of gods and men sharing in *logos* "which is law by nature" (ὅς ἐστι φύσει νόμος); and Diogenes Laertius 7.128, which cites Chrysippus for the thesis that justice, *nomos*, and *orthos logos* exist by nature, not merely by convention.

[9]*Kathēkonta* are actions that reason prevails upon us to do in accordance with nature and that, once done, admit of a rational defense (D. L. 7.107–9; cf. Arius 85.12.15; Plut. *De comm. not.* 1069e). Yet morally they may be either virtuous or vicious, depending upon the agent's disposition: if he acts out of certain knowledge, then his actions are virtuous—they are *katorthōmata;* otherwise, they are vicious from the standpoint of morality even if they do accord with nature. The evidence is collected in *SVF* 1.230–32, 3.491–523, and the subject may be studied in the section on "proper functions" in A. A. Long and D. N. Sedley, *The Hellenistic Philosophers* (Cambridge, 1987), 1:359–68; on Cicero's usage see J. M. Rist, *Stoic Philosophy* (Cambridge, 1969), pp. 97–111. The evidence for Chrysippus' *On Virtuous Actions* is collected by von Arnim in *SVF* 3.674. For the meaning of the distinction between *kathēkonta* and *katorthōmata*, see especially G. B. Kerferd, "What Does the Wise Man Know?" in *The Stoics*, ed. J. M. Rist (Berkeley, 1978), pp. 125–36, and B. Inwood, *Ethics and Human Action in Early Stoicism* (Oxford, 1985), pp. 213–15. It is said (D. L. 7.25) that Zeno was the first to use the term *kathēkon* and to write on the subject.

[10]Thus "living according to virtue" is the only example we are offered of an ἀεὶ καθῆκον (D. L. 7.108–9).

[11]*Katorthōmata* thus include all the virtues and indeed "everything done according to right reason" (Arius 96.18–97.14; cf. 85.18–86.12, 93.14–18; Sex. Emp. *Math.* 11.200–207).

[12]So Chrysippus in his *On Law* (ap. Plut. *De Stoic. repugn.* 1037c–d = *SVF* 3.520) and in his *Demonstrations on Justice* (ap. 1041a–b = *SVF* 3.297); cf. Plut. *De Stoic. repugn.* 1038a; Cic. *Leg.* 2.8, 1.18–19; Arius 96.10–16 (cf. 96.17–97.14), 102.4–10. That only the sage is capable of performing *katorthōmata:* Cic. *Fin.* 4.15; cf. Arius 96.10–16, 102.4–10. The

One might suppose then that actions belonging to this special class of *katorthōmata* might admit of codification in a manner comparable, for example, to Aquinas' class of primary precepts. But even brief consideration of the nature of *katorthōmata* shows that this cannot be the case. For they do not represent a class distinct from *kathēkonta* because the agent's actions admit of a different external description, but rather because of a difference in his motivation: the *kathēkonta* of ordinary human beings become *katorthōmata* when performed by the sage, whose perfectly rational and consistent disposition guarantees the moral infallibility of all his actions.[13] Put simply, natural law prescribes the intensional rather than the extensional characteristics of virtuous actions.[14] And these intensional characteristics do not admit of codification in moral rules: for *katorthōmata* are entirely circumstance dependent, in the sense that "special circumstances" may require justified exception to *kathēkonta* in order to remain consistent with the higher will of Zeus, and no moral rules can substitute for the sage's right reason in guiding their performance.[15] Thus the early Stoics clearly do not conceive of natural law as being constituted by a code of moral rules comparable, for instance, to Aquinas' code of primary and secondary precepts. To the contrary, they advance a dispositional rather than a rule-following model of natural law,[16] and a correspondingly different account of the content of the moral conduct prescribed by it: in their theory, it pre-

---

content of natural law corresponds not to a set of moral rules or precepts but to the sage's distinctive moral attributes; put differently, natural law prescribes the intensional rather than the extensional characteristics of virtuous actions. When we speak of actions that accord with natural law, we refer to his *katorthōmata;* conversely, *katorthōmata* specify the content of the moral conduct natural law enjoins. To act in accordance with natural law, then, means to perform actions that accord with nature (*kathēkonta*) with the mental disposition that enables one to know infallibly why a given course of action does indeed accord with nature.

[13]The distinctive features of the sage's rational disposition are set forth by Cicero in *De finibus* 3.16–25, a text that seems consistent with our other evidence for Chrysippus on this point (*ap.* Stob. *Ecl.* 5.906.18–907.5 = *SVF* 3.510; see my remarks in *AJP* 113 [1992]: 117–18).

[14]Curiously, the question of whether natural law prescribes *katorthōmata* or *kathēkonta* is not faced by Striker 1986, 1991 (above, note 1), who, without considering the evidence from *On Law* (*ap.* Plut. *De Stoic. repugn.* 1037c–d = *SVF* 3.520) discussed below, seems to assume that natural law is constituted by a code of moral rules. Similarly neglecting this text, M. Schofield, *The Stoic Idea of the City* (Cambridge, 1991), pp. 67–74, in his account of natural law as prescriptive reason, does not even broach the problem of the moral content of nature's prescriptions for human beings. Mitsis (above, note 1) faces the problem squarely: attempting to discredit Plutarch's text as reliable evidence for *On Law*, he argues that Stoic natural law provides other injunctions or prescriptions in addition to *katorthōmata*.

[15]See section 3 below for the doctrine of "special circumstances" as it pertains to Zeno's *Republic*.

[16]In drawing this contrast I do not mean to suggest that Aquinas takes no account of intensionalist considerations: he clearly regards them as necessary to the perfection of virtue (q. 91 a. 4) but treats them in his account of virtue rather than of natural law.

scribes not a determinate class of actions but a certain rational disposition with which one is to act, namely, the perfectly rational and
consistent disposition which enables the sage to apprehend and act in
accordance with the provident order of nature. One consequence is
that early Stoic usage of *nomos* is radically revisionary: it refers not to a
code of moral rules or to positive legislation but rather is identical with
the sage's right reason.[17]

These preliminary remarks suggest the complexity of the problem
we face in attempting to understand the origins of natural law theory.
While there is clear evidence that the early Stoic scholarchs first originated this theory, there also is clear evidence that they did not understand it in a manner at all comparable to that of the later tradition. In
fact, we know very little concerning the origin, early form, and philosophical motivation of the theory of natural law. Accordingly, if we
wish to understand this theory and its development, we need to give
renewed consideration to the context in which it was first developed
and presented. Although the fact has remained for all intents and
purposes unnoticed in the scholarly discussion, astonishingly enough,
Zeno's *Republic* is the founding work of the natural law tradition—it
represents the first attempt, in other words, to specify the way of life of
a community governed according to natural law.[18] In what follows I
shall undertake to show that careful attention to this work in its literary

[17]So Chrysippus *ap.* D. L. 7.87–88; Cleanthes, *SVF* 1.537.3, 12–13, 20–25; Plut. *De
Stoic. repugn.* 1038; Cic. *Leg.* 1.18–19, 2.8. Early Stoic usage is not univocal: *nomos* also
serves to refer to the causal nexus of fate (Arius *ap.* Euseb. *Praep. evang.* 15.15 = *SVF*
2.528; cf. Chrysippus *ap.* Plut. *De Stoic. repugn.* 1050c–d), which the sage apprehends in
"following nature." For the Stoic thesis of the similarity of the mind of god and man, see
Cic. *Nat. d.* 2.58; Arius 96.10–17.

[18]Schofield (above, note 14), pp. 93–103, proposes a different account of the origins of
natural law theory: he argues that Chrysippus undertook "to adapt Zeno's conception of
a community of sages to the notion of the community of rational beings who are citizens
of the universe" and that his idea of the cosmic city (set forth in *De nat.* 3) "mediates the
transition from republicanism to natural law theory." This hypothesis seems to me implausible on at least three independent grounds: (1) although he tries (unsuccessfully:
see below, note 44) to discredit Plutarch *De virtute Alexandri* 329a–b as a credible source
of information about Zeno's *Republic*, even Schofield admits that *koinos nomos* in this text
is "incontrovertibly Stoic" and "a key principle of Zeno's *Republic*": hence there is no reason to suppose that natural law theory required the mediation of Chrysippean doctrine
on the cosmic city; (2) Schofield's characterization of Zeno's theory as "republicanism"
rather than "natural law" rests upon an unargued but highly questionable reading of
Zeno's Platonic target (see section 2 below); and (3) the role assigned to Chrysippus' account of the cosmic city in this hypothesis is rendered unlikely by the "irresistible conjecture" (see below, note 76) that Chrysippus was developing "an original Zenonian
treatment of these themes": hence it is more economical and plausible to suppose that
Zeno himself developed the doctrine of *koinos nomos* in the context of the cosmic city, as
argued in section 2 below.

and philosophical context will clarify the original form and motivation of the theory of natural law.

My first objective, then, is to identify the philosophical problems which Zeno sought to resolve by developing the theory of natural law that he presents in his *Republic*.[19] This theory, I shall argue, is intended to provide improved answers to questions Plato considered in his *Republic* and *Laws* by making more precise and explicit the teaching on natural justice Plato gives to Socrates. Zeno's account of the institutional arrangements of his best regime, moreover, is intended to show how Plato misconceives the way of life that accords with natural justice. In fact, these institutional arrangements seem intended to discharge the conditions for the best regime laid down by the Athenian Stranger in book 5 of the *Laws* (739 c–e), so well does Zeno's polity of sages correspond to Plato's "city of gods or children of gods."[20] Zeno's *Republic* thus belongs to a continuing tradition of discussion about the best way in which to answer the conventionalist challenge—the most powerful exposition of which is that of Glaucon and Adeimantus at the outset of book 2 of Plato's *Republic*—to show that justice is naturally choiceworthy in itself, independently of its rewards and consequences. In offering an account of the way of life that accords with natural law, Zeno sides with other Socratics—Plato included—in holding that justice is natural, rooted somehow in man's rational nature, and not merely conventional in origin,[21] though Zeno's position differs quite radically from that of his predecessors.

[19]The evidence for Zeno's *Republic* is assembled in *SVF* 1.259–71 and in Philodemus *De Stoicis*, in the edition of T. Dorandi, *CErc* 12 (1982): 91–133; for the modern discussion, see A. Dyroff, *Die Ethik der alten Stoa* (Berlin, 1897), pp. 206–19; N. Festa, *I frammenti degli Stoici antici* (Bari, 1932), 1:9–25; H. C. Baldry, " 'Zeno's Ideal State," *JHS* 79 (1959): 3–15; Rist (above, note 9), pp. 54–80; M. Isnardi-Parente, "La politica della Stoa antica," *Sandalion* 3 (1980): 67–98; J. Mansfeld, "Diogenes Laertius on Stoic Philosophy," in *Diogene Laerzio: Storico del penserio antico*, a special issue of *Elenchos* 7 (1986): 328–51; A. Erskine, *The Hellenistic Stoa: Political Thought and Action* (Ithaca, N.Y., 1990), pp. 9–42; P. A. Vander Waerdt, "Politics and Philosophy in Stoicism," *OSAP* 9 (1991): 185–211; Schofield (above, note 14).

[20]I take it that the regime of the *Laws*, "second-best" by virtue of its abandonment of radical communism, is a practical version of the best regime of the *Republic*, as the Athenian Stranger himself suggests (739a–e, 711a–712a, 875c–d; cf. Arist. *Pol.* 1265a1–9, 1264b26–28, 1265b31–1266a6); therefore it presupposes the same scheme of education and the rule of the same philosophy (cf. H. Cherniss, *Gnomon* 25 [1953]: 377–79; T. L. Pangle, *The Laws of Plato* [New York, 1980], pp. 376–77, 459–62, 504, 509–10; A. Laks, "Legislation and Demiurgy: On the Relationship between Plato's *Republic* and *Laws*," *CA* 9 [1990]: 209–29).

[21]For the Stoic position, cf. D. L. 7.128; *SVF* 3.314. The locus classicus of classical conventionalism is *Laws* 889e–890a; cf. 891c–892c, 966c–968a; Arist. *Soph. el.* 1137a7–18; Heraclitus B102 DK; Pl. *Rep.* 338c (Thrasymachus), 358b–362c (Glaucon); *Grg.* 482c–486d (Callicles); and Antiphon fr. B44 DK; the best analysis of it remains L. Strauss, *Natural Right and History* (Chicago, 1953), pp. 97–115; see also C. H. Kahn, "The Origins of

My thesis that Zeno's agenda in his *Republic* is anti-Platonic is not a novelty: Plutarch reports that Zeno "wrote in reply to Plato's *Republic*" (*De Stoic. repugn.* 1034e–f = *SVF* 1.260); there is clear evidence that the early Stoics gave close attention to the text of Plato's *Republic*, as witnessed, for example, by the substantial fragments of Chrysippus' extensive book in refutation of Plato's teaching on natural justice;[22] ancient writers commonly associate Zeno's best regime with Plato's (e.g., *SVF* 1.261–63); and modern scholars have long recognized that certain features of Zeno's polity—such as its community of women (D. L. 7.131, 33) or abolition of currency for exchange or foreign travel (D. L. 7.33, contradicting *Leg.* 742a–b; cf. *Rep.* 371b, 417a–b)—bear some relation to the "city in speech" the Platonic Socrates constructs in the *Republic*. But so far there is no cogent account of how the philosophical intention of Zeno's *Republic*, as opposed to isolated points of detail, represents a reply to Plato.[23] My objective is to explain exactly how the early Stoic theory of natural law represents an attempt to improve upon Plato's answer to Glaucon's challenge. In developing my case I shall also draw upon the testimonia of Chrysippus' polemic against Plato on natural justice.[24] In working with such fragmentary material as we

---

Social Contract Theory," in *The Sophists and Their Legacy*, ed. G. B. Kerferd, *Hermes Einzelschriften* 44 (Wiesbaden, 1981), pp. 92–108. It is important to bear in mind that conventionalism is compatible not only with a view that sees the pursuit of one's self-interest as the human good but also with one like Epicurus', which sees the social contract as providing the conditions necessary for the pursuit of philosophy (cf. P. A. Vander Waerdt, "The Justice of the Epicurean Wise Man," *CQ* n.s. 38 [1987]: 402–22; P. Mitsis, *Epicurus' Ethical Theory: The Pleasures of Invulnerability* [Ithaca, N.Y., 1988], pp. 59–90).

[22]The fragments of this work show that the early Stoics gave close attention to analysis of the text of the *Republic:* thus Chrysippus denounces Cephalus (*Rep.* 330d–331b) for making fear of the gods a deterrent from injustice, likening this argument to the "bogey and hobgoblin with which women try to keep little children from mischief" (*De Stoic. repugn.* 1040a–b); and he says that the notion of "doing oneself injustice is absurd, for injustice exists in relation to another and not to oneself" (1041b–c), so rejecting the analogy between psychic and political justice on which the entire argument of the *Republic* rests.

[23]Thus Erskine (above, note 19), pp. 30–33, for instance, fails to consider how Zeno's doctrines are grounded in his theory of natural law, and how this theory represents a reply to Plato. Schofield (above, note 14), pp. 22–56, develops, on the basis of parallels with Plato, an interpretation of Zeno's *Republic* according to which it represents a communistic "community in the ordinary sense of the word": but his account fails to take into account the complexities in assessing whether Plato's "best city in speech" represents a practical political model (see section 2 below). Inasmuch as Schofield relies on unargued assertions concerning Plato's project to establish Zeno's, his interpretation of the latter's *Republic* stands or falls with his interpretation of the former's. In section 2 below I have offered a very different account of their intention (note that Schofield, pp. 22–24, offers no argument against the interpretation he categorizes as [b]).

[24]Plut. *De Stoic. repugn.* 1040a (cf. H. Cherniss [p. 467n. b of the Loeb edition], *Moralia* XIII, pt. 2 [Cambridge, Mass., 1976] ad loc.) = *SVF* 3.313; fragments are preserved at 1040d, 1041b, and *De comm. not.* 1070e–f; a fragment of his *Exhortations* against the companion dialogue *Cleitophon* 408a is preserved at *De Stoic. repugn.* 1039d–1040a. (These

have in the case of the early Stoics, one often can only conjecture the target or original context of a particular doctrine. But I hope that this parallel evidence, illustrating as it does the care the early Stoics gave to study and refutation of Plato's political writings, will lend added plausibility to my thesis.

Although it has remained relatively neglected by modern scholars, Zeno's *Republic* was arguably the most famous and controversial of all Hellenistic philosophical works, and it provoked considerable controversy even within the Stoa: some later Stoics rejected the *Republic* as spurious; others subjected it to censorship; still others attempted to discount it as the product of Zeno's youth.[25] This controversy arose in large part from Zeno's apparent advocacy of such Cynic tenets as the permissibility—under certain "special circumstances" (D. L. 7.122), I shall argue later—of incest (*SVF* 1.256) and cannibalism (*SVF* 1.254). Since the *Republic* was an early work,[26] reportedly written under the influence of the Cynic Crates (D. L. 7.4), scholars have tended to focus their attention on these Cynic affiliations.[27] It is equally clear, however, that by the time he wrote the *Republic* Zeno had decisively broken with

excerpts are based on careful study of Chrysippus' book: Plutarch's *Concerning Justice against Chrysippus*, Lamprias no. 59.) Other early Stoic writing against Plato includes Persaeus' refutation of the *Laws* in seven books (D. L. 7.36).

[25]Cf. Philod. *De Stoic.*, cols. 2–7, with Dorandi (above, note 19), pp. 92–97, and Mansfeld (above, note 19), pp. 321–23, 343–51. The authenticity of the *Republic* is guaranteed by Chrysippus, who cites the work as Zeno's (D. L. 7.33–34) and defends some of its most controversial contents (cannibalism [*SVF* 3.747–53; cf. Cleanthes, *SVF* 1.584], incest [*SVF* 3.743–46, 753], the community of women and children [*SVF* 3.728, 744–45]). For censorship of Zeno's *Republic*, see the story about Athenodorus' deletions in Diogenes Laertius 7.34; also Clem Al. *Strom.* 5.9 = *SVF* 1.43: "The Stoics say that the first Zeno wrote certain things that they are reluctant to give to their pupils to read unless they have first proven themselves to be genuine philosophers."

[26]Erskine (above, note 19), pp. 9–15, has cleverly attempted to discredit the evidence on which this view is based, but I believe that Diogenes Laertius 7.4 remains an insuperable difficulty for his view; see Vander Waerdt (above, note 19), pp. 193–94. The suggestion of Rist (above, note 9), pp. 71–72, that Zeno composed the *Republic* before he realized the importance of nature in ethical context faces the difficulty that its political doctrines are intelligible only in light of the theory of natural law. (Philodemus *De Stoicis*, col. 14, neatly refutes opponents who question the authenticity of Zeno's *Republic* by pointing out that it is compatible with the theory of the *telos*, which, they also hold, made him the founder of Stoicism.)

[27]See esp. Rist (above, note 9) and Mansfeld (above, note 19); also M. Fisch, "Alexander and the Stoics," *AJP* 58 (1937): 132–34; D. B. Dudley, *A History of Cynicism* (London, 1937). Philodemus' *De Stoicis* provides detailed evidence of the controversy within the Stoa over the status of Zeno's Cynic leanings (the Cynics retained a separate identity well into the Imperial period; see J. L. Moles, "*Honestius quam Ambitiosius?* An Exploration of the Cynic's Attitude toward Moral Corruption in His Fellow Men," *JHS* 103 [1983]: 103–23; C. E. Manning, "School Philosophy and Popular Philosophy in the Roman Empire," *ANRW* II.36.5 [Berlin, forthcoming]); a Stoic could adopt radically different moral postures depending upon his attitude toward this question.

the Cynics, above all by holding that the study of nature is essential for virtue. If this break is due to the influence of Zeno's teacher, the Academic Polemon,[28] as John Rist has well argued,[29] then we can trace to Zeno's intellectual biography the decisive preoccupation with Platonism that we shall find in his theory. In any case, even before Zeno's time the Cynic Diogenes wrote a dialogue in reply to Plato's *Republic*,[30] and Zeno too regarded its teaching as the main competitor to his own.

Our subject thus is a case study in the intellectual origins of Stoic philosophy. Since we possess no complete book by an early Stoic, and since the extant fragments are largely preserved in later doxography, which is itself influenced by subsequent philosophical developments, it is often difficult to identify the specific problems and debates that led to the development of the early scholarchs' position. But recent scholarship has made it increasingly clear that philosophical debate during the Hellenistic period was dominated by disputes among a variety of philosophical movements over the interpretation of Socrates' heritage, each movement tracing its ancestry to Socrates and claiming to expound the authentic version of his philosophy.[31]

The early Stoics certainly participated prominently in this debate. Philodemus reports that some members of the school traced their lineage to Socrates through the succession Socrates–Antisthenes–Diogenes–Zeno, and, accordingly, that they actually wished to be called Socratics (*De Stoic.*, cols. 12–13). The Stoics' attempt to construct a Socratic pedigree for themselves is eloquently witnessed by their stories about Zeno's conversion to philosophy—it is reported, for instance, that he first began to associate with the Cynic Crates after reading book 2 of Xenophon's *Memorabilia* in a bookshop; when he enquired where such men as Socrates could be found, the proprietor told him to follow Crates (D. L. 7.2–3). About the meaning of Socrates' heritage, however, there was considerable controversy even within the Stoa: thus Ariston's difference with Chrysippus over such questions as the unity

---

[28]Cf. D. L. 7.2; Cic. *Acad.* 1.35; *Fin.* 4.3; Numen. fr. 25 des Places.

[29]"Zeno and Stoic Consistency," *Phronesis* 22 (1977): 161–74.

[30]For its title: D. L. 6.80; its apparent contents: D. L. 6.72–73, 103 (many antecedents of Stoic thought); anecdotes about Diogenes and Plato: D. L. 6.24–26, 40–41. For the heated debate within the Stoa over the authenticity of Diogenes' *Republic* (Chrysippus is said to have cited it as his in nine different books), see Philod. *De Stoic.* cols. 15.14–16 fin., which reports that certain contemporary Stoics (τινες τῶν καθ' ἡμᾶς, col. 15.13) denied that Diogenes ever wrote a *Republic*—apparently in order to disarm the charge that Zeno's *Republic* borrowed significantly from the Cynics. Philodemus' refutation is accepted, among others, by G. Giannantoni, *Socratis et Socraticorum Reliquiae*[2] (Naples, 1990), 3:416–17; M. O. Goulet-Cazé, *L'ascèse cynique* (Paris, 1986), pp. 85–90.

[31]E.g., A. A. Long, "Socrates in Hellenistic Philosophy," *CQ* n.s. 39 (1988): 150–71; Julia Annas' essay in Chapter 12; Gisela Striker's essay in Chapter 9; and the further studies cited below in notes 32–33.

of virtue and the status of the "indifferents," and the value of rules of conduct for moral progressors stems in part from disagreement over how best to interpret certain Socratic premises and doctrines to which both subscribed.[32] Hence it is not surprising that the early Stoics were especially concerned to discredit other Socratics who offered rival portraits of Socrates and of his significance. Their debate with Arcesilaus and the skeptical Academy over the existence and character of the cognitive impression, which persisted until the end of the Hellenistic period, is the best-known example.[33] In the case of our subject, both Plato and Zeno understand Socrates to hold that justice is somehow rooted in man's rational nature, but they construe this position in quite different ways, Zeno's theory of natural law representing an attempt to discredit Plato's interpretation of this Socratic position.

Since the scattered fragments of Zeno's *Republic* do not allow us to reconstruct its original order of exposition,[34] we will proceed as follows. First, I will argue that the purpose of Zeno's work is to illustrate the way of life that accords with natural law, and that this explains some of the peculiar social and institutional features of his polity of sages. Next, in section 2, I will try to show that Zeno's purpose in offering an account of his best regime, a "dream or image of a philosopher's well-regulated regime" (Plut., *De virt. Alex.* 329a–b), corresponds quite closely to Plato's purpose in constructing his "city in speech" in his *Republic*. Third, I will suggest that Zeno's theory of natural law represents an attempted improvement over Plato's teaching on natural justice in the *Republic* (section 3). Finally, in section 4, I will argue that the institutional arrangements of Zeno's best regime are best explained as a deliberate response to Plato's paradox of the rule of the philosopher-kings.

1. Natural Law in Zeno's Polity of Sages

Our best guide to the interpretation of Zeno's *Republic* is provided by Plutarch in a famous passage whose language is saturated with Platonic allusions—allusions, I shall try to show, that reflect Zeno's attempt to

[32]See A. M. Ioppolo, *Aristone di Chio e lo Stoicismo antico* (Naples, 1980); M. Schofield, "Ariston of Chios and the Unity of Virtue," *AP* 4 (1984): 83–96; Striker 1991 (above, note 1), pp. 14–24; J. Annas, *The Morality of Happiness* (Oxford, 1993).

[33]See M. Frede, "Stoics and Sceptics on Clear and Distinct Impressions," in *The Skeptical Tradition,* ed. M. F. Burnyeat (Berkeley, 1983), pp. 65–93.

[34]Our only clue is furnished by Cassius' report that Zeno began with a denunciation of traditional education (D. L. 7.32). Cassius' *laudationes* provide precise line references for the doctrines he cites, but there is no reason to assume that he summarizes Zeno's own line of argument.

refine Plato's teaching on natural justice in the *Republic* and *Laws* by
making it more precise and consistent:

καὶ μὴν ἡ πολὺ θαυμαζομένη πολιτεία τοῦ . . . Ζήνωνος εἰς ἓν τοῦτο συντ-
είνει κεφάλαιον, ἵνα μὴ κατὰ πόλεις μηδὲ κατὰ δήμους οἰκῶμεν, ἰδίοις
ἕκαστοι διωρισμένοι δικαίοις, ἀλλὰ πάντας ἀνθρώπους ἡγώμεθα δημό-
τας καὶ πολίτας, εἰς δὲ βίος ᾖ καὶ κόσμος, ὥσπερ ἀγέλης συννόμου νόμῳ
κοινῷ συντρεφομένης. τοῦτο Ζήνων μὲν ἔγραψεν ὥσπερ ὄναρ ἢ εἴδωλον
εὐνομίας φιλοσόφου καὶ πολιτείας ἀνατυπωσάμενος.

The much-admired *Republic* of Zeno . . . is aimed at this one main point,
that we should not dwell in cities or peoples,[35] each one marked out by its
own principles of justice, but we should regard all human beings as our
fellow members of the populace and fellow-citizens, and there should be
one way of life[36] and order,[37] like that of a herd[38] grazing together[39] and

---

[35]For this translation and Stoic parallels, see Schofield (above, note 14), p. 104 n. 1.

[36]Schofield (above, note 14), p. 109, claims: "The relatively few texts which deal with
the teachings of the early Stoics on the relations of the wise with each other do not claim
that they lead a single way of life." But he is overlooking Cleanthes' account of how evil
human beings, by neglecting the "one eternal *logos*," are deprived of all the good things
they desire; they fail to see the *koinos nomos* of god, "being obedient to which they would
have a good life [βίον ἐσθλόν] with *nous*" (*SVF* 1.537.21–25): it is hard to imagine a closer
parallel to Zeno's claim that one way of life follows from living according to the *koinos
nomos*. Moreover, Chrysippus' extensive work *On Lives* in four books (we possess ten fragments listed by von Arnim, *SVF* 3:194) clearly considered alternative candidates for
the single best way of life for a human being.

[37]Schofield (above, note 14), p. 109: "I am unable to find in texts representing the
views of the early Stoics any subsequent use of *kosmos* in the sense of an ordering of
society. The expression seems to be used exclusively of the physical universe, even
if the universe so designated is sometimes viewed *as* a cosmic city or society." On the
interpretation proposed below, κόσμος here refers to the *megalopolis* and is to be
construed both as the physical universe and as an ordering of society (see below,
note 72). For the latter sense of *kosmos*, see Cleanthes' *Hymn* (*SVF* 1.537.19): Zeus has
the power of "putting in order what is disorderly" (κοσμεῖν τἄκοσμα; cf. the morally
loaded sense of *kosmos* in line 28). The following line indicates unequivocally that *kosmos*
here bears the sense of an ordering of society ("you have fitted together into one all
good things with the evil"), although Cleanthes may mean to evoke the cosmic order
as well.

[38]Schofield (above, note 14), pp. 107–8, calls this comparison "the most questionable
feature" of Plutarch's report, but it is attested in a variety of later Stoic texts (esp. Hi-
erocles, col. 11.14, συναγελαστικὸν ζῷον, with Cic. *Fin.* 3.62–63 and the discussion of
S. G. Pembroke, "*Oikeiōsis*," in *Problems in Stoicism*, ed A. A. Long [London, 1971], pp.
125–27 with pp. 144–45 nn. 61–63; Plut. *De comm. not.* 1065f, with reference to the cosmic city; Clem. Al. *Strom.* 2.420 = *SVF* 3.332, where regime is defined as a τροφὴ
ἀνθρώπων καλὴ κατὰ κοινωνίαν and law giving as a science that cares for the human
herd, ἀνθρώπων ἀγέλης. Its prominence in the Platonic targets (esp. *Minos* 318a, 321c;
Plt. 265b–268d, 274b–276d; cf. Xen. *Cyr.* 1.1.2; J. B. Skemp, *Plato's Statesman* [London,
1952], pp. 52–66) against which Zeno is writing makes it entirely plausible that he would
have adopted it.

[39]σύννομος, *Leg.* 666e; cf. συννομή, *Plt.* 268; and Plut. *De comm. not.* 1065f (discussed
below).

nurtured[40] by a common[41] law.[42] Zeno wrote this, picturing as it were a dream or image of a philosopher's well-regulated regime.[43] (*De virt. Alex.* 329a–b = *SVF* 1.262)

Zeno's injunction that there should be one way of life and order, nurtured as it were by a common law (*nomos koinos*), clearly alludes to the Stoic theory that the human *telos* is to live in rational consistency with nature.[44] Since Zeno is attested to have identified the *koinos nomos* or *orthos logos* as the canon or standard that human beings follow in living according to nature,[45] we may safely assume that the "one way of life and order" which Zeno advocates in the passage from Plutarch just quoted accords with natural law as understood in this early Stoic theory.[46]

Let us begin our exegesis of this passage with a problem concerning the citizen body of the best regime: Plutarch states that we should regard "all human beings" as our fellow citizens, and this text has become the principal document in the dossier of those who see Zeno as advocating a universal world-state.[47] It is hard to reconcile this view, how-

[40]συντρέφεται, *Leg.* 752c; echoed in the τροφή and τροφός of *Plt.* 268a, c; 276d.

[41]*Koinos* here means common *not* to all mankind but rather to those who perfectly embody human nature: so Chrysippus in his *On Ends* (D. L. 7.87) identifies *koinos nomos* with right reason, in his theory possessed only by the sage; Cleanthes in his *Hymn to Zeus* states that the wicked do not follow the *koinos nomos* (*SVF* 1.537.24). Hence *koinos* is to be understood as "general" or "basic" rather than "universally shared." That this is its sense in early Stoic epistemological contexts is argued by D. Obbink, "What All Men Believe—Must Be True: Common Conceptions and *consensio omnium* in Aristotle and Hellenistic Philosophy," *OSAP* 10 (1992): 193–231, who shows that the doctrine of κοιναὶ ἔννοιαι was originally quite independent of the *consensus* argument, with which it is often conflated in the doxography. But Zeno may also characterize law as "common" here in agreement with Plato *Laws* 875a that the true art of politics must care for the common rather than private interest: what Zeno thinks that might entail is taken up in section 4 below.

[42]The Athenian Stranger similarly plays on *nomos* in the sense of "pasturing" in criticizing the Cretan regime for keeping its young "like colts grazing in a herd" (*Leg.* 666e; see also *Minos* 317d–318a): Zeno's appropriation of the herd image to characterize his "one way of life and order" may thus be a rejoinder to Plato's criticism of the analogy.

[43]For the adaptation of Platonic language here, see section 2 below.

[44]Schofield (above, note 14), pp. 104–11, attempts to impugn the credibility of this text, but with no more success than the predecessors refuted by Baldry (above, note 19), pp. 12–13, and Erskine (above, note 19), pp. 18–22, as argued in the preceding notes.

[45]See Cic. *Nat. d.* 1.36, quoted above in note 8.

[46]In my view Zeno, Cleanthes, and Chrysippus all shared a consistent and mutually reinforcing doctrine of natural law, so that—in the absence of countervailing evidence, and with due caution—we may draw upon Chrysippus and Cleanthes to aid in the interpretation of the *Republic*. The evidence that supports this assumption is set forth in my forthcoming book, cited above, note 1.

[47]Against this thesis of W. W. Tarn's ("Alexander, Cynics, and Stoics," *AJP* 60 [1939]: 41–70; *Alexander the Great* [Cambridge, 1940]), see the compelling replies of M. Fisch ("Alexander and the Stoics," *AJP* 58 [1937]: 59–82, 129–51) and E. Badian ("Alexander the Great and the Unity of Mankind," *Historia* 7 [1958]: 425–44).

ever, with other evidence that clearly restricts citizenship in this regime to Stoic sages. Zeno's statements that only σπουδαῖοι are citizens (D. L. 7.32–33; cf. 7.121–22) and that there should be a community of women *among* sages (D. L. 7.33, 131) are otherwise difficult to explain, given that his regime admits no distinctions of social class. If virtue is the sole criterion for ties of kinship, friendship, and citizenship (D. L. 7.122–24), and if the sage acts rightly in everything he does, all nonsages wrongly in everything (Arius 113.18–23 = SVF 3.529), then it is clear that the sage alone is capable of living in a community governed by the common law.[48] Moreover, if Zeno agreed with Chrysippus in holding that natural law prescribes virtuous actions, the *katorthōmata* that only sages are capable of performing (see above, note 12), then he would have every motivation to find the vast majority of humankind incapable of living in accordance with the *koinos nomos*.[49] Just as citizenship in the best regime extends only to sages, so does the capacity to live in accordance with the *koinos nomos*.[50] In view of such considerations, Plutarch's "all human beings" is best understood to refer to those capable of living according to the common law—that is, to all wise human beings.[51]

[48]Similar reasoning applies to the sage's singular knowledge of good and evil, which makes him alone fit to rule—as Chrysippus wrote in vindicating Zeno's use of the term "king" to designate the sage who has the freedom and capacity for independent action. For the classification of the forms of rule in Diogenes Laertius 7.121–22, see Erskine (above, note 19). If I am right in suggesting that Zeno's polity depicts the way of life of the *megalopolis*, which admits only gods and sages to its membership, then there is additional reason to suppose that he restricted citizenship in his polity to sages.

[49]Although we have no explicit evidence concerning how Zeno conceived of the moral content of natural law's prescriptions, the motivation of his polity of sages emerges much more clearly if we take him to agree with Chrysippus on this point. Zeno holds that the sage acts rightly in everything he does, everyone else wrongly (Arius 113.18–23 = SVF 3.529): hence he is unlikely to have held nonsages capable of participating in the *koinos nomos*.

[50]In his account of the rule of sages during the *saeculum aureum* (Sen. *Ep*. 90 = Posidonius fr. 284 Edelstein and Kidd; cf. I. G. Kidd's *Commentary* [Cambridge, 1988], 2:960–71), Posidonius appears to provide an interesting adaptation of Zenonian ideas in explaining the genealogy of law: the first human beings and their uncorrupted followers followed one man—the *sapiens*—as leader and law ("*primi mortalium . . . eundum habebant et ducem et legem*," *Ep*. 90.4); only when vice arose, bringing with it tyranny, did there arise a need for positive laws, which originally were framed by *sapientes*.

[51]This follows a suggestion of O. Murray, *CR* 80 (1966): 368; cf. Baldry (above, note 19), pp. 6–7; Rist (above, note 9), pp. 64–65; Erskine (above, note 19), p. 20 (who suggests that Polybius 6.56.10 may refer to Zeno's *Republic*); the contrary arguments of Moles (above, note 27), do not seem to me persuasive. Note that Plutarch identifies "all" as the morally good at *De virtute Alexandri* 329c. It has recently been proposed that "in restricting 'citizenship' to the wise (D. L. 7.33), Zeno meant simply that only they would actively govern; any number of others, though excluded from political office as 'inferiors', would still be members of society" (S. A. White, *JHP* 30 [1992]: 295), but there is no evidence that Zeno admitted distinctions of class in his best regime; to the contrary, the "one way of life and order" he advocates effectively abolishes any ruling class.

This interpretation also has the advantage of easily accounting for the Zenonian doctrines that attracted hostile criticism in antiquity. Most of our evidence for the controversy generated by the *Republic* dates from the first century B.C., when Philodemus undertook in his *De Stoicis* to refute Stoic attempts to explain or explain away Zeno's apparent advocacy of various Cynic doctrines.[52] But it is likely that these controversies go back to the earliest period of the Stoa, for Chrysippus in his *On Republic* seems to have undertaken a comprehensive defense of these Cynic doctrines.[53]

Zeno's critics appear to have taken proposals he advanced for his polity of sages and applied them to the case of ordinary human beings. Take for example the information provided in our most extensive report concerning the *Republic*, Cassius the skeptic's denunciation of Zeno preserved in Diogenes Laertius 7.32–34: (1) Zeno begins the *Republic* by rejecting the educational curriculum (*engkyklion paideian*) as useless;[54] (2) he declares all who are not morally good (*spoudaioi*)—even family members—foes, enemies, slaves, and aliens;[55] (3) he presents only the morally good as citizens, friends, relations, and free men;[56] (4) he advocates the community of women (*among sages:* D. L. 7.131);[57] (5) he prohibits the building of temples, law courts, and gymnasia;[58] (6) he abolishes currency;[59] finally, (7) he orders men and women to wear the same clothes and to keep no part of their body completely covered (D. L. 7.32–34).[60] This litany of criticism is not surprising

[52]Schofield (above, note 14), pp. 20–21, conjectures that Cassius the skeptic compiled his attack on Zeno during the same period.

[53]For instance, his *On Republic* defended the community of women (D. L. 7.121) and incest (D. L. 7.188); his defense of cannibalism (*SVF* 3.474–52) is also well attested. He praised Diogenes the Cynic for masturbating in public while saying to bystanders: "Would that I could rub hunger out of my belly in this way" (Plut. *De Stoic. repugn.* 1044b = *SVF* 3.706), and quoted him on the uselessness of weapons (*ap.* Philod. *De Stoic.*, cols. 15.31–16.4).

[54]For the Cynic antecedent, see D. L. 6.73, 103–4, with Mansfeld (above, note 19), pp. 328–51. Chrysippus appears not to follow Zeno on this point (D. L. 7.129 = *SVF* 3.738; cf. Arius 67.5–12 = *SVF* 3.294), but see below, note 61.

[55]There is good Cynic precedent for this in Antisthenes' claims that only the *spoudaioi* are friends (D. L. 6.12, quoting Diocles).

[56]See D. L. 6.12.

[57]Diogenes the Cynic advocated that women be held in common (D. L. 6.72), a view that Chrysippus also endorsed (D. L. 7.131). The Platonic antecedent is discussed below.

[58]This appears to be an anti-Platonic provision, for Plato in the *Laws* makes specific provision for temples (758a, 771a, 778b–c), law courts (766d, 778d), and gymnasia (778)—as Dyroff (above, note 19), p. 210, pointed out.

[59]This too specifically contradicts the *Laws* (742a–b; cf. *Rep.* 371b, 417a–b), but it may also have a cynic antecedent in Diogenes the Cynic's injunction "Deface the coinage" (D. L. 6.20–21, 71), on which see now *SSR*, 4:423–33.

[60]Cf. Philod. *De Stoic.*, col. 19.12–14. These rules on dress reflect Cynic practice (e.g., the case of Crates' wife Hipparchia: D. L. 6.97) as well as Plato's *Republic* (452a–b, 457 a–b), both discussed in section 4 below. Schofield (above, note 14), pp. 3–21, has

if Zeno's proposals are taken to apply to ordinary human life. But it is easily answered once one recognizes that these proposals rather relate to a community of sages. As regards (1), the sage certainly finds the traditional educational curriculum useless, promoting as it does ends that accord not with nature but with the conventions of ordinary political communities.[61] As for (2) and (3), it is a well-known Stoic doctrine that only sages are genuinely free, everyone else (φαῦλοι) being incapable of independent action (αὐτοπραγία) and therefore slaves; they are the only true kings, because they alone have "knowledge of good and evil" (D. L. 7.121–22); they alone are friends, holding everything in common, on account of their likeness to one another (D. L. 7.124). The rest (4–7) represent examples—to which we will return in section 4—of Zeno's attempt to abolish all merely conventional features of civic life, as required by his injunction that we live according to natural law, undivided by the conventions of ordinary communities. In each of these cases, it is the sage's right reason, enabling him to attain man's natural end of living in rational consistency with nature, that confers upon him citizenship in Zeno's best regime.

Cassius' report makes clear that the "one way of life and order" of Zeno's polity of the wise presupposes the abolition of the conventional distinctions upon which ordinary political life relies. What then does Zeno propose to put in place of these distinctions? One striking and apparently paradoxical feature of his polity is that it appears to admit no code of positive laws, no rulers, and no class distinctions. The only

---

recently argued (following C. Wachsmuth, "Stichometrisches und Bibliothekarisches," *RhM* 34 [1879]: 38–51 at pp. 39–42; Mansfeld [above, note 19], pp. 344–46) that Diogenes Laertius 7.32–34 and the criticism of Chrysippus at 7.187–89 derive from Cassius as a common source, and he offers an elaborate hypothesis concerning Cassius' project in an attempt to defend the MSS ἀντιτεθῆναι (were set in opposition) rather than Richards' emendation ἀνατεθῆναι (were replaced) at 7.34. My reservations are the following: (1) there is no evidence that the text on which Schofield relies to reconstruct a Pyrrhonist antithesis, Sextus Empiricus *Outlines of Pyrrhonism* 3.245–48 = *Against the Professors* 11.189–94, derives from Cassius; (2) of the six topics on which Schofield attempts to find antithetical conflict, he finds none in two, and I find none of the other four compelling (e.g., Zeno's abolition of coinage in his polity of sages need not conflict with Chrysippus' enquiry into ways of making money in ordinary communities)—see also B. Inwood, *Bryn Mawr Classical Review* 3.2 (1992): 208–13; (3) in the context of Athenodorus' deletion of passages criticized by the Stoics, the proposed emendation at 7.34 makes much better sense of the passage than the MSS reading; (4) there is no hint of antithetical opposition within 7.32–34 or 7.187–89, so we would have to suppose that Diogenes (or his source) detached Zeno's doctrines from their antithetical context—yet Diogenes' very point in retailing this information is to convey what Zeno's critics said. Schofield's hypothesis that Diogenes based his report at 7.32–34 on a Pyrrhonist antithesis thus seems to me implausible and poorly supported.

[61]Zeno's doctrine would be consistent with Chrysippus' endorsement of *engkyklia mathēmata* (D. L. 7.129 = *SVF* 3.738) if we took the latter's statement to refer to moral progressors.

law in force in Zeno's polity is to act in rational consistency with nature, in accordance with the common law (*koinos nomos*) in which human beings share in virtue of their natural capacity to act in accordance with right reason and divine providence. This law presupposes the abolition of the laws and customs of actual Greek cities; yet it appears not to replace them with anything. Why does a regime governed according to natural law admit no code of positive legislation?

The distinctive features of the early Stoic theory of natural law sketched at the outset help to disarm this apparent paradox. If Zeno's understanding of *koinos nomos* is consistent with that of Cleanthes (*SVF* 1.537.24) and Chrysippus (D. L. 7.87–88; *SVF* 3.314, 520)—and we have no reason to doubt their doctrinal consistency on this point—then the *nomos* that nurtures human beings who seek to live in accordance with Zeno's "one way of life and order" is identical with the sage's right reason, which enables him to act infallibly in rational consistency with nature. This law has three features that are especially relevant here: (1) it is constituted by the sage's rational disposition, not by a code of rules or legislation; (2) it prescribes *katorthōmata,* actions whose moral correctness is guaranteed by the disposition with which they are performed; and (3) its prescription is sufficient to ensure the agent's attainment of his natural end, namely, "living consistently" or "consistently with nature."[62]

These features of Stoic natural law together explain why Zeno's polity of sages admits no code of positive legislation. Not only does positive law have no place within the framework of the first feature, a dispositional rather than rule-following model of natural law,[63] but the second ensures that there is no need in Stoic theory for a positive code of law, or for a judiciary applying and interpreting it, to correct the generality of law in the name of equity and so to guarantee moral correctness or justice in particular circumstances.[64] The prescriptions of Stoic natural law, *katorthōmata,* represent the sage's application of his rational disposition to the moral demands of particular circumstances: they are actions that are reasonable in the circumstances in which they are performed, and they are performed by agents whose moral moti-

---

[62]Like most recent commentators, I take these two formulations of the end attested for Zeno (Arius 75.11–76.8, 77.16–27; D. L. 7.87), as well as the formulations of his immediate successors, as consistent and mutually reinforcing attempts to express a single doctrine.

[63]Contrast, for example, the place of positive or human law in Aquinas' theory of natural law (*Summa theologiae* I.ii, q. 94).

[64]As opposed, for instance, to Platonic and Aristotelian teachings that insist that a wise statesman is necessary to correct law's generality for the sake of equity. It is only at a later period in the Stoa, when law comes to be treated in relation to inferior regimes, that equity features in Stoic discussions of justice: see Erskine (above, note 19), pp. 152–53.

vation is always correct. Thus, in specifying the intensional rather than the extensional features of virtuous actions, the Stoic theory has no need to bridge the gap that emerges, for example, in competing natural right theories such as Plato's or Aristotle's, between law's generality and the contingent particularity of moral action. Finally, as regards the third feature, the sufficiency of natural law for happiness ensures that the absence of a place for a code of positive law in the Stoic theory of natural law is not accidental: if natural law provides comprehensive guidance in obtaining man's natural end, there is no constructive function such a law code could perform.

The peculiar institutional features of Zeno's best regime follow directly from this conception of natural law. Since all its citizens are sages, there is no need of social classes, rulers, or judicial institutions to enforce correct conduct. Nor is there need of regulations to govern the treatment of property: the sages' friendship, made possible by their unique virtue and similarity to one another, enables them to hold everything in common, and so eliminates the causes of internal dissension that divide ordinary political communities;[65] and, in any case, knowledge alone legitimates property rights (D. L. 7.125), so that conventional regulations would prove not merely superfluous but contrary to nature. The citizens' knowledge of natural law ensures that they will infallibly act rationally, consistently, and harmoniously in accordance with nature in all particular circumstances, without any external constraint or direction, undivided by the differing principles of justice that divide ordinary political communities.[66] Since they can regard all of their fellow citizens as sages, they have no need of merely conventional, hence arbitrary, distinctions that have no foundation in natural law, such as status based upon birth and citizenship or private property. A positive code of law—whose generality would in any case require justified exception in special circumstances[67]—could serve no useful pur-

---

[65]D. L. 7.124. This text does not specifically cite the *Republic*, but it appears to be consistent with Athenaeus' report (561c = *SVF* 1.263) that Eros is a god who brings about friendship, freedom, and concord (ὁμόνοια); in any case, it reports a subject, namely, the relation between friendship and community of property among sages, that will certainly have figured in Zeno's book (taking him to show how his polity can meet the conditions the Athenian Stranger stipulates for the best regime: see section 4 below).

[66]*Homonoia* as a fundamental feature of Zeno's regime is attested by Athenaeus' report about Eros (561c = *SVF* 1.263), and it is defined by later Stoics as a "knowledge of common goods" (see Arius 93.19–94.6, 106.12–17, 108.15–18). Chrysippus wrote *On Concord*, in which he defended Zeno's usage of "free" and "slave" (see Ath. 267b; D. L. 7.121): these terms feature in Zeno's *Republic*, and it is likely that Chrysippus undertook to explain in this work the relationship between moral freedom and *homonoia*. For Zeno's Platonic precedent, see, for instance, *Rep.* 431d–432a.

[67]Hence the doctrine that the sage will violate even the most widely held moral prohibitions (e.g., against cannibalism) in order to act in rational consistency with nature (D. L. 7.125; Plut. *De Stoic. repugn.* 1038a): see section 4 below.

pose in a community whose citizens infallibly choose the correct course of action in all circumstances.

2. The Intention of Zeno's Best Regime

Now that we have seen that the theory of natural law accounts for some of the peculiar social and institutional features of Zeno's best regime, let us consider how this theory represents an attempted improvement over Plato's teaching in the *Republic*. Our first question is this: What was Zeno's intention in offering an account of the way of life of a regime whose citizenship is restricted to sages? It is not at all clear what relevance this account is supposed to bear to ordinary political life. Since Zeno's regime excludes the vast majority of humankind from its citizenship, and since natural law cannot be codified in moral rules or positive legislation to guide nonsages, the way of life Zeno depicts cannot be reproduced elsewhere, in any citizen body not composed entirely of sages. And if the sage is in fact as rare as the Ethiopians' phoenix, with only one or two known examples,[68] then Zeno's polity is not one that could ever be realized in deed.

A plausible interpretation of Zeno's intention emerges, I suggest, if we consider it in light of Plato's best "city in speech" to which it is a response. Socrates' avowed purpose in constructing the regime ruled by philosopher-kings is to provide a "pattern laid up in heaven" (*Rep.* 592a–b; cf. 472c–e; *Leg.* 702a–b; Cic. *Rep.* 2.52) by seeing which one can found such a regime within one's soul.[69] This regime exemplifies the way of life that accords with natural justice, but it serves as a pattern for psychic justice—not as a political proposal that can be brought to realization in the absence of some "divine chance" (592a; cf. 499b–c, 501e–502b; *Leg.* 711d–712a).[70] I suggest that the status of Zeno's pol-

[68]Alex. *Aphr. De fato* 199.14–22 = *SVF* 3.658; cf. Plut. *De Stoic repugn.* 1048e; *De comm. not.* 1076b–c; Sext. Emp. *Math.* 7.432–35; Diogenian. *ap.* Euseb. *Praep. evang.* 6.264b = *SVF* 3.668; Cic. *Nat. d.* 3.79.

[69]Recently M. F. Burnyeat has argued that Plato presents his "best city in speech" as a practical political teaching: see "The Practicability of Plato's Ideally Just City," in *On Justice*, ed. K. Boudouris (Athens, 1989), pp. 94–105; but, among many considerations, the "second-best" regime developed by the Athenian Stranger explicitly calls into question the practicability of the first regime, which presupposes a radical communism that the Athenian Stranger repeatedly indicates is contrary to human nature (cf. *Leg.* 739c, 740a, 773b); in addition Burnyeat does not consider the evidence within the *Republic* (e.g., 592a–b), which suggests that its practical realization is not Socrates' concern.

[70]For this interpretation of the *Republic*, see, for instance, L. Strauss, *The City and Man* (Chicago, 1964), pp. 50–138, esp. pp. 121–28; D. Clay, "Reading the *Republic*," in *Platonic Writings/Platonic Readings*, ed. C. Griswold (London, 1988), pp. 19–33, 269–72; for the support Aristotle gives this reading: P. A. Vander Waerdt, "Kingship and Philosophy in Aristotle's Best Regime," *Phronesis* 30 (1985): 249–73.

ity of the wise is similar: that Zeno characterized his polity as "a dream
or image" because it was intended to clarify the conditions, however
unlikely or impossible, that would have to obtain in order to secure the
realization of a way of life that accords with natural law.[71] In support
of this, I suggest that the polity Zeno depicts in his *Republic* is none
other than the *megalopolis*—the community of gods and sages, founded
in rationality, that exemplifies the way of life that accords with natural law.

What I propose, in other words, is that we consider Zeno's polity in
light of the distinction, accepted by Stoics of all periods, between the
two communities into which human beings are born—the natural and
the conventional[72]. As Seneca puts it, "one, which is great and truly
common, embracing gods and men, in which we look neither to this
corner nor to that but measure the boundaries of our city by the sun;[73]
the other, the one to which we have been assigned by the accident of
our birth."[74] Although our sources for the Stoic distinction between
man's two communities are principally late and doxographical, there is
every reason to suppose that it goes back to Zeno. For Chrysippus, in
his *On Nature* 3, argues that "the cosmos of the wise is one, its citizenship being held by gods and human beings together,"[75] and Cleanthes'
praise of the *koinos nomos* in his *Hymn to Zeus* (*ap.* Stob. *Ecl.* 1.1.12 =
SVF 1.537) also presupposes that man participates in community with
the gods through his rationality. These parallel treatments by Chrysippus and Cleanthes have led to the "irresistible conjecture" that these
authors "sought to develop an original Zenonian treatment of these

---

[71]That Plutarch's language at *De virtute Alexandri* 329b reflects Zeno's own is supported not only by the numerous parallels in the latter's Platonic target but also by Philodemus' ἀδυνατοὺς ὑποθέσεις (*De Stoic.*, col. 12.9).

[72]For the Stoic doctrine of the natural community of gods and human beings, in which
the latter share by virtue of their rationality, see, in addition to Chrysippus *De natura* 3,
quoted in the text, Diogenes of Babylon, *SVF* 3.117 (on pp. 241–42); Arius *ap.* Euseb.
Praep. evang. 15.15.3–5 = *SVF* 2.528 and *ap.* Stob. *Ecl.* 2.103.11–23, quoting Cleanthes;
Sen. *De otio* 4.1; Cic. *Nat. d.* 2.78–79, 153–55; Plut. *De comm. not.* 1065f; Dio Chrys. *Or.*
36.20–25; M. Aurelius *Med.* (e.g., 8.2). Some of these later texts take human rationality,
rather than the perfected rationality of the sage, as the criterion for membership in the
megalopolis, but *De natura* 3 makes clear that Chrysippus took the latter view.

[73]This formulation is consistent with Zeno's injunction that we regard all human beings as our fellow citizens (Plut. *De virt. Alex.* 329a–b).

[74]Sen. *De otio* 4.1:1 "duas res publicas amino complectamur, alterm magnam et vere
publicam qua di atque homines continentur, in qua non ad hunc angulum respicimus aut
ad illum sed terminos civitatis nostrae cum sole metimur, alteram cui nos adscripsit
condicio nascendi." Seneca goes on to characterize service to the first community by enquiring into such questions as what virtue is, whether it is one or many, whether our
world is unique, and so on.

[75]Chrysippus *De nat.* 3 *ap.* Philod. *De pietate*, col. 7.21–27 (text in A. Henrichs, "Die
Kritik der stoischen Theologie im *P. Herc.* 1428," *CErc* 4 [1974]: 18).

themes."[76] Aristocles' account of Zeno's cosmology (*ap.* Euseb. *Praep. evang.* 15.816d = *SVF* 1.98), which develops an analogy between the causal nexus of fate that orders the cosmos and a well-ordered political regime, provides some independent evidence to support this conjecture.

If we now consider Zeno's project in the *Republic* in light of this distinction between man's two communities, it seems clear that the "one way of life and order" he there advocates corresponds to the *megalopolis.* This natural community of gods and human beings is a regime that knows no boundaries and whose citizenship is determined by rational participation in the provident design of nature. A doxographical report by Arius Didymus makes the connection between natural law and the cosmic city explicit:

ὁ κόσμος οἱονεὶ πόλις ἐστὶν ἐκ θεῶν καὶ ἀνθρώπων συνεστῶσα, τῶν μὲν θεῶν τὴν ἡγεμονίαν ἐχόντων, τῶν δὲ ἀνθρώπων ὑποτεταγμένων. κοινωνίαν δ' ὑπάρχειν πρὸς ἀλλήλους διὰ τὸ λόγου μετέχειν, ὅς ἐστι φύσει νόμος· τὰ δ' ἄλλα πάντα γεγονέναι τούτων ἕνεκα.

The world is like a city consisting of gods and men, with the gods serving as the rulers and men as their subjects. They are members of a community because of their participation in reason, which is natural law; and everything else is created for their sake. (*ap.* Euseb. *Praep. evang.* 15.15.3–5 = *SVF* 2.528)

Arius does not refer to Zeno's *Republic* in this passage, but a variety of considerations converge to show that this work is to be read in light of the doctrine here reported.[77] There is first of all the Stoics' position that the cosmos alone is properly a city, and that those on earth, though so called, are not really cities.[78] Cleanthes, Chrysippus, and Diogenes

[76]So Schofield (above, note 14), p. 81, failing to recognize that the admission that Zeno himself developed the doctrine of the cosmic city undermines his claim that it was Chrysippus who first grafted the theory of natural law onto the doctrine of the cosmic city.

[77]The argument by which the Stoics move from the premise that gods and humans share rationality in common to the conclusion that they share right reason, hence law, in common is set out in Cicero (*Nat. d.* 2.78–79, 153–55; *Leg.* 1.23; cf. Plut. *De comm. not.* 1065f). On the *megalopolis,* see also Philo (*De Joseph.* = *SVF* 3.323), who characterizes it as using one regime and law—further evidence that the cosmic city is the community united by natural law.

[78]See esp. Clem. Al. *Strom.* 4.26 = *SVF* 3.327 and Philod. *De Stoic.,* col. 20.4–6, who reports that the Cynics and Stoics held that "we should not consider any of the cities or laws we know to be a city or law." There may be a Cynic precedent in Diogenes' position that the only correct regime is the one in the cosmos (D. L. 6.72; cf. *SSR,* 4:537–50 [Nota

of Babylon all maintain that only a group of morally good human beings united by natural law constitutes a true city.[79] Diogenes explicitly
states that "there is no *nomos* or *polis* among the ἄφρόνες" in contrast to
the community of gods and sages.[80] The early Stoics' radical depreca-
tion of existing political communities would appear to rule out the possibility that Zeno's best regime could belong to the second community,
which has no natural status.[81] Some reason for thinking that it specifically describes the *megalopolis* is provided by Plutarch's use of the herd
analogy in *De virtute Alexandri* 329a–b, an analogy that is strikingly paralleled in his description (*De comm. not.* 1065f) of the cosmic city: he
reports that Zeus fashioned the cosmos "as a town common to gods and
human beings who are to graze together [συννομησόμενον] with justice
and virtue harmoniously and blissfully." This text may well represent
an unrecognized allusion to Zeno's *Republic:* although not identical, the
language and thought are entirely consistent with the report of *De virtute Alexandri* 329a–b;[82] the grazing image—rare in Stoic texts (see
above, note 38), hence unlikely to have been fabricated by Plutarch—
serves in both passages to characterize the way of life of those who live
justly or in accordance with the *koinos nomos;* and the association of natural law with the cosmic city, attested by Arius in the text quoted above,
provides independent reason for supposing that this passage accurately specifies the membership of the "herd" grazing in Zeno's polity
of the wise. Such an interpretation is entirely consistent with our other
evidence for early Stoic political thought. Since natural law enjoins the
abolition of all conventional boundaries and distinctions, as Zeno stipulates in his *Republic,* no ordinary political regime can promote a way

50], with literature on Cynic cosmopolitanism cited at p. 545. n.20; Schofield [above,
note 14], pp. 143–45, argues inconclusively against the reliability of Diogenes Laertius
6.72 with respect to its information about Diogenes).

[79]Cf. Arius 103.11–23, quoting Cleanthes; Clem. Al. *Strom.* 4.26 = *SVF* 3.327; Dio
Chrys. *Or.* 36.20–25; Diogenian. *ap.* Euseb. *Praep. evang.* 6.264b = *SVF* 3.324; D. L.
7.122; Diogenes of Babylon, *SVF* 3.117, pp. 241–42 (see next note).

[80]*P. Herc.* 1506, col. 8 = Philod. *De rhet.* 2, p. 211 Sudhaus = *SVF* 3.117; for a new
text and full discussion of this papyrus, see D. Obbink and P. A. Vander Waerdt, "Diogenes of Babylon: The Stoic Sage in the City of Fools," *GRBS* 32 (1991): 355–96.

[81]"By nature there is no fatherland," says Ariston (Plut. *De exil.* 600e = *SVF* 1.371),
"just as there is no house or cultivated field, smithy or doctor's surgery; but each one of
these comes to be so, or rather is so named and called, always in relation to the occupant
and user."

[82]Thus ἄστυ κοινόν picks up εἰς κόσμος (*asty,* although unusual, does not provide
grounds for objection to the credentials of this text: the Stoics use a variety of terms to
refer to the cosmic city and often qualify their description with ὡσανεί, quasi, "as it
were": see, for instance, Arius *ap.* Euseb. *Praep. evang.* 15.817.6; M. Aurelius *Med.* 4.3.2,
4.4; Cic. *Fin.* 3.64; *Nat. d.* 2.78, 154); θεῶν καὶ ἀνθρώπων specifies the membership of
the herd referred to in 329a–b; μετὰ δικῆς καὶ ἀρετῆς expresses νόμῳ κοινῷ; ὁμολ-
ογαομένως picks up the negative injunction not to live divided and of course features in
Zeno's definition of the end (Arius 75.11–76.8, 77.16–27; D. L. 7.87).

of life that accords with it. Only in the cosmic city may one become κοσμοπολίτης (Philo *De mundi opificio* 142 = *SVF* 3.337)—a citizen of the cosmos who lives according to natural law, unfettered by the conventions of ordinary political communities.[83] The Stoic must conduct his search for happiness, and for the attainment of his natural perfection, in the first community in which he shares by virtue of his rationality, and this is the community Zeno apparently undertook to describe in his *Republic*.[84]

This is one reason why the early Stoic scholarchs take so little interest in questions that loom large in the political thought of the other heirs of Socrates, such as the relative merits of different forms of regime. There is in fact no evidence that any of the early scholarchs sought to promote any particular regime.[85] Cicero praises the early Stoics' political writings for their keen insight but states that they are not intended for practical political use ("nam veteres verbo tenus acute illi quidem, sed non ad hunc usum popularem atque civilem de re publica disserebant," *Leg.* 3.14). The absence of any early Stoic teaching on the forms of regime lends strong support to Cicero's perception of a fundamental difference between the writings of the early scholarchs and of later Stoics, beginning with Diogenes of Babylon, who attempted to clarify the practical implications of the early scholarchs' teachings. In seeking to construct a political philosophy that would be comparable to that of Plato and Aristotle in scope and intention, they shifted attention from

---

[83]There is of course good precedent for the doctrine of the sage as *kosmopolitēs* in Diogenes (see also Crates *ap.* D. L. 6.98), but Zeno's incorporation of it into the *megalopolis* presumably goes much farther and marks a significant departure from Cynic thought. See also the evidence for later Stoic views set out in G. R. Stanton, "The Cosmopolitan Ideas of Epictetus and Marcus Aurelius," *Phronesis* 13 (1968): 183–95.

[84]My suggestion that Zeno depicts the *megalopolis* as his model of this hypothetical regime helps to explain our evidence that Zeno spoke of a city or cities in his *Republic* (D. L. 7.33; Ath. 561c) without having to gather all or most of the sages in the world together in a single place (hence the expedient sometimes adopted of transporting Zeno's polity into some future golden age). The Stoic doctrine of the mutual benefits sages confer upon one another even when they are not together (see Plut. *De Stoic. repugn.* 1068f–1069a, 1076a–b; cf. Cherniss ad loc.) may well originate in an attempt to explain how the sages' friendship and community may benefit them even though they are scattered throughout the inhabited world.

[85]The report of Diogenes Laertius (7.131) that the Stoics advocate the mixed regime is best explained as referring to a later period in the school's history, when the relative merits of different forms of regime were being debated (some evidence is collected in F. E. Devine, "Stoicism on the Best Regime," *JHI* 31 [1970]: 323–36). Cicero *De legibus* 3.13–16 provides sufficient evidence that the early scholarchs did not provide clear guidance in applying their theory of natural law to actual political communities. Chrysippus holds that we should attach ourselves not to just any regime but to the right one (Sen. *De otio* 8.1 = *SVF* 3.695; cf. *Ep.* 68.2)—but only the natural community of gods and human beings meets this requirement.

man's first community to his second and adopted a very different attitude toward the second.[86] For the early scholarchs, on the other hand, man's first, natural community remained the center of attention.

When we consider Zeno's polity of the wise in light of this background, there is good reason to suppose that his purpose in the *Republic* is not to describe a political community whose practical realization he considers possible but rather the way of life that characterizes the first natural community, in which the wise share by virtue of their rationality. This interpretation has clear advantages. It enables us to preserve the link between natural law and the cosmic city that is an integral part of our doxography.[87] It takes account of the striking similarities between *De virtute Alexandri* 329a–b and *De communibus notitiis contra Stoicos* 1065f. It explains how Zeno undertook to found a community that recognizes no merely conventional boundaries, as he enjoins in the *Republic*. Moreover, as a community that exists nowhere on earth, it might quite readily be characterized as "a dream or image of a philosopher's well-regulated regime."

If the foregoing suggestions are correct, then Zeno's regime in promoting life in accordance with natural law prescribes conduct of which only members of the *megalopolis*, sages and gods, are capable. The way of life he describes, accordingly, is not intended—as his ancient critics presumed—to provide specific recommendations for existing regimes to imitate.[88] It would be pointless, after all, for such regimes to transform their way of life to adopt practices such as the abolition of currency or the community of women, when their citizens are incapable of achieving the rational consistency and harmony that natural law requires. Thus the practical purpose of Zeno's best regime—unlike Aristotle's, for example—cannot be to provide a model that can ever be realized anywhere indeed. Its relevance to political life in the ordinary sense must be sought elsewhere.

In the passage we quoted earlier, Plutarch states that Zeno's *Republic* pictures "a dream or image of a philosopher's well-regulated regime" (*De virt. Alex.* 329a–b). This language certainly supports our claim that Zeno's polity is a hypothetical model of the truly just community. But Plutarch's language also brings Plato to mind. When Socrates in *Republic* 4 obtains Glaucon's assent to this argument that justice both within

---

[86]See Vander Waerdt (above, note 19), esp. pp. 204–11. Erskine (above, note 19) offers a very different reconstruction of early Stoic political philosophy.

[87]Arius' report (106.12–20) that every *phaulos* is at enmity with the gods—enmity being defined as lack of harmony with the affairs of life—may well derive ultimately from an explanation of why nonsages cannot belong to the *megalopolis*.

[88]Pace Baldry (above, note 19), p. 5; Erskine (above, note 19), pp. 9–42.

the city and within the individual soul consists in the parts of each minding their own business, he says: "then that dream of ours has reached its perfect fulfillment" (443b).[89] The dream to which he refers is the first part of the "noble lie" in book 3, in which Socrates attempts to persuade the citizens that the god fashioned the class distinctions between guardians, auxiliaries, and the farmers and craftsmen by mixing into their souls gold, silver, and iron and bronze respectively (414d–415b). His lie consists in attempting to persuade the citizens that "the rearing and education we gave them were like dreams"; in truth the god was fashioning them under the earth. Inasmuch as the noble lie is the origin both of the threefold class division and of the communism (the second part of the lie) of the guardian class, this dream is central to the foundation of Socrates' best "city in speech" (cf. *Leg.* 663d–e).[90] It would be entirely appropriate for Zeno, in offering his rival depiction of the way of life that accords with natural justice, to present his own polity—whose citizens live in common without the divisions of social class and legal compulsion—as likewise a "dream" whose realization depends upon on divine providence. Chrysippus' attack (*ap.* Plut. *De Stoic. repugn.* 1041b–c = *SVF* 3.288) on the Platonic distinction between psychic and political justice provides independent evidence that the early Stoics took a particular interest in this aspect of the Platonic teaching.

In any case, Zeno's polity certainly resembles Plato's in that it appears to depict a hypothetical model of a regime the conditions for whose realization seem impossible. The purpose of his model may well be similar. As we saw earlier, Socrates and Glaucon eventually come to the conclusion in book 9 that it does not matter whether the best regime can actually come into being; it is rather a paradigm laid up in heaven for the man who wishes to found the just city within his own soul. Similarly, Zeno may have intended to provide a hypothetical model of the truly just life as a pattern for the man who wishes to live in rational consistency with nature. Such a hypothetical model might also serve to guide the wise in living out their lives happily in inferior regimes.[91] There may be a trace of this Zenonian claim in later texts that specify how the actions of sages benefit one another even in cases in which they are not living in proximity to one another.[92] In that case, the depiction of the way of life of the natural community in which hu-

---

[89]For the sense in which Socrates understands this dream, see 476c–d.

[90]For discussion, see C. Page, "The Truth about Lies in Plato's Republic," *AP* 11 (1991): 1–33.

[91]Cf. Chrysippus' remarks on political participation cited below, note 113.

[92]See Plut. *De comm. not.* 1068f–1069a (= *SVF* 3.627) with the further evidence assembled by Cherniss ad loc.

mans share by virtue of their rationality could provide a model of how the sage may live happily outside the *megalopolis*.

If the foregoing suggestions are correct, we are now in a better position to assess the controversy surrounding the status of Zeno's best regime. Plutarch, in the context surrounding the passage quoted earlier, takes Zeno to have accomplished in words what Alexander accomplished in deeds, and some modern scholars have supposed by this analogy that Zeno advocated a universal world-state.[93] Such a view, of course, overlooks the basic difference between man's first and second political communities, failing to recognize that Zeno's polity of the wise belongs to the first. Once one sees that natural law gives man access to the true polity, the natural community he shares with the gods, it becomes clear that Zeno's purpose in the *Republic* is not to provide a model for a world-state, but to describe how an individual may attain his natural end and perfection in the true polity governed by natural law, even while living out his life in inferior regimes.

3. Natural Law and Conventionalism

It is time now to consider how Plato and Zeno set out to answer the conventionalist challenge in developing their teachings on natural justice. I suggest that Zeno's conception of natural law as identical with the sage's right reason represents in part an attempt to draw out the implications of Plato's own reasoning in answering this challenge in the *Republic*. More particularly, Zeno seeks to exploit his insight (put most succinctly at *Statesman* 294a–295e) that the very generality of law makes it fallible, and that in consequence its proper application always depends upon a wise statesman who can discern the just course of action even in exceptional circumstances.[94] If this is so, however, then such fallible laws cannot by themselves constitute an answer to the challenge to show that justice is naturally choiceworthy, given that they always admit of exception. The only infallibly correct law, by the Platonic Socrates' own reasoning, is that laid down by a wise statesman in application of his right reason to a particular circumstance. Accordingly, in identifying natural law with the sage's right reason, Zeno is merely making explicit the reasoning that Plato himself displays in seeking to answer the conventionalist challenge. In that case, his theory represents an attempt, constructed in opposition to Plato in an effort to

---

[93]See the studies cited above, note 47.

[94]This point emerges with particular clarity in the *Minos*, where it is said that "law wishes to be the discovery of being" (315a; cf. 316b, 317d), and Minos is adduced as a lawgiver whose understanding of being enabled him to found unshakable laws (321b).

improve his view, to explain exactly how justice is founded in one's rational nature, so providing the nonarbitrary standard necessary to answer the conventionalist challenge.[95]

This challenge is put most powerfully by Glaucon and Adeimantus at the beginning of *Republic* 2. They hold that justice originates in a compact of advantage to refrain from mutual harm; but since its origin lies in human agreement, having no basis in man's rational nature as such, they fear that man will violate it whenever it is possible and in his self-interest to do so. They confront Socrates with the case of two men, each of whom possesses Gyges' ring—a just man who suffers from a reputation for injustice and an unjust man who reaps the benefits of a just reputation—and they demand that Socrates prove that the just life is superior independently of or even (in the former case) in spite of its rewards and consequences.

Now an answer to this challenge does not obviously require one to identify the origin of justice through the construction of a political regime. But the strategy Socrates chooses in reply is to construct a series of cities in speech—the city of pigs, which is transformed by the introduction of unnecessary desires into the feverish city, which in turn is purged and transformed into the city ruled by the philosopher-king. The assumption on which this strategy rests is that justice within the city and the soul is exactly analogous, such that to identify where justice originates in the city will enable one to discern its origin within the human soul.[96] His purpose in constructing the best city in speech is to provide a natural standard for the just life that will prove its superiority over the unjust life.

The founding and maintenance of Socrates' best regime relies upon its philosopher-guardians, whose educational program equips them with the knowledge that enables them to act infallibly in the city's best interests. But in the course of founding his city, Socrates also lays down a great deal of positive legislation that serves to regulate all aspects of its way of life. Some of these laws—such as the provisions establishing the community of women and children (457b–d) and the festivals at which procreation may take place (459d–460b)—serve to establish the form of the regime itself, by regulating the class structure on which its way of life rests. But other laws cannot possibly be supposed to be

---

[95]See above, note 21.

[96]There is an important difference in the two argumentative strategies Socrates employs here, well brought out by Clay (above, note 70), pp. 24–25. There is no evidence that Zeno sought to give an account of natural law either as part of a genetic account of the origin of the city or as a projection of such an account on the human soul (note Chrysippus' rejection of the analogy between psychic and political justice, *ap.* Plut. *De Stoic. repugn.* 1041b–c).

foundational in this sense—so, for example, the law that while on a military campaign "no one whom he [the man of exceptional valor] wants to kiss be permitted to refuse, so that if a man happens to love someone, either male or female, he would be more eager to win the rewards of valor" (468b–c); or the law that the guardians are not to waste the property of Greek—as opposed to barbarian—opponents at war (471b–c; cf. *Leg.* 629d). Such laws seem intended to promote natural justice as Socrates conceives it by abolishing conventional practices especially inimical to it. But they seem to establish other conventions that cannot be claimed invariably to accord with nature. Thus the code of positive law that Socrates lays down for his guardians encompasses much more than provisions to establish its class structure and educational program.

Socrates distinguishes between laws the guardians must obey and laws they are allowed to imitate at their own discretion without explaining how to draw the lines of demarcation (458b–c). This presents a difficulty that the Stoics, I suggest, are concerned to resolve. If the guardians are necessary in part to apply the laws properly (such as in the case of marriage regulations), and to make the exceptions to general practice necessary in particular cases, then Socrates' code of positive legislation is not in itself a dictate of natural justice. It relies for its application and sanction on the knowledge of good and evil possessed by the philosophers who are to rule this regime. Thus we cannot speak of any law or principle of natural justice independent of philosophic knowledge.

If this is so, then we can see why Zeno chose to identify natural law—the common law in which human beings share by virtue of their rationality—with the sage's rational disposition, for the only prescriptions that may be said infallibly to accord with nature are those that represent the application of his right reason to particular circumstances. In taking this step, Zeno could easily have supposed that he was simply making explicit and precise the reasoning Socrates himself displays in searching for natural justice in the *Republic*.

The Platonic Socrates is well aware of the force of the argument that there is no provision of positive law that does not admit of exception in extreme or unusual cases.[97] He uses it to dispose both of Polemarchus' definition of justice as giving to each what is owed (331e–334d) and of

---

[97]Similarly, Aristotle holds that all right is changeable (*Eth. Nic.* 1134b18–1135a6; cf. ps.-Arist. *Mag. mor.* 1194b30–1195a8), apparently because there is no principle of justice that does not admit of exception in an extreme case; cf. Strauss (above, note 70), pp. 157–63, who rejects both the Thomistic and Averoistic readings, and, for a challenging critique of Strauss's position, J. M. Finnis, "Aristotle, Aquinas, and Moral Absolutes," *Catholica: International Quarterly Selection* 12 (Winter 1990): 7–15.

Thrasymachus' definition of it as the advantage of the stronger (338d–340c).[98] Yet the Platonic Socrates clearly holds that the just man whose soul is properly ordered is one who will not engage in acts of injustice; and when he makes this claim in book 4, he cites some of the same examples (filching a deposit, thefts) that he used in book 1 to demonstrate that there are certain circumstances that require exception to positive laws or moral rules. His philosopher-guardian represents a ruler who (in accordance with Thrasymachus' postulate) acts infallibly in accordance with the requirements of his art of ruling—though in his subjects' interests rather than his own.

My suggestion that the Stoics in identifying natural law with the sage's right reason seek to make explicit Plato's own reasoning in the *Republic* presupposes that in their view too there are no moral rules that do not admit of exception and hence cannot represent invariable or immutable principles of natural justice. And, in fact, the Stoics criticized Plato on precisely this point. In the book he wrote against Plato's teaching on natural justice, Chrysippus denounced him for holding (in the classification of goods that opens *Republic* 2, 357c)[99] that health is good, arguing that justice and all the other virtues are annulled by this position (Plut. *De Stoic. repugn.* 1040d = *SVF* 3.157; cf. Cherniss ad loc.). The point of his objection is that virtue alone is good; hence no moral rule to the effect "pursue health as a good" can stand without exception.

It is easy to see why the early Stoics take this view: they hold that providence has ordained the natural course of events down to the smallest detail, such that even events apparently contrary to our individual nature—as, in this case, illness—in fact accord with nature. As Chrysippus says in the first book of his *On Nature,*

οὕτω δὲ τῆς τῶν ὅλων οἰκονομίας προαγούσης, ἀναγκαῖον κατὰ ταύτην, ὡς ἄν ποτ' ἔχωμεν, ἔχειν ἡμᾶς, εἴτε παρὰ φύσιν τὴν ἰδίαν νοσοῦντες εἴτε πεπηρωμένοι εἴτε γραμματικοὶ γεγονότες ἢ μουσικοί.

Since the organization of the universe as a whole proceeds in this way, it is necessarily in conformity with this organization that we are in whatever state we may be, whether contrary to our individual nature we are ill or

---

[98]It seems likely, in fact, that Socrates was accustomed to using this strategy as a regular feature of his practice as a moral educator, for in *Memorabilia* 4—a text that provides a paradigm case of the stages of Socratic moral teaching—Socrates deflates Euthydemus' boast to be as just as any man by showing him that he is unable to identify certain actions as either invariably just or unjust. See Donald Morrison's discussion in Chapter 7 of this volume.

[99]Cf. *Leg.* 631c, 661a–d; *Lysis* 218e–219a; *Grg.* 452a–b, 504c.

are maimed or have become grammarians or musicians. (Plut. *De Stoic. re-pugn.* 1050a = *SVF* 2.937)

The occasional divergence between the rational determinism of nature and man's individual nature to which Chrysippus here refers ensures that there are no "natural laws" that by themselves guide us to virtue. While health, to continue our example, belongs to the class of naturally preferred things (D. L. 7.105–7) and hence is generally pursued as "according to nature," it sometimes accords with nature's provident design for us to be ill (cf. Chrysippus *ap.* Epictetus *Diss.* 2.6.9 = *SVF* 3.191); in such "special circumstances" illness is what is best for us, even though, in most cases, it is contrary to our individual natures.[100] The unorthodox Stoic Ariston, who held in opposition to Chrysippus that there is no class of preferred indifferents, provides an even clearer example (*ap.* Sext. Emp. *Math.* 11.64–67 = *SVF* 1.361): "If healthy men had to serve a tyrant and be destroyed for this reason, while the sick had to be released from service and, therewith also, from destruction, the sage would rather choose sickness in this circumstance than health."[101] Thus, contrary to what Plato implies, health is not simply good; there is no moral rule of general validity "Act so as to be healthy," because it requires the sage's right reason to determine, in any given case, whether health or illness accords with nature.

The doctrine of "special circumstances" provides the context in which to consider the place of cannibalism in Zeno's *Republic.* Zeno's critics took this practice—as well as incest, not specifically attested for the *Republic* but probably treated there[102]—to be recommendations to follow in ordinary practice. Yet Diogenes Laertius 7.121 (a passage that also quotes the *Republic*) states: "The sage will even taste of human flesh under stress of circumstances [κατὰ περίστασιν]." I suggest that Zeno considered incest and cannibalism as test cases of moral prohibitions that might be thought to apply without exception. His argument in reply would be that there may indeed be certain "special circumstances"—namely, when there is a divergence between the common nature and the individual nature—in which these practices would accord with nature.[103] Thus he does not advocate incest or cannibalism but

---

[100]For Chrysippus' account of the sense in which human illness comes about through nature, see Gell. *NA* 7.1.1–13 = *SVF* 2.1169–70.

[101]This example is borrowed from Xenophon *Memorabilia* 4.2.32.

[102]This conjecture is based on the apparent prominence of the test case of incest in the defense of Zeno's views by Chrysippus in his *On Republic* (D. L. 7.188; see above, note 53).

[103]For the doctrine of special circumstances (περιστατικά: D. L. 7.109), see G. Nebel, "Der Begriff des *kathēkon* in der alten Stoa," *Philologus* 70 (1935): 439–60 at pp. 457–58, with the qualifications noted by N. P. White, "Two Notes on Stoic Terminology," *AJP* 99

merely insists that they do not constitute immutable moral prohibitions, hence exceptions to the principle that the sage's right reason is circumstance-dependent. If this interpretation is correct, and the doctrine of *kathēkonta kata peristasin* represents Zeno's way of integrating his Cynic training into his theory of natural law,[104] then we have clear evidence that the problem of how to construct a moral theory that takes full account of the absence of any invariable or exceptionless moral rules dates to the founding work of the Stoa.[105]

If we now turn to consider how the early Stoics' theory of natural law constitutes an answer to Glaucon's challenge, we can easily see that it meets all of the requirements the Platonic Socrates himself accepted as standing in need of answer. Since the Stoics hold that virtue alone is

---

(1978): 111–15. This class of *kathēkonta* clearly goes back to the earliest stages of Stoicism, as the citation from Zeno's *Republic* at Diogenes Laertius 7.121 shows, and therefore does not (as Nebel suggests) originate in Ariston's controversy with Chrysippus over the usefulness of *praecepta*. Origen, *Contra Celsum* 4.45 = *SVF* 3.743 states that the Stoics considered incest a *kathēkon kata peristasin*, offering as a hypothesis the case in which the human race has entirely perished except for a man and his daughter, whose duty it is to preserve the race. Debate over the status of *kathēkonta kata peristasin* continued in the controversy, discussed above, over Zeno's apparent endorsement of Cynic tenets in his *Republic*. Posidonius devoted a section of his *On Appropriate Action* to *Peri tou kata peristasin kathēkontos*, which Cicero was keen to see in composing his *De officiis* (see *Att.* 16.11; cf. 4.8a.2). While none of our evidence explicitly concerned with *kathēkonta kata peristasin* specifies what conditions must obtain to give rise to "special circumstances," I propose that we link this class of *kathēkonta* with the divergences between the common nature and human nature that Chrysippus (*ap.* Epictetus *Diss.* 2.6.9 = *SVF* 3.191) cites as grounds for overriding the preferred indifferent of health. This interpretation has the advantage of providing clear criteria for the appropriateness of this class.

[104]For Cynic precedent, see the report of Diogenes' position on cannibalism in Diogenes Laertius 6.72–73. It has been objected to me that the doctrine of *kathēkonta kata peristasin* may have been formulated by later Stoics in an effort to explain away features of Zeno's *Republic* that they found embarrassing. Certainly not all of our evidence restricts incest to "special circumstances": so, for example, Sextus has preserved evidence that Zeno defended the relationship between Jocasta and Oedipus (*Pyr.* 3.205, 246; *Math.* 11.191 = *SVF* 1.256), perhaps following the Cynic mock tragedy *Oedipus*, which is reported to have sanctioned incest; and Sextus also preserves evidence that Chrysippus treated incest as indifferent (*Pyr.* 1.160; 3.205, 246–48). Yet to say that incest is indifferent is entirely compatible with restricting its appropriateness to special circumstances, while the case of Oedipus could well be adduced as a paradigm of a divergence between human and cosmic nature. The question of the sense in which Zeno meant to endorse the Cynic tenets he discusses became so disputed in school polemic that it is no surprise that later writers—especially skeptics like Sextus—suppress mention of the conditions restricting its appropriateness.

[105]It has been suggested to me that Zeno's injunction against building temples of the gods (e.g., Plut. *De Stoic. repugn.* 1034b; other evidence in *SVF* 1.164–65) represents an exceptionless moral rule. Yet the Stoics' participation in religious ritual cited by Plutarch suggests that they may have considered temples appropriate under certain circumstances: once again, we should not assume that provisions suitable for a polity of sages are invariably appropriate in other cases.

good, all other objects of choice being indifferent, they have no difficulty in satisfying the first demand, to show that justice is naturally good independently of its wages and consequences. They answer the second demand, to show that man is so constituted as to require justice to attain his natural perfection, by their normative account of man's development as a rational animal (set out most fully in Cicero *De finibus* 3.16–21).[106] This account explains how he gradually learns to perform *kathēkonta*—including, of course, acts of justice—so perfecting his capacity to act in accordance with nature, until his disposition finally is firmly fixed, his irrational impulses are transformed into rational ones, and his sole motivation is to act in accordance with the provident order of nature. On this theory one can become a sage only through repeated, habitual acts of justice; and once one attains the knowledge of good and evil necessary to transform *kathēkonta* into *katorthōmata*, acts of justice will be a regular result of the sage's integral virtue. Finally, as for the third demand, to show that other-regarding virtues have a natural root in man's constitution such that he can achieve happiness only by practicing them, the Stoic doctrine of οἰκείωσις provides a much clearer (not to say truer) basis than anything in Plato of why other-regarding virtue is an essential component of happiness and of how social duties are rooted in man's nature (cf. Cic. *Off.* 1.22).[107] Thus there is every reason to suppose that the Stoic theory, like Plato's, is intended to answer the conventionalist challenge, and that in working out their position the Stoics sought to improve on Plato's answers.

4. The Institutional Arrangements of the Best Regime: Zeno versus Plato

We are now in a position to consider how the social and institutional arrangements of Zeno's polity attempt to improve upon those of Plato's best regime. Zeno's account of the way of life that accords with the *koinos nomos* appears to fulfill the fundamental Platonic principle that the things of friends be held common to the greatest extent possible (see esp. *Leg.* 739c–e). In sketching the institutional arrangements best suited to discharge this requirement in his polity of sages, Zeno undertakes to resolve difficulties in the Platonic account by rendering it more precise and consistent. I want to consider three examples to illustrate

---

[106]On Stoic doctrines of moral evolution, see Inwood (above, note 9), pp. 182–215; M. Frede, "The Stoic Doctrine of the Affections of the Soul," in *The Norms of Nature*, ed. M. Schofield and G. Striker (Cambridge, 1986), pp. 93–110.

[107]The origins of the doctrine of social *oikeiōsis* are notoriously obscure, but I have adduced evidence in support of tracing it back to Zeno himself in "Hermarchus and the Epicurean Genealogy of Morals," *TAPA* 118 (1988): 87–106 at pp. 104–6.

this point. My first suggestion is that in restricting citizenship to sages, thereby abolishing class differences, Zeno seeks to disarm the conflict of interest Plato's philosopher-kings face in being compelled (contrary to the "one man, one job" principle, 370b) to undertake two jobs—that of ruler as well as philosopher.

The argument of Plato's *Republic* culminates—in its "third wave"— when Glaucon once again demands to know whether it is possible for the just city to come into being. Socrates replies: the smallest change capable of bringing about its realization would be the conjunction of political power and philosophy—unless philosophers rule as kings or kings philosophize, there will be no rest from evils for cities nor for the human race (473c–e). This would require a radical change on the part of both cities and philosophers: the cities would have to become willing to accept the philosophers' rule, and the philosophers would have to become willing to rule. The only way for Socrates to effect the latter is to compel the philosophers, unwilling and contrary to their own interest, to descend once again into the cave and submit to the necessity of ruling over the city (499b–c, 500d, 519c–520e, 521b, 539e–540b). When Glaucon objects that he does them an injustice by depriving them of the better life that is available to them, Socrates has recourse to the notion of justice as paying one's debts that he had rejected in book 1: he argues that it is just for the philosophers to repay their debt to the city for nourishing their education by consenting to return to the cave (519d–520d; cf. 419a–421c; *Leg.* 903c–d). But, whether just or not, the very fact that the philosophers must be *compelled* to rule points up the fundamental difficulty (which Aristotle criticizes in *Politics* 1264b15–23) in Socrates' attempt to secure the city's happiness at the expense of its best class: it is entirely against the philosophers' interest to rule, since the sole source of the philosophers' happiness consists in the activity of philosophizing.[108] Even if a city could be persuaded to accept their rule, they would resist the return to the cave, which would destroy their happiness. Indeed, it would appear that the chief reason the just city cannot be realized in deed, that it serves as a "pattern laid up in heaven" for the person who wishes to found the just city within his own soul, is that the only person who is just, wise, and happy—the philosopher—has no interest in ruling voluntarily.[109]

---

[108]Gazing upon the sun as they do, they believe that they dwell on the Isles of the Blessed (519c), and would rather undergo anything whatever than return to their former condition among the prisoners in the cave (516c–d; cf. 514b–515c); once they have seen the idea of the good they are unwilling to return to the human things, as their souls always yearn to spend their time above, in the sunlight (517b–d; cf. 500b–d, 592a–b)— one would pity the soul returned to the darkness of the cave from the light of the sun (518b).

[109]Cf. above, note 70.

Now Zeno's central objection to the Platonic paradox of the rule of the philosopher-kings cannot very well be its impossibility, given that his own polity has the same feature. But he may well have aimed to resolve the problem to which Aristotle draws attention in his criticism in *Politics* 2: that in attempting to make the city as a whole happy Socrates destroys the happiness of the guardian class; that the city as a whole cannot be happy unless all or at least some of its parts are happy; and that if the guardians are not happy, no one else will be, certainly not the artisans or multitude (1264b15–23; cf. 1329a22–24). In other words, in sacrificing the happiness of his philosophers to the necessity of ruling, Plato founds a regime none of whose citizens are happy.

If we consider why Zeno restricted membership in his polity to sages, we can now see that he may have done so in an attempt to resolve this Platonic paradox.[110] The problem of motivating the wise to rule thereby does not even arise,[111] because Zeno's polity has no distinctions of social class and a citizen body that has no need of rulers or of the compulsion of positive law to enforce correct conduct. Zeno could well have held that such a position is required by the Platonic "one man, one job" principle: if the necessity of ruling and guarding the city against internal and external enemies conflicts with this central Platonic tenet, then one way of resolving the dilemma is to remove the necessity of ruling by restricting citizenship to those who live in accordance with the *koinos nomos* and have no need of being ruled. This solution also has the advantage of making possible a community of friends that may genuinely hold its possessions in common without resorting to the distinctions of class that Plato admits and that leads him to admit private property outside of the guardian class. Zeno's restriction of citizenship in his best regime to sages thus may represent an anti-Platonic rejoinder intended to resolve a dilemma at the heart of Plato's teaching on natural justice.

Moreover, if the question of ruling were to arise (e.g., for the sage who lives in an inferior regime), the Stoics face none of Plato's difficulties in explaining why the sage would take part in politics. Chrysippus in particular explicitly rejects the view that philosophers should

---

[110]The Stoics do of course agree with Plato that only the wise are fit to rule, because "a ruler must have knowledge of what is good and evil, and no inferior man has this" (D. L. 7.121–22). In restricting the citizen body of his best regime to sages, Zeno also renders moot the difficulties (emphasized by Aristotle in *Politics* 2) that arise from the fact that only Plato's guardian class practices communism and community of women: Zeno's citizens are able to live as friends holding everything in common (D. L. 7.124; cf. 33) without excluding some citizens in the regime from sharing in this way of life.

[111]Zeno in fact objects to the very notion of the compulsion of philosophers; he says: "Someone could sooner immerse a bladder filled with air than compel any morally good man against his will to do anything he does not want" (*ap.* Philo *Quod omnis probus liber sit* 97 = *SVF* 1.218); hence the Stoic objection to Plato's dictum that the philosophers, being absorbed in the pursuit of truth, would rule only under compulsion (Cic. *Off.* 1.28).

particularly follow the scholarly life (Plut. *De Stoic. repugn.* 1033c–d = *SVF* 3.702), suggesting that such a life, properly understood, would be dedicated to hedonism.[112] It is easy to see why Chrysippus took this position. Since virtue consists partly in rational consistency with one's nature, and since one's nature is social as well as rational, even the sage must discharge the social *kathēkonta* if he is to remain consistent with himself and his surroundings (*SVF* 3.694–700; cf. Arius 109.14–20). The external appearance of his actions, after all, does not differ from that of the conventionally virtuous man: what differs is the rational disposition with which he performs all his actions.[113] Thus Zeno faces none of Plato's problems in explaining why his sages would engage in such political activity as might be necessary.[114]

This brings us to a second way in which Zeno may seek to improve upon the way of life of Plato's best regime. Zeno appears to hold that Plato radically misconstrues the conditions necessary for the realization of natural justice. This regime, after all, originates in an act of injustice: when the city of pigs is transformed by the introduction of unnecessary desires into the feverish city, one of its first acts is the conquest of its neighbors' land in order to provide for excess production (373d–e). Moreover, it does not distinguish friends from enemies strictly on the basis of virtue, but on the purely arbitrary ground of birth and citizenship. Socrates holds that there is a natural difference in the treatment due to barbarians as distinguished from fellow Greeks: the former are "enemies by nature," while the latter are "by nature friends"; accordingly, Socrates objects to the enslavement of the latter but not of the former (469b–471b).[115]

---

[112]Cherniss *ad* 1033d (p. 417 n. 3) refers this passage to the Epicureans and Peripatetics, but there seems to be no reason to exclude Plato as a target here.

[113]Chrysippus' interest in this subject is well attested by his *On Lives* (*testimonia* collected by von Arnim, *SVF* 3.194), in which he considered inter alia the three preferred ways of making a living—association with kings, participation in politics, σοφιστεία (see esp. Plut. *De Stoic. repugn.* 1043b–c = *SVF* 3.691, 1043e and 1047f = *SVF* 3.693; Arius 109.10–110.8; and the criticism at D. L. 7.189). Diogenes Laertius 7.121 cites Chrysippus *On Lives* 1 for the view that the sage will take part in politics if nothing hinders him; for Stoic reflection on the political life see Arius 94.8–17, 109.10–20, 143.24–144.21; Cic. *Fin.* 3.68; and for abstention from political life, Arius 111.3–9 and Sen. *De otio* 3.2. Chrysippus' statement in his *On Rhetoric* that the sage will speak in public and participate in ruling *just as if* he considered wealth to be a good (Plut. *De Stoic. repugn.* 1034b = *SVF* 3.698) provides some indication of how he will conduct himself in practical politics.

[114]For an appraisal of the Stoic position on political participation, see Vander Waerdt (above, note 19), pp. 202–3.

[115]Chrysippus (*ap.* Philod. *De Stoic.*, cols. 15.31–16.4) quotes Diogenes the Cynic on the uselessness of weapons (cf. D. L. 6.70–71, 85): if Chrysippus here as elsewhere in his *On Republic* is defending a Cynic tenet also advanced by Zeno in his *Republic* (so, for example, Baldry [above, note 19], p. 10 and n. 12), then we may suppose that Zeno undertook in this work to abolish external warfare altogether—thus eliminating one of the central preoccupations of Plato's philosopher-guardians.

For Zeno, on the other hand, natural justice requires the eradication of all merely conventional boundaries (Plut. *De virt. Alex.* 329a–b; cf. Cic. *Rep.* 3.33). To sanction different treatment merely on the basis of ethnic origin would seem flagrantly to violate natural law. Here again Zeno's view represents an attempt to improve upon the Platonic Socrates' by construing the requirements of his teaching on justice strictly. More particularly, Zeno seeks to avoid an apparent contradiction in it: while the citizens of Plato's best regime are required to treat each according to his due, such that one's position within the regime is determined by the quality of one's soul (those with golden souls become philosopher-guardians, and so forth), foreigners are excluded from any share in this regime by mere accident of birth, irrespective of their natural character and attainments. Thus, solely for conventional reasons, they cannot share in the way of life that Plato holds to accord with nature.[116] Zeno's best regime, to the contrary, is a community whose citizenship is determined solely by rationality; only the virtuous may belong to it, and the sole basis for ties of kinship, friendship, and so forth is virtue (D. L. 7.122–24). In enjoining that we not be divided by the differing principles of justice of conventional communities, Zeno appears once again to aim to disarm a difficulty that appears to threaten the internal consistency of the Platonic account of natural justice.

Our final example of how Zeno seeks to improve upon Plato's teaching by making the implications of his own reasoning more precise is the community of women, which both Plato (451c–456b) and Zeno (D. L. 7.33, 131) advocate. Following Antisthenes, Zeno takes the position that men and women have the same capacity to attain virtue.[117] Accordingly, he regards gender-based social distinctions as merely conventional, not founded in nature—hence his view that men and women are to wear the same clothing (D. L. 7.33), following the precedent set by Crates' wife Hipparchia (D. L. 6.93, 97; cf. Epictetus *Diss.* 3.22, 76).[118] This is a feature of Plato's community of women (*Rep.* 452a–b, 457a–b), but Zeno differs fundamentally from him on its motivation.

[116]The guardians' θυμός (375a–376c) presumably is responsible for the different attitude they take toward fellow citizens and foreigners; for the political problem posed by *thymos*, cf. Vander Waerdt (above, note 70).

[117]This is an inference from Zeno's injunction concerning dress (D. L. 7.33), but the doctrine is securely attested for the early scholarchs: see Chrysippus *ap.* Philod. *De pietate*, col. 5.8–11, Cleanthes *On the Thesis That Virtue Is the Same in Both a Man and a Woman* (D. L. 7.175), and Lactantius' report in *Divinae institutiones* 3.25 that the Stoics held that women should philosophize, apparently because their capacity for virtue is identical. For equality in sexual relations, see Zeno *ap.* Sext. Emp. *Pyr.* 3.245 = *Math.* 11.190.

[118]Cf. Rist (above, note 9), pp. 65–67.

In Plato's regime, women are held to be equal to men in all important matters except strength and sex (451d, 456a), and the female guardians are to share in the same educational program. But Socrates has to *legislate* this equality (cf. 452c, 453d, 456b–c, 457a–c), which he thinks most will regard as ridiculous. Thus the Platonic Socrates has to resort to the compulsion of positive law to establish the natural equality of the sexes. From Zeno's point of view, however, Socrates' guardians are mere progressors toward virtue—they are apparently unable, without the compulsion of legislation, to maintain these egalitarian arrangements. For Zeno's best regime, on the other hand, there is no need of law to enforce the natural equality of women: since all his citizens are wise, it will arise naturally.[119] Thus the extraordinary conventions Socrates has to institute in order to bring about the best regime in which natural justice may come to light have no place in Zeno's polity of the wise. Since Zeno's citizens live according to natural law, they have no need to resort to the compulsion of conventional legislation to live happily.

If we now compare, in light of these examples, the most succinct Platonic account of the practices necessary for the realization of the best regime, that of the Athenian Stranger in *Laws* 5 (739c–e), with the institutional arrangements of Zeno's polity of sages, we can see that this polity exemplifies each element in the Stranger's program. That program rests upon the principle that the best regime should embody to the greatest possible extent the maxim that "the things of friends are common," and the Stranger enumerates as provisions to realize this end (1) the community of women and children, (2) the community of property, and (3) every device to exclude the "private." We have seen that Zeno's polity of sages exemplifies all these proposals: for (1) see Diogenes Laertius 7.33, 133; for (2) Diogenes Laertius 7.33 (abolition of coinage for internal exchange or travel), 7.124 with Athenaeus 561c (the friendship of sages provides a community of things in life), and Diogenes Laertius 7.125 (knowledge alone legitimates property rights); and for (3) Diogenes Laertius 7.33 (men and women should wear the same clothing). These striking programmatic similarities provide strong reason for thinking that Zeno developed his account of the *koinos nomos* in an attempt to show how one could satisfy Plato's conditions for the realization of the best regime—if one jettisoned the inconsistent Platonic program of positive legislation administered by

---

[119]The same may be said for Socrates' attempt to foster unity through conventions—such as calling all children "mine" and so forth—intended to foster a community of pleasure and pain (*Rep.* 462b; cf. *Leg.* 739c–e). Zeno holds that this kind of civic concord arises naturally, through the work of Eros, which provides friendship, concord, and freedom (Ath. 561c = *SVF* 1.263; cf. D. L. 7.130).

philosophically informed statesmen, and replaced it with a polity of sages whose morally infallible right reason renders unnecessary all recourse to codes of law, judicial institutions, and instruments of social compulsion. Thus there is every reason to suppose that Zeno, in elaborating the theory of natural law in his *Republic,* sought to improve the Platonic account of natural justice by making it more precise and consistent.

It has long been recognized that the theory of natural law originated in an attempt to resolve the Socratic problem of how to elaborate a teaching on natural justice that would adequately answer the problem posed by conventionalism.[120] What has not been recognized is the extent to which the early Stoics modeled their theory, and their account of the relation between politics and philosophy, on Plato's. They not only appropriated his problems but sought to improve upon the answers he had given to them. If the interpretation of Zeno's *Republic* we have offered in this chapter is correct, some of the most distinctive features of the early Stoic position—its identification of natural law with the sage's right reason, its restriction of citizenship in the *megalopolis* to sages, and its vision of a polity without laws, social classes, or judicial institutions—represent attempts to refine the Platonic teaching on natural justice by making it more precise and consistent.[121]

[120]So, among others, Strauss (above, note 21), pp. 138–42 and, less clearly, Striker 1986 (above, note 1).

[121]In preparing this essay for publication, I have benefited from the many helpful comments and suggestions I received from audiences at the conference "The Socratic Movement" at Duke University in April 1990; at the conference "Ancient Greek Philosophy" at the University of Sydney in July 1990; at the University of Newcastle, New South Wales, and at the University of Aukland in September 1990; at Cornell University in March 1991; at the University of Glasgow in June 1992; and at the conference "Die praktische Philosophie der Stoiker" at the Universität Bern in October 1992. I am especially grateful to my commentator on the last occasion, Phillip Mitsis, for his challenging and thoughtful response to my account of the origins of natural law theory, as well as to Diskin Clay, Michael Frede, and Gerhard Seel for their helpful criticism.

[12]

Plato the Skeptic

Julia Annas

From about 273 B.C., when Arcesilaus of Pitane took over its head-ship, until it petered out in the first century B.C., Plato's school, the Academy, practiced and taught a form of skepticism. This is surpris-ing; even more so is the fact that the Academy regarded skeptical phi-losophizing as philosophizing in the spirit of Plato, doing what Plato did. Modern scholars tend to regard this as so surprising as to be an aberration, but it was not so regarded in antiquity. Middle Platonists like Plutarch respected and defended the skeptical New Academy.[1] The Neoplatonist commentators, though they disagreed with the thesis that Plato was a skeptic, thought of it as a familiar thesis requiring refutation.[2] Even a hostile figure like Numenius, who regards the New Academy as a ghastly mistake, pays it the compliment of exten-sive attention.[3]

It is worth seriously asking just what the members of the New Acad-emy were doing when they represented their own skeptical practice as being in the Platonic tradition. The evidence is extensive enough, and ancient skepticism rich and interesting enough, for it to be worth our

[1]See J. Glucker, *Antiochus and the Late Academy, Hypomnemata* 56 (Göttingen 1976), chap. 6; P. Donini, "Lo scetticiso accademico, Aristotele e l'unità della tradizione platon-ica secondo Plutarco," in *Storiografia e dossografia nella filosofia antica,* ed. G. Cambiano (Turin, 1986), pp. 203–26.

[2]This will be discussed below.

[3]Numen. *On the Revolt of the Academy from Plato,* frs. 24–28 des Places.

while to reconstruct the way that the New Academy read Plato, even if it is in the end a way that we do not share.[4]

We are faced with two distinct bodies of evidence. One has to do with Arcesilaus and his concern with the figure of Socrates and Socratic practice. The other deals with Plato as a whole, without distinguishing between Socrates and Plato, and focuses on arguments in and features of the middle and late dialogues. This material ascribes a milder form of skepticism to Plato and probably derives from Philo's later Academy. I shall deal with these two bodies of evidence separately.

1. Socrates and Skepticism

Arcesilaus, as has been recently stressed, was the inventor of the skeptical Socrates; hitherto Socrates had been an important figure in Hellenistic philosophy, but not in the role of a skeptic. Socrates served as inspiration to the Cynics with their marketplace moralizing, and to the more rigorous and argumentative Stoics.[5] Arcesilaus represented his own skeptical philosophizing as a revival of Socratic practice; the interesting question is what he was relying on in this attempt to re-claim Socrates as an uncommitted enquirer rather than as a dog-matic moralist.

It was not Socrates' profession of ignorance.[6] On this point Arcesi-laus seems, rather surprisingly, to have got Socrates wrong. Arcesilaus thought that Socrates claimed to know that he knew nothing (Cic. *Varro* 45; cf. 16; *Luc.* 74). But Socrates never says this; he merely says that he knows nothing. The strongest expression he uses is that he is aware of not having knowledge (σύνοιδα ἐμαυτῷ, Ap. 21b4–5). But this is not a claim to knowledge on this score. In any case, Arcesilaus criticized Socrates on this point, taking an avowal of knowledge that one does not know to be negative dogmatism, a flaw in an otherwise skeptical Soc-rates. So this cannot be Arcesilaus' ground.

Some brief but very informative passages make it clear what the point of connection was that Arcesilaus made. They all come from

---

[4]I have been greatly helped by recent work by M. Frede ("The Sceptic's Two Kinds of Assent and the Question of the Possibility of Knowledge," in *Philosophy in History,* ed. R. Rorty et al. [Cambridge, 1984], pp. 225–78), M. Burnyeat ("Carneades Was No Proba-bilist" [forthcoming]), and P. Woodruff ("The Skeptical Side of Plato's Method," *Revue internationale de philosophie* 156–57 [1986]: 22–37).

[5]The varied influence of Socrates is lucidly discussed by A. A. Long in "Socrates in Hellenistic Philosophy," *CQ* n.s. 38 (1988): 150–71.

[6]Despite Cicero *Varro* 44, where it is said that Arcesilaus started his attacks not out of competitiveness but because of the same obscurity in things that led Socrates to his con-fession of ignorance. For Democritus, Anaxagoras, Empedocles, and "nearly all the an-cients" are added; no special reference to Socrates can be in mind.

Cicero, who had studied in the Academy and speaks knowledgeably about its practices.[7] At *De oratore* 3.67 we find the following:

> First [in contrast to his predecessors in the Academy, who had made no radical changes of teaching method] Arcesilaus, Polemon's pupil, seized on the following in particular out of various writings of Plato and from the Socratic conversations: that nothing sure can be apprehended by either the senses or the mind. He is said to have employed an outstandingly attractive style of speaking in rejecting any judgments of the mind or senses, and to have been the first to set up the practice—though this was highly Socratic—of not showing what he thought but of arguing against what anyone else said that they thought.

And at *De finibus* 2.2 Cicero says that we can see from Plato how Socrates made fun of the sophists:

> He [Socrates] had the practice of drawing out his interlocutors' beliefs by conversation and questioning, so as to say what he thought in response to their replies. This custom was abandoned by his successors, but Arcesilaus revived it and instituted the following practice: those who wished to hear him should not ask him questions but should themselves tell him what they thought: when they had told him, he would argue against it.[8]

Here we find two points: that Arcesilaus took the results of Socratic practice to be negative, and that he revived what he took to be the Socratic practice of ad hominem arguing. Since Arcesilaus criticized Socrates for negative dogmatism, his conclusion that neither the senses nor the mind can grasp anything sure cannot have been itself a piece of dogma but must represent, in the usual skeptical fashion, his own personal state of conviction on the matter. More interesting is the information about method. Arcesilaus' own practice, as we find definitively argued by P. Coussin and others,[9] was to argue only from his oppo-

---

[7]I shall concentrate on Cicero's evidence. There are some fragments from other sources connecting Arcesilaus with Socrates, but they are all inconclusive. They are coupled by Plutarch as having written nothing, and Plutarch tells us that Socrates was one of the respectable ancestors for his philosophizing sought by Arcesilaus, the others being Parmenides and Heraclitus (see fr. 1d Mette). Lactantius (fr. 14b Mette) says that Arcesilaus "auctore Socrate suscepit hanc sententiam, ut adfirmaret sciri nihil posse"; this seems to be derivative from Cicero *De oratore* 3.67 (immediately below).

[8]Cf. *Fin.* 5.10; *De or.* 3.80; *Nat. d.* 1.11.

[9]Couissin's classic article. "Le stoïcisme de la nouvelle Académie," *Revue d'histoire de la philosophie* 3 (1929) 241–76, is reprinted in English in *The Skeptical Tradition*, ed. M. F. Burnyeat (Berkeley, 1983), pp. 31–63. For some modifications to the Couissin view, see A. M. Ioppolo, *Opinione e scienza: Il dibattito tra Stoici e Accademici nel III e nel II secolo a.C.* (Naples, 1986), with my discussion, "The Heirs of Socrates," *Phronesis* 33 (1988): 100–112.

nent's premises. His way of arguing, that is, was entirely ad hominem. What these passages tell us is that this is what he took Socrates to have done as well. I shall follow through seriously this idea: How might Arcesilaus have tried to show that Socrates' practice was indeed totally ad hominem like his own, and how might he have dealt with certain obvious difficulties?

A few words of caution. In good skeptical spirit I shall be arguing here from as few premises as possible, and so in two respects shall be minimizing my position on Arcesilaus. First, we know more about Arcesilaus' skeptical strategies than just what the two passages above tell us. We know, for example, that he was prominent for leading himself and others to ἐποχή, suspension of judgment, on various theses.[10] But in what follows I shall make no use of this; we have no evidence that Arcesilaus claimed that Socrates suspended judgment, and indeed it is hard to see how anyone might have thought this. Similarly with the rest of our evidence; none of it is directly relevant to the point I shall work from, namely, Arcesilaus' known commitment to ad hominem argument, arguing only from what the interlocutor provides without committing oneself to the truth of the premises, or indeed the validity of the argument.

Second, there is more to Arcesilaus' skepticism than his appeal to Socrates, and the nature of his position is at many points controversial. He was influenced in a Socratic direction by his predecessors in the Academy.[11] He was obviously influenced by desire to oppose the Stoics.[12] And he had *some* relation to Pyrrho, the prototypical skeptic. It has been argued by David Sedley that Arcesilaus had a considerable debt to Pyrrho, which he concealed;[13] more recently Fernanda Decleva Caizzi has argued that he would be aware of Pyrrho only as a figurehead, and a rather eccentric one at that, and aware of skeptical arguments only through Timon, after his own skeptical debut.[14] It is an important question how we are to link and to estimate all these influences, but I shall pass it by here, since nothing that I say hinges on having any particular answer to it. Arcesilaus had many interests; but he was first and foremost the head of the Academy, who saw himself as in

---

[10]See Cic. *Varro* 45ff.; *Luc.* 59; Sext. Emp. *Pyr.* 1.232–34; Numen. frs. 25.75–82, 26.104–11 des Places. Cf. P. Couissin, "L'origine et l'évolution de l'epochē," *REG* 42 (1929): 373–97.

[11]See A. A. Long, "Diogenes Laertius' *Life of Arcesilaus*," in *Diogene Laerzio: Storico del pensiero antico*, a special volume of *Elenchos* 7 (1986): 429–49.

[12]As is stressed most forcefully in Couissin's articles cited above.

[13]"The Motivation of Greek Scepticism," in *The Skeptical Tradition*, ed. M. F. Burnyeat (Berkeley, 1983), pp. 9–29.

[14]"Pirroniani ed Accademici nel III secolo a.C.," in *Aspects de la philosophie hellénistique*, Fondation Hardt, Entretiens sur l'antiquité classique 32 (1986), pp. 147–83.

some way a follower of Plato.[15] We would expect him to have some attitude to Plato, whose books we know he read,[16] and to Socrates. Clarification of his attitude to Socrates and to ad hominem arguing is bound to tell us something important about how he and the rest of the skeptical Academy saw themselves as inheritors of Plato's tradition, whatever other influences they also felt.

Finally, I shall write, for the sake of clarity, as though Arcesilaus were a skeptic searching for a pedigree—as though, that is, he already had a skeptical practice and then claimed that this could be found in Socrates. But this is not to claim that this is the only possible *genetic* account. Nothing I say is meant to preclude the thesis that it was reading the Socratic dialogues that made a skeptic out of Arcesilaus in the first place and gave him the ideas that he then used to interpret Socrates as a skeptic.[17]

What would Arcesilaus have to do to make his interpretation of Socrates plausible? He would have to show first that Socrates does argue ad hominem in the way a skeptic would. He would also have to cope with certain obvious features of Plato's Socrates that stand in the way of such an interpretation; for in Plato's Socratic dialogues Socrates represents himself always as searching for the truth, indeed, for knowledge of the truth. He often seems to argue from beliefs that he shares with the interlocutor, rather than being noncommittal as to the truth of those beliefs. And, most of all, Socrates has firm and passionately held beliefs of a moral kind—that virtue is a kind of skill, that you have to have it to be happy, and so on. How then can he be a skeptic?

We can best see how Arcesilaus could have coped with these points if we renew our focus on the star evidence, namely, the ascription by Arcesilaus to Socrates of ad hominem arguing. Why would a skeptic make ad hominem arguing prominent anyway? Ancient skeptics (of all kinds) do not see their task as negative—as that of challenging everybody's claims to know anything, or the claims of one area of enquiry vis-à-vis those of another. The ancient skeptic is σκεπτικός, enquiring—he is primarily a seeker after truth. Far from doubting whether there is any knowledge, the ancient skeptic is always eager to find some. Cicero, defending the cause of the later Academy, of which he saw himself as a member, says:

> We desire to discover the truth without any dispute and attempt this with the greatest attention and effort. For even though all our cognition is

---

[15]This is stressed by Ioppolo (above, note 9) and by Long (above, note 5).
[16]D. L. 4.32–33; *Index Academicorum*, col. 19.13–16.
[17]As is suggested by Long (above, note 5).

blocked by many obstructions, and even though there is so much obscurity in the things themselves and weakness on the part of our judgments that both the most ancient and the most learned philosophers have rightly distrusted their ability to discover what they desired, still they did not give in, and neither shall we get worn out and abandon our effort to search things out. (*Luc.* 7)[18]

But—and there is a big but—knowledge and even true beliefs are hard to come by. Claims to knowledge or to true belief tend to be challenged by opponents (especially in philosophy). The skeptics are impressed by these challenges and if none is available produce some themselves and carry on meeting responses and modifications with fresh challenges. But they do not do so because of any commitment to the idea that there is no knowledge or true belief (or to the idea that there is, but we can never get any). Rather, the skeptic keeps arguing because the difficulties are genuine. He is (at least in principle) open-minded; he wants to have knowledge or at least true belief; it is just that there do always seem to be problems that have not been successfully met. The skeptic sees his opponent, the dogmatist, as the person who gives in too soon, who makes a claim to knowledge or true belief and then through laziness or stupidity or complacency fails to see the problems involved. Hence for the skeptic the main danger is "rash assent," premature commitment to a claim about the way things are. This was certainly Arcesilaus' view, as we can see from Cicero *Varro* 45, where it is said to be his view that knowledge is so hard to come by that Socrates was wrong even to say that he knew that he did not know; so no one should make any assertion or affirmation or assent to the ways things appear to one. One must always hold back one's rashness from every slip, since it is rash to assent to what is false or unclear, and a disgrace to do either of these things. And so the skeptic goes round doing the dogmatist the service of pointing out the problems that his rash assent overlooked—not in the negative spirit of showing that there is no truth here, or that if there is, we can't get it, but (at least in principle) in the cooperative spirit of searching for some truth that isn't problematic. The skeptic, then, is distinguished from the dogmatist *not* by his goal of searching for truth but by the fact that he is *still* searching, because still aware of the difficulties. The dogmatist is just the one who has given up.[19]

---

[18]Cf. *Fin.* 1.2–3 and *Luc.* 127; the latter is somewhat reminiscent of the passages about knowledge in *Republic* 5–7.

[19]Cf. Sext. Emp. *Pyr.* 1.1; although this is a Pyrrhonist statement, there is no reason why the Academics should not share it, especially since they were following Plato's recommended practice of enquiry and were not committed to gaining peace of mind through skepticism. (Cf. next note.)

Given that ancient skeptics are enquiring after truth and prepared to challenge any claim across the board, it is not surprising that ancient skeptical reasoning will be ad hominem, that is, will use only premises granted by the opponent. We may find this startling, but for the ancient skeptic the main danger is rash assent, and ad hominem reasoning is ideally suited to remove this in two ways. First, you directly attack the opponent's rash assent. You take what he accepts and show him that there are problems *just from this:* having located a problem in his beliefs, you get him to give up those beliefs. And second, you do this without committing *yourself.* If your argument depends on beliefs of yours, that makes it vulnerable to objections that can be brought against those beliefs. The fewer beliefs of yours your argument rests on, the harder it is for the opponent to avoid by rejecting or attacking those beliefs. Hence for the ancient skeptic, purely ad hominem reasoning is the most, not the least, serious kind; it is the most relevant, least vulnerable, and most effective.

We can now see right off that in ascribing to Socrates his own skeptical practice, Arcesilaus was not denying that Socrates was seriously seeking after truth, nor ascribing a disreputable mode of arguing to him. Rather, he was ascribing to Socrates the most serious and wholehearted way, according to an ancient skeptic, of seeking for the truth. We may not agree, of course; we may well think that it is feasible to search for the truth in more positive ways, and that the skeptic is overestimating the difficulties. The point here, however, is that this interpretation makes sense in its own terms; it is the skeptical interpretation of Socrates that we are trying to understand.

It is worth noting here that the Academic skeptics did consistently think of themselves as searching for the truth. The Pyrrhonist skeptics complicated this matter by their claims that enquiring after the truth in the rigorous skeptical manner will in fact lead to peace of mind, and that this will bring about a happy life. This creates the problem that it is hard to take this thought seriously without compromising the search for truth; and though the trick can be turned, it is useful for our purposes that the Academic skeptics at any rate never saw themselves as seeking anything but the truth.[20]

We can also see how Socrates might well be seen as someone aware of the need to combat rash assent, for Socrates' interlocutors are typically not people who are wrong or ignorant. Rather, they are typically complacent or pretentious people who, if they have the right beliefs, have them unreflectively and for the wrong reasons. In *De finibus* 2.1–2, quoted in part above, Cicero prefaces his account of Arcesi-

---

[20]Cf. G. Striker, "Über den Unterschied zwischen den Pyrrhonern und den Akademikern," *Phronesis* 26 (1981): 153–71.

laus reviving Socratic practice with a reminder of how Plato's Socrates makes fun of the sophists. Socrates' deflation of pompous sophists makes it indeed plausible to see him as someone who characteristically attacks those whose rash assent has outrun their grasp of what they are talking about.

It is, however, one thing to see what might make this interpretation plausible to Arcesilaus; it is another to ask, when we step back and examine it on our own account, the question that is bound to occur to us: *Does* Socrates in the Socratic dialogues *in fact* argue ad hominem—solely, that is, from the interlocutor's premises?

Sometimes he uncontroversially does so. There is a striking example in the *Hippias minor.* In this short dialogue Socrates forces the complacent sophist Hippias to the conclusion that the good person is the person who does wrong willingly. Even Hippias sees that this conclusion can't be right; Socrates contents himself with pointing out that the argument has forced them to it, so that they are in a state of "wandering around." On the usual reading of Plato, the *Hippias minor* has always seemed a rather pointless dialogue. Why does Socrates argue for a conclusion that he patently doesn't believe? But clearly Socrates is not arguing *for* anything. He picks on Hippias, a vain and complacent person who is a particularly good example of what was later to be called rash assent, premature pontificating. Hippias is led by clever manipulation of his incautious beliefs into absurdity. It is left to him (or rather the dialogue ends, and it is left to the reader) to work out what has gone wrong, and either to avoid the conclusion by repairing the argument or to avoid coming out with the offending belief in the future.

In the *Hipparchus*[21] Socrates presses a friend on the nature of "loving gain." When the friend gets puzzled, Socrates offers him various exits and points out that it is like making moves in a game of draughts (229e): he can retract premise A or premise B or premise C. It is up to him, in other words; the problems come from the moves that he has made. The friend picks one option, but this leads to a dead end. Again, it is left to the reader to work out what other moves he could have made and whether they might have worked better.

In other dialogues we can find smaller pieces of ad hominem reasoning. One of the most striking is the initial series of arguments against Polemarchus in *Republic* 1. Socrates shows Polemarchus that as he conceives of justice, it is not much use (332c–333a), and worse, that the just man is a kind of thief (333e–334b). The argument does seem

---

[21]The reasons for not regarding this dialogue as genuine are feeble. See P. Friedlaender, *Plato,* trans. H. Meyerhoff (New York, 1964), 2:119–28 and 339–42. Philosophers often object to its historical section, but ancient historians (including the *Cambridge Ancient History*) do not share these doubts.

to show that, says Polemarchus unhappily (334a). When Socrates goes on to show that on Polemarchus' view of justice it will be just to injure those who do no injustice, Polemarchus protests (334d): there must be something wrong with the argument if it shows that, he says, and adjusts his view accordingly to avoid the unwelcome conclusion.

In all of this Socrates commits himself to no beliefs of his own in the course of the discussion. He goes along with the interlocutor, drawing out beliefs that he is committed to. To reject the conclusion the interlocutor has to fault *his own* argument or reject one of *his own* beliefs; he can't do so by attacking any of Socrates' beliefs, since Socrates has put forward no beliefs relevant to the matter in hand. This is most blatantly obvious, of course, in the *Hippias minor* and *Republic* 1; nobody has seriously supposed that Socrates really thinks that the good person is the one who can willingly do wrong, or that the just person is a kind of thief.

We, again, stepping back, may think that this is not the whole story. In the *Hippias minor* Socrates is troubled and seems to point to the need for further investigation.[22] In *Republic* 1 Socrates goes on to add an argument with Polemarchus that argues from very Socratic premises. That is, once we widen the context of these arguments, we can find reason to doubt that merely ad hominem argument is all that is going on. But this does not, of course, undermine the claim that there is a perfectly good ad hominem reading of them, which is not forced and which would fit Arcesilaus' picture of an ad hominem Socrates.

It is also hard to think that Arcesilaus did not appeal to a dialogue that is clearly late but is deliberately Socratic in form—the *Theaetetus*. Here we find that ad hominem reasoning has been raised to a feature of Socratic methodology. The point is made explicit by the imagery of Socrates as the barren midwife and by the constant repetition of the point that Socrates is not putting forward any of his own ideas but is merely drawing ideas out of Theaetetus to see whether they work or not. All that happens is that Theaetetus offers various definitions of knowledge; none of them work; and so he is cured of any complacency on the subject. Socrates gets Theaetetus to see that all his definitions must be rejected because they lead to unacceptable results; he does not himself put forward any beliefs, still less use them to refute Theaetetus. The obviously reasonable way to read the *Theaetetus* is to see Socrates as arguing in it wholly ad hominem, though there is a his-

---

[22]Alan Code has pointed out to me that Socrates puts in a major qualification to his own acceptance of the offensive conclusion; at 376b4–6 Socrates says that the good person will be none other than the person who goes wrong and does shameful and wrong things willingly—*if there is such a person.*

tory of attempts to find a hidden doctrinal agenda by those who dislike the ad hominem reading.[23]

Still, this kind of ad hominem reasoning is not the norm in the Socratic dialogues. Certainly they all display Socrates knocking down an opponent's claim without putting anything positive in its place. Only in a very few cases, however, is the reasoning ad hominem in the sense that all the premises are supplied by the interlocutor, with Socrates uncommitted. In nearly all arguments Socrates does seem to hold beliefs; indeed he uses them to reject the interlocutor's suggestion, which is shown to conflict with beliefs that are retained, and that Socrates shares. Laches' suggestion that courage is standing firm, for example, founders because there can be bravery in retreat (190e–191c). The suggestion that it is endurance with knowledge, with which he concurs, founders because people can show more, not less, courage in taking risks when they lack knowledge and skill than in running risks when they have it (193b–c). In all this there is no suggestion that Socrates does not share the belief in question. Indeed, if he does not, it is hard to see how he could share enough beliefs about courage with the interlocutor for them to have a serious discussion as to what it is. And the usual form a "Socratic elenchus" takes is that of Socrates using beliefs he and his interlocutors share to show the interlocutor that he has a problem. This is the normal form of a "Socratic elenchus," whatever further problems remain as to its structure.

If Socrates makes trouble for his interlocutors by appealing to beliefs that they both hold, then he holds, and argues from, some beliefs. If so,

[23]It seems as though this was first attempted by Middle Platonists against the skeptical Academy's reading. The anonymous commentator on the dialogue (plausibly redated by H. A. S. Tarrant to the first century B.C. in "The Date of Anon. *In Theaetetum*," *CQ* n.s. 33 [1983]: 161–87) claims that Plato did hold beliefs (col. 55.8–13) against those who claim on the basis of passages like 150c that "Plato is an Academic, holding no beliefs" (col. 54.38: ἐκ τοιούτων λέξεών τινες οἴονται ᾿Ακαδημαϊκὸν τὸν Πλάτωνα ὡς οὐδὲν δογματίζοντα). The Neoplatonists also read the dialogue this way. The sixth-century anonymous *Introduction to Platonic Philosophy*, ed. L. G. Westerink (Amsterdam, 1962), says that Plato does not demolish all accounts of knowledge in the *Theaetetus*, since he does not himself accept that the soul is like a blank tablet, but thinks of it as needing only purification to attain (nonempirical) truth. Something similar seems to lie behind the odd "Platonic" arguments retailed by other Neoplatonist commentators against the "skeptical" claims that knowledge is impossible because everything is in flux (a confused version of the first part of the *Theaetetus*): these are to the effect that Plato accepts what is said about flux, but restricts it to the perceptible realm, above which the soul rises to grasp truth (Ammon. *In Cat. prooemium* 2.17–3.8; Olympiodorus *Prolegomena* 4.20–5.6; Philoponus *In Cat. prooemium* 2.8–24, in an incomplete and especially confused version). The most influential modern version, which revives many of the Neoplatonist readings, is that of Cornford; more recently John McDowell's translation and notes express a more moderate view but still hold that Plato is committed to some beliefs (about perception, for example) that are not presented in the dialogue but explain why some conclusions are rejected in it.

it would seem that Arcesilaus must be wrong; purely ad hominem reasoning is not characteristic of the Socratic dialogues, even if it occasionally occurs. Given this, the prospects of an overall skeptical reading of these dialogues may well seem dim; and we might feel inclined to reject Arcesilaus' reading as hopelessly selective and unbalanced, and to take the few passages of undeniably ad hominem reasoning in other ways. On its own, after all, it hardly implies skepticism. Perhaps Socrates uses it against Hippias in a spirit of personal spite, to make Hippias himself look silly. Perhaps he similarly wants to make Polemarchus look foolish; and perhaps he uses it in the *Theaetetus* in a manipulative way, so that Theaetetus' suggestions all founder while the preferred view waits in the wings.

It is possible, I believe, to see how Arcesilaus might have dealt with this, and to do so by turning to the source of his third difficulty: the fact that Socrates holds definite and passionate beliefs, particularly moral beliefs. No one can read the Socratic dialogues and fail to get the impression that Socrates believes, and is as committed as anyone could be to believing, certain theses: that virtue is a kind of skill, that you have to have virtue to be happy, that it is better to suffer than to do wrong, and so on. Prima facie these form another stumbling block in the way of the skeptical interpretation. But Arcesilaus may have been struck by two points about these beliefs.

First, the fact that Socrates has these beliefs emerges in a curiously oblique way from his arguments with others. We get the impression, for example, that Socrates believes that the virtues are some kind of unity (I deliberately leave it indeterminate just what kind, since nothing I say hangs on this) because he attacks arguments to show that the virtues are distinct (in the *Protagoras*) and because some of the arguments he employs (for example, at the end of the *Euthyphro* and the *Laches*) point that way. But Socrates never clearly formulates these beliefs (or their relationships) in any authoritative way. Nor does he ever put them forward as objects for reasoned debate. We have to work out the structure and exact content of Socrates' ethics for ourselves to a great extent.

Second, and as a consequence of this, Socrates never *argues to or from* his substantial moral beliefs. He sometimes claims, notably in the *Gorgias*, that an interlocutor is committed to them, but he never puts forward his own beliefs on his own account either to be examined or as premises to be argued from. Rather, he goes around examining *other people's* beliefs and seeing what *they* lead to.

But now we get an interesting result, for Socrates tends to appeal to commonsense beliefs that, if these strong Socratic theses are correct, are not true. For example, if Socrates thinks that all the virtues form a unity, then he can hardly share the assumption that founds many of the arguments in the *Laches,* that courage is a distinct virtue with its own nature and province. If he is committed to thinking that virtue is in its essence knowledge, then he can hardly endorse the thought that the unskilled divers risking their necks because they don't know what they are doing are actually braver than the skilled. And so if he is committed to these Socratic theses, then the arguments in the *Laches,* in which beliefs are tested against other beliefs that are retained, can be taken as ad hominem after all: Socrates is feeding the interlocutor premises that he does not himself share. And what goes for the *Laches* clearly goes for the majority of Socratic arguments. Much Socratic argument seems to rest on assumptions that Socrates cannot straightforwardly share if he accepts the strong Socratic theses. Put somewhat crudely: the more substantial we make Socrates' moral beliefs, the easier it becomes to read his arguments as ad hominem, directed against the interlocutor but neither supportive of nor dependent on Socrates' own convictions. Socrates has convictions but does not bring them into explicit relation with his argumentative practice, which remains negative and directed at the views of others. We can, then, see how Arcesilaus could come to treat all, not just a few, Socratic arguments as ad hominem—namely, by treating Socrates as committed to the strong Socratic theses and then explicitly severing them from Socratic argumentative practice.

Arcesilaus' interpretation of the Socratic dialogues thus turns out to be wholly compatible with the undeniable fact that Socrates is presented as committed to substantial dogmatic theses about the unity of virtue and so on; in fact it rests on this, for it is only if we take seriously Socrates' commitment to the substantial theses that we see how to read the arguments in a way that does not have Socrates share the commonsense beliefs that he uses to discomfit the interlocutor. The interlocutor is being shown that his beliefs get him into trouble because of commonsense beliefs that he has; but Socrates, on the skeptical reading, is not committed to those beliefs. He is always arguing from what the other person accepts.

Three points are worth stressing here. First, to treat all of Socrates" arguments as ad hominem is in no way to downgrade the seriousness of those arguments. They serve a serious and useful purpose in demonstrating what is wrong with various people's rash assents. We have seen that this is a genuinely important matter.

Second, the seriousness of Socrates' *practice* is not undermined either. For it need not matter whether he himself shares the objections he brings to an interlocutor's thesis. What matters is that the interlocutor be freed from rash assent and come to see what the problems are; and this will not happen until he copes with the objections. Any philosopher will sometimes find herself in the position of urging objections she does not share, just because it is important that her partner in discussion face these objections for herself. One can quite consistently find objections important, and find it important that the interlocutor face them, without sharing them; to reject this is surely to have a naive view of the complexity of philosophy. It must be said that this can lead to a kind of concealment: one urges the objections without coming out and saying that one does not share them. But it is not clear that this is objectionable in itself; it depends on the purpose. Usually the purpose will be pedagogical; and Socrates certainly appears always in the position of a teacher, or at least in that of someone who has reflected more, and more effectively, than the interlocutor. A passage in the *Theaetetus* brings this out clearly. In the argument about the role of the senses and the mind in perception at 184–86 Socrates begins by feeding ideas rather openly to Theaetetus and then checks himself at 184e and insists that Theaetetus answer for himself only in response to questions. Theaetetus duly limits himself to answering questions and is led to see for himself the crucial point that it is the mind by itself that deals with the "common things" the argument has brought in. Socrates' response (185e) is delighted: he thought that himself, he says, but he wanted Theaetetus to agree to it for himself. Here Plato is loudly making the point that although Socrates does hold the relevant belief, it is essential to the way he argues that Theaetetus come to discover it for himself, since the whole dialogue examines Theaetetus' beliefs, without bringing those of Socrates into it. Presumably this is the aspect of Socratic method that Cicero has in mind when he talks of Academics following Socrates in concealing their own views.[24]

Third, such an interpretation does not downgrade the seriousness and importance of Socrates' commitment to the substantial theses either. We may think that if they are neither based on nor answerable to Socratic arguments, they must be arbitrary and might as well be held on whim. But this is not so. Compare here the "digression" in the *Theaetetus*. Consistently elsewhere in the dialogue Socrates refuses to put forward any beliefs, limiting himself to testing Theaetetus' suggestions; this point is stressed to the point of tedium. But in the passage 172b–177c he expresses, eloquently and at length, his opinion that values are not, as Protagoras would have it, relative to the conditions of human life: rather there are objective standards, which form the basis of the

---

[24]*Tusc.* 5.11. Socrates produces through Plato and others many schools "e quibus nos potissimum consecuti sumus, quo Socratem usum arbitrabamur, ut nostram ipsi sententiam tegeremus, errore alios levaremus et in omni disputatione quid esset simillimum veri quaereremus." He ascribes this to Carneades, not to Arcesilaus, but there seems no problem in reading this feature back.

good person's happiness and the evil person's misery. These ideas are put forward with a confidence that recalls the *Republic;* Plato has no doubt or qualification, even though he underlines the fact that these are counterintuitive ideas, which will seem silly to most people, for whom the ideal of the successful life is totally different. How can this be reconciled with the ad hominem nature of the rest of the dialogue? The passage is clearly marked as a digression, independent of the argument, which Socrates and Theodorus leave at the digression's start and return to at the end (173b, 177b–c). Socrates clearly has convictions, of a definite and counterintuitive kind; but when examining the views of others he keeps his own beliefs out of it. It is clear how Arcesilaus would have welcomed the *Theaetetus* as evidence for a Socrates arguing ad hominem, and easy to see how he would extend this interpretation to the early dialogues: Socrates' substantial moral beliefs could be treated as having the status of the digression in the *Theaetetus*—passionately held, definite, and counterintuitive, *but not part of the argument.*

I have suggested how Arcesilaus' interpretation of the Socratic dialogues might be made out as viable. Socrates constantly searches for truth but does not claim to know any; he has strongly held views but does not assert these as reasoned, defensible theses; he limits his philosophical activity to arguing against the rash beliefs of others, showing them how their own premises land them in difficulties. This does make the activity of Socrates sound like the activity of Arcesilaus. There is, of course, an important difference. Arcesilaus did not believe, passionately or not, that virtue is needed for the happy life, and so on. Or rather, he *may* very well have followed Socrates in believing these things, but he certainly did not assert them. As Couissin says of him, "Himself a critic of the ideas of other men, he was unwilling to lay himself open to criticism, and so he kept his thoughts to himself."[25]

I hope to have shown, working cautiously from what we have good evidence for, how Arcesilaus would have claimed Socrates as a skeptic, and how he would have met the most obvious difficulties: Socrates' quest for truth, the use of shared premises, and Socrates' firm moral convictions. We have seen how the third, which might well seem the worst problem from a skeptic's point of view, can actually turn to advantage in dealing with the second difficulty.

I turn now from trying to make out Arcesilaus' case to raising two questions that we, who are not members of the skeptical Academy, are bound to raise. First, all this has served to show how a skeptic might account for the role of Socrates in the Socratic dialogues and

[25]Couissin (above, note 9), p. 40.

the *Theaetetus.* None of this applies to the *Republic* or other middle period dialogues, which clearly offer no handle to the form of interpretation I have been laying out.[26] But Arcesilaus was head of *Plato's*
Academy. Ariston's famous lampoon represented him as a monstrous
Chimaera with *Plato,* not Socrates, in front, Pyrrho behind, and so
on—clearly a reference to his official position as head of Plato's school.
Surely he must have had some way of coping with the *Republic,* to take
only the most obvious case?

Arcesilaus can hardly have ignored this problem; we know, for example, that he studied "Plato's books," which can hardly have been limited to the dialogues convenient for him. Annoyingly, we have no good
evidence on this matter. We do have evidence of a different kind for the
skeptical Academy's interpretation of Plato, which I shall present below
in section 2; but it is best to keep this distinct from our evidence for
Arcesilaus. Perhaps Arcesilaus merely tried to play down the contrast
between Socrates and Plato, by concentrating on a selective reading of
the dialogues and simply not paying much attention to inconvenient
ones like the *Republic.* If this sounds implausible, we should recall that
similarly selective and biased interpretations of Hume have been current in much of the twentieth century without raising general complaint. Certainly Antiochus, when he made a break with the skeptical
Academy, insisted that there was a sharp divergence between Socrates
and Plato and may have been controverting Academic orthodoxy in so
doing. Antiochus' view is clear in Cicero *Varro* 15ff.: Socrates asserted
nothing himself and merely refuted others and spent his time in exhorting others to virtue. (Note that Antiochus finds no problem in seeing Socrates as a moralist with convictions but no reasoned asserted
views.) Plato, however, produced a definite body of philosophical doctrine and a system, which Socrates would not have approved. Antiochus, then, draws the distinction in the strongest possible terms (which
many, incidentally, would agree with today); possibly when he got so
angry with Philo over the *Sosus* incident it was because Philo had explicitly come out and denied any such sharp opposition.[27]

If Antiochus was reacting against an Academic habit of selectively
reading Plato in a Socratic way, this makes more significant a passage
from the anonymous commentary on the *Theaetetus* (dating probably to

---

[26]Even among the early dialogues the *Crito* might be thought to be an obvious stumbling block; Socrates points out to Crito that their argument depends on a substantial
Socratic premise (49d–e), and this is based on argument (49a–b). However, Socrates
does not show us these arguments. And the *Crito* is in other ways odd; the Laws do not
argue with Socrates but simply order him around and tell him without argument that he
has to accept some very contentious theses.

[27]Cic. *Luc.* 11ff. See J. Dillon, *The Middle Platonists* (London, 1977), pp. 54–59. Gregory Vlastos emphasized this point to me.

the first century B.C.); the commentator remarks of the midwife passage and others like it that these passages were taken by some to show that "*Plato* [not Socrates] is an Academic, holding no beliefs" (col. 54.38). Further speculation is perhaps not useful, because of the lack of evidence. We remain, however, with a feeling of dissatisfaction, wishing we had something more definite. Second, and more important, can we seriously accept such an interpretation of Socrates? I have done my best to show that Arcesilaus' skeptical Socrates is not an aberration. We are dealing not with a silly, farfetched fantasy but with an interpretation that makes good sense on its own terms. Can we share it?

We have seen that Arcesilaus is quite entitled to hold that all Socratic argument can be seen as ad hominem. But he can only do this by taking Socrates not to share the beliefs he uses to create trouble for the interlocutors. He can do this by stressing Socrates' commitment to substantial Socratic convictions, particularly moral ones; for if he holds these, he does not straightforwardly share the interlocutor's beliefs. Arcesilaus, then, has no trouble in ascribing positive, firm, and even passionate beliefs, even of a counterintuitive nature, to Socrates. But he can do so only at the cost of doing what I called severing them from Socratic argumentative practice. A skeptic can have views and convictions, all right, and can even put them forward with passion. What he cannot do without compromising his skepticism is to put them forward as reasoned theses, to be argued to or argued from. The skeptical interpretation of Socrates only works, then, if we see Socrates' positive beliefs as held in intellectual isolation from his negative argumentative practice. A skeptic keeps his own beliefs out of it when examining those of others; Socrates will only be like Arcesilaus if his positive beliefs bear as little relation to his negative questioning of others' views as did those of Arcesilaus (whatever *they* were).

I have argued that we can indeed find this separation of conviction and argument in the *Theaetetus*, where it is actually not just accepted but explicitly emphasized as a point of methodology. Socrates, argumentatively the barren midwife, has convictions as firm and as counterintuitive as what we find in the *Republic;* and this is quite consistent, for the convictions are in a "digression" explicitly kept out of the argument. Arcesilaus, I suggested, must have read the Socratic dialogues in this way also. Can we? Here the answer can be brief: no. This point can be briefly made, for it is surely not necessary to make it at length. Socrates' methods of arguing in the Socratic dialogues are elusive and hard to systematize; they do not always seem the same, and Socratic methods are often puzzlingly indirect. But nothing warrants us in finding such a radical disjunction of argument and conviction as we find in the *Theaetetus*. We must build up the structure of Socratic ethics with caution and allow for flexibility and anomaly, but it is perverse to deny that it is there, to see in the early dialogues nothing but positive conviction and unconnected ad hominem argument.[28]

It is no accident that at several points in reconstructing Arcesilaus' skeptical Socrates I have had to appeal to the *Theaetetus*. It is plausible to see this dialogue as central for Arcesilaus; we can see from the anonymous commentary on the dialogue that it seems to have been the skeptical Academy's star text, and it seems to be the source of much in the direction and concerns of a great deal of Hellenistic epistemology. The problems come in reading the Socratic dialogues in the light of the *Theaetetus*, for in them Socrates does not appear as a barren midwife; his own ideas stand in a relation to his arguments that is complex and elusive but real. There are problems in interpreting the elenchus, but they cannot be brushed aside by the thought that there is no problem, that we have nothing but ad hominem arguments here, which themselves show nothing systematic about Socrates' own views.

All this raises a considerable irony. If Arcesilaus' skeptical Socrates can be found in the *Theaetetus*, while we cannot read the *Theaetetus'* methodology back into the early Socratic dialogues, then Arcesilaus has failed to show us a skeptical Socrates, but he has shown us a skeptical Plato. *But* he has shown us a skeptical Plato in just the dialogue where Plato harks back to the Socratic dialogues. And this leaves us with a new twist to the old "Socratic problem"; but that is another story.

2. Plato and Skepticism

Cicero in the part of *Varro* that has been preserved first presents Varro putting forward Antiochus' view of the history of the Old Academy. Antiochus, as already stressed above, draws a sharp distinction between Socrates, who argued without coming to systematic or positive results, and Plato, who did, and who in the Antiochean view was the fountainhead of the entire Old Academic, Peripatetic, and Stoic sys-

[28]It is at least worth a mention that scholars who emphasize the "literary" aspects of the Socratic dialogues are often implicitly accepting something like Arcesilaus' view, particularly if they stress the characters of Socrates' interlocutors and Socrates' occasionally dubious-seeming ways of arguing. If an argument is ad hominem, then fully to understand it we must know about what the interlocutor thinks, and focus on the actual moves and why they are made, rather than seeing the argument as part of a built-up "Socratic ethics." Much recent focus on "the dialogue form" and treatment of Socratic arguments piecemeal with stress on the particular context implicitly revives Arcesilaus' Socrates. The Academy may even have stressed these literary aspects themselves, since we know that an interest in oratory developed in the Academy, and Socratic arguments provide much material for studying how to (and how not to) convince various types of people.

tems, a body of ideas Antiochus proposed to renew and resystematize. Cicero begins his reply on behalf of the legitimacy of the skeptical Academy by defending Arcesilaus as a genuine Socratic enquirer and then, just before the text breaks off, relates him to Plato. He concedes that the skeptical Academy can be called the New Academy to contrast it with what went before—nonetheless, he says, it can be called old if we are prepared to make Plato a member of the Old Academy, for in Plato's books "nothing is assented to; there are many arguments on both sides of a question, and on all matters there is much enquiry, but nothing firm is said."[29]

Cicero is talking about the whole New Academy, from Arcesilaus to Carneades (and possibly beyond), but he makes no allusion to the Socratic practice that I have argued distinguished Arcesilaus' methods. Rather, he is presenting a Plato who is not, as Antiochus claims, a producer of systematic doctrines but can be seen as a skeptic of a kind, a real precursor of the New Academy. We can see from this exchange, incomplete as it is, how both dogmatists and skeptics claimed that Plato really belonged in their tradition, and what Cicero says indicates how the skeptics might have done it. Because the speech breaks off, we cannot tell how this kind of claim about Plato was related to the evidence about Arcesilaus' Socratic practice; in any case we shall see that there are good reasons for keeping the two separate.

There are three claims made here: that in Plato's works nothing is assented to, that he often argues on both sides of a question, and that he presents enquiry rather than firm statement. How are we to distinguish the first from the third? Most plausibly, the first concerns the form of Plato's writing: claims made in the dialogues are not prefaced by expressions of certainty but are put forward with hesitations and hedges. The third claims that in fact what is being done in the dialogues is enquiry rather than the putting forward of statements.[30]

These claims reappear in fuller form and with some additions in an anonymous Neoplatonist commentator in the school of Olympiodorus, who is dated by the editor, L. G. Westerink, to the sixth century A.D. In his *Introduction to Platonic Philosophy* the commentator puts forward and discusses five arguments for considering Plato a skeptic. The Neoplatonist commentators in general feel the need to rebut the claim that Plato was a skeptic, but usually they do so very briefly, in the course of listing the skeptics along with other schools of philosophy in a standard

---

[29]"cuius in libris nihil adfirmatur et in utramque partem multa disseruntur, de omnibus quaeritur, nihil certi dicitur," *Varro* 46.

[30]There is some support for this in the way the arguments are organized in the Neoplatonist commentator discussed below.

introduction to Plato or Aristotle.[31] Further, they seem not very interested in skepticism, confusing Academic and Pyrrhonist positions and often muddling them in with material about Protagoras and flux from the first part of the *Theaetetus*.[32] Anonymous, however, is not only much fuller than the others but much clearer; he explicitly mentions the New Academy and lays out clearly five arguments that could plausibly have been put forward in the New Academy. We should be cautious,[33] but we should also consider Anonymous an important source on this issue.

The five arguments are as follows:

[First,] in his discussion of things, they say, he uses certain adverbs indicating ambivalence and doubt—such as "probably" and "perhaps" and "maybe"; and that is a mark not of one who knows but of one who fails to apprehend any precise knowledge. . . . Second, they argue that inasmuch as he tries to establish contrary views about the same things, he clearly extols inapprehensibility [*akatalēpsia*][34]—for example, he tries to establish contraries when discussing friendship in the *Lysis*, temperance in the *Charmides*, piety in the *Euthyphro*. . . . Third, they say that he thinks that there is no such thing as knowledge, as is clear from the fact that he refutes every account of knowledge in the *Theaetetus*, as well as number; how can we say that someone like this extols apprehension? . . . Their fourth argument is this: if Plato thinks that knowledge is twofold, one sort coming through perception and the other through thought, and if he says that each sort falls down, it is clear that he extols inapprehensibility. For he says, "We do not see or hear anything accurately; our senses make errors"; and again he says of objects of thought that "our soul is entangled with this evil, the body, and cannot think of anything." . . . This is their

[31]Anonymous does so in an introduction to Platonic philosophy; Olympiodorus, Ammonius, Elias, Philoponus, and Simplicius all do so in their introductions to Aristotle's *Categories*.

[32]Philoponus calls the founder of the skeptics Pyrrho and does not seem to realize that it is the skeptical *Academy* that is in question. Elias, Ammonius, Philoponus, and Olympiodorus all refer to ἀκαταληψία, characteristic of the New Academy. Ammonius, Philoponus, and Olympiodorus all add considerations about flux that are evidently a confused reminiscence of the first part of the *Theaetetus*. Sometimes skepticism is assimilated to Protagoreanism, sometimes clearly distinguished from it. Plato's alleged arguments against skepticism often include a "self-refutation" argument deriving from the *Theaetetus*' self-refutation argument against Protagoras. Clearly by this period there was little serious interest in getting right just what skepticism is.

[33]Anonymous talks of "the New Academy" and *akatalēpsia* and uses "Academic" correctly for "skeptic." But he also uses ἐφεκτικοί, a word employed by the other commentators for skeptics in general.

[34]The Academic skeptics argued against the Stoics, who thought that there could be "apprehension" (κατάληψις), which we can take to be knowledge of particular facts (as opposed to ἐπιστήμη or knowledge proper, systematic understanding of a body of beliefs). What is being ascribed to Plato here is a rebuttal of claims to knowledge (not a claim that there is no knowledge).

fifth argument: they say that he himself says in his dialogue, "I know nothing and I teach nothing; all that I do is raise problems." See how he says in his own words that he has no apprehension.[35]

There is overlap between Cicero and Anonymous. Both mention the arguments that Plato uses expressions appropriate to doubt and hesitation, and that he argues on both sides of some questions. These are the most interesting arguments, and I shall concentrate on them; the others can be dismissed more quickly.

Cicero's third argument is too general to lend itself to detailed discussion. He is pointing to a very general feature of the Platonic dialogues: although they are full of very definite and strongly held claims, they have two features that distinguish them from most works of philosophy. They are all in the dialogue form; Plato never speaks in his own voice, and so all the dialogues are in form reports of enquiry carried on by two or more people, not reports of conclusions argued for and arrived at by Plato. The total effect is to distance Plato from his works, and to present them to us as discussions that are to stimulate us to continue them, rather than as reports of doctrines for us to assimilate. This is in general true; Plato is certainly different in this regard from Epicurus, say. But it is not so clearly true of some of the late dialogues; and it has certainly not stopped generations of scholars and philosophers, from the Middle Platonists to Paul Shorey, from finding in Plato a system of doctrines. This kind of consideration, then, cannot be decisive.

Anonymous' third argument appeals to the *Theaetetus,* taken to express Platonic rather than distinctively Socratic views. We have already seen why the *Theaetetus* was a star dialogue for skeptical interpretations of Plato. But one dialogue on its own, whether taken as Socratic or Platonic, cannot determine how we interpret all Plato's writings. Anonymous himself claims that Plato does not share the assumptions about knowledge that the arguments in the *Theaetetus* rest on—a move found tempting, as we have seen, from the Neoplatonists to Cornford (see above, note 23).

The fifth argument appeals to passages in the dialogues where Socrates (taken as unproblematically representing Plato) denies that he has any knowledge or that he teaches; he merely raises problems.

[35]Anon., ed. Westerink, pp. 205–6 Hermann. The translation is that in J. Annas and J. Barnes, *The Modes of Scepticism* (Cambridge, 1986), p. 13, with some additions by Annas. The reader should be warned that the position taken in the present essay is a divergence by Annas from the Annas-Barnes position on this issue in the book. That position is further defended by H. Maconi in a review of A. M. Ioppolo, *Opinione e scienza,* in *OSAP* 6 (1988): 231–54.

Despite the claim to be giving Plato's own words, Anonymous does not give any passage verbatim—though shortly afterward he says that "Plato" says that he knows nothing except one small thing, "giving and receiving an argument," by which he means dialectic; and this indicates that the passage he mainly has in mind is *Theaetetus* 161b. There, Socrates, asked by Theodorus for a refutation of a statement just made, says that he is not a bag of arguments; what goes on in a Socratic conversation is just that Socrates draws out arguments from his interlocutors. The only knowledge he has is this small item, the ability to do this.[36] Since it is the *Theaetetus* that is mainly in mind, we can object again that we are not entitled to interpret all the dialogues in the light of this one. Anonymous cites from other dialogues passages that show that dialectic is sometimes conceived of as a way to knowledge, not merely as the raising of problems and examination of the views of others. He adds the interesting claim that when Socrates says that he knows nothing he is not denying that he has any knowledge but denying that he has the kind that only the gods can have. Measured against the divine ideal, he has nothing; but in human terms he can have quite a lot. Recently Gregory Vlastos defended a similar interpretation of Socrates' profession of ignorance;[37] and possibly Anonymous is extending the point to Plato, who in the *Timaeus* stresses that the account he is giving is the best that mortals can do, but far from the exact truth.[38]

The fourth argument seems to have the *Phaedo* in view, this being the dialogue where Plato both disparages the senses most violently and expresses most strongly the view that the soul is hindered and clogged in its search for philosophical knowledge by its connection with the body. The alternative as posed by Anonymous' source is Hellenistic in form, and reminiscent of many of Sextus' arguments: knowledge must come empirically, through the senses, or by thinking, through the soul or mind; if neither is feasible, there is no knowledge. But Anonymous himself points out intelligently why this posing of the alternatives does not capture what Plato is saying, for even in the *Phaedo* Plato does not say that the senses are cognitively useless; they represent to us the way perceived objects are like, all right, and their limitation is that they do not on their own convey the essences (οὐσίαι) of things. Knowledge for Plato requires grasp of a thing's essence, and this can be done only by

---

[36]ἐγὼ δὲ οὐδὲν ἐπίσταμαι πλέον πλὴν βραχέος, ὅσον λόγον παρ' ἑτέρου σοφοῦ λαβεῖν καὶ ἀποδέξασθαι μετρίως. Anonymous simplifies this to πλὴν ὀλίγου τινος, καὶ τοῦτο τοῦ λαμβάνειν λόγον καὶ διδόναι.

[37]"Socrates' Disavowal of Knowledge," *PQ* 35 (1985): 1–31.

[38]Cf. *Ti.* 29b–d. At 40d–e he appeals to the "sons of gods" for the stories about the gods; this seems to be ironical, but it turns up, apparently seriously, as a ground for taking Plato to be a skeptic, at Diogenes Laertius 9.72.

thought. In the *Phaedo* this is the task of the mind when it is "purified" and freed from the body, and Plato stresses the difficulty of doing this; but he is setting the standards for knowledge high, not denying that it can ever be attained. (We could say the same of the programme of *Republic* 5–7. Plato is sketching an ideal of knowledge that nobody, as things are, will in fact attain. We can see how the skeptical Academy might put stress on this latter point and take Plato's message to us to be that the best we can ever achieve is to carry on enquiring. But it is equally legitimate to take the force of these books to be that since there is knowledge, we should strive for the ideal conditions in which we could come near to attaining it.)

The two most interesting arguments are the two that Cicero and Anonymous share. Of course the more surprising is the argument that Plato is a skeptic because he often argues to establish both sides of an issue. What is in question is a familiar skeptical strategy. The skeptic picks on an interlocutor's rash assertion that something is F. He argues convincingly against it being F. Then he argues equally convincingly *for* its being F. The interlocutor is thus brought to a state of "equipollence" (ἰσοσθένεια): every ground for holding it to be F is matched by an equally strong ground for holding it to be not-F. The result is *epochē*, suspension of judgment: the interlocutor finds that as a matter of fact he can now no longer assert either that it is F or that it is not-F; he has become detached from any commitment on the matter (even if it still *appears* to him more plausible that it is F). The skeptic's aim is to do this for every case of rash assent (his own included).[39]

But how could anyone ascribe this mode of arguing to Plato? In the Socratic dialogues Socrates often reduces his interlocutor to bafflement, admission of defeat, or silence but never to suspension of judgment. However, the argument here does not particularly concern the Socratic dialogues, and the key is to be found in the form of words that the skeptic uses to describe the results of argument. The skeptic in a state of equipollence declares that the thing is "no more F than not-F"; he makes it clear that he is not making a claim about the thing, saying that it is both, or neither; he is simply recording his own mental condition of equipollence on the matter. The skeptic uses the phrase "no more" (οὐ μᾶλλον) in a skeptical sense (cf. Sex. Emp. *Pyr.* 1.188–91).

Plato sometimes uses the *ou mallon* description of the upshot of an argument (*Tht.* 182e10, 181e5–7; *Meno* 78e6; *Rep.* 340b3–5); but it cannot be given the skeptical reading, for Plato is describing not equipollence but the result that the thing in question has been shown to be not-F. But he does recognize skeptical argument to equipollence, and

---

[39]On these features of skeptical reasoning, see Annas and Barnes (above, note 35).

the use of "no more F than not-F" to describe the result. He does not, however, describe it approvingly. In *Republic.* 7, discussing the undesirable effects of premature practice of dialectic, he says that if you get used to refuting people too soon, you will acquire the view that anything is "no more fine than foul, and the same with just and good and whatever else is esteemed" (538d6–e2). Plato finds it dangerous to think, as the Pyrrhonist skeptics at least later did, that on any matter one should expect the arguments pro and con to come out even. Thinking this, for Plato, makes you irresponsible, aggressive, and negative in argument.

However, this happens when you do dialectic *too soon,* with the wrong attitudes. Finding that there is as much to be said con as pro *can* be salutary; for, as we find in a famous passage of *Republic* 7 (523–25), some things stir the mind to think while others do not. Our experience never reports that a finger is also the opposite of a finger, and so we are not stirred to wonder what a finger is. But some concepts do—and the concepts that have this desirable feature of getting us to start thinking are those that have opposites, precisely because it is only in these cases that we can find that there is as much to be said for a thing's being not-F as for its being F. It is when something "is seen to be no more one than many" that we think and ask ourselves what is one, and what is many. It turns out, then, that equipollence can be no bad thing—the resulting intellectual discomfort stirs us to think in a way that leads us out of the original problem. The premature dialectician is wrong not in arguing to equipollence but in remaining satisfied with the resulting discomfort rather than enquiring farther.

On this point no ancient skeptic would disagree with Plato; as stressed, ancient skeptics are enquirers and think that finding difficulties should stir us to enquire more.[40] The skeptic parts company only when Plato announces what the mind discovers—intellectually graspable essences or forms that, when we understand them, take the sting out of the original problem as to the "contradictions in perception." For the skeptic, this is the typical fault of dogmatism: giving up too soon, staying complacently satisfied when there are further problems to enquire into. But for Plato, insistence on further enquiry, when one has found intellectually satisfying results, is immature; it is to avoid just this that he insists that the guardians do years of study before launching on to dialectic. So though we can find Plato arguing to equipollence, it is not for him, as it is for the skeptics, part of an ongoing enquiry; it is limited to cases where the senses provide grounds for equipollence, and it leads us to use our minds to grasp forms. In keep-

[40]In a way compatible with suspending judgment on the original problem, of course.

ing with this, when he uses the form of words "no more F than not-F," he does not, unlike his premature dialecticians, give it the skeptical reading: things that are no more F than not-F are *both* F and not-F, a cognitive deficiency not shared by forms. Burying one's parents is no more fine than foul—that is, it is both (*Hip. ma.* 293b5–8); shame is no more good than bad—that is, it is both (*Chrm.* 161b1–2); the many beautifuls, justs, and so on at *Republic* 5, 479a–b are no more beautiful than ugly, just than unjust, and so on—that is, they are both, and belief or δόξα is the state of mind of finding them to be both.

The so-called argument from opposites has attracted a great deal of attention in recent Platonic scholarship, and much attention has been paid to the fact that in the passages where Plato argues for forms he does so from the inadequacies, in their application to empirical things, of terms that have opposites. One result of this is that forms will be generated only for terms that have opposites; yet Plato nowhere welcomes or even recognizes such a limitation. The role of opposites in these passages becomes more comprehensible, I think, if we see Plato as making a nonskeptical application of a form of argument that, if applied in a different spirit, leads to equipollence and suspension of judgment—as indeed we find it doing in later skeptics like Sextus.[41]

However, our result is that while Plato does sometimes argue on both sides of an issue and even urge that we be led to equipollence, this has no tendency to show him to be a skeptic; he rejects the skeptical attitude to this kind of argument and uses it in his own case to establish the conclusion that there are forms that the mind can grasp—a quintessentially dogmatic conclusion. Thus members of the skeptical Academy were on weak ground here: they were pointing to a form of argument shared by Plato and by the skeptics but not to any real community of application. We find here a skeptical root of Plato's major metaphysical claim, something certainly of interest and arguably often neglected, but we do not find a skeptical Plato.

The final argument appears, in Anonymous' version, initially puzzling. First, it seems to ignore the obvious: Plato's works are in dialogue form, and expressions of doubt indicate the interlocutor's attitude, not Plato's. We are presumably to take him to refer to Socrates' statements and to have in mind the middle and later dialogues, where Socrates is represented as putting forward definite and positive statements, but usually with some disclaimer of this kind. Why, however, should such

---

[41]I have, in considering this argument, freely used Pyrrhonist sources, since they are the only informative ones. We know that among the Academic skeptics Arcesilaus at least argued to *epochē*, and it has been argued by Couissin (above, note 10) that the Academy was the source of the notion of suspension of judgment, but it is not clear exactly how it fits in with known Academy practice. I have therefore used the explicit and lucid account of equipollence and suspension in Sextus.

qualifications as "probably" and "perhaps" show that Plato is a skeptic of any kind? Surely a dogmatist can qualify his claims without becoming a skeptic?

Once again we find that skeptics made a distinctive use of these phrases. Sextus tells us that the skeptic uses phrases like these not merely to qualify an assertion and make it more modest, as a dogmatist would, but rather to indicate that the skeptic is not really asserting anything but merely indicating what appears to him to be the case, but without commitment to its truth.[42] That is why I have taken Anonymous' first argument, about the use of certain phrases, to be the same as the first point mentioned in Cicero, that in Plato nothing is asserted; use of certain words indicates skepticism only if the words are used to convey a skeptical detachment from what is put forward. This argument, then, amounts to the claim that however dogmatic in content are statements that we can find in Plato, they are put forward with qualifications that distance the speaker (and author, here fused) from commitment to their truth.

Is there anything in this claim about Plato? It seems clearly aimed at the middle and later, rather than the Socratic, dialogues, since only in the former does Socrates put forward definite and positive statements that look like Platonic doctrine. It is certainly true that we find this kind of verbal qualification, and the bolder the metaphysical claim, the more insistent the qualification. In the *Phaedo,* for example, Socrates never says that he know that the soul is immortal; he puts this forward as the thesis that has stood up best to argument and that he cannot help accepting as true, even though he never convinces all the interlocutors. In the *Republic* the account of the Form of the Good, and with it the ambitious metaphysical sketch of the central books, is said by Socrates to be only his own poor and inadequate beliefs on the subject, far from knowledge (506 b–d).

But is Plato indicating skeptical detachment, or merely a modest attitude to doctrine? Certainly Anonymous retorts that Plato employs these expressions for accuracy, not to indicate real hesitation; and this was in general the Neoplatonist response, especially as regards the *Phaedo.*[43] In the absence of other, unmistakable signs that an author is a skeptic, use of these expressions is surely most naturally taken to indicate not detachment from the content of what is asserted but simply a qualifi-

---

[42]Sext. Emp. *Pyr.* 1.194–95. Sextus cites the expressions τάχα, ἔξεστι, and ἐνδέχεται; Anonymous, the expressions εἰκός, ἴσως, and τάχ᾽ὡς οἶμαι. Again I am using a Pyrrhonist source to illuminate Academic practice, for lack of good Academic sources on this; I do not think it misleading.

[43]Olympiodorus in his commentary on *Phaedo* 69d5 tells us that Ammonius wrote a monograph on this passage to refute the idea that Socrates is really in doubt about the soul. In his note on 72d7 Olympiodorus repeats the point that Socrates' expressions of doubt do not express real doubt on the issue.

cation of a modest kind, either as to things being exactly as claimed or as to one's certainty on the topic. If there were such powerful independent arguments for the Plato of the middle dialogues really being a skeptic, then the well-marked hesitation of Socrates when coming out with strong metaphysical statements could be taken in a way consistent with skepticism. Plato would then be seen as an enquirer, who works out various positions by argument and puts them forward not as fixed doctrines for pupils to learn but as what seems the best position reached by argument so far. The qualifications would indicate that however convinced Socrates is of the soul's immortality or the importance of the Good, these positions are provisional, in that the argument is still going on: Socrates puts forward one side but is aware that there are difficulties that can be raised on the other. The dialogues, even the "metaphysical" ones, do not present us with doctrines but invite us to continue the arguments. This is undoubtedly an attractive picture of Plato's middle dialogues (and one that in fact has more influence on the actual philosophical activity of most modern scholars than the doctrinal Plato). But it cannot on its own convince us to read Plato this way. We can see how the skeptical Academy, especially when it had established a long tradition of nondoctrinal philosophical activity, would read Plato this way, to bring him into their own tradition (although in fact they did not continue Plato's own arguments very much, as far as we know; they concentrated on contemporary philosophy, and on arguing with their own most powerful contemporaries, the Stoics). But we, with no such motive, are not likely to find this the best reading of the *Phaedo* and the *Republic*.[44]

The reasonable conclusion, then, is that the arguments in Cicero and Anonymous are too weak or inconclusive to make it plausible to read Plato as a skeptic. We can see the lines on which the skeptical Academy read Plato's middle and later dialogues; and while they emphasize a stimulus to further enquiry, and a qualification of his claims, which are often missed in studying Plato, the interpretation is just not plausible as an attempt to show that Plato is never dogmatic, never wants us to accept doctrines that he has argued for. Here Sextus appears to be right (*Pyr.* 1.221–23): to show that Plato is a skeptic one has to show that he never puts forward doctrines, and that is an implausible position. Showing that here and there he advocates further enquiry, or that he hedges his claims, is not to the point.

---

[44]This is not to say, of course, that we must read Plato as simply enquiring, or simply reporting doctrines. Any sensitive reading of the *Phaedo* will find in it the stimulus to further examination of the issues. But it will also find much that Plato is committed to; and a skeptical reading has to make Plato consistently reject presentation of doctrine.

There is one further point of interest about this final argument, however. It turns up in a confrontation between the *late* Academy and Antiochus; and we can see how it is compatible with a weaker form of skepticism than that of Arcesilaus. Arcesilaus' version of Socratic practice involves detachment from all beliefs; but by the time of the late Academy under Philo Academics had, by dint of constant argument on various issues, settled into the view that some positions were more strongly supported by argument than others: continued debate just did not turn up as good considerations on the other side. An Academic skeptic could thus take the line that some beliefs were more convincing or plausible than others, in the sense that any reasonable person, exposed to all the arguments, would come down on their side rather than on that of the opposite. But it now became hard to distinguish this kind of modified skeptic from a suitably modest and qualified dogmatist, who put forward his claims with the backing of powerful argument, but without claiming that they were certainly true. In this situation the only thing that distinguished a skeptic from a Stoic, say, on some topic, was that the former would insist that despite finding the position convincing and supported by the best available argument, he would still detach himself from commitment to its truth—something that even the most modest Stoic would not do. In this context the skeptics' use of expressions to distance themselves from commitment to the truth of what they asserted would acquire a special importance. And it may be that the ascription of this skeptical use of expressions of doubt to Plato represents the weaker skepticism of the late Academy under Philo. While it is consistent with Arcesilaus' revival of Socratic method, it does not seem to belong in the same climate of skepticism. And, while dating or even tracing developments in the skeptical Academy is hazardous, it at least appears to me to be the case that the skeptical Academy began with a return to a skeptical version of Socratic practice, and that it was probably only later, when their skepticism had become considerably mitigated, that they claimed the Plato of the middle dialogues as a skeptical ancestor.

In conclusion, we have found that the skeptical Academy's attempt to see itself as the true heir of Plato was not silly or farfetched; it made sense of both skepticism and Plato. But it is in the end too selective to be convincing as a reading of Plato as a whole; and it is more complex and involves more varied conceptions of skepticism than sometimes thought.[45]

---

[45] A distant ancestor of this essay was read at an Oxford seminar that Jonathan Barnes and I gave. Since then it has gone through many versions; parts of some of these were read at the University of Texas, the Los Angeles area colloquium in ancient philosophy

Afterword

I wrote the paper that eventually became "Plato the Skeptic" in 1985, and over the years since then I have noticed a definite shift in its reception, from bafflement at the very idea of conjoining "Plato" and "skeptic" to a readier acceptance of the idea that one strand in the Platonic tradition might have been a skeptical one. This has been due partly to the diffusion of improved understanding of ancient skepticism and partly to an increased willingness, on the part of scholars, to take seriously a variety of approaches to Plato. One aspect of the latter has been a greater readiness to open up "the Socratic question" and to take seriously perspectives on Socrates other than Plato's. One result of this, in turn, is that we can achieve a better understanding of both Socrates and the Hellenistic schools, by noting what happens in cases where a Hellenistic movement of thought, like the skeptics or Stoics or Cynics, takes as a model Socrates, as distinguished from, or even opposed to, Plato. In the case of the Academic skeptics the matter is complex and difficult, and Christopher Shields's essay is a welcome contribution to the debate that is improving our understanding of these intellectual links.

Shields is sympathetic to the case that we can plausibly motivate Arcesilaus' claim to be in the tradition of Socrates, for we can see why Arcesilaus could reasonably claim to find, in Socratic practice, the idea that philosophy consists in continued enquiry, in the habit of arguing ad hominem (that is, arguing from the opponent's premises rather than from a substantial position of his own), and in the striking absence of any attempt to argue systematically from or to Socrates' substantial moral beliefs. Here we get a complication, however; Shields focuses on the Socratic dialogues, explicitly leaving out of account "the clearly post-Socratic *Theaetetus*" (his note 8). However, if one does this, then it is hardly surprising that Socrates' practice looks somewhat different from the explicitly skeptical procedure of Arcesilaus, for, as I stress in my essay, in the Socratic dialogues Socrates, while not in the process of developing a system of his moral beliefs, does not appear to be committed to a clear separation between positive position and negative

(Pomona), and the Berkeley conference in ancient philosophy. I am most grateful to the audiences on all these occasions for comments, and also to Jonathan Barnes, Lesley Brown, Myles Burnyeat, Alan Code, Stephen Everson, Gail Fine, and James Lesher. My greatest debt is to Gregory Vlastos, whose extensive and generous comments stimulated much reshaping and great improvement, and whose discussions greatly deepened my sense of what is at stake in the attempt to see Plato as part of a skeptical tradition. Whatever value the paper has is due to him.

argument.[46] "Socratic ethics" is as difficult as it is because the reader of the dialogues tends to feel impelled to systematize the Socratic theses in some way, and furthermore to feel that one purpose of the dialogue form is to impel the reader to do just this.[47]

In the *Theaetetus*, on the other hand, we do find unmistakable indications that separation of negative argument and positive position is explicitly part of a deliberate methodology. Socrates is the barren midwife; he consistently refuses to be drawn on his own views in an argument, limiting himself to drawing out and criticizing those of Theaetetus, and in the "digression" he heavily underlines the point that the positive views he puts forward are not part of the argument. If one thought that Socratic practice led to a position that was recognizably skeptical and recognizably Socratic, one would surely see the *Theaetetus* as the place where this position can be found. Socrates is not here committed to holding any strong methodological positions of his own, but he is surely committed to a position that quite clearly severs doctrine from argument and impels the reader to continue the argument rather than to systematize doctrine. The members of the Academy seem to have concentrated on the *Theaetetus*,[48] and it is surely reasonable to regard the *Theaetetus* as giving them their picture of Socratic practice, against which they measured their own.

But we cannot, of course, take the *Theaetetus* to be evidence for Socratic practice without opening up "the Socratic question." Shields does not consider the *Theaetetus*, because it is "clearly post-Socratic," thus apparently taking the view that the Socratic dialogues are evidence for the views of the historical Socrates, whereas later dialogues are evidence rather for the different views of Plato. This would undoubtedly be regarded as an uncontroversial approach by many scholars.

I would myself stress that while the *Theaetetus* is without a doubt a later dialogue, it is equally clearly a Socratic dialogue; Plato has deliberately harked back to the format and style of the earlier Socratic dialogues. This surely has something to do with the fact that in the *Theaetetus* Socrates appears not as the devotee of collection and division, nor as the exponent of elaborate metaphysical ideas, but as the barren midwife. The later dialogue gives us Plato's later thoughts

---

[46]This is the basis of Vlastos' reservations about there being a real intellectual link between Socrates and Arcesilaus.

[47]However, there are many deep problems in doing this, problems to which the dialogues do not themselves indicate solutions. How, for example, are we to combine the thesis that virtue is a skill with the thesis that virtue is sufficient for happiness? Which thesis are we to pick, if any, as the Socratic refutand of the *Hippias minor*? How seriously does Socrates take the hedonism in the *Protagoras*? And so on.

[48]Judging from the comment of the anonymous commentator; see above.

about Socratic methodology, and they are presented as a development of the earlier methodology in a way that collection and division, say, are not. If we think that the Socratic dialogues give us a reliable account of the views of the historical Socrates, then the *Theaetetus* gives us Plato's view of a direction in which Socrates' methodology might go. If we are not so sanguine about distinguishing Socratic from Platonic elements in Plato, then we can take it that both the earlier dialogues and the later give us Plato's interpretation of one way that Socrates' methodology might develop. Either way, the *Theaetetus* gives us a statement by Plato about Socratic method that is more radical than what we find in the Socratic dialogues. And, whether we, like the anonymous commentator on the dialogue, take this to hold for Plato as well as for Socrates, or not, we certainly find a methodology that can reasonably be called skeptical; ad hominem argument and refusal to argue to or from one's own position are here at the level of self-conscious method. I would, then, take it to be the *Theaetetus* that Arcesilaus might legitimately have in mind as an expression of Socratic method, even though it is more radical than the Socratic dialogues; and the *Theaetetus* can certainly be interpreted in a skeptical way.

There remains, however, one large problem in particular, on which Shields focuses much of his essay: some of our evidence ascribes *epochē* to Arcesilaus, and this is a definitely un-Socratic feature.[49] According to Shields, Arcesilaus is committed to (E), the principle that all judgment should be suspended. This is a straightforward normative principle and at once raises the question of what Arcesilaus' grounds were for holding it, and how he could hold it consistently with his skepticism. According to Shields, (E) is grounded by (U), the principle that everything is "undiscerned" (not reliably ascertained), and is held as a second-order judgment whose objects are various first-order judgments. Shields gives an interesting defense of the claim that what distinguishes Arcesilaus' position is precisely his holding of these general principles; for it is this that enables him to go beyond Socrates' case-by-case procedure to develop *general* skeptical strategies. Arcesilaus has reason to believe in advance that his dogmatic opponents will fail; he "can and does expect his opponents to join him in *epochē*."

One point can be raised even before we focus on the status of *epochē* itself. This position makes Socrates more of a genuine *skeptikos* or enquirer than Arcesilaus; whatever the form one's general regulative principles take, they certainly provide a set of substantial prior constraints on the way that one will enquire. They do not, of course, pre-

---

[49]I emphasize this myself (above, note 9), pp. 106–8, in a discussion review of Ioppolo's *Opinione e scienza* (above, note 9).

vent enquiry, but it is a little hard to see why, on this view, Cicero should represent the Academy as continuing the Platonic tireless search for truth.[50] Commitment to (E) goes far beyond the mere recognition that there are a number of obstacles to enquiry, as Cicero admits. Socrates is on this view the one who is not committed beforehand to judging that the outcome of enquiry and debate must come out one way rather than another.

Shields is right to press the point about *epochē*, however. Much of our evidence about Arcesilaus ascribes *epochē* to him. But does this compel us to hold that he held the normative principle (E)? This is not so clear. Sextus' evidence is suspect here, since he regularly contrasts Pyrrhonist with Academic skepticism in a way that misrepresents the latter. Even Shields's star passage, Cicero's description in his own person of Arcesilaus' "innovations" at *Varro* 43–46, seems to me less than conclusive. Arcesilaus is represented as maintaining that one "should" (*oportere*) not assent; but this need mean only that suspension of judgment is what will in fact follow, if (of course) one follows the argument through properly. Similarly elliptical references to suspension of judgment are common in Sextus, and it would be wrong to conclude on the basis of them that Sextus is committed to something like (E). Further, *epochē* is introduced, whatever its status, on the basis of the claim that nothing can be reliably known; but in the context this looks less like Arcesilaus' own claim than like a response to the position of Zeno, which is just said to have started the Academic debate in the first place. Again, Sextus offers numerous passages where the skeptic appears at first to be committed to a position, but where closer inspection shows that this is really half of a dialectical argument whose other side is being taken for granted in the context. So this passage does not seem to me to support the claim that Arcesilaus endorsed (E) as a substantial principle.

In what way, then, was Arcesilaus committed to *epochē*? I am still inclined to believe that as the result of argumentative practice he found himself accepting that equipollence and suspension of judgment in fact came about, for those who followed through the argument and were not blinkered by doctrine.[51] Thus any assertions of his about *epochē* would presumably be like the apparent assertions about his own and others' assents, which he ascribed to the effects of nature, in the absence of rational grounds.[52] Nature here seems to play the role that the Pyrrhonists assign to the appearances: it is what explains our acting in the absence of *belief* that things are a certain way. If this is the status of

[50]*Luc.* 7; see above.
[51]See Annas (above, note 9), pp. 106–8.
[52]D. L. 4.36.

Arcesilaus' acceptance of *epochē*, then clearly it does not have to be grounded on anything like a belief that everything is undiscerned. Nor does Arcesilaus face a problem of consistency. His attacks on the Stoics will be not be "motivated by a philosophical argument about the possibility of knowledge" but rather will be the product of irritation by dogmatic pretensions, as Socrates was irritated by the sophists.

It remains true that *epochē* is an un-Socratic idea, and that despite much scholarship it is hard to decide what is its likely original home. Both Pyrrho and the Stoa have been suggested as the sources of *epochē* for Arcesilaus; that this is possible says much about the state of the evidence. Further, Shields is clearly right to insist that there are difficulties in the idea that one can accept a principle in a way that is weaker than believing it but stronger than merely doing what does in fact conform to it. I do not think that the problem is insuperable for the Academics, although I think that the use that the Pyrrhonists make of the contrast between being and appearing is more effective in this context.[53] And finally, Shields is surely correct in insisting that the traditional choice between Arcesilaus the closet dogmatist and Arcesilaus the mere dialectician is too simplistic. There are, as he points out, more possibilities, and further discussion is bound to take account of these. Shields's discussion takes us farther into the puzzle of the skeptical Academy, and the way in which, in a very changed philosophical climate, they harked back to Socrates as their intellectual forebear.

[53]R. Bett, "Carneades' Distinction between Assent and Approval," *Monist* 73 (1990): 3–20, indicates some responses that could be made to the type of criticism that Shields offers.

[13]

Socrates among the Skeptics

Christopher J. Shields

"How Arcesilaus and Carneades could have associated their systematic adherence to ἐποχή with Socrates' ringing affirmations we shall never know: our information about them is all too scant." So claims Gregory Vlastos.[1] Yet Arcesilaus evidently looks to Socratic dialectic and to Socratic avowals of ignorance as legitimating sources of his own extreme skepticism. Indeed, according to Cicero, Arcesilaus views Socrates as his primary source of skeptical inspiration:[2] "Arcesilaus first drew this particular lesson most powerfully from various books of Plato and from Socrates' talk: nothing is certain" (Cic. *De or.* 3.67; cf. *Fin.* 2.2, 5.10; *Acad.* 1.44ff.; *Nat. d.* 1.11). When looking at the Socrates of Plato's early dialogues,[3] however, Vlastos and others find only a Socrates

---

[1] *Socrates: Ironist and Moral Philosopher* (Ithaca, N.Y., 1991), p. 5. Vlastos is responding both to Grote, who had accepted Cicero's linkage of Arcesilaus and Carneades to Socrates, and to his earlier self, who thought Socrates' method of investigation "quite compatible with suspended judgment as to the material truth of any of its conclusions." For Vlastos' earlier views, see especially his introduction to *Plato's Protagoras*, trans. B. Jowett, rev. M. Ostwald (Indianapolis, 1956), p. xxxi. See also G. Grote, *Plato and Other Companions of Socrates* (London, 1865), 1:239.

[2] His more proximate sources of inspiration must surely have been Timon and, through him, Pyrrho. For an overview of the lines of transmission, see D. N. Sedley, "The Protagonists," in *Doubt and Dogmatism* (Oxford, 1980), pp. 1–19.

[3] I accept the conventional picture of the early or "Socratic" dialogues as including the *Apology*, the *Euthyphro*, the *Charmides*, the *Laches*, the *Lysis*, the *Hippias minor*, the *Euthydemus*, the *Gorgias*, and the *Ion*. I also accept the *Hippias major*, sometimes thought to be spurious, as early. I sometimes cite evidence from the *Protagoras* and the *Meno*, which I regard as transitional dialogues, but which therefore touch base in important respects

unwilling to claim certain knowledge on his own behalf, and not one unwilling to embrace a form of elenctic propositional knowledge.[4] According to such critics, when Socrates insists that he has no knowledge, he means only that he has no knowledge of a specifiable sort:[5] perhaps he has no *certain* knowledge, no *expert* knowledge,[6] or no knowledge within a particular sphere of inquiry, such as moral theory. This would be compatible with his nevertheless having knowledge of other sorts: perhaps he knows some things without being certain of them, has the sort of knowledge nonexperts can have, or indeed has no knowledge of moral matters, even though he has knowledge in subjects other than morality, perhaps psychology or logic. Such a Socrates is not a skeptic, or at least not the sort of skeptic Arcesilaus advertises himself to be. If this is correct, and if Cicero is right to attribute Socratic inspiration to him, then the suggestion lies near that Arcesilaus relies on Socrates only disingenuously, that he misrepresents the historical Socrates in an effort to forge a philosophical lineage where none exists.

This at any rate seems to be the view some of Arcesilaus' contemporaries took of the matter. In an anti-Epicurean tract dedicated to refuting the principal arguments of Epicurus' pupil Colotes, Plutarch defends Arcesilaus against the charge of promoting himself as trading in novelties:

ὁ δ' Ἀρκεσίλαος τοσοῦτον ἀπέδει τοῦ καινοτομίας τινὰ δόξαν ἀγαπᾶν καί ὑποποιεῖσθαί ⟨τι⟩ τῶν παλαιῶν ὥστε ἐγκαλεῖν τοὺς τότε σοφιστὰς ὅτι προστρίβεται Σωκράτει καὶ Πλάτωνι καὶ Παρμενίδῃ καὶ Ἡρακλείτῳ τὰ περὶ τῆς ἐποχῆς δόγματα καὶ τῆς ἀκαταληψίας οὐδὲν δεομένοις, ἀλλ' οἷον ἀναγωγὴν καὶ βεβαίωσιν αὐτῶν εἰς ἄνδρας ἐνδόξους ποιούμενος.

But Arcesilaus was so far from welcoming a reputation as an innovator or as assuming something from the ancients that contemporary wise men charged that he inflicted[7] his views about suspension [*epochē*] and the lack

---

with the earlier Socratic dialogues. The Socratic dialogues comprise a thematically related family, characterized chiefly by their preoccupation with ethical matters and their aporetic character. It is precisely this aporetic character that at least initially lends credence to a picture of Socrates as skeptical.

[4]G. Vlastos, "Socrates' Disavowal of Knowledge," *PQ* 35 (1985): 1–31.

[5]I do not here entertain the irrefutable (but I believe utterly implausible) suggestion that Socratic avowals of ignorance are without exception simply intended as ironic. Nor do I entertain the much more plausible suggestion that Socrates engages in "complex irony" of the sort Vlastos (above, note 1) attributes to him. See Vlastos, chap. 1 and additional note 1.1.

[6]For this sort of view, see P. Woodruff, "Expert Knowledge in the *Apology* and *Laches:* What a General Needs to Know," *PBACAP* (1987): 79–115.

[7]The sophists, in this rendering, accuse him of "inflicting" (*prostribein*) his views on the ancients; this term might more neutrally be rendered as "imparted" or "attached"; Einarson and De Lacy have "foisted" in the Loeb (*Plutarch's Moralia* 14.277). They are jus-

of cataleptic assent on Socrates, Plato, Parmenides, and Heraclitus, although they needed nothing [of the sort]; but Arcesilaus wanted to make his view secure by referring it back to reputable men. (*Adv. Col.* 1121e–1122a)

Does Arcesilaus misleadingly or even disingenuously attempt to "secure" his view by casting it back to the ancients?

It would certainly be a mistake to condemn Arcesilaus too quickly, particularly with respect to potential Socratic inspiration.[8] Arcesilaus' claims surely find some root in Socrates' repeated professions of ignorance, or at least in his repeated tendency to highlight his own epistemic inadequacies. Thus Socrates says rather directly in the *Meno:* "I do not know anything about virtue" (71b3). Elsewhere Socrates offers a remark we might have expected from Arcesilaus himself. In the *Gorgias*, Socrates informs Callicles: "I do not say what I say as one who knows" but rather as one merely searching along with others (506a3–6; cf. 509a4–6).[9] Moreover, Plato's Socrates does not mirror in every detail the Socrates we find represented in other quarters of the doxography, most notably in Xenophon. The complaint of a disingenuous Arcesilaus, as mooted, relies on a specific reading of the early Platonic dialogues, without reference to other strands of the Socratic tradition.

Even so, there is ample reason to suppose that Arcesilaus would have relied most heavily on Plato's dialogues for his picture of Socrates;[10] and I am doubtful that non-Platonic sources portray a more stridently

---

tified in the more trenchant choice, since the context is almost certain to have been reproachful and antagonistic. In any case, according to Plutarch, some of Arcesilaus' contemporaries read him as attributing *epochē* to Socrates.

[8]I have learned this lesson best from Julia Annas. See her "Platon le sceptique," *Revue de métaphysique et de morale* 2 (1990): 267–91. Annas concludes: "we have discovered that the attempt of the skeptical Academy to think of itself as Plato's authentic heir was neither stupid nor far-fetched; there was sense to it with regard to skepticism as well as with regard to Plato. In the final analysis, it is too selective to constitute a convincing reading of Plato in his entirety, but it is more complex and it takes in more varied conceptions of skepticism than we used to think." Annas discusses the Platonic corpus more fully than I have undertaken here, considering in some detail, for example, the clearly post-Socratic *Theaetetus;* I will concentrate my remarks on her section "Socrate et le scepticisme," pp. 268–81. Although I have not been entirely persuaded by her case, our final views have much in common, and my own thinking on Arcesilaus' relation to Socrates is deeply indebted to her excellent discussion. I thank her for allowing me to see her essay in manuscript form.

[9]For a review of the main evidence concerning Socrates' avowals of ignorance, see Vlastos (above, note 1), pp. 21–44, 82–86.

[10]Diogenes at any rate reports Arcesilaus as having acquired Plato's books (D.L. 4.32), and a broad education within the Platonic tradition would certainly have been required for his election to succeed Crates as head of the Academy. For a succinct, compelling account of Arcesilaus' relation to Socrates that focuses primarily on the Socrates in Plato's dialogues, see A. A. Long, "Socrates in Hellenistic Philosophy," *CQ* n.s. 38 (1988): 150–71 at pp. 156–60.

skeptical Socrates than we have in Plato himself.[11] In any case, there remains the independent question of whether Plato's Socrates, taken in isolation from other portions of the doxography, actually manifests the skeptical qualities Arcesilaus is claimed to have attributed to him. I will focus on two related questions. First, we must ask whether the Socrates of Plato's early dialogues practices a brand of Arcesilaun skepticism. Then, if, as I will argue, he does not, we have a further question: is Arcesilaus to be convicted on the charge of misrepresentation his contemporaries leveled against him? I will argue that the complexity of this second question precludes any simple answer.[12] On the account I will offer, Socratic skepticism is far more limited in its goals and results than Arcesilaun skepticism. We accordingly cannot regard Arcesilaus in any straightforward sense as taking up the mantle of Socratic dialectic. Still, this observation falls short of any charge of misrepresentation. Although Socratic dialectic does not license the trenchant form of skepticism Arcesilaus practices, it does not follow that Arcesilaus has simply misunderstood or misconstrued the character of that dialectic. Rather, he selectively focuses on certain strands in Socratic practice and develops them in the interscholastic dialectical context of his own day. I therefore disagree with Vlastos' insistence that we will never know how Arcesilaus could associate his adherence to *epochē* with Socrates. Although agreeing with him that Socrates never practices Arcesilaun skepticism—or anything approaching it—I nevertheless believe there is a wholly plausible account of how Arcesilaus could legitimately view his own methodology as developing from Socratic dialectic. My

[11]Some evidence for this conclusion can be found in J. Glucker, *Antiochus and the Late Academy,* Hypomnemata 56 (Göttingen, 1978), pp. 31–64. In what follows I am indebted to Glucker's study and to H.-J. Krämer, *Platonismus und hellenistische Philosophie* (Berlin, 1971). Krämer endeavors to establish that Arcesilaus derives much of his dialectical method from late Plato and the early Academy. This is surely closer to the mark than A. Weische's argument that Arcesilaus derived his skepticism and skeptical methodology from the Peripatetic school as it flourished under Theophrastus (*Cicero und die Neue Akademie* [Münster, 1961]), but since I will be concerned principally with the Socrates of the early Platonic dialogues, I will not undertake to discuss this view. As will become evident, I am most sympathetic with P. Couissin's contention that Arcesilaus' skepticism develops primarily with an eye toward refuting Zeno's Stoic dogmatism ("Le Stoïcisme de la nouvelle Académie," *Revue d'histoire de la philosophie* 3 [1929]: 241–76). I will disagree, however, with Couissin's claim that Arcesilaus argues wholly ad hominem, where this entails his not holding any of the theses he employs in his ad hominem arguments. In my view, he argues ad hominem while advancing the substantive skeptical theses he endorses. See section 3 below.

[12]For this reason M. Frede's contention that "Arcesilaus and his followers thought of themselves as just following Socratic practice" presents an unduly simple picture of the situation ("The Sceptic's Two Kinds of Assent and the Question of the Possibility of Knowledge," in *Essays in Ancient Philosophy* [Minneapolis, 1987], p. 204; the essay appeared originally in *Philosophy in History,* ed. R. Rorty et al. [Cambridge, 1984]; all page references are to the 1987 reprint). I discuss Frede's views in greater detail below in section 3.

answer to the second question will, therefore, be twofold: if Arcesilaus regards Socrates' elenctic procedure in Plato's early dialogues as fully skeptical, then he misunderstands or misconstrues that practice; yet by extending certain Socratic practices, and by situating them in a theoretical context that must be regarded as more self-consciously skeptical in its aims than the context we have recounted in Plato's early dialogues, Arcesilaus can without shame claim to be an heir of Socrates.

My principal argument for distinguishing Socratic dialectic and Arcesilaun skepticism turns on the generality of the premises required for motivating the form of skepticism practiced in the Academy under Arcesilaus: Socratic dialectic never employs or presupposes the general, modal premises necessary for generating a nearly universal commitment to *epochē* of the sort, I will argue, Arcesilaus urges. Hence Arcesilaus could not be justified in claiming to find an exponent of his practice in Socrates. Even so, Arcesilaus is no less justified than his Stoic opponents in claiming Socratic parentage.

1. Two Pictures of Arcesilaus the Skeptic

Possibly reacting to the codifying tendencies of Speusippus and Xenocrates, as well as to the Stoic dogmatizing of Zeno, Arcesilaus ushered in a new—or from his perspective renewed—age of skepticism as head of the Academy.[13] In particular, Arcesilaus fastened upon a pair of principles that came to be more or less definitive of the so-called New Academy. When Varro calls for an explanation and defense of Arcesilaus' "innovations" in the Academy,[14] Cicero complies, but only after noting that the doctrines are not new but really quite old:

> cum Zenone . . . ut accepimus Arcesilas sibi omne certamen instituit, non pertinacia aut studio vincendi ut quidem mihi videtur, sed earum rerum obscuritate quae ad confessionem ignorationis adduxerant Socratem, et iam ante Socratem Democritum Anaxagoram Empedoclem omnes paene

---

[13]It is unlikely that Numenius could be right in passing Arcesilas off as a Pyrrhonist in an Academician's clothing. To be sure, his views on the suspension of judgment approach Pyrrho's; but Numenius is clearly a hostile source with a transparent agenda of his own.

[14]Varro says: "tuae sunt nunc partes . . . qui ab antiquorum ratione desciscis et ea quae ab Arcesila novata sunt probas, docere quod et qua de causa discidium factum sit, ut videamus satisne ista sit iusta defectio" ("It now falls to you, who have turned away from the thinking of the ancients and who approve of the innovations of Arcesilaus, to recount what the schism was and why it occurred, so that we may judge whether your desertion is sufficiently justified," *Acad.* 1.43).

veteres, qui nihil cognosci nihil percipi nihil sciri posse dixerunt, angustos sensus, imbecillos animos, brevia curricula vitae, et (ut Democritus) in profundo veritatem esse demersam, opinionibus et institutis omnia teneri, nihil veritati relinqui, deinceps omnia tenebris circumfusa esse dixerunt. itaque Arcesilas negabat esse quicquam quod sciri posset, ne illud quidem ipsum quod Socrates sibi reliquisset, ut nihil scire se sciret; sic omnia latere censebat in occulto, neque esse quicquam quod cerni aut intellegi posset. quibus de causis nihil oportere neque profiteri neque affirmare quemquam neque assensione approbare, cohibereque semper et ab omni lapsu continere temeritatem, quae tum esset insignis cum aut falsa aut incognita res approbaretur, neque hoc quicquam esse turpius quam cognitioni et perceptioni assensionem approbationemque praecurrere.

As we have heard, Arcesilaus began his entire struggle with Zeno not out of obstinacy or desire for victory, as it seems to me at any rate, but because of the obscurity of the things that had brought Socrates to an admission of ignorance, and before him already, Democritus, Anaxagoras, Empedocles, and almost all the ancients, who said that nothing could be grasped or cognized or known, because, they said, the senses are limited, the mind feeble, the course of life short, and because (as Democritus says) truth has been submerged in an abyss, with everything in the grip of opinions and conventions, nothing left for truth and everything in turn surrounded by darkness. So Arcesilaus denied that anything could be known, not even the one thing Socrates had retained for himself—the knowledge that he knew nothing. Such was the extent of the obscurity in which everything lurked, on his assessment, and there was nothing that could be discerned or understood. For these reasons, he said, no one should maintain or assert anything or give it the acceptance of assent, but should always curb his rashness to accept something false or undiscerned, and nothing was more reprehensible than for assent and acceptance to run ahead of cognition and grasp. (*Acad.* 1.43–4)

Of the two central principles Cicero attributes to Arcesilaus, the first is clearly the most fundamental. It is the principal ground for skepticism in the New Academy and involves the claim that nothing is discerned or reliably ascertained (*incognita*):[15]

(U) Everything is undiscerned.

The second is a principle of suspension:

(E) All judgment should be suspended (everyone should strive for *epochē*).

[15]The rendering of *incognita* is rather difficult. J. Reid provides some useful remarks in *The Academica of Cicero* (London, 1885), p. 189 n. 21.

As stated, (E) is straightforwardly a normative principle; and Arcesilaus evidently presumes that (U) underwrites its normative force. Thus (U) and (E) are related, both ultimately resting on whatever reasons Arcesilaus has for advancing (U).

Before investigating the grounds of (U), however, it is necessary to appreciate that in attributing these theses to Arcesilaus, Cicero is at odds with a second interpretive tradition, one that undercuts his view by denying that Arcesilaus subscribed to any positive doctrines whatsoever; and if he holds to no positive doctrines whatsoever, he hardly adheres to (E) and (U). Cicero's view has not gained widespread approval: the preponderance of contemporary interpretation favors a view recorded in the *Index Academicorum* according to which "he asserted nothing but only refuted the other schools" (*Ind. Ac.* 20.2–4). On this account, Arcesilaus is at root a thoroughgoing dialectician: he has no positive doctrines of his own but orchestrates the premises of others so as to display their absurd consequences. As Numenius reports,

Τὸν δ' οὖν Ζήνωνα ὁ Ἀρκεσίλαος ἀντίτεχνον καὶ ἀξιόνικον ὑπάρχοντα θεωρῶν τούς παρ' ἐκείνου ἀποφερομένους λόγους καθῄρει καί οὐδὲν ὤκνει.... τὸ δὲ δόγμα τοῦτο αὐτοῦ πρώτου εὐρομένου καὐτὸ καὶ τὸ ὄνομα βλέπων εὐδοκιμοῦν ἐν ταῖς Ἀθήναις, τὴν καταληπτικὴν φαντασίαν, πάσῃ μηχανῇ ἐχρῆτο ἐπ' αὐτήν.

Arcesilaus, seeing that Zeno was his rival and that he was capable of overcoming him, set himself straightaway to demolish the arguments that he brought up.... Seeing that both the doctrine of the cataleptic *phantasia* and its name, which Zeno had been the first to discover, were highly regarded in Athens, Arcesilaus employed every means to assail it. (*ap.* Euseb. *Praep. evang.* 14. 6. 12–13)

Numenius adopts an arch attitude toward Arcesilaus and dismisses him as a mere sophistical gamesman (see esp. Euseb. *Praep. evang.* 14. 6. 2). He is therefore inclined to dismiss any positive contribution he might have made; Numenius, in fact, prefers to represent him as a clever but parasitic confounder of others (cf. D. L. 4. 37, 47).

On this approach, Arcesilaus is mute about his own beliefs: he does not for his own part advocate even *epochē*. Rather, he points out to the Stoic dogmatizers that in their own terms—namely, by embracing the very premises they profess to embrace—they should practice *epochē*. Since the Stoic sage will refuse to assent to anything uncertain, and since, despite the Stoics' confident commitment to the cataleptic *phantasia*, nothing is certain, the sage will necessarily assent to nothing. Thus if Arcesilaus can show not only that no *phantasia* is grasped cataleptically but also that the Stoic sage is bound to agree in virtue of other commitments he has made, then he will have to concede (E) and will necessarily suspend all judgment.

If Arcesilaus is this sort of dialectician, he might or might not himself accept (E). He could, as far as our sources go, accept the very argument he urges on the Stoics, that is, that nothing is certain, and that if nothing is certain, judgment should be suspended. Or it may be the case that he himself rejects (E), that he thinks that although the Stoics must accept (E), given their epistemology, none of his own commitments have this consequence.[16] He could do this in either of two ways: he could himself deny the claim that nothing is certain; or he could more indirectly allow that nothing is certain, but deny the alleged connection between uncertainty and suspension. (As we have seen, [E] is after all a normative principle, and one whose credentials remain obscure.) In either case, it will be possible for Arcesilaus himself to be a dogmatist: it is consistent with the dialectical interpretation that Arcesilaus himself accept some principles as certain, without accepting the normative arguments that, by his lights at any rate, the Stoics must accept. Thus he may be a dogmatist who is not susceptible to the skeptical arguments he wields against his fellow dogmatists.

On the other hand, Arcesilaus might regard his dialectical argument as cutting both ways, so that he endorses the *epochē* he urges on the Stoics. Hence there seem to be four possible characterizations of Arcesilaus, dividing along the question of whether he himself endorses (E). If he endorses (E), he may do so (1) for the very reasons he offers the Stoics, or (2) for reasons altogether independent of those reasons. If he refrains from endorsing (E), this may be due to his (3) in principle endorsing nothing, or (4) his endorsing nothing that commends (E) to him. According to this last alternative, Arcesilaus may himself be a complete dogmatist, and one whose dogmatism is superior to the Stoic variety. Of course, no one ascribes (4) to Arcesilaus; but the reluctance we have seen in this regard should not incline us to attribute (3) to him, so that he is what we may call a *mere* dialectician, a dialectician who never advocates any position but merely demonstrates how the dogmatism of others undermines itself; for Arcesilaus could equally be a *committed* dialectician, who endorses (E) for general reasons, including perhaps those reasons he thinks should move the Stoics to accept it.

It is worth remembering that if we do not regard Arcesilaus as in some sense endorsing or accepting (E), nothing precludes his being a dogmatist. I say this because scholars too often assume that since Arcesilaus cannot himself accept (E), he must therefore be a mere di-

---

[16]I owe this point to R. J. Hankinson.

alectical catalyst operating on Stoic inferential processes. Two considerations undermine this approach. First, it is unclear why Arcesilaus cannot accept (E); second, even if he does accept (E), it does not follow that he does so because he holds to no opinions whatsoever: he may accept (E) for the simple reason that it follows from other positions he endorses. Hence, although no evidence supports (4), we should not reject this interpretation on the grounds that Arcesilaus could be a critic of the Stoics only by being himself agnostic. This will be a point of some significance when we come to assess the ways in which Arcesilaus is and is not Socratic.

In short, if Arcesilaus is not a closet dogmatist, he may be either a committed or a mere dialectician. He may himself reject (E), reject Stoic positions he sees as leading to (E), and may indeed refrain from endorsing any proposition whatsoever. Conversely, he may be a committed dialectician who accepts arguments leading to (E), perhaps the very arguments he thinks the Stoics must accept.

This is a point worth reviewing, since there is ample reason for supposing that Arcesilaus is not a mere dialectician: the dominant ancient doxography represents him as advocating *epochē*, and therefore as endorsing (E). In addition to the passage from Cicero's *Academica* already quoted, we have several from Diogenes Laertius:

> Arcesilaus founded the Middle Academy. And he was the first to hold his assertions in check; he did so because of the contrariety of arguments. (4.28)

Similarly:

> He never wrote a book, because of his suspension of judgment about everything. (4.32)

Sextus represents him much the same way. He regards him as virtually a fellow Pyrrhonist, on the grounds that

> he is never found asserting anything concerning whether anything obtains or not, nor does he privilege anything over anything else in terms of credibility or otherwise but suspends judgment about everything. He also holds that the end is *epochē*, which is accompanied as we have said, by ἀταραξία. (*Pyr.* 1.232)

Finally, Plutarch says, quite simply:

> These [the Academics in Arcesilaus' circle] were the ones to suspend judgment about everything. (*Adv. Col.* 1120c)

These sources uniformly read him as advocating *epochē*, and so as endorsing (E), and not merely as prodding the Stoics to do so. Indeed, no mention is made in these contexts of his being a narrowly focused anti-Stoic antagonist. Consequently, we should presume he endorsed (E) unless some overriding reason prohibits our doing so.

The principal reason adduced to override this presumption seems to be a worry about pragmatic inconsistency: does not (E), if true, commend skepticism about (E)? Should not, then, the defender of (E) suspend judgment about (E)? If so, no one moved by (E)-like considerations should judge (E) to be true; and no one not moved by (E)-like considerations will want to judge that (E) is true. Hence no one should judge that (E) is true.

Although as the skeptical Academy developed under Carneades a number of ingenious strategies responding to this line of argument came to be employed, no source attests a response owing directly to Arcesilaus himself.[17] Even so, Michael Frede attempts to develop a strategy available to Arcesilaus for meeting this form of argumentation. He is right to do so, in my view, since there is absolutely no reason Arcesilaus must be read as a mere dialectician in the face of this argument. But this is not Frede's motivation: he thinks Arcesilaus is a mere dialectician,[18] and wonders how it is possible for him to urge the Stoics to endorse *epochē*. To encourage the Stoics to advocate *epochē* seems already to endorse the principle *that* epochē *should be endorsed by the Stoics.* And this seems precluded by (E). Hence Frede needs to show how the dialectical Arcesilaus can engage in even this kind of interchange.

Frede's strategy for reconciling a commitment to (E) with any form of adherence to (E) or any kind of recommendation that (E) be endorsed comes up short in several crucial respects, and in respects illuminating for our appreciation of how Arcesilaus was and was not Socratic. Noticing that Sextus and others distinguish two types of assent (*Pyr.* 1.13; cf. 2.26, 104; 3.6, 13, 29, 81, 135, 167), Frede suggests that there is a "purely passive" form of assent,[19] unlike the form of assent precluded by (E). Thus Arcesilaus may assent to (E), in the purely passive way, without properly endorsing (E), or assenting to (E) in a way that would involve him in making the judgment that (E) is true. Since (E) pre-

---

[17]See P. A. Vander Waerdt, "Colotes and the Epicurean Refutation of Skepticism," *GRBS* 30 (1989): 225–69 at pp. 228–44, 245 n. 54, and 253–66.

[18]Frede (above, note 12), p. 204, claims: "Arcesilaus and his followers thought of themselves as just following Socratic practice. . . . In fact . . . they went one step further: they not only did not want to be committed to the truth of the premises and the conclusion of their arguments, they also did not want to be committed to the validity of their arguments."

[19]Frede (above, note 12), p. 208.

cludes only this form of assent, there is no inconsistency on Arcesilaus' part; he may be a mere dialectician and still urge (E) upon the Stoics.

Since there is no evidence that Arcesilaus ever took up this strategy, and since there is no evidence that "Arcesilaus and this followers . . . did not want to be committed to the validity of their arguments,"[20] Frede's point must just be that this would have been a coherent position for them to adopt. If it is coherent, then we can at least recognize as a possibility that Arcesilaus is a mere dialectician who never himself assents to (E). But is this a coherent point of view?

Frede initially likens purely passive assent to the sort of assent one would give to a tyrant merely by failing actively to oppose him. If a tyrant comes onto the scene and issues the decree that all inhabitants must pay a certain tribute, then I may pay that tribute without ever assenting to the proposition that the tribute should be paid. This is not, however, a terribly apt metaphor: I may not agree that the tyrant is entitled to the payment, and I may not be pleased that the world is such that some hypothetical necessity compels me to render payment, but at some point I endorse the hypothetical proposition "If thus and such (e.g., if I am to remain alive), I must render payment." It is precisely because I believe the truth of the conditional and desire the state of affairs specified in its antecedent that I render payment. On the other hand, if Frede means only that my acts may *conform* to the rules of a tyrant without my being aware of those rules, then it is hardly appropriate to regard me as having assented to them, however "passively." If a man in a New York subway decrees to no one in particular: "Henceforth, every person in America will tie his left shoe before his right each time he puts on a pair of shoes," and a woman in Montana in fact proceeds in just this way each morning, then her actions conform to his decree without her ever having assented to it.

The problem with a notion of purely passive assent is, of course, that assent seems a mental *action*. If I conform without such a mental action, I do not assent; if I perform a mental action of any sort, then I am not purely passive in my assent. Perhaps for reasons of this sort Frede proceeds to explicate the notion of noncommittal assent in a distinct, nonequivalent way. He rightly wonders how somebody "could be said to have the view that *p* without thinking that it is the case that *p* or that it is true that *p*."[21] One would have thought it analytic that if S has the view that *p*, then S thinks it is the case that *p* and thinks that *p* is true. After all, it would be a strange person who would say: "In my view it is raining outside," but, when asked whether it is the case that it is raining

[20] Frede (above, note 12), p. 208.
[21] Frede (above, note 12), p. 208.

outside or whether in her view it is true that it is raining outside, went on to insist: "Well, wait a minute, I certainly don't want to commit myself to any of *that*."[22] This would be to say: "In my view it is raining, but I don't think it is the case that it is raining," or "Yes, in my view it is raining, but I don't think it's true that it is raining." This hardly seems to be of any service to Arcesilaus.

Frede suggests a way of trying to deal with this problem. He points out that it is entirely possible for someone to have the view that *p* without ever, as a separate mental act, assenting to the proposition that *p is true* or to the proposition *that p is the case*.[23] This might happen in either of two ways: one's "acquiescence in the impression" might be sufficient for action without one's ever entertaining the proposition *that p is true;* or one might never even entertain *p* at all, as when a carpenter completes a project working with oak without at any time in the course of the project entertaining the notion that oak needs thus and such tending. Still, it will be fair to say that the proposition governed the carpenter's action, even though there is no point at which the carpenter so much as entertained it. Without entertaining it, the carpenter *had the view* without *assenting* to it.

As for the first case, it is of course true that one can assent to a given proposition *p* without ever, as a separate mental act, stopping to assent to the proposition *that p is true*. Yet this would be a curious place for a skeptic to rest her case. After all, I can be a complete, unrepentant dogmatist by defending such propositions as

1. the Principle of the Excluded Middle,
2. that universals exist,
3. that I have complete apodeictic certainty of my own existence,
4. that a good person lives in conformity with nature,
5. that happiness consists in the realization of one's fully human capacities,

and many more like them, without ever, as separate mental acts, stopping to defend the propositions *that (1) is true, that (2) is true,* and so forth. If assent in every case required this further act, then hardly anyone would fail to be a skeptic. Therefore, if Frede's first case proves anything, it proves much more than he can want.

---

[22]Of course, a philosopher might want to deny that truth is a predicate, and so to hold that strictly and literally it is never the case that *p is true*. But all that is required here is what S. Schiffer calls the pleonastic sense of truth, where this carries no ontological commitments whatsoever (*Remnants of Meaning* [Cambridge, Mass., 1987], pp. 139–78 and 211–64).

[23]Frede (above, note 12), p. 208.

Frede's second case suffers a similar defect. Of course I can act on some belief I have never entertained. As Frede points out, dispositional craft knowledge seems an especially good case of just this phenomenon. A carpenter, one would expect, could articulate, with some degree of confidence, the principles that guide her work even if she does not always call them forth to consciousness while working, and even if, as Frede claims, it would be positively disruptive for her to do so. Do we say, then, that while working she "passively" assented to them without the sort of assent required for full-blown nonskeptical assent? Once again, if the carpenter merely conforms to the principle by accident, she has not assented; but if she, upon reflection, can articulate and acknowledge the principle, then her assent has been unconscious but not therefore passive. If rich assent requires conscious assent, then we assent to precious little.

This becomes most clear when we focus on the proposition in question, namely, (E). The skeptic may have been governed in his actions by (E) even though he never explicitly called (E) forth to consciousness for assent. (It must be said, however, that it is a little difficult to determine what actions [E] may govern—beyond the acts of trying to enjoin one's opponents to subscribe to [E].) Does this show that the skeptic has assented only passively in the proposed way? It does not seem so. If I offer you arguments requiring the truth of modus ponens even though I have never heard of modus ponens (and most people who use it have not) and so have never consciously assented to it as such, my argument's employment of the principle entails that I endorse it. Otherwise, I could not offer you the arguments I offer you. Either my action-governing endorsement of (E) carries a commitment to (E), in which case I have all the assent that it is needed for dogmatism, or (E) is idle as a principle structuring my action. I may have accidentally conformed to (E) thus far; but, as we have seen, conformity alone is not sufficient for assent of any kind. Hence Frede's second account of "passive assent" fails. Consequently, he has not provided Arcesilaus any way of being a mere dialectician. He therefore provides no coherent explanation of how Arcesilaus can enjoin the Stoics to endorse (E) without himself assenting to some principle or other, if only *that the Stoics, given their own views, should assent to (E).*

Like Frede, I think Arcesilaus must respond to the following argument: he must either assent to some principle or other, or refrain from claiming that the Stoics must accept (E). Unlike Frede, I do not make the historical claim that Arcesilaus took up the strategy I will offer him: there is simply no evidence concerning how Arcesilaus responded or would have responded to this argument. Still, we can see that Arcesilaus can respond to this argument, and so we will not be entitled to claim, as some have claimed, that he *must* be some form of mere dialectician who proceeds by distinguishing between types of assent. If he can consistently endorse (E), we may agree with the dominant ancient doxography that represents him as doing just that.

There is certainly nothing inconsistent in Arcesilaus' endorsing (E), as long as we allow that (E) ranges over first-order judgments, while it is itself a second-order judgment whose objects are all first-order judgments. If (E) is a regulative principle that directs withholding assent for all nonregulative principles, there is nothing self-defeating or pragmatically inconsistent about it at all. Arcesilaus can in principle, then, endorse (E) without violating its purport. Consequently, it would be an error to regard him—on logical grounds—as precluded from endorsing (E). Hence one may enquire into his grounds for accepting (E).

But something stronger can be said. If we grant that Arcesilaus can be a committed dialectician, noting that he can accept (E) without contradicting the dictates of (E), and so without immediately refuting his own skeptical position, we allow that no point of logic decides the issue. But when we reflect on his own practice, we see that he seems to have recognized some such point: insofar as he urges the Stoics to accept (E), he must, unless he is the rank gamesman Numenius accuses him of being, regard it as possible to endorse (E) without self-contradiction; and he must think it is possible to come to realize (E) on the basis of argumentation, since this is precisely what he offers the Stoics. After all, if he does not think it is possible to advocate (E), then in encouraging the Stoics to embrace (E), Arcesilaus must intend to induce the Stoics to endorse a proposition he recognizes as self-contradictory. If this is his tack, Numenius will be right to accuse him of a particularly shabby form of intellectual chicanery. But there is no reason to believe that this is his tack, and so no reason to read him in this light. His proddings of the Stoics could as easily have been applied to himself, and he could as easily have adopted the practice of a committed dialectician. If I am right about this, and Arcesilaus turns out to be a committed rather than a mere dialectician, he will emerge as practicing a type of thoroughgoing skepticism in which it is impossible to implicate Socrates.[24]

What basis could he have for being a committed dialectician? As we saw, Cicero clearly represents (E) as an inferred principle, one that should follow directly from the straightforwardly epistemological thesis (U), that everything is undiscerned. The root of Arcesilaus' skepticism must, consequently, be sought in (U).

[24]For a fuller argument for the conclusion that Arcesilaus is what I am calling a committed dialectician, see A. Ioppolo, *Opinione e scienze: Il dibattito tra Stoici e Accademici nel III e nel II secolo a.C.* (Naples, 1986). See also A. J. Hankinson, "Arcesilaus," in *The Arguments of the Sceptics* (London, forthcoming). My understanding of Arcesilaus' skepticism is indebted to Hankinson's excellent discussion.

The grounds for (U), however, emerge only by reference to Arcesilaus' anti-Stoicism. It will, accordingly, be possible to determine the degree of Arcesilaus' skepticism more exactly only by looking to the dialectical context in which it developed. This context is provided by Zeno's attempts to formulate a criterion for a cataleptic *phantasia*. Diogenes reports the Stoic position as follows:

τῆς δὲ φαντασίας τὴν μὲν καταληπτικήν, τὴν, δὲ ἀκατάληπτον· καταληπτικὴν μέν, ἣν κριτήριον εἶναι τῶν πραγμάτων φασίν, τὴν γινομένην ἀπὸ ὑπάρχοντος κατ' αὐτὸ τὸ ὑπάρχον ἐναπεσφραγισμένην καὶ ἐναπομεμαγμένην· ἀκατάληπτον δὲ ἢ τὴν μὴ ἀπὸ ὑπάρχοντος, ἢ ἀπὸ ὑπάρχοντος μέν, μὴ κατ' αὐτὸ δὲ τὸ ὑπάρχον· τὴν μὴ τρανῆ μηδὲ ἔκτυπον.

Among *phantasiai*, one is cataleptic, the other noncataleptic. The cataleptic, which they say is the criterion of things, is that which comes from something existent and is in accordance with the existing thing itself, having been stamped and imprinted; the noncataleptic either comes from something nonexistent or if from something existent, then not in accordance with the existent thing; and it is neither clear nor distinct. (7.46)

This report suggests the following definition:

p is a cataleptic *phantasia* iff: (1) *p* is produced from an existent object; (2) *p* is in accordance with the object that produces it; (3) *p* is imprinted by the object with which it is in accordance; and (4) *p* is clear and distinct.

Each of these conditions builds on the previous one. (1) is the most straightforward: if *p* is not produced by something that exists, then one cannot grasp it cataleptically; since cataleptic *phantasiai* should guarantee accuracy, no *phantasia* of a hallucination could be cataleptic. But this is clearly not sufficient: (2) makes clear that a distorted *phantasia* of an existing object cannot be cataleptic. That Orestes has a *phantasia* caused by Electra is not sufficient. If Orestes perceives Electra to be one of the Furies, then his *phantasia* cannot be cataleptic. Although this should clearly be ruled out, it is less clear what should be ruled *in* by the phrase "in accordance with" [κατά]. Commentators universally treat this as a form of representation, although there is ample reason to doubt that this can be the entire story within the Chrysippean and post-Chrysippean Stoic semantic theory.[25] Even so, as a simplifying assumption for the present discussion, we can interpret (2) as holding minimally that a *phantasia* can be cataleptic only if it is broadly isomorphic with some existent object. And as (3) brings out, even this cannot be sufficient. If Electra causes an impression of Chrysothemis in Orestes,

[25]See my "Truth Evaluability of Stoic *Phantasiai*," *JHP* 31 (1993): 1–22.

then Orestes will not have grasped it cataleptically. A *phantasia* is cataleptic only if it is caused *by* the existent object of which it is a *phantasia*. There is a further question about whether the *phantasia* must be caused *in the right way* or *along a nondeviant path*.[26] But in any case, the existent object with which the *phantasia* is broadly isomorphic must minimally be directly causally responsible for its having been imprinted.

Diogenes indirectly provides a fourth condition, one echoed in Sextus (*Math.* 7.257). In differentiating noncataleptic from cataleptic *phantasiai*, Diogenes notes the former are not clear and distinct. The purport would seem to be (although there is no entailment here) that cataleptic *phantasiai are* clear and distinct. If so, the conditions are significantly more exclusive than sometimes thought. Clause 4 states a psychological criterion, and one that will provide additional ammunition to Arcesilaus: beyond having a *phantasia* isomorphic with and caused in the right way by some existent object, the sage must be in a position to notice some manifestation of the epistemological primary afforded by all and only cataleptic *phantasiai*. This psychological criterion is therefore evidently not reducible to any of the previous three. Presumably a nonsage could have a *phantasia* meeting conditions 1, 2, and 3 without grasping it cataleptically. Consequently, a given perceiver may be able to have a *phantasia* that meets the intrinsic conditions for being cataleptic without having the right doxastic system for appreciating it, perhaps because the perceiver in question lacks the right sorts of second-order beliefs about that *phantasia*, namely, that it is clear and distinct.[27]

If this is correct, the Stoics may be quite circumspect both about the intrinsic nature of cataleptic *phantasiai* and about the sorts of perceivers capable of recognizing them to be such.[28] This would make Arcesi-

---

[26]It is unclear what the Stoics will say about deviant causal chains resulting in *phantasiai* that are broadly isomorphic with the existent entities ultimately responsible for them. There are two sorts of cases here: (1) Odysseus' visage may be distorted by abnormal perceptual conditions and then be accidentally reassembled by a defect in Eumaios' sense faculty; or (2) Odysseus may disguise himself as a beggar and then be misperceived by Eumaios (again because of a defect in his perceptual apparatus) as Odysseus. Clause 3 of the definition may or may not be intended to rule out such cases.

[27]Sextus (*Math.* 7.252) further supports the contention that a *phantasia*'s being cataleptic is at least partly a function of the perceiver: there Sextus likens the sage to a craftsman: "He who has a cataleptic impression fastens on the objective difference of things with the skill of a craftsman, since an impression of this kind has a special characteristic of its own compared with other impressions." Hence although there clearly are intrinsic differences between cataleptic and noncataleptic *phantasiai*, only a skilled perceiver may be in a position to notice the difference.

[28]Sextus *Math.* 7.257 is most naturally read as suggesting that cataleptic *phantasia* present themselves as such and can hardly be ignored; even so, he may mean only to the sage, in which case the point about the systemic psychological condition obtains.

laus' skeptical chores in some ways easier, but also in some ways more difficult. On the one hand, it will be relatively easy for Arcesilaus to claim that no one could meet such stringent requirements; but it will be more difficult for him to provide counterexamples of someone's meeting the criteria without having certain knowledge. That is, he may accept the Stoic definition of cataleptic *phantasiai* as apt and concede that someone capable of having such *phantasiai* would be in a secure epistemological position, only to point out that no human could be in such a godlike position. Thus, although the doxography here is somewhat indeterminate, one may conjecture that the Arcesilaun strategy was two-pronged: after having first cooked up counterexamples to the Stoics' initial definitions, Arcesilaus then pointed out that the revised definition was so demanding that no human could satisfy its conditions. Evidently for this sort of reason, Sextus' *Against The Professors* 7.252 has "They added 'of such a type as could not come from something nonexistent' because the Academics did not suppose, as the Stoics did, that an impression could be found in all respects similar to it." If we take this emendation, we may add a fifth clause to our definition of cataleptic *phantasiai:* (5) it is of such a type that could not have come from something nonexistent. As R. J. Hankinson observes in a forthcoming article, this clause "has an uncomfortable air of trivial stipulation about it." It has, moreover, the effect of rendering the definition unsatisfiable, since (5) requires, together with (4), that a perceiver be in a position to surmise from a *phantasia*'s intrinsic features that it could not possibly have come from a nonexistent object. Arcesilaus can press this point to his advantage and, simultaneously, to the Stoic's dialectical disadvantage by in effect forcing them to concede that because cataleptic *phantasiai* are so hard to come by, even the sage cannot grasp them. And if the sage cannot grasp them, he must, by the Stoics' own account, suspend judgment.

Many of the skeptical arguments Cicero recounts seem to adopt just this strategy. For example:

> quaesivit de Zenone fortasse quid futurum esset si nec percipere quicquam posset sapiens nec opinari sapientis esset. ille credo nihil opinaturum, quoniam esset quod percipi posset. quid ergo id esset? visum credo. quale igitur visum? tum illum ita definisse: ex eo quod esset sicut esset inpressum et signatum et effictum. post requisitum etiamne si eius modi esset visum verum quale vel falsum. hic Zenonem vidisse acute nullum esse visum quod percipi posset, si id tale esset ab eo quod est cuius modi ab eo quod non est posset esse. recte consensit Aresilas ad definitionem additum, neque enim falsum percipi posse neque verum si esset tale quale vel falsum; incubuit autem in eas disputationes ut doceret nullum tale esse visum a vero ut non eisudem modi etiam a falso possit esse.

[Arcesilaus]might have asked of Zeno what would happen if the sage could not apprehend anything, and if it also belonged to the sage not to form opinions. Zeno, I believe, would reply that he would not form opinions because he could apprehend anything [any impression]. . . . What would it be [that he would apprehend]? An impression, I believe, that was impressed, sealed, and reproduced from something that is just as it is. Arcesilaus then asked if this held even if there were a true impression of exactly the same form as a false one. Here Zeno was acute enough to see that if an impression proceeding from something that was such that there could be an impression of something that was not of exactly the same form, then there was no impression that could be apprehended. Arcesilaus agreed that this addition to the definition was justified, since one could not apprehend an impression if a true one were such as a false one could be. He argued forcefully, however, in order to show that no impression coming from what is was such that no impression coming from what is not could not be of the same form. (*Acad.* 2.77–78)

If "no impression coming from what is was such that no impression coming from what was not could not be of the same form," then no sage would ever be in a position to discriminate between cataleptic and noncataleptic *phantasiai* in virtue of their intrinsic marks. Thus the argument runs:[29]

1. A *phantasia* is cataleptic only if it meets clauses 1–5.
2. It is impossible for anything to satisfy clauses 1–5.
3. Therefore, cataleptic *phantasiai* are impossible.
4. The sage assents only to cataleptic *phantasiai*.
5. Therefore, it is impossible for the sage to assent to anything.
6. Necessarily, if one assents to nothing, one suspends judgment.
7. Therefore, "it will follow even according to the Stoics that the sage will suspend judgment" (*Math.* 7.155).

Taking (6) here as analytic, if the Stoics assert (4) and concede (1), the only room for dispute concerns (2).

The argument for (2) is precisely the argument for (U), the principle that everything is undiscerned, and it is just this argument Arcesilaus seems to regard as Socratically inspired. According to Cicero (*Acad.* 1.43–46, 2.66–67), then, Arcesilaus has really two distinct Socratic postures: he views himself as engaging in Socratic dialectic, and he accepts Socratic avowals of ignorance as evidence for a Socratic commitment to (U). Do Socratic avowals contain any such generic point?

---

[29]Cf. *Acad.* 2.66–67: " 'If the sage ever assents to anything, he will sometimes also opine; but he will never opine, therefore he will never assent to anything.' Arcesilaus used to accept this argument, for he endorsed both the leading and the additional premise."

This much seems clear: Socrates certainly practiced a form of dialectic and elenctic refutation, and he certainly seeks to highlight his own epistemic inadequacies. But it is not yet clear whether Arcesilaus' form of elenctic refutation is appropriately regarded as Socratic; and it is even less clear whether Socrates' professions of ignorance in any way approach the positive form of skepticism Arcesilaus practices, in either motivation or consequence.

2. Socrates' Skeptical Demeanor: The Case for Arcesilaus

Socrates reports bewilderment upon learning from Chaerephon of the oracle at Delphi's assessment of his wisdom:

> When I heard of this reply I asked myself: Whatever does the god mean? What is his riddle? I am very conscious that I am not wise at all; what then does he mean by saying that I am the wisest? For surely he does not lie; it is not legitimate for him to do so. (*Ap.* 21b)

Although the god had replied only that no one was wiser than Socrates, and consequently said nothing to entail that Socrates was himself at all wise, Socrates' response clearly suggests that he understood the god's message, at least rhetorically, as a mandate to prove his own intellectual inferiority. For him, the oracle's message was a command to enquire into the bases of his fellows' opinions, to learn from them where possible, and to expose their ignorance where necessary.

He reports a surprising lack of success (*Ap.* 21c–e). He continuously refutes his fellow citizens and cannot understand how this is possible. After all, he knows little or nothing, and so cannot justifiably regard himself as rivaling the wisest. Still, this hardly sounds like the self-portrait of a confirmed skeptic, one who approaches Arcesilaus' boundless zeal for refutation dedicated to imparting *epochē*. How, then, can Arcesilaus claim to be Socratic?

In a recent reevaluation of Socrates' and Plato's positions in the skeptical Academy, Julia Annas argues forcefully for a modified vindication of Arcesilaus' claims to Socratic lineage.[30] She points out, quite reasonably, that like Arcesilaus, Socrates is a searcher, but not one who ever claims to have found the truth; that although Socrates has some strongly held views (e.g., about the relationship between knowledge and virtue), he never asserts them as the dogmatic conclusions of philosophical arguments; and, most important, that Socrates confines him-

---

[30]Annas (above, note 8).

self to arguing against the ill-considered beliefs of others by engaging them elenctically in an effort to teach them how their premature convictions land them in difficulties, including incoherences of the worst kind. Although Annas does not press the point, one reasonable response to Socratic cross-examination is simply to admit one's ignorance, and to back off from belief, which for many interlocutors will approach a form of *epochē*.[31] From this perspective, Socrates' practice really does seem to foreshadow that of Arcesilaus. Consequently, the case Annas sketches merits a careful consideration.

Socrates is bound to seem dogmatic in comparison with, say, a fullblown skeptic of Carneades' ilk. Whatever else he holds, Socrates fairly clearly accepts some substantive theses—for example, that virtue is akin to a craft, and that only craftsmen (vs. mere practitioners) can provide accounts of what they do (*Ap.* 22b9–e1; *Grg.* 465a, 501a; *Cri.* 47c8–48a1; *Lach.* 184e11–185e6), that without knowledge one cannot be virtuous (*Ap.* 29d2–30a2; *Lach.* 193d11–e6)—and he evidently holds to some regulative or methodological principles as well—for instance, that knowledge of definitions is logically prior to knowledge of instances of the definition (*Euthphr.* 6e3–6, 4d9–5d1, 15d4–e1; *Lach.* 189e3–190b1, 190b7–c2; *Hi. ma.* 288a8–9; *Meno* 73c6–8).[32] He seems actively interested in debunking the views of others in favor of his own, and so to have more in common with the Stoic than the skeptic. In any case, Socrates hardly seems interested in the radical skepticism practiced in the skeptical Academy. For these reasons, the suggestion that he is the fountainhead of this sort of skeptical philosophy seems a flat nonstarter.

Annas responds, correctly I think, that Arcesilaus could certainly appeal to Socrates as equally σκεπτικός, as seeking and enquiring after the truth.[33] An ancient skeptic, or enquirer, wants to attain knowledge; he does not decide in advance that knowledge is impossible; he is, rather, ever attuned to the intractable difficulties that seem to crop up whenever we move toward epistemological closure. His goal is the goal of every philosopher: he seeks the truth. Unlike the dogmatist, however, he does not stop enquiring prematurely. He does not lazily fail to

---

[31] In fact, Socrates' interlocutors do not arrive at *epochē*. Some never realize they have been refuted, or at least never admit their ignorance (Laches, *Lach.* 194a8–b4; Nicias, *Lach.* 200b2–c1; Euthyphro, *Euthphr.* 15e3–4; Hippias, *Hi. mi.* 304a5–b4; Critias, *Chrm.* 169c3–d1); some admit ignorance, but the dialogue ends (Charmides, *Chrm.* 176a6–b1; Ion, *Ion* 541e–542b2); and some conversations are simply interrupted.

[32] On the so-called Socratic fallacy (the label originates with P. Geach, "Plato's *Euthyphro:* An Analysis and Commentary," *Monist* 50 [1966]), see now H. Benson, "The Priority of Definition and the Socratic Elenchus," *OSAP* 8 (1990): 19–65.

[33] She cites Cicero *Lucullus* 7, where Cicero claims on behalf of the Academy that the true skeptic never abandons the search for the truth.

trace the absurd consequences of the positions he has adopted. On the contrary, he is the true philosopher, ever seeking the truth, never resting comfortably on apparent truths. This is precisely Arcesilaus' disposition: he holds knowledge to be so difficult to attain that he criticized Socrates for holding that he knew only that he was ignorant (*Acad.* 1.45). Thus one cannot justifiably criticize Arcesilaus on the grounds that he, unlike Socrates, does not seek the truth.[34]

I say this is correct, but only as far as it goes. Arcesilaus could legitimately view himself as a Socratic fellow seeker; and he could legitimately point out that he, like Socrates, simply took it upon himself to point out the flaws inherent in the hastily drawn, complacent conclusions of the dogmatists. Even so, there seem to be two salient differences. First, even if we grant that both Arcesilaus and Socrates are truth seekers, their motivations for engaging in elenctic cross-examination are not in all ways the same. Socrates, by his own account, is on a divine mission to make sense of a perplexing oracle (*Ap.* 21b). He wants to know how no one could be wiser. Arcesilaus, by contrast, is motivated by a philosophical argument about the possibility of knowledge. He maintains (U) and infers (E); Socrates never endorses (U) and indeed never even suggests (E).

Moreover, we need to sort out their individual modal commitments. Arcesilaus has an argument, developed in response to Stoic dogmatizing, with the conclusion that cataleptic *phantasiai* are impossible. Socrates never endorses this modal conclusion. He, like Arcesilaus, continues to notice that dogmatists stop enquiring too soon; but he never offers a general argument to the effect that any cessation of enquiry is necessarily too soon. He reports that he is continually surprised by his discovery of the inadequacies of his interlocutors' positions. Arcesilaus has a theory driving his enquiry that makes this anything but surprising. That the dogmatists end up with philosophical difficulties is entirely predictable: they could not have done otherwise. Socrates' interlocutors should not have ceased enquiring—if they ever began to enquire in the first place—but as far as he is concerned, they certainly could have stopped and would have been entitled to stop if they had reached the appropriate conclusions. Socrates' skeptical credentials are accordingly considerably more modest than those of Arcesilaus.

There is a further problem. Annas worries that Socrates has strong moral convictions, and that he evidently argues to and from them in

---

[34] Annas (above, note 8), pp. 272–73: "The skeptic is thus distinguished from the dogmatist not by his aim (the search for truth) but by the fact that he is still searching, because he remains mindful of the difficulties. The dogmatist is simply someone who has given that up."

the Platonic dialogues. This would present a problem, since, on her interpretation, Arcesilaus is a pure skeptic who argues exclusively ad hominem. If Socrates, by contrast, argues in more than ad hominem ways, he will not qualify as an Arcesilaun skeptic. If Socrates accepts dogmatic theses and uses them to confound his interlocutors, he will be nothing more than a dogmatist setting out to refute his opponents, and therefore not a skeptic at all.

Socrates clearly argues ad hominem in some dialogues. The *Hippias minor* traces a convoluted argument forcing Hippias to conclude that the good person does wrong willingly. This cannot be Socrates' view; he thinks that a good person will never do wrong willingly. So the dialogue must be an exercise in refutation, implicitly leaving the reader the homework assignment of determining which belief or beliefs lead to such a ridiculous conclusion. Socrates does not share Hippias' beliefs and evidently has a covert appreciation of the problem in advance that positions him to orchestrate the sophist's thrashing.

Even so, examples of such extreme dialectic are rare in the Socratic dialogues. Socrates regularly introduces reasonable beliefs to confound his opponents. Laches realizes that courage cannot be equated with standing firm in battle, since this is sometimes foolish (*Lach.* 190e–191c). Euthyphro has a formal insight when he sees that an account of piety must do more than cite possible instances of piety (*Euthphr.* 5e–6a; cf. *Meno* 71e). Socrates has this belief, communicates it to Euthyphro, and congratulates him when he returns a definition of the right form (*Euthphr.* 7a). This prompts Annas to respond that Socrates' beliefs emerge only obliquely. He does not offer them as the conclusions of arguments, or even as premises of original arguments that proceed detached from his interlocutor's points of view. More important, his trademark theses (e.g., that knowledge is necessary and sufficient for virtue; that virtue is a craft; that suffering wrong is to be preferred to committing it) are not reasonable, at least not to untutored common sense. They are, on the contrary, deeply counterintuitive, and so are never at play in refutations of the proponents of unreflective, commonsense morality.[35] Hence, she concludes, his own theses are detached from his philosophical practice, isolated from his dialectical practice by their pronounced outlandishness. Thus, where Socrates offers commonsense opinions, he argues ad hominem, and where he offers his own convictions, he does not argue at all.

This line of argumentation invites some questions. But we can grant it for the moment in order to enquire whether it has the desired outcome. Annas' thought is that Socrates really does argue ad hominem,

[35]Annas (above, note 8), p. 277.

when he argues, and has insulated opinions that do not inform his philosophical practice. He is, therefore, close to her picture of an Arcesilaun skeptic. Yet we have seen reason to doubt this picture of Arcesilaus. Arcesilaus does argue ad hominem, but nothing precludes his endorsing the premises of the arguments leading to *epochē*.[36] His arguments simultaneously undermine Stoic dogmatism and advance skeptical theses. Hence if Socrates argues exclusively ad hominem, he will not be the active sort of skeptic Arcesilaus evidently is. If Annas' conception of Socrates is apt, then he is not Arcesilaun, and Arcesilaus will have no business claiming skeptical solidarity with him.

What is worse, if we grant that Socrates does have positive views, however insulated from his elenctic practice, he will have to respond to the very argument Arcesilaus mounts against the Stoics. Arcesilaus himself endorses some second-order theses about the conditions of knowledge and their unfulfillability. Socrates, on Annas' account, endorses substantive theses in moral philosophy. It does not matter that he never avails himself of them in refuting others; it matters only that he assents to them, for whatever private reasons, and that he is therefore bound to respond to Arcesilaun arguments. Their alleged insulation does not render them immune from skeptical refutation. Hence, even on this supposition, Socrates looks still less skeptical than Stoic.

In my view, then, Annas is certainly correct to point out that Arcesilaus was not foolish, or disingenuous, in claiming Socratic heritage. Still, as I have suggested, nothing in Socrates entails anything approaching (E); and if (E) is essential to Arcesilaun skepticism, Socrates cannot legitimately be regarded as the sort of Academician Arcesilaus is alleged to have considered him.

3. Dialectical and Skeptical Strategies

The foregoing suggests three principal differences between Arcesilaus and the Socrates of Plato's early dialogues: (1) Arcesilaus is an active skeptic, who employs self-consciously skeptical strategies to refute his opponents, while Socrates never actively relies on a self-conscious skeptical methodology; (2) Arcesilaus employs general skeptical argu-

---

[36]As suggested, we may view him as arguing more disjunctively: either the Stoic definitions of cataleptic *phantasiai* are open to clear, intuitive counterexamples, in which case they provide no general reason for thinking that anything is certain, or they are airtight definitions but are so demanding that no one could ever satisfy them, in which case the Stoics positively prove that no one can know anything certain. In the second instance, we may read Arcesilaus as hypothetically joining the dogmatist, in order to show how dogmatism itself leads to *epochē*.

ments with strong modal commitments, while Socrates proceeds piecemeal, never relying on any inchoate trope or general skeptical
argument; consequently, (3) Socrates cannot expect in advance to refute his opponents, since he has no general reason for believing that
they will succumb to a general argument he will deploy, while Arcesilaus can and does expect his opponents to join him in *epochē*. I will comment more fully on each of these points of difference.

First, Arcesilaus may be *skeptikos* just like Socrates. But he is also a
skeptic and is therefore committed to developing and refining skeptical
strategies. This he does, and with a skeptical game plan in mind. He
needs to determine which premises his opponents accept or must accept, and to show them how their own presuppositions lead them down
the path to *epochē*. In this respect, his negative strategy precisely mirrors the positive strategy employed by Aquinas in the *Summa contra
Gentiles*. Aquinas needs to convince the Arabs that their own first principles, largely Aristotelian, commit them to belief in a Christian God.
That Aquinas himself shares these principles does not entail that he is
arguing in anything but an ad hominem way. Arcesilaus, unlike Aquinas, pushes toward a form of disbelief, toward suspension, or *epochē*.
Socrates shares neither of their strategies, since his dominant goal, if
we believe him, is to prove the oracle wrong.

This is a point, I think, worth emphasizing, since it seems often to go
unnoticed in this context. When Aquinas argues ad hominem against
the Arabs, nothing precludes his endorsing both the premises and the
conclusions he claims they must accept. The force of such ad hominem
arguing will be to force one's opponents to come to appreciate the consequences of their own views, consequences they seem to have missed
for themselves. When Arcesilaus pressures the Stoics, this may be because he sees that they accept principles that yield a conclusion he
finds inescapable, namely, (E). Nothing about the content of (E) precludes his endorsing (E), and so nothing prohibits him from arguing as
a committed dialectician. He may, then, proceed as Aquinas does by arguing ad hominem even while employing premises he accepts for conclusions he embraces.

Second, Arcesilaus' goal carries with it the need for general skeptical
arguments, for arguments of nearly universal applicability. Any such
argument requires modal premises about the necessary conditions of
cataleptic assent, and about the possibilities of satisfying those conditions. This is just the sort of argument we find in Arcesilaus developing
in response to Stoic accounts of the cataleptic *phantasia*. General modal
arguments are, however, altogether absent in Socrates. He proceeds on
a case-by-case basis, consistently refuting his interlocutors, but never
claiming to have a general strategy for doing so. Socratic dialectic is not
suited for such strident skepticism, because it is not sufficiently gen-

eral. Here, perhaps, is the single most important difference between Socratic and Arcesilaun skepticism: Socrates never develops and never has any reason to develop the general modal arguments required for the campaigns of the skeptical Academy spearheaded by Arcesilaus.

Third, since Socrates has no general skeptical position, and since he has no tropelike method for pushing his opponents toward *epochē*, he has himself no reason to suppose that *epochē* is inevitable, and never commends it to anyone. He continues searching for real definitions, for essences, and casts aside failed definitions with a philosophical adroitness that never calls upon general skeptical principles. Since he has no reason to suppose in advance that he will not eventually uncover the essences he seeks, he has no reason to suppose his enquiry will end in *epochē*. Arcesilaus can and does have this expectation. He can have this expectation only if he has developed skeptical strategies at his disposal. These are precisely the strategies in response to Stoic dogmatism.

The Socrates of Plato's early dialogues modestly—and perhaps at times ironically—downplays his evident substantive and methodological command of the moral issues he pursues and the framework he fashions for pursuing them. Noticing this, Arcesilaus seizes an opportunity to portray himself as springing from the same skeptical stock as Socrates. On one portrait of Arcesilaus, according to which he is a willy-nilly skeptic who never commits himself to any general skeptical theses, this will not be terribly wide of the mark. We have found this portrait inaccurate: Arcesilaus develops a distinctive and important form of skeptical refutation, one perfectly general and employing modal premises altogether absent in Socrates' elenctic method. Arcesilaus self-consciously uses this skeptical strategy to nudge his dogmatic adversaries toward *epochē;* Socrates, by contrast, leads his interlocutors toward aporia, with the express aim of advancing the enquiry. As Vlastos points out, in contrasting the Socrates of the Socratic dialogues with the Socrates of the Platonic dialogues,

> Socrates' enquiries display a pattern of investigation whose rationale he does not investigate. They are constrained by rules he does not undertake to justify. In marked contrast to the "Socrates" who speaks for Plato in the middle dialogues, who refers frequently to "method" [μέθοδος] he follows (either systematically or for some particular purpose in a special context), the "Socrates" who speaks for Socrates in Plato's earlier dialogues never uses this word and never discusses his method of investigation. He never troubles to say why his way of searching is the way to discover the truth or even to say what this way of searching is. He has no name for it.[37]

[37]"The Socratic Elenchus," *OSAP* 1 (1983): 27–28.

The same contrast extends to Arcesilaus, who too has a method, skeptical to be sure, but a method nonetheless. Socrates' Socrates, Plato's Socrates, and Arcesilaus' Socrates all engage in dialectic: the first piecemeal, the second two for articulated theoretical purposes, and within the contexts of larger and self-consciously enunciated methodologies. Arcesilaus did not need to be Socrates' heir to be a powerful and innovative skeptic, and we may wonder why he evidently felt compelled to claim Socrates as his intellectual progenitor. But we cannot fairly regard him as a rogue in search of a pedigree to which he has no claim: if we focus exclusively on certain Socratic practices while ignoring others, and regard Arcesilaus as extending and generalizing those practices in response to the dialectical challenges of his own day, we can endorse Cicero's contention that Arcesilaus looked first to Socrates.[38]

[38]This article is most heavily indebted to Julia Annas, whose related essay in this volume helped me rethink some of the main issues discussed. It is also indebted to Jim Hankinson's forthcoming treatment of the skeptical strategies available to Arcesilaus; I thank him for allowing me to see his work in manuscript form. I have also received extremely helpful written comments from Phillip Mitsis and the editor of this volume. I thank them both for their guidance.

[14]

The Socratic Origins of the
Cynics and the Cyrenaics

Voula Tsouna McKirahan

Within several centuries after Socrates' death his most intimate followers had come to be known as Socratics, a label that is probably of Peripatetic origin,[1] and that has passed into modern scholarly usage typically accompanied by the modifier Minor.[2] This label covers a variety of personalities with diverse interests, and it intimates that their common feature is that they developed Socrates' philosophical teaching in various ways. Implicit in the modern usage is the conviction that these Socratics—excepting Plato and perhaps Xenophon—were of minor intellectual vigor and lacking in originality, a belief that has been challenged in scholarship both recent and dated.[3]

The extent to which the philosophical views of the Socratics are indebted to Socrates is in truth difficult to determine. There are two

---

[1]On the origins of this label, see J. Glucker, *Antiochus and the Late Academy, Hypomnemata* 56 (Göttingen, 1978). In identifying Socrates' closest followers, the Alexandrians could take their cue from Plato *Phaedo* 59b. Some Hellenistic thinkers who traced their intellectual pedigree to Socrates are willing to be called Socratics: so, for example, in the case of the Stoics: Philod. *De Stoic.*, cols. 12–13, in the edition of T. Dorandi, *CErc* 12 (1982): 91–133.

[2]As in the account of P. Merlan, "Minor Socratics," *JHP* 10 (1972): 143–52.

[3]On the Cynics, see, among others, M. -O. Goulet-Cazé, *L'ascèse cynique* (Paris, 1986), esp. pp. 141–58, 190–91; and H. D. Rankin, *Antisthenes Sokratikos* (Amsterdam, 1986), esp. pp. 179–88. Rankin places part of Antisthenes' importance precisely in the fact that he influenced the development of the Greek concept of liberty in Roman times. On the Cyrenaics, see, for instance, K. Döring, *Die Sokratesschuler Aristipp und die Kyrenaiker* (Stuttgart, 1988); V. Tsouna, "Les philosophes cyrénaiques et leur théorie de la connaissance" (Thèse de doctorat, Paris, 1988), esp. pp. 102 ff.

main reasons for this. First, the fact that Socrates wrote nothing left philosophers, from antiquity to the present, with the problem of assessing evidence on him from sources as different as Plato, Xenophon, and Aristotle.[4] The task of those who seek the authentic Socrates in the Platonic writings alone is not any easier; for the Socrates of the elenctic dialogues differs methodologically and philosophically from the central personage of the middle and late dialogues.[5] So in order to define the Socratic character of the doctrines of the Socratics with clarity and completeness, one must first give a full account of what one takes to be the philosophy of the historical Socrates. Second, the surviving evidence on these thinkers is of a peculiar nature. Few fragments from their writings survive. For the most part our information comes from historiographies of the Hellenistic era read and excerpted by later writers, and these are composed from a perspective that is considerably different from modern conceptions of the history of philosophy.

In view of these factors, I have chosen to avoid general talk about the Socratics and to undertake instead a very specific task. My discussion is centered on two members of the Socratic circle, Antisthenes and Aristippus.[6] Four points are generally made in the scholarship concerning them: (1) both are Socratics who, after meeting Socrates, abandoned their previous intellectual activities and consecrated themselves to the development of Socratic ethics; (2) in a way both failed in this task—thus their achievement is minor in comparison with Plato's; (3) their doctrines are diametrically opposed to one another's, especially so far as their views on pleasure and politics are concerned; and (4) the philosophical impact that they are supposed to have had as the founders of the Cynic and Cyrenaic sects respectively is sheer invention on the part of Hellenistic historiographers.

My own discussion focuses on these four points. In section 1, I argue that Antisthenes was not an antihedonist and that his doctrines of pleasure and of self-sufficiency can reasonably be characterized as Socratic. I also suggest that he participated in an important way and in his own right in philosophical discussions and debates; as an example, I refer to his attempt to moderate Socratic intellectualism, and, more generally, to some features of his intellectual presence on the Athenian scene. In

[4]For the problems involved in assessing the relative merits of our sources on Socrates see, for example, A. R. Lacey, "Our Knowledge of Socrates," in *The Philosophy of Socrates,* ed. G. Vlastos (New York, 1971), pp. 22–49; and the Introduction to this volume.

[5]In this I follow G. Vlastos, *Socrates: Ironist and Moral Philosopher* (Ithaca, N.Y., 1991), pp. 45–80.

[6]The collection of fragments that I shall mainly use for textual evidence is G. Giannantoni, *Socratis et Socraticorum Reliquiae*[2], 4 vols. (Naples, 1990). In cases where Giannantoni gives too much or too little of the context with the result that the testimonium is unclear, I cite the original source.

section 2, I maintain that Aristippus was not a hedonist and that his few surviving ethical views are distinctly Socratic. Despite our meager evidence, we do get a glimpse of a philosopher with a good sense of dialectical argumentation who can stand on his own ground intellectually. In section 3, I discuss the alleged contrast between Antisthenes' and Aristippus' doctrines on political participation. I argue first that the contrast should be minimized, and second that these political views are much closer to one another than either of them is to the political attitude of Socrates.

It remains to explain how I deal with the problem of determining what counts as a Socratic view. It will become clear, I hope, that not much in the way of an overall interpretation of Socrates is needed for my argument. For the most part, I work with the evidence from the early Plato and from Xenophon and try to stick to rather uncontroversial features of the historical Socrates attested usually by more than one main source and discussed exhaustively by classical scholars: Socratic intellectualism; exclusive interest in ethics; the sufficiency of virtue for happiness; moderation and self-mastery with respect to bodily pleasures and material goods, in private as well as in public life; criticism of politicians and political institutions but commitment to obeying the laws. I have tried to assist the reader by adding references to the Platonic and Xenophontic passages on Socrates where I thought it necessary.

I discuss to some extent in section 4 the difficulties presented by the nature of the evidence on Antisthenes and Aristippus. There I refer to some features of the Hellenistic historiography on the Socratics, and I focus on the writers mentioned by Diogenes Laertius in his chapters on Antisthenes and Aristippus. I venture a few remarks concerning our attitude toward ancient historiography and especially toward the "succession" genre.[7] And I argue that the line of succession that starts from Socrates and passes from Antisthenes to the Cynics and from them to the Stoics makes a claim that, though historically debatable, is philosophically legitimate.

1. Antisthenes as a Socratic

Sources as early as Xenophon attest to Antisthenes' fascination with Socrates' personality and teaching and to his presence in the Socratic

[7]The literary genre of the successions, which is probably of Peripatetic origin, consists in providing a rigid schematization of the history of ancient philosophy by outlining uninterrupted historical connections between various schools and by tracing the successive generations of philosophers of each school or sect. On this subject see esp. Glucker

circle.[8] Many features of his ethics—such as the invulnerability of acquired virtue and its sufficiency for happiness, the importance of
philosophical education, the emphasis on the supremacy of the moral
law, and perhaps the view that virtue secures some kind of immortality
for the soul—suggest that Antisthenes and Socrates were interested in
a common array of ethical themes and that they adopted similar philosophical solutions with regard to many of them. In this section I focus
on two interrelated features of Antisthenean ethics that argue forcefully for its Socratic character: a certain detachment from worldly
goods and a disciplined enjoyment of plain pleasures.[9]

These characteristics emerge in various anecdotes that bear on Antisthenes' appointment as the founder of the Cynic sect: a barefoot,
poorly dressed, middle-aged man, carrying a staff and a wallet, who
walks every day from his residence in Piraeus to Athens in order to
converse with Socrates.[10] The anecdotes may well be historically false
and influenced by the display of beggary and poverty of later Cynics.[11]
The early sources, however, confirm that Antisthenes did not care
much about material comforts but focused his attention on the promotion of his philosophical education and practical virtue through his
association with Socrates. In Xenophon's account (*Symp.* 34–44), Antisthenes is reported to enjoy some rudimentary material goods (a
house, a bed with bedclothes, simple food and drink) and to determine
his wealth not in material terms but in terms of his leisure to pursue
what is worth pursuing. So Antisthenes did not do away altogether
with the material side of life but only with luxuries that may distract
one's attention from the goods that really matter. In that respect, his
attitude is truly Socratic, according not only to Xenophon's portrayal
but also to that of the early Platonic dialogues,[12] for the Platonic Socra-

---

(above, note 1); J. Mejer, *Diogenes Laertius and His Hellenistic Background*, Hermes Einzelschriften 40 (Wiesbaden, 1978); also section 4 below.

[8]For Xenophon's portrayal of Antisthenes, see esp. *Mem.* 2.1–5; *Symp.* 2.4–7, 4.34–45.
Plato testifies that he was present among other close friends of Socrates in his last hour
(*Phd.* 59b). For Antisthenes' closeness to Socrates, see Xen. *Mem.* 3.11.17.

[9]See the brief and lucid discussion of the topic in W. K. C. Guthrie, *The Sophists* (Cambridge, 1971), pp. 209–18, 304–11.

[10]*SSR* 5.a.12, 15, 22.

[11]This is connected to the question of whether Antisthenes was the founder of Cynicism, which is a widely debated issue. See, for example, *SSR*, 3:203–11 n. 24, and Giannantoni's conclusion: "Dovrano essere interpretate come invenzione posteriori anche
tutte le notizie che tendano ad attribuire gia ad Antistene gli elementi essenziali dell' ab-
bigliamento e del modo di vivere cinico" (*SSR*, 3:211). On the other side of the debate,
see, among others, E. Zeller, *Die Philosophie der Griechen* (Leipzig, 1923), 2.1:28off. See
also Giannantoni's summary presentation and criticism of scholarly views on the subject
in *SSR*, cited above.

[12]For a persuasive interpretation of Socrates' attitude toward the nonmoral goods see
Vlastos (above, note 5), pp. 224–31. Vlastos' views are grounded in solid textual evidence

tes is not an ascetic. Socrates removes the worldly goods from the top of his hierarchy of values, makes them conditional upon the virtue of the individual, and claims that if one has the wisdom to use them properly, then things like wealth, strength, state honors, or high offices are indeed goods rather than intermediaries between good and evil.[13] But if Socrates does not reject all material goods, he certainly does not go out of his way to acquire or to increase them.[14]

Enjoyment of various goods is related to pleasure, and pleasure is not unconditionally condemned either by Antisthenes or by his teacher. It is unnecessary to broach here the subject of the pleasures of the soul or of the mind, inasmuch as most members of the Socratic circle endorse mental pleasures—whether this implies hedonism, moderate hedonism, or no hedonism at all. I shall confine my discussion to bodily pleasures, which are invariably associated with the enjoyment of worldly goods, for it is precisely in respect of these pleasures that Antisthenes is traditionally said to deviate from the Socratic norm by professing an extreme asceticism never advocated by his mentor.

Several ancient authors report that Antisthenes adopted a thoroughly negative view of bodily pleasure. Aristotle's anonymous reference to "those who think that no pleasure is a good either in itself or incidentally" (*Eth. Nic.* 7.11, 1152b8–10) is often taken to refer to Antisthenes.[15] According to Diogenes Laertius (6.2, 9.101) he believed that toil (which involves pain) is a good, while pleasure is an evil. By the second century A.D. the proverbial saying "I prefer to go mad than to feel pleasure," which is also attributed to him, completes the picture of a personality for whom virtue and pleasure are irremediably incompatible.

But a closer look at the fragments indicates that this picture is not quite adequate, for there is a completely different tradition of various late sources attesting a moderate attitude according to which Antisthenes did not discard all pleasures unqualifiedly but only some of them.[16] Stobaeus reports that Antisthenes was agreeable to pleasures

---

mostly from the early Platonic dialogues. See, for instance, *Ap.* 30a–b; *Grg.* 467e–468b4, 499c–500a; *Euthd.* 279a–b; *Meno.* 78c; also Xen. *Mem.* 1.3.5–15.

[13]In Socratic scholarship the attitude of Socrates toward material goods is often connected to his views on pleasure. For an interesting discussion of the topic see the essay by Harold Tarrant in Chapter 4 of this volume.

[14]The minor importance of nonmoral goods in Socratic ethics is signaled by the Socratic thesis that virtue is both necessary and sufficient for happiness. For an engaging perspective on this subject, see Vlastos (above, note 5), pp. 200–232; and, for the Stoics' development of this thesis, see the essay by Gisela Striker in Chapter 9.

[15]Giannantoni, for instance, includes that passage in the fragments of Antisthenes (*SSR* 5.a.118) and attributes to him the expressions "I would rather go mad then feel pleasure" and "I would shoot Aphrodite" (*SSR*, 3:358 n.39).

[16]The same kind of incompatibility between an ascetic and mildly hedonistic tradition occurs in the evidence on Diogenes. See K. von Fritz, "Quellen Untersuchungen zu

resulting from hard effort but hostile to the "easy" pleasures (*SSR* 5.a. 126)—a statement in the light of which we may read Diogenes Laertius' passage as implying a similar position. Athenaeus reproduces the even more positive view that pleasures for which one has no reason to repent are good (*SSR* 5.a.127). Both texts are compatible with Xenophon's much earlier evidence, which depicts Antisthenes as susceptible to the simple pleasures of life. At the same time, Xenophon's Antisthenes objects to intense pleasures on the grounds that these may be harmful (*Symp.* 4.37–39). It is reasonable to assume that intense pleasures are the ones that come about effortlessly, the "easy" pleasures, and that they are the ones about which we may repent in the future.

Xenophon's testimony should be preferred because it is earliest, it derives from his firsthand acquaintance with Antisthenes, and it provides details about the kind of pleasures he accepted (i.e., bodily pleasures produced by the satisfaction of basic needs). As such it fits well the Socratic side of Antisthenes, for no matter what position one takes regarding the controversial subject of Socratic hedonism, Socrates clearly does not dismiss all bodily pleasures but only those that may result in enslavement of the soul; there are some bodily pleasures that produce nonmoral goods (Pl. *Grg.* 499c–500a) and that are not objectionable provided that they are coupled with virtue.[17]

Still, we need to explain why some fragments assign an obsessive antihedonism to Antisthenes. None of them comes from an early source. As I have already pointed out, Aristotle does not refer to Antisthenes by name in the passage in the *Nicomachean Ethics* just quoted (7.11, 1152b8–10), whereas he does identify him and his followers when he criticizes Antisthenes' logic. The commentator who introduces the name of Antisthenes is very cautious. He makes clear that he is not the one who thinks that Aristotle has Antisthenes in mind, but others do (φασι, *SSR* 5.a.120). Besides, the immediate context in the *Nicomachean Ethics*, a discussion of the sufficiency of virtue for happiness irrespective of the pains or pleasures involved, can refer to Socrates as readily as to Antisthenes. I see no philosophical reason to assume that Aristotle criticizes here the latter's tenets rather than the former's. As to the late sources on our subject, we need to recall that

---

Leben und Philosophie des Diogenes von Sinope," *Philologus Supplbd.* 18, Heft 2 (1926): 1–97 at pp. 42ff.; Goulet-Cazé (above, note 3), pp. 77–84.

[17]See above, note 12. See also Plato *Laws* 660e–661a, where various nonmoral or moral goods are considered as goods only if they are acquired or performed with justice. (This theme occurs in several places in Plato's later dialogues.) Again, see Xenophon *Memorabilia* 4.1.5, where wealth, a nonmoral good, is not rejected on its own account but only if accompanied by lack of education and therefore of the possibility "to distinguish between things useful and things harmful."

the thesis that bodily pleasure is to be rejected unqualifiedly belongs to some of the Cynics, and that by the end of the Hellenistic era, if not earlier, Antisthenes was considered the founder of their sect. Hence it is not surprising that Cynic dicta were attributed to him, and the notorious "I prefer to go mad than to feel pleasure" is probably one such case.[18]

Turning now to the question of how "minor" a thinker Antisthenes was, we should examine first how much he simply repeated Socrates' views, and second, what position he occupies on the intellectual spectrum of fifth- and fourth-century Athens. Despite the undoubtedly Socratic aspects of his doctrine, it would be a mistake to accept the view of some scholars that Antisthenes limited his intellectual activities, during Socrates' lifetime, merely to reproducing the latter's views and to developing the particular aspects of Socratic teaching that suited him best after his teacher's death,[19] for there is evidence that Antisthenes did not uncritically embrace all that Socrates said. An example is Antisthenes' conception of virtue, which differs from the Socratic view. Socrates' beliefs that virtue is knowledge and that nobody does wrong willingly are attested many times in the early Platonic dialogues[20] and also by Aristotle.[21] For Socrates, right action results from knowledge of what is good, and once one has that knowledge human weakness cannot inhibit one from acting virtuously. It follows that the kind of physical or mental exercises that aim to develop self-control are irrelevant to moral action, strictly speaking, although Socrates may have recommended them for nonmoral purposes.[22] There certainly is an intellectualist component in Antisthenes' thought, for according to him the fool can become wise, therefore virtuous, by means of education, and once virtue is acquired, it cannot be lost (D.L. 6.12, 13, 105).[23] Virtue depends upon a μάθησις, or teaching, on the nature of the good and the bad, on the nature of pleasure and pain, and we have every reason to believe that this *mathēsis* is theoretical in the first place. But on the other hand, Antisthenes claimed that virtue consists in deeds and fur-

---

[18]I am in complete agreement with Tarrant's view (see Chapter 4) that Antisthenes' ethics is compatible with an enlightened hedonism that consists in allowing for the enjoyment of pleasure only when pleasure is the appropriate response to a particular situation.

[19]See, for example, G. Grote, *Plato and the Other Companions of Socrates*[3] (London, 1875), 2:504–6; Guthrie (above note 9), p. 306; Goulet-Cazé (above, note 3), pp. 141–50.

[20]See *Ap.* 26a; *Lach.* 194d; *Lysis* 210d; *Prt.* 357aff.; *Chrm.* 174bff.; also *Hi. ma.* 296c; *Grg.* 488a.

[21]See *Eth. Eud.* 1.5, 1216b1–25.

[22]See Xen. *Symp.* 2.17; Pl. *Symp.* 219cff.

[23]Similarly, vice can be "unlearned," and this constitutes a μάθημα, or lesson (*SSR* 5.87).

ther that virtue is sufficient for happiness *provided that the Socratic strength is added to it* (D.L. 6.11). Strength here is strength of character or strength of will by means of which one overcomes one's weaknesses and thus performs virtuous deeds.[24] So knowledge is no longer a sufficient condition for virtue unless strength is present.

We have no way to find out how Antisthenes' position on the nature of virtue was initially formed. It may have been developed by Antisthenes *before* he met Socrates, which would imply that this affinity of views between the two philosophers was a motive and not a consequence of Antisthenes' adherence to the Socratic circle. It may equally well have been the outcome of interaction between Antisthenes, the other Socratics, and Socrates himself. Antisthenes may have reached it while Socrates was still alive or, alternatively, after Socrates' death. We simply do not have adequate evidence to determine the origin of Antisthenes' doctrine. Nevertheless, it seems virtually certain that Antisthenes' doctrine is not a simple repetition of a Socratic belief. His conception of virtue is less counterintuitive than the one entailed by Socratic intellectualism, and from that point of view it might appear as a significant improvement over the latter, although in strictly philosophical terms it probably is not. One may even wonder whether some philosophers did in truth consider Antisthenes' introduction of the notion of strength as an improvement over the Socratic position, for Cynics, Stoics, and before them Xenophon developed doctrines in which knowledge obtained by means of reason coexists with the requirement of intellectual and physical exercise as a means to self-control.[25] On account of both his philosophical contribution and his influence I suggest that it is awkward to consider Antisthenes as a minor thinker in the ordinary sense of the term.

Another result of the assumption that Antisthenes was completely subdued to the personality of Socrates is the widespread belief that after he met Socrates, Antisthenes devoted himself exclusively to ethics. It may be true that he had a strong interest in ethics, and it is likely that he developed it further after he joined the Socratics. But there is no significant indication that Antisthenes, during the years of his companionship with Socrates, composed only ethical treatises or that he disclaimed his previous works. Nor does Antisthenes' practice as a teacher support the hypothesis in question. Whether he was teaching in the gymnasium of Cynosarges (*SSR* 5.a.22, 23) and whether this would im-

---

[24]The point has been made by Goulet-Cazé (above, note 3), pp. 142ff. Her claim that Antisthenes was the first Socratic to appeal to the ideal of strength of character thus emphasizes the moral importance of exercise or training (ἄσκησις).

[25]On this see the major contribution of Goulet-Cazé (above, note 3) to the analysis of the notion of *askēsis*.

ply the existence of an organized school[26] is dubious.[27] But he certainly had a number of pupils and followers who are identified as a separate sect and who presumably embraced both the Antisthenean doctrine and mode of life. There is no reason to assume that this teaching consisted solely of ethical topics; on the contrary, Aristotle refers explicitly to the logic of "the Antistheneans" (*SSR* 5.a.150), Epictetus cites his principle that "the beginning of education is the examination of names" (*SSR* 5.a.160), and Stobaeus reports an anecdote in which Antisthenes offers lessons in rhetoric or alternatively in philosophy according to the needs and capacities of each pupil (*SSR* 5.a.173). There is some evidence that Antisthenes charged fees for his teaching.[28] If this was indeed the case, it is likely that he offered to teach a variety of subjects that were in demand, not only ethics. Again, no source suggests that Antisthenes abandoned these activities upon becoming Socrates' friend: to the contrary, the story that he advised his own students to follow Socrates implies that he continued his teaching during his Socratic days. It is doubtful that he could secure his living from family money, and yet Xenophon attests that he lived in decent, although not luxurious, conditions (*SSR* 5.a.82), which implies some income.

Looking into details of the preserved lists of Antisthenes' writings (*SSR* 5.a.41), we find a prolific author who is attested to have treated a variety of subjects: logic, epistemology and metaphysics, grammar and literature, rhetoric, political philosophy and religion, as well as ethics. In this respect, Antisthenes displays the wide intellectual interests characteristic of the sophistic period. The overlap between his interests and those of the sophists, on the one hand, and of Socrates, on the other, has led D. B. Dudley to propose the following interpretation of Antisthenes' philosophy:

> The impression left by an examination of what are known to have been his doctrines in various departments of knowledge is that there is little here that is original. His logical position was that of the Neo-Eleatics; the influence of Socrates is paramount in his ethics; his political views are a synthesis compounded of the Socratic idea of the *sophos*, the Sophistic

[26]Cf. *SSR* 5.a.150, where Aristotle refers to Antisthenes' pupils as οἱ Ἀντισθένειοι; and *SSR* 5.a.26, which distinguishes the doctrine of the Antistheneans from that of the Cynics.

[27]On this see F. Decleva Caizzi, *Antisthenis Fragmenta* (Milan, 1966), pp. 119ff.; and *SSR*, 3:203–11 n. 24.

[28]*SSR* 5.a.169. *SSR* 5.a.170 can be considered valid evidence for the claim that Antisthenes charged fees for his teaching only if one assumes, together with Giannantoni, that Antisthenes is indeed a target of attack in Isocrates *Against the Sophists* 13.1–6. However, Giannantoni dismisses the probability of Antisthenes charging fees on the grounds of Xenophon *Symposium* 4.43 (*SSR*, 3:205).

opposition between *nomos* and *physis* and the reactions of a "Socratic man" to the events of contemporary history. In his interest in names one may suspect the influence of Prodicus; that of Gorgias is undoubted on his style and his rhetorical studies; in Homeric "interpretation" he followed the already popular method of allegory.[29]

In other words, Antisthenes' doctrine is nothing but an eclectic amalgam of the philosophy of Socrates and of the sophists, and the philosopher is characterized as "a typical minor figure of that time of intellectual ferment."[30] This interpretation is typical of a whole generation of scholars discussing Antisthenes;[31] hence brief comment on it is in order.

The way in which Dudley reaches his rather depressing conclusion is, I believe, objectionable on three separate grounds.

First, methodologically: philosophical evaluation should not rely completely on the chronological priority of one doctrine over another. Originality, for instance, is not only a matter of which doctrine came first but also of when it acquired argumentative coherence and completeness. Even if Dudley is right in claiming that Antisthenes did not come up with a radically new set of tenets, it does not follow that his philosophical contribution in discussing already familiar topics was unoriginal.

Second, historically: Antisthenes received a good deal of attention from major and minor philosophical figures of the Greek world,[32] not only as a result of his relation to Socrates but also in his own right. Aristotle, for instance, discusses his metaphysical and logical views on substances, composite substances, and definitions and cites "the fable of Antisthenes" in order to illustrate one of his own tenets in the *Politics* (*SSR* 5.a.68); Aristotelian commentators reproduce and criticize his thesis on the impossibility of contradiction (*SSR* 5.a.153, 155) and his theory of universals (*SSR* 5.a.149), and none of them connects these subjects to the sophists or the Neo-Eleatics. Antisthenes also was praised for his literary virtues (*SSR* 5.a.50), his argumentative skill (*SSR* 5.a.22), and his qualities as a teacher of philosophy and rhetoric.[33]

Third, and most important, philosophically: despite the lack of substantial evidence on the subject, there are some examples that point in

---

[29]*A History of Cynicism* (London, 1937), p. 14.

[30]Dudley (above, note 29).

[31]It must be noticed that some recent scholarly works contain a sympathetic and thorough account of Antisthenes' doctrine: see Goulet-Cazé (above, note 3); Rankin (above, note 3).

[32]*SSR* 5.a.68. Dudley (above, note 29), p. 14, admits that Antisthenes was popular in ancient times and attributes this popularity to his being a writer of *Socratic Discourses*.

[33]Various anecdotes and repartees are related to the subject of Antisthenes as a teacher.

a direction different from Dudley's account of Antisthenean doctrine along eclectic lines. Consider three cases involving Antisthenes' logic, metaphysics, and theory of language. First, Antisthenes shares the sophistic view that falsehood is impossible (*SSR* 5.a.152, 155) as well as its corollary, the impossibility of contradiction. But unlike Gorgias or Protagoras, he provides support for that thesis by arguing that each object can be described only by one λόγος, that is, that there is only one *logos* proper to each thing (Arist. *Metaph.* Δ5, 1024b32–34; D.L. 6.3); since contradiction requires that there be two *logoi* about the same thing and, furthermore, that one of them be true and the other false, it follows that contradiction is impossible.[34] Second, the thesis that essences are not further analyzable and therefore cannot be defined is ascribed to Antisthenes and his school on the authority of Aristotle, who criticizes it vigorously (*Metaph.* H3, 1043b23ff.); it has no exact precedent in the sophistic tradition.[35] Third, the doctrine of the natural affinity between names and objects is associated both with Antisthenes and with the sophist Lycophron; but there is no further evidence of influence either way, nor do we know enough to assert that the content of the doctrine was identical in the two cases. These three examples indicate that there is a range of common interests between Antisthenes and some of the sophists.[36] But Antisthenes seems inclined to go farther than reproducing standard paradoxes and illustrating familiar topics for familiar purposes. Rather, he is interested in the philosophical foundations of sophistic tenets and seems to appreciate genuine philosophical investigation for its own merits.

2. Aristippus as a Socratic

It is harder to assess Aristippus' philosophy than Antisthenes': the hostility of most sources,[37] the occasional confusion between Aristippus and his grandson,[38] and the habit of many late authors to ascribe

---

[34]On this see, for example, C. M. Gillespie, "The Logic of Antisthenes," *AGP* 26 (1913): 479–500; V. Celluprica, "Antistene: Logico o sofista," *Elenchos* 8 (1987): 285–328.

[35]See, however, the doctrine referred to by Plato in *Theaetetus* 201c–202c, with J. Mac-Dowell's commentary, *Plato's Theaetetus* (Oxford, 1973), pp. 231–39; and M. F. Burnyeat, "The Material and Sources of Plato's Dream," *Phronesis* 15 (1970): 101–22.

[36]Cf. Guthrie (above, note 9), pp. 209–18, 304–11.

[37]See, for instance, the anecdotes in *SSR* 4.a.5, 6, 7, 27–43, 44–48.

[38]Many modern scholars have expressed the suspicion that ancient authors often fell victims of the synonymy between the two Aristippi and failed to distinguish them from each other. This claim is usually attached to views about who is the real founder of the Cyrenaic doctrine. Cf., for example, Grote (above, note 19), 3:549; E. Mannebach, *Aristippi et Cyrenaicorum Fragmenta* (Leiden, 1961), pp. 114–18.

philosophical tenets to the Cyrenaics in general rather than to each Cyrenaic separately are the principal reasons.[39] Looking at the evidence, we can see that there are two categories of testimony on Aristippean ethics, one that attributes to him a straightforward hedonism and one that does not consider him a hedonist at all. According to the former, Aristippus was the first Cyrenaic to define the moral end as a smooth movement (*SSR* 4.a.175) that results in a pleasure of the body, is confined strictly to the present, and is very short-lived (*SSR* 4.a.174). Pleasure must be distinguished from happiness (εὐδαιμονία), which is the sum of particular pleasures, present as well as past and future ones, extended over one's lifetime (*SSR* 4.a.173, 174). It is pleasure and not happiness that is pursued for its own sake (*SSR* 4.a.172). (Authors in this tradition often add venomous comments about the way in which Aristippus uses hedonism as an alibi for his self-indulgence.)[40]

On the other hand, Aristocles denies that Aristippus defined pleasure as the only thing that is intrinsically good, and there is further information that he never lectured defending a particular moral end (*SSR* 4.a.173), whether pleasure or anything else—a piece of evidence that fits perfectly with Aristippus' distaste for a didactic tone in teaching or speaking (Arist. *Rh.* 2.23, 1398b31–32). Instead, Aristippus believes that pleasure is to be sought and enjoyed not unconditionally but only if it does not endanger our self-control (*SSR* 4.a.86, 87, 95–98). The latter is the result of philosophical education, together with the acquisition of internal freedom, self-awareness,[41] and the promotion of the well-being of the soul by means of study (μελέτη) and endurance (καρτερία).[42] These goods are not instrumental to the enjoyment of pleasure but valuable in themselves. If one obtains them, one may securely savor bodily pleasures; if one does not obtain them, one presumably should not pursue bodily pleasures, for they would hinder the promotion of virtue in the soul. It is obvious that the testimonies concerning hedonism imply an unbridgeable gap between Socratic and Aristippean ethics, while the nonhedonistic evidence does not. Leaving aside speculations about the origin of the two traditions, I want to argue for accepting the latter.

First, as already mentioned, Eusebius reports Aristocles' outright declaration that Aristippus was not a hedonist, only thought to be so

[39]It is noteworthy that the extended fragments on Cyrenaic epistemology are attributed to the Cyrenaics in general and not to Aristippus or to his grandson.

[40]*SSR* 4.a.53, 54, 96, 99, 201. See also Socrates' attack on the identification of happiness with pleasure in Plato *Gorgias* 494e, which served as a basis for considering Aristippus' alleged hedonism as thoroughly anti-Socratic. (There is no indication that this passage in the *Gorgias* has Aristippus as a specific target.)

[41]Cf. Pl. *Ap.* 38a for the importance ascribed to it by Socrates.

[42]*SSR* 4.a.2, 5, 55, 56, 105, 107, 124, 130.

on the grounds of his intemperance (πάνυ ὑγρὸς καὶ φιλήδονος, *SSR* 4.a.173). Since Eusebius' source or sources on the Cyrenaics are excellent, as indicated by his accurate presentation of the very unusual tenets of Cyrenaic epistemology, we have good reason to trust his testimony. Second, it is undoubtedly true that the Cyrenaics who came after Aristippus developed a hedonistic theory in which the moral end was the momentary present pleasure. Their ethics was backed by an elaborate epistemology that claims that the only knowledge accessible to us is the knowledge of our undergoings (πάθη).[43] The ethical claim that momentary pleasure is the good has an irrefutable character precisely in virtue of the fact that pleasure is an undergoing and therefore is self-evident.[44] But no text on Cyrenaic epistemology mentions Aristippus. Instead, the most plausible candidate as the founder of the doctrine is Aristippus' grandson, usually called Aristippus the Mother-taught. If Aristippus were a hedonist, his ethics would lack the epistemological basis for its central claim and thus would appear trivial. On the other hand, in the nonhedonistic tradition Aristippus' ethical theory is firmly based on beliefs common to the members of the Socratic circle, is coherent and intuitively persuasive. Third, no author indicates that Aristippus worked out what sort of activities were acceptable as a means to the end of enjoying pleasure. If Aristippus were a hedonist pursuing exclusively the pleasure of the present and showing indifference to its implications in the longer run, he would be committed to the view that any activity that provides pleasure would do. But then he could hardly be acceptable as a companion of Socrates. It is one thing for Socrates to count against Aristippus his excessive joie de vivre, but it would be another to consider him outright immoral, and there is no evidence that Socrates so considered him. Fourth, the view that pleasure is μονό-χρονος (*SSR* 4.a.174), taken together with the belief that momentary pleasure is the end, appears incompatible with the importance attrib-

---

[43]On Cyrenaic epistemology, see Döring (above, note 3), pp. 8–32; V. Tsouna McKirahan, "The Cyrenaic Theory of Knowledge," *OSAP* 10 (1992): 161–92.

[44]On this see T. H. Irwin, "Aristippus against Happiness," *Monist* 74 (1991): 62–66. In this closely argued article, Irwin claims that the rejection of eudaimonism by Aristippus and the Cyrenaics is based on doubts about personal identity. The notion of happiness entails beliefs about temporally extended collections of individual impressions. It also is based on the assumption that we are temporally extended persons, which again involves belief in temporally extended collections. But according to the Cyrenaics such beliefs are unsupported, since they are not about individual affections. So skepticism about collections of individual impressions that extends to skepticism about a persisting self is at the basis of Aristippus' rejection of eudaimonism. This fascinating and highly philosophical interpretation is, I believe, incompatible with the evidence on the Socratic aspect of Aristippus. Interests such as education, endurance, or self-control make sense only if one perceives oneself and others as persisting selves who admit of moral improvement. That of course does not affect Irwin's argument, for even if it does not apply to Aristippus, it can be argued that it applies to the Cyrenaics who came after him.

uted to long-lasting activities such as philosophy or painful efforts such as endurance. If we believe the claim of the testimonies concerning hedonism, it follows that not only must we discard Aristocles as a witness but also that we must disbelieve all texts that attribute to Aristippus Socratic features. And this, first, is not economical, and, second, it leaves unexplained the presence of Aristippus in the Socratic circle.

If, on the other hand, we accept the nonhedonistic portrayal of Aristippus' doctrine, and we assume that one interprets the evidence on Socrates (including Platonic dialogues such as the *Protagoras*, the *Gorgias*, and the *Hippias major*) along nonhedonist lines,[45] as I am inclined to do,[46] then we infer that Aristippus and Socrates differ on the subject of pleasure with respect to its practical implications, not in their respective definitions of the moral end. For Socrates, control over bodily pleasure dictates a life of moderation, while for Aristippus it does not. One piece of evidence on this topic is particularly helpful in tracing the limits of Aristippus' Socraticism in the matter of pleasure and its entailments. It is an argument between Aristippus and Socrates reported by Xenophon (*Mem.* 2.1.11–34) on the undesirability of a voluptuous life and on the implications of such a life for one's civic existence. I shall come back to the details of the argument in section 3; here I refer only to the parts of it that are relevant to Aristippus' views on pleasure.

I argue for two points regarding the passage from Xenophon. First, it provides direct evidence for the claim that Aristippus was a eudaimonist and not a hedonist. Second, Socrates' argument leaves unscathed Aristippus' belief that is morally right for one to enjoy various pleasures.

Socrates intends to rebuke Aristippus for being too keen on savoring various bodily pleasures; so he offers him two alternatives. Either Aristippus will be a ruler, in which case he must acquire self-restraint, or he will be ruled, subordinate or slave, in which case he can immerse himself in pleasures but also risk undergoing serious pains. Socrates' assumption must be that Aristippus will choose the former and thus that he will be committed to moderation. He proves wrong in his expectation, for part of Aristippus' answer is that he aims at the easiest and pleasantest life (ῥᾷστά τε καὶ ἥδιστα βιοτεύειν, *Mem.* 2.1.9) and that he wishes to live a life of freedom that leads to happiness (πρὸς εὐδαιμονίαν ἄγειν, 2.1.11). But this indicates that Aristippus does not seek pleasures for their own sake but presumably views them as a means to or a component of happiness. Also, he does not look at the momentary pleasures of the present but at his life as a whole (*bioteuein*). Besides, it

---

[45]There is a vast bibliography on the subject: see Harold Tarrant's essay in the present volume (Chapter 4), which contains an interpretation of the Platonic evidence on Socrates according to which he is presented as a kind of intellectual hedonist.

[46]I shall not argue for it here, for purposes of brevity and coherence.

seems that Socrates addresses his rebellious interlocutor on the assumption that he is not a hedonist of the kind that other Cyrenaics turned out to be, for his questions as to what political role Aristippus wishes to play or as to how he plans to live his life, as well as his final exhortation that Aristippus think these matters over and show some care for his life in the future (2.1.34), presuppose that Socrates conceives of Aristippus' life as a whole and that Aristippus shares that way of looking at his own life.

Independent evidence tells us that Aristippus indulged in pleasures but at the same time made sure that he was in control of his experiences and that pleasure did not master him instead (SSR 4.a.86–87, 95–98). In order to succeed in rendering him more temperate, Socrates should argue that self-discipline entails moderation and that it is incompatible with satisfying unnecessary desires. Instead, he puts forward a utilitarian argument in which moderation in pleasure is instrumental to the end of ruling. Aristippus admits that if one is interested in becoming a ruler, then one should cultivate moderation. But he is not interested in becoming a ruler, and so does not need to become temperate. However, Socrates continues with his argument and keeps missing the point. We are left to wonder whether Aristippus is finally right: although pleasure is not the moral end, it is an important constituent of happiness. And one can be self-disciplined without abstaining from pleasure either partially or totally.

It is hard to assess Aristippus' overall philosophical importance on the basis of the available evidence and thus to assess the question of how "minor" he was. Traditionally he is depicted as one of the most minor figures of the Socratic circle—someone whose questionable charm consists in vulgar wit, social rudeness, opportunism, and unscrupulousness. However, there are some indications that such a portrayal is unfounded. The titles of his works (SSR 4.a.144), if indeed they are genuine,[47] show that his primary interest was in ethical questions (SSR 4.a.166). It may be that he mostly dealt with practical ethics, but we are also allowed to glimpse a theoretical argument to the effect that every object is associated with a moral end, and therefore objects that are morally neutral do not exist (SSR 4.a.171). On account of this argument he dismissed the study of mathematics (SSR 4.a.170–71) and perhaps also of natural science.[48] On the other hand, some titles of his books indicate an interest in rhetoric. Linguistic morphology and semantics should be added to his topics of discussion (SSR 4.a.149), al-

[47]SSR 4.a.144. According to Diogenes Laertius (2.84), Sosicrates believed that Aristippus wrote nothing at all.
[48]SSR 4.a.167–68. However, it must be noticed that according to Sextus the Cyrenaic theory is divided into five sections, one of which is natural science and another logic.

though it is unknown whether he had any grammatical, semantic, or linguistic theory of his own. History and perhaps literature complete the list of his interests.[49] Whether or not Aristippus showed any originality in any of these subjects, his intellectual activity was not restricted to the thoughtless adoption of a few Socratic tenets or to the reproduction of Socratic mannerisms but extended to familiar topics of Greek intellectual tradition. Nor can his knowledge of the latter have been completely superficial, for he taught in the competitive environment of Athenian culture for a substantial fee and fairly successfully (*SSR* 4.a.1, 3, 7, 23), a fact that is diligently exploited by various authors for polemic purposes.

3. Antisthenes and Aristippus on Political Participation

The assumption that Antisthenes was a sworn antihedonist, while the Cyrenean was a sybaritic hedonist, and that consequently neither was a Socratic in his ethics[50] lies behind the long-standing belief that their doctrines were diametrically opposed, and not only in strictly ethical matters.[51] In the following passage Saint Augustine epitomizes two points of contrast on which I now focus my discussion:

> Did not Aristippus flourish there [at Athens], who saw the highest good in the pleasure of the body, and there too Antisthenes, who asserted that man becomes happy rather by superior character—two distinguished philosophers, both Socratic, yet they located the highest life in realms so different and contradictory that, while one said that the wise man should shun politics, the other said that he should serve the state? Yet each mustered his flock of disciples to follow his own sectarian philosophy. (*De civ. d.* 18.41)

In view of our discussion in sections 1 and 2 of the two philosophers' positions on pleasure, it is clear that so sharp a contrast between their ethics is unjustified. Antisthenes welcomes certain bodily pleasures,

---

[49]Aristippus is reported to have written a history of his homeland, Libya (D.L. 2.83). He wrote in two dialects, Attic and Doric: this may indicate an interest in literature, but it could also be the result of having been educated as a Cyrenean gentleman of independent means—in which case it does not constitute evidence of special scholarly knowledge.

[50]This thesis has survived into recent scholarship: thus Vlastos (above, note 5), pp. 204–5, 208, holds that for Aristippus virtue is desirable only as an instrumental means to happiness and that happiness is identical with pleasure, while for Antisthenes virtue is the sole constituent of and identical with happiness. I too used to hold that view; cf. my doctoral thesis (above, note 3).

[51]Cf. Harold Tarrant's essay in Chapter 4.

provided that they are of the right kind, amount, and intensity, just as Aristippus accepts pleasure, provided that the conditions of self-awareness and self-control obtain. Antisthenes is not an unqualified enemy of pleasure, nor is Aristippus an unconditional lover of it. Since both gave priority to the development and protection of virtue in the soul, and both stressed the importance of self-discipline, they are in these respects close to Socratic morality, and there is no room for the dramatic difference envisaged by both ancient and modern commentators. Nor is there much sense in trying to assess whether the hedonism of the Cyrenean or the asceticism of Antisthenes represents more faithfully the Socratic spirit.[52]

The second point on which Saint Augustine concentrates, namely, participation in politics, is another pillar of the sharp distinction traditionally drawn between Antisthenes and Aristippus: the former is considered a pure Socratic in his civic loyalty and his commitment to serve the state,[53] while the latter is depicted as a cosmopolitan whose lack of civic bonds is scandalous and alienates him from Socrates.[54]

The few surviving fragments of Antisthenes' political thought display a preoccupation with political incompetence and corruption, its results for the city-state, the relation between vice and power, and the need for good political criteria (*SSR* 5.a.71, 73, 76). He treated the problematic topic of virtues and their connection to the civic good and stressed the uncontroversial character of justice as the highest virtue both in the individual and in the state (*SSR* 5.a.78). Diogenes Laertius (6.11) attributes to him the tenet that "the wise person will be guided in his public deeds not by the established laws but by the law of virtue,"[55] while a passage in Stobaeus summarizes Antisthenes' attitude toward practical politics as an equilibrium between excessive involvement in and total abstention from political life (*SSR* 5.a.70).

---

[52]Most modern scholars agree that although Antisthenes' asceticism carries some features of Socratic morality to the extreme, it is the closest approximation to the teaching of Socrates. See, among others, Grote (above, note 19); Giannantoni, *SSR* 3:348–61 n. 39. For an exhaustive bibliography, see esp. *SSR* 3:348–61 nn. 1–48; see also Goulet-Cazé's discussion (above, note 3), pp. 141–45, of Antisthenes' intellectualism and its Socratic provenance.

[53]The Socrates of the early Platonic dialogues declares that he abstains from politics (*Ap.* 31c–32a; *Grg.* 473e), and yet he claims that he is the only Athenian to engage in true political art (*Grg.* 521d). These two claims are not contradictory; cf. Vlastos (above, note 5), pp. 240–41, who argues that Socrates did not have any political theory despite his critical attitude toward the politics of his day and despite his strong commitment to the laws of the Athenian state. See also R. Kraut, *Socrates and the State* (Princeton, 1984), with Vlastos' review in *TLS* 24 (August 1984).

[54]Cf. J. Humbert, *Socrate et les petits Socratiques* (Paris, 1967), pp. 246–47, 261–63.

[55]For a parallel of Antisthenes with the Platonic Socrates regarding the priority of the moral laws over the laws of the state see *Apology* 29d, where Socrates declares that he will obey the god rather than the Athenians, much as he cherishes them.

These texts have been taken to indicate a refusal to become a pro-
tagonist on the Athenian political scene and also a wholehearted acceptance of the bonds of Athenian citizenship.[56] These features are
shared by the Platonic and Xenophontic Socrates;[57] as I shall argue,
neither should be assigned to Antisthenes.

While Antisthenes' political thought undeniably displays certain
Socratic characteristics, there appear to be important differences between the two philosophers on the question of political practice.
Socrates was not a professional politician but participated in politics by
his own choice and in his capacity as an Athenian citizen. While his attitude toward the application of Athenian laws in his own case is controversial, it is clear that his criticisms of political principles as well as of
powerful individuals did not undermine his acceptance of his jury's
verdict of death. Part of this was due to his awareness of the rights and
obligations of his citizenship, as emerges mainly from the evidence in
the *Crito*.

None of this was the case with Antisthenes. He was the son of a
Thracian slave (*SSR* 5.a.1–6) and probably, therefore, not an Athenian
citizen.[58] If so, his participation in politics (in Athens anyway), either as
a politician or as a layman, was excluded. Thus he could not go so close
to politics "as to get burned" but also did not go so far from it "as to feel
chilly" (*SSR* 5.a.70), since he benefited from provisions in the Athenian
constitution protecting people of his status. In this contingent situation
he was unlikely to feel "the slave" or "the offspring" of the laws (Pl. *Cri.*
50e) of any particular city. He was not allowed "to persuade" them
(51c) by means of a public speech, he had no "agreement" or "contract"
with them (51e–52a), and if he had been in Socrates' place, perhaps he
would have done what "the meanest slave would do" (52d): escape
from prison and from a morally unjust death. His attacks on the politicians of the day are expected from a moral philosopher,[59] concern
Athens only incidentally, and constitute no evidence for a particular
psychological involvement with the city of Athens. His thoughts on the
relation between virtue and politics are a familiar topic among Socratics and sophists and are by no means the exclusive property of an Athenian. The implication of his dictum that the public deeds of the wise
should be dictated by the moral rather than the civic law seems to me

---

[56]Humbert (above, note 54), p. 247.

[57]For Xenophon, see David O'Connor's essay in Chapter 6 of this volume. He discusses Socrates' political attitude in terms of a paradox created by his view that political
control is something desirable and by his rejection of the conventional means of political
control.

[58]Cf. Sen. *Constant.* 18.5; Guthrie (above, note 9), p. 306 n. 1; and Humbert (above,
note 54), p. 247.

[59]His attacks on Alcibiades are notorious for their violence.

straightforward: if the former happens to conflict with the latter, so much the worse for the civic law.[60] This does not express any commitment to the laws of a city, whatever these are, or any particular loyalty to the laws of Athens. It may be that Antisthenes allowed for the wise man to serve the state, as St. Augustine reports, provided that the appropriate moral conditions obtain. But this is not to say that involvement in politics is an unconditional moral obligation.

Our main source on Aristippus' political stance is Xenophon *Memorabilia* 2.1. The context of the argument is rhetoric,[61] and the argument itself, at least according to its author, is initiated by Socrates and has a didactic purpose (2.1.34). Socrates' assumption is that there are two and only two possible roles that one can undertake in politics, that of ruling and that of "never putting himself forward" (2.1.1), which Socrates equates with being ruled (2.1.10). He argues that either of these roles requires a particular type of moral education regarding matters of pleasure and pain: in the case of "those fitting to be rulers" the educational objective should be self-restraint, endurance, and temperance.[62] So far as the ruled are concerned, the implication is that they may indulge in satisfying intemperate desires or indeed that they should be encouraged to do so because then they are easily amenable to obeying their leaders.

The first step of the argument deploys along familiar lines: by a series of questions and answers Socrates leads Aristippus to conclude that men who restrain themselves regarding pleasure are fit to be rulers,[63] while the intemperate can have no claim to political power (2.1.2–7). So far the reader has no reason to suspect that Socrates' interlocutor will challenge the exhaustive and exclusive disjunction that in a political society either one is a ruler or one is ruled (2.1.12). Then Socrates directs the argument to Aristippus himself and asks him the following question: "Have you ever thought in which of these two categories you would classify yourself?" (2.1.7). Socrates' expectation seems to be that Aristippus will opt for one of the two alternatives; in either case his answer would enable Socrates to make his point that lack of moderation regarding bodily pleasures is to be avoided. If Aristippus answers that he is or wants to be a ruler, and since he has admitted that only the temperate are fit to be rulers, it follows that he should

[60]Humbert (above, note 54), pp. 246–47, draws precisely the opposite conclusion.

[61]Cf. David O'Connor's essay in Chapter 6. O'Connor interprets Aristippus' political position in the *Memorabilia* as a distorted imitation of Socratic self-sufficiency such that in the doctrine of Aristippus self-sufficiency becomes alienation.

[62]These are to be distinguished from the mastery over pleasure that Aristippus professes and that I refer to as self-control.

[63]See also *Mem.* 1.5.1.

"exercise restraint with respect to food and drink and lust and sleep and chill and heat and toil" (2.11.1). On the other hand, if he claims to be among the ruled, Socrates will misleadingly equate that condition with political subordination (2.1.10) and slavery (2.1.12) and will enumerate the evils that make these states undesirable (2.1.12–13).

Aristippus' dialectical move is to attach the bipolar scheme of ruling or being ruled to the political condition of citizenship by granting that point to Socrates (2.1.12), to detach himself from that condition (2.1.13), and to introduce a third possibility, namely, an apolitical stance "that leads neither through ruling nor through slavery but through freedom" to happiness (2.1.11). Thus Aristippus can decline to be a ruler and yet can avoid being ruled, for Socrates himself considers citizenship as the necessary condition for these alternatives to be exhaustive (2.1.12), and Aristippus removes this condition by his claim that he is a foreigner in every land (2.1.13).[64] So the liberty he claims for himself has a peculiar meaning: it is not freedom *in* the city but *from* the city. This point is confirmed by Saint Augustine: part of "the highest life" as defined by the Cyrenean is the voluntary abstention from the politics of any particular city.[65]

Aristippus' position makes sense as a political option in view of his own nationality. For a Cyrenean whose native land was a theater of turmoil long after the fall of the Battiads and that, despite its wealth, lacked political and cultural identity, indifference to politics is an understandable attitude of practical and psychological self-defense. However, we must not lose perspective of the fact that the argument in Xenophon is a moral argument. If we are to believe Xenophon, Socrates' motivation was to make Aristippus admit the moral and practical value of temperance, not to make him spell out his political stance. Similarly, Aristippus' disavowal of civic bonds appears like a means to the end of enjoying an easy and pleasant life. That does not mean that Aristippus was not serious about his political views. But it does mean

---

[64]The word ξένος may mean "foreigner" or "a stranger receiving hospitality and protection qua stranger." If we take it in this second sense in 2.1.13, it may provide the beginning of an answer to Socrates' argument in 2.1.14–15 that strangers are vulnerable to all kinds of injuries precisely because they do not have the protections that citizenship offers. Aristippus might question the truth of this remark by reminding Socrates that strangers are customarily well received and courteously treated.

[65]I prefer to avoid the term *cosmopolitan* in referring to Aristippus' stance—first, because Aristippus' position is different from the Cynic thesis in significant respects, and the word is usually associated with Cynicism; second, because its modern use may lead to confusion. According to modern usage, cosmopolitanism denotes an eclectic mentality accompanied by smooth manners, social grace and flexibility, and a good deal of skepticism regarding moral matters. The political implications of the modern attitude are only incidental to the extent that one's political beliefs are part of one's character and behavior.

that, at least in this argument, which is also our main surviving passage on the matter, politics for Aristippus is subordinate to ethics. In that light it seems unjustified to contrast sharply the political views and behavior of Antisthenes with those of Aristippus, for neither proposes an unqualified acceptance or rejection of political ties, neither develops a political theory for its own sake, and neither is a citizen in the standard Greek meaning of the word.

4. Ancient Historiography and the Foundation of the Cynic and Cyrenaic Schools

Early in ancient historiography Socrates and his companions were conceived as a group. This is indicated by the surviving titles and fragments of works such as *The Socratics* by Phanias and a homonymous composition by Idomeneus. It is also indicated by the locus that the various Socratics occupy in compilations of a biographical or doxographical nature, such as Hermippus' and Diocles' *Lives,* Heraclides', Sotion's, and Sosicrates' books *On the Successions,* and Hippobotus' book *On the Sects.* These writings examine the personalities and doctrines of each of the Socratics, one after the other, as members of one school whose founder was Socrates. Thus in Heraclides, for instance, Aristippus is treated right after Socrates, and Antisthenes comes right after Aristippus. The same holds of Sosicrates' book on the successions of the philosophers. Overschematic though it may be, the classification of Antisthenes and Aristippus in the same Socratic group would be trivial and unproblematic were it not for two interrelated reasons: first, the Hellenistic historiographers considered Antisthenes and Aristippus as the founders of the Cynic and Cyrenaic schools respectively. Second, they treated these two schools under the heading of the Socratics in view of the fact that their founders were Socratics. Antisthenes' and Aristippus' identity as Socratics was as strong as their Cynic or Cyrenaic character in the eyes of several ancient scholars, a fact that renders their classification a tricky matter. In book 7 of his treatise, for instance, Sotion treats Antisthenes together with the Cynics and not with Socrates. Similarly, a few centuries later, Diogenes Laertius locates him in book 6 of his *Lives* despite his explicit intention to place him in book 2, after Xenophon (2.47). It follows that the relations between the Socratics, on the one hand, and the Cyrenaics, on the other, are viewed as a problem for the ancient historiographers in their attempts to classify the Greek philosophers.

The matter of who founded the Cynic and Cyrenaic schools is to the moderns at least as much of a problem as it was to the ancients, but of quite a different nature, for it is not conceived as a question of taxonomy but as a historical and philosophical question. And it cannot be decided until the reliability of our sources has been ascertained. So those who argued that Antisthenes determined the foundational principles of Cynicism relied heavily on the evidence from Hellenistic sources and especially on the tradition of the successions that claims the existence of a Cynic school as well as an uninterrupted sequence from Socrates to Antisthenes to Diogenes and down to Zeno.[66] On the other hand, the consensus in most recent scholarship is to consider the Hellenistic sources as artificial, antiphilosophical, and therefore completely unreliable.[67] For example, it is noticed that, for historical reasons, the teacher-pupil relationship between Antisthenes and Diogenes that the successions assert cannot be true,[68] nor is it true that a Cynic school ever existed. Cynicism was a way of living rather than a doctrine, and its teaching, if teaching there was, was performed by example and not by lecturing within the bounds of an educational institution. The debate on Aristippus follows a similar pattern. Either the testimony of the successions is considered sound, and Aristippus is consequently appointed as the first Cyrenaic hedonist,[69] or it is completely dismissed on historical grounds, with the result that the existence of a Cyrenaic school appears doubtful, and the leadership of Aristippus even more so.[70]

My purpose here is not to question a moderate skepticism with respect to the uncritical use of historiographical sources. Together with Dudley, I am persuaded that Antisthenes did not found a school where Cynicism was formally taught and that he was probably not the teacher of Diogenes. Following E. Mannebach, I find no reason to assume that Aristippus organized an institution called the Cyrenaic school or that he was the first to formulate the hedonistic sensationalism of Cyrenaic philosophy. I focus, however, on the information that we do get from our Hellenistic sources rather than on that which we do not get and suggest that this information is not altogether irrelevant to our interests as historians of philosophy. I argue briefly for the following points. First, the anecdotal material of the Hellenistic sources sometimes embodies, illustrates, or explains philosophical tenets. Second, the claim of the successions to continuity, although often historically unfounded, can be philosophically enlightening.

[66]This attitude occurs mostly in the scholarly writings of the nineteenth century. See *SSR* 3:206 nn. 12–13.

[67]See *SSR* 3:206 nn. 12–13.

[68]See, for instance, Dudley (above, note 29), pp. 1–17.

[69]Philosophically, this view was supported by reference to the Platonic dialogues. For a complete bibliography on this see G. Giannantoni, *I Cirenaici* (Florence, 1958), pp. 123ff. For a cautious approach, see M. Gigante, *PP* 16 (1961): 392–96.

[70]See Mannebach (above, note 38), pp. 86–93; and *SSR* 3:157–59.

Anecdotes, apophthegms, and repartees are standard elements of Hellenistic biography. Their aim is to advance the description of the character and personality of a philosopher by reference to particular episodes that supposedly display them.[71] Nowadays the personalia of a philosopher of the past would leave a systematic philosopher glacially indifferent. The reason is, I think, that we conceive of philosophy as a purely intellectual enterprise that does not, and probably should not, affect all aspects of our behavior. But this does not appear to be the case in Hellenistic historiography. Systematic and doxographical accounts of a doctrine are often accompanied by anecdotal material that displays, as it were, the philosophy in action. Take some examples from Diogenes Laertius: Antisthenes' anticonformism is illustrated by the remark "If both his parents were Athenians, he would not have been so brave" (6.1), or by his reaction to Plato's slandering: "It is the privilege of a king to do good and be ill spoken of" (6.3). His intellectualist belief that once virtue is acquired, it cannot be lost is displayed in his retort to the accusation that he intermingles with evil men: "Doctors attend their patients without getting the fever themselves" (6.6). Some writers describe (mistakenly, as argued above) his attitude toward pleasure by referring to the apophthegm "I prefer to be mad than to feel pleasure" (6.3). Aristippus' *Life* in Diogenes Laertius contains abundant material to choose from. Perhaps the most familiar example is his retort "I possess Lais, but I am not possessed by her" (2.75), which refers to his belief in enjoying and yet mastering pleasure. He complies with Dionysus' desire to see him dressed in women's clothes and comments that "even amid Bacchic festivals a prudent soul will not be corrupted" (2.78), thus agreeing with Antisthenes on the invulnerability of virtue. The humanity and freedom that he attaches to philosophical education are contained in his reply to a father who complains about Aristippus' high fee by saying that for such an amount he can buy a slave. Aristippus answers: "By all means do so, and you will have two" (2.72). It is also typical of anecdotes in a *Life* to illustrate the character and views of a philosopher in an unfavorable light. In Diogenes Laertius, Aristippus indeed receives preferential treatment. Of the sources mentioned by Diogenes in the lengthy doxographical part of this life many are hostile, as we can detect from the material they present.[72] But this does not invalidate my point. As with any other kind of source, the Hellenistic sources on the Socratics may be accurate or not, friendly or not, rich with material or meager, and it is up to the ancient excerpter or to

---

[71] See Mejer (above, note 7), pp. 61ff.

[72] See the references to Phanias, Xenophon, Theodorus, and Plato (whose unique mention of Aristippus is at *Phaedo* 59c). On the other hand, Sotion, Bion, and Diocles are favorable to him.

the modern reader to evaluate them. My point is simply that insofar as their anecdotal features rely on or report philosophical views, they must not be dismissed a priori simply because of their peculiar form.

My second point concerns the attempt of Hellenistic writers to establish uninterrupted successions of philosophers by classifying them along the lines of teacher-pupil relationships. Like any overschematization, the successions admittedly have weak points, especially concerning chronological and biographical details. For instance, Diogenes may never have met Antisthenes,[73] and it is debatable whether the Cyrenaic Antipater was ever the pupil of Theodorus.[74] In the case of Aristippus and the Cyrenaic succession, however, the historicity of the claim that Aristippus was in a sense the founder of the sect seems obvious insofar as the beginnings of the sect were a family affair in which the pattern of teacher and pupil was probably preserved for three generations (D.L. 2.72, 86; SSR 4.b.1–6).[75] Antisthenes' case is more interesting than Aristippus' for the historian of philosophy, for apart from biographical reasons supporting the Cynic-Stoic succession, which are probably false, Diogenes Laertius—or indeed his source—gives proper doxographical reasons for the philosophical continuity of these thinkers, since he groups Antisthenes together with the Cynics and Zeno on account of doctrinal affinities. "Antisthenes led the way to the impassibility of Diogenes (ἀπάθεια), the continence of Crates (ἐγκράτεια), and the capacity for endurance of Zeno (καρτερία)" (D.L. 6.15). The claim is perfectly arguable. To give some examples having to do with themes treated in this essay, neither Antisthenes nor Crates believed that all pleasures are against nature, and nothing would hinder the former from subscribing to Crates' attack on theoretical hedonism (SSR 5.h.45). Antisthenes' practical morality stresses self-sufficiency and moderation as defined later by Crates, as well as the ideal of endurance encountered later in the philosophy of Zeno. One may also appeal to anti-intellectualist elements of Antisthenean ethics, which approach Cynicism, and appeal to the belief that virtue is sufficient for happiness, which is shared by all the philosophers of the succession from Socrates to Zeno. The idea that what is good is τὸ οἰκεῖον (Xen. *Mem.* 3.8.1–7) and the notion of a cosmic providence (*Mem.* 4.3)—if in-

---

[73]Dudley (above, note 29), pp. 2–3. Wilamowitz, *Platon* (Berlin, 1920), 2:162ff.; SSR 3: n. 24, and nn. 11–31 for bibliography on the matter. For an ancient source see Julian *Or.* 9.187c; and on this Caizzi (above, note 27), p. 123.

[74]On the problems connected with the Cyrenaic succession see Tsouna (above, note 3), pp. 20–37.

[75]The story of the beginnings of the Cyrenaic succession sounds all the more plausible because the two male figures in it bear the same name, and it was customary for the grandson to be named after his grandfather.

deed they should be attributed to Antisthenes[76]—have a Stoic ring (though this is more farfetched).[77]

I have suggested that we reestablish some trust in the surviving evidence on the Socratics and that we diminish our skepticism regarding the philosophical and historical value of the Hellenistic sources. This attitude toward the sources seems to me to favor the interpretation that Antisthenes and Aristippus are in the senses indicated above the founders of the Cynic and Cyrenaic sects. To some readers this approach may appear tedious as well as philosophically indifferent. I have suggested that it is neither. It rather seems a necessary step toward reconstructing a persuasive picture of the Socratic movement and its philosophical contributions.[78]

[76]On the first Xenophontic passage, see F. Decleva Caizzi, *Studi Urbanati* (1964): 86ff.
[77]I do not imply that they are identical with any Stoic concepts at close inspection.
[78]I thank Jacques Brunschwig, Richard McKirahan, and the editor of the present volume for their comments. Gregory Vlastos read the last version of this paper, which I dedicate to his memory.

Contributors

Julia Annas is Professor of Philosophy at the University of Arizona at Tucson. She previously taught at St. Hugh's College, Oxford, and Columbia University. She was a Junior Fellow of the Center for Hellenic Studies during 1983–84, and she became a Senior Fellow in 1993. Founding editor of *Oxford Studies in Ancient Philosophy*, she has published a translation with commentary on Aristotle's *Metaphysics M–N* (Oxford, 1976), a commentary on Plato's *Republic* (Oxford, 1979), *The Modes of Scepticism* (Cambridge, 1986), and *The Hellenistic Philosophy of Mind* (Berkeley, 1991), as well as numerous articles on a wide range of subjects in ancient philosophy. She recently completed a book on Hellenistic ethics entitled *The Morality of Happiness* (Oxford, 1993).

Diskin Clay is R. J. R. Nabisco Professor of Classical Studies at Duke University. He previously taught at Johns Hopkins University and the C.U.N.Y. Graduate Center. His books include *Lucretius and Epicurus* (Ithaca, N.Y., 1983), *The Philosophical Inscription of Diogenes of Oenoanda* (*ANRW* II.36.4 [Berlin, 1990]), and a new edition of John Locke's *Questions Concerning the Law of Nature* (Ithaca, N.Y., 1990). He is also the author of many articles on Greek literature and philosophy. Formerly editor of the *American Journal of Philology*, he is completing books on Dante and on Plato.

Joseph G. DeFilippo is Assistant Professor of Classics at the University of North Dakota. He previously taught at Cornell University. He is the author of articles on Apuleius and Plato and is currently at work on a monograph on Aristotle's theology.

Charles H. Kahn is Professor of Philosophy at the University of Pennsylvania. His books include *Anaximander and the Origins of Greek Cosmology* (New York, 1963), *The Verb "To Be" in Ancient Greek* (Leiden, 1973), and *Heraclitus* (Cambridge, 1979). He has also published many articles on a wide range of subjects in ancient philosophy. He recently completed *Plato and the Socratic Dialogue* (Cambridge, forthcoming).

Voula Tsouna McKirahan is a Fellow of the National Endowment for the Humanities during 1994–95. Her publications include articles on Epicureanism and skepticism, a forthcoming edition of *P.Herc.* 1251 (the *Ethica Comparetti*), and a monograph on Cyrenaic epistemology.

Phillip T. Mitsis is Director of the Onassis Center at New York University. He previously was Mellon Chair in Classics at Cornell University and Visiting Professor of Philosophy at the University of Pittsburgh for the Spring semester, 1994. He was a Fellow of the National Humanities Center during 1987–88 and of the Howard Foundation during 1989–90. He has published *Epicurus' Ethical Theory: The Pleasures of Invulnerability* (Ithaca, N.Y., 1988), and he is at work on a translation with philosophical commentary on Cicero's *De finibus* 1–2 for the Clarendon Later Ancient Philosophers series.

Donald R. Morrison is Associate Professor of Philosophy at Rice University. He previously taught at Harvard University and the University of Massachusetts at Amherst, and he was a von Humboldt Fellow at the Freie Universität, Berlin, during 1986–87 and at Universität Konstanz during 1994. He has published a bibliography of Xenophon's Socratic writings as well as articles on ancient skepticism and on Aristotle's metaphysics.

David K. O'Connor is Associate Professor of Philosophy at the University of Notre Dame. He was a Fellow of the National Endowment for the Humanities and a Visiting Scholar at Duke University during 1988–89. His articles on Aristotle and Epicurus seek to explore the resources classical moral philosophy offers to contemporary theory.

Thomas L. Pangle is Professor of Political Science at the University of Toronto. He has also taught at Yale University, Dartmouth College, and the University of Chicago. He was a Guggenheim Fellow during 1981–82 and a Constitutional Fellow of the National Endowment for the Humanities during 1985–86. His books include *Montesquieu's Philosophy of Liberalism*

(Chicago, 1973), a translation of Plato's *Laws* with commentary (New York, 1980), and *The Spirit of Modern Republicanism: The Moral Vision of the American Founders and the Philosophy of Locke* (Chicago, 1988). He has edited *The Roots of Political Philosophy: Ten Forgotten Socratic Dialogues* (Ithaca, N.Y., 1987) and has published numerous articles on classical political philosophy, on Nietzsche, and on the philosophical foundations of the American founding. He recently completed *The Ennobling of Democracy: The Challenge of the Post-Modern Era* (Baltimore, forthcoming).

Christopher J. Shields is Associate Professor of Philosophy at the University of Colorado at Boulder. During 1988–89 he was a von Humboldt Fellow at the Johannes Gutenberg-Universität, Mainz and during 1992–93 a Visiting Fellow at Corpus Christi College, Oxford. His publications on Aristotle, Stoicism, Aquinas, and Leibniz fall in the fields of epistemology, philosophical psychology, and ethics. He is currently at work on a book on Aristotle's philosophy of language and mind.

John A. Stevens is Assistant Professor of Classics at East Carolina University, Greenville. He previously taught at New York University. He recently completed his dissertation on the chorus in Seneca's drama at Duke University.

Gisela Striker is George Martin Lane Professor of Philosophy and the Classics at Harvard University. She previously taught at Universität Göttingen and Columbia University. She is the author of monographs on Plato's *Philebus* and on Hellenistic epistemology, and the coeditor of *The Norms of Nature: Studies in Hellenistic Ethics* (Cambridge, 1986). During 1990–91 she was a Fellow of the Wissenschaftskolleg zu Berlin, working on a translation with commentary on Aristotle's *Prior Analytics* for publication by the Berlin Academy.

Harold A. S. Tarrant is Professor of Classics at the University of Newcastle, New South Wales. He previously taught at the University of Sydney. He is the author of many studies on the history of Platonism and on Hellenistic epistemology, including *Platonism or Scepticism? The Philosophy of the Fourth Academy* (Cambridge, 1985), *Thrasyllan Platonism* (Ithaca, N.Y., 1993), and articles on the Aristophanic and the Platonic Socrates. He recently completed *The Last Days of Socrates* for Penguin Books (London, 1993).

Paul A. Vander Waerdt is Planning and Development Officer at the East Bay Center for the Performing Arts in Richmond, California, a Development Consultant to the University of California at San Francisco AIDS Health Project, and a Member of the Board of Managers of the Buchanan

YMCA in San Francisco. He previously taught classical studies and philosophy at Duke University. His publications on Aristotle and Hellenistic philosophy fall principally in the fields of philosophical psychology, ethics, and political philosophy. He is author of *The Theory of Natural Law in Antiquity* (Ithaca, N.Y., forthcoming). He has edited a collection of essays entitled "Tradition and Innovation in Epicureanism," which appeared in *Greek, Roman and Byzantine Studies* 30 (1989), and he coedited *The School of Hellas* (Oxford, 1991). During 1990–91 he was a Fellow of the National Endowment for the Humanities, and during 1992–93 a Visiting Fellow of Clare Hall, Cambridge.

Index